JOHN MUIR

JOHN MUIR

NATURE WRITINGS

The Story of My Boyhood and Youth
My First Summer in the Sierra
The Mountains of California
Stickeen
Selected Essays

THE LIBRARY OF AMERICA

Distributed to the trade in the United States
by Penguin Books USA Inc
and in Canada by Penguin Books Canada Ltd.

Library of Congress Catalog Number: 96-9664
For cataloging information, see end of Index.
ISBN: 1-883011-24-8

First Printing
The Library of America—92

508.74
MUI

Manufactured in the United States of America

WILLIAM CRONON
SELECTED THE CONTENTS AND
WROTE THE NOTES FOR THIS VOLUME

Contents

THE STORY OF
MY BOYHOOD AND YOUTH

Contents

Illustrations

John Muir

I

A BOYHOOD IN SCOTLAND

EARLIEST RECOLLECTIONS—THE "DANDY DOCTOR"
TERROR—DEEDS OF DARING—THE SAVAGERY OF
BOYS—SCHOOL AND FIGHTING—BIRDS'-NESTING.

WHEN I was a boy in Scotland I was fond of everything
that was wild, and all my life I've been growing fonder
and fonder of wild places and wild creatures. Fortunately
around my native town of Dunbar, by the stormy North Sea,
there was no lack of wildness, though most of the land lay in
smooth cultivation. With red-blooded playmates, wild as myself, I loved to wander in the fields to hear the birds sing, and
along the seashore to gaze and wonder at the shells and sea-
weeds, eels and crabs in the pools among the rocks when the
tide was low; and best of all to watch the waves in awful
storms thundering on the black headlands and craggy ruins
of the old Dunbar Castle when the sea and the sky, the waves
and the clouds, were mingled together as one. We never
thought of playing truant, but after I was five or six years old
I ran away to the seashore or the fields almost every Saturday,
and every day in the school vacations except Sundays, though
solemnly warned that I must play at home in the garden and
back yard, lest I should learn to think bad thoughts and say
bad words. All in vain. In spite of the sure sore punishments
that followed like shadows, the natural inherited wildness in
our blood ran true on its glorious course as invincible and
unstoppable as stars.

My earliest recollections of the country were gained on
short walks with my grandfather when I was perhaps not over
three years old. On one of these walks grandfather took me
to Lord Lauderdale's gardens, where I saw figs growing
against a sunny wall and tasted some of them, and got as many
apples to eat as I wished. On another memorable walk in a
hayfield, when we sat down to rest on one of the haycocks I
heard a sharp, prickly, stinging cry, and, jumping up eagerly,
called grandfather's attention to it. He said he heard only the

wind, but I insisted on digging into the hay and turning it over until we discovered the source of the strange exciting sound,—a mother field mouse with half a dozen naked young hanging to her teats. This to me was a wonderful discovery. No hunter could have been more excited on discovering a bear and her cubs in a wilderness den.

I was sent to school before I had completed my third year. The first schoolday was doubtless full of wonders, but I am not able to recall any of them. I remember the servant washing my face and getting soap in my eyes, and mother hanging a little green bag with my first book in it around my neck so I would not lose it, and its blowing back in the sea-wind like a flag. But before I was sent to school my grandfather, as I was told, had taught me my letters from shop signs across the street. I can remember distinctly how proud I was when I had spelled my way through the little first book into the second, which seemed large and important, and so on to the third. Going from one book to another formed a grand triumphal advancement, the memories of which still stand out in clear relief.

The third book contained interesting stories as well as plain reading- and spelling-lessons. To me the best story of all was "Llewellyn's Dog," the first animal that comes to mind after the needle-voiced field mouse. It so deeply interested and touched me and some of my classmates that we read it over and over with aching hearts, both in and out of school and shed bitter tears over the brave faithful dog, Gelert, slain by his own master, who imagined that he had devoured his son because he came to him all bloody when the boy was lost, though he had saved the child's life by killing a big wolf. We have to look far back to learn how great may be the capacity of a child's heart for sorrow and sympathy with animals as well as with human friends and neighbors. This auld-lang-syne story stands out in the throng of old schoolday memories as clearly as if I had myself been one of that Welsh hunting-party—heard the bugles blowing, seen Gelert slain, joined in the search for the lost child, discovered it at last happy and smiling among the grass and bushes beside the dead, mangled wolf, and wept with Llewellyn over the sad fate of his noble, faithful dog friend.

Another favorite in this book was Southey's poem "The Inchcape Bell," a story of a priest and a pirate. A good priest in order to warn seamen in dark stormy weather hung a big bell on the dangerous Inchcape Rock. The greater the storm and higher the waves, the louder rang the warning bell, until it was cut off and sunk by wicked Ralph the Rover. One fine day, as the story goes, when the bell was ringing gently, the pirate put out to the rock, saying, "I'll sink that bell and plague the Abbot of Aberbrothok." So he cut the rope, and down went the bell "with a gurgling sound; the bubbles rose and burst around," etc. Then "Ralph the Rover sailed away; he scoured the seas for many a day; and now, grown rich with plundered store, he steers his course for Scotland's shore." Then came a terrible storm with cloud darkness and night darkness and high roaring waves. "Now where we are," cried the pirate, "I cannot tell, but I wish I could hear the Inchcape bell." And the story goes on to tell how the wretched rover "tore his hair," and "curst himself in his despair," when "with a shivering shock" the stout ship struck on the Inchcape Rock, and went down with Ralph and his plunder beside the good priest's bell. The story appealed to our love of kind deeds and of wildness and fair play.

A lot of terrifying experiences connected with these first schooldays grew out of crimes committed by the keeper of a low lodging-house in Edinburgh, who allowed poor homeless wretches to sleep on benches or the floor for a penny or so a night, and, when kind Death came to their relief, sold the bodies for dissection to Dr. Hare of the medical school. None of us children ever heard anything like the original story. The servant girls told us that "Dandy Doctors," clad in long black cloaks and supplied with a store of sticking-plaster of wondrous adhesiveness, prowled at night about the country lanes and even the town streets, watching for children to choke and sell. The Dandy Doctor's business method, as the servants explained it, was with lightning quickness to clap a sticking-plaster on the face of a scholar, covering mouth and nose, preventing breathing or crying for help, then pop us under his long black cloak and carry us to Edinburgh to be sold and sliced into small pieces for folk to learn how we were made. We always mentioned the name "Dandy Doctor" in a fearful whisper, and never dared venture out of doors after dark. In the short winter days it got dark before school closed, and in cloudy weather we sometimes had difficulty in finding our way home unless a servant with a lantern was sent for us; but during the Dandy Doctor period the school was closed earlier, for if detained until the usual hour the teacher could not get us to leave the schoolroom. We would rather stay all night supperless than dare the mysterious doctors supposed to be lying in wait for us. We had to go up a hill called the Davel Brae that lay between the schoolhouse and the main street. One evening just before dark, as we were running up the hill, one of the boys shouted, "A Dandy Doctor! A Dandy Doctor!" and we all fled pellmell back into the schoolhouse to the astonishment of Mungo Siddons, the teacher. I can remember to this day the amused look on the good dominie's face as he stared and tried to guess what had got into us, until one of the older boys breathlessly explained that there was an awful big Dandy Doctor on the Brae and we couldna gang hame. Others corroborated the dreadful news. "Yes! We saw him, plain as onything, with his lang black cloak to hide us in, and some of us thought we saw a sticken-plaister ready in his hand." We were in such a state of fear and trembling that the teacher saw he wasn't going to get rid of us without going himself as leader. He went only a short distance, however, and turned us over to the care of the two biggest scholars, who led us to the top of the Brae and then left us to scurry home and dash into the door like pursued squirrels diving into their holes.

Just before school skaled (closed), we all arose and sang the fine hymn "Lord, dismiss us with Thy blessing." In the spring when the swallows were coming back from their winter homes we sang—

> "Welcome, welcome, little stranger,
>   Welcome from a foreign shore;
>   Safe escaped from many a danger . . ."

and while singing we all swayed in rhythm with the music. "The Cuckoo," that always told his name in the spring of the year, was another favorite song, and when there was nothing in particular to call to mind any special bird or animal, the songs we sang were widely varied, such as

> "The whale, the whale is the beast for me,
> Plunging along through the deep, deep sea."

But the best of all was "Lord, dismiss us with Thy blessing," though at that time the most significant part I fear was the first three words.

With my school lessons father made me learn hymns and Bible verses. For learning "Rock of Ages" he gave me a penny, and I thus became suddenly rich. Scotch boys are seldom spoiled with money. We thought more of a penny those economical days than the poorest American schoolboy thinks of a dollar. To decide what to do with that first penny was an extravagantly serious affair. I ran in great excitement up and down the street, examining the tempting goodies in the shop windows before venturing on so important an investment. My playmates also became excited when the wonderful news got abroad that Johnnie Muir had a penny, hoping to obtain a taste of the orange, apple, or candy it was likely to bring forth.

At this time infants were baptized and vaccinated a few days after birth. I remember very well a fight with the doctor when my brother David was vaccinated. This happened, I think, before I was sent to school. I couldn't imagine what the doctor, a tall, severe-looking man in black, was doing to my brother, but as mother, who was holding him in her arms, offered no objection, I looked on quietly while he scratched the arm until I saw blood. Then, unable to trust even my mother, I managed to spring up high enough to grab and bite the doctor's arm, yelling that I wasna gan to let him hurt my bonnie brither, while to my utter astonishment mother and the doctor only laughed at me. So far from complete at times is sympathy between parents and children, and so much like wild beasts are baby boys, little fighting, biting, climbing pagans.

Father was proud of his garden and seemed always to be trying to make it as much like Eden as possible, and in a corner of it he gave each of us a little bit of ground for our very own in which we planted what we best liked, wondering how the hard dry seeds could change into soft leaves and flowers and find their way out to the light; and, to see how they were coming on, we used to dig up the larger ones, such as peas and beans, every day. My aunt had a corner assigned to her in our garden which she filled with lilies, and we all looked with the utmost respect and admiration at that precious lily-bed and wondered whether when we grew up we should ever be rich enough to own one anything like so grand. We imagined that each lily was worth an enormous sum of money and never dared to touch a single leaf or petal of them. We really stood in awe of them. Far, far was I then from the wild lily gardens of California that I was destined to see in their glory.

When I was a little boy at Mungo Siddons's school a flower-show was held in Dunbar, and I saw a number of the exhibitors carrying large handfuls of dahlias, the first I had ever seen. I thought them marvelous in size and beauty and, as in the case of my aunt's lilies, wondered if I should ever be rich enough to own some of them.

Although I never dared to touch my aunt's sacred lilies, I have good cause to remember stealing some common flowers from an apothecary, Peter Lawson, who also answered the purpose of a regular physician to most of the poor people of the town and adjacent country. He had a pony which was considered very wild and dangerous, and when he was called out of town he mounted this wonderful beast, which, after standing long in the stable, was frisky and boisterous, and often to our delight reared and jumped and danced about from side to side of the street before he could be persuaded to go ahead. We boys gazed in awful admiration and wondered how the druggist could be so brave and able as to get on and stay on that wild beast's back. This famous Peter loved flowers and had a fine garden surrounded by an iron fence, through the bars of which, when I thought no one saw me, I oftentimes snatched a flower and took to my heels. One day Peter discovered me in this mischief, dashed out into the street and caught me. I screamed that I wouldna steal any more if he would let me go. He didn't say anything but just dragged me along to the stable where he kept the wild pony, pushed me in right back of its heels, and shut the door. I was screaming, of course, but as soon as I was imprisoned the fear of being kicked quenched all noise. I hardly dared breathe. My only hope was in motionless silence. Imagine the agony I endured! I did not steal any more of his flowers. He was a good hard judge of boy nature.

I was in Peter's hands some time before this, when I was about two and a half years old. The servant girl bathed us small folk before putting us to bed. The smarting soapy scrubbings of the Saturday nights in preparation for the Sabbath were particularly severe, and we all dreaded them. My sister Sarah, the next older than me, wanted the long-legged stool I was sitting on awaiting my turn, so she just tipped me off. My chin struck on the edge of the bath-tub, and, as I was talking at the time, my tongue happened to be in the way of my teeth when they were closed by the blow, and a deep gash was cut on the side of it, which bled profusely. Mother came running at the noise I made, wrapped me up, put me in the servant girl's arms and told her to run with me through the garden and out by a back way to Peter Lawson to have something done to stop the bleeding. He simply pushed a wad of cotton into my mouth after soaking it in some brown astringent stuff, and told me to be sure to keep my mouth shut and all would soon be well. Mother put me to bed, calmed my fears, and told me to lie still and sleep like a gude bairn. But just as I was dropping off to sleep I swallowed the bulky wad of medicated cotton and with it, as I imagined, my tongue also. My screams over so great a loss brought mother, and when she anxiously took me in her arms and inquired what was the matter, I told her that I had swallowed my tongue. She only laughed at me, much to my astonishment, when I expected that she would bewail the awful loss her boy had sustained. My sisters, who were older than I, oftentimes said when I happened to be talking too much, "It's a pity you hadn't swallowed at least half of that long tongue of yours when you were little."

It appears natural for children to be fond of water, although the Scotch method of making every duty dismal contrived to make necessary bathing for health terrible to us. I well remember among the awful experiences of childhood being taken by the servant to the seashore when I was between two and three years old, stripped at the side of a deep pool in the rocks, plunged into it among crawling crawfish and slippery wriggling snake-like eels, and drawn up gasping and shrieking only to be plunged down again and again. As the time approached for this terrible bathing, I used to hide in the darkest corners of the house, and oftentimes a long search was required to find me. But after we were a few years older, we enjoyed bathing with other boys as we wandered along the shore, careful, however, not to get into a pool that had an invisible boy-devouring monster at the bottom of it. Such pools, miniature maelstroms, were called "sookin-in-goats" and were well known to most of us. Nevertheless we never ventured into any pool on strange parts of the coast before we had thrust a stick into it. If the stick were not pulled out of our hands, we boldly entered and enjoyed plashing and ducking long ere we had learned to swim.

One of our best playgrounds was the famous old Dunbar Castle, to which King Edward fled after his defeat at Bannockburn. It was built more than a thousand years ago, and though we knew little of its history, we had heard many mysterious stories of the battles fought about its walls, and firmly believed that every bone we found in the ruins belonged to an ancient warrior. We tried to see who could climb highest on the crumbling peaks and crags, and took chances that no cautious mountaineer would try. That I did not fall and finish my rock-scrambling in those adventurous boyhood days seems now a reasonable wonder.

Among our best games were running, jumping, wrestling, and scrambling. I was so proud of my skill as a climber that when I first heard of hell from a servant girl who loved to tell its horrors and warn us that if we did anything wrong we would be cast into it, I always insisted that I could climb out of it. I imagined it was only a sooty pit with stone walls like those of the castle, and I felt sure there must be chinks and cracks in the masonry for fingers and toes. Anyhow the terrors of the horrible place seldom lasted long beyond the telling; for natural faith casts out fear.

Most of the Scotch children believe in ghosts, and some under peculiar conditions continue to believe in them all through life. Grave ghosts are deemed particularly dangerous, and many of the most credulous will go far out of their way to avoid passing through or near a graveyard in the dark. After being instructed by the servants in the nature, looks, and habits of the various black and white ghosts, boowuzzies, and witches we often speculated as to whether they could run fast, and tried to believe that we had a good chance to get away from most of them. To improve our speed and wind, we often took long runs into the country. Tam o' Shanter's mare outran a lot of witches,—at least until she reached a place of safety beyond the keystone of the bridge,—and we thought perhaps we also might be able to outrun them.

Our house formerly belonged to a physician, and a servant girl told us that the ghost of the dead doctor haunted one of the unoccupied rooms in the second story that was kept dark on account of a heavy window-tax. Our bedroom was adjacent to the ghost room, which had in it a lot of chemical apparatus,—glass tubing, glass and brass retorts, test-tubes, flasks, etc.,—and we thought that those strange articles were still used by the old dead doctor in compounding physic. In the long summer days David and I were put to bed several hours before sunset. Mother tucked us in carefully, drew the curtains of the big old-fashioned bed, and told us to lie still and sleep like gude bairns; but we were usually out of bed, playing games of daring called "scootchers," about as soon as our loving mother reached the foot of the stairs, for we couldn't lie still, however hard we might try. Going into the ghost room was regarded as a very great scootcher. After venturing in a few steps and rushing back in terror, I used to dare David to go as far without getting caught.

The roof of our house, as well as the crags and walls of the old castle, offered fine mountaineering exercise. Our bedroom was lighted by a dormer window. One night I opened it in search of good scootchers and hung myself out over the slates, holding on to the sill, while the wind was making a balloon of my nightgown. I then dared David to try the adventure, and he did. Then I went out again and hung by one hand, and David did the same. Then I hung by one finger, being careful not to slip, and he did that too. Then I stood on the sill and examined the edge of the left wall of the window, crept up the slates along its side by slight finger-holds, got astride of the roof, sat there a few minutes looking at the scenery over the garden wall while the wind was howling and threatening to blow me off, then managed to slip down, catch hold of the sill, and get safely back into the room. But before attempting this scootcher, recognizing its dangerous character, with commendable caution I warned David that in case I should happen to slip I would grip the rain-trough when I was going over the eaves and hang on, and that he must then run fast downstairs and tell father to get a ladder for me, and tell him to be quick because I would soon be tired hanging dangling in the wind by my hands. After my return from this capital scootcher, David, not to be outdone, crawled up to the top of the window-roof, and got bravely astride of it; but in trying to return he lost courage and began to greet (to cry), "I canna get doon. Oh, I canna get doon." I leaned out of the window and shouted encouragingly, "Dinna greet, Davie, dinna greet, I'll help ye doon. If you greet, fayther will hear, and gee us baith an awfu' skelping." Then, standing on the sill and holding on by one hand to the window-casing, I directed him to slip his feet down within reach, and, after securing a good hold, I jumped inside and dragged him in by his heels. This finished scootcher-scrambling for the night and frightened us into bed.

In the short winter days, when it was dark even at our early bedtime, we usually spent the hours before going to sleep playing voyages around the world under the bed-clothing. After mother had carefully covered us, bade us good-night and gone downstairs, we set out on our travels. Burrowing like moles, we visited France, India, America, Australia, New Zealand, and all the places we had ever heard of; our travels never ending until we fell asleep. When mother came to take a last look at us, before she went to bed, to see that we were covered, we were oftentimes covered so well that she had difficulty in finding us, for we were hidden in all sorts of positions where sleep happened to overtake us, but in the morning we always found ourselves in good order, lying straight like gude bairns, as she said.

Some fifty years later, when I visited Scotland, I got one of my Dunbar schoolmates to introduce me to the owners of our old home, from whom I obtained permission to go upstairs to examine our bedroom window and judge what sort of adventure getting on its roof must have been, and with all my after experience in mountaineering, I found that what I had done in daring boyhood was now beyond my skill.

Boys are often at once cruel and merciful, thoughtlessly hard-hearted and tender-hearted, sympathetic, pitiful, and kind in ever changing contrasts. Love of neighbors, human or animal, grows up amid savage traits, coarse and fine. When father made out to get us securely locked up in the back yard to prevent our shore and field wanderings, we had to play away the comparatively dull time as best we could. One of our amusements was hunting cats without seriously hurting them. These sagacious animals knew, however, that, though not very dangerous, boys were not to be trusted. One time in particular I remember, when we began throwing stones at an experienced old Tom, not wishing to hurt him much, though he was a tempting mark. He soon saw what we were up to, fled to the stable, and climbed to the top of the hay manger. He was still within range, however, and we kept the stones flying faster and faster, but he just blinked and played possum without wincing either at our best shots or at the noise we made. I happened to strike him pretty hard with a good-sized pebble, but he still blinked and sat still as if without feeling. "He must be mortally wounded," I said, "and now we must kill him to put him out of pain," the savage in us rapidly growing with indulgence. All took heartily to this sort of cat mercy and began throwing the heaviest stones we could manage, but that old fellow knew what characters we were, and just as we imagined him mercifully dead he evidently thought the play was becoming too serious and that it was time to retreat; for suddenly with a wild whirr and gurr of energy he launched himself over our heads, rushed across the yard in a blur of speed, climbed to the roof of another building and over the garden wall, out of pain and bad company, with all his lives wideawake and in good working order.

After we had thus learned that Tom had at least nine lives, we tried to verify the common saying that no matter how far cats fell they always landed on their feet unhurt. We caught one in our back yard, not Tom but a smaller one of manageable size, and somehow got him smuggled up to the top story of the house. I don't know how in the world we managed to let go of him, for as soon as we opened the window and held him over the sill he knew his danger and made violent efforts to scratch and bite his way back into the room; but we determined to carry the thing through, and at last managed to drop him. I can remember to this day how the poor creature in danger of his life strained and balanced as he was falling and managed to alight on his feet. This was a cruel thing for even wild boys to do, and we never tried the experiment again, for we sincerely pitied the poor fellow when we saw him creeping slowly away, stunned and frightened, with a swollen black and blue chin.

Again—showing the natural savagery of boys—we delighted in dog-fights, and even in the horrid red work of slaughter-houses, often running long distances and climbing over walls and roofs to see a pig killed, as soon as we heard the desperately earnest squealing. And if the butcher was good-natured, we begged him to let us get a near view of the mysterious insides and to give us a bladder to blow up for a foot-ball.

But here is an illustration of the better side of boy nature. In our back yard there were three elm trees and in the one nearest the house a pair of robin-redbreasts had their nest. When the young were almost able to fly, a troop of the celebrated "Scottish Grays," visited Dunbar, and three or four of the fine horses were lodged in our stable. When the soldiers were polishing their swords and helmets, they happened to notice the nest, and just as they were leaving, one of them climbed the tree and robbed it. With sore sympathy we watched the young birds as the hard-hearted robber pushed them one by one beneath his jacket,—all but two that jumped out of the nest and tried to fly, but they were easily caught as they fluttered on the ground, and were hidden away with the rest. The distress of the bereaved parents, as they hovered and screamed over the frightened crying children they so long had loved and sheltered and fed, was pitiful to see; but the shining soldier rode grandly away on his big gray horse, caring only for the few pennies the young songbirds would bring and the beer they would buy, while we all, sisters and brothers, were crying and sobbing. I remember, as if it happened this day, how my heart fairly ached and choked me. Mother put us to bed and tried to comfort us, telling us that the little birds would be well fed and grow big, and soon learn to sing in pretty cages; but again and again we rehearsed the sad story of the poor bereaved birds and their frightened children, and could not be comforted. Father came into the room when we were half asleep and still sobbing, and I heard mother telling him that, "a' the bairns' hearts were broken over the robbing of the nest in the elm."

After attaining the manly, belligerent age of five or six years, very few of my schooldays passed without a fist fight, and half a dozen was no uncommon number. When any classmate of our own age questioned our rank and standing as fighters, we always made haste to settle the matter at a quiet place on the Davel Brae. To be a "gude fechter" was our highest ambition, our dearest aim in life in or out of school. To be a good scholar was a secondary consideration, though we tried hard to hold high places in our classes and gloried in being Dux. We fairly reveled in the battle stories of glorious William Wallace and Robert the Bruce, with which every breath of Scotch air is saturated, and of course we were all going to be soldiers. On the Davel Brae battleground we often managed to bring on something like real war, greatly more exciting than personal combat. Choosing leaders, we divided into two armies. In winter damp snow furnished plenty of ammunition to make the thing serious, and in summer sand and grass sods. Cheering and shouting some battle-cry such as "Bannockburn! Bannockburn! Scotland forever! The Last War in India!" we were led bravely on. For heavy battery work we stuffed our Scotch blue bonnets with snow and sand, sometimes mixed with gravel, and fired them at each other as cannon-balls.

Of course we always looked eagerly forward to vacation days and thought them slow in coming. Old Mungo Siddons gave us a lot of gooseberries or currants and wished us a happy time. Some sort of special closing-exercises—singing, recitations, etc.—celebrated the great day, but I remember only the berries, freedom from school work, and opportunities for runaway rambles in the fields and along the wave-beaten seashore.

An exciting time came when at the age of seven or eight years I left the auld Davel Brae school for the grammar school.

Of course I had a terrible lot of fighting to do, because a new scholar had to meet every one of his age who dared to challenge him, this being the common introduction to a new school. It was very strenuous for the first month or so, establishing my fighting rank, taking up new studies, especially Latin and French, getting acquainted with new classmates and the master and his rules. In the first few Latin and French lessons the new teacher, Mr. Lyon, blandly smiled at our comical blunders, but pedagogical weather of the severest kind quickly set in, when for every mistake, everything short of perfection, the taws was promptly applied. We had to get three lessons every day in Latin, three in French, and as many in English, besides spelling, history, arithmetic, and geography. Word lessons in particular, the wouldst-couldst-shouldst-have-loved kind, were kept up, with much warlike thrashing, until I had committed the whole of the French, Latin, and English grammars to memory, and in connection with reading-lessons we were called on to recite parts of them with the rules over and over again, as if all the regular and irregular incomprehensible verb stuff was poetry. In addition to all this, father made me learn so many Bible verses every day that by the time I was eleven years of age I had about three fourths of the Old Testament and all of the New by heart and by sore flesh. I could recite the New Testament from the beginning of Matthew to the end of Revelation without a single stop. The dangers of cramming and of making scholars study at home instead of letting their little brains rest were never heard of in those days. We carried our school-books home in a strap every night and committed to memory our next day's lessons before we went to bed, and to do that we had to bend our attention as closely on our tasks as lawyers on great million-dollar cases. I can't conceive of anything that would now enable me to concentrate my attention more fully than when I was a mere stripling boy, and it was all done by whipping,— thrashing in general. Old-fashioned Scotch teachers spent no time in seeking short roads to knowledge, or in trying any of the new-fangled psychological methods so much in vogue nowadays. There was nothing said about making the seats easy or the lessons easy. We were simply driven pointblank against our books like soldiers against the enemy, and sternly ordered,

"Up and at 'em. Commit your lessons to memory!" If we failed in any part, however slight, we were whipped; for the grand, simple, all-sufficing Scotch discovery had been made that there was a close connection between the skin and the memory, and that irritating the skin excited the memory to any required degree.

Fighting was carried on still more vigorously in the high school than in the common school. Whenever any one was challenged, either the challenge was allowed or it was decided by a battle on the seashore, where with stubborn enthusiasm we battered each other as if we had not been sufficiently battered by the teacher. When we were so fortunate as to finish a fight without getting a black eye, we usually escaped a thrashing at home and another next morning at school, for other traces of the fray could be easily washed off at a well on the church brae, or concealed, or passed as results of playground accidents; but a black eye could never be explained away from downright fighting. A good double thrashing was the inevitable penalty, but all without avail; fighting went on without the slightest abatement, like natural storms; for no punishment less than death could quench the ancient inherited belligerence burning in our pagan blood. Nor could we be made to believe it was fair that father and teacher should thrash us so industriously for our good, while begrudging us the pleasure of thrashing each other for our good. All these various thrashings, however, were admirably influential in developing not only memory but fortitude as well. For if we did not endure our school punishments and fighting pains without flinching and making faces, we were mocked on the playground, and public opinion on a Scotch playground was a powerful agent in controlling behavior; therefore we at length managed to keep our features in smooth repose while enduring pain that would try anybody but an American Indian. Far from feeling that we were called on to endure too much pain, one of our playground games was thrashing each other with whips about two feet long made from the tough, wiry stems of a species of polygonum fastened together in a stiff, firm braid. One of us handing two of these whips to a companion to take his choice, we stood up close together and thrashed each other on the legs until one succumbed to the intolerable pain and thus lost the game. Nearly all of our playground games were strenuous,—shin-battering shinny, wrestling, prisoners' base, and dogs and hares,—all augmenting in no slight degree our lessons in fortitude. Moreover, we regarded our punishments and pains of every sort as training for war, since we were all going to be soldiers. Besides single combats we sometimes assembled on Saturdays to meet the scholars of another school, and very little was required for the growth of strained relations, and war. The immediate cause might be nothing more than a saucy stare. Perhaps the scholar stared at would insolently inquire, "What are ye glowerin' at, Bob?" Bob would reply, "I'll look where I hae a mind and hinder me if ye daur." "Weel, Bob," the outraged stared-at scholar would reply, "I'll soon let ye see whether I daur or no!" and give Bob a blow on the face. This opened the battle, and every good scholar belonging to either school was drawn into it. After both sides were sore and weary, a strong-lunged warrior would be heard above the din of battle shouting, "I'll tell ye what we'll dae wi' ye. If ye'll let us alane we'll let ye alane!" and the school war ended as most wars between nations do; and some of them begin in much the same way.

Notwithstanding the great number of harshly enforced rules, not very good order was kept in school in my time. There were two schools within a few rods of each other, one for mathematics, navigation, etc., the other, called the grammar school, that I attended. The masters lived in a big freestone house within eight or ten yards of the schools, so that they could easily step out for anything they wanted or send one of the scholars. The moment our master disappeared, perhaps for a book or a drink, every scholar left his seat and his lessons, jumped on top of the benches and desks or crawled beneath them, tugging, rolling, wrestling, accomplishing in a minute a depth of disorder and din unbelievable save by a Scottish scholar. We even carried on war, class against class, in those wild, precious minutes. A watcher gave the alarm when the master opened his house-door to return, and it was a great feat to get into our places before he entered, adorned in awful majestic authority, shouting "Silence!" and striking resounding blows with his cane on a desk or on some unfortunate scholar's back.

Forty-seven years after leaving this fighting school, I returned on a visit to Scotland, and a cousin in Dunbar introduced me to a minister who was acquainted with the history of the school, and obtained for me an invitation to dine with the new master. Of course I gladly accepted, for I wanted to see the old place of fun and pain, and the battleground on the sands. Mr. Lyon, our able teacher and thrasher, I learned, had held his place as master of the school for twenty or thirty years after I left it, and had recently died in London, after preparing many young men for the English Universities. At the dinner-table, while I was recalling the amusements and fights of my old schooldays, the minister remarked to the new master, "Now, don't you wish that you had been teacher in those days, and gained the honor of walloping John Muir?" This pleasure so merrily suggested showed that the minister also had been a fighter in his youth. The old freestone school building was still perfectly sound, but the carved, ink-stained desks were almost whittled away.

The highest part of our playground back of the school commanded a view of the sea, and we loved to watch the passing ships and, judging by their rigging, make guesses as to the ports they had sailed from, those to which they were bound, what they were loaded with, their tonnage, etc. In stormy weather they were all smothered in clouds and spray, and showers of salt scud torn from the tops of the waves came flying over the playground wall. In those tremendous storms many a brave ship foundered or was tossed and smashed on the rocky shore. When a wreck occurred within a mile or two of the town, we often managed by running fast to reach it and pick up some of the spoils. In particular I remember visiting the battered fragments of an unfortunate brig or schooner that had been loaded with apples, and finding fine unpitiful sport in rushing into the spent waves and picking up the red-cheeked fruit from the frothy, seething foam.

All our school-books were extravagantly illustrated with drawings of every kind of sailing-vessel, and every boy owned some sort of craft whittled from a block of wood and trimmed with infinite pains,—sloops, schooners, brigs, and full-rigged ships, with their sails and string ropes properly adjusted and named for us by some old sailor. These precious toy craft with lead keels we learned to sail on a pond near the town. With the sails set at the proper angle to the wind, they made fast straight voyages across the pond to boys on the other side, who readjusted the sails and started them back on the return voyages. Oftentimes fleets of half a dozen or more were started together in exciting races.

Our most exciting sport, however, was playing with gunpowder. We made guns out of gas-pipe, mounted them on sticks of any shape, clubbed our pennies together for powder, gleaned pieces of lead here and there and cut them into slugs, and, while one aimed, another applied a match to the touchhole. With these awful weapons we wandered along the beach and fired at the gulls and solan-geese as they passed us. Fortunately we never hurt any of them that we knew of. We also dug holes in the ground, put in a handful or two of powder, tamped it well around a fuse made of a wheat-stalk, and, reaching cautiously forward, touched a match to the straw. This we called making earthquakes. Oftentimes we went home with singed hair and faces well peppered with powder-grains that could not be washed out. Then, of course, came a correspondingly severe punishment from both father and teacher.

Another favorite sport was climbing trees and scaling gardenwalls. Boys eight or ten years of age could get over almost any wall by standing on each other's shoulders, thus making living ladders. To make walls secure against marauders, many of them were finished on top with broken bottles imbedded in lime, leaving the cutting edges sticking up; but with bunches of grass and weeds we could sit or stand in comfort on top of the jaggedest of them.

Like squirrels that begin to eat nuts before they are ripe, we began to eat apples about as soon as they were formed, causing, of course, desperate gastric disturbances to be cured by castor oil. Serious were the risks we ran in climbing and squeezing through hedges, and, of course, among the country folk we were far from welcome. Farmers passing us on the roads often shouted by way of greeting: "Oh, you vagabonds! Back to the toon wi' ye. Gang back where ye belang. You're up to mischief, Ise warrant. I can see it. The gamekeeper'll catch ye, and maist like ye'll a' be hanged some day."

Breakfast in those auld-lang-syne days was simple oatmeal

porridge, usually with a little milk or treacle, served in wooden dishes called "luggies," formed of staves hooped together like miniature tubs about four or five inches in diameter. One of the staves, the lug or ear, a few inches longer than the others, served as a handle, while the number of luggies ranged in a row on a dresser indicated the size of the family. We never dreamed of anything to come after the porridge, or of asking for more. Our portions were consumed in about a couple of minutes; then off to school. At noon we came racing home ravenously hungry. The midday meal, called dinner, was usually vegetable broth, a small piece of boiled mutton, and barley-meal scone. None of us liked the barley scone bread, therefore we got all we wanted of it, and in desperation had to eat it, for we were always hungry, about as hungry after as before meals. The evening meal was called "tea" and was served on our return from school. It consisted, as far as we children were concerned, of half a slice of white bread without butter, barley scone, and warm water with a little milk and sugar in it, a beverage called "content," which warmed but neither cheered nor inebriated. Immediately after tea we ran across the street with our books to Grandfather Gilrye, who took pleasure in seeing us and hearing us recite our next day's lessons. Then back home to supper, usually a boiled potato and piece of barley scone. Then family worship, and to bed.

Our amusements on Saturday afternoons and vacations depended mostly on getting away from home into the country, especially in the spring when the birds were calling loudest. Father sternly forbade David and me from playing truant in the fields with plundering wanderers like ourselves, fearing we might go on from bad to worse, get hurt in climbing over walls, caught by gamekeepers, or lost by falling over a cliff into the sea. "Play as much as you like in the back yard and garden," he said, "and mind what you'll get when you forget and disobey." Thus he warned us with an awfully stern countenance, looking very hard-hearted, while naturally his heart was far from hard, though he devoutly believed in eternal punishment for bad boys both here and hereafter. Nevertheless, like devout martyrs of wildness, we stole away to the seashore or the green, sunny fields with almost religious regularity, taking advantage of opportunities when father was very busy, to join our companions, oftenest to hear the birds sing and hunt their nests, glorying in the number we had discovered and called our own. A sample of our nest chatter was something like this: Willie Chisholm would proudly exclaim—"I ken (know) seventeen nests, and you, Johnnie, ken only fifteen."

"But I wouldna gie my fifteen for your seventeen, for five of mine are larks and mavises. You ken only three o' the best singers."

"Yes, Johnnie, but I ken six goldies and you ken only one. Maist of yours are only sparrows and linties and robin-redbreasts."

Then perhaps Bob Richardson would loudly declare that he "kenned mair nests than onybody, for he kenned twenty-three, with about fifty eggs in them and mair than fifty young birds—maybe a hundred. Some of them naething but raw gorblings but lots of them as big as their mithers and ready to flee. And aboot fifty craw's nests and three fox dens."

"Oh, yes, Bob, but that's no fair, for naebody counts craw's nests and fox holes, and then you live in the country at Belle-haven where ye have the best chance."

"Yes, but I ken a lot of bumbee's nests, baith the red-legged and the yellow-legged kind."

"Oh, wha cares for bumbee's nests!"

"Weel, but here's something! Ma father let me gang to a fox hunt, and man, it was grand to see the hounds and the lang-legged horses lowpin the dykes and burns and hedges!"

The nests, I fear, with the beautiful eggs and young birds, were prized quite as highly as the songs of the glad parents, but no Scotch boy that I know of ever failed to listen with enthusiasm to the songs of the skylarks. Oftentimes on a broad meadow near Dunbar we stood for hours enjoying their marvelous singing and soaring. From the grass where the nest was hidden the male would suddenly rise, as straight as if shot up, to a height of perhaps thirty or forty feet, and, sustaining himself with rapid wing-beats, pour down the most delicious melody, sweet and clear and strong, overflowing all bounds, then suddenly he would soar higher again and again, ever higher and higher, soaring and singing until lost to sight even on perfectly clear days, and oftentimes in cloudy weather "far in the downy cloud," as the poet says.

To test our eyes we often watched a lark until he seemed a faint speck in the sky and finally passed beyond the keenest-sighted of us all. "I see him yet!" we would cry, "I see him yet!" "I see him yet!" "I see him yet!" as he soared. And finally only one of us would be left to claim that he still saw him. At last he, too, would have to admit that the singer had soared beyond his sight, and still the music came pouring down to us in glorious profusion, from a height far above our vision, requiring marvelous power of wing and marvelous power of voice, for that rich, delicious, soft, and yet clear music was distinctly heard long after the bird was out of sight. Then, suddenly ceasing, the glorious singer would appear, falling like a bolt straight down to his nest, where his mate was sitting on the eggs.

It was far too common a practice among us to carry off a young lark just before it could fly, place it in a cage, and fondly, laboriously feed it. Sometimes we succeeded in keeping one alive for a year or two, and when awakened by the spring weather it was pitiful to see the quivering imprisoned soarer of the heavens rapidly beating its wings and singing as though it were flying and hovering in the air like its parents. To keep it in health we were taught that we must supply it with a sod of grass the size of the bottom of the cage, to make the poor bird feel as though it were at home on its native meadow,—a meadow perhaps a foot or at most two feet square. Again and again it would try to hover over that miniature meadow from its miniature sky just underneath the top of the cage. At last, conscience-stricken, we carried the beloved prisoner to the meadow west of Dunbar where it was born, and, blessing its sweet heart, bravely set it free, and our exceeding great reward was to see it fly and sing in the sky.

In the winter, when there was but little doing in the fields, we organized running-matches. A dozen or so of us would start out on races that were simply tests of endurance, running on and on along a public road over the breezy hills like hounds, without stopping or getting tired. The only serious trouble we ever felt in these long races was an occasional stitch in our sides. One of the boys started the story that sucking raw eggs was a sure cure for the stitches. We had hens in our back yard, and on the next Saturday we managed to swallow a couple of eggs apiece, a disgusting job, but we would do almost anything to mend our speed, and as soon as we could get away after taking the cure we set out on a ten or twenty mile run to prove its worth. We thought nothing of running right ahead ten or a dozen miles before turning back; for we knew nothing about taking time by the sun, and none of us had a watch in those days. Indeed, we never cared about time until it began to get dark. Then we thought of home and the thrashing that awaited us. Late or early, the thrashing was sure, unless father happened to be away. If he was expected to return soon, mother made haste to get us to bed before his arrival. We escaped the thrashing next morning, for father never felt like thrashing us in cold blood on the calm holy Sabbath. But no punishment, however sure and severe, was of any avail against the attraction of the fields and woods. It had other uses, developing memory, etc., but in keeping us at home it was of no use at all. Wildness was ever sounding in our ears, and Nature saw to it that besides school lessons and church lessons some of her own lessons should be learned, perhaps with a view to the time when we should be called to wander in wildness to our heart's content. Oh, the blessed enchantment of those Saturday runaways in the prime of the spring! How our young wondering eyes reveled in the sunny, breezy glory of the hills and the sky, every particle of us thrilling and tingling with the bees and glad birds and glad streams! Kings may be blessed; we were glorious, we were free,— school cares and scoldings, heart thrashings and flesh thrashings alike, were forgotten in the fullness of Nature's glad wildness. These were my first excursions,—the beginnings of lifelong wanderings.

II

A NEW WORLD

STORIES OF AMERICA—GLORIOUS NEWS—CROSSING
THE ATLANTIC—THE NEW HOME—A BAPTISM IN NA-
TURE—NEW BIRDS—THE ADVENTURES OF WATCH—
SCOTCH CORRECTION—MARAUDING INDIANS.

OUR grammar-school reader, called, I think, "Maccou-
lough's Course of Reading," contained a few natural-
history sketches that excited me very much and left a deep
impression, especially a fine description of the fish hawk and
the bald eagle by the Scotch ornithologist Wilson, who had
the good fortune to wander for years in the American woods
while the country was yet mostly wild. I read his description
over and over again, till I got the vivid picture he drew by
heart,—the long-winged hawk circling over the heaving
waves, every motion watched by the eagle perched on the top
of a crag or dead tree; the fish hawk poising for a moment to
take aim at a fish and plunging under the water; the eagle
with kindling eye spreading his wings ready for instant flight
in case the attack should prove successful; the hawk emerging
with a struggling fish in his talons, and proud flight; the eagle
launching himself in pursuit; the wonderful wing-work in the
sky, the fish hawk, though encumbered with his prey, circling
higher, higher, striving hard to keep above the robber eagle;
the eagle at length soaring above him, compelling him with a
cry of despair to drop his hard-won prey; then the eagle steady-
ing himself for a moment to take aim, descending swift as a
lightning-bolt, and seizing the falling fish before it reached
the sea.

Not less exciting and memorable was Audubon's wonderful
story of the passenger pigeon, a beautiful bird flying in vast
flocks that darkened the sky like clouds, countless millions
assembling to rest and sleep and rear their young in certain
forests, miles in length and breadth, fifty or a hundred nests
on a single tree; the overloaded branches bending low and
often breaking; the farmers gathering from far and near,

29

beating down countless thousands of the young and old birds from their nests and roosts with long poles at night, and in the morning driving their bands of hogs, some of them brought from farms a hundred miles distant, to fatten on the dead and wounded covering the ground.

In another of our reading-lessons some of the American forests were described. The most interesting of the trees to us boys was the sugar maple, and soon after we had learned this sweet story we heard everybody talking about the discovery of gold in the same wonder-filled country.

One night, when David and I were at grandfather's fireside solemnly learning our lessons as usual, my father came in with news, the most wonderful, most glorious, that wild boys ever heard. "Bairns," he said, "you needna learn your lessons the nicht, for we're gan to America the morn!" No more grammar, but boundless woods full of mysterious good things; trees full of sugar, growing in ground full of gold; hawks, eagles, pigeons, filling the sky; millions of birds' nests, and no gamekeepers to stop us in all the wild, happy land. We were utterly, blindly glorious. After father left the room, grandfather gave David and me a gold coin apiece for a keepsake, and looked very serious, for he was about to be deserted in his lonely old age. And when we in fullness of young joy spoke of what we were going to do, of the wonderful birds and their nests that we should find, the sugar and gold, etc., and promised to send him a big box full of that tree sugar packed in gold from the glorious paradise over the sea, poor lonely grandfather, about to be forsaken, looked with downcast eyes on the floor and said in a low, trembling, troubled voice, "Ah, poor laddies, poor laddies, you'll find something else ower the sea forbye gold and sugar, birds' nests and freedom fra lessons and schools. You'll find plenty hard, hard work." And so we did. But nothing he could say could cloud our joy or abate the fire of youthful, hopeful, fearless adventure. Nor could we in the midst of such measureless excitement see or feel the shadows and sorrows of his darkening old age. To my schoolmates, met that night on the street, I shouted the glorious news, "I'm gan to Amaraka the morn!" None could believe it. I said, "Weel, just you see if I am at the skule the morn!"

Next morning we went by rail to Glasgow and thence joyfully sailed away from beloved Scotland, flying to our fortunes on the wings of the winds, care-free as thistle seeds. We could not then know what we were leaving, what we were to encounter in the New World, nor what our gains were likely to be. We were too young and full of hope for fear or regret, but not too young to look forward with eager enthusiasm to the wonderful schoolless bookless American wilderness. Even the natural heart-pain of parting from grandfather and grandmother Gilrye, who loved us so well, and from mother and sisters and brother was quickly quenched in young joy. Father took with him only my sister Sarah (thirteen years of age), myself (eleven), and brother David (nine), leaving my eldest sister, Margaret, and the three youngest of the family, Daniel, Mary, and Anna, with mother, to join us after a farm had been found in the wilderness and a comfortable house made to receive them.

In crossing the Atlantic before the days of steamships, or even the American clippers, the voyages made in old-fashioned sailing-vessels were very long. Ours was six weeks and three days. But because we had no lessons to get, that long voyage had not a dull moment for us boys. Father and sister Sarah, with most of the old folk, stayed below in rough weather, groaning in the miseries of seasickness, many of the passengers wishing they had never ventured in "the auld rockin'creel," as they called our bluff-bowed, wave-beating ship, and, when the weather was moderately calm, singing songs in the evenings,—"The Youthful Sailor Frank and Bold," "Oh, why left I my hame, why did I cross the deep," etc. But no matter how much the old tub tossed about and battered the waves, we were on deck every day, not in the least seasick, watching the sailors at their rope-hauling and climbing work; joining in their songs, learning the names of the ropes and sails, and helping them as far as they would let us; playing games with other boys in calm weather when the deck was dry, and in stormy weather rejoicing in sympathy with the big curly-topped waves.

The captain occasionally called David and me into his cabin and asked us about our schools, handed us books to read, and seemed surprised to find that Scotch boys could read and pronounce English with perfect accent and knew so much Latin and French. In Scotch schools only pure English was taught, although not a word of English was spoken out of school. All through life, however well educated, the Scotch spoke Scotch among their own folk, except at times when unduly excited on the only two subjects on which Scotchmen get much excited, namely religion and politics. So long as the controversy went on with fairly level temper, only gude braid Scots was used, but if one became angry, as was likely to happen, then he immediately began speaking severely correct English, while his antagonist, drawing himself up, would say: "Weel, there's na use pursuing this subject ony further, for I see ye hae gotten to your English."

As we neared the shore of the great new land, with what eager wonder we watched the whales and dolphins and porpoises and seabirds, and made the good-natured sailors teach us their names and tell us stories about them!

There were quite a large number of emigrants aboard, many of them newly married couples, and the advantages of the different parts of the New World they expected to settle in were often discussed. My father started with the intention of going to the backwoods of Upper Canada. Before the end of the voyage, however, he was persuaded that the States offered superior advantages, especially Wisconsin and Michigan, where the land was said to be as good as in Canada and far more easily brought under cultivation; for in Canada the woods were so close and heavy that a man might wear out his life in getting a few acres cleared of trees and stumps. So he changed his mind and concluded to go to one of the Western States.

On our wavering westward way a grain-dealer in Buffalo told father that most of the wheat he handled came from Wisconsin; and this influential information finally determined my father's choice. At Milwaukee a farmer who had come in from the country near Fort Winnebago with a load of wheat agreed to haul us and our formidable load of stuff to a little town called Kingston for thirty dollars. On that hundred-mile journey, just after the spring thaw, the roads over the prairies were heavy and miry, causing no end of lamentation, for we often got stuck in the mud, and the poor farmer sadly declared that never, never again would he be tempted to try to haul such a cruel, heart-breaking, wagon-breaking, horse-killing load, no, not for a hundred dollars. In leaving Scotland, father, like many other home-seekers, burdened himself with far too much luggage, as if all America were still a wilderness in which little or nothing could be bought. One of his big iron-bound boxes must have weighed about four hundred pounds, for it contained an old-fashioned beam-scales with a complete set of cast-iron counterweights, two of them fifty-six pounds each, a twenty-eight, and so on down to a single pound. Also a lot of iron wedges, carpenter's tools, and so forth, and at Buffalo, as if on the very edge of the wilderness, he gladly added to his burden a big cast-iron stove with pots and pans, provisions enough for a long siege, and a scythe and cumbersome cradle for cutting wheat, all of which he succeeded in landing in the primeval Wisconsin woods.

A land-agent at Kingston gave father a note to a farmer by the name of Alexander Gray, who lived on the border of the settled part of the country, knew the section-lines, and would probably help him to find a good place for a farm. So father went away to spy out the land, and in the mean time left us children in Kingston in a rented room. It took us less than an hour to get acquainted with some of the boys in the village; we challenged them to wrestle, run races, climb trees, etc., and in a day or two we felt at home, carefree and happy, notwithstanding our family was so widely divided. When father returned he told us that he had found fine land for a farm in sunny open woods on the side of a lake, and that a team of three yoke of oxen with a big wagon was coming to haul us to Mr. Gray's place.

We enjoyed the strange ten-mile ride through the woods very much, wondering how the great oxen could be so strong and wise and tame as to pull so heavy a load with no other harness than a chain and a crooked piece of wood on their necks, and how they could sway so obediently to right and left past roadside trees and stumps when the driver said *haw* and *gee*. At Mr. Gray's house, father again left us for a few days to build a shanty on the quarter-section he had selected four or five miles to the westward. In the mean while we enjoyed our freedom as usual, wandering in the fields and meadows, looking at the trees and flowers, snakes and birds and squirrels. With the help of the nearest neighbors the little shanty was built in less than a day after the rough bur-oak logs for the walls and the white-oak boards for the floor and roof were got together.

To this charming hut, in the sunny woods, overlooking a flowery glacier meadow and a lake rimmed with white water-lilies, we were hauled by an ox-team across trackless carex swamps and low rolling hills sparsely dotted with round-headed oaks. Just as we arrived at the shanty, before we had time to look at it or the scenery about it, David and I jumped down in a hurry off the load of household goods, for we had discovered a blue jay's nest, and in a minute or so we were up the tree beside it, feasting our eyes on the beautiful green eggs and beautiful birds,—our first memorable discovery. The handsome birds had not seen Scotch boys before and made a desperate screaming as if we were robbers like themselves; though we left the eggs untouched, feeling that we were already beginning to get rich, and wondering how many more nests we should find in the grand sunny woods. Then we ran along the brow of the hill that the shanty stood on, and down to the meadow, searching the trees and grass tufts and bushes, and soon discovered a bluebird's and a woodpecker's nest, and began an acquaintance with the frogs and snakes and turtles in the creeks and springs.

This sudden plash into pure wildness—baptism in Nature's warm heart—how utterly happy it made us! Nature streaming into us, wooingly teaching her wonderful glowing lessons, so unlike the dismal grammar ashes and cinders so long thrashed into us. Here without knowing it we still were at school; every wild lesson a love lesson, not whipped but charmed into us. Oh, that glorious Wisconsin wilderness! Everything new and pure in the very prime of the spring when Nature's pulses were beating highest and mysteriously keeping time with our own! Young hearts, young leaves, flowers, animals, the winds and the streams and the sparkling lake, all wildly, gladly rejoicing together!

Next morning, when we climbed to the precious jay nest to take another admiring look at the eggs, we found it empty. Not a shell-fragment was left, and we wondered how in the

world the birds were able to carry off their thin-shelled eggs
either in their bills or in their feet without breaking them, and
how they could be kept warm while a new nest was being
built. Well, I am still asking these questions. When I was on
the Harriman Expedition I asked Robert Ridgway, the emi-
nent ornithologist, how these sudden flittings were accomplished, and he frankly confessed that he didn't know, but

Muir's Lake (Fountain Lake) and the Garden Meadow
Sketched from the roof of the Bur-Oak Shanty

guessed that jays and many other birds carried their eggs in
their mouths; and when I objected that a jay's mouth seemed
too small to hold its eggs, he replied that birds' mouths were
larger than the narrowness of their bills indicated. Then I
asked him what he thought they did with the eggs while a

new nest was being prepared. He didn't know; neither do I to this day. A specimen of the many puzzling problems presented to the naturalist.

We soon found many more nests belonging to birds that were not half so suspicious. The handsome and notorious blue jay plunders the nests of other birds and of course he could not trust us. Almost all the others—brown thrushes, bluebirds, song sparrows, kingbirds, hen-hawks, nighthawks, whip-poor-wills, woodpeckers, etc.—simply tried to avoid being seen, to draw or drive us away, or paid no attention to us.

We used to wonder how the woodpeckers could bore holes so perfectly round, true mathematical circles. We ourselves could not have done it even with gouges and chisels. We loved to watch them feeding their young, and wondered how they could glean food enough for so many clamorous, hungry, unsatisfiable babies, and how they managed to give each one its share; for after the young grew strong, one would get his head out of the door-hole and try to hold possession of it to meet the food-laden parents. How hard they worked to support their families, especially the red-headed and speckledy woodpeckers and flickers; digging, hammering on scaly bark and decaying trunks and branches from dawn to dark, coming and going at intervals of a few minutes all the livelong day!

We discovered a hen-hawk's nest on the top of a tall oak thirty or forty rods from the shanty and approached it cautiously. One of the pair always kept watch, soaring in wide circles high above the tree, and when we attempted to climb it, the big dangerous-looking bird came swooping down at us and drove us away.

We greatly admired the plucky kingbird. In Scotland our great ambition was to be good fighters, and we admired this quality in the handsome little chattering flycatcher that whips all the other birds. He was particularly angry when plundering jays and hawks came near his home, and took pains to thrash them not only away from the nest-tree but out of the neighborhood. The nest was usually built on a bur oak near a meadow where insects were abundant, and where no undesirable visitor could approach without being discovered. When a hen-hawk hove in sight, the male immediately set off after him, and it was ridiculous to see that great, strong bird hurrying away as fast as his clumsy wings would carry him, as soon as he saw the little, waspish kingbird coming. But the kingbird easily overtook him, flew just a few feet above him, and with a lot of chattering, scolding notes kept diving and striking him on the back of the head until tired; then he alighted to rest on the hawk's broad shoulders, still scolding and chattering as he rode along, like an angry boy pouring out vials of wrath. Then, up and at him again with his sharp bill; and after he had thus driven and ridden his big enemy a mile or so from the nest, he went home to his mate, chuckling and bragging as if trying to tell her what a wonderful fellow he was.

This first spring, while some of the birds were still building their nests and very few young ones had yet tried to fly, father hired a Yankee to assist in clearing eight or ten acres of the best ground for a field. We found new wonders every day and often had to call on this Yankee to solve puzzling questions. We asked him one day if there was any bird in America that the kingbird couldn't whip. What about the sandhill crane? Could he whip that long-legged, long-billed fellow?

"A crane never goes near kingbirds' nests or notices so small a bird," he said, "and therefore there could be no fighting between them." So we hastily concluded that our hero could whip every bird in the country except perhaps the sandhill crane.

We never tired listening to the wonderful whip-poor-will. One came every night about dusk and sat on a log about twenty or thirty feet from our cabin door and began shouting "Whip poor Will! Whip poor Will!" with loud emphatic earnestness. "What's that? What's that?" we cried when this startling visitor first announced himself. "What do you call it?"

"Why, it's telling you its name," said the Yankee. "Don't you hear it and what he wants you to do? He says his name is 'Poor Will' and he wants you to whip him, and you may if you are able to catch him." Poor Will seemed the most wonderful of all the strange creatures we had seen. What a wild, strong, bold voice he had, unlike any other we had ever heard on sea or land!

A near relative, the bull-bat, or nighthawk, seemed hardly less wonderful. Towards evening scattered flocks kept the sky lively as they circled around on their long wings a hundred feet or more above the ground, hunting moths and beetles, interrupting their rather slow but strong, regular wing-beats at short intervals with quick quivering strokes while uttering keen, squeaky cries something like *pfee, pfee*, and every now and then diving nearly to the ground with a loud ripping, bellowing sound, like bull-roaring, suggesting its name; then turning and gliding swiftly up again. These fine wild gray birds, about the size of a pigeon, lay their two eggs on bare ground without anything like a nest or even a concealing bush or grass-tuft. Nevertheless they are not easily seen, for they are colored like the ground. While sitting on their eggs, they depend so much upon not being noticed that if you are walking rapidly ahead they allow you to step within an inch or two of them without flinching. But if they see by your looks that you have discovered them, they leave their eggs or young, and, like a good many other birds, pretend that they are sorely wounded, fluttering and rolling over on the ground and gasping as if dying, to draw you away. When pursued we were surprised to find that just when we were on the point of overtaking them they were always able to flutter a few yards farther, until they had led us about a quarter of a mile from the nest; then, suddenly getting well, they quietly flew home by a roundabout way to their precious babies or eggs, o'er a' the ills of life victorious, bad boys among the worst. The Yankee took particular pleasure in encouraging us to pursue them.

Everything about us was so novel and wonderful that we could hardly believe our senses except when hungry or while father was thrashing us. When we first saw Fountain Lake Meadow, on a sultry evening, sprinkled with millions of lightning-bugs throbbing with light, the effect was so strange and beautiful that it seemed far too marvelous to be real. Looking from our shanty on the hill, I thought that the whole wonderful fairy show must be in my eyes; for only in fighting, when my eyes were struck, had I ever seen anything in the least like it. But when I asked my brother if he saw anything strange in the meadow he said, "Yes, it's all covered with shaky fire-sparks." Then I guessed that it might be something outside of us, and applied to our all-knowing Yankee to explain it. "Oh, it's nothing but lightnin'-bugs," he said, and kindly led us down the hill to the edge of the fiery meadow, caught a few of the wonderful bugs, dropped them into a cup, and carried them to the shanty, where we watched them throbbing and flashing out their mysterious light at regular intervals, as if each little passionate glow were caused by the beating of a heart. Once I saw a splendid display of glow-worm light in the foothills of the Himalayas, north of Calcutta, but glorious as it appeared in pure starry radiance, it was far less impressive than the extravagant abounding, quivering, dancing fire on our Wisconsin meadow.

Partridge drumming was another great marvel. When I first heard the low, soft, solemn sound I thought it must be made by some strange disturbance in my head or stomach, but as all seemed serene within, I asked David whether he heard anything queer. "Yes," he said, "I hear something saying *boomp, boomp, boomp,* and I'm wondering at it." Then I was half satisfied that the source of the mysterious sound must be in something outside of us, coming perhaps from the ground or from some ghost or bogie or woodland fairy. Only after long watching and listening did we at last discover it in the wings of the plump brown bird.

The love-song of the common jack snipe seemed not a whit less mysterious than partridge drumming. It was usually heard on cloudy evenings, a strange, unearthly, winnowing, spiritlike sound, yet easily heard at a distance of a third of a mile. Our sharp eyes soon detected the bird while making it, as it circled high in the air over the meadow with wonderfully strong and rapid wing-beats, suddenly descending and rising, again and again, in deep, wide loops; the tones being very low and smooth at the beginning of the descent, rapidly increasing to a curious little whirling storm-roar at the bottom, and gradually fading lower and lower until the top was reached. It was long, however, before we identified this mysterious wing-singer as the little brown jack snipe that we knew so well and had so often watched as he silently probed the mud around the edges of our meadow stream and spring-holes, and made short zigzag flights over the grass uttering only little short, crisp quacks and chucks.

The love-songs of the frogs seemed hardly less wonderful than those of the birds, their musical notes varying from the

sweet, tranquil, soothing peeping and purring of the hylas to
the awfully deep low-bass blunt bellowing of the bullfrogs.
Some of the smaller species have wonderfully clear, sharp
voices and told us their good Bible names in musical tones
about as plainly as the whip-poor-will. *Isaac, Isaac; Yacob, Yacob; Israel, Israel;* shouted in sharp, ringing, far-reaching
tones, as if they had all been to school and severely drilled in
elocution. In the still, warm evenings, big bunchy bullfrogs
bellowed, *Drunk! Drunk! Drunk! Jug o' rum! Jug o' rum!*
and early in the spring, countless thousands of the commonest
species, up to the throat in cold water, sang in concert, making a mass of music, such as it was, loud enough to be heard
at a distance of more than half a mile.

Far, far apart from this loud marsh music is that of the many
species of hyla, a sort of soothing immortal melody filling the
air like light.

We reveled in the glory of the sky scenery as well as that of
the woods and meadows and rushy, lily-bordered lakes. The
great thunderstorms in particular interested us, so unlike any
seen in Scotland, exciting awful, wondering admiration. Gazing awe-stricken, we watched the upbuilding of the sublime
cloud-mountains,—glowing, sun-beaten pearl and alabaster
cumuli, glorious in beauty and majesty and looking so firm
and lasting that birds, we thought, might build their nests
amid their downy bosses; the black-browed storm-clouds
marching in awful grandeur across the landscape, trailing
broad gray sheets of hail and rain like vast cataracts, and ever
and anon flashing down vivid zigzag lightning followed by
terrible crashing thunder. We saw several trees shattered, and
one of them, a punky old oak, was set on fire, while we wondered why all the trees and everybody and everything did not
share the same fate, for oftentimes the whole sky blazed. After
sultry storm days, many of the nights were darkened by
smooth black apparently structureless cloud-mantles which at
short intervals were illumined with startling suddenness to a
fiery glow by quick, quivering lightning-flashes, revealing the
landscape in almost noonday brightness, to be instantly
quenched in solid blackness.

But those first days and weeks of unmixed enjoyment and
freedom, reveling in the wonderful wildness about us, were

soon to be mingled with the hard work of making a farm. I was first put to burning brush in clearing land for the plough. Those magnificent brush fires with great white hearts and red flames, the first big, wild outdoor fires I had ever seen, were wonderful sights for young eyes. Again and again, when they were burning fiercest so that we could hardly approach near enough to throw on another branch, father put them to awfully practical use as warning lessons, comparing their heat with that of hell, and the branches with bad boys. "Now, John," he would say,—"now, John, just think what an awful thing it would be to be thrown into that fire:—and then think of hellfire, that is so many times hotter. Into that fire all bad boys, with sinners of every sort who disobey God, will be cast as we are casting branches into this brush fire, and although suffering so much, their sufferings will never never end, because neither the fire nor the sinners can die." But those terrible fire lessons quickly faded away in the blithe wilderness air; for no fire can be hotter than the heavenly fire of faith and hope that burns in every healthy boy's heart.

Soon after our arrival in the woods some one added a cat and puppy to the animals father had bought. The cat soon had kittens, and it was interesting to watch her feeding, protecting, and training them. After they were able to leave their nest and play, she went out hunting and brought in many kinds of birds and squirrels for them, mostly ground squirrels (spermophiles), called "gophers" in Wisconsin. When she got within a dozen yards or so of the shanty, she announced her approach by a peculiar call, and the sleeping kittens immediately bounced up and ran to meet her, all racing for the first bite of they knew not what, and we too ran to see what she brought. She then lay down a few minutes to rest and enjoy the enjoyment of her feasting family, and again vanished in the grass and flowers, coming and going every half-hour or so. Sometimes she brought in birds that we had never seen before, and occasionally a flying squirrel, chipmunk, or big fox squirrel. We were just old enough, David and I, to regard all these creatures as wonders, the strange inhabitants of our new world.

The pup was a common cur, though very uncommon to us, a black and white short-haired mongrel that we named

"Watch." We always gave him a pan of milk in the evening just before we knelt in family worship, while daylight still lingered in the shanty. And, instead of attending to the prayers, I too often studied the small wild creatures playing around us. Field mice scampered about the cabin as though it had been built for them alone, and their performances were very amusing. About dusk, on one of the calm, sultry nights so grateful to moths and beetles, when the puppy was lapping his milk, and we were on our knees, in through the door came a heavy broad-shouldered beetle about as big as a mouse, and after it had droned and boomed round the cabin two or three times, the pan of milk, showing white in the gloaming, caught its eyes, and, taking good aim, it alighted with a slanting, glinting plash in the middle of the pan like a duck alighting in a lake. Baby Watch, having never before seen anything like that beetle, started back, gazing in dumb astonishment and fear at the black sprawling monster trying to swim. Recovering somewhat from his fright, he began to bark at the creature, and ran round and round his milk-pan, wouf-woufing, gurring, growling, like an old dog barking at a wild-cat or a bear. The natural astonishment and curiosity of that boy dog getting his first entomological lesson in this wonderful world was so immoderately funny that I had great difficulty in keeping from laughing out loud.

Snapping turtles were common throughout the woods, and we were delighted to find that they would snap at a stick and hang on like bull-dogs; and we amused ourselves by introducing Watch to them, enjoying his curious behavior and theirs in getting acquainted with each other. One day we assisted one of the smallest of the turtles to get a good grip of poor Watch's ear. Then away he rushed, holding his head sidewise, yelping and terror-stricken, with the strange buglike reptile biting hard and clinging fast,—a shameful amusement even for wild boys.

As a playmate Watch was too serious, though he learned more than any stranger would judge him capable of, was a bold, faithful watch-dog, and in his prime a grand fighter, able to whip all the other dogs in the neighborhood. Comparing him with ourselves, we soon learned that although he could not read books he could read faces, was a good judge of character, always knew what was going on and what we were about to do, and liked to help us. We could run nearly as fast as he could, see about as far, and perhaps hear as well, but in sense of smell his nose was incomparably better than ours. One sharp winter morning when the ground was covered with snow, I noticed that when he was yawning and stretching himself after leaving his bed he suddenly caught the scent of something that excited him, went round the corner of the house, and looked intently to the westward across a tongue of land that we called West Bank, eagerly questioning the air with quivering nostrils, and bristling up as though he felt sure that there was something dangerous in that direction and had actually caught sight of it. Then he ran toward the Bank, and I followed him, curious to see what his nose had discovered. The top of the Bank commanded a view of the north end of our lake and meadow, and when we got there we saw an Indian hunter with a long spear, going from one muskrat cabin to another, approaching cautiously, careful to make no noise, and then suddenly thrusting his spear down through the house. If well aimed, the spear went through the poor beaver rat as it lay cuddled up in the snug nest it had made for itself in the fall with so much far-seeing care, and when the hunter felt the spear quivering, he dug down the mossy hut with his tomahawk and secured his prey,—the flesh for food, and the skin to sell for a dime or so. This was a clear object lesson on dogs' keenness of scent. That Indian was more than half a mile away across a wooded ridge. Had the hunter been a white man, I suppose Watch would not have noticed him.

When he was about six or seven years old, he not only became cross, so that he would do only what he liked, but he fell on evil ways, and was accused by the neighbors who had settled around us of catching and devouring whole broods of chickens, some of them only a day or two out of the shell. We never imagined he would do anything so grossly undoglike. He never did at home. But several of the neighbors declared over and over again that they had caught him in the act, and insisted that he must be shot. At last, in spite of tearful protests, he was condemned and executed. Father examined the poor fellow's stomach in search of sure evidence, and discovered the heads of eight chickens that he had de-

voured at his last meal. So poor Watch was killed simply because his taste for chickens was too much like our own. Think
of the millions of squabs that preaching, praying men and
women kill and eat, with all sorts of other animals great and
small, young and old, while eloquently discoursing on the
coming of the blessed peaceful, bloodless millennium! Think
of the passenger pigeons that fifty or sixty years ago filled the
woods and sky over half the continent, now exterminated by
beating down the young from the nests together with the
brooding parents, before they could try their wonderful
wings; by trapping them in nets, feeding them to hogs, etc.
None of our fellow mortals is safe who eats what we eat, who
in any way interferes with our pleasures, or who may be used
for work or food, clothing or ornament, or mere cruel, sport-
ish amusement. Fortunately many are too small to be seen,
and therefore enjoy life beyond our reach. And in looking
through God's great stone books made up of records reaching
back millions and millions of years, it is a great comfort to
learn that vast multitudes of creatures, great and small and
infinite in number, lived and had a good time in God's love
before man was created.

The old Scotch fashion of whipping for every act of dis-
obedience or of simple, playful forgetfulness was still kept up
in the wilderness, and of course many of those whippings fell
upon me. Most of them were outrageously severe, and utterly
barren of fun. But here is one that was nearly all fun.

Father was busy hauling lumber for the frame house that
was to be got ready for the arrival of my mother, sisters, and
brother, left behind in Scotland. One morning, when he was
ready to start for another load, his ox-whip was not to be
found. He asked me if I knew anything about it. I told him
I didn't know where it was, but Scotch conscience compelled
me to confess that when I was playing with it I had tied it to
Watch's tail, and that he ran away, dragging it through the
grass, and came back without it. "It must have slipped off his
tail," I said, and so I didn't know where it was. This honest,
straightforward little story made father so angry that he exclaimed with heavy, foreboding emphasis: "The very deevil's
in that boy!" David, who had been playing with me and was
perhaps about as responsible for the loss of the whip as I was,

said never a word, for he was always prudent enough to hold his tongue when the parental weather was stormy, and so escaped nearly all punishment. And, strange to say, this time I also escaped, all except a terrible scolding, though the thrashing weather seemed darker than ever. As if unwilling to let the sun see the shameful job, father took me into the cabin where the storm was to fall, and sent David to the woods for a switch. While he was out selecting the switch, father put in the spare time sketching my play-wickedness in awful colors, and of course referred again and again to the place prepared for bad boys. In the midst of this terrible word-storm, dreading most the impending thrashing, I whimpered that I was only playing because I couldn't help it; didn't know I was doing wrong; wouldn't do it again, and so forth. After this miserable dialogue was about exhausted, father became impatient at my brother for taking so long to find the switch; and so was I, for I wanted to have the thing over and done with. At last, in came David, a picture of open-hearted innocence, solemnly dragging a young bur-oak sapling, and handed the end of it to father, saying it was the best switch he could find. It was an awfully heavy one, about two and a half inches thick at the butt and ten feet long, almost big enough for a fence-pole. There wasn't room enough in the cabin to swing it, and the moment I saw it I burst out laughing in the midst of my fears. But father failed to see the fun and was very angry at David, heaved the bur-oak outside and passionately demanded his reason for fetching "sic a muckle rail like that instead o' a switch? Do ye ca' that a switch? I have a gude mind to thrash you instead o' John." David, with demure, downcast eyes, looked preternaturally righteous, but as usual prudently answered never a word.

It was a hard job in those days to bring up Scotch boys in the way they should go; and poor overworked father was determined to do it if enough of the right kind of switches could be found. But this time, as the sun was getting high, he hitched up old Tom and Jerry and made haste to the Kingston lumber-yard, leaving me unscathed and as innocently wicked as ever; for hardly had father got fairly out of sight among the oaks and hickories, ere all our troubles, hell-threatenings, and exhortations were forgotten in the fun we had lassoing a stubborn old sow and laboriously trying to teach her to go reasonably steady in rope harness. She was the first hog that father bought to stock the farm, and we boys regarded her as a very wonderful beast. In a few weeks she had a lot of pigs, and of all the queer, funny, animal children we had yet seen, none amused us more. They were so comic in size and shape, in their gait and gestures, their merry sham fights, and the false alarms they got up for the fun of scampering back to their mother and begging her in most persuasive little squeals to lie down and give them a drink.

After her darling short-snouted babies were about a month old, she took them out to the woods and gradually roamed farther and farther from the shanty in search of acorns and roots. One afternoon we heard a rifle-shot, a very noticeable thing, as we had no near neighbors, as yet. We thought it must have been fired by an Indian on the trail that followed the right bank of the Fox River between Portage and Packwaukee Lake and passed our shanty at a distance of about three quarters of a mile. Just a few minutes after that shot was heard, along came the poor mother rushing up to the shanty for protection, with her pigs, all out of breath and terror-stricken. One of them was missing, and we supposed of course that an Indian had shot it for food. Next day, I discovered a blood-puddle where the Indian trail crossed the outlet of our lake. One of father's hired men told us that the Indians thought nothing of levying this sort of blackmail whenever they were hungry. The solemn awe and fear in the eyes of that old mother and those little pigs I never can forget; it was as unmistakable and deadly a fear as I ever saw expressed by any human eye, and corroborates in no uncertain way the oneness of all of us.

III

LIFE ON A WISCONSIN FARM

HUMANITY IN OXEN—JACK, THE PONY—LEARNING
TO RIDE—NOB AND NELL—SNAKES—MOSQUITOES
AND THEIR KIN—FISH AND FISHING—CONSIDER-
ING THE LILIES—LEARNING TO SWIM—A NARROW
ESCAPE FROM DROWNING AND A VICTORY—
ACCIDENTS TO ANIMALS.

COMING direct from school in Scotland while we were still hopefully ignorant and far from tame,—notwithstanding the unnatural profusion of teaching and thrashing lavished upon us,—getting acquainted with the animals about us was a never-failing source of wonder and delight. At first my father, like nearly all the backwoods settlers, bought a yoke of oxen to do the farm work, and as field after field was cleared, the number was gradually increased until we had five yoke. These wise, patient, plodding animals did all the ploughing, logging, hauling, and hard work of every sort for the first four or five years, and, never having seen oxen before, we looked at them with the same eager freshness of conception as we did at the wild animals. We worked with them, sympathized with them in their rest and toil and play, and thus learned to know them far better than we should had we been only trained scientific naturalists. We soon learned that each ox and cow and calf had individual character. Old white-faced Buck, one of the second yoke of oxen we owned, was a notably sagacious fellow. He seemed to reason sometimes almost like ourselves. In the fall we fed the cattle lots of pumpkins and had to split them open so that mouthfuls could be readily broken off. But Buck never waited for us to come to his help. The others, when they were hungry and impatient, tried to break through the hard rind with their teeth, but seldom with success if the pumpkin was full grown. Buck never wasted time in this mumbling, slavering way, but crushed them with his head. He went to the pile, picked out a good one, like a boy choosing an orange or apple, rolled it down on to the open ground, deliberately kneeled in front of it, placed his broad, flat brow on top of it, brought his weight hard down and crushed it, then quietly arose and went on with his meal in comfort. Some would call this "instinct," as if so-called "blind instinct" must necessarily make an ox stand on its head to break pumpkins when its teeth got sore, or when nobody came with an axe to split them. Another fine ox showed his skill when hungry by opening all the fences that stood in his way to the corn-fields.

The humanity we found in them came partly through the expression of their eyes when tired, their tones of voice when hungry and calling for food, their patient plodding and pulling in hot weather, their long-drawn-out sighing breath when exhausted and suffering like ourselves, and their enjoyment of rest with the same grateful looks as ours. We recognized their kinship also by their yawning like ourselves when sleepy and evidently enjoying the same peculiar pleasure at the roots of their jaws; by the way they stretched themselves in the morning after a good rest; by learning languages,—Scotch, English, Irish, French, Dutch,—a smattering of each as required in the faithful service they so willingly, wisely rendered; by their intelligent, alert curiosity, manifested in listening to strange sounds; their love of play; the attachments they made; and their mourning, long continued, when a companion was killed.

When we went to Portage, our nearest town, about ten or twelve miles from the farm, it would oftentimes be late before we got back, and in the summer-time, in sultry, rainy weather, the clouds were full of sheet lightning which every minute or two would suddenly illumine the landscape, revealing all its features, the hills and valleys, meadows and trees, about as fully and clearly as the noonday sunshine; then as suddenly the glorious light would be quenched, making the darkness seem denser than before. On such nights the cattle had to find the way home without any help from us, but they never got off the track, for they followed it by scent like dogs. Once, father, returning late from Portage or Kingston, compelled Tom and Jerry, our first oxen, to leave the dim track, imagining they must be going wrong. At last they stopped and refused to go farther. Then father unhitched them from the wagon, took hold of Tom's tail, and was thus led straight to the shanty. Next morning he set out to seek his wagon and found it on the brow of a steep hill above an impassable swamp. We learned less from the cows, because we did not enter so far into their lives, working with them, suffering heat and cold, hunger and thirst, and almost deadly weariness with them; but none with natural charity could fail to sympathize with them in their love for their calves, and to feel that it in no way differed from the divine mother-love of a woman in thoughtful, self-sacrificing care; for they would brave every danger, giving their lives for their offspring. Nor could we fail to sympathize with their awkward, blunt-nosed baby calves, with such beautiful, wondering eyes looking out on the world and slowly getting acquainted with things, all so strange to them, and awkwardly learning to use their legs, and play and fight.

Before leaving Scotland, father promised us a pony to ride when we got to America, and we saw to it that this promise was not forgotten. Only a week or two after our arrival in the woods he bought us a little Indian pony for thirteen dollars from a store-keeper in Kingston who had obtained him from a Winnebago or Menominee Indian in trade for goods. He was a stout handsome bay with long black mane and tail, and, though he was only two years old, the Indians had already taught him to carry all sorts of burdens, to stand without being tied, to go anywhere over all sorts of ground fast or slow, and to jump and swim and fear nothing,—a truly wonderful creature, strangely different from shy, skittish, nervous, superstitious civilized beasts. We turned him loose, and, strange to say, he never ran away from us or refused to be caught, but behaved as if he had known Scotch boys all his life; probably because we were about as wild as young Indians.

One day when father happened to have a little leisure, he said, "Noo, bairns, rin doon the meadow and get your powny and learn to ride him." So we led him out to a smooth place near an Indian mound back of the shanty, where father directed us to begin. I mounted for the first memorable lesson, crossed the mound, and set out at a slow walk along the wagon-track made in hauling lumber; then father shouted: "Whup him up, John, whup him up! Make him gallop; gallopin' is easier and better than walkin' or trottin'." Jack was willing, and away he sped at a good fast gallop. I managed to keep my balance fairly well by holding fast to the mane, but could not keep from bumping up and down, for I was plump and elastic and so was Jack; therefore about half of the time I was in the air.

After a quarter of a mile or so of this curious transportation, I cried, "Whoa, Jack!" The wonderful creature seemed to understand Scotch, for he stopped so suddenly I flew over his head, but he stood perfectly still as if that flying method of dismounting were the regular way. Jumping on again, I bumped and bobbed back along the grassy, flowery track, over the Indian mound, cried, "Whoa, Jack!" flew over his head, and alighted in father's arms as gracefully as if it were all intended for circus work.

After going over the course five or six times in the same free, picturesque style, I gave place to brother David, whose performances were much like my own. In a few weeks, however, or a month, we were taking adventurous rides more than a mile long out to a big meadow frequented by sandhill cranes, and returning safely with wonderful stories of the great long-legged birds we had seen, and how on the whole journey away and back we had fallen off only five or six times. Gradually we learned to gallop through the woods without roads of any sort, bareback and without rope or bridle, guiding only by leaning from side to side or by slight knee pressure. In this free way we used to amuse ourselves, riding at full speed across a big "kettle" that was on our farm, without holding on by either mane or tail.

These so-called "kettles" were formed by the melting of large detached blocks of ice that had been buried in moraine material thousands of years ago when the ice-sheet that covered all this region was receding. As the buried ice melted, of course the moraine material above and about it fell in, forming hopper-shaped hollows, while the grass growing on their sides and around them prevented the rain and wind from filling them up. The one we performed in was perhaps seventy or eighty feet wide and twenty or thirty feet deep; and without a saddle or hold of any kind it was not easy to keep from slipping over Jack's head in diving into it, or over his tail climbing out. This was fine sport on the long summer Sundays when we were able to steal away before meeting-time without being seen. We got very warm and red at it, and oftentimes poor Jack, dripping with sweat like his riders, seemed to have been boiled in that kettle.

In Scotland we had often been admonished to be bold, and this advice we passed on to Jack, who had already got many a wild lesson from Indian boys. Once, when teaching him to jump muddy streams, I made him try the creek in our meadow at a place where it is about twelve feet wide. He jumped bravely enough, but came down with a grand splash hardly more than halfway over. The water was only about a foot in depth, but the black vegetable mud half afloat was unfathomable. I managed to wallow ashore, but poor Jack sank deeper and deeper until only his head was visible in the black abyss, and his Indian fortitude was desperately tried. His foundering so suddenly in the treacherous gulf recalled the story of the Abbot of Aberbrothok's bell, which went down with a gurgling sound while bubbles rose and burst around. I had to go to father for help. He tied a long hemp rope brought from Scotland around Jack's neck, and Tom and Jerry seemed to have all they could do to pull him out. After which I got a solemn scolding for asking the "puir beast to jump intil sic a saft bottomless place."

We moved into our frame house in the fall, when mother with the rest of the family arrived from Scotland, and, when the winter snow began to fly, the bur-oak shanty was made into a stable for Jack. Father told us that good meadow hay was all he required, but we fed him corn, lots of it, and he grew very frisky and fat. About the middle of winter his long hair was full of dust and, as we thought, required washing. So, without taking the frosty weather into account, we gave him a thorough soap and water scouring, and as we failed to get him rubbed dry, a row of icicles formed under his belly. Father happened to see him in this condition and angrily asked what we had been about. We said Jack was dirty and we had washed him to make him healthy. He told us we ought to be ashamed of ourselves, "soaking the puir beast in cauld water at this time o' year"; that when we wanted to clean him we should have sense enough to use the brush and curry-comb.

In summer Dave or I had to ride after the cows every evening about sundown, and Jack got so accustomed to bringing in the drove that when we happened to be a few minutes late he used to go off alone at the regular time and bring them

Our First Wisconsin Home
On the hill near the shanty built in the summer of 1849

home at a gallop. It used to make father very angry to see Jack chasing the cows like a shepherd dog, running from one to the other and giving each a bite on the rump to keep them on the run, flying before him as if pursued by wolves. Father would declare at times that the wicked beast had the deevil in him and would be the death of the cattle. The corral and barn were just at the foot of a hill, and he made a great display of the drove on the home stretch as they walloped down that hill with their tails on end.

One evening when the pell-mell Wild West show was at its wildest, it made father so extravagantly mad that he ordered me to "Shoot Jack!" I went to the house and brought the gun, suffering most horrible mental anguish, such as I suppose unhappy Abraham felt when commanded to slay Isaac. Jack's life was spared, however, though I can't tell what finally became of him. I wish I could. After father bought a span of work horses he was sold to a man who said he was going to ride him across the plains to California. We had him, I think, some five or six years. He was the stoutest, gentlest, bravest little horse I ever saw. He never seemed tired, could canter all day with a man about as heavy as himself on his back, and feared nothing. Once fifty or sixty pounds of beef that was tied on his back slid over his shoulders along his neck and weighed down his head to the ground, fairly anchoring him; but he stood patient and still for half an hour or so without making the slightest struggle to free himself, while I was away getting help to untie the pack-rope and set the load back in its place.

As I was the eldest boy I had the care of our first span of work horses. Their names were Nob and Nell. Nob was very intelligent, and even affectionate, and could learn almost anything. Nell was entirely different; balky and stubborn, though we managed to teach her a good many circus tricks; but she never seemed to like to play with us in anything like an affectionate way as Nob did. We turned them out one day into the pasture, and an Indian, hiding in the brush that had sprung up after the grass fires had been kept out, managed to catch Nob, tied a rope to her jaw for a bridle, rode her to Green Lake, about thirty or forty miles away, and tried to sell her for fifteen dollars. All our hearts were sore, as if one of the family had been lost. We hunted everywhere and could not at first imagine what had become of her. We discovered her track where the fence was broken down, and, following it for a few miles, made sure the track was Nob's; and a neighbor told us he had seen an Indian riding fast through the woods on a horse that looked like Nob. But we could find no farther trace of her until a month or two after she was lost, and we had given up hope of ever seeing her again. Then we learned that she had been taken from an Indian by a farmer at Green Lake because he saw that she had been shod and had worked in harness. So when the Indian tried to sell her the farmer said: "You are a thief. That is a white man's horse. You stole her."

"No," said the Indian, "I brought her from Prairie du Chien and she has always been mine."

The man, pointing to her feet and the marks of the harness, said: "You are lying. I will take that horse away from you and put her in my pasture, and if you come near it I will set the dogs on you." Then he advertised her. One of our neighbors happened to see the advertisement and brought us the glad news, and great was our rejoicing when father brought her home. That Indian must have treated her with terrible cruelty, for when I was riding her through the pasture several years afterward, looking for another horse that we wanted to catch, as we approached the place where she had been captured she stood stock still gazing through the bushes, fearing the Indian might still be hiding there ready to spring; and she was so excited that she trembled, and her heartbeats were so loud that I could hear them distinctly as I sat on her back, *boomp*, *boomp*, *boomp*, like the drumming of a partridge. So vividly had she remembered her terrible experiences.

She was a great pet and favorite with the whole family, quickly learned playful tricks, came running when we called, seemed to know everything we said to her, and had the utmost confidence in our friendly kindness.

We used to cut and shock and husk the Indian corn in the fall, until a keen Yankee stopped overnight at our house and among other labor-saving notions convinced father that it was better to let it stand, and husk it at his leisure during the winter, then turn in the cattle to eat the leaves and trample down the stalks, so that they could be ploughed under in the spring. In this winter method each of us took two rows and husked into baskets, and emptied the corn on the ground in piles of fifteen to twenty basketfuls, then loaded it into the wagon to be hauled to the crib. This was cold, painful work, the temperature being oftentimes far below zero and the ground covered with dry, frosty snow, giving rise to miserable crops of chilblains and frosted fingers,—a sad change from the merry Indian-summer husking, when the big yellow pumpkins covered the cleared fields;—golden corn, golden pumpkins, gathered in the hazy golden weather. Sad change, indeed, but we occasionally got some fun out of the nipping, shivery work from hungry prairie chickens, and squirrels and mice that came about us.

The piles of corn were often left in the field several days, and while loading them into the wagon we usually found field mice in them,—big, blunt-nosed, strong-scented fellows that we were taught to kill just because they nibbled a few grains of corn. I used to hold one while it was still warm, up to Nob's nose for the fun of seeing her make faces and snort at the smell of it; and I would say: "Here, Nob," as if offering her a lump of sugar. One day I offered her an extra fine, fat, plump specimen, something like a little woodchuck, or musk-rat, and to my astonishment, after smelling it curiously and doubtfully, as if wondering what the gift might be, and rubbing it back and forth in the palm of my hand with her upper lip, she deliberately took it into her mouth, crunched and munched and chewed it fine and swallowed it, bones, teeth, head, tail, everything. Not a single hair of that mouse was wasted. When she was chewing it she nodded and grunted, as though critically tasting and relishing it.

My father was a steadfast enthusiast on religious matters, and, of course, attended almost every sort of church-meeting, especially revival meetings. They were occasionally held in summer, but mostly in winter when the sleighing was good and plenty of time available. One hot summer day father drove Nob to Portage and back, twenty-four miles over a sandy road. It was a hot, hard, sultry day's work, and she had evidently been over-driven in order to get home in time for one of these meetings. I shall never forget how tired and wilted she looked that evening when I unhitched her; how she drooped in her stall, too tired to eat or even to lie down. Next morning it was plain that her lungs were inflamed; all the dreadful symptoms were just the same as my own when I had pneumonia. Father sent for a Methodist minister, a very energetic, resourceful man, who was a blacksmith, farmer, butcher, and horse-doctor as well as minister; but all his gifts and skill were of no avail. Nob was doomed. We bathed her head and tried to get her to eat something, but she couldn't eat, and in about a couple of weeks we turned her loose to let her come around the house and see us in the weary suffering and loneliness of the shadow of death. She tried to follow us children, so long her friends and workmates and playmates. It was awfully touching. She had several hemorrhages, and in the forenoon of her last day, after she had had one of her dreadful spells of bleeding and gasping for breath, she came to me trembling, with beseeching, heartbreaking looks, and after I had bathed her head and tried to soothe and pet her, she lay down and gasped and died. All the family gathered about her, weeping, with aching hearts. Then dust to dust.

She was the most faithful, intelligent, playful, affectionate, human-like horse I ever knew, and she won all our hearts. Of the many advantages of farm life for boys one of the greatest is the gaining a real knowledge of animals as fellow-mortals, learning to respect them and love them, and even to win some of their love. Thus godlike sympathy grows and thrives and spreads far beyond the teachings of churches and schools, where too often the mean, blinding, loveless doctrine is taught that animals have neither mind nor soul, have no rights that we are bound to respect, and were made only for man, to be petted, spoiled, slaughtered, or enslaved.

At first we were afraid of snakes, but soon learned that most of them were harmless. The only venomous species seen on our farm were the rattlesnake and the copperhead, one of each. David saw the rattler, and we both saw the copperhead. One day, when my brother came in from his work, he reported that he had seen a snake that made a queer buzzy noise with its tail. This was the only rattlesnake seen on our farm, though we heard of them being common on limestone hills eight or ten miles distant. We discovered the copperhead when we were ploughing, and we saw and felt at the first long, fixed, half-charmed, admiring stare at him that he was an awfully dangerous fellow. Every fibre of his strong, lithe, quivering body, his burnished copper-colored head, and above all his fierce, able eyes, seemed to be overflowing full of deadly power, and bade us beware. And yet it is only fair to say that this terrible, beautiful reptile showed no disposition to hurt us until we threw clods at him and tried to head him off from a log fence into which he was trying to escape. We were barefooted and of course afraid to let him get very near, while we vainly battered him with the loose sandy clods of the freshly ploughed field to hold him back until we could get a stick. Looking us in the eyes after a moment's pause, he probably saw we were afraid, and he came right straight at us, snapping and looking terrible, drove us out of his way, and won his fight.

Out on the open sandy hills there were a good many thick burly blow snakes, the kind that puff themselves up and hiss. Our Yankee declared that their breath was very poisonous and that we must not go near them. A handsome ringed species common in damp, shady places was, he told us, the most wonderful of all the snakes, for if chopped into pieces, however small, the fragments would wriggle themselves together again, and the restored snake would go on about its business as if nothing had happened. The commonest kinds were the striped slender species of the meadows and streams, good swimmers, that lived mostly on frogs.

Once I observed one of the larger ones, about two feet long, pursuing a frog in our meadow, and it was wonderful to see how fast the legless, footless, wingless, finless hunter could run. The frog, of course, knew its enemy and was making desperate efforts to escape to the water and hide in the marsh mud. He was a fine, sleek yellow muscular fellow and was springing over the tall grass in wide-arching jumps. The green-striped snake, gliding swiftly and steadily, was keeping the frog in sight and, had I not interfered, would probably have tired out the poor jumper. Then, perhaps, while digesting and enjoying his meal, the happy snake would himself be swallowed frog and all by a hawk. Again, to our astonishment, the small specimens were attacked by our hens. They pursued and pecked away at them until they killed and devoured them, oftentimes quarreling over the division of the spoil, though it was not easily divided.

We watched the habits of the swift-darting dragonflies, wild bees, butterflies, wasps, beetles, etc., and soon learned to discriminate between those that might be safely handled and the

pinching or stinging species. But of all our wild neighbors the
mosquitoes were the first with which we became very intimately acquainted.

The beautiful meadow lying warm in the spring sunshine,
outspread between our lily-rimmed lake and the hill-slope that
our shanty stood on, sent forth thirsty swarms of the little
gray, speckledy, singing, stinging pests; and how tellingly they
introduced themselves! Of little avail were the smudges that
we made on muggy evenings to drive them away; and amid
the many lessons which they insisted upon teaching us we
wondered more and more at the extent of their knowledge,
especially that in their tiny, flimsy bodies room could be found
for such cunning palates. They would drink their fill from
brown, smoky Indians, or from old white folk flavored with
tobacco and whiskey, when no better could be had. But the
surpassing fineness of their taste was best manifested by their
enthusiastic appreciation of boys full of lively red blood, and
of girls in full bloom fresh from cool Scotland or England.
On these it was pleasant to witness their enjoyment as they
feasted. Indians, we were told, believed that if they were brave
fighters they would go after death to a happy country abounding in game, where there were no mosquitoes and no cowards.
For cowards were driven away by themselves to a miserable
country where there was no game fit to eat, and where the
sky was always dark with huge gnats and mosquitoes as big as
pigeons.

We were great admirers of the little black water-bugs. Their
whole lives seemed to be play, skimming, swimming, swirling,
and waltzing together in little groups on the edge of the lake
and in the meadow springs, dancing to music we never could
hear. The long-legged skaters, too, seemed wonderful fellows,
shuffling about on top of the water, with air-bubbles like little
bladders tangled under their hairy feet; and we often wished
that we also might be shod in the same way to enable us to
skate on the lake in summer as well as in icy winter. Not less
wonderful were the boatmen, swimming on their backs, pulling themselves along with a pair of oar-like legs.

Great was the delight of brothers David and Daniel and
myself when father gave us a few pine boards for a boat, and
it was a memorable day when we got that boat built and

launched into the lake. Never shall I forget our first sail over the gradually deepening water, the sunbeams pouring through it revealing the strange plants covering the bottom, and the fishes coming about us, staring and wondering as if the boat were a monstrous strange fish.

The water was so clear that it was almost invisible, and when we floated slowly out over the plants and fishes, we seemed to be miraculously sustained in the air while silently exploring a veritable fairyland.

We always had to work hard, but if we worked still harder we were occasionally allowed a little spell in the long summer evenings about sundown to fish, and on Sundays an hour or two to sail quietly without fishing-rod or gun when the lake was calm. Therefore we gradually learned something about its inhabitants,—pickerel, sunfish, black bass, perch, shiners, pumpkin-seeds, ducks, loons, turtles, muskrats, etc. We saw the sunfishes making their nests in little openings in the rushes where the water was only a few feet deep, ploughing up and shoving away the soft gray mud with their noses, like pigs, forming round bowls five or six inches in depth and about two feet in diameter, in which their eggs were deposited. And with what beautiful, unweariable devotion they watched and hovered over them and chased away prowling spawn-eating enemies that ventured within a rod or two of the precious nest!

The pickerel is a savage fish endowed with marvelous strength and speed. It lies in wait for its prey on the bottom, perfectly motionless like a waterlogged stick, watching everything that moves, with fierce, hungry eyes. Oftentimes when we were fishing for some other kinds over the edge of the boat, a pickerel that we had not noticed would come like a bolt of lightning and seize the fish we had caught before we could get it into the boat. The very first pickerel that I ever caught jumped into the air to seize a small fish dangling on my line, and, missing its aim, fell plump into the boat as if it had dropped from the sky.

Some of our neighbors fished for pickerel through the ice in midwinter. They usually drove a wagon out on the lake, set a large number of lines baited with live minnows, hung a loop of the lines over a small bush planted at the side of each hole, and watched to see the loops pulled off when a fish had taken the bait. Large quantities of pickerel were often caught in this cruel way.

Our beautiful lake, named Fountain Lake by father, but Muir's Lake by the neighbors, is one of the many small glacier lakes that adorn the Wisconsin landscapes. It is fed by twenty or thirty meadow springs, is about half a mile long, half as wide, and surrounded by low finely-modeled hills dotted with oak and hickory, and meadows full of grasses and sedges and many beautiful orchids and ferns. First there is a zone of green, shining rushes, and just beyond the rushes a zone of white and orange water-lilies fifty or sixty feet wide forming a magnificent border. On bright days, when the lake was rippled by a breeze, the lilies and sun-spangles danced together in radiant beauty, and it became difficult to discriminate between them.

On Sundays, after or before chores and sermons and Bible-lessons, we drifted about on the lake for hours, especially in lily time, getting finest lessons and sermons from the water and flowers, ducks, fishes, and muskrats. In particular we took Christ's advice and devoutly "considered the lilies"—how they grow up in beauty out of gray lime mud, and ride gloriously among the breezy sun-spangles. On our way home we gathered grand bouquets of them to be kept fresh all the week. No flower was hailed with greater wonder and admiration by the European settlers in general—Scotch, English, and Irish—than this white water-lily (*Nymphæa odorata*). It is a magnificent plant, queen of the inland waters, pure white, three or four inches in diameter, the most beautiful, sumptuous, and deliciously fragrant of all our Wisconsin flowers. No lily garden in civilization we had ever seen could compare with our lake garden.

The next most admirable flower in the estimation of settlers in this part of the new world was the pasque-flower or wind-flower (*Anemone patens* var. *Nuttalliana*). It is the very first to appear in the spring, covering the cold gray-black ground with cheery blossoms. Before the axe or plough had touched the "oak openings" of Wisconsin, they were swept by running fires almost every autumn after the grass became dry. If from any cause, such as early snowstorms or late rains, they happened to escape the autumn fire besom, they were likely to be burned in the spring after the snow melted. But whether burned in the spring or fall, ashes and bits of charred twigs and grass stems made the whole country look dismal. Then, before a single grass-blade had sprouted, a hopeful multitude of large hairy, silky buds about as thick as one's thumb came to light, pushing up through the black and gray ashes and cinders, and before these buds were fairly free from the ground they opened wide and displayed purple blossoms about two inches in diameter, giving beauty for ashes in glorious abundance. Instead of remaining in the ground waiting for warm weather and companions, this admirable plant seemed to be in haste to rise and cheer the desolate landscape. Then at its leisure, after other plants had come to its help, it spread its leaves and grew up to a height of about two or three feet. The spreading leaves formed a whorl on the ground, and another about the middle of the stem as an involucre, and on the top of the stem the silky, hairy long-tailed seeds formed a head like a second flower. A little church was established among the earlier settlers and the meetings at first were held in our house. After working hard all the week it was difficult for boys to sit still through long sermons without falling asleep, especially in warm weather. In this drowsy trouble the charming anemone came to our help. A pocketful of the pungent seeds industriously nibbled while the discourses were at their dullest kept us awake and filled our minds with flowers.

The next great flower wonders on which we lavished admiration, not only for beauty of color and size, but for their curious shapes, were the cypripediums, called "lady's-slippers" or "Indian moccasins." They were so different from the familiar flowers of old Scotland. Several species grew in our meadow and on shady hillsides,—yellow, rose-colored, and some nearly white, an inch or more in diameter, and shaped exactly like Indian moccasins. They caught the eye of all the European settlers and made them gaze and wonder like children. And so did calopogon, pogonia, spiranthes, and many other fine plant people that lived in our meadow. The beautiful Turk's-turban (*Lilium superbum*) growing on streambanks was rare in our neighborhood, but the orange lily grew in abundance on dry ground beneath the bur-oaks and often brought Aunt Ray's lily-bed in Scotland to mind. The butter-fly-weed, with its brilliant scarlet flowers, attracted flocks of butterflies and made fine masses of color. With autumn came a glorious abundance and variety of asters, those beautiful plant stars, together with goldenrods, sunflowers, daisies, and liatris of different species, while around the shady margin of the meadow many ferns in beds and vaselike groups spread their beautiful fronds, especially the osmundas (*O. claytoniana, regalis,* and *cinnamomea*) and the sensitive and ostrich ferns.

Early in summer we feasted on strawberries, that grew in rich beds beneath the meadow grasses and sedges as well as in the dry sunny woods. And in different bogs and marshes, and around their borders on our own farm and along the Fox River, we found dewberries and cranberries, and a glorious profusion of huckleberries, the fountain-heads of pies of wondrous taste and size, colored in the heart like sunsets. Nor were we slow to discover the value of the hickory trees yielding both sugar and nuts. We carefully counted the different kinds on our farm, and every morning when we could steal a few minutes before breakfast after doing the chores, we visited the trees that had been wounded by the axe, to scrape off and enjoy the thick white delicious syrup that exuded from them, and gathered the nuts as they fell in the mellow Indian summer, making haste to get a fair share with the sapsuckers and squirrels. The hickory makes fine masses of color in the fall, every leaf a flower, but it was the sweet sap and sweet nuts that first interested us. No harvest in the Wisconsin woods was ever gathered with more pleasure and care. Also, to our delight, we found plenty of hazelnuts, and in a few places abundance of wild apples. They were desperately sour, and we used to fill our pockets with them and dare each other to eat one without making a face,—no easy feat.

One hot summer day father told us that we ought to learn to swim. This was one of the most interesting suggestions he had ever offered, but precious little time was allowed for trips to the lake, and he seldom tried to show us how. "Go to the frogs," he said, "and they will give you all the lessons you need. Watch their arms and legs and see how smoothly they kick themselves along and dive and come up. When you want to dive, keep your arms by your side or over your head, and kick, and when you want to come up, let your legs drag and paddle with your hands."

We found a little basin among the rushes at the south end of the lake, about waist-deep and a rod or two wide, shaped like a sunfish's nest. Here we kicked and plashed for many a lesson, faithfully trying to imitate frogs; but the smooth, comfortable sliding gait of our amphibious teachers seemed hopelessly hard to learn. When we tried to kick frog-fashion, down went our heads as if weighted with lead the moment our feet left the ground. One day it occurred to me to hold my breath as long as I could and let my head sink as far as it liked without paying any attention to it, and try to swim under the water instead of on the surface. This method was a great success, for at the very first trial I managed to cross the basin without touching bottom, and soon learned the use of my limbs. Then, of course, swimming with my head above water soon became so easy that it seemed perfectly natural. David tried the plan with the same success. Then we began to count the number of times that we could swim around the basin without stopping to rest, and after twenty or thirty rounds failed to tire us, we proudly thought that a little more practice would make us about as amphibious as frogs.

On the fourth of July of this swimming year one of the Lawson boys came to visit us, and we went down to the lake to spend the great warm day with the fishes and ducks and turtles. After gliding about on the smooth mirror water, telling stories and enjoying the company of the happy creatures about us, we rowed to our bathing-pool, and David and I went in for a swim, while our companion fished from the boat a little way out beyond the rushes. After a few turns in the pool, it occurred to me that it was now about time to try deep water. Swimming through the thick growth of rushes and lilies was somewhat dangerous, especially for a beginner, because one's arms and legs might be entangled among the long, limber stems; nevertheless I ventured and struck out boldly enough for the boat, where the water was twenty or thirty feet deep. When I reached the end of the little skiff I raised my right hand to take hold of it to surprise Lawson, whose back was toward me and who was not aware of my approach; but I failed to reach high enough, and, of course, the weight of my arm and the stroke against the over-leaning stern of the boat shoved me down and I sank, struggling, frightened and confused. As soon as my feet touched the bottom, I slowly rose to the surface, but before I could get breath enough to call for help, sank back again and lost all control of myself. After sinking and rising I don't know how many times, some water got into my lungs and I began to drown. Then suddenly my mind seemed to clear. I remembered that I could swim under water, and, making a desperate struggle toward the shore, I reached a point where with my toes on the bottom I got my mouth above the surface, gasped for help, and was pulled into the boat.

This humiliating accident spoiled the day, and we all agreed to keep it a profound secret. My sister Sarah had heard my cry for help, and on our arrival at the house inquired what had happened. "Were you drowning, John? I heard you cry you couldna get oot." Lawson made haste to reply, "Oh, no! He was juist haverin (making fun)."

I was very much ashamed of myself, and at night, after calmly reviewing the affair, concluded that there had been no reasonable cause for the accident, and that I ought to punish myself for so nearly losing my life from unmanly fear. Accordingly at the very first opportunity, I stole away to the lake by myself, got into my boat, and instead of going back to the old swimming-bowl for further practice, or to try to do sanely and well what I had so ignominiously failed to do in my first adventure, that is, to swim out through the rushes and lilies, I rowed directly out to the middle of the lake, stripped, stood up on the seat in the stern, and with grim deliberation took a header and dove straight down thirty or forty feet, turned easily, and, letting my feet drag, paddled straight to the surface with my hands as father had at first directed me to do. I then swam round the boat, glorying in my suddenly acquired confidence and victory over myself, climbed into it, and dived again, with the same triumphant success. I think I went down four or five times, and each time as I made the dive-spring shouted aloud, "Take that!" feeling that I was getting most gloriously even with myself.

Never again from that day to this have I lost control of myself in water. If suddenly thrown overboard at sea in the dark, or even while asleep, I think I would immediately right myself in a way some would call "instinct," rise among the waves, catch my breath, and try to plan what would better be done. Never was victory over self more complete. I have been a good swimmer ever since. At a slow gait I think I could swim all day in smooth water moderate in temperature. When I was a student at Madison, I used to go on long swimming-journeys, called exploring expeditions, along the south shore of Lake Mendota, on Saturdays, sometimes alone, sometimes with another amphibious explorer by the name of Fuller.

My adventures in Fountain Lake call to mind the story of a boy who in climbing a tree to rob a crow's nest fell and broke his leg, but as soon as it healed compelled himself to climb to the top of the tree he had fallen from.

Like Scotch children in general we were taught grim self-denial, in season and out of season, to mortify the flesh, keep our bodies in subjection to Bible laws, and mercilessly punish ourselves for every fault imagined or committed. A little boy, while helping his sister to drive home the cows, happened to use a forbidden word. "I'll have to tell fayther on ye," said the horrified sister. "I'll tell him that ye said a bad word." "Weel," said the boy, by way of excuse, "I couldna help the word comin' into me, and it's na waur to speak it oot than to let it rin through ye."

A Scotch fiddler playing at a wedding drank so much whis-key that on the way home he fell by the roadside. In the morning he was ashamed and angry and determined to punish himself. Making haste to the house of a friend, a gamekeeper, he called him out, and requested the loan of a gun. The alarmed gamekeeper, not liking the fiddler's looks and voice, anxiously inquired what he was going to do with it. "Surely," said he, "you're no gan to shoot yoursel." "No-o," with char-acteristic candor replied the penitent fiddler, "I dinna think that I'll juist exactly kill mysel, but I'm gaun to tak a dander doon the burn (brook) wi' the gun and gie mysel a deevil o' a fleg (fright)."

One calm summer evening a red-headed woodpecker was drowned in our lake. The accident happened at the south end, opposite our memorable swimming-hole, a few rods from the place where I came so near being drowned years before. I had returned to the old home during a summer vacation of the State University, and, having made a beginning in botany, I was, of course, full of enthusiasm and ran eagerly to my beloved pogonia, calopogon, and cypripedium gardens, osmunda ferneries, and the lake lilies and pitcher-plants. A little before sundown the day-breeze died away, and the lake, reflecting the wooded hills like a mirror, was dimpled and dotted and streaked here and there where fishes and turtles were poking out their heads and muskrats were sculling themselves along with their flat tails making glittering tracks. After lingering a while, dreamily recalling the old, hard, half-happy days, and watching my favorite red-headed woodpeckers pursuing moths like regular flycatchers, I swam out through the rushes and up the middle of the lake to the north end and back, gliding slowly, looking about me, enjoying the scenery as I would in a saunter along the shore, and studying the habits of the animals as they were explained and recorded on the smooth glassy water.

On the way back, when I was within a hundred rods or so of the end of my voyage, I noticed a peculiar plashing disturbance that could not, I thought, be made by a jumping fish or any other inhabitant of the lake; for instead of low regular out-circling ripples such as are made by the popping up of a head, or like those raised by the quick splash of a leaping fish, or diving loon or muskrat, a continuous struggle was kept up for several minutes ere the outspreading, interfering ring-waves began to die away. Swimming hastily to the spot to try to discover what had happened, I found one of my woodpeckers floating motionless with outspread wings. All was over. Had I been a minute or two earlier, I might have saved him. He had glanced on the water I suppose in pursuit of a moth, was unable to rise from it, and died struggling, as I nearly did at this same spot. Like me he seemed to have lost his mind in blind confusion and fear. The water was warm, and had he kept still with his head a little above the surface, he would sooner or later have been wafted ashore. The best aimed flights of birds and man "gang aft agley," but this was the first case I had witnessed of a bird losing its life by drowning.

Doubtless accidents to animals are far more common than is generally known. I have seen quails killed by flying against our house when suddenly startled. Some birds get entangled in hairs of their own nests and die. Once I found a poor snipe in our meadow that was unable to fly on account of difficult egg-birth. Pitying the poor mother, I picked her up out of the grass and helped her as gently as I could, and as soon as the egg was born she flew gladly away. Oftentimes I have thought it strange that one could walk through the woods and mountains and plains for years without seeing a single blood-spot. Most wild animals get into the world and out of it without being noticed. Nevertheless we at last sadly learn that they are all subject to the vicissitudes of fortune like ourselves. Many birds lose their lives in storms. I remember a particularly severe Wisconsin winter, when the temperature was many degrees below zero and the snow was deep, preventing the quail, which feed on the ground, from getting anything like enough of food, as was pitifully shown by a flock I found on our farm frozen solid in a thicket of oak sprouts. They were in a circle about a foot wide, with their heads outward, packed close together for warmth. Yet all had died without a struggle, perhaps more from starvation than frost. Many small birds lose their lives in the storms of early spring, or even summer. One mild spring morning I picked up more than a score out of the grass and flowers, most of them darling singers that had perished in a sudden storm of sleety rain and hail.

In a hollow at the foot of an oak tree that I had chopped down one cold winter day, I found a poor ground squirrel frozen solid in its snug grassy nest, in the middle of a store of nearly a peck of wheat it had carefully gathered. I carried it home and gradually thawed and warmed it in the kitchen, hoping it would come to life like a pickerel I caught in our lake through a hole in the ice, which, after being frozen as hard as a bone and thawed at the fireside, squirmed itself out of the grasp of the cook when she began to scrape it, bounced off the table, and danced about on the floor, making wonderful springy jumps as if trying to find its way back home to the lake. But for the poor spermophile nothing I could do in the way of revival was of any avail. Its life had passed away without the slightest struggle, as it lay asleep curled up like a ball, with its tail wrapped about it.

IV

A PARADISE OF BIRDS

BIRD FAVORITES—THE PRAIRIE CHICKENS—WATER-
FOWL—A LOON ON THE DEFENSIVE—
PASSENGER PIGEONS.

THE Wisconsin oak openings were a summer paradise for song birds, and a fine place to get acquainted with them; for the trees stood wide apart, allowing one to see the happy homeseekers as they arrived in the spring, their mating, nest-building, the brooding and feeding of the young, and, after they were full-fledged and strong, to see all the families of the neighborhood gathering and getting ready to leave in the fall. Excepting the geese and ducks and pigeons nearly all our summer birds arrived singly or in small draggled flocks, but when frost and falling leaves brought their winter homes to mind they assembled in large flocks on dead or leafless trees by the side of a meadow or field, perhaps to get acquainted and talk the thing over. Some species held regular daily meetings for several weeks before finally setting forth on their long southern journeys. Strange to say, we never saw them start. Some morning we would find them gone. Doubtless they migrated in the night time. Comparatively few species remained all winter, the nuthatch, chickadee, owl, prairie chicken, quail, and a few stragglers from the main flocks of ducks, jays, hawks, and bluebirds. Only after the country was settled did either jays or bluebirds winter with us.

The brave, frost-defying chickadees and nuthatches stayed all the year wholly independent of farms and man's food and affairs.

With the first hints of spring came the brave little bluebirds, darling singers as blue as the best sky, and of course we all loved them. Their rich, crispy warbling is perfectly delightful, soothing and cheering, sweet and whisperingly low, Nature's fine love touches, every note going straight home into one's heart. And withal they are hardy and brave, fearless fighters in defense of home. When we boys approached their knot-hole nests, the bold little fellows kept scolding and diving at us and tried to strike us in the face, and oftentimes we were afraid they would prick our eyes. But the boldness of the little housekeepers only made us love them the more.

None of the bird people of Wisconsin welcomed us more heartily than the common robin. Far from showing alarm at the coming of settlers into their native woods, they reared their young around our gardens as if they liked us, and how heartily we admired the beauty and fine manners of these graceful birds and their loud cheery song of *Fear not, fear not, cheer up, cheer up.* It was easy to love them for they reminded us of the robin redbreast of Scotland. Like the bluebirds they dared every danger in defense of home, and we often wondered that birds so gentle could be so bold and that sweet-voiced singers could so fiercely fight and scold.

Of all the great singers that sweeten Wisconsin one of the best known and best loved is the brown thrush or thrasher, strong and able without being familiar, and easily seen and heard. Rosy purple evenings after thunder-showers are the favorite song-times, when the winds have died away and the steaming ground and the leaves and flowers fill the air with fragrance. Then the male makes haste to the top-most spray of an oak tree and sings loud and clear with delightful enthusiasm until sundown, mostly I suppose for his mate sitting on the precious eggs in a brush heap. And how faithful and watchful and daring he is! Woe to the snake or squirrel that ventured to go nigh the nest! We often saw him diving on them, pecking them about the head and driving them away as bravely as the kingbird drives away hawks. Their rich and varied strains make the air fairly quiver. We boys often tried to interpret the wild ringing melody and put it into words.

After the arrival of the thrushes came the bobolinks, gushing, gurgling, inexhaustible fountains of song, pouring forth floods of sweet notes over the broad Fox River meadows in wonderful variety and volume, crowded and mixed beyond description, as they hovered on quivering wings above their hidden nests in the grass. It seemed marvelous to us that birds so moderate in size could hold so much of this wonderful song stuff. Each one of them poured forth music enough for a whole flock, singing as if its whole body, feathers and all, were made up of music, flowing, glowing, bubbling melody interpenetrated here and there with small scintillating prickles and spicules. We never became so intimately acquainted with the bobolinks as with the thrushes, for they lived far out on the broad Fox River meadows, while the thrushes sang on the tree-tops around every home. The bobolinks were among the first of our great singers to leave us in the fall, going apparently direct to the rice-fields of the Southern States, where they grew fat and were slaughtered in countless numbers for food. Sad fate for singers so purely divine.

One of the gayest of the singers is the redwing blackbird. In the spring, when his scarlet epaulets shine brightest, and his little modest gray wife is sitting on the nest, built on rushes in a swamp, he sits on a nearby oak and devotedly sings almost all day. His rich simple strain is *baumpalee, baumpalee,* or *bob-alee* as interpreted by some. In summer, after nesting cares are over, they assemble in flocks of hundreds and thousands to feast on Indian corn when it is in the milk. Scattering over a field, each selects an ear, strips the husk down far enough to lay bare an inch or two of the end of it, enjoys an exhilarating feast, and after all are full they rise simultaneously with a quick birr of wings like an old-fashioned church congregation fluttering to their feet when the minister after giving out the hymn says, "Let the congregation arise and sing." Alighting on nearby trees, they sing with a hearty vengeance, bursting out without any puttering prelude in gloriously glad concert, hundreds or thousands of exulting voices with sweet gurgling *baumpalees* mingled with chippy vibrant and exploding globules of musical notes, making a most enthusiastic, indescribable joy-song, a combination unlike anything to be heard elsewhere in the bird kingdom; something like bagpipes, flutes, violins, pianos, and human-like voices all bursting and bubbling at once. Then suddenly some one of the joyful congregation shouts Chirr! Chirr! and all stop as if shot.

The sweet-voiced meadowlark with its placid, simple song of *peery-eery-ódical* was another favorite, and we soon learned to admire the Baltimore oriole and its wonderful hanging nests, and the scarlet tanager glowing like fire amid the green leaves.

But no singer of them all got farther into our hearts than

the little speckle-breasted song sparrow, one of the first to arrive and begin nest-building and singing. The richness, sweetness, and pathos of this small darling's song as he sat on a low bush often brought tears to our eyes.

The little cheery, modest chickadee midget, loved by every innocent boy and girl, man and woman, and by many not altogether innocent, was one of the first of the birds to attract our attention, drawing nearer and nearer to us as the winter advanced, bravely singing his faint silvery, lisping, tinkling notes ending with a bright *dee, dee, dee!* however frosty the weather.

The nuthatches, who also stayed all winter with us, were favorites with us boys. We loved to watch them as they traced the bark-furrows of the oaks and hickories head downward, deftly flicking off loose scales and splinters in search of insects, and braving the coldest weather as if their little sparks of life were as safely warm in winter as in summer, unquenchable by the severest frost. With the help of the chickadees they made a delightful stir in the solemn winter days, and when we were out chopping we never ceased to wonder how their slender naked toes could be kept warm when our own were so painfully frosted though clad in thick socks and boots. And we wondered and admired the more when we thought of the little midgets sleeping in knot-holes when the temperature was far below zero, sometimes thirty-five degrees below, and in the morning, after a minute breakfast of a few frozen insects and hoarfrost crystals, playing and chatting in cheery tones as if food, weather, and everything was according to their own warm hearts. Our Yankee told us that the name of this darling was Devil-downhead.

Their big neighbors the owls also made good winter music, singing out loud in wild, gallant strains bespeaking brave comfort, let the frost bite as it might. The solemn hooting of the species with the widest throat seemed to us the very wildest of all the winter sounds.

Prairie chickens came strolling in family flocks about the shanty, picking seeds and grasshoppers like domestic fowls, and they became still more abundant as wheat- and corn-fields were multiplied, but also wilder, of course, when every shotgun in the country was aimed at them. The booming of the males during the mating-season was one of the loudest and strangest of the early spring sounds, being easily heard on calm mornings at a distance of a half or three fourths of a mile. As soon as the snow was off the ground, they assembled in flocks of a dozen or two on an open spot, usually on the side of a ploughed field, ruffled up their feathers, inflated the curious colored sacks on the sides of their necks, and strutted about with queer gestures something like turkey gobblers, uttering strange loud, rounded, drumming calls,—*boom! boom! boom!* interrupted by choking sounds. My brother Daniel caught one while she was sitting on her nest in our corn-field. The young are just like domestic chicks, run with the mother as soon as hatched, and stay with her until autumn, feeding on the ground, never taking wing unless disturbed. In winter, when full-grown, they assemble in large flocks, fly about sun-down to selected roosting-places on tall trees, and to feeding-places in the morning,—unhusked corn-fields, if any are to be found in the neighborhood, or thickets of dwarf birch and willows, the buds of which furnish a considerable part of their food when snow covers the ground.

The wild rice-marshes along the Fox River and around Puc-away Lake were the summer homes of millions of ducks, and in the Indian summer, when the rice was ripe, they grew very fat. The magnificent mallards in particular afforded our Yan-kee neighbors royal feasts almost without price, for often as many as a half-dozen were killed at a shot, but we seldom were allowed a single hour for hunting and so got very few. The autumn duck season was a glad time for the Indians also, for they feasted and grew fat not only on the ducks but on the wild rice, large quantities of which they gathered as they glided through the midst of the generous crop in canoes, bending down handfuls over the sides, and beating out the grain with small paddles.

The warmth of the deep spring fountains of the creek in our meadow kept it open all the year, and a few pairs of wood ducks, the most beautiful, we thought, of all the ducks, wintered in it. I well remember the first specimen I ever saw. Father shot it in the creek during a snowstorm, brought it into the house, and called us around him, saying: "Come, bairns, and admire the work of God displayed in this bonnie bird. Naebody but God could paint feathers like these. Juist look at the colors, hoo they shine, and hoo fine they overlap and blend thegether like the colors o' the rainbow." And we all agreed that never, never before had we seen so awfu' bonnie a bird. A pair nested every year in the hollow top of an oak stump about fifteen feet high that stood on the side of the meadow, and we used to wonder how they got the fluffy young ones down from the nest and across the meadow to the lake when they were only helpless, featherless midgets; whether the mother carried them to the water on her back or in her mouth. I never saw the thing done or found anybody who had until this summer, when Mr. Holabird, a keen observer, told me that he once saw the mother carry them from the nest tree in her mouth, quickly coming and going to a nearby stream, and in a few minutes get them all together and proudly sail away.

Sometimes a flock of swans were seen passing over at a great height on their long journeys, and we admired their clear bugle notes, but they seldom visited any of the lakes in our neighborhood, so seldom that when they did it was talked of for years. One was shot by a blacksmith on a millpond with a long-range Sharp's rifle, and many of the neighbors went far to see it.

The common gray goose, Canada honker, flying in regular harrow-shaped flocks, was one of the wildest and wariest of all the large birds that enlivened the spring and autumn. They seldom ventured to alight in our small lake, fearing, I suppose, that hunters might be concealed in the rushes, but on account of their fondness for the young leaves of winter wheat when they were a few inches high, they often alighted on our fields when passing on their way south, and occasionally even in our corn-fields when a snowstorm was blowing and they were hungry and wing-weary, with nearly an inch of snow on their backs. In such times of distress we used to pity them, even while trying to get a shot at them. They were exceedingly cautious and circumspect; usually flew several times round the adjacent thickets and fences to make sure that no enemy was near before settling down, and one always stood on guard, relieved from time to time, while the flock was feeding. Therefore there was no chance to creep up on them unobserved;

you had to be well hidden before the flock arrived. It was the ambition of boys to be able to shoot these wary birds. I never got but two, both of them at one so-called lucky shot. When I ran to pick them up, one of them flew away, but as the poor fellow was sorely wounded he didn't fly far. When I caught him after a short chase, he uttered a piercing cry of terror and despair, which the leader of the flock heard at a distance of about a hundred rods. They had flown off in frightened disorder, of course, but had got into the regular harrow-shape order when the leader heard the cry, and I shall never forget how bravely he left his place at the head of the flock and hurried back screaming and struck at me in trying to save his companion. I dodged down and held my hands over my head, and thus escaped a blow of his elbows. Fortunately I had left my gun at the fence, and the life of this noble bird was spared after he had risked it in trying to save his wounded friend or neighbor or family relation. For so shy a bird boldly to attack a hunter showed wonderful sympathy and courage. This is one of my strangest hunting experiences. Never before had I regarded wild geese as dangerous, or capable of such noble self-sacrificing devotion.

The loud clear call of the handsome bob-whites was one of the pleasantest and most characteristic of our spring sounds, and we soon learned to imitate it so well that a bold cock often accepted our challenge and came flying to fight. The young run as soon as they are hatched and follow their parents until spring, roosting on the ground in a close bunch, heads out ready to scatter and fly. These fine birds were seldom seen when we first arrived in the wilderness, but when wheat-fields supplied abundance of food they multiplied very fast, although oftentimes sore pressed during hard winters when the snow reached a depth of two or three feet, covering their food, while the mercury fell to twenty or thirty degrees below zero. Occasionally, although shy on account of being persistently hunted, under pressure of extreme hunger in the very coldest weather when the snow was deepest they ventured into barnyards and even approached the doorsteps of houses, searching for any sort of scraps and crumbs, as if piteously begging for food. One of our neighbors saw a flock come creeping up through the snow, unable to fly, hardly able to walk, and while approaching the door several of them actually fell down and died; showing that birds, usually so vigorous and apparently independent of fortune, suffer and lose their lives in extreme weather like the rest of us, frozen to death like settlers caught in blizzards. None of our neighbors perished in storms, though many had feet, ears, and fingers frost-nipped or solidly frozen.

As soon as the lake ice melted, we heard the lonely cry of the loon, one of the wildest and most striking of all the wilderness sounds, a strange, sad, mournful, unearthly cry, half laughing, half wailing. Nevertheless the great northern diver, as our species is called, is a brave, hardy, beautiful bird, able to fly under water about as well as above it, and to spear and capture the swiftest fishes for food. Those that haunted our lake were so wary none was shot for years, though every boy hunter in the neighborhood was ambitious to get one to prove his skill. On one of our bitter cold New Year holidays I was surprised to see a loon in the small open part of the lake at the mouth of the inlet that was kept from freezing by the warm spring water. I knew that it could not fly out of so small a place, for these heavy birds have to beat the water for half a mile or so before they can get fairly on the wing. Their narrow, finlike wings are very small as compared with the weight of the body and are evidently made for flying through water as well as through the air, and it is by means of their swift flight through the water and the swiftness of the blow they strike with their long, spear-like bills that they are able to capture the fishes on which they feed. I ran down the meadow with the gun, got into my boat, and pursued that poor winter-bound straggler. Of course he dived again and again, but had to come up to breathe, and I at length got a quick shot at his head and slightly wounded or stunned him, caught him, and ran proudly back to the house with my prize. I carried him in my arms; he didn't struggle to get away or offer to strike me, and when I put him on the floor in front of the kitchen stove, he just rested quietly on his belly as noiseless and motionless as if he were a stuffed specimen on a shelf, held his neck erect, gave no sign of suffering from any wound, and though he was motionless, his small black eyes seemed to be ever keenly watchful. His formidable bill, very sharp, three or three and a half inches long, and shaped like a pickaxe, was held perfectly level. But the wonder was that he did not struggle or make the slightest movement. We had a tortoise-shell cat, an old Tom of great experience, who was so fond of lying under the stove in frosty weather that it was difficult even to poke him out with a broom; but when he saw and smelled that strange big fishy, black and white, speckledy bird, the like of which he had never before seen, he rushed wildly to the farther corner of the kitchen, looked back cautiously and suspiciously, and began to make a careful study of the handsome but dangerous-looking stranger. Becoming more and more curious and interested, he at length advanced a step or two for a nearer view and nearer smell; and as the wonderful bird kept absolutely motionless, he was encouraged to venture gradually nearer and nearer until within perhaps five or six feet of its breast. Then the wary loon, not liking Tom's looks in so near a view, which perhaps recalled to his mind the plundering minks and muskrats he had to fight when they approached his nest, prepared to defend himself by slowly, almost imperceptibly drawing back his long pickaxe bill, and without the slightest fuss or stir held it level and ready just over his tail. With that dangerous bill drawn so far back out of the way, Tom's confidence in the stranger's peaceful intentions seemed almost complete, and, thus encouraged, he at last ventured forward with wondering, questioning eyes and quivering nostrils until he was only eighteen or twenty inches from the loon's smooth white breast. When the beautiful bird, apparently as peaceful and inoffensive as a flower, saw that his hairy yellow enemy had arrived at the right distance, the loon, who evidently was a fine judge of the reach of his spear, shot it forward quick as a lightning-flash, in marvelous contrast to the wonderful slowness of the preparatory poising, backward motion. The aim was true to a hair-breadth. Tom was struck right in the centre of his forehead, between the eyes. I thought his skull was cracked. Perhaps it was. The sudden astonishment of that outraged cat, the virtuous indignation and wrath, terror, and pain, are far beyond description. His eyes and screams and desperate retreat told all that. When the blow was received, he made a noise that I never heard a cat make before or since; an awfully deep, condensed, screechy,

explosive *Wuck!* as he bounced straight up in the air like a
bucking bronco; and when he alighted after his spring, he
rushed madly across the room and made frantic efforts to
climb up the hard-finished plaster wall. Not satisfied to get
the width of the kitchen away from his mysterious enemy, for
the first time that cold winter he tried to get out of the house,
anyhow, anywhere out of that loon-infested room. When he
finally ventured to look back and saw that the barbarous bird
was still there, tranquil and motionless in front of the stove,
he regained command of some of his shattered senses and
carefully commenced to examine his wound. Backed against
the wall in the farthest corner, and keeping his eye on the
outrageous bird, he tenderly touched and washed the sore
spot, wetting his paw with his tongue, pausing now and then
as his courage increased to glare and stare and growl at his
enemy with looks and tones wonderfully human, as if saying:
"You confounded fishy, unfair rascal! What did you do that
for? What had I done to you? Faithless, legless, long-nosed
wretch!" Intense experiences like the above bring out the humanity that is in all animals. One touch of nature, even a cat-
and-loon touch, makes all the world kin.

It was a great memorable day when the first flock of passenger pigeons came to our farm, calling to mind the story
we had read about them when we were at school in Scotland.
Of all God's feathered people that sailed the Wisconsin sky,
no other bird seemed to us so wonderful. The beautiful wanderers flew like the winds in flocks of millions from climate to
climate in accord with the weather, finding their food—
acorns, beechnuts, pine-nuts, cranberries, strawberries, huckleberries, juniper berries, hackberries, buckwheat, rice, wheat,
oats, corn—in fields and forests thousands of miles apart. I
have seen flocks streaming south in the fall so large that they
were flowing over from horizon to horizon in an almost continuous stream all day long, at the rate of forty or fifty miles
an hour, like a mighty river in the sky, widening, contracting,
descending like falls and cataracts, and rising suddenly here
and there in huge ragged masses like high-plashing spray.
How wonderful the distances they flew in a day—in a year—
in a lifetime! They arrived in Wisconsin in the spring just after
the sun had cleared away the snow, and alighted in the woods

to feed on the fallen acorns that they had missed the previous autumn. A comparatively small flock swept thousands of acres perfectly clean of acorns in a few minutes, by moving straight ahead with a broad front. All got their share, for the rear constantly became the van by flying over the flock and alighting in front, the entire flock constantly changing from rear to front, revolving something like a wheel with a low buzzing wing roar that could be heard a long way off. In summer they feasted on wheat and oats and were easily approached as they rested on the trees along the sides of the field after a good full meal, displaying beautiful iridescent colors as they moved their necks backward and forward when we went very near them. Every shotgun was aimed at them and everybody feasted on pigeon pies, and not a few of the settlers feasted also on the beauty of the wonderful birds. The breast of the male is a fine rosy red, the lower part of the neck behind and along the sides changing from the red of the breast to gold, emerald green and rich crimson. The general color of the upper parts is grayish blue, the under parts white. The extreme length of the bird is about seventeen inches; the finely modeled slender tail about eight inches, and extent of wings twenty-four inches. The females are scarcely less beautiful. "Oh, what bonnie, bonnie birds!" we exclaimed over the first that fell into our hands. "Oh, what colors! Look at their breasts, bonnie as roses, and at their necks aglow wi' every color juist like the wonderfu' wood ducks. Oh, the bonnie, bonnie creatures, they beat a'! Where did they a' come fra, and where are they a' gan? It's awfu' like a sin to kill them!" To this some smug, practical old sinner would remark: "Aye, it's a peety, as ye say, to kill the bonnie things, but they were made to be killed, and sent for us to eat as the quails were sent to God's chosen people, the Israelites, when they were starving in the desert ayont the Red Sea. And I must confess that meat was never put up in neater, handsomer-painted packages."

In the New England and Canada woods beechnuts were their best and most abundant food, farther north, cranberries and huckleberries. After everything was cleaned up in the north and winter was coming on, they went south for rice, corn, acorns, haws, wild grapes, crab-apples, sparkle-berries, etc. They seemed to require more than half of the continent for feeding-grounds, moving from one table to another, field to field, forest to forest, finding something ripe and wholesome all the year round. In going south in the fine Indian-summer weather they flew high and followed one another, though the head of the flock might be hundreds of miles in advance. But against head winds they took advantage of the inequalities of the ground, flying comparatively low. All followed the leader's ups and downs over hill and dale though far out of sight, never hesitating at any turn of the way, vertical or horizontal that the leaders had taken, though the largest flocks stretched across several States, and belts of different kinds of weather.

There were no roosting- or breeding-places near our farm, and I never saw any of them until long after the great flocks were exterminated. I therefore quote, from Audubon's and Pokagon's vivid descriptions.

"Toward evening," Audubon says, "they depart for the roosting-place, which may be hundreds of miles distant. One on the banks of Green River, Kentucky, was over three miles wide and forty long."

"My first view of it," says the great naturalist, "was about a fortnight after it had been chosen by the birds, and I arrived there nearly two hours before sunset. Few pigeons were then to be seen, but a great many persons with horses and wagons and armed with guns, long poles, sulphur pots, pine pitch torches, etc., had already established encampments on the borders. Two farmers had driven upwards of three hundred hogs a distance of more than a hundred miles to be fattened on slaughtered pigeons. Here and there the people employed in plucking and salting what had already been secured were sitting in the midst of piles of birds. Dung several inches thick covered the ground. Many trees two feet in diameter were broken off at no great distance from the ground, and the branches of many of the tallest and largest had given way, as if the forest had been swept by a tornado.

"Not a pigeon had arrived at sundown. Suddenly a general cry arose—'Here they come!' The noise they made, though still distant, reminded me of a hard gale at sea passing through the rigging of a close-reefed ship. Thousands were soon knocked down by the pole-men. The birds continued to pour in. The fires were lighted and a magnificent as well as terrifying sight presented itself. The pigeons pouring in alighted everywhere, one above another, until solid masses were formed on the branches all around. Here and there the perches gave way with a crash, and falling destroyed hundreds beneath, forcing down the dense groups with which every stick was loaded; a scene of uproar and conflict. I found it useless to speak or even to shout to those persons nearest me. Even the reports of the guns were seldom heard, and I was made aware of the firing only by seeing the shooters reloading. None dared venture within the line of devastation. The hogs had been penned up in due time, the picking up of the dead and wounded being left for the next morning's employment. The pigeons were constantly coming in and it was after midnight before I perceived a decrease in the number of those that arrived. The uproar continued all night, and anxious to know how far the sound reached I sent off a man who, returning two hours after, informed me that he had heard it distinctly three miles distant.

"Toward daylight the noise in some measure subsided; long before objects were distinguishable the pigeons began to move off in a direction quite different from that in which they had arrived the evening before, and at sunrise all that were able to fly had disappeared. The howling of the wolves now reached our ears, and the foxes, lynxes, cougars, bears, coons, opossums, and polecats were seen sneaking off, while eagles and hawks of different species, accompanied by a crowd of vultures, came to supplant them and enjoy a share of the spoil.

"Then the authors of all this devastation began their entry amongst the dead, the dying and mangled. The pigeons were picked up and piled in heaps until each had as many as they could possible dispose of, when the hogs were let loose to feed on the remainder.

"The breeding-places are selected with reference to abundance of food, and countless myriads resort to them. At this period the note of the pigeon is coo coo coo, like that of the domestic species but much shorter. They caress by billing, and during incubation the male supplies the female with food. As the young grow, the tyrant of creation appears to disturb the peaceful scene, armed with axes to chop down the squab-laden trees, and the abomination of desolation and destruction produced far surpasses even that of the roosting places."

Pokagon, an educated Indian writer, says: "I saw one nesting-place in Wisconsin one hundred miles long and from three to ten miles wide. Every tree, some of them quite low and scrubby, had from one to fifty nests on each. Some of the nests overflow from the oaks to the hemlock and pine woods. When the pigeon hunters attack the breeding-places they sometimes cut the timber from thousands of acres. Millions are caught in nets with salt or grain for bait, and schooners, sometimes loaded down with the birds, are taken to New York where they are sold for a cent apiece."

V

YOUNG HUNTERS

AMERICAN HEAD-HUNTERS—DEER—A RESURRECTED
WOODPECKER—MUSKRATS—FOXES AND BADGERS—
A PET COON—BATHING—SQUIRRELS—
GOPHERS—A BURGLARIOUS SHRIKE.

IN the older eastern States it used to be considered great
sport for an army of boys to assemble to hunt birds, squirrels, and every other unclaimed, unprotected live thing of
shootable size. They divided into two squads, and, choosing
leaders, scattered through the woods in different directions,
and the party that killed the greatest number enjoyed a supper
at the expense of the other. The whole neighborhood seemed
to enjoy the shameful sport especially the farmers afraid of
their crops. With a great air of importance, laws were enacted
to govern the gory business. For example, a gray squirrel must
count four heads, a woodchuck six heads, common red squirrel two heads, black squirrel ten heads, a partridge five heads,
the larger birds, such as whip-poor-wills and nighthawks two
heads each, the wary crows three, and bob-whites three. But
all the blessed company of mere songbirds, warblers, robins,
thrushes, orioles, with nuthatches, chickadees, blue jays,
woodpeckers, etc., counted only one head each. The heads of
the birds were hastily wrung off and thrust into the game-
bags to be counted, saving the bodies only of what were called
game, the larger squirrels, bob-whites, partridges, etc. The
blood-stained bags of the best slayers were soon bulging full.
Then at a given hour all had to stop and repair to the town,
empty their dripping sacks, count the heads, and go rejoicing
to their dinner. Although, like other wild boys, I was fond of
shooting, I never had anything to do with these abominable
head-hunts. And now the farmers having learned that birds
are their friends wholesale slaughter has been abolished.

We seldom saw deer, though their tracks were common.
The Yankee explained that they traveled and fed mostly at
night, and hid in tamarack swamps and brushy places in the

daytime, and how the Indians knew all about them and could find them whenever they were hungry.

Indians belonging to the Menominee and Winnebago tribes occasionally visited us at our cabin to get a piece of bread or some matches, or to sharpen their knives on our grindstone, and we boys watched them closely to see that they didn't steal Jack. We wondered at their knowledge of animals when we saw them go direct to trees on our farm, chop holes in them with their tomahawks and take out coons, of the existence of which we had never noticed the slightest trace. In winter, after the first snow, we frequently saw three or four Indians hunting deer in company, running like hounds on the fresh, exciting tracks. The escape of the deer from these noiseless, tireless hunters was said to be well-nigh impossible; they were followed to the death.

Most of our neighbors brought some sort of gun from the old country, but seldom took time to hunt, even after the first hard work of fencing and clearing was over, except to shoot a duck or prairie chicken now and then that happened to come in their way. It was only the less industrious American settlers who left their work to go far a-hunting. Two or three of our most enterprising American neighbors went off every fall with their teams to the pine regions and cranberry marshes in the northern part of the State to hunt and gather berries. I well remember seeing their wagons loaded with game when they returned from a successful hunt. Their loads consisted usually of half a dozen deer or more, one or two black bears, and fifteen or twenty bushels of cranberries; all solidly frozen. Part of both the berries and meat was usually sold in Portage; the balance furnished their families with abundance of venison, bear grease, and pies.

Winter wheat is sown in the fall, and when it is a month or so old the deer, like the wild geese, are very fond of it, especially since other kinds of food are then becoming scarce. One of our neighbors across the Fox River killed a large number, some thirty or forty, on a small patch of wheat, simply by lying in wait for them every night. Our wheat-field was the first that was sown in the neighborhood. The deer soon found it and came in every night to feast, but it was eight or nine years before we ever disturbed them. David then killed one deer, the only one killed by any of our family. He went out shortly after sundown at the time of full moon to one of our wheat-fields, carrying a double-barreled shotgun loaded with buckshot. After lying in wait an hour or so, he saw a doe and her fawn jump the fence and come cautiously into the wheat. After they were within sixty or seventy yards of him, he was surprised when he tried to take aim that about half of the moon's disc was mysteriously darkened as if covered by the edge of a dense cloud. This proved to be an eclipse. Nevertheless, he fired at the mother, and she immediately ran off, jumped the fence, and took to the woods by the way she came. The fawn danced about bewildered, wondering what had become of its mother, but finally fled to the woods. David fired at the poor deserted thing as it ran past him but happily missed it. Hearing the shots, I joined David to learn his luck. He said he thought he must have wounded the mother, and when we were strolling about in the woods in search of her we saw three or four deer on their way to the wheat-field, led by a fine buck. They were walking rapidly, but cautiously halted at intervals of a few rods to listen and look ahead and scent the air. They failed to notice us, though by this time the moon was out of the eclipse shadow and we were standing only about fifty yards from them. I was carrying the gun. David had fired both barrels but when he was reloading one of them he happened to put the wad intended to cover the shot into the empty barrel, and so when we were climbing over the fence the buckshot had rolled out, and when I fired at the big buck I knew by the report that there was nothing but powder in the charge. The startled deer danced about in confusion for a few seconds, uncertain which way to run until they caught sight of us, when they bounded off through the woods. Next morning we found the poor mother lying about three hundred yards from the place where she was shot. She had run this distance and jumped a high fence after one of the buckshot had passed through her heart.

Excepting Sundays we boys had only two days of the year to ourselves, the 4th of July and the 1st of January. Sundays were less than half our own, on account of Bible lessons, Sunday-school lessons and church services; all the others were labor days, rain or shine, cold or warm. No wonder, then, that our two holidays were precious and that it was not easy to decide what to do with them. They were usually spent on the highest rocky hill in the neighborhood, called the Observatory; in visiting our boy friends on adjacent farms to hunt, fish, wrestle, and play games; in reading some new favorite book we had managed to borrow or buy; or in making models of machines I had invented.

One of our July days was spent with two Scotch boys of our own age hunting redwing blackbirds then busy in the corn-fields. Our party had only one single-barreled shotgun, which, as the oldest and perhaps because I was thought to be the best shot, I had the honor of carrying. We marched through the corn without getting sight of a single redwing, but just as we reached the far side of the field, a red-headed woodpecker flew up, and the Lawson boys cried: "Shoot him! Shoot him! he is just as bad as a blackbird. He eats corn!" This memorable woodpecker alighted in the top of a white oak tree about fifty feet high. I fired from a position almost immediately beneath him, and he fell straight down at my feet. When I picked him up and was admiring his plumage, he moved his legs slightly, and I said, "Poor bird, he's no deed yet and we'll hae to kill him to put him oot o' pain,"—sincerely pitying him, after we had taken pleasure in shooting him. I had seen servant girls wringing chicken necks, so with desperate humanity I took the limp unfortunate by the head, swung him around three or four times thinking I was wringing his neck, and then threw him hard on the ground to quench the last possible spark of life and make quick death doubly sure. But to our astonishment the moment he struck the ground he gave a cry of alarm and flew right straight up like a rejoicing lark into the top of the same tree, and perhaps to the same branch he had fallen from, and began to adjust his ruffled feathers, nodding and chirping and looking down at us as if wondering what in the bird world we had been doing to him. This of course banished all thought of killing, as far as that revived woodpecker was concerned, no matter how many ears of corn he might spoil, and we all heartily congratulated him on his wonderful, triumphant resurrection from three kinds of death,—shooting, neck-wringing, and destructive concussion. I suppose only one pellet had touched him, glancing on his head.

Another extraordinary shooting-affair happened one summer morning shortly after daybreak. When I went to the stable to feed the horses I noticed a big white-breasted hawk on a tall oak in front of the chicken-house, evidently waiting for a chicken breakfast. I ran to the house for the gun, and when I fired he fell about halfway down the tree, caught a branch with his claws, hung back downward and fluttered a few seconds, then managed to stand erect. I fired again to put him out of pain, and to my surprise the second shot seemed to restore his strength instead of killing him, for he flew out of the tree and over the meadow with strong and regular wing-beats for thirty or forty rods apparently as well as ever, but died suddenly in the air and dropped like a stone.

We hunted muskrats whenever we had time to run down to the lake. They are brown bunchy animals about twenty-three inches long, the tail being about nine inches in length, black in color and flattened vertically for sculling, and the hind feet are half-webbed. They look like little beavers, usually have from ten to a dozen young, are easily tamed and make interesting pets. We liked to watch them at their work and at their meals. In the spring when the snow vanishes and the lake ice begins to melt, the first open spot is always used as a feeding-place, where they dive from the edge of the ice and in a minute or less reappear with a mussel or a mouthful of pontederia or water-lily leaves, climb back on to the ice and sit up to nibble their food, handling it very much like squirrels or marmots. It is then that they are most easily shot, a solitary hunter oftentimes shooting thirty or forty in a single day. Their nests on the rushy margins of lakes and streams, far from being hidden like those of most birds, are conspicuously large, and conical in shape like Indian wigwams. They are built of plants—rushes, sedges, mosses, etc.—and ornamented around the base with mussel-shells. It was always pleasant and interesting to see them in the fall as soon as the nights began to be frosty, hard at work cutting sedges on the edge of the meadow or swimming out through the rushes, making long glittering ripples as they sculled themselves along, diving where the water is perhaps six or eight feet deep and re-appearing in a minute or so with large mouthfuls of the weedy tangled plants gathered from the bottom, returning to their big wigwams, climbing up and depositing their loads where most needed to make them yet larger and firmer and warmer, foreseeing the freezing weather just like ourselves when we banked up our house to keep out the frost.

They lie snug and invisible all winter but do not hibernate. Through a channel carefully kept open they swim out under the ice for mussels, and the roots and stems of water-lilies, etc., on which they feed just as they do in summer. Sometimes the oldest and most enterprising of them venture to orchards near the water in search of fallen apples; very seldom, how-ever, do they interfere with anything belonging to their mortal enemy man. Notwithstanding they are so well hidden and protected during the winter, many of them are killed by In-dian hunters, who creep up softly and spear them through the thick walls of their cabins. Indians are fond of their flesh, and so are some of the wildest of the white trappers. They are easily caught in steel traps, and after vainly trying to drag their feet from the cruel crushing jaws, they sometimes in their agony gnaw them off. Even after having gnawed off a leg they are so guileless that they never seem to learn to know and fear traps, for some are occasionally found that have been caught twice and have gnawed off a second foot. Many other animals suffering excruciating pain in these cruel traps gnaw off their legs. Crabs and lobsters are so fortunate as to be able to shed their limbs when caught or merely frightened, apparently without suffering any pain, simply by giving themselves a little shivery shake.

The muskrat is one of the most notable and widely distrib-uted of American animals, and millions of the gentle, indus-trious, beaver-like creatures are shot and trapped and speared every season for their skins, worth a dime or so,—like shoot-ing boys and girls for their garments.

Surely a better time must be drawing nigh when godlike human beings will become truly humane, and learn to put their animal fellow mortals in their hearts instead of on their backs or in their dinners. In the mean time we may just as well as not learn to live clean, innocent lives instead of slimy, bloody ones. All hale, red-blooded boys are savage, the best and boldest the savagest, fond of hunting and fishing. But when thoughtless childhood is past, the best rise the highest above all this bloody flesh and sport business, the wild foundational animal dying out day by day, as divine uplifting, transfiguring charity grows in.

Hares and rabbits were seldom seen when we first settled in the Wisconsin woods, but they multiplied rapidly after the animals that preyed upon them had been thinned out or exterminated, and food and shelter supplied in grain-fields and log fences and the thickets of young oaks that grew up in pastures after the annual grass fires were kept out. Catching hares in the winter-time, when they were hidden in hollow fence-logs, was a favorite pastime with many of the boys whose fathers allowed them time to enjoy the sport. Occasionally a stout, lithe hare was carried out into an open snow-covered field, set free, and given a chance for its life in a race with a dog. When the snow was not too soft and deep, it usually made good its escape, for our dogs were only fat, short-legged mongrels. We sometimes discovered hares in standing hollow trees, crouching on decayed punky wood at the bottom, as far back as possible from the opening, but when alarmed they managed to climb to a considerable height if the hollow was not too wide, by bracing themselves against the sides.

Foxes, though not uncommon, we boys held steadily to work seldom saw, and as they found plenty of prairie chickens for themselves and families, they did not often come near the farmer's hen-roosts. Nevertheless the discovery of their dens was considered important. No matter how deep the den might be, it was thoroughly explored with pick and shovel by sport-loving settlers at a time when they judged the fox was likely to be at home, but I cannot remember any case in our neighborhood where the fox was actually captured. In one of the dens a mile or two from our farm a lot of prairie chickens were found and some smaller birds.

Badger dens were far more common than fox dens. One of our fields was named Badger Hill from the number of badger holes in a hill at the end of it, but I cannot remember seeing a single one of the inhabitants.

On a stormy day in the middle of an unusually severe winter, a black bear, hungry, no doubt, and seeking something to eat, came strolling down through our neighborhood from the northern pine woods. None had been seen here before, and it caused no little excitement and alarm, for the European settlers imagined that these poor, timid, bashful bears were as dangerous as man-eating lions and tigers, and that they would pursue any human being that came in their way. This species is common in the north part of the State, and few of our enterprising Yankee hunters who went to the pineries in the fall failed to shoot at least one of them.

We saw very little of the owlish, serious-looking coons, and no wonder, since they lie hidden nearly all day in hollow trees and we never had time to hunt them. We often heard their curious, quavering, whinnying cries on still evenings, but only once succeeded in tracing an unfortunate family through our corn-field to their den in a big oak and catching them all. One of our neighbors, Mr. McRath, a Highland Scotchman, caught one and made a pet of it. It became very tame and had perfect confidence in the good intentions of its kind friend and master. He always addressed it in speaking to it as a "little man." When it came running to him and jumped on his lap or climbed up his trousers, he would say, while patting its head as if it were a dog or a child, "Coonie, ma mannie, Coonie, ma mannie, hoo are ye the day? I think you're hungry,"—as the comical pet began to examine his pockets for nuts and bits of bread,—"Na, na, there's nathing in my pooch for ye the day, my wee mannie, but I'll get ye something." He would then fetch something it liked,—bread, nuts, a carrot, or perhaps a piece of fresh meat. Anything scattered for it on the floor it felt with its paw instead of looking at it, judging of its worth more by touch than sight.

The outlet of our Fountain Lake flowed past Mr. McRath's door, and the coon was very fond of swimming in it and searching for frogs and mussels. It seemed perfectly satisfied to stay about the house without being confined, occupied a comfortable bed in a section of a hollow tree, and never wandered far. How long it lived after the death of its kind master I don't know.

I suppose that almost any wild animal may be made a pet,

simply by sympathizing with it and entering as much as possible into its life. In Alaska I saw one of the common gray mountain marmots kept as a pet in an Indian family. When its master entered the house it always seemed glad, almost like a dog, and when cold or tired it snuggled up in a fold of his blanket with the utmost confidence.

We have all heard of ferocious animals, lions and tigers, etc., that were fed and spoken to only by their masters, becoming perfectly tame; and, as is well known, the faithful dog that follows man and serves him, and looks up to him and loves him as if he were a god, is a descendant of the blood-thirsty wolf or jackal. Even frogs and toads and fishes may be tamed, provided they have the uniform sympathy of one person, with whom they become intimately acquainted without the distracting and varying attentions of strangers. And surely all God's people, however serious and savage, great or small, like to play. Whales and elephants, dancing, humming gnats, and invisibly small mischievous microbes,—all are warm with divine radium and must have lots of fun in them.

As far as I know, all wild creatures keep themselves clean. Birds, it seems to me, take more pains to bathe and dress themselves than any other animals. Even ducks, though living so much in water, dip and scatter cleansing showers over their backs, and shake and preen their feathers as carefully as landbirds. Watching small singers taking their morning baths is very interesting, particularly when the weather is cold. Alighting in a shallow pool, they oftentimes show a sort of dread of dipping into it, like children hesitating about taking a plunge, as if they felt the same kind of shock, and this makes it easy for us to sympathize with the little feathered people.

Occasionally I have seen from my study-window red-headed linnets bathing in dew when water elsewhere was scarce. A large Monterey cypress with broad branches and innumerable leaves on which the dew lodges in still nights made favorite bathing-places. Alighting gently, as if afraid to waste the dew, they would pause and fidget as they do before beginning to plash in pools, then dip and scatter the drops in showers and get as thorough a bath as they would in a pool. I have also seen the same kind of baths taken by birds on the boughs of silver firs on the edge of a glacier meadow, but nowhere have I seen the dew-drops so abundant as on the Monterey cypress; and the picture made by the quivering wings and irised dew was memorably beautiful. Children, too, make fine pictures plashing and crowing in their little tubs. How widely different from wallowing pigs, bathing with great show of comfort and rubbing themselves dry against rough-barked trees!

Some of our own species seem fairly to dread the touch of water. When the necessity of absolute cleanliness by means of frequent baths was being preached by a friend who had been reading Combe's Physiology, in which he had learned something of the wonders of the skin with its millions of pores that had to be kept open for health, one of our neighbors remarked: "Oh! that's unnatural. It's well enough to wash in a tub maybe once or twice a year, but not to be paddling in the water all the time like a frog in a spring-hole." Another neighbor, who prided himself on his knowledge of big words, said with great solemnity: "I never can believe that man is amphibious!"

Natives of tropic islands pass a large part of their lives in water, and seem as much at home in the sea as on the land; swim and dive, pursue fishes, play in the waves like surf-ducks and seals, and explore the coral gardens and groves and sea-weed meadows as if truly amphibious. Even the natives of the far north bathe at times. I once saw a lot of Eskimo boys ducking and plashing right merrily in the Arctic Ocean.

It seemed very wonderful to us that the wild animals could keep themselves warm and strong in winter when the temperature was far below zero. Feeble-looking rabbits scud away over the snow, lithe and elastic, as if glorying in the frosty, sparkling weather and sure of their dinners. I have seen gray squirrels dragging ears of corn about as heavy as themselves out of our field through loose snow and up a tree, balancing them on limbs and eating in comfort with their dry, electric tails spread airily over their backs. Once I saw a fine hardy fellow go into a knot-hole. Thrusting in my hand I caught him and pulled him out. As soon as he guessed what I was up to, he took the end of my thumb in his mouth and sunk his teeth right through it, but I gripped him hard by the neck, carried him home, and shut him up in a box that contained about half a bushel of hazel- and hickory-nuts, hoping that he would not be too much frightened and discouraged to eat while thus imprisoned after the rough handling he had suffered. I soon learned, however, that sympathy in this direction was wasted, for no sooner did I pop him in than he fell to with right hearty appetite, gnawing and munching the nuts as if he had gathered them himself and was very hungry that day. Therefore, after allowing time enough for a good square meal, I made haste to get him out of the nut-box and shut him up in a spare bedroom, in which father had hung a lot of selected ears of Indian corn for seed. They were hung up by the husks on cords stretched across from side to side of the room. The squirrel managed to jump from the top of one of the bed-posts to the cord, cut off an ear, and let it drop to the floor. He then jumped down, got a good grip of the heavy ear, carried it to the top of one of the slippery, polished bed-posts, seated himself comfortably, and, holding it well balanced, deliberately pried out one kernel at a time with his long chisel teeth, ate the soft, sweet germ, and dropped the hard part of the kernel. In this masterly way, working at high speed, he demolished several ears a day, and with a good warm bed in a box made himself at home and grew fat. Then naturally, I suppose, free romping in the snow and tree-tops with companions came to mind. Anyhow he began to look for a way of escape. Of course he first tried the window, but found that his teeth made no impression on the glass. Next he tried the sash and gnawed the wood off level with the glass; then father happened to come upstairs and discovered the mischief that was being done to his seed corn and window and immediately ordered him out of the house.

The flying squirrel was one of the most interesting of the little animals we found in the woods, a beautiful brown creature, with fine eyes and smooth, soft fur like that of a mole or field mouse. He is about half as long as the gray squirrel, but his wide-spread tail and the folds of skin along his sides that form the wings make him look broad and flat, something like a kite. In the evenings our cat often brought them to her kittens at the shanty, and later we saw them fly during the day from the trees we were chopping. They jumped and glided off smoothly and apparently without effort, like birds, as soon as they heard and felt the breaking shock of the strained fibres at the stump, when the trees they were in began to totter and groan. They can fly, or rather glide, twenty or thirty yards from the top of a tree twenty or thirty feet high to the foot of another, gliding upward as they reach the trunk, or if the distance is too great they alight comfortably on the ground and make haste to the nearest tree, and climb just like the wingless squirrels.

Every boy and girl loves the little fairy, airy striped chipmunk, half squirrel, half spermophile. He is about the size of a field mouse, and often made us think of linnets and song sparrows as he frisked about gathering nuts and berries. He likes almost all kinds of grain, berries, and nuts,—hazel-nuts, hickory-nuts, strawberries, huckleberries, wheat, oats, corn,— he is fond of them all and thrives on them. Most of the hazel bushes on our farm grew along the fences as if they had been planted for the chipmunks alone, for the rail fences were their favorite highways. We never wearied watching them, especially when the hazel-nuts were ripe and the little fellows were sitting on the rails nibbling and handling them like tree-squirrels. We used to notice too that, although they are very neat animals, their lips and fingers were dyed red like our own, when the strawberries and huckleberries were ripe. We could always tell when the wheat and oats were in the milk by seeing the chipmunks feeding on the ears. They kept nibbling at the wheat until it was harvested and then gleaned in the stubble, keeping up a careful watch for their enemies,—dogs, hawks, and shrikes. They are as widely distributed over the continent as the squirrels, various species inhabiting different regions on the mountains and lowlands, but all the different kinds have the same general characteristics of light, airy cheerfulness and good nature.

Before the arrival of farmers in the Wisconsin woods the small ground squirrels, called "gophers," lived chiefly on the seeds of wild grasses and weeds, but after the country was cleared and ploughed no feasting animal fell to more heartily on the farmer's wheat and corn. Increasing rapidly in numbers and knowledge, they became very destructive, especially in the spring when the corn was planted, for they learned to trace the rows and dig up and eat the three or four seeds in each hill about as fast as the poor farmers could cover them. And unless great pains were taken to diminish the numbers of the cunning little robbers, the fields had to be planted two or three times over, and even then large gaps in the rows would be found. The loss of the grain they consumed after it was ripe, together with the winter stores laid up in their burrows, amounted to little as compared with the loss of the seed on which the whole crop depended.

One evening about sundown, when my father sent me out with the shotgun to hunt them in a stubble field, I learned something curious and interesting in connection with these mischievous gophers, though just then they were doing no harm. As I strolled through the stubble watching for a chance for a shot, a shrike flew past me and alighted on an open spot at the mouth of a burrow about thirty yards ahead of me. Curious to see what he was up to, I stood still to watch him. He looked down the gopher hole in a listening attitude, then looked back at me to see if I was coming, looked down again and listened, and looked back at me. I stood perfectly still, and he kept twitching his tail, seeming uneasy and doubtful about venturing to do the savage job that I soon learned he had in his mind. Finally, encouraged by my keeping so still, to my astonishment he suddenly vanished in the gopher hole.

A bird going down a deep narrow hole in the ground like a ferret or a weasel seemed very strange, and I thought it would be a fine thing to run forward, clap my hand over the hole, and have the fun of imprisoning him and seeing what he would do when he tried to get out. So I ran forward but stopped when I got within a dozen or fifteen yards of the hole, thinking it might perhaps be more interesting to wait and see what would naturally happen without my interference. While I stood there looking and listening, I heard a great disturbance going on in the burrow, a mixed lot of keen squeaking, shrieking, distressful cries, telling that down in the dark something terrible was being done. Then suddenly out popped a half-grown gopher, four and a half or five inches long, and, without stopping a single moment to choose a way of escape, ran screaming through the stubble straight away from its home, quickly followed by another and another, until some half-dozen were driven out, all of them crying and running in different directions as if at this dreadful time home, sweet home, was the most dangerous and least desirable of any place in the wide world. Then out came the shrike, flew above the runaway gopher children, and, diving on them, killed them one after another with blows at the back of the skull. He then seized one of them, dragged it to the top of a small clod so as to be able to get a start, and laboriously made out to fly with it about ten or fifteen yards, when he alighted to rest. Then he dragged it to the top of another clod and flew with it about the same distance, repeating this hard work over and over again until he managed to get one of the gophers on to the top of a log fence. How much he ate of his hard-won prey, or what he did with the others, I can't tell, for by this time the sun was down and I had to hurry home to my chores.

VI

THE PLOUGHBOY

THE CROPS—DOING CHORES—THE SIGHTS AND
SOUNDS OF WINTER—ROAD-MAKING—THE SPIRIT-
RAPPING CRAZE—TUBERCULOSIS AMONG THE SET-
TLERS—A CRUEL BROTHER—THE RIGHTS OF THE
INDIANS—PUT TO THE PLOUGH AT THE AGE OF
TWELVE—IN THE HARVEST-FIELD—OVER-INDUSTRY
AMONG THE SETTLERS—RUNNING THE BREAKING-
PLOUGH—DIGGING A WELL—CHOKE-DAMP—
LINING BEES.

AT FIRST, wheat, corn, and potatoes were the principal
crops we raised; wheat especially. But in four or five
years the soil was so exhausted that only five or six bushels an
acre, even in the better fields, was obtained, although when
first ploughed twenty and twenty-five bushels was about the
ordinary yield. More attention was then paid to corn, but
without fertilizers the corn-crop also became very meagre. At
last it was discovered that English clover would grow on even
the exhausted fields, and that when ploughed under and
planted with corn, or even wheat, wonderful crops were
raised. This caused a complete change in farming methods;
the farmers raised fertilizing clover, planted corn, and fed the
crop to cattle and hogs.

But no crop raised in our wilderness was so surprisingly rich
and sweet and purely generous to us boys and, indeed, to
everybody as the watermelons and muskmelons. We planted
a large patch on a sunny hill-slope the very first spring, and it
seemed miraculous that a few handfuls of little flat seeds
should in a few months send up a hundred wagon-loads of
crisp, sumptuous, red-hearted and yellow-hearted fruits covering all the hill. We soon learned to know when they were
in their prime, and when over-ripe and mealy. Also that if a
second crop was taken from the same ground without fertilizing it, the melons would be small and what we called soapy;
that is, soft and smooth, utterly uncrisp, and without a trace

97

of the lively freshness and sweetness of those raised on virgin soil. Coming in from the farm work at noon, the half-dozen or so of melons we had placed in our cold spring were a glorious luxury that only weary barefooted farm boys can ever know.

Spring was not very trying as to temperature, and refreshing rains fell at short intervals. The work of ploughing commenced as soon as the frost was out of the ground. Corn- and potato-planting and the sowing of spring wheat was comparatively light work, while the nesting birds sang cheerily, grass and flowers covered the marshes and meadows and all the wild, uncleared parts of the farm, and the trees put forth their new leaves, those of the oaks forming beautiful purple masses as if every leaf were a petal; and with all this we enjoyed the mild soothing winds, the humming of innumerable small insects and hylas, and the freshness and fragrance of everything. Then, too, came the wonderful passenger pigeons streaming from the south, and flocks of geese and cranes, filling all the sky with whistling wings.

The summer work, on the contrary, was deadly heavy, especially harvesting and corn-hoeing. All the ground had to be hoed over for the first few years, before father bought cultivators or small weed-covering ploughs, and we were not allowed a moment's rest. The hoes had to be kept working up and down as steadily as if they were moved by machinery. Ploughing for winter wheat was comparatively easy, when we walked barefooted in the furrows, while the fine autumn tints kindled in the woods, and the hillsides were covered with golden pumpkins.

In summer the chores were grinding scythes, feeding the animals, chopping stove-wood, and carrying water up the hill from the spring on the edge of the meadow, etc. Then breakfast, and to the harvest or hay-field. I was foolishly ambitious to be first in mowing and cradling, and by the time I was sixteen led all the hired men. An hour was allowed at noon for dinner and more chores. We stayed in the field until dark, then supper, and still more chores, family worship, and to bed; making altogether a hard, sweaty day of about sixteen or seventeen hours. Think of that, ye blessed eight-hour-day laborers!

In winter father came to the foot of the stairs and called us at six o'clock to feed the horses and cattle, grind axes, bring in wood, and do any other chores required, then breakfast, and out to work in the mealy, frosty snow by daybreak, chopping, fencing, etc. So in general our winter work was about as restless and trying as that of the long-day summer. No matter what the weather, there was always something to do. During heavy rains or snowstorms we worked in the barn, shelling corn, fanning wheat, thrashing with the flail, making axe-handles or ox-yokes, mending things, or sprouting and sorting potatoes in the cellar.

No pains were taken to diminish or in any way soften the natural hardships of this pioneer farm life; nor did any of the Europeans seem to know how to find reasonable ease and comfort if they would. The very best oak and hickory fuel was embarrassingly abundant and cost nothing but cutting and common sense; but instead of hauling great heart-cheering loads of it for wide, open, all-welcoming, climate-changing, beauty-making, Godlike ingle-fires, it was hauled with weary heart-breaking industry into fences and waste places to get it out of the way of the plough, and out of the way of doing good. The only fire for the whole house was the kitchen stove, with a fire-box about eighteen inches long and eight inches wide and deep,—scant space for three or four small sticks, around which in hard zero weather all the family of ten persons shivered, and beneath which in the morning we found our socks and coarse, soggy boots frozen solid. We were not allowed to start even this despicable little fire in its black box to thaw them. No, we had to squeeze our throbbing, aching, chilblained feet into them, causing greater pain than toothache, and hurry out to chores. Fortunately the miserable chilblain pain began to abate as soon as the temperature of our feet approached the freezing-point, enabling us in spite of hard work and hard frost to enjoy the winter beauty,—the wonderful radiance of the snow when it was starry with crystals, and the dawns and the sunsets and white noons, and the cheery, enlivening company of the brave chickadees and nuthatches.

The winter stars far surpassed those of our stormy Scotland in brightness, and we gazed and gazed as though we had

never seen stars before. Oftentimes the heavens were made
still more glorious by auroras, the long lance rays, called
"Merry Dancers" in Scotland, streaming with startling tremulous motion to the zenith. Usually the electric auroral light
is white or pale yellow, but in the third or fourth of our Wisconsin winters there was a magnificently colored aurora that
was seen and admired over nearly all the continent. The whole
sky was draped in graceful purple and crimson folds glorious
beyond description. Father called us out into the yard in front
of the house where we had a wide view, crying, "Come!
Come, mother! Come, bairns! and see the glory of God. All
the sky is clad in a robe of red light. Look straight up to the
crown where the folds are gathered. Hush and wonder and
adore, for surely this is the clothing of the Lord Himself, and
perhaps He will even now appear looking down from his high
heaven." This celestial show was far more glorious than anything we had ever yet beheld, and throughout that wonderful
winter hardly anything else was spoken of.

We even enjoyed the snowstorms, the thronging crystals,
like daisies, coming down separate and distinct, were very different from the tufted flakes we enjoyed so much in Scotland,
when we ran into the midst of the slow-falling feathery throng
shouting with enthusiasm: "Jennie's plucking her doos! Jennie's plucking her doos (doves)!"

Nature has many ways of thinning and pruning and trimming her forests,—lightning-strokes, heavy snow, and storm-
winds to shatter and blow down whole trees here and there
or break off branches as required. The results of these methods I have observed in different forests, but only once have I
seen pruning by rain. The rain froze on the trees as it fell and
grew so thick and heavy that many of them lost a third or
more of their branches. The view of the woods after the storm
had passed and the sun shone forth was something never to
be forgotten. Every twig and branch and rugged trunk was
encased in pure crystal ice, and each oak and hickory and
willow became a fairy crystal palace. Such dazzling brilliance,
such effects of white light and irised light glowing and flashing
I had never seen before, nor have I since. This sudden change
of the leafless woods to glowing silver was, like the great aurora, spoken of for years, and is one of the most beautiful of

the many pictures that enriches my life. And besides the great shows there were thousands of others even in the coldest weather manifesting the utmost fineness and tenderness of beauty and affording noble compensation for hardship and pain.

One of the most striking of the winter sounds was the loud roaring and rumbling of the ice on our lake, from its shrinking and expanding with the changes of the weather. The fishermen who were catching pickerel said that they had no luck when this roaring was going on above the fish. I remember how frightened we boys were when on one of our New Year holidays we were taking a walk on the ice and heard for the first time the sudden rumbling roar beneath our feet and running on ahead of us, creaking and whooping as if all the ice eighteen or twenty inches thick was breaking.

In the neighborhood of our Wisconsin farm there were extensive swamps consisting in great part of a thick sod of very tough carex roots covering thin, watery lakes of mud. They originated in glacier lakes that were gradually overgrown. This sod was so tough that oxen with loaded wagons could be driven over it without cutting down through it, although it was afloat. The carpenters who came to build our frame house, noticing how the sedges sunk beneath their feet, said that if they should break through, they would probably be well on their way to California before touching bottom. On the contrary, all these lake-basins are shallow as compared with their width. When we went into the Wisconsin woods there was not a single wheel-track or cattle-track. The only man-made road was an Indian trail along the Fox River between Portage and Packwauckee Lake. Of course the deer, foxes, badgers, coons, skunks, and even the squirrels had well-beaten tracks from their dens and hiding-places in thickets, hollow trees, and the ground, but they did not reach far, and but little noise was made by the soft-footed travelers in passing over them, only a slight rustling and swishing among fallen leaves and grass.

Corduroying the swamps formed the principal part of road-making among the early settlers for many a day. At these annual road-making gatherings opportunity was offered for discussion of the news, politics, religion, war, the state of the crops, comparative advantages of the new country over the old, and so forth, but the principal opportunities, recurring every week, were the hours after Sunday church services. I remember hearing long talks on the wonderful beauty of the Indian corn; the wonderful melons, so wondrous fine for "sloken a body on hot days"; their contempt for tomatoes, so fine to look at with their sunny colors and so disappointing in taste; the miserable cucumbers the "Yankee bodies" ate, though tasteless as rushes; the character of the Yankees, etcetera. Then there were long discussions about the Russian war, news of which was eagerly gleaned from Greeley's "New York Tribune"; the great battles of the Alma, the charges at Balaklava and Inkerman; the siege of Sebastopol; the military genius of Todleben; the character of Nicholas; the character of the Russian soldier, his stubborn bravery, who for the first time in history withstood the British bayonet charges; the probable outcome of the terrible war; the fate of Turkey, and so forth.

Very few of our old-country neighbors gave much heed to what are called spirit-rappings. On the contrary, they were regarded as a sort of sleight-of-hand humbug. Some of these spirits seem to be stout able-bodied fellows, judging by the weights they lift and the heavy furniture they bang about. But they do no good work that I know of; never saw wood, grind corn, cook, feed the hungry, or go to the help of poor anxious mothers at the bedsides of their sick children. I noticed when I was a boy that it was not the strongest characters who followed so-called mediums. When a rapping-storm was at its height in Wisconsin, one of our neighbors, an old Scotchman, remarked, "Thay puir silly medium-bodies may gang to the deil wi' their rappin' speerits, for they dae nae gude, and I think the deil's their fayther."

Although in the spring of 1849 there was no other settler within a radius of four miles of our Fountain Lake farm, in three or four years almost every quarter-section of government land was taken up, mostly by enthusiastic home-seekers from Great Britain, with only here and there Yankee families from adjacent states, who had come drifting indefinitely westward in covered wagons, seeking their fortunes like winged seeds; all alike striking root and gripping the glacial drift soil as naturally as oak and hickory trees; happy and hopeful, establishing homes and making wider and wider fields in the hospitable wilderness. The axe and plough were kept very busy; cattle, horses, sheep, and pigs multiplied; barns and corn-cribs were filled up, and man and beast were well fed; a schoolhouse was built, which was used also for a church; and in a very short time the new country began to look like an old one.

Comparatively few of the first settlers suffered from serious accidents. One of our neighbors had a finger shot off, and on a bitter, frosty night had to be taken to a surgeon in Portage, in a sled drawn by slow, plodding oxen, to have the shattered stump dressed. Another fell from his wagon and was killed by the wheel passing over his body. An acre of ground was reserved and fenced for graves, and soon consumption came to fill it. One of the saddest instances was that of a Scotch family from Edinburgh, consisting of a father, son, and daughter, who settled on eighty acres of land within half a mile of our place. The daughter died of consumption the third year after their arrival, the son one or two years later, and at last the father followed his two children. Thus sadly ended bright hopes and dreams of a happy home in rich and free America.

Another neighbor, I remember, after a lingering illness died of the same disease in mid-winter, and his funeral was attended by the neighbors in sleighs during a driving snowstorm when the thermometer was fifteen or twenty degrees below zero. The great white plague carried off another of our near neighbors, a fine Scotchman, the father of eight promising boys, when he was only about forty-five years of age. Most of those who suffered from this disease seemed hopeful and cheerful up to a very short time before their death, but Mr. Reid, I remember, on one of his last visits to our house, said with brave resignation: "I know that never more in this world can I be well, but I must just submit. I must just submit."

One of the saddest deaths from other causes than consumption was that of a poor feeble-minded man whose brother, a sturdy blacksmith and preacher, etc., was a very hard taskmaster. Poor half-witted Charlie was kept steadily at work,—although he was not able to do much, for his body was about as feeble as his mind. He never could be taught the right use of an axe, and when he was set to chopping down trees for firewood he feebly hacked and chipped round and round them, sometimes spending several days in nibbling down a tree that a beaver might have gnawed down in half the time. Occasionally when he had an extra large tree to chop, he would go home and report that the tree was too tough and strong for him and that he could never make it fall. Then his brother, calling him a useless creature, would fell it with a few well-directed strokes, and leave Charlie to nibble away at it for weeks trying to make it into stove-wood.

The brawny blacksmith minister punished his feeble brother without any show of mercy for every trivial offense or mistake or pathetic little shortcoming. All the neighbors pitied him, especially the women, who never missed an opportunity to give him kind words, cookies, and pie; above all, they bestowed natural sympathy on the poor imbecile as if he were an unfortunate motherless child. In particular, his nearest neighbors, Scotch Highlanders, warmly welcomed him to their home and never wearied in doing everything that tender sympathy could suggest. To those friends he ran away at every opportunity. But after years of suffering from overwork and punishment his feeble health failed, and he told his Scotch friends one day that he was not able to work any more or do anything that his brother wanted him to do, that he was beaten every day, and that he had come to thank them for their kindness and to bid them good-bye, for he was going to drown himself in Muir's lake. "Oh, Charlie! Charlie!" they cried, "you mustn't talk that way. Cheer up! You will soon be stronger. We all love you. Cheer up! Cheer up! And always come here whenever you need anything."

"Oh, no!" he pathetically replied, "I know you love me, but I can't cheer up any more. My heart's gone, and I want to die."

Next day, when Mr. Anderson, a carpenter whose house was on the west shore of our lake, was going to a spring he saw a man wade out through the rushes and lily-pads and throw himself forward into deep water. This was poor Charlie. Fortunately, Mr. Anderson had a skiff close by, and as the distance was not great he reached the broken-hearted imbecile in time to save his life, and after trying to cheer him took him home to his brother. But even this terrible proof of despair failed to soften the latter. He seemed to regard the attempt at suicide simply as a crime calculated to bring the reproach of the neighbors upon him. One morning, after receiving another beating, Charlie was set to work chopping firewood in front of the house, and after feebly swinging his axe a few times he pitched forward on his face and died on the wood-pile. The unnatural brother then walked over to the neighbor who had saved Charlie from drowning, and after talking on ordinary affairs, crops, the weather, etc., said in a careless tone: "I have a little job of carpenter work for you, Mr. Anderson." "What is it, Mr. ——?" "I want you to make a coffin." "A coffin!" said the startled carpenter. "Who is dead?" "Charlie," he coolly replied. All the neighbors were in tears over the poor child man's fate. But, strange to say, in all that excessively law-abiding neighborhood none was bold enough or kind enough to break the blacksmith's jaw.

The mixed lot of settlers around us offered a favorable field for observation of the different kinds of people of our own race. We were swift to note the way they behaved, the differences in their religion and morals, and in their ways of drawing a living from the same kind of soil under the same general conditions; how they protected themselves from the weather; how they were influenced by new doctrines and old ones seen in new lights in preaching, lecturing, debating, bringing up their children, etc., and how they regarded the Indians, those first settlers and owners of the ground that was being made into farms.

I well remember my father's discussing with a Scotch neighbor, a Mr. George Mair, the Indian question as to the rightful ownership of the soil. Mr. Mair remarked one day that it was pitiful to see how the unfortunate Indians, children of Nature, living on the natural products of the soil, hunting, fishing, and even cultivating small corn-fields on the most fertile spots, were now being robbed of their lands and pushed ruthlessly back into narrower and narrower limits by alien races who were cutting off their means of livelihood. Father replied that surely it could never have been the intention of God to allow Indians to rove and hunt over so fertile a country and hold it forever in unproductive wildness, while Scotch and Irish and

English farmers could put it to so much better use. Where an Indian required thousands of acres for his family, these acres in the hands of industrious, God-fearing farmers would support ten or a hundred times more people in a far worthier manner, while at the same time helping to spread the gospel.

Mr. Mair urged that such farming as our first immigrants were practicing was in many ways rude and full of the mistakes of ignorance, yet, rude as it was, and ill-tilled as were most of our Wisconsin farms by unskillful, inexperienced settlers who had been merchants and mechanics and servants in the old countries, how should we like to have specially trained and educated farmers drive us out of our homes and farms, such as they were, making use of the same argument, that God could never have intended such ignorant, unprofitable, devastating farmers as we were to occupy land upon which scientific farmers could raise five or ten times as much on each acre as we did? And I well remember thinking that Mr. Mair had the better side of the argument. It then seemed to me that, whatever the final outcome might be, it was at this stage of the fight only an example of the rule of might with but little or no thought for the right or welfare of the other fellow if he were the weaker; that "they should take who had the power, and they should keep who can," as Wordsworth makes the marauding Scottish Highlanders say.

Many of our old neighbors toiled and sweated and grubbed themselves into their graves years before their natural dying days, in getting a living on a quarter-section of land and vaguely trying to get rich, while bread and raiment might have been serenely won on less than a fourth of this land, and time gained to get better acquainted with God.

I was put to the plough at the age of twelve, when my head reached but little above the handles, and for many years I had to do the greater part of the ploughing. It was hard work for so small a boy; nevertheless, as good ploughing was exacted from me as if I were a man, and very soon I had to become a good ploughman, or rather ploughboy. None could draw a straighter furrow. For the first few years the work was particularly hard on account of the tree-stumps that had to be dodged. Later the stumps were all dug and chopped out to make way for the McCormick reaper, and because I proved to be the best chopper and stump-digger I had nearly all of it to myself. It was dull, hard work leaning over on my knees all day, chopping out those tough oak and hickory stumps, deep down below the crowns of the big roots. Some, though fortunately not many, were two feet or more in diameter.

And as I was the eldest boy, the greater part of all the other hard work of the farm quite naturally fell on me. I had to split rails for long lines of zigzag fences. The trees that were tall enough and straight enough to afford one or two logs ten feet long were used for rails, the others, too knotty or cross-grained, were disposed of in log and cordwood fences. Making rails was hard work and required no little skill. I used to cut and split a hundred a day from our short, knotty oak timber, swinging the axe and heavy mallet, often with sore hands, from early morning to night. Father was not successful as a rail-splitter. After trying the work with me a day or two, he in despair left it all to me. I rather liked it, for I was proud of my skill, and tried to believe that I was as tough as the timber I mauled, though this and other heavy jobs stopped my growth and earned for me the title "Runt of the family."

In those early days, long before the great labor-saving machines came to our help, almost everything connected with wheat-raising abounded in trying work,—cradling in the long, sweaty dog-days, raking and binding, stacking, thrashing,—and it often seemed to me that our fierce, over-industrious way of getting the grain from the ground was too closely connected with grave-digging. The staff of life, naturally beautiful, oftentimes suggested the grave-digger's spade. Men and boys, and in those days even women and girls, were cut down while cutting the wheat. The fat folk grew lean and the lean leaner, while the rosy cheeks brought from Scotland and other cool countries across the sea faded to yellow like the wheat. We were all made slaves through the vice of over-industry. The same was in great part true in making hay to keep the cattle and horses through the long winters. We were called in the morning at four o'clock and seldom got to bed before nine, making a broiling, seething day seventeen hours long loaded with heavy work, while I was only a small stunted boy; and a few years later my brothers David and Daniel and my older sisters had to endure about as much as I did. In the harvest dog-days and dog-nights and dog-mornings, when we arose from our clammy beds, our cotton shirts clung to our backs as wet with sweat as the bathing-suits of swimmers, and remained so all the long, sweltering days. In mowing and cradling, the most exhausting of all the farm work, I made matters worse by foolish ambition in keeping ahead of the hired men. Never a warning word was spoken of the dangers of over-work. On the contrary, even when sick we were held to our tasks as long as we could stand. Once in harvest-time I had the mumps and was unable to swallow any food except milk, but this was not allowed to make any difference, while I staggered with weakness and sometimes fell headlong among the sheaves. Only once was I allowed to leave the harvest-field—when I was stricken down with pneumonia. I lay gasping for weeks, but the Scotch are hard to kill and I pulled through. No physician was called, for father was an enthusiast, and always said and believed that God and hard work were by far the best doctors.

None of our neighbors were so excessively industrious as father; though nearly all of the Scotch, English, and Irish worked too hard, trying to make good homes and to lay up money enough for comfortable independence. Excepting small garden-patches, few of them had owned land in the old country. Here their craving land-hunger was satisfied, and they were naturally proud of their farms and tried to keep them as neat and clean and well-tilled as gardens. To accomplish this without the means for hiring help was impossible. Flowers were planted about the neatly kept log or frame houses; barnyards, granaries, etc., were kept in about as neat order as the homes, and the fences and corn-rows were rigidly straight. But every uncut weed distressed them; so also did every ungathered ear of grain, and all that was lost by birds and gophers; and this overcarefulness bred endless work and worry.

As for money, for many a year there was precious little of it in the country for anybody. Eggs sold at six cents a dozen in trade, and five-cent calico was exchanged at twenty-five cents a yard. Wheat brought fifty cents a bushel in trade. To get cash for it before the Portage Railway was built, it had to be hauled to Milwaukee, a hundred miles away. On the other hand, food was abundant,—eggs, chickens, pigs, cattle, wheat, corn, potatoes, garden vegetables of the best, and wonderful melons as luxuries. No other wild country I have ever known extended a kinder welcome to poor immigrants. On the arrival in the spring, a log house could be built, a few acres ploughed, the virgin sod planted with corn, potatoes, etc., and enough raised to keep a family comfortably the very first year; and wild hay for cows and oxen grew in abundance on the numerous meadows. The American settlers were wisely content with smaller fields and less of everything, kept indoors during excessively hot or cold weather, rested when tired, went off fishing and hunting at the most favorable times and seasons of the day and year, gathered nuts and berries, and in general tranquilly accepted all the good things the fertile wilderness offered.

After eight years of this dreary work of clearing the Fountain Lake farm, fencing it and getting it in perfect order, building a frame house and the necessary outbuildings for the cattle and horses,—after all this had been victoriously accomplished, and we had made out to escape with life,—father bought a half-section of wild land about four or five miles to the eastward and began all over again to clear and fence and break up other fields for a new farm, doubling all the stunting, heartbreaking chopping, grubbing, stump-digging, rail-splitting, fence-building, barn-building, house-building, and so forth.

By this time I had learned to run the breaking plough. Most of these ploughs were very large, turning furrows from eighteen inches to two feet wide, and were drawn by four or five yoke of oxen. They were used only for the first ploughing, in breaking up the wild sod woven into a tough mass, chiefly by the cordlike roots of perennial grasses, reinforced by the taproots of oak and hickory bushes, called "grubs," some of which were more than a century old and four or five inches in diameter. In the hardest ploughing on the most difficult ground, the grubs were said to be as thick as the hair on a dog's back. If in good trim, the plough cut through and turned over these grubs as if the century-old wood were soft like the flesh of carrots and turnips; but if not in good trim the grubs promptly tossed the plough out of the ground. A stout Highland Scot, our neighbor, whose plough was in bad order and who did not know how to trim it, was vainly trying to keep it in the ground by main strength, while his son, who was driving and merrily whipping up the cattle, would cry encouragingly, "Haud her in, fayther! Haud her in!"

"But hoo i' the deil can I haud her in when she'll no *stop* in?" his perspiring father would reply, gasping for breath between each word. On the contrary, with the share and coulter sharp and nicely adjusted, the plough, instead of shying at every grub and jumping out, ran straight ahead without need of steering or holding, and gripped the ground so firmly that it could hardly be thrown out at the end of the furrow.

Our breaker turned a furrow two feet wide, and on our best land, where the sod was toughest, held so firm a grip that at the end of the field my brother, who was driving the oxen, had to come to my assistance in throwing it over on its side to be drawn around the end of the landing; and it was all I could do to set it up again. But I learned to keep that plough in such trim that after I got started on a new furrow I used to ride on the crossbar between the handles with my feet resting comfortably on the beam, without having to steady or steer it in any way on the whole length of the field, unless we had to go round a stump, for it sawed through the biggest grubs without flinching.

The growth of these grubs was interesting to me. When an acorn or hickory-nut had sent up its first season's sprout, a few inches long, it was burned off in the autumn grass fires; but the root continued to hold on to life, formed a callus over the wound and sent up one or more shoots the next spring. Next autumn these new shoots were burned off, but the root and calloused head, about level with the surface of the ground, continued to grow and send up more new shoots; and so on, almost every year until very old, probably far more than a century, while the tops, which would naturally have become tall broad-headed trees, were only mere sprouts seldom more than two years old. Thus the ground was kept open like a prairie, with only five or six trees to the acre, which had escaped the fire by having the good fortune to grow on a bare spot at the door of a fox or badger den, or between straggling grass-tufts wide apart on the poorest sandy soil.

The uniformly rich soil of the Illinois and Wisconsin prairies produced so close and tall a growth of grasses for fires that no tree could live on it. Had there been no fires, these fine prairies, so marked a feature of the country, would have been covered by the heaviest forests. As soon as the oak openings in our neighborhood were settled, and the farmers had prevented running grass-fires, the grubs grew up into trees and formed tall thickets so dense that it was difficult to walk through them and every trace of the sunny "openings" vanished.

We called our second farm Hickory Hill, from its many fine hickory trees and the long gentle slope leading up to it. Compared with Fountain Lake farm it lay high and dry. The land was better, but it had no living water, no spring or stream or meadow or lake. A well ninety feet deep had to be dug, all except the first ten feet or so in fine-grained sandstone. When the sandstone was struck, my father, on the advice of a man who had worked in mines, tried to blast the rock; but from lack of skill the blasting went on very slowly, and father decided to have me do all the work with mason's chisels, a long, hard job, with a good deal of danger in it. I had to sit cramped in a space about three feet in diameter, and wearily chip, chip, with heavy hammer and chisels from early morning until dark, day after day, for weeks and months. In the morning, father and David lowered me in a wooden bucket by a windlass, hauled up what chips were left from the night before, then went away to the farm work and left me until noon, when they hoisted me out for dinner. After dinner I was promptly lowered again, the forenoon's accumulation of chips hoisted out of the way, and I was left until night.

One morning, after the dreary bore was about eighty feet deep, my life was all but lost in deadly choke-damp,—carbonic acid gas that had settled at the bottom during the night. Instead of clearing away the chips as usual when I was lowered to the bottom, I swayed back and forth and began to sink under the poison. Father, alarmed that I did not make any noise, shouted, "What's keeping you so still?" to which he got no reply. Just as I was settling down against the side of the wall, I happened to catch a glimpse of a branch of a bur-oak tree which leaned out over the mouth of the shaft. This sud-

The Hickory Hill House, built in 1857

denly awakened me, and to father's excited shouting I feebly murmured, "Take me out." But when he began to hoist he found I was not in the bucket and in wild alarm shouted, "Get in! Get in the bucket and hold on! Hold on!" Somehow I managed to get into the bucket, and that is all I remembered until I was dragged out, violently gasping for breath.

One of our near neighbors, a stone mason and miner by the name of William Duncan, came to see me, and after hearing the particulars of the accident he solemnly said: "Weel, Johnnie, it's God's mercy that you're alive. Many a companion of mine have I seen dead with choke-damp, but none that I ever saw or heard of was so near to death in it as you were and escaped without help." Mr. Duncan taught father to throw water down the shaft to absorb the gas, and also to drop a bundle of brush or hay attached to a light rope, dropping it again and again to carry down pure air and stir up the poison. When, after a day or two, I had recovered from the shock, father lowered me again to my work, after taking the precaution to test the air with a candle and stir it up well with a brush-and-hay bundle. The weary hammer-and-chisel-chipping went on as before, only more slowly, until ninety feet down, when at last I struck a fine, hearty gush of water. Constant dropping wears away stone. So does constant chipping, while at the same time wearing away the chipper. Father never spent an hour in that well. He trusted me to sink it straight and plumb, and I did, and built a fine covered top over it, and swung two iron-bound buckets in it from which we all drank for many a day.

The honey-bee arrived in America long before we boys did, but several years passed ere we noticed any on our farm. The introduction of the honey-bee into flowery America formed a grand epoch in bee history. This sweet humming creature, companion and friend of the flowers, is now distributed over the greater part of the continent, filling countless hollows in rocks and trees with honey as well as the millions of hives prepared for them by honey-farmers, who keep and tend their flocks of sweet winged cattle, as shepherds keep sheep,—a charming employment, "like directing sunbeams," as Thoreau says. The Indians call the honey-bee the white man's fly; and though they had long been acquainted with several species of

bumblebees that yielded more or less honey, how gladly surprised they must have been when they discovered that, in the
hollow trees where before they had found only coons or squirrels, they found swarms of brown flies with fifty or even a
hundred pounds of honey sealed up in beautiful cells. With
their keen hunting senses they of course were not slow to
learn the habits of the little brown immigrants and the best
methods of tracing them to their sweet homes, however well
hidden. During the first few years none were seen on our
farm, though we sometimes heard father's hired men talking
about "lining bees." None of us boys ever found a bee tree,
or tried to find any until about ten years after our arrival in
the woods. On the Hickory Hill farm there is a ridge of moraine material, rather dry, but flowery with goldenrods and
asters of many species, upon which we saw bees feeding in the
late autumn just when their hives were fullest of honey, and
it occurred to me one day after I was of age and my own
master that I must try to find a bee tree. I made a little box
about six inches long and four inches deep and wide; bought
half a pound of honey, went to the goldenrod hill, swept a
bee into the box and closed it. The lid had a pane of glass in
it so I could see when the bee had sucked its fill and was ready
to go home. At first it groped around trying to get out, but,
smelling the honey, it seemed to forget everything else, and
while it was feasting I carried the box and a small sharp-
pointed stake to an open spot, where I could see about me,
fixed the stake in the ground, and placed the box on the flat
top of it. When I thought that the little feaster must be about
full, I opened the box, but it was in no hurry to fly. It slowly
crawled up to the edge of the box, lingered a minute or two
cleaning its legs that had become sticky with honey, and when
it took wing, instead of making what is called a bee-line for
home, it buzzed around the box and minutely examined it as
if trying to fix a clear picture of it in its mind so as to be able
to recognize it when it returned for another load, then circled
around at a little distance as if looking for something to locate
it by. I was the nearest object, and the thoughtful worker
buzzed in front of my face and took a good stare at me, and
then flew up on to the top of an oak on the side of the open
spot in the centre of which the honey-box was. Keeping a

keen watch, after a minute or two of rest or wing-cleaning, I saw it fly in wide circles round the tops of the trees nearest the honey-box, and, after apparently satisfying itself, make a bee-line for the hive. Looking endwise on the line of flight, I saw that what is called a bee-line is not an absolutely straight line, but a line in general straight made of many slight, wavering, lateral curves. After taking as true a bearing as I could, I waited and watched. In a few minutes, probably ten, I was surprised to see that bee arrive at the end of the outleaning limb of the oak mentioned above, as though that was the first point it had fixed in its memory to be depended on in retracing the way back to the honey-box. From the tree-top it came straight to my head, thence straight to the box, entered without the least hesitation, filled up and started off after the same preparatory dressing and taking of bearings as before. Then I took particular pains to lay down the exact course so I would be able to trace it to the hive. Before doing so, however, I made an experiment to test the worth of the impression I had that the little insect found the way back to the box by fixing telling points in its mind. While it was away, I picked up the honey-box and set it on the stake a few rods from the position it had thus far occupied, and stood there watching. In a few minutes I saw the bee arrive at its guide-mark, the overleaning branch on the tree-top, and thence came bouncing down right to the spaces in the air which had been occupied by my head and the honey-box, and when the cunning little honey-gleaner found nothing there but empty air it whirled round and round as if confused and lost; and although I was standing with the open honey-box within fifty or sixty feet of the former feasting-spot, it could not, or at least did not, find it.

Now that I had learned the general direction of the hive, I pushed on in search of it. I had gone perhaps a quarter of a mile when I caught another bee, which, after getting loaded, went through the same performance of circling round and round the honey-box, buzzing in front of me and staring me in the face to be able to recognize me; but as if the adjacent trees and bushes were sufficiently well known, it simply looked around at them and bolted off without much dressing, indicating, I thought, that the distance to the hive was not great. I followed on and very soon discovered it in the bottom log of a corn-field fence, but some lucky fellow had discovered it before me and robbed it. The robbers had chopped a large hole in the log, taken out most of the honey, and left the poor bees late in the fall, when winter was approaching, to make haste to gather all the honey they could from the latest flowers to avoid starvation in the winter.

VII

KNOWLEDGE AND INVENTIONS

HUNGRY FOR KNOWLEDGE—BORROWING BOOKS—
PATERNAL OPPOSITION—SNATCHED MOMENTS—
EARLY RISING PROVES A WAY OUT OF DIFFICUL-
TIES—THE CELLAR WORKSHOP—INVENTIONS—
AN EARLY-RISING MACHINE—NOVEL CLOCKS—
HYGROMETERS, ETC.—A NEIGHBOR'S ADVICE.

I LEARNED arithmetic in Scotland without understanding any of it, though I had the rules by heart. But when I was about fifteen or sixteen years of age, I began to grow hungry for real knowledge, and persuaded father, who was willing enough to have me study provided my farm work was kept up, to buy me a higher arithmetic. Beginning at the beginning, in one summer I easily finished it without assistance, in the short intervals between the end of dinner and the afternoon start for the harvest- and hay-fields, accomplishing more without a teacher in a few scraps of time than in years in school before my mind was ready for such work. Then in succession I took up algebra, geometry, and trigonometry and made some little progress in each, and reviewed grammar. I was fond of reading, but father had brought only a few religious books from Scotland. Fortunately, several of our neighbors had brought a dozen or two of all sorts of books, which I borrowed and read, keeping all of them except the religious ones carefully hidden from father's eye. Among these were Scott's novels, which, like all other novels, were strictly forbidden, but devoured with glorious pleasure in secret. Father was easily persuaded to buy Josephus' "Wars of the Jews," and D'Aubigné's "History of the Reformation," and I tried hard to get him to buy Plutarch's Lives, which, as I told him, everybody, even religious people, praised as a grand good book; but he would have nothing to do with the old pagan until the graham bread and anti-flesh doctrines came suddenly into our backwoods neighborhood, making a stir something like phrenology and spirit-rappings, which were as mysterious in their attacks as influenza. He then thought it possible that Plutarch might be turned to account on the food question by revealing what those old Greeks and Romans ate to make them strong; and so at last we gained our glorious Plutarch. Dick's "Christian Philosopher," which I borrowed from a neighbor, I thought I might venture to read in the open, trusting that the word "Christian" would be proof against its cautious condemnation. But father balked at the word "Philosopher," and quoted from the Bible a verse which spoke of "philosophy falsely so-called." I then ventured to speak in defense of the book, arguing that we could not do without at least a little of the most useful kinds of philosophy.

"Yes, we can," he said with enthusiasm, "the Bible is the only book human beings can possibly require throughout all the journey from earth to heaven."

"But how," I contended, "can we find the way to heaven without the Bible, and how after we grow old can we read the Bible without a little helpful science? Just think, father, you cannot read your Bible without spectacles, and millions of others are in the same fix; and spectacles cannot be made without some knowledge of the science of optics."

"Oh!" he replied, perceiving the drift of the argument, "there will always be plenty of worldly people to make spectacles."

To this I stubbornly replied with a quotation from the Bible with reference to the time coming when "all shall know the Lord from the least even to the greatest," and then who will make the spectacles? But he still objected to my reading that book, called me a contumacious quibbler too fond of disputation, and ordered me to return it to the accommodating owner. I managed, however, to read it later.

On the food question father insisted that those who argued for a vegetable diet were in the right, because our teeth showed plainly that they were made with reference to fruit and grain and not for flesh like those of dogs and wolves and tigers. He therefore promptly adopted a vegetable diet and requested mother to make the bread from graham flour instead of bolted flour. Mother put both kinds on the table, and meat also, to let all the family take their choice, and while father was insisting on the foolishness of eating flesh, I came to her help by calling father's attention to the passage in the Bible which told the story of Elijah the prophet who, when he was pursued by enemies who wanted to take his life, was hidden by the Lord by the brook Cherith, and fed by ravens; and surely the Lord knew what was good to eat, whether bread or meat. And on what, I asked, did the Lord feed Elijah? On vegetables or graham bread? No, he directed the ravens to feed his prophet on flesh. The Bible being the sole rule, father at once acknowledged that he was mistaken. The Lord never would have sent flesh to Elijah by the ravens if graham bread were better.

I remember as a great and sudden discovery that the poetry of the Bible, Shakespeare, and Milton was a source of inspiring, exhilarating, uplifting pleasure; and I became anxious to know all the poets, and saved up small sums to buy as many of their books as possible. Within three or four years I was the proud possessor of parts of Shakespeare's, Milton's, Cowper's, Henry Kirke White's, Campbell's, and Akenside's works, and quite a number of others seldom read nowadays. I think it was in my fifteenth year that I began to relish good literature with enthusiasm, and smack my lips over favorite lines, but there was desperately little time for reading, even in the winter evenings,—only a few stolen minutes now and then. Father's strict rule was, straight to bed immediately after family worship, which in winter was usually over by eight o'clock. I was in the habit of lingering in the kitchen with a book and candle after the rest of the family had retired, and considered myself fortunate if I got five minutes' reading before father noticed the light and ordered me to bed; an order that of course I immediately obeyed. But night after night I tried to steal minutes in the same lingering way, and how keenly precious those minutes were, few nowadays can know. Father failed perhaps two or three times in a whole winter to notice my light for nearly ten minutes, magnificent golden blocks of time, long to be remembered like holidays or geological periods. One evening when I was reading Church history father was particularly irritable, and called out with hope-killing emphasis, "*John, go to bed!* Must I give you a separate order every night to get you to go to bed? Now, I will have no irregularity in the family; you *must* go when the rest go, and without my having to tell you." Then, as an after-thought, as if judging that his words and tone of voice were too severe for so pardonable an offense as reading a religious book he unwarily added: "If you *will* read, get up in the morning and read. You may get up in the morning as early as you like."

That night I went to bed wishing with all my heart and soul that somebody or something might call me out of sleep to avail myself of this wonderful indulgence; and next morning to my joyful surprise I awoke before father called me. A boy sleeps soundly after working all day in the snowy woods, but that frosty morning I sprang out of bed as if called by a trumpet blast, rushed downstairs, scarce feeling my chilblains, enormously eager to see how much time I had won; and when I held up my candle to a little clock that stood on a bracket in the kitchen I found that it was only one o'clock. I had gained five hours, almost half a day! "Five hours to myself!" I said, "five huge, solid hours!" I can hardly think of any other event in my life, any discovery I ever made that gave birth to joy so transportingly glorious as the possession of these five frosty hours.

In the glad, tumultuous excitement of so much suddenly acquired time-wealth, I hardly knew what to do with it. I first thought of going on with my reading, but the zero weather would make a fire necessary, and it occurred to me that father might object to the cost of fire-wood that took time to chop. Therefore, I prudently decided to go down cellar, and begin work on a model of a self-setting sawmill I had invented. Next morning I managed to get up at the same gloriously early hour, and though the temperature of the cellar was a little below the freezing point, and my light was only a tallow candle the mill work went joyfully on. There were a few tools in a corner of the cellar,—a vise, files, a hammer, chisels, etc., that father had brought from Scotland, but no saw excepting a coarse crooked one that was unfit for sawing dry hickory or oak. So I made a fine-tooth saw suitable for my work out of a strip of steel that had formed part of an old-fashioned corset, that cut the hardest wood smoothly. I also made my own bradawls, punches, and a pair of compasses, out of wire and old files.

My workshop was immediately under father's bed, and the

filing and tapping in making cogwheels, journals, cams, etc., must, no doubt, have annoyed him, but with the permission he had granted in his mind, and doubtless hoping that I would soon tire of getting up at one o'clock, he impatiently waited about two weeks before saying a word. I did not vary more than five minutes from one o'clock all winter, nor did I feel any bad effects whatever, nor did I think at all about the subject as to whether so little sleep might be in any way injurious; it was a grand triumph of will-power over cold and common comfort and work-weariness in abruptly cutting down my ten hours' allowance of sleep to five. I simply felt that I was rich beyond anything I could have dreamed of or hoped for. I was far more than happy. Like Tam o'Shanter I was glorious, "O'er a' the ills o' life victorious."

Father, as was customary in Scotland, gave thanks and asked a blessing before meals, not merely as a matter of form and decent Christian manners, for he regarded food as a gift derived directly from the hands of the Father in heaven. Therefore every meal to him was a sacrament requiring conduct and attitude of mind not unlike that befitting the Lord's Supper. No idle word was allowed to be spoken at our table, much less any laughing or fun or story-telling. When we were at the breakfast-table, about two weeks after the great golden time-discovery, father cleared his throat preliminary, as we all knew, to saying something considered important. I feared that it was to be on the subject of my early rising, and dreaded the withdrawal of the permission he had granted on account of the noise I made, but still hoping that, as he had given his word that I might get up as early as I wished, he would as a Scotchman stand to it, even though it was given in an unguarded moment and taken in a sense unreasonably far-reaching. The solemn sacramental silence was broken by the dreaded question:—

"John, what time is it when you get up in the morning?"

"About one o'clock," I replied in a low, meek, guilty tone of voice.

"And what kind of a time is that, getting up in the middle of the night and disturbing the whole family?"

I simply reminded him of the permission he had freely granted me to get up as early as I wished.

"I *know* it," he said, in an almost agonized tone of voice, "I *know* I gave you that miserable permission, but I never imagined that you would get up in the middle of the night."

To this I cautiously made no reply, but continued to listen for the heavenly one-o'clock call, and it never failed.

After completing my self-setting sawmill I dammed one of the streams in the meadow and put the mill in operation. This

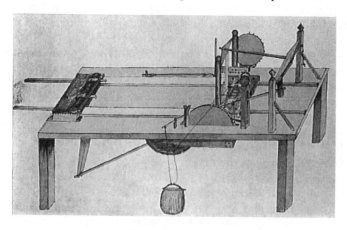

Self-Setting Sawmill
Model built in cellar

invention was speedily followed by a lot of others,—water-wheels, curious doorlocks and latches, thermometers, hygrometers, pyrometers, clocks, a barometer, an automatic contrivance for feeding the horses at any required hour, a lamp-lighter and fire-lighter, an early-or-late-rising machine, and so forth.

After the sawmill was proved and discharged from my mind, I happened to think it would be a fine thing to make a time-keeper which would tell the day of the week and the day of the month, as well as strike like a common clock and point out the hours; also to have an attachment whereby it could be connected with a bedstead to set me on my feet at any hour in the morning; also to start fires, light lamps, etc. I had learned the time laws of the pendulum from a book, but with this exception I knew nothing of timekeepers, for I had never seen the inside of any sort of clock or watch. After long brooding, the novel clock was at length completed in my mind, and was tried and found to be durable and to work well and look well before I had begun to build it in wood. I carried small parts of it in my pocket to whittle at when I was out at work on the farm, using every spare or stolen moment within reach without father's knowing anything about it. In the middle of summer, when harvesting was in progress, the novel time-machine was nearly completed. It was hidden upstairs in a spare bedroom where some tools were kept. I did the making and mending on the farm, but one day at noon, when I happened to be away, father went upstairs for a hammer or something and discovered the mysterious machine back of the bedstead. My sister Margaret saw him on his knees examining it, and at the first opportunity whispered in my ear, "John, fayther saw that thing you're making upstairs." None of the family knew what I was doing, but they knew very well that all such work was frowned on by father, and kindly warned me of any danger that threatened my plans. The fine invention seemed doomed to destruction before its time-ticking commenced, though I thought it handsome, had so long carried it in my mind, and like the nest of Burns's wee mousie it had cost me mony a weary whittling nibble. When we were at dinner several days after the sad discovery, father began to clear his throat to speak, and I feared the doom of martyrdom was about to be pronounced on my grand clock.

"John," he inquired, "what is that thing you are making upstairs?"

I replied in desperation that I didn't know what to call it.

"What! You mean to say you don't know what you are trying to do?"

"Oh, yes," I said, "I know very well what I am doing."

"What, then, is the thing for?"

"It's for a lot of things," I replied, "but getting people up early in the morning is one of the main things it is intended for; therefore it might perhaps be called an early-rising machine."

After getting up so extravagantly early, all the last memorable winter to make a machine for getting up perhaps still earlier seemed so ridiculous that he very nearly laughed. But after controlling himself and getting command of a sufficiently solemn face and voice he said severely, "Do you not think it is very wrong to waste your time on such nonsense?"

"No," I said meekly, "I don't think I'm doing any wrong."

"Well," he replied, "I assure you I do; and if you were only half as zealous in the study of religion as you are in contriving and whittling these useless, nonsensical things, it would be infinitely better for you. I want you to be like Paul, who said that he desired to know nothing among men but Christ and Him crucified."

To this I made no reply, gloomily believing my fine machine was to be burned, but still taking what comfort I could in realizing that anyhow I had enjoyed inventing and making it.

After a few days, finding that nothing more was to be said, and that father after all had not had the heart to destroy it, all necessity for secrecy being ended, I finished it in the half-hours that we had at noon and set it in the parlor between two chairs, hung moraine boulders that had come from the direction of Lake Superior on it for weights, and set it running. We were then hauling grain into the barn. Father at this period devoted himself entirely to the Bible and did no farm work whatever. The clock had a good loud tick, and when he heard it strike, one of my sisters told me that he left his study, went to the parlor, got down on his knees and carefully examined the machinery, which was all in plain sight, not being enclosed in a case. This he did repeatedly, and evidently seemed a little proud of my ability to invent and whittle such a thing, though careful to give no encouragement for anything more of the kind in future.

But somehow it seemed impossible to stop. Inventing and whittling faster than ever, I made another hickory clock, shaped like a scythe to symbolize the scythe of Father Time. The pendulum is a bunch of arrows symbolizing the flight of time. It hangs on a leafless mossy oak snag showing the effect of time, and on the snath is written, "All flesh is grass." This, especially the inscription, rather pleased father, and, of course, mother and all my sisters and brothers admired it. Like the first it indicates the days of the week and month, starts fires and beds at any given hour and minute, and, though made more than fifty years ago, is still a good timekeeper.

My mind still running on clocks, I invented a big one like a town clock with four dials, with the time-figures so large they could be read by all our immediate neighbors as well as ourselves when at work in the fields, and on the side next the house the days of the week and month were indicated. It was to be placed on the peak of the barn roof. But just as it was all but finished, father stopped me, saying that it would bring too many people around the barn. I then asked permission to put it on the top of a black-oak tree near the house. Studying the larger main branches, I thought I could secure a sufficiently rigid foundation for it, while the trimmed sprays and leaves would conceal the angles of the cabin required to shelter the works from the weather, and the two-second pendu-

Clock. The star hand rising and setting with the sun all the year.
Invented by the author in his boyhood

lum, fourteen feet long, could be snugly encased on the side of the trunk. Nothing about the grand, useful timekeeper, I argued, would disfigure the tree, for it would look something like a big hawk's nest. "But that," he objected, "would draw still bigger bothersome trampling crowds about the place, for who ever heard of anything so queer as a big clock on the top of a tree?" So I had to lay aside its big wheels and cams and rest content with the pleasure of inventing it, and looking at it in my mind and listening to the deep solemn throbbing of its long two-second pendulum with its two old axes back to back for the bob.

One of my inventions was a large thermometer made of an iron rod, about three feet long and five eighths of an inch in

Barometer
Invented by the author in his boyhood

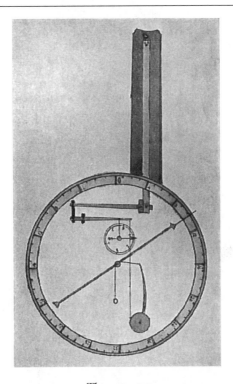

Thermometer

diameter, that had formed part of a wagon-box. The expansion and contraction of this rod was multiplied by a series of levers made of strips of hoop iron. The pressure of the rod against the levers was kept constant by a small counterweight, so that the slightest change in the length of the rod was instantly shown on a dial about three feet wide multiplied about thirty-two thousand times. The zero-point was gained by packing the rod in wet snow. The scale was so large that the big black hand on the white-painted dial could be seen distinctly and the temperature read while we were ploughing in the field below the house. The extremes of heat and cold caused the hand to make several revolutions. The number of these revolutions was indicated on a small dial marked on the larger one. This thermometer was fastened on the side of the

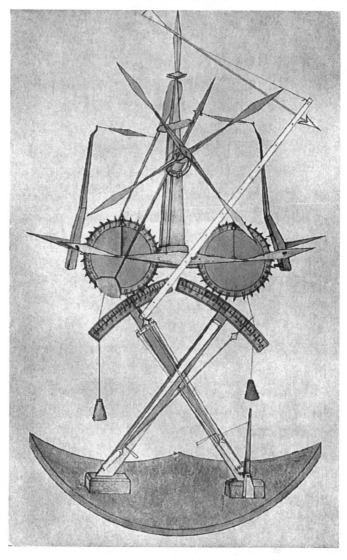

*Combined Thermometer, Hygrometer, Barometer, and Pyrometer
Invented by the author in his boyhood*

house, and was so sensitive that when any one approached it within four or five feet the heat radiated from the observer's body caused the hand of the dial to move so fast that the motion was plainly visible, and when he stepped back, the hand moved slowly back to its normal position. It was regarded as a great wonder by the neighbors and even by my own all-Bible father.

Boys are fond of the books of travelers, and I remember that one day, after I had been reading Mungo Park's travels in Africa, mother said: "Weel, John, maybe you will travel like Park and Humboldt some day." Father overheard her and cried out in solemn deprecation, "Oh, Anne! dinna put sic notions in the laddie's heed." But at this time there was precious little need of such prayers. My brothers left the farm when they came of age, but I stayed a year longer, loath to leave home. Mother hoped I might be a minister some day; my sisters that I would be a great inventor. I often thought I should like to be a physician, but I saw no way of making money and getting the necessary education, excepting as an inventor. So, as a beginning, I decided to try to get into a big shop or factory and live a while among machines. But I was naturally extremely shy and had been taught to have a poor opinion of myself, as of no account, though all our neighbors encouragingly called me a genius, sure to rise in the world. When I was talking over plans one day with a friendly neighbor, he said: "Now, John, if you wish to get into a machine-shop, just take some of your inventions to the State Fair, and you may be sure that as soon as they are seen they will open the door of any shop in the country for you. You will be welcomed everywhere." And when I doubtingly asked if people would care to look at things made of wood, he said, "Made of wood! Made of wood! What does it matter what they're made of when they are so out-and-out original. There's nothing else like them in the world. That is what will attract attention, and besides they're mighty handsome things anyway to come from the backwoods." So I was encouraged to leave home and go at his direction to the State Fair when it was being held in Madison.

VIII

THE WORLD AND THE UNIVERSITY

LEAVING HOME—CREATING A SENSATION IN PAR-
DEEVILLE—A RIDE ON A LOCOMOTIVE—AT THE
STATE FAIR IN MADISON—EMPLOYMENT IN A
MACHINE-SHOP AT PRAIRIE DU CHIEN—BACK TO
MADISON—ENTERING THE UNIVERSITY—TEACHING
SCHOOL—FIRST LESSON IN BOTANY—MORE INVEN-
TIONS—THE UNIVERSITY OF THE WILDERNESS.

WHEN I told father that I was about to leave home, and
inquired whether, if I should happen to be in need of
money, he would send me a little, he said, "No; depend entirely on yourself." Good advice, I suppose, but surely need-
lessly severe for a bashful, home-loving boy who had worked
so hard. I had the gold sovereign that my grandfather had
given me when I left Scotland, and a few dollars, perhaps ten,
that I had made by raising a few bushels of grain on a little
patch of sandy abandoned ground. So when I left home to
try the world I had only about fifteen dollars in my pocket.

Strange to say, father carefully taught us to consider ourselves very poor worms of the dust, conceived in sin, etc., and
devoutly believed that quenching every spark of pride and self-
confidence was a sacred duty, without realizing that in so doing he might at the same time be quenching everything else.
Praise he considered most venomous, and tried to assure me
that when I was fairly out in the wicked world making my
own way I would soon learn that although I might have
thought him a hard taskmaster at times, strangers were far
harder. On the contrary, I found no lack of kindness and
sympathy. All the baggage I carried was a package made up
of the two clocks and a small thermometer made of a piece of
old washboard, all three tied together, with no covering or
case of any sort, the whole looking like one very complicated
machine.

The aching parting from mother and my sisters was, of

course, hard to bear. Father let David drive me down to Pardeeville, a place I had never before seen, though it was only nine miles south of the Hickory Hill home. When we arrived at the village tavern, it seemed deserted. Not a single person was in sight. I set my clock baggage on the rickety platform. David said good-bye and started for home, leaving me alone in the world. The grinding noise made by the wagon in turning short brought out the landlord, and the first thing that caught his eye was my strange bundle. Then he looked at me and said, "Hello, young man, what's this?"

"Machines," I said, "for keeping time and getting up in the morning, and so forth."

"Well! Well! That's a mighty queer get-up. You must be a Down-East Yankee. Where did you get the pattern for such a thing?"

"In my head," I said.

Some one down the street happened to notice the landlord looking intently at something and came up to see what it was. Three or four people in that little village formed an attractive crowd, and in fifteen or twenty minutes the greater part of the population of Pardeeville stood gazing in a circle around my strange hickory belongings. I kept outside of the circle to avoid being seen, and had the advantage of hearing the remarks without being embarrassed. Almost every one as he came up would say, "What's that? What's it for? Who made it?" The landlord would answer them all alike, "Why, a young man that lives out in the country somewhere made it, and he says it's a thing for keeping time, getting up in the morning, and something that I didn't understand. I don't know what he meant." "Oh, no!" one of the crowd would say, "that can't be. It's for something else—something mysterious. Mark my words, you'll see all about it in the newspapers some of these days." A curious little fellow came running up the street, joined the crowd, stood on tiptoe to get sight of the wonder, quickly made up his mind, and shouted in crisp, confident, cock-crowing style, "I know what that contraption's for. It's a machine for taking the bones out of fish."

This was in the time of the great popular phrenology craze, when the fences and barns along the roads throughout the country were plastered with big skull-bump posters, headed,

"Know Thyself," and advising everybody to attend school-house lectures to have their heads explained and be told what they were good for and whom they ought to marry. My mechanical bundle seemed to bring a good deal of this phrenology to mind, for many of the onlookers would say, "I wish I could see that boy's head,—he must have a tremendous bump of invention." Others complimented me by saying, "I wish I had that fellow's head. I'd rather have it than the best farm in the State."

I stayed overnight at this little tavern, waiting for a train. In the morning I went to the station, and set my bundle on the platform. Along came the thundering train, a glorious sight, the first train I had ever waited for. When the conductor saw my queer baggage, he cried, "Hello! What have we here?"

"Inventions for keeping time, early rising, and so forth. May I take them into the car with me?"

"You can take them where you like," he replied, "but you had better give them to the baggage-master. If you take them into the car they will draw a crowd and might get broken."

So I gave them to the baggage-master and made haste to ask the conductor whether I might ride on the engine. He good-naturedly said: "Yes, it's the right place for you. Run ahead, and tell the engineer what I say." But the engineer bluntly refused to let me on, saying: "It don't matter what the conductor told you. *I* say you can't ride on my engine."

By this time the conductor, standing ready to start his train, was watching to see what luck I had, and when he saw me returning came ahead to meet me.

"The engineer won't let me on," I reported.

"Won't he?" said the kind conductor. "Oh! I guess he will. You come down with me." And so he actually took the time and patience to walk the length of that long train to get me on to the engine.

"Charlie," said he, addressing the engineer, "don't you ever take a passenger?"

"Very seldom," he replied.

"Anyhow, I wish you would take this young man on. He has the strangest machines in the baggage-car I ever saw in my life. I believe he could make a locomotive. He wants to see the engine running. Let him on." Then in a low whisper he told me to jump on, which I did gladly, the engineer of-fering neither encouragement nor objection.

As soon as the train was started, the engineer asked what the "strange thing" the conductor spoke of really was.

"Only inventions for keeping time, getting folk up in the morning, and so forth," I hastily replied, and before he could ask any more questions I asked permission to go outside of the cab to see the machinery. This he kindly granted, adding, "Be careful not to fall off, and when you hear me whistling for a station you come back, because if it is reported against me to the superintendent that I allow boys to run all over my engine I might lose my job."

Assuring him that I would come back promptly, I went out and walked along the foot-board on the side of the boiler, watching the magnificent machine rushing through the land-scapes as if glorying in its strength like a living creature. While seated on the cow-catcher platform, I seemed to be fairly fly-ing, and the wonderful display of power and motion was en-chanting. This was the first time I had ever been on a train, much less a locomotive, since I had left Scotland. When I got to Madison, I thanked the kind conductor and engineer for my glorious ride, inquired the way to the Fair, shouldered my inventions, and walked to the Fair Ground.

When I applied for an admission ticket at a window by the gate I told the agent that I had something to exhibit.

"What is it?" he inquired.

"Well, here it is. Look at it."

When he craned his neck through the window and got a glimpse of my bundle, he cried excitedly, "Oh! *you* don't need a ticket,—come right in."

When I inquired of the agent where such things as mine should be exhibited, he said, "You see that building up on the hill with a big flag on it? That's the Fine Arts Hall, and it's just the place for your wonderful invention."

So I went up to the Fine Arts Hall and looked in, wonder-ing if they would allow wooden things in so fine a place.

I was met at the door by a dignified gentleman, who greeted me kindly and said, "Young man, what have we got here?"

"Two clocks and a thermometer," I replied.

"Did you make these? They look wonderfully beautiful and novel and must, I think, prove the most interesting feature of the fair."

"Where shall I place them?" I inquired.

"Just look around, young man, and choose the place you like best, whether it is occupied or not. You can have your pick of all the building, and a carpenter to make the necessary shelving and assist you every way possible!"

So I quickly had a shelf made large enough for all of them, went out on the hill and picked up some glacial boulders of the right size for weights, and in fifteen or twenty minutes the clocks were running. They seemed to attract more attention than anything else in the hall. I got lots of praise from the crowd and the newspaper-reporters. The local press reports were copied into the Eastern papers. It was considered wonderful that a boy on a farm had been able to invent and make such things, and almost every spectator foretold good fortune. But I had been so lectured by my father above all things to avoid praise that I was afraid to read those kind newspaper notices, and never clipped out or preserved any of them, just glanced at them and turned away my eyes from beholding vanity. They gave me a prize of ten or fifteen dollars and a diploma for wonderful things not down in the list of exhibits.

Many years later, after I had written articles and books, I received a letter from the gentleman who had charge of the Fine Arts Hall. He proved to be the Professor of English Literature in the University of Wisconsin at this Fair time, and long afterward he sent me clippings of reports of his lectures. He had a lecture on me, discussing style, etcetera, and telling how well he remembered my arrival at the Hall in my shirt-sleeves with those mechanical wonders on my shoulder, and so forth, and so forth. These inventions, though of little importance, opened all doors for me and made marks that have lasted many years, simply, I suppose, because they were original and promising.

I was looking around in the mean time to find out where I should go to seek my fortune. An inventor at the Fair, by the name of Wiard, was exhibiting an iceboat he had invented to run on the upper Mississippi from Prairie du Chien to St.

Paul during the winter months, explaining how useful it would be thus to make a highway of the river while it was closed to ordinary navigation by ice. After he saw my inventions he offered me a place in his foundry and machine-shop in Prairie du Chien and promised to assist me all he could. So I made up my mind to accept his offer and rode with him to Prairie du Chien in his iceboat, which was mounted on a flat car. I soon found, however, that he was seldom at home and that I was not likely to learn much at his small shop. I found a place where I could work for my board and devote my spare hours to mechanical drawing, geometry, and physics, making but little headway, however, although the Pelton family, for whom I worked, were very kind. I made up my mind after a few months' stay in Prairie du Chien to return to Madison, hoping that in some way I might be able to gain an education.

At Madison I raised a few dollars by making and selling a few of those bedsteads that set the sleepers on their feet in the morning,—inserting in the footboard the works of an ordinary clock that could be bought for a dollar. I also made a few dollars addressing circulars in an insurance office, while at the same time I was paying my board by taking care of a pair of horses and going errands. This is of no great interest except that I was thus winning my bread while hoping that something would turn up that might enable me to make money enough to enter the State University. This was my ambition, and it never wavered no matter what I was doing. No University, it seemed to me, could be more admirably situated, and as I sauntered about it, charmed with its fine lawns and trees and beautiful lakes, and saw the students going and coming with their books, and occasionally practising with a theodolite in measuring distances, I thought that if I could only join them it would be the greatest joy of life. I was desperately hungry and thirsty for knowledge and willing to endure anything to get it.

One day I chanced to meet a student who had noticed my inventions at the Fair and now recognized me. And when I said, "You are fortunate fellows to be allowed to study in this beautiful place. I wish I could join you." "Well, why don't you?" he asked. "I haven't money enough," I said. "Oh, as to money," he reassuringly explained, "very little is required. I presume you're able to enter the Freshman class, and you can board yourself as quite a number of us do at a cost of about a dollar a week. The baker and milkman come every day. You can live on bread and milk." Well, I thought, maybe I have money enough for at least one beginning term. Anyhow I couldn't help trying.

With fear and trembling, overladen with ignorance, I called on Professor Stirling, the Dean of the Faculty, who was then Acting President, presented my case, and told him how far I had got on with my studies at home, and that I hadn't been to school since leaving Scotland at the age of eleven years, excepting one short term of a couple of months at a district school, because I could not be spared from the farm work. After hearing my story, the kind professor welcomed me to the glorious University—next, it seemed to me, to the Kingdom of Heaven. After a few weeks in the preparatory department I entered the Freshman class. In Latin I found that one of the books in use I had already studied in Scotland. So, after an interruption of a dozen years, I began my Latin over again where I had left off; and, strange to say, most of it came back to me, especially the grammar which I had committed to memory at the Dunbar Grammar School.

During the four years that I was in the University, I earned enough in the harvest-fields during the long summer vacations to carry me through the balance of each year, working very hard, cutting with a cradle four acres of wheat a day, and helping to put it in the shock. But, having to buy books and paying, I think, thirty-two dollars a year for instruction, and occasionally buying acids and retorts, glass tubing, bell-glasses, flasks, etc., I had to cut down expenses for board now and then to half a dollar a week.

One winter I taught school ten miles north of Madison, earning much-needed money at the rate of twenty dollars a month, "boarding round," and keeping up my University work by studying at night. As I was not then well enough off to own a watch, I used one of my hickory clocks, not only for keeping time, but for starting the school fire in the cold mornings, and regulating class-times. I carried it out on my shoulder to the old log schoolhouse, and set it to work on a little shelf nailed to one of the knotty, bulging logs. The winter was very cold, and I had to go to the schoolhouse and start the fire about eight o'clock to warm it before the arrival of the scholars. This was a rather trying job, and one that my clock might easily be made to do. Therefore, after supper one evening I told the head of the family with whom I was boarding that if he would give me a candle I would go back to the schoolhouse and make arrangements for lighting the fire at eight o'clock, without my having to be present until time to open the school at nine. He said, "Oh! young man, you have some curious things in the school-room, but I don't think you can do that." I said, "Oh, yes! It's easy," and in hardly more than an hour the simple job was completed. I had only to place a teaspoonful of powdered chlorate of potash and sugar on the stove-hearth near a few shavings and kindling, and at the required time make the clock, through a simple arrangement, touch the inflammable mixture with a drop of sulphuric acid. Every evening after school was dismissed, I shoveled out what was left of the fire into the snow, put in a little kindling, filled up the big box stove with heavy oak wood, placed the lighting arrangement on the hearth, and set the clock to drop the acid at the hour of eight; all this requiring only a few minutes.

The first morning after I had made this simple arrangement I invited the doubting farmer to watch the old squat schoolhouse from a window that overlooked it, to see if a good smoke did not rise from the stovepipe. Sure enough, on the minute, he saw a tall column curling gracefully up through the frosty air, but instead of congratulating me on my success he solemnly shook his head and said in a hollow, lugubrious voice, "Young man, you will be setting fire to the schoolhouse." All winter long that faithful clock fire never failed, and by the time I got to the schoolhouse the stove was usually red-hot.

At the beginning of the long summer vacations I returned to the Hickory Hill farm to earn the means in the harvest-fields to continue my University course, walking all the way to save railroad fares. And although I cradled four acres of wheat a day, I made the long, hard, sweaty day's work still longer and harder by keeping up my study of plants. At the noon hour I collected a large handful, put them in water to keep them fresh, and after supper got to work on them and sat up till after midnight, analyzing and classifying, thus leaving only four hours for sleep; and by the end of the first year, after taking up botany, I knew the principal flowering plants of the region.

I received my first lesson in botany from a student by the name of Griswold, who is now County Judge of the County of Waukesha, Wisconsin. In the University he was often laughed at on account of his anxiety to instruct others, and his frequently saying with fine emphasis, "Imparting instruction is my greatest enjoyment." One memorable day in June, when I was standing on the stone steps of the north dormitory, Mr. Griswold joined me and at once began to teach. He reached up, plucked a flower from an overspreading branch of a locust tree, and, handing it to me, said, "Muir, do you know what family this tree belongs to?"

"No," I said, "I don't know anything about botany."

"Well, no matter," said he, "what is it like?"

"It's like a pea flower," I replied.

"That's right. You're right," he said, "it belongs to the Pea Family."

"But how can that be," I objected, "when the pea is a weak, clinging, straggling herb, and the locust a big, thorny hardwood tree?"

"Yes, that is true," he replied, "as to the difference in size, but it is also true that in all their essential characters they are alike, and therefore they must belong to one and the same family. Just look at the peculiar form of the locust flower; you see that the upper petal, called the banner, is broad and erect, and so is the upper petal of the pea flower; the two lower petals, called the wings, are outspread and wing-shaped; so are those of the pea; and the two petals below the wings are united on their edges, curve upward, and form what is called the keel, and so you see are the corresponding petals of the pea flower. And now look at the stamens and pistils. You see that nine of the ten stamens have their filaments united into a sheath around the pistil, but the tenth stamen has its filament free. These are very marked characters, are they not? And, strange to say, you will find them the same in the tree and in the vine. Now look at the ovules or seeds of the locust, and you will see that they are arranged in a pod or legume like those of the pea. And look at the leaves. You see the leaf of the locust is made up of several leaflets, and so also is the leaf of the pea. Now taste the locust leaf."

I did so and found that it tasted like the leaf of the pea. Nature has used the same seasoning for both, though one is a straggling vine, the other a big tree.

"Now, surely you cannot imagine that all these similar characters are mere coincidences. Do they not rather go to show that the Creator in making pea vine and locust tree had the same idea in mind, and that plants are not classified arbitrarily? Man has nothing to do with their classification. Nature has attended to all that, giving essential unity with boundless variety, so that the botanist has only to examine plants to learn the harmony of their relations."

This fine lesson charmed me and sent me flying to the woods and meadows in wild enthusiasm. Like everybody else I was always fond of flowers, attracted by their external beauty and purity. Now my eyes were opened to their inner beauty, all alike revealing glorious traces of the thoughts of God, and leading on and on into the infinite cosmos. I wandered away at every opportunity, making long excursions round the lakes, gathering specimens and keeping them fresh in a bucket in my room to study at night after my regular class tasks were learned; for my eyes never closed on the plant glory I had seen.

Nevertheless, I still indulged my love of mechanical inventions. I invented a desk in which the books I had to study were arranged in order at the beginning of each term. I also made a bed which set me on my feet every morning at the hour determined on, and in dark winter mornings just as the bed set me on the floor it lighted a lamp. Then, after the minutes allowed for dressing had elapsed, a click was heard and the first book to be studied was pushed up from a rack below the top of the desk, thrown open, and allowed to remain there the number of minutes required. Then the machinery closed the book and allowed it to drop back into its stall, then moved the rack forward and threw up the next in order, and so on, all the day being divided according to the times of recitation, and time required and allotted to each study. Besides this, I thought it would be a fine thing in the summer-time when the sun rose early, to dispense with the clock-controlled bed machinery, and make use of sunbeams instead. This I did simply by taking a lens out of my small spy-glass, fixing it on a frame on the sill of my bedroom window, and pointing it to the sunrise; the sunbeams focused on a thread burned it through, allowing the bed machinery to put me on my feet. When I wished to arise at any given time after sunrise, I had only to turn the pivoted frame that held the lens the requisite number of degrees or minutes. Thus I took Emerson's advice and hitched my dumping-wagon bed to a star.

I also invented a machine to make visible the growth of plants and the action of the sunlight, a very delicate contrivance, enclosed in glass. Besides this I invented a barometer and a lot of novel scientific apparatus. My room was regarded as a sort of show place by the professors, who oftentimes brought visitors to it on Saturdays and holidays. And when, some eighteen years after I had left the University, I was sauntering over the campus in time of vacation, and spoke to a man who seemed to be taking some charge of the grounds, he informed me that he was the janitor; and when I inquired what had become of Pat, the janitor in my time, and a favorite with the students, he replied that Pat was still alive and well, but now too old to do much work. And when I pointed to the dormitory room that I long ago occupied, he said: "Oh! then I know who you are," and mentioned my name. "How comes it that you know my name?" I inquired. He explained that "Pat always pointed out that room to newcomers and told long stories about the wonders that used to be in it." So long had the memory of my little inventions survived.

Although I was four years at the University, I did not take the regular course of studies, but instead picked out what I thought would be most useful to me, particularly chemistry, which opened a new world, and mathematics and physics, a little Greek and Latin, botany and geology. I was far from satisfied with what I had learned, and should have stayed longer. Anyhow I wandered away on a glorious botanical and geological excursion, which has lasted nearly fifty years and is

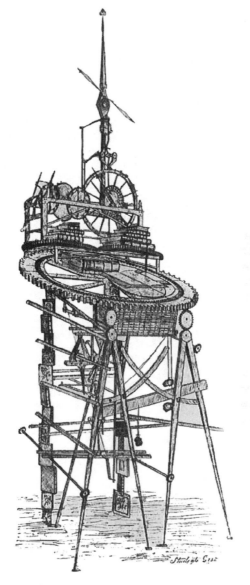

My Desk
made and used at the Wisconsin State University

not yet completed, always happy and free, poor and rich, without thought of a diploma or of making a name, urged on and on through endless, inspiring, Godful beauty.

From the top of a hill on the north side of Lake Mendota I gained a last wistful, lingering view of the beautiful University grounds and buildings where I had spent so many hungry and happy and hopeful days. There with streaming eyes I bade my blessed Alma Mater farewell. But I was only leaving one University for another, the Wisconsin University for the University of the Wilderness.

Index

MY FIRST SUMMER
IN THE SIERRA

TO
THE SIERRA CLUB OF CALIFORNIA
FAITHFUL DEFENDER OF THE
PEOPLE'S PLAYGROUNDS

Contents

Illustrations

Chapter I

IN the great Central Valley of California there are only two seasons—spring and summer. The spring begins with the first rain-storm, which usually falls in November. In a few months the wonderful flowery vegetation is in full bloom, and by the end of May it is dead and dry and crisp, as if every plant had been roasted in an oven.

Then the lolling, panting flocks and herds are driven to the high, cool, green pastures of the Sierra. I was longing for the mountains about this time, but money was scarce and I couldn't see how a bread supply was to be kept up. While I was anxiously brooding on the bread problem, so troublesome to wanderers, and trying to believe that I might learn to live like the wild animals, gleaning nourishment here and there from seeds, berries, etc., sauntering and climbing in joyful independence of money or baggage, Mr. Delaney, a sheepowner, for whom I had worked a few weeks, called on me, and offered to engage me to go with his shepherd and flock to the headwaters of the Merced and Tuolumne Rivers—the very region I had most in mind. I was in the mood to accept work of any kind that would take me into the mountains whose treasures I had tasted last summer in the Yosemite region. The flock, he explained, would be moved gradually higher through the successive forest belts as the snow melted, stopping for a few weeks at the best places we came to. These I thought would be good centers of observation from which I might be able to make many telling excursions within a radius of eight or ten miles of the camps to learn something of the plants, animals, and rocks; for he assured me that I should be left perfectly free to follow my studies. I judged, however, that I was in no way the right man for the place, and freely explained my shortcomings, confessing that I was wholly unacquainted with the topography of the upper mountains, the streams that would have to be crossed, and the wild sheepeating animals, etc.; in short that, what with bears, coyotes, rivers, cañons, and thorny, bewildering chaparral, I feared that half or more of his flock would be lost. Fortunately these shortcomings seemed insignificant to Mr. Delaney. The main thing, he said, was to have a man about the camp whom he could trust to see that the shepherd did his duty, and he assured me that the difficulties that seemed so formidable at a distance would vanish as we went on; encouraging me further by saying that the shepherd would do all the herding, that I could study plants and rocks and scenery as much as I liked, and that he would himself accompany us to the first main camp and make occasional visits to our higher ones to replenish our store of provisions and see how we prospered. Therefore I concluded to go, though still fearing, when I saw the silly sheep bouncing one by one through the narrow gate of the home corral to be counted, that of the two thousand and fifty many would never return.

I was fortunate in getting a fine St. Bernard dog for a companion. His master, a hunter with whom I was slightly acquainted, came to me as soon as he heard that I was going to spend the summer in the Sierra and begged me to take his favorite dog, Carlo, with me, for he feared that if he were compelled to stay all summer on the plains the fierce heat might be the death of him. "I think I can trust you to be kind to him," he said, "and I am sure he will be good to you. He knows all about the mountain animals, will guard the camp, assist in managing the sheep, and in every way be found able and faithful." Carlo knew we were talking about him, watched our faces, and listened so attentively that I fancied he understood us. Calling him by name, I asked him if he was willing to go with me. He looked me in the face with eyes expressing wonderful intelligence, then turned to his master, and after permission was given by a wave of the hand toward me and a farewell patting caress, he quietly followed me as if he perfectly understood all that had been said and had known me always.

June 3, 1869. This morning provisions, camp-kettles, blankets, plant-press, etc., were packed on two horses, the flock headed for the tawny foothills, and away we sauntered in a cloud of dust: Mr. Delaney, bony and tall, with sharply hacked profile like Don Quixote, leading the pack-horses, Billy, the proud shepherd, a Chinaman and a Digger Indian to assist in driving for the first few days in the brushy foothills, and myself with notebook tied to my belt.

The home ranch from which we set out is on the south side of the Tuolumne River near French Bar, where the foothills of metamorphic gold-bearing slates dip below the stratified deposits of the Central Valley. We had not gone more than a mile before some of the old leaders of the flock showed by the eager, inquiring way they ran and looked ahead that they were thinking of the high pastures they had enjoyed last summer. Soon the whole flock seemed to be hopefully excited, the mothers calling their lambs, the lambs replying in tones wonderfully human, their fondly quavering calls interrupted now and then by hastily snatched mouthfuls of withered grass. Amid all this seeming babel of baas as they streamed over the hills every mother and child recognized each other's voice. In case a tired lamb, half asleep in the smothering dust, should fail to answer, its mother would come running back through the flock toward the spot whence its last response was heard, and refused to be comforted until she found it, the one of a thousand, though to our eyes and ears all seemed alike.

The flock traveled at the rate of about a mile an hour, outspread in the form of an irregular triangle, about a hundred yards wide at the base, and a hundred and fifty yards long, with a crooked, ever-changing point made up of the strongest foragers, called the "leaders," which, with the most active of those scattered along the ragged sides of the "main body," hastily explored nooks in the rocks and bushes for grass and leaves; the lambs and feeble old mothers dawdling in the rear were called the "tail end."

About noon the heat was hard to bear; the poor sheep panted pitifully and tried to stop in the shade of every tree they came to, while we gazed with eager longing through the dim burning glare toward the snowy mountains and streams, though not one was in sight. The landscape is only wavering foothills roughened here and there with bushes and trees and outcropping masses of slate. The trees, mostly the blue oak (*Quercus Douglasii*), are about thirty to forty feet high, with pale blue-green leaves and white bark, sparsely planted on the thinnest soil or in crevices of rocks beyond the reach of grass fires. The slates in many places rise abruptly through the tawny grass in sharp lichen-covered slabs like tombstones in deserted burying-grounds. With the exception of the oak and four or five species of manzanita and ceanothus, the vegetation of the foothills is mostly the same as that of the plains. I saw this region in the early spring, when it was a charming landscape garden full of birds and bees and flowers. Now the scorching weather makes everything dreary. The ground is full of cracks, lizards glide about on the rocks, and ants in amazing numbers, whose tiny sparks of life only burn the brighter with the heat, fairly quiver with unquenchable energy as they run in long lines to fight and gather food. How it comes that they do not dry to a crisp in a few seconds' exposure to such sun-fire is marvelous. A few rattlesnakes lie coiled in out-of-the-way places, but are seldom seen. Magpies and crows, usually so noisy, are silent now, standing in mixed flocks on the ground beneath the best shade trees, with bills wide open and wings drooped, too breathless to speak; the quails also are trying to keep in the shade about the few tepid alkaline water-holes; cottontail rabbits are running from shade to shade among the ceanothus brush, and occasionally the long-eared hare is seen cantering gracefully across the wider openings.

After a short noon rest in a grove, the poor dust-choked flock was again driven ahead over the brushy hills, but the dim roadway we had been following faded away just where it was most needed, compelling us to stop to look about us and get our bearings. The Chinaman seemed to think we were lost, and chattered in pidgin English concerning the abundance of "litty stick" (chaparral), while the Indian silently scanned the billowy ridges and gulches for openings. Pushing through the thorny jungle, we at length discovered a road trending toward Coulterville, which we followed until an hour before sunset, when we reached a dry ranch and camped for the night.

Camping in the foothills with a flock of sheep is simple and easy, but far from pleasant. The sheep were allowed to pick what they could find in the neighborhood until after sunset, watched by the shepherd, while the others gathered wood, made a fire, cooked, unpacked and fed the horses, etc. About dusk the weary sheep were gathered on the highest open spot near camp, where they willingly bunched close together, and after each mother had found her lamb and suckled it, all lay down and required no attention until morning.

Supper was announced by the call, "Grub!" Each with a tin plate helped himself direct from the pots and pans while chatting about such camp studies as sheep-feed, mines, coyotes, bears, or adventures during the memorable gold days of pay dirt. The Indian kept in the background, saying never a word, as if he belonged to another species. The meal finished, the dogs were fed, the smokers smoked by the fire, and under the influences of fullness and tobacco the calm that settled on their faces seemed almost divine, something like the mellow meditative glow portrayed on the countenances of saints. Then suddenly, as if awakening from a dream, each with a sigh or a grunt knocked the ashes out of his pipe, yawned, gazed at the fire a few moments, said, "Well, I believe I'll turn in," and straightway vanished beneath his blankets. The fire smouldered and flickered an hour or two longer; the stars shone brighter; coons, coyotes, and owls stirred the silence here and there, while crickets and hylas made a cheerful, continuous music, so fitting and full that it seemed a part of the very body of the night. The only discordance came from a snoring sleeper, and the coughing sheep with dust in their throats. In the starlight the flock looked like a big gray blanket.

June 4. The camp was astir at daybreak; coffee, bacon, and beans formed the breakfast, followed by quick dish-washing and packing. A general bleating began about sunrise. As soon as a mother ewe arose, her lamb came bounding and bunting for its breakfast, and after the thousand youngsters had been suckled the flock began to nibble and spread. The restless wethers with ravenous appetites were the first to move, but dared not go far from the main body. Billy and the Indian and the Chinaman kept them headed along the weary road, and allowed them to pick up what little they could find on a breadth of about a quarter of a mile. But as several flocks had already gone ahead of us, scarce a leaf, green or dry, was left; therefore the starving flock had to be hurried on over the bare, hot hills to the nearest of the green pastures, about twenty or thirty miles from here.

The pack-animals were led by Don Quixote, a heavy rifle over his shoulder intended for bears and wolves. This day has been as hot and dusty as the first, leading over gently sloping brown hills, with mostly the same vegetation, excepting the strange-looking Sabine pine (*Pinus Sabiniana*), which here forms small groves or is scattered among the blue oaks. The trunk divides at a height of fifteen or twenty feet into two or more stems, outleaning or nearly upright, with many straggling branches and long gray needles, casting but little shade. In general appearance this tree looks more like a palm than a pine. The cones are about six or seven inches long, about five in diameter, very heavy, and last long after they fall, so that the ground beneath the trees is covered with them. They make fine resiny, light-giving camp-fires, next to ears of Indian corn the most beautiful fuel I've ever seen. The nuts, the Don tells me, are gathered in large quantities by the Digger Indians for food. They are about as large and hard-shelled as hazelnuts—food and fire fit for the gods from the same fruit.

June 5. This morning a few hours after setting out with the crawling sheep-cloud, we gained the summit of the first well-defined bench on the mountain-flank at Pino Blanco. The Sabine pines interest me greatly. They are so airy and strangely palm-like I was eager to sketch them, and was in a fever of excitement without accomplishing much. I managed to halt long enough, however, to make a tolerably fair sketch of Pino Blanco peak from the southwest side, where there is a small field and vineyard irrigated by a stream that makes a pretty fall on its way down a gorge by the roadside.

After gaining the open summit of this first bench, feeling the natural exhilaration due to the slight elevation of a thousand feet or so, and the hopes excited concerning the outlook to be obtained, a magnificent section of the Merced Valley at what is called Horseshoe Bend came full in sight—a glorious wilderness that seemed to be calling with a thousand songful voices. Bold, down-sweeping slopes, feathered with pines and clumps of manzanita with sunny, open spaces between them, make up most of the foreground; the middle and background present fold beyond fold of finely modeled hills and ridges rising into mountain-like masses in the distance, all covered with a shaggy growth of chaparral, mostly adenostoma,

Horseshoe Bend, Merced River

*On second bench. Edge of the main forest belt, above Coulterville,
near Greeley's Mill*

planted so marvelously close and even that it looks like soft, rich plush without a single tree or bare spot. As far as the eye can reach it extends, a heaving, swelling sea of green as regular and continuous as that produced by the heaths of Scotland. The sculpture of the landscape is as striking in its main lines as in its lavish richness of detail; a grand congregation of massive heights with the river shining between, each carved into smooth, graceful folds without leaving a single rocky angle exposed, as if the delicate fluting and ridging fashioned out of metamorphic slates had been carefully sandpapered. The whole landscape showed design, like man's noblest sculptures. How wonderful the power of its beauty! Gazing awe-stricken, I might have left everything for it. Glad, endless work would then be mine tracing the forces that have brought forth its features, its rocks and plants and animals and glorious weather. Beauty beyond thought everywhere, beneath, above, made and being made forever. I gazed and gazed and longed and admired until the dusty sheep and packs were far out of sight, made hurried notes and a sketch, though there was no need of either, for the colors and lines and expression of this divine landscape-countenance are so burned into mind and heart they surely can never grow dim.

The evening of this charmed day is cool, calm, cloudless, and full of a kind of lightning I have never seen before—white glowing cloud-shaped masses down among the trees and bushes, like quick-throbbing fireflies in the Wisconsin meadows rather than the so-called "wild fire." The spreading hairs of the horses' tails and sparks from our blankets show how highly charged the air is.

June 6. We are now on what may be called the second bench or plateau of the Range, after making many small ups and downs over belts of hill-waves, with, of course, corresponding changes in the vegetation. In open spots many of the lowland compositæ are still to be found, and some of the Mariposa tulips and other conspicuous members of the lily family; but the characteristic blue oak of the foothills is left below, and its place is taken by a fine large species (*Quercus Californica*) with deeply lobed deciduous leaves, picturesquely divided trunk, and broad, massy, finely lobed and modeled head. Here also at a height of about twenty-five hundred feet we come to the edge of the great coniferous forest, made up mostly of yellow pine with just a few sugar pines. We are now in the mountains and they are in us, kindling enthusiasm, making every nerve quiver, filling every pore and cell of us. Our flesh-and-bone tabernacle seems transparent as glass to the beauty about us, as if truly an inseparable part of it, thrilling with the air and trees, streams and rocks, in the waves of the sun,—a part of all nature, neither old nor young, sick nor well, but immortal. Just now I can hardly conceive of any bodily condition dependent on food or breath any more than the ground or the sky. How glorious a conversion, so complete and wholesome it is, scarce memory enough of old bondage days left as a standpoint to view it from! In this newness of life we seem to have been so always.

Through a meadow opening in the pine woods I see snowy peaks about the head-waters of the Merced above Yosemite. How near they seem and how clear their outlines on the blue air, or rather *in* the blue air; for they seem to be saturated with it. How consuming strong the invitation they extend! Shall I be allowed to go to them? Night and day I'll pray that I may, but it seems too good to be true. Some one worthy will go, able for the Godful work, yet as far as I can I must drift about these love-monument mountains, glad to be a servant of servants in so holy a wilderness.

Found a lovely lily (*Calochortus albus*) in a shady adenostoma thicket near Coulterville, in company with *Adiantum Chilense*. It is white with a faint purplish tinge inside at the base of the petals, a most impressive plant, pure as a snow crystal, one of the plant saints that all must love and be made so much the purer by it every time it is seen. It puts the roughest mountaineer on his good behavior. With this plant the whole world would seem rich though none other existed. It is not easy to keep on with the camp cloud while such plant people are standing preaching by the wayside.

During the afternoon we passed a fine meadow bounded by stately pines, mostly the arrowy yellow pine, with here and there a noble sugar pine, its feathery arms outspread above the spires of its companion species in marked contrast; a glorious tree, its cones fifteen to twenty inches long, swinging like tassels at the ends of the branches with superb ornamental effect. Saw some logs of this species at the Greeley Mill. They are round and regular as if turned in a lathe, excepting the butt cuts, which have a few buttressing projections. The fragrance of the sugary sap is delicious and scents the mill and lumber yard. How beautiful the ground beneath this pine thickly strewn with slender needles and grand cones, and the piles of cone-scales, seed-wings and shells around the instep of each tree where the squirrels have been feasting! They get the seeds by cutting off the scales at the base in regular order, following their spiral arrangement, and the two seeds at the base of each scale, a hundred or two in a cone, must make a good meal. The yellow pine cones and those of most other species and genera are held upside down on the ground by the Douglas squirrel, and turned around gradually until stripped, while he sits usually with his back to a tree, probably for safety. Strange to say, he never seems to get himself smeared with gum, not even his paws or whiskers—and how cleanly and beautiful in color the cone-litter kitchen-middens he makes.

We are now approaching the region of clouds and cool streams. Magnificent white cumuli appeared about noon above the Yosemite region,—floating fountains refreshing the glorious wilderness,—sky mountains in whose pearly hills and dales the streams take their rise,—blessing with cooling shadows and rain. No rock landscape is more varied in sculpture, none more delicately modeled than these landscapes of the sky; domes and peaks rising, swelling, white as finest marble and firmly outlined, a most impressive manifestation of world building. Every rain-cloud, however fleeting, leaves its mark, not only on trees and flowers whose pulses are quickened, and on the replenished streams and lakes, but also on the rocks are its marks engraved whether we can see them or not.

I have been examining the curious and influential shrub *Adenostoma fasciculata*, first noticed about Horseshoe Bend. It is very abundant on the lower slopes of the second plateau near Coulterville, forming a dense, almost impenetrable growth that looks dark in the distance. It belongs to the rose family, is about six or eight feet high, has small white flowers in racemes eight to twelve inches long, round needle-like leaves, and reddish bark that becomes shreddy when old. It grows on sun-beaten slopes, and like grass is often swept away by running fires, but is quickly renewed from the roots. Any trees that may have established themselves in its midst are at length killed by these fires, and this no doubt is the secret of the unbroken character of its broad belts. A few manzanitas, which also rise again from the root after consuming fires, make out to dwell with it, also a few bush compositæ—baccharis and linosyris, and some liliaceous plants, mostly calochortus and brodiæa, with deepset bulbs safe from fire. A multitude of birds and "wee, sleekit, cow'rin', tim'rous beasties" find good homes in its deepest thickets, and the open bays and lanes that fringe the margins of its main belts offer shelter and food to the deer when winter storms drive them down from their high mountain pastures. A most admirable plant! It is now in bloom, and I like to wear its pretty fragrant racemes in my buttonhole.

Azalea occidentalis, another charming shrub, grows beside cool streams hereabouts and much higher in the Yosemite region. We found it this evening in bloom a few miles above Greeley's Mill, where we are camped for the night. It is closely related to the rhododendrons, is very showy and fragrant, and everybody must like it not only for itself but for the shady alders and willows, ferny meadows, and living water associated with it.

Another conifer was met to-day—incense cedar (*Libocedrus decurrens*), a large tree with warm yellow-green foliage in flat plumes like those of arborvitæ, bark cinnamon-colored, and as the boles of the old trees are without limbs they make striking pillars in the woods where the sun chances to shine on them—a worthy companion of the kingly sugar and yellow pines. I feel strangely attracted to this tree. The brown close-grained wood, as well as the small scale-like leaves, is fragrant, and the flat over-lapping plumes make fine beds, and must shed the rain well. It would be delightful to be storm-bound beneath one of these noble, hospitable, inviting old trees, its broad sheltering arms bent down like a tent, incense rising from the fire made from its dry fallen branches, and a hearty wind chanting overhead. But the weather is calm to-night, and our camp is only a sheep camp. We are near the North Fork of the Merced. The night wind is telling the wonders of the upper mountains, their snow fountains and gardens, forests and groves; even their topography is in its tones. And the stars, the everlasting sky lilies, how bright they are now that we have climbed above the lowland dust! The horizon is bounded and adorned by a spiry wall of pines, every tree harmoniously related to every other; definite symbols, divine hieroglyphics written with sunbeams. Would I could understand them! The stream flowing past the camp through ferns and lilies and alders makes sweet music to the ear, but the pines marshaled around the edge of the sky make a yet sweeter music to the eye. Divine beauty all. Here I could stay tethered forever with just bread and water, nor would I be lonely; loved friends and neighbors, as love for everything increased, would seem all the nearer however many the miles and mountains between us.

June 7. The sheep were sick last night, and many of them are still far from well, hardly able to leave camp, coughing, groaning, looking wretched and pitiful, all from eating the leaves of the blessed azalea. So at least say the shepherd and the Don. Having had but little grass since they left the plains, they are starving, and so eat anything green they can get. "Sheep-men" call azalea "sheep-poison," and wonder what the Creator was thinking about when he made it—so desperately does sheep business blind and degrade, though supposed to have a refining influence in the good old days we read of. The California sheep owner is in haste to get rich, and often does, now that pasturage costs nothing, while the climate is so favorable that no winter food supply, shelter-pens, or barns are required. Therefore large flocks may be kept at slight expense, and large profits realized, the money invested doubling, it is claimed, every other year. This quickly acquired wealth usually creates desire for more. Then indeed the wool is drawn close down over the poor fellow's eyes, dimming or shutting out almost everything worth seeing.

As for the shepherd, his case is still worse, especially in winter when he lives alone in a cabin. For, though stimulated at times by hopes of one day owning a flock and getting rich like his boss, he at the same time is likely to be degraded by the life he leads, and seldom reaches the dignity or advantage—or disadvantage—of ownership. The degradation in his case has for cause one not far to seek. He is solitary most of the year, and solitude to most people seems hard to bear. He seldom has much good mental work or recreation in the way of books. Coming into his dingy hovel-cabin at night, stupidly weary, he finds nothing to balance and level his life with the universe. No, after his dull drag all day after the sheep, he must get his supper; he is likely to slight this task and try to satisfy his hunger with whatever comes handy. Perhaps no bread is baked; then he just makes a few grimy flapjacks in his unwashed frying-pan, boils a handful of tea, and perhaps fries a few strips of rusty bacon. Usually there are dried peaches or apples in the cabin, but he hates to be bothered with the cooking of them, just swallows the bacon and flapjacks, and depends on the genial stupefaction of tobacco for the rest. Then to bed, often without removing the clothing worn during the day. Of course his health suffers, reacting on his mind; and seeing nobody for weeks or months, he finally becomes semi-insane or wholly so.

The shepherd in Scotland seldom thinks of being anything but a shepherd. He has probably descended from a race of shepherds and inherited a love and aptitude for the business almost as marked as that of his collie. He has but a small flock to look after, sees his family and neighbors, has time for reading in fine weather, and often carries books to the fields with which he may converse with kings. The oriental shepherd, we read, called his sheep by name; they knew his voice and followed him. The flocks must have been small and easily managed, allowing piping on the hills and ample leisure for reading and thinking. But whatever the blessings of sheep-culture in other times and countries, the California shepherd, as far as I've seen or heard, is never quite sane for any considerable time. Of all Nature's voices baa is about all he hears. Even the howls and ki-yis of coyotes might be blessings if well heard, but he hears them only through a blur of mutton and wool, and they do him no good.

The sick sheep are getting well, and the shepherd is discoursing on the various poisons lurking in these high pastures—azalea, kalmia, alkali. After crossing the North Fork of the Merced we turned to the left toward Pilot Peak, and made a considerable ascent on a rocky, brush-covered ridge to

Brown's Flat, where for the first time since leaving the plains the flock is enjoying plenty of green grass. Mr. Delaney intends to seek a permanent camp somewhere in the neighborhood, to last several weeks.

Before noon we passed Bower Cave, a delightful marble palace, not dark and dripping, but filled with sunshine, which pours into it through its wide-open mouth facing the south. It has a fine, deep, clear little lake with mossy banks embowered with broad-leaved maples, all under ground, wholly unlike anything I have seen in the cave line even in Kentucky, where a large part of the State is honeycombed with caves. This curious specimen of subterranean scenery is located on a belt of marble that is said to extend from the north end of the Range to the extreme south. Many other caves occur on the belt, but none like this, as far as I have learned, combining as it does sunny outdoor brightness and vegetation with the crystalline beauty of the underworld. It is claimed by a Frenchman, who has fenced and locked it, placed a boat on the lakelet and seats on the mossy bank under the maple trees, and charges a dollar admission fee. Being on one of the ways to the Yosemite Valley, a good many tourists visit it during the travel months of summer, regarding it as an interesting addition to their Yosemite wonders.

Poison oak or poison ivy (*Rhus diversiloba*), both as a bush and a scrambler up trees and rocks, is common throughout the foothill region up to a height of at least three thousand feet above the sea. It is somewhat troublesome to most travelers, inflaming the skin and eyes, but blends harmoniously with its companion plants, and many a charming flower leans confidingly upon it for protection and shade. I have oftentimes found the curious twining lily (*Stropholirion Californicum*) climbing its branches, showing no fear but rather congenial companionship. Sheep eat it without apparent ill effects; so do horses to some extent, though not fond of it, and to many persons it is harmless. Like most other things not apparently useful to man, it has few friends, and the blind question, "Why was it made?" goes on and on with never a guess that first of all it might have been made for itself.

Brown's Flat is a shallow fertile valley on the top of the divide between the North Fork of the Merced and Bull Creek, commanding magnificent views in every direction. Here the adventurous pioneer David Brown made his headquarters for many years, dividing his time between gold-hunting and bear-hunting. Where could lonely hunter find a better solitude? Game in the woods, gold in the rocks, health and exhilaration in the air, while the colors and cloud furniture of the sky are ever inspiring through all sorts of weather. Though sternly practical, like most pioneers, old David seems to have been uncommonly fond of scenery. Mr. Delaney, who knew him well, tells me that he dearly loved to climb to the summit of a commanding ridge to gaze abroad over the forest to the snow-clad peaks and sources of the rivers, and over the fore-ground valleys and gulches to note where miners were at work or claims were abandoned, judging by smoke from cabins and camp-fires, the sounds of axes, etc.; and when a rifle-shot was heard, to guess who was the hunter, whether Indian or some poacher on his wide domain. His dog Sandy accompanied him everywhere, and well the little hairy mountaineer knew and loved his master and his master's aims. In deer-hunting he had but little to do, trotting behind his master as he slowly made his way through the wood, careful not to step heavily on dry twigs, scanning open spots in the chaparral, where the game loves to feed in the early morning and towards sunset; peering cautiously over ridges as new outlooks were reached, and along the meadowy borders of streams. But when bears were hunted, little Sandy became more important, and it was as a bear-hunter that Brown became famous. His hunting method, as described by Mr. Delaney, who had passed many a night with him in his lonely cabin and learned his stories, was simply to go slowly and silently through the best bear pastures, with his dog and rifle and a few pounds of flour, until he found a fresh track and then follow it to the death, paying no heed to the time required. Wherever the bear went he followed, led by little Sandy, who had a keen nose and never lost the track, however rocky the ground. When high open points were reached, the likeliest places were carefully scanned. The time of year enabled the hunter to determine approximately where the bear would be found,—in the spring and early summer on open spots about the banks of streams and springy places eating grass and clover and lupines, or in dry meadows feasting on strawberries; toward the end of summer, on dry ridges, feasting on manzanita berries, sitting on his haunches, pulling down the laden branches with his paws, and pressing them together so as to get good compact mouthfuls however much mixed with twigs and leaves; in the Indian summer, beneath the pines, chewing the cones cut off by the squirrels, or occasionally climbing a tree to gnaw and break off the fruitful branches. In late autumn, when acorns are ripe, Bruin's favorite feeding-grounds are groves of the California oak in park-like cañon flats. Always the cunning hunter knew where to look, and seldom came upon Bruin unawares. When the hot scent showed the dangerous game was nigh, a long halt was made, and the intricacies of the topography and vegetation leisurely scanned to catch a glimpse of the shaggy wanderer, or to at least determine where he was most likely to be.

"Whenever," said the hunter, "I saw a bear before it saw me I had no trouble in killing it. I just studied the lay of the land and got to leeward of it no matter how far around I had to go, and then worked up to within a few hundred yards or so, at the foot of a tree that I could easily climb, but too small for the bear to climb. Then I looked well to the condition of my rifle, took off my boots so as to climb well if necessary, and waited until the bear turned its side in clear view when I could make a sure or at least a good shot. In case it showed fight I climbed out of reach. But bears are slow and awkward with their eyes, and being to leeward of them they could not scent me, and I often got in a second shot before they noticed the smoke. Usually, however, they run when wounded and hide in the brush. I let them run a good safe time before I ventured to follow them, and Sandy was pretty sure to find them dead. If not, he barked and drew their attention, and occasionally rushed in for a distracting bite, so that I was able to get to a safe distance for a final shot. Oh, yes, bear-hunting is safe enough when followed in a safe way, though like every other business it has its accidents, and little doggie and I have had some close calls. Bears like to keep out of the way of men as a general thing, but if an old, lean, hungry mother with cubs met a man on her own ground she would, in my opinion, try to catch and eat him. This would be only fair play anyhow, for we eat them, but nobody hereabout has been used for bear grub that I know of."

Brown had left his mountain home ere we arrived, but a considerable number of Digger Indians still linger in their cedar-bark huts on the edge of the flat. They were attracted in the first place by the white hunter whom they had learned to respect, and to whom they looked for guidance and protection against their enemies the Pah Utes, who sometimes made raids across from the east side of the Range to plunder the stores of the comparatively feeble Diggers and steal their wives.

Chapter II

JUNE 8. The sheep, now grassy and good-natured, slowly nibbled their way down into the valley of the North Fork of the Merced at the foot of Pilot Peak Ridge to the place selected by the Don for our first central camp, a picturesque hopper-shaped hollow formed by converging hill slopes at a bend of the river. Here racks for dishes and provisions were made in the shade of the river-bank trees, and beds of fern fronds, cedar plumes, and various flowers, each to the taste of its owner, and a corral back on the open flat for the wool.

June 9. How deep our sleep last night in the mountain's heart, beneath the trees and stars, hushed by solemn-sounding waterfalls and many small soothing voices in sweet accord whispering peace! And our first pure mountain day, warm, calm, cloudless,—how immeasurable it seems, how serenely wild! I can scarcely remember its beginning. Along the river, over the hills, in the ground, in the sky, spring work is going on with joyful enthusiasm, new life, new beauty, unfolding, unrolling in glorious exuberant extravagance,—new birds in their nests, new winged creatures in the air, and new leaves, new flowers, spreading, shining, rejoicing everywhere.

The trees about the camp stand close, giving ample shade for ferns and lilies, while back from the bank most of the sunshine reaches the ground, calling up the grasses and flowers in glorious array, tall bromus waving like bamboos, starry compositæ, monardella, Mariposa tulips, lupines, gilias, violets, glad children of light. Soon every fern frond will be unrolled, great beds of common pteris and woodwardia along the river, wreaths and rosettes of pellæa and cheilanthes on sunny rocks. Some of the woodwardia fronds are already six feet high.

A handsome little shrub, *Chamæbatia foliolosa*, belonging to the rose family, spreads a yellow-green mantle beneath the sugar pines for miles without a break, not mixed or roughened with other plants. Only here and there a Washington lily may be seen nodding above its even surface, or a bunch or two of tall bromus as if for ornament. This fine carpet shrub begins to appear at, say, twenty-five hundred or three thousand feet above sea level, is about knee high or less, has brown branches, and the largest stems are only about half an inch in diameter. The leaves, light yellow green, thrice pinnate and finely cut, give them a rich ferny appearance, and they are dotted with minute glands that secrete wax with a peculiar pleasant odor that blends finely with the spicy fragrance of the pines. The flowers are white, five eighths of an inch in diameter, and look like those of the strawberry. Am delighted with this little bush. It is the only true carpet shrub of this part of the Sierra. The manzanita, rhamnus, and most of the species of ceanothus make shaggy rugs and border fringes rather than carpets or mantles.

The sheep do not take kindly to their new pastures, perhaps from being too closely hemmed in by the hills. They are never fully at rest. Last night they were frightened, probably by bears or coyotes prowling and planning for a share of the grand mass of mutton.

June 10. Very warm. We get water for the camp from a rock basin at the foot of a picturesque cascading reach of the river where it is well stirred and made lively without being beaten into dusty foam. The rock here is black metamorphic slate, worn into smooth knobs in the stream channels, contrasting with the fine gray and white cascading water as it glides and glances and falls in lace-like sheets and braided overfolding currents. Tufts of sedge growing on the rock knobs that rise above the surface produce a charming effect, the long elastic leaves arching over in every direction, the tips of the longest drooping into the current, which dividing against the projecting rocks makes still finer lines, uniting with the sedges to see how beautiful the happy stream can be made. Nor is this all, for the giant saxifrage also is growing on some of the knob rock islets, firmly anchored and displaying their broad, round, umbrella-like leaves in showy groups by themselves, or above the sedge tufts. The flowers of this species (*Saxifraga peltata*) are purple, and form tall glandular racemes that are in bloom before the appearance of the leaves. The fleshy root-stocks grip the rock in cracks and hollows, and thus enable the plant to hold on against occasional floods,—a marked species em-

ployed by Nature to make yet more beautiful the most interesting portions of these cool clear streams. Near camp the
trees arch over from bank to bank, making a leafy tunnel full
of soft subdued light, through which the young river sings
and shines like a happy living creature.

Heard a few peals of thunder from the upper Sierra, and
saw firm white bossy cumuli rising back of the pines. This was
about noon.

June 11. On one of the eastern branches of the river discovered some charming cascades with a pool at the foot of each
of them. White dashing water, a few bushes and tufts of carex
on ledges leaning over with fine effect, and large orange lilies
assembled in superb groups on fertile soil-beds beside the
pools.

There are no large meadows or grassy plains near camp to
supply lasting pasture for our thousands of busy nibblers. The
main dependence is ceanothus brush on the hills and tufted
grass patches here and there, with lupines and pea-vines
among the flowers on sunny open spaces. Large areas have
already been stripped bare, or nearly so, compelling the poor
hungry wool bundles to scatter far and wide, keeping the
shepherds and dogs at the top of their speed to hold them
within bounds. Mr. Delaney has gone back to the plains, taking the Indian and Chinaman with him, leaving instruction to
keep the flock here or hereabouts until his return, which he
promised would not be long delayed.

How fine the weather is! Nothing more celestial can I conceive. How gently the winds blow! Scarce can these tranquil
air-currents be called winds. They seem the very breath of
Nature, whispering peace to every living thing. Down in the
camp dell there is no swaying of tree-tops; most of the time
not a leaf moves. I don't remember having seen a single lily
swinging on its stalk, though they are so tall the least breeze
would rock them. What grand bells these lilies have! Some of
them big enough for children's bonnets. I have been sketching them, and would fain draw every leaf of their wide shining
whorls and every curved and spotted petal. More beautiful,
better kept gardens cannot be imagined. The species is *Lilium
pardalinum*, five to six feet high, leaf-whorls a foot wide,

flowers about six inches wide, bright orange, purple spotted in the throat, segments revolute—a majestic plant.

June 12. A slight sprinkle of rain—large drops far apart, falling with hearty pat and plash on leaves and stones and into the mouths of the flowers. Cumuli rising to the eastward. How beautiful their pearly bosses! How well they harmonize with the upswelling rocks beneath them. Mountains of the sky, solid-looking, finely sculptured, their richly varied topography wonderfully defined. Never before have I seen clouds so substantial looking in form and texture. Nearly every day toward noon they rise with visible swelling motion as if new worlds were being created. And how fondly they brood and hover over the gardens and forests with their cooling shadows and showers, keeping every petal and leaf in glad health and heart. One may fancy the clouds themselves are plants, springing up in the skyfields at the call of the sun, growing in beauty until they reach their prime, scattering rain and hail like berries and seeds, then wilting and dying.

The mountain live oak, common here and a thousand feet or so higher, is like the live oak of Florida, not only in general appearance, foliage, bark, and wide-branching habit, but in its tough, knotty, unwedgeable wood. Standing alone with plenty of elbow room, the largest trees are about seven to eight feet in diameter near the ground, sixty feet high, and as wide or wider across the head. The leaves are small and undivided, mostly without teeth or wavy edging, though on young shoots some are sharply serrated, both kinds being found on the same tree. The cups of the medium-sized acorns are shallow, thick walled, and covered with a golden dust of minute hairs. Some of the trees have hardly any main trunk, dividing near the ground into large wide-spreading limbs, and these, dividing again and again, terminate in long, drooping, cordlike branchlets, many of which reach nearly to the ground, while a dense canopy of short, shining, leafy branchlets forms a round head which looks something like a cumulus cloud when the sunshine is pouring over it.

A marked plant is the bush poppy (*Dendromecon rigidum*), found on the hot hillsides near camp, the only woody member of the order I have yet met in all my walks. Its flowers are

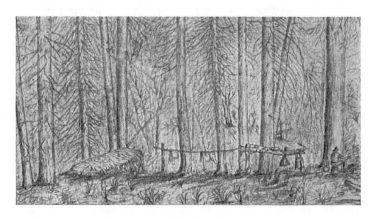

Camp, north fork of the Merced

Mountain Live Oak (Quercus chrysolepis), eight feet in diameter

bright orange yellow, an inch to two inches wide, fruit-pods three or four inches long, slender and curving,—height of bushes about four feet, made up of many slim, straight branches, radiating from the root,—a companion of the manzanita and other sun-loving chaparral shrubs.

June 13. Another glorious Sierra day in which one seems to be dissolved and absorbed and sent pulsing onward we know not where. Life seems neither long nor short, and we take no more heed to save time or make haste than do the trees and stars. This is true freedom, a good practical sort of immortality. Yonder rises another white skyland. How sharply the yellow pine spires and the palm-like crowns of the sugar pines are outlined on its smooth white domes. And hark! the grand thunder billows booming, rolling from ridge to ridge, followed by the faithful shower.

A good many herbaceous plants come thus far up the mountains from the plains, and are now in flower, two months later than their lowland relatives. Saw a few columbines to-day. Most of the ferns are in their prime,—rock ferns on the sunny hillsides, cheilanthes, pellæa, gymnogramme; woodwardia, aspidium, woodsia along the stream banks, and the common *Pteris aquilina* on sandy flats. This last, however common, is here making shows of strong, exuberant, abounding beauty to set the botanist wild with admiration. I measured some scarce full grown that are more than seven feet high. Though the commonest and most widely distributed of all the ferns, I might almost say that I never saw it before. The broad-shouldered fronds held high on smooth stout stalks growing close together, overleaning and overlapping, make a complete ceiling, beneath which one may walk erect over several acres without being seen, as if beneath a roof. And how soft and lovely the light streaming through this living ceiling, revealing the arching branching ribs and veins of the fronds as the framework of countless panes of pale green and yellow plant-glass nicely fitted together—a fairyland created out of the commonest fern-stuff.

The smaller animals wander about as if in a tropical forest. I saw the entire flock of sheep vanish at one side of a patch and reappear a hundred yards farther on at the other, their progress betrayed only by the jerking and trembling of the fronds; and strange to say very few of the stout woody stalks were broken. I sat a long time beneath the tallest fronds, and never enjoyed anything in the way of a bower of wild leaves more strangely impressive. Only spread a fern frond over a man's head and worldly cares are cast out, and freedom and beauty and peace come in. The waving of a pine tree on the top of a mountain,—a magic wand in Nature's hand,—every devout mountaineer knows its power; but the marvelous beauty value of what the Scotch call a breckan in a still dell, what poet has sung this? It would seem impossible that any one, however incrusted with care, could escape the Godful influence of these sacred fern forests. Yet this very day I saw a shepherd pass through one of the finest of them without betraying more feeling than his sheep. "What do you think of these grand ferns?" I asked. "Oh, they're only d——d big brakes," he replied.

Lizards of every temper, style, and color dwell here, seemingly as happy and companionable as the birds and squirrels. Lowly, gentle fellow mortals, enjoying God's sunshine, and doing the best they can in getting a living, I like to watch them at their work and play. They bear acquaintance well, and one likes them the better the longer one looks into their beautiful, innocent eyes. They are easily tamed, and one soon learns to love them, as they dart about on the hot rocks, swift as dragon-flies. The eye can hardly follow them; but they never make long-sustained runs, usually only about ten or twelve feet, then a sudden stop, and as sudden a start again; going all their journeys by quick, jerking impulses. These many stops I find are necessary as rests, for they are short-winded, and when pursued steadily are soon out of breath, pant pitifully, and are easily caught. Their bodies are more than half tail, but these tails are well managed, never heavily dragged nor curved up as if hard to carry; on the contrary, they seem to follow the body lightly of their own will. Some are colored like the sky, bright as bluebirds, others gray like the lichened rocks on which they hunt and bask. Even the horned toad of the plains is a mild, harmless creature, and so are the snake-like species which glide in curves with true snake motion, while their small, undeveloped limbs drag as useless appendages. One specimen fourteen inches long which I observed closely made no use whatever of its tender, sprouting limbs, but glided with all the soft, sly ease and grace of a snake. Here comes a little, gray, dusty fellow who seems to know and trust me, running about my feet, and looking up cunningly into my face. Carlo is watching, makes a quick pounce on him, for the fun of the thing I suppose; but Liz has shot away from his paws like an arrow, and is safe in the recesses of a clump of chaparral. Gentle saurians, dragons, descendants of an ancient and mighty race, Heaven bless you all and make your virtues known! for few of us know as yet that scales may cover fellow creatures as gentle and lovable as feathers, or hair, or cloth.

Mastodons and elephants used to live here no great geological time ago, as shown by their bones, often discovered by miners in washing gold-gravel. And bears of at least two species are here now, besides the California lion or panther, and wild cats, wolves, foxes, snakes, scorpions, wasps, tarantulas; but one is almost tempted at times to regard a small savage black ant as the master existence of this vast mountain world. These fearless, restless, wandering imps, though only about a quarter of an inch long, are fonder of fighting and biting than any beast I know. They attack every living thing around their homes, often without cause as far as I can see. Their bodies are mostly jaws curved like ice-hooks, and to get work for these weapons seems to be their chief aim and pleasure. Most of their colonies are established in living oaks somewhat decayed or hollowed, in which they can conveniently build their cells. These are chosen probably because of their strength as opposed to the attacks of animals and storms. They work both day and night, creep into dark caves, climb the highest trees, wander and hunt through cool ravines as well as on hot, unshaded ridges, and extend their highways and byways over everything but water and sky. From the foothills to a mile above the level of the sea nothing can stir without their knowledge; and alarms are spread in an incredibly short time, without any howl or cry that we can hear. I can't understand the need of their ferocious courage; there seems to be no common sense in it. Sometimes, no doubt, they fight in defense of their homes, but they fight anywhere and always wherever they can find anything to bite. As soon as a vulnerable spot is discovered on man or beast, they stand on their heads and sink their jaws, and though torn limb from limb, they will yet hold on and die biting deeper. When I contemplate this fierce creature so widely distributed and strongly intrenched, I see that much remains to be done ere the world is brought under the rule of universal peace and love.

On my way to camp a few minutes ago, I passed a dead pine nearly ten feet in diameter. It has been enveloped in fire from top to bottom so that now it looks like a grand black pillar set up as a monument. In this noble shaft a colony of large jet-black ants have established themselves, laboriously cutting tunnels and cells through the wood, whether sound or decayed. The entire trunk seems to have been honeycombed, judging by the size of the talus of gnawed chips like sawdust piled up around its base. They are more intelligent looking than their small, belligerent, strong-scented brethren, and have better manners, though quick to fight when required. Their towns are carved in fallen trunks as well as in those left standing, but never in sound, living trees or in the ground. When you happen to sit down to rest or take notes near a colony, some wandering hunter is sure to find you and come cautiously forward to discover the nature of the intruder and what ought to be done. If you are not too near the town and keep perfectly still he may run across your feet a few times, over your legs and hands and face, up your trousers, as if taking your measure and getting comprehensive views, then go in peace without raising an alarm. If, however, a tempting spot is offered or some suspicious movement excites him, a bite follows, and such a bite! I fancy that a bear or wolf bite is not to be compared with it. A quick electric flame of pain flashes along the outraged nerves, and you discover for the first time how great is the capacity for sensation you are possessed of. A shriek, a grab for the animal, and a bewildered stare follow this bite of bites as one comes back to consciousness from sudden eclipse. Fortunately, if careful, one need not be bitten oftener than once or twice in a lifetime. This wonderful electric species is about three fourths of an inch long. Bears are fond of them, and tear and gnaw their home-logs to pieces, and roughly devour the eggs, larvæ, parent ants, and the rotten or sound wood of the cells, all in one spicy acid hash. The Digger Indians also are fond of the larvæ and even of the perfect ants, so I have been told by old mountaineers. They bite off and reject the head, and eat the tickly acid body with keen relish. Thus are the poor biters bitten, like every other biter, big or little, in the world's great family.

There is also a fine, active, intelligent-looking red species, intermediate in size between the above. They dwell in the ground, and build large piles of seed husks, leaves, straw, etc., over their nests. Their food seems to be mostly insects and plant leaves, seeds and sap. How many mouths Nature has to fill, how many neighbors we have, how little we know about them, and how seldom we get in each other's way! Then to think of the infinite numbers of smaller fellow mortals, invisibly small, compared with which the smallest ants are as mastodons.

June 14. The pool-basins below the falls and cascades hereabouts, formed by the heavy down-plunging currents, are kept nicely clean and clear of detritus. The heavier parts of the material swept over the falls are heaped up a short distance in front of the basins in the form of a dam, thus tending, together with erosion, to increase their size. Sudden changes, however, are effected during the spring floods, when the snow is melting and the upper tributaries are roaring loud from "bank to brae." Then boulders that have fallen into the channels, and which the ordinary summer and winter currents were unable to move, are suddenly swept forward as by a mighty besom, hurled over the falls into these pools, and piled up in a new dam together with part of the old one, while some of the smaller boulders are carried farther down stream and variously lodged according to size and shape, all seeking rest where the force of the current is less than the resistance they are able to offer. But the greatest changes made in these relations of fall, pool, and dam are caused, not by the ordinary spring floods, but by extraordinary ones that occur at irregular intervals. The testimony of trees growing on flood boulder deposits shows that a century or more has passed since the last master flood came to awaken everything movable to go swirling and dancing on wonderful journeys. These floods may occur during the summer, when heavy thunder-showers, called "cloud-bursts," fall on wide, steeply inclined stream basins furrowed by converging channels, which suddenly gather the waters together into the main trunk in booming torrents of enormous transporting power, though short lived.

One of these ancient flood boulders stands firm in the middle of the stream channel, just below the lower edge of the pool dam at the foot of the fall nearest our camp. It is a nearly cubical mass of granite about eight feet high, plushed with mosses over the top and down the sides to ordinary high-water mark. When I climbed on top of it to-day and lay down to rest, it seemed the most romantic spot I had yet found— the one big stone with its mossy level top and smooth sides standing square and firm and solitary, like an altar, the fall in front of it bathing it lightly with the finest of the spray, just enough to keep its moss cover fresh; the clear green pool beneath, with its foam-bells and its half circle of lilies leaning forward like a band of admirers, and flowering dogwood and alder trees leaning over all in sun-sifted arches. How sooth-ingly, restfully cool it is beneath that leafy, translucent ceiling, and how delightful the water music—the deep bass tones of the fall, the clashing, ringing spray, and infinite variety of small low tones of the current gliding past the side of the boulder-island, and glinting against a thousand smaller stones down the ferny channel! All this shut in; every one of these influ-ences acting at short range as if in a quiet room. The place seemed holy, where one might hope to see God.

After dark, when the camp was at rest, I groped my way back to the altar boulder and passed the night on it,—above the water, beneath the leaves and stars,—everything still more impressive than by day, the fall seen dimly white, singing Na-ture's old love song with solemn enthusiasm, while the stars peering through the leaf-roof seemed to join in the white wa-ter's song. Precious night, precious day to abide in me forever. Thanks be to God for this immortal gift.

June 15. Another reviving morning. Down the long moun-tain-slopes the sunbeams pour, gilding the awakening pines, cheering every needle, filling every living thing with joy. Rob-ins are singing in the alder and maple groves, the same old song that has cheered and sweetened countless seasons over almost all of our blessed continent. In this mountain hollow they seem as much at home as in farmers' orchards. Bullock's

oriole and the Louisiana tanager are here also, with many warblers and other little mountain troubadours, most of them
now busy about their nests.

Discovered another magnificent specimen of the goldcup
oak six feet in diameter, a Douglas spruce seven feet, and a
twining lily (*Stropholirion*), with stem eight feet long, and
sixty rose-colored flowers.

Sugar pine cones are cylindrical, slightly tapered at the end
and rounded at the base. Found one to-day nearly twenty-
four inches long and six in diameter, the scales being open.
Another specimen nineteen inches long; the average length of
full-grown cones on trees favorably situated is nearly eighteen
inches. On the lower edge of the belt at a height of about
twenty-five hundred feet above the sea they are smaller, say a
foot to fifteen inches long, and at a height of seven thousand
feet or more near the upper limits of its growth in the Yosemite region they are about the same size. This noble tree is an
inexhaustible study and source of pleasure. I never weary of
gazing at its grand tassel cones, its perfectly round bole one
hundred feet or more without a limb, the fine purplish color
of its bark, and its magnificent outsweeping, down-curving
feathery arms forming a crown always bold and striking and
exhilarating. In habit and general port it looks somewhat like
a palm, but no palm that I have yet seen displays such majesty
of form and behavior either when poised silent and thoughtful
in sunshine, or wide-awake waving in storm winds with every
needle quivering. When young it is very straight and regular
in form like most other conifers; but at the age of fifty to one
hundred years it begins to acquire individuality, so that no
two are alike in their prime or old age. Every tree calls for
special admiration. I have been making many sketches, and
regret that I cannot draw every needle. It is said to reach a
height of three hundred feet, though the tallest I have measured falls short of this stature sixty feet or more. The diameter
of the largest near the ground is about ten feet, though I've
heard of some twelve feet thick or even fifteen. The diameter
is held to a great height, the taper being almost imperceptibly
gradual. Its companion, the yellow pine, is almost as large.
The long silvery foliage of the younger specimens forms magnificent cylindrical brushes on the top shoots and the ends of

the upturned branches, and when the wind sways the needles all one way at a certain angle every tree becomes a tower of white quivering sun-fire. Well may this shining species be called the silver pine. The needles are sometimes more than a foot long, almost as long as those of the long-leaf pine of Florida. But though in size the yellow pine almost equals the sugar pine, and in rugged enduring strength seems to surpass it, it is far less marked in general habit and expression, with its regular conventional spire and its comparatively small cones clustered stiffly among the needles. Were there no sugar pine,

Sugar Pine

then would this be the king of the world's eighty or ninety species, the brightest of the bright, waving, worshiping multitude. Were they mere mechanical sculptures, what noble objects they would still be! How much more throbbing, thrilling, overflowing, full of life in every fiber and cell, grand glowing silver-rods—the very gods of the plant kingdom, living their sublime century lives in sight of Heaven, watched and loved and admired from generation to generation! And how many other radiant resiny sun trees are here and higher up,—libocedrus, Douglas spruce, silver fir, sequoia. How rich our inheritance in these blessed mountains, the tree pastures into which our eyes are turned!

Now comes sundown. The west is all a glory of color transfiguring everything. Far up the Pilot Peak Ridge the radiant host of trees stand hushed and thoughtful, receiving the Sun's good-night, as solemn and impressive a leave-taking as if sun and trees were to meet no more. The daylight fades, the color spell is broken, and the forest breathes free in the night breeze beneath the stars.

June 16. One of the Indians from Brown's Flat got right into the middle of the camp this morning, unobserved. I was seated on a stone, looking over my notes and sketches, and happening to look up, was startled to see him standing grim and silent within a few steps of me, as motionless and weather-stained as an old tree-stump that had stood there for centuries. All Indians seem to have learned this wonderful way of walking unseen,—making themselves invisible like certain spiders I have been observing here, which, in case of alarm, caused, for example, by a bird alighting on the bush their webs are spread upon, immediately bounce themselves up and down on their elastic threads so rapidly that only a blur is visible. The wild Indian power of escaping observation, even where there is little or no cover to hide in, was probably slowly acquired in hard hunting and fighting lessons while trying to approach game, take enemies by surprise, or get safely away when compelled to retreat. And this experience transmitted through many generations seems at length to have become what is vaguely called instinct.

How smooth and changeless seems the surface of the mountains about us! Scarce a track is to be found beyond the range of the sheep except on small open spots on the sides of the streams, or where the forest carpets are thin or wanting. On the smoothest of these open strips and patches deer tracks may be seen, and the great suggestive footprints of bears, which, with those of the many small animals, are scarce enough to answer as a kind of light ornamental stitching or embroidery. Along the main ridges and larger branches of the river Indian trails may be traced, but they are not nearly as distinct as one would expect to find them. How many centuries Indians have roamed these woods nobody knows, probably a great many, extending far beyond the time that Columbus touched our shores, and it seems strange that heavier marks have not been made. Indians walk softly and hurt the landscape hardly more than the birds and squirrels, and their brush and bark huts last hardly longer than those of wood rats, while their more enduring monuments, excepting those wrought on the forests by the fires they made to improve their hunting grounds, vanish in a few centuries.

How different are most of those of the white man, especially on the lower gold region—roads blasted in the solid rock, wild streams dammed and tamed and turned out of their channels and led along the sides of cañons and valleys to work in mines like slaves. Crossing from ridge to ridge, high in the air, on long straddling trestles as if flowing on stilts, or down and up across valleys and hills, imprisoned in iron pipes to strike and wash away hills and miles of the skin of the mountain's face, riddling, stripping every gold gully and flat. These are the white man's marks made in a few feverish years, to say nothing of mills, fields, villages, scattered hundreds of miles along the flank of the Range. Long will it be ere these marks are effaced, though Nature is doing what she can, replanting, gardening, sweeping away old dams and flumes, leveling gravel and boulder piles, patiently trying to heal every raw scar. The main gold storm is over. Calm enough are the gray old miners scratching a bare living in waste diggings here and there. Thundering underground blasting is still going on to feed the pounding quartz mills, but their influence on the landscape is light as compared with that of the pick-and-shovel storms waged a few years ago. Fortunately for Sierra scenery the gold-bearing slates are mostly restricted to the foothills.

The region about our camp is still wild, and higher lies the snow about as trackless as the sky.

Only a few hills and domes of cloudland were built yesterday and none at all to-day. The light is peculiarly white and thin, though pleasantly warm. The serenity of this mountain weather in the spring, just when Nature's pulses are beating highest, is one of its greatest charms. There is only a moderate breeze from the summits of the Range at night, and a slight breathing from the sea and the lowland hills and plains during the day, or stillness so complete no leaf stirs. The trees hereabouts have but little wind history to tell.

Sheep, like people, are ungovernable when hungry. Excepting my guarded lily gardens, almost every leaf that these hoofed locusts can reach within a radius of a mile or two from camp has been devoured. Even the bushes are stripped bare, and in spite of dogs and shepherds the sheep scatter to all points of the compass and vanish in dust. I fear some are lost, for one of the sixteen black ones is missing.

June 17. Counted the wool bundles this morning as they bounced through the narrow corral gate. About three hundred are missing, and as the shepherd could not go to seek them, I had to go. I tied a crust of bread to my belt, and with Carlo set out for the upper slopes of the Pilot Peak Ridge, and had a good day, notwithstanding the care of seeking the silly runaways. I went out for wool, and did not come back shorn. A peculiar light circled around the horizon, white and thin like that often seen over the auroral corona, blending into the blue of the upper sky. The only clouds were a few faint flossy pencilings like combed silk. I pushed direct to the boundary of the usual range of the flock, and around it until I found the outgoing trail of the wanderers. It led far up the ridge into an open place surrounded by a hedge-like growth of ceanothus chaparral. Carlo knew what I was about, and eagerly followed the scent until we came up to them, huddled in a timid, silent bunch. They had evidently been here all night and all the forenoon, afraid to go out to feed. Having escaped restraint, they were, like some people we know of, afraid of their freedom, did not know what to do with it, and seemed glad to get back into the old familiar bondage.

June 18. Another inspiring morning, nothing better in any

world can be conceived. No description of Heaven that I have ever heard or read of seems half so fine. At noon the clouds occupied about .05 of the sky, white filmy touches drawn delicately on the azure.

The high ridges and hilltops beyond the woolly locusts are now gay with monardella, clarkia, coreopsis, and tall tufted grasses, some of them tall enough to wave like pines. The lupines, of which there are many ill-defined species, are now mostly out of flower, and many of the compositæ are beginning to fade, their radiant corollas vanishing in fluffy pappus like stars in mist.

We had another visitor from Brown's Flat to-day, an old Indian woman with a basket on her back. Like our first caller from the village, she got fairly into camp and was standing in plain view when discovered. How long she had been quietly looking on, I cannot say. Even the dogs failed to notice her stealthy approach. She was on her way, I suppose, to some wild garden, probably for lupine and starchy saxifrage leaves and rootstocks. Her dress was calico rags, far from clean. In every way she seemed sadly unlike Nature's neat well-dressed animals, though living like them on the bounty of the wilderness. Strange that mankind alone is dirty. Had she been clad in fur, or cloth woven of grass or shreddy bark, like the juniper and libocedrus mats, she might then have seemed a rightful part of the wilderness; like a good wolf at least, or bear. But from no point of view that I have found are such debased fellow beings a whit more natural than the glaring tailored tourists we saw that frightened the birds and squirrels.

June 19. Pure sunshine all day. How beautiful a rock is made by leaf shadows! Those of the live oak are particularly clear and distinct, and beyond all art in grace and delicacy, now still as if painted on stone, now gliding softly as if afraid of noise, now dancing, waltzing in swift, merry swirls, or jumping on and off sunny rocks in quick dashes like wave embroidery on seashore cliffs. How true and substantial is this shadow beauty, and with what sublime extravagance is beauty thus multiplied! The big orange lilies are now arrayed in all their glory of leaf and flower. Noble plants, in perfect health, Nature's darlings.

June 20. Some of the silly sheep got caught fast in a tangle of chaparral this morning, like flies in a spider's web, and had to be helped out. Carlo found them and tried to drive them from the trap by the easiest way. How far above sheep are intelligent dogs! No friend and helper can be more affectionate and constant than Carlo. The noble St. Bernard is an honor to his race.

The air is distinctly fragrant with balsam and resin and mint,—every breath of it a gift we may well thank God for. Who could ever guess that so rough a wilderness should yet be so fine, so full of good things. One seems to be in a majestic domed pavilion in which a grand play is being acted with scenery and music and incense,—all the furniture and action so interesting we are in no danger of being called on to endure one dull moment. God himself seems to be always doing his best here, working like a man in a glow of enthusiasm.

June 21. Sauntered along the river-bank to my lily gardens. The perfection of beauty in these lilies of the wilderness is a never-ending source of admiration and wonder. Their rhizomes are set in black mould accumulated in hollows of the metamorphic slates beside the pools, where they are well watered without being subjected to flood action. Every leaf in the level whorls around the tall polished stalks is as finely finished as the petals, and the light and heat required are measured for them and tempered in passing through the branches of over-leaning trees. However strong the winds from the noon rainstorms, they are securely sheltered. Beautiful hypnum carpets bordered with ferns are spread beneath them, violets too, and a few daisies. Everything around them sweet and fresh like themselves.

Cloudland to-day is only a solitary white mountain; but it is so enriched with sunshine and shade, the tones of color on its big domed head and bossy outbulging ridges, and in the hollows and ravines between them, are ineffably fine.

June 22. Unusually cloudy. Besides the periodical shower-bearing cumuli there is a thin, diffused, fog-like cloud overhead. About .75 in all.

June 23. Oh, these vast, calm, measureless mountain days, inciting at once to work and rest! Days in whose light everything seems equally divine, opening a thousand windows to show us God. Nevermore, however weary, should one faint by the way who gains the blessings of one mountain day;

whatever his fate, long life, short life, stormy or calm, he is rich forever.

June 24. Our regular allowance of clouds and thunder. Shepherd Billy is in a peck of trouble about the sheep; he declares that they are possessed with more of the evil one than any other flock from the beginning of the invention of mutton and wool to the last batch of it. No matter how many are missing, he will not, he says, go a step to seek them, because, as he reasons, while getting back one wanderer he would probably lose ten. Therefore runaway hunting must be Carlo's and mine. Billy's little dog Jack is also giving trouble by leaving camp every night to visit his neighbors up the mountain at Brown's Flat. He is a common-looking cur of no particular breed, but tremendously enterprising in love and war. He has cut all the ropes and leather straps he has been tied with, until his master in desperation, after climbing the brushy mountain again and again to drag him back, fastened him with a pole attached to his collar under his chin at one end, and to a stout sapling at the other. But the pole gave good leverage, and by constant twisting during the night, the fastening at the sapling end was chafed off, and he set out on his usual journey, dragging the pole through the brush, and reached the Indian settlement in safety. His master followed, and making no allowance, gave him a beating, and swore in bad terms that next evening he would "fix that infatuated pup" by anchoring him unmercifully to the heavy cast-iron lid of our Dutch oven, weighing about as much as the dog. It was linked directly to his collar close up under the chin, so that the poor fellow seemed unable to stir. He stood quite discouraged until after dark, unable to look about him, or even to lie down unless he stretched himself out with his front feet across the lid, and his head close down between his paws. Before morning, however, Jack was heard far up the height howling Excelsior, cast-iron anchor to the contrary notwithstanding. He must have walked, or rather climbed, erect on his hind legs, clasping the heavy lid like a shield against his breast, a formidable ironclad condition in which to meet his rivals. Next night, dog, pot-lid, and all, were tied up in an old bean-sack, and thus at last angry Billy gained the victory. Just before leaving home, Jack was bitten in the lower jaw by a rattlesnake, and for a week or so his head and neck were swollen to more than double the normal size; nevertheless he ran about as brisk and lively as ever, and is now completely recovered. The only treatment he got was fresh milk—a gallon or two at a time forcibly poured down his sore, poisoned throat.

June 25. Though only a sheep-camp, this grand mountain hollow is home, sweet home, every day growing sweeter, and I shall be sorry to leave it. The lily gardens are safe as yet from the trampling flock. Poor, dusty, raggedy, famishing creatures, I heartily pity them. Many a mile they must go every day to gather their fifteen or twenty tons of chaparral and grass.

June 26. Nuttall's flowering dogwood makes a fine show when in bloom. The whole tree is then snowy white. The involucres are six to eight inches wide. Along the streams it is a good-sized tree thirty to fifty feet high, with a broad head when not crowded by companions. Its showy involucres attract a crowd of moths, butterflies, and other winged people about it for their own, and, I suppose, the tree's advantage. It likes plenty of cool water, and is a great drinker like the alder, willow, and cottonwood, and flourishes best on stream banks, though it often wanders far from streams in damp shady glens beneath the pines, where it is much smaller. When the leaves ripen in the fall, they become more beautiful than the flowers, displaying charming tones of red, purple, and lavender. Another species grows in abundance as a chaparral shrub on the shady sides of the hills, probably *Cornus sessilis*. The leaves are eaten by the sheep.—Heard a few lightning strokes in the distance, with rumbling, mumbling reverberations.

June 27. The beaked hazel (*Corylus rostrata*, var. *Californica*) is common on cool slopes up toward the summit of the Pilot Peak Ridge. There is something peculiarly attractive in the hazel, like the oaks and heaths of the cool countries of our forefathers, and through them our love for these plants has, I suppose, been transmitted. This species is four or five feet high, leaves soft and hairy, grateful to the touch, and the delicious nuts are eagerly gathered by Indians and squirrels. The sky as usual adorned with white noon clouds.

June 28. Warm, mellow summer. The glowing sunbeams make every nerve tingle. The new needles of the pines and firs are nearly full grown and shine gloriously. Lizards are glinting about on the hot rocks; some that live near the camp are more than half tame. They seem attentive to every movement on our part, as if curious to simply look on without suspicion of harm, turning their heads to look back, and making a variety of pretty gestures. Gentle, guileless creatures with beautiful eyes, I shall be sorry to leave them when we leave camp.

June 29. I have been making the acquaintance of a very interesting little bird that flits about the falls and rapids of the main branches of the river. It is not a water-bird in structure, though it gets its living in the water, and never leaves the streams. It is not web-footed, yet it dives fearlessly into deep swirling rapids, evidently to feed at the bottom, using its wings to swim with under water just as ducks and loons do. Sometimes it wades about in shallow places, thrusting its head under from time to time in a jerking, nodding, frisky way that is sure to attract attention. It is about the size of a robin, has short crisp wings serviceable for flying either in water or air, and a tail of moderate size slanted upward, giving it, with its nodding, bobbing manners, a wrennish look. Its color is plain bluish ash, with a tinge of brown on the head and shoulders. It flies from fall to fall, rapid to rapid, with a solid whir of wing-beats like those of a quail, follows the windings of the stream, and usually alights on some rock jutting up out of the current, or on some stranded snag, or rarely on the dry limb of an overhanging tree, perching like regular tree birds when it suits its convenience. It has the oddest, daintiest mincing manners imaginable; and the little fellow can sing too, a sweet, thrushy, fluty song, rather low, not the least boisterous, and much less keen and accentuated than from its vigorous briskness one would be led to look for. What a romantic life this little bird leads on the most beautiful portions of the streams, in a genial climate with shade and cool water and spray to temper the summer heat. No wonder it is a fine singer, considering the stream songs it hears day and night. Every breath the little poet draws is part of a song, for all the air about the rapids and falls is beaten into music, and its first lessons must begin before it is born by the thrilling and quivering of the eggs in unison with the tones of the falls. I have not yet found its nest, but it must be near the streams, for it never leaves them.

June 30. Half cloudy, half sunny, clouds lustrous white. The tall pines crowded along the top of the Pilot Peak Ridge look like six-inch miniatures exquisitely outlined on the satiny sky. Average cloudiness for the day about .25. No rain. And so this memorable month ends, a stream of beauty unmeasured, no more to be sectioned off by almanac arithmetic than sun-radiance or the currents of seas and rivers—a peaceful, joyful stream of beauty. Every morning, arising from the death of sleep, the happy plants and all our fellow animal creatures great and small, and even the rocks, seemed to be shouting, "Awake, awake, rejoice, rejoice, come love us and join in our song. Come! Come!" Looking back through the stillness and romantic enchanting beauty and peace of the camp grove, this June seems the greatest of all the months of my life, the most truly, divinely free, boundless like eternity, immortal. Everything in it seems equally divine—one smooth, pure, wild glow of Heaven's love, never to be blotted or blurred by anything past or to come.

July 1. Summer is ripe. Flocks of seeds are already out of their cups and pods seeking their predestined places. Some will strike root and grow up beside their parents, others flying on the wings of the wind far from them, among strangers. Most of the young birds are full feathered and out of their nests, though still looked after by both father and mother, protected and fed and to some extent educated. How beautiful the home life of birds! No wonder we all love them.

I like to watch the squirrels. There are two species here, the large California gray and the Douglas. The latter is the brightest of all the squirrels I have ever seen, a hot spark of life, making every tree tingle with his prickly toes, a condensed nugget of fresh mountain vigor and valor, as free from disease as a sunbeam. One cannot think of such an animal ever being weary or sick. He seems to think the mountains belong to him, and at first tried to drive away the whole flock of sheep as well as the shepherd and dogs. How he scolds, and what faces he makes, all eyes, teeth, and whiskers! If not so comically small, he would indeed be a dreadful fellow. I should like to know more about his bringing up, his life in the home

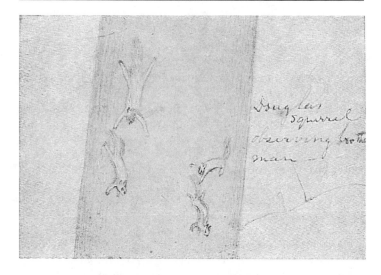

Douglas Squirrel observing Brother Man

knot-hole, as well as in the treetops, throughout all seasons. Strange that I have not yet found a nest full of young ones. The Douglas is nearly allied to the red squirrel of the Atlantic slope, and may have been distributed to this side of the continent by way of the great unbroken forests of the north.

The California gray is one of the most beautiful, and, next to the Douglas, the most interesting of our hairy neighbors. Compared with the Douglas he is twice as large, but far less lively and influential as a worker in the woods and he manages to make his way through leaves and branches with less stir than his small brother. I have never heard him bark at anything except our dogs. When in search of food he glides silently from branch to branch, examining last year's cones, to see whether some few seeds may not be left between the scales, or gleans fallen ones among the leaves on the ground, since none of the present season's crop is yet available. His tail floats now behind him, now above him, level or gracefully curled like a wisp of cirrus cloud, every hair in its place, clean and shining and radiant as thistle-down in spite of rough, gummy work. His whole body seems about as unsubstantial as his tail. The little Douglas is fiery, peppery, full of brag and fight and show, with movements so quick and keen they almost sting the onlooker, and the harlequin gyrating show he makes of himself turns one giddy to see. The gray is shy, and oftentimes stealthy in his movements, as if half expecting an enemy in every tree and bush, and back of every log, wishing only to be let alone apparently, and manifesting no desire to be seen or admired or feared. The Indians hunt this species for food, a good cause for caution, not to mention other enemies—hawks, snakes, wild cats. In woods where food is abundant they wear paths through sheltering thickets and over prostrate trees to some favorite pool where in hot and dry weather they drink at nearly the same hour every day. These pools are said to be narrowly watched, especially by the boys, who lie in ambush with bow and arrow, and kill without noise. But, in spite of enemies, squirrels are happy fellows, forest favorites, types of tireless life. Of all Nature's wild beasts, they seem to me the wildest. May we come to know each other better.

The chaparral-covered hill-slope to the south of the camp, besides furnishing nesting-places for countless merry birds, is the home and hiding-place of the curious wood rat (*Neotoma*), a handsome, interesting animal, always attracting attention wherever seen. It is more like a squirrel than a rat, is much larger, has delicate, thick, soft fur of a bluish slate color, white on the belly; ears large, thin, and translucent; eyes soft, full, and liquid; claws slender, sharp as needles; and as his limbs are strong, he can climb about as well as a squirrel. No rat or squirrel has so innocent a look, is so easily approached, or expresses such confidence in one's good intentions. He seems too fine for the thorny thickets he inhabits, and his hut also is as unlike himself as may be, though softly furnished inside. No other animal inhabitant of these mountains builds houses so large and striking in appearance. The traveler coming suddenly upon a group of them for the first time will not be likely to forget them. They are built of all kinds of sticks, old rotten pieces picked up anywhere, and green prickly twigs bitten from the nearest bushes, the whole mixed with miscellaneous odds and ends of everything movable, such as bits of cloddy earth, stones, bones, deerhorn, etc., piled up in a conical mass as if it were got ready for burning. Some of these curious cabins are six feet high and as wide at the base, and a dozen or more of them are occasionally grouped together, less perhaps for the sake of society than for advantages of food and shelter. Coming through the dense shaggy thickets of some lonely hillside, the solitary explorer happening into one of these strange villages is startled at the sight, and may fancy himself in an Indian settlement, and begin to wonder what kind of reception he is likely to get. But no savage face will he see, perhaps not a single inhabitant, or at most two or three seated on top of their wigwams, looking at the stranger with the mildest of wild eyes, and allowing a near approach. In the center of the rough spiky hut a soft nest is made of the inner fibers of bark chewed to tow, and lined with feathers and the down of various seeds, such as willow and milkweed. The delicate creature in its prickly, thick-walled home suggests a tender flower in a thorny involucre. Some of the nests are built in trees thirty or forty feet from the ground, and even in garrets, as if seeking the company and protection of man, like swallows and linnets, though accustomed to the wildest solitude. Among house-keepers Neotoma has the reputation of a thief, because he carries away everything transportable to his queer hut,—knives, forks, combs, nails, tin cups, spectacles, etc.,—merely, however, to strengthen his fortifications, I guess. His food at home, as far as I have learned, is nearly the same as that of the squirrels—nuts, berries, seeds, and sometimes the bark and tender shoots of the various species of ceanothus.

July 2. Warm, sunny day, thrilling plants and animals and rocks alike, making sap and blood flow fast, and making every particle of the crystal mountains throb and swirl and dance in glad accord like star-dust. No dullness anywhere visible or thinkable. No stagnation, no death. Everything kept in joyful rhythmic motion in the pulses of Nature's big heart.

Pearl cumuli over the higher mountains—clouds, not with a silver lining, but all silver. The brightest, crispest, rockiest-looking clouds, most varied in features and keenest in outline I ever saw at any time of year in any country. The daily building and unbuilding of these snowy cloud-ranges—the highest Sierra—is a prime marvel to me, and I gaze at the stupendous white domes, miles high, with ever fresh admiration. But in the midst of these sky and mountain affairs a change of diet is pulling us down. We have been out of bread a few days, and begin to miss it more than seems reasonable, for we have plenty of meat and sugar and tea. Strange we should feel food-poor in so rich a wilderness. The Indians put us to shame, so do the squirrels,—starchy roots and seeds and bark in abundance, yet the failure of the meal sack disturbs our bodily balance, and threatens our best enjoyments.

July 3. Warm. Breeze just enough to sift through the woods and waft fragrance from their thousand fountains. The pine and fir cones are growing well, resin and balsam dripping from every tree, and seeds are ripening fast, promising a fine harvest. The squirrels will have bread. They eat all kinds of nuts long before they are ripe, and yet never seem to suffer in stomach.

Chapter III

A BREAD FAMINE

JULY 4. The air beyond the flock range, full of the essences of the woods, is growing sweeter and more fragrant from day to day, like ripening fruit.

Mr. Delaney is expected to arrive soon from the lowlands with a new stock of provisions, and as the flock is to be moved to fresh pastures we shall all be well fed. In the mean time our stock of beans as well as flour has failed—everything but mutton, sugar, and tea. The shepherd is somewhat demoralized, and seems to care but little what becomes of his flock. He says that since the boss has failed to feed him he is not rightly bound to feed the sheep, and swears that no decent white man can climb these steep mountains on mutton alone. "It's not fittin' grub for a white man really white. For dogs and coyotes and Indians it's different. Good grub, good sheep. That's what I say." Such was Billy's Fourth of July oration.

July 5. The clouds of noon on the high Sierra seem yet more marvelously, indescribably beautiful from day to day as one becomes more wakeful to see them. The smoke of the gunpowder burned yesterday on the lowlands, and the eloquence of the orators has probably settled or been blown away by this time. Here every day is a holiday, a jubilee ever sounding with serene enthusiasm, without wear or waste or cloying weariness. Everything rejoicing. Not a single cell or crystal unvisited or forgotten.

July 6. Mr. Delaney has not arrived, and the bread famine is sore. We must eat mutton a while longer, though it seems hard to get accustomed to it. I have heard of Texas pioneers living without bread or anything made from the cereals for months without suffering, using the breast-meat of wild turkeys for bread. Of this kind they had plenty in the good old days when life, though considered less safe, was fussed over the less. The trappers and fur traders of early days in the Rocky Mountain regions lived on bison and beaver meat for months. Salmon-eaters, too, there are among both Indians and whites who seem to suffer little or not at all from the want of bread. Just at this moment mutton seems the least desirable of food, though of good quality. We pick out the leanest bits, and down they go against heavy disgust, causing nausea and an effort to reject the offensive stuff. Tea makes matters worse, if possible. The stomach begins to assert itself as an independent creature with a will of its own. We should boil lupine leaves, clover, starchy petioles, and saxifrage rootstocks like the Indians. We try to ignore our gastric troubles, rise and gaze about us, turn our eyes to the mountains, and climb doggedly up through brush and rocks into the heart of the scenery. A stifled calm comes on, and the day's duties and even enjoyments are languidly got through with. We chew a few leaves of ceanothus by way of luncheon, and smell or chew the spicy monardella for the dull headache and stomach-ache that now lightens, now comes muffling down upon us and into us like fog. At night more mutton, flesh to flesh, down with it, not too much, and there are the stars shining through the cedar plumes and branches above our beds.

July 7. Rather weak and sickish this morning, and all about a piece of bread. Can scarce command attention to my best studies, as if one couldn't take a few days' saunter in the God-ful woods without maintaining a base on a wheat-field and gristmill. Like caged parrots we want a cracker, any of the hundred kinds—the remainder biscuit of a voyage around the world would answer well enough, nor would the wholesomeness of saleratus biscuit be questioned. Bread without flesh is a good diet, as on many botanical excursions I have proved. Tea also may easily be ignored. Just bread and water and delightful toil is all I need,—not unreasonably much, yet one ought to be trained and tempered to enjoy life in these brave wilds in full independence of any particular kind of nourishment. That this may be accomplished is manifest, as far as bodily welfare is concerned, in the lives of people of other climes. The Eskimo, for example, gets a living far north of the wheat line, from oily seals and whales. Meat, berries, bitter weeds, and blubber, or only the last, for months at a time; and yet these people all around the frozen shores of our continent are said to be hearty, jolly, stout, and brave. We hear, too, of fish-eaters, carnivorous as spiders, yet well enough as far as stomachs are concerned, while we are so ridiculously helpless, making wry faces over our fare, looking sheepish in digestive distress amid rumbling, grumbling sounds that might well pass for smothered baas. We have a large supply of sugar, and this evening it occurred to me that these belligerent stomachs might possibly, like complaining children, be coaxed with candy. Accordingly the frying-pan was cleansed, and a lot of sugar cooked in it to a sort of wax, but this stuff only made matters worse.

Man seems to be the only animal whose food soils him, making necessary much washing and shield-like bibs and napkins. Moles living in the earth and eating slimy worms are yet as clean as seals or fishes, whose lives are one perpetual wash. And, as we have seen, the squirrels in these resiny woods keep themselves clean in some mysterious way; not a hair is sticky, though they handle the gummy cones, and glide about apparently without care. The birds, too, are clean, though they seem to make a good deal of fuss washing and cleaning their feathers. Certain flies and ants I see are in a fix, entangled and sealed up in the sugar-wax we threw away, like some of their ancestors in amber. Our stomachs, like tired muscles, are sore with long squirming. Once I was very hungry in the Bonaventure graveyard near Savannah, Georgia, having fasted for several days; then the empty stomach seemed to chafe in much the same way as now, and a somewhat similar tenderness and aching was produced, hard to bear, though the pain was not acute. We dream of bread, a sure sign we need it. Like the Indians, we ought to know how to get the starch out of fern and saxifrage stalks, lily bulbs, pine bark, etc. Our education has been sadly neglected for many generations. Wild rice would be good. I noticed a leersia in wet meadow edges, but the seeds are small. Acorns are not ripe, nor pine nuts, nor filberts. The inner bark of pine or spruce might be tried. Drank tea until half intoxicated. Man seems to crave a stimulant when anything extraordinary is going on, and this is the only one I use. Billy chews great quantities of tobacco, which I suppose helps to stupefy and moderate his misery. We look and listen for the Don every hour. How beautiful upon the mountains his big feet would be!

In the warm, hospitable Sierra, shepherds and mountain

men in general, as far as I have seen, are easily satisfied as to
food supplies and bedding. Most of them are heartily content
to "rough it," ignoring Nature's fineness as bothersome or
unmanly. The shepherd's bed is often only the bare ground
and a pair of blankets, with a stone, a piece of wood, or a
pack-saddle for a pillow. In choosing the spot, he shows less
care than the dogs, for they usually deliberate before making
up their minds in so important an affair, going from place to
place, scraping away loose sticks and pebbles, and trying for
comfort by making many changes, while the shepherd casts
himself down anywhere, seemingly the least skilled of all rest
seekers. His food, too, even when he has all he wants, is usually far from delicate, either in kind or cooking. Beans, bread
of any sort, bacon, mutton, dried peaches, and sometimes potatoes and onions, make up his bill-of-fare, the two latter articles being regarded as luxuries on account of their weight as
compared with the nourishment they contain; a half-sack or
so of each may be put into the pack in setting out from the
home ranch and in a few days they are done. Beans are the
main standby, portable, wholesome, and capable of going far,
besides being easily cooked, although curiously enough a
great deal of mystery is supposed to lie about the bean-pot.
No two cooks quite agree on the methods of making beans
do their best, and, after petting and coaxing and nursing the
savory mess,—well oiled and mellowed with bacon boiled into
the heart of it,—the proud cook will ask, after dishing out a
quart or two for trial, "Well, how do you like *my* beans?" as
if by no possibility could they be like any other beans cooked
in the same way, but must needs possess some special virtue
of which he alone is master. Molasses, sugar, or pepper may
be used to give desired flavors; or the first water may be
poured off and a spoonful or two of ashes or soda added to
dissolve or soften the skins more fully, according to various
tastes and notions. But, like casks of wine, no two potfuls are
exactly alike to every palate. Some are supposed to be spoiled
by the moon, by some unlucky day, by the beans having been
grown on soil not suitable; or the whole year may be to blame
as not favorable for beans.

Coffee, too, has its marvels in the camp kitchen, but not
so many, and not so inscrutable as those that beset the bean-

pot. A low, complacent grunt follows a mouthful drawn in with a gurgle, and the remark cast forth aimlessly, "That's good coffee." Then another gurgling sip and repetition of the judgment, "*Yes, sir*, that *is* good coffee." As to tea, there are but two kinds, weak and strong, the stronger the better. The only remark heard is, "That tea's weak," otherwise it is good enough and not worth mentioning. If it has been boiled an hour or two or smoked on a pitchy fire, no matter,—who cares for a little tannin or creosote? they make the black beverage all the stronger and more attractive to tobacco-tanned palates.

Sheep-camp bread, like most California camp bread, is baked in Dutch ovens, some of it in the form of yeast powder biscuit, an unwholesome sticky compound leading straight to dyspepsia. The greater part, however, is fermented with sour dough, a handful from each batch being saved and put away in the mouth of the flour sack to inoculate the next. The oven is simply a cast-iron pot, about five inches deep and from twelve to eighteen inches wide. After the batch has been mixed and kneaded in a tin pan the oven is slightly heated and rubbed with a piece of tallow or pork rind. The dough is then placed in it, pressed out against the sides, and left to rise. When ready for baking a shovelful of coals is spread out by the side of the fire and the oven set upon them, while another shovelful is placed on top of the lid, which is raised from time to time to see that the requisite amount of heat is being kept up. With care good bread may be made in this way, though it is liable to be burned or to be sour, or raised too much, and the weight of the oven is a serious objection.

At last Don Delaney comes doon the lang glen—hunger vanishes, we turn our eyes to the mountains, and to-morrow we go climbing toward cloudland.

Never while anything is left of me shall this first camp be forgotten. It has fairly grown into me, not merely as memory pictures, but as part and parcel of mind and body alike. The deep hopper-like hollow, with its majestic trees through which all the wonderful nights the stars poured their beauty. The flowery wildness of the high steep slope toward Brown's Flat, and its bloom-fragrance descending at the close of the still days. The embowered river-reaches with their multitude of voices making melody, the stately flow and rush and glad exulting onsweeping currents caressing the dipping sedge-leaves and bushes and mossy stones, swirling in pools, dividing against little flowery islands, breaking gray and white here and there, ever rejoicing, yet with deep solemn undertones re-calling the ocean—the brave little bird ever beside them, sing-ing with sweet human tones among the waltzing foam-bells, and like a blessed evangel explaining God's love. And the Pilot Peak Ridge, its long withdrawing slopes gracefully modeled and braided, reaching from climate to climate, feathered with trees that are the kings of their race, their ranks nobly mar-shaled to view, spire above spire, crown above crown, waving their long, leafy arms, tossing their cones like ringing bells—blessed sun-fed mountaineers rejoicing in their strength, every tree tuneful, a harp for the winds and the sun. The hazel and buckthorn pastures of the deer, the sun-beaten brows purple and yellow with mint and golden-rods, carpeted with cham-œbatia, humming with bees. And the dawns and sunrises and sundowns of these mountains days,—the rose light creeping higher among the stars, changing to daffodil yellow, the level beams bursting forth, streaming across the ridges, touching pine after pine, awakening and warming all the mighty host to do gladly their shining day's work. The great sun-gold noons, the alabaster cloud-mountains, the landscape beaming with consciousness like the face of a god. The sunsets, when the trees stood hushed awaiting their good-night blessings. Divine, enduring, unwastable wealth.

Chapter IV

TO THE HIGH MOUNTAINS

JULY 8. Now away we go toward the topmost mountains. Many still, small voices, as well as the noon thunder, are calling, "Come higher." Farewell, blessed dell, woods, gardens, streams, birds, squirrels, lizards, and a thousand others. Farewell. Farewell.

Up through the woods the hoofed locusts streamed beneath a cloud of brown dust. Scarcely were they driven a hundred yards from the old corral ere they seemed to know that at last they were going to new pastures, and rushed wildly ahead, crowding through gaps in the brush, jumping, tumbling like exulting hurrahing flood-waters escaping through a broken dam. A man on each flank kept shouting advice to the leaders, who in their famishing condition were behaving like Gadarene swine; two other drivers were busy with stragglers, helping them out of brush tangles; the Indian, calm, alert, silently watched for wanderers likely to be overlooked; the two dogs ran here and there, at a loss to know what was best to be done, while the Don, soon far in the rear, was trying to keep in sight of his troublesome wealth.

As soon as the boundary of the old eaten-out range was passed the hungry horde suddenly became calm, like a mountain stream in a meadow. Thenceforward they were allowed to eat their way as slowly as they wished, care being taken only to keep them headed toward the summit of the Merced and Tuolumne divide. Soon the two thousand flattened paunches were bulged out with sweet-pea vines and grass, and the gaunt, desperate creatures, more like wolves than sheep, became bland and governable, while the howling drivers changed to gentle shepherds, and sauntered in peace.

Toward sundown we reached Hazel Green, a charming spot on the summit of the dividing ridge between the basins of the Merced and Tuolumne, where there is a small brook flowing through hazel and dogwood thickets beneath magnificent silver firs and pines. Here, we are camped for the night, our big fire, heaped high with rosiny logs and branches, is blazing like

Divide between the Tuolumne and the Merced, below Hazel Green

a sunrise, gladly giving back the light slowly sifted from the sunbeams of centuries of summers; and in the glow of that old sunlight how impressively surrounding objects are brought forward in relief against the outer darkness! Grasses, larkspurs, columbines, lilies, hazel bushes, and the great trees form a circle around the fire like thoughtful spectators, gazing and listening with human-like enthusiasm. The night breeze is cool, for all day we have been climbing into the upper sky, the home of the cloud mountains we so long have admired. How sweet and keen the air! Every breath a blessing. Here the sugar pine reaches its fullest development in size and beauty and number of individuals, filling every swell and hollow and down-plunging ravine almost to the exclusion of other species. A few yellow pines are still to be found as companions, and in the coolest places silver firs; but noble as these are, the sugar pine is king, and spreads long protecting arms above them while they rock and wave in sign of recognition.

We have now reached a height of six thousand feet. In the forenoon we passed along a flat part of the dividing ridge that is planted with manzanita (*Arctostaphylos*), some specimens the largest I have seen. I measured one, the bole of which is four feet in diameter and only eighteen inches high from the ground, where it dissolves into many wide-spreading branches forming a broad round head about ten or twelve feet high, covered with clusters of small narrow-throated pink bells. The leaves are pale green, glandular, and set on edge by a twist of the petiole. The branches seem naked; for the chocolate-colored bark is very smooth and thin, and is shed off in flakes that curl when dry. The wood is red, close-grained, hard, and heavy. I wonder how old these curious tree-bushes are, probably as old as the great pines. Indians and bears and birds and fat grubs feast on the berries, which look like small apples, often rosy on one side, green on the other. The Indians are said to make a kind of beer or cider out of them. There are many species. This one, *Arctostaphylos pungens*, is common hereabouts. No need have they to fear the wind, so low they are and steadfastly rooted. Even the fires that sweep the woods seldom destroy them utterly, for they rise again from the root, and some of the dry ridges they grow on are seldom touched by fire. I must try to know them better.

I miss my river songs to-night. Here Hazel Creek at its topmost springs has a voice like a bird. The wind-tones in the great trees overhead are strangely impressive, all the more because not a leaf stirs below them. But it grows late, and I must to bed. The camp is silent; everybody asleep. It seems extravagant to spend hours so precious in sleep. "He giveth his beloved sleep." Pity the poor beloved needs it, weak, weary, forspent; oh, the pity of it, to sleep in the midst of eternal, beautiful motion instead of gazing forever, like the stars.

July 9. Exhilarated with the mountain air, I feel like shouting this morning with excess of wild animal joy. The Indian lay down away from the fire last night, without blankets, having nothing on, by way of clothing, but a pair of blue overalls and a calico shirt wet with sweat. The night air is chilly at this elevation, and we gave him some horse-blankets, but he didn't seem to care for them. A fine thing to be independent of clothing where it is so hard to carry. When food is scarce, he can live on whatever comes in his way—a few berries, roots, bird eggs, grasshoppers, black ants, fat wasp or bumblebee larvæ, without feeling that he is doing anything worth mention, so I have been told.

Our course to-day was along the broad top of the main ridge to a hollow beyond Crane Flat. It is scarce at all rocky, and is covered with the noblest pines and spruces I have yet seen. Sugar pines from six to eight feet in diameter are not uncommon, with a height of two hundred feet or even more. The silver firs (*Abies concolor* and *A. magnifica*) are exceedingly beautiful, especially the *magnifica*, which becomes more abundant the higher we go. It is of great size, one of the most notable in every way of the giant conifers of the Sierra. I saw specimens that measured seven feet in diameter and over two hundred feet in height, while the average size for what might be called full-grown mature trees can hardly be less than one hundred and eighty or two hundred feet high and five or six feet in diameter; and with these noble dimensions there is a symmetry and perfection of finish not to be seen in any other tree, hereabout at least. The branches are whorled in fives mostly, and stand out from the tall, straight, exquisitely tapered bole in level collars, each branch regularly pinnated like the fronds of ferns, and densely clad with leaves all around the branchlets, thus giving them a singularly rich and sumptuous appearance. The extreme top of the tree is a thick blunt shoot pointing straight to the zenith like an admonishing finger. The cones stand erect like casks on the upper branches. They are about six inches long, three in diameter, blunt, velvety, and cylindrical in form, and very rich and precious looking. The seeds are about three quarters of an inch long, dark reddish brown with brilliant iridescent purple wings, and when ripe, the cone falls to pieces, and the seeds thus set free at a height of one hundred and fifty or two hundred feet have a good send off and may fly considerable distances in a good breeze; and it is when a good breeze is blowing that most of them are shaken free to fly.

The other species, *Abies concolor*, attains nearly as great a height and thickness as the *magnifica*, but the branches do not form such regular whorls, nor are they so exactly pinnated or richly leaf-clad. Instead of growing all around the branchlets, the leaves are mostly arranged in two flat horizontal rows. The cones and seeds are like those of the *magnifica* in form but less than half as large. The bark of the *magnifica* is reddish purple and closely furrowed, that of the *concolor* gray and widely furrowed. A noble pair.

At Crane Flat we climbed a thousand feet or more in a

distance of about two miles, the forest growing more dense and the silvery *magnifica* fir forming a still greater portion of the whole. Crane Flat is a meadow with a wide sandy border lying on the top of the divide. It is often visited by blue cranes to rest and feed on their long journeys, hence the name. It is about half a mile long, draining into the Merced, sedgy in the middle, with a margin bright with lilies, columbines, larkspurs, lupines, castilleia, then an outer zone of dry, gently sloping ground starred with a multitude of small flowers—eunanus, mimulus, gilia, with rosettes of spraguea, and tufts of several species of eriogonum and the brilliant zauschneria. The noble forest wall about it is made up of the two silver firs and the yellow and sugar pines, which here seem to reach their highest pitch of beauty and grandeur; for the elevation, six thousand feet or a little more, is not too great for the sugar and yellow pines or too low for the *magnifica* fir, while the *concolor* seems to find this elevation the best possible. About a mile from the north end of the flat there is a grove of *Sequoia gigantea*, the king of all the conifers. Furthermore, the Douglas spruce (*Pseudotsuga Douglasii*) and *Libocedrus decurrens*, and a few two-leaved pines, occur here and there, forming a small part of the forest. Three pines, two silver firs, one Douglas spruce, one sequoia,—all of them, except the two-leaved pine, colossal trees,—are found here together, an assemblage of conifers unrivaled on the globe.

We passed a number of charming garden-like meadows lying on top of the divide or hanging like ribbons down its sides, imbedded in the glorious forest. Some are taken up chiefly with the tall white-flowered *Veratrum Californicum*, with boat-shaped leaves about a foot long, eight or ten inches wide, and veined like those of cypripedium,—a robust, hearty, liliaceous plant, fond of water and determined to be seen. Columbine and larkspur grow on the dryer edges of the meadows, with a tall handsome lupine standing waist-deep in long grasses and sedges. Castilleias, too, of several species make a bright show with beds of violets at their feet. But the glory of these forest meadows is a lily (*L. parvum*). The tallest are from seven to eight feet high with magnificent racemes of ten to twenty or more small orange-colored flowers; they stand out free in open ground, with just enough grass and other companion plants about them to fringe their feet, and show them off to best advantage. This is a grand addition to my lily acquaintances,—a true mountaineer, reaching prime vigor and beauty at a height of seven thousand feet or there-abouts. It varies, I find, very much in size even in the same meadow, not only with the soil, but with age. I saw a specimen that had only one flower, and another within a stone's throw had twenty-five. And to think that the sheep should be allowed in these lily meadows! after how many centuries of Nature's care planting and watering them, tucking the bulbs in snugly below winter frost, shading the tender shoots with clouds drawn above them like curtains, pouring refreshing rain, making them perfect in beauty, and keeping them safe by a thousand miracles; yet, strange to say, allowing the trampling of devastating sheep. One might reasonably look for a wall of fire to fence such gardens. So extravagant is Nature with her choicest treasures, spending plant beauty as she spends sunshine, pouring it forth into land and sea, garden and desert. And so the beauty of lilies falls on angels and men, bears and squirrels, wolves and sheep, birds and bees, but as far as I have seen, man alone, and the animals he tames, destroy these gardens. Awkward, lumbering bears, the Don tells me, love to wallow in them in hot weather, and deer with their sharp feet cross them again and again, sauntering and feeding, yet never a lily have I seen spoiled by them. Rather, like gardeners, they seem to cultivate them, pressing and dibbling as required. Anyhow not a leaf or petal seems misplaced.

The trees round about them seem as perfect in beauty and form as the lilies, their boughs whorled like lily leaves in exact order. This evening, as usual, the glow of our camp-fire is working enchantment on everything within reach of its rays. Lying beneath the firs, it is glorious to see them dipping their spires in the starry sky, the sky like one vast lily meadow in bloom! How can I close my eyes on so precious a night?

July 10. A Douglas squirrel, peppery, pungent autocrat of the woods, is barking overhead this morning, and the small forest birds, so seldom seen when one travels noisily, are out on sunny branches along the edge of the meadow getting warm, taking a sun bath and dew bath—a fine sight. How charming the sprightly confident looks and ways of these little feathered people of the trees! They seem sure of dainty, wholesome breakfasts, and where are so many breakfasts to come from? How helpless should we find ourselves should we try to set a table for them of such buds, seeds, insects, etc., as would keep them in the pure wild health they enjoy! Not a headache or any other ache amongst them, I guess. As for the irrepressible Douglas squirrels, one never thinks of their breakfasts or the possibility of hunger, sickness or death; rather they seem like stars above chance or change, even though we may see them at times busy gathering burrs, working hard for a living.

On through the forest ever higher we go, a cloud of dust dimming the way, thousands of feet trampling leaves and flowers, but in this mighty wilderness they seem but a feeble band, and a thousand gardens will escape their blighting touch. They cannot hurt the trees, though some of the seedlings suffer, and should the woolly locusts be greatly multiplied, as on account of dollar value they are likely to be, then the forests, too, may in time be destroyed. Only the sky will then be safe, though hid from view by dust and smoke, incense of a bad sacrifice. Poor, helpless, hungry sheep, in great part misbegotten, without good right to be, semi-manufactured, made less by God than man, born out of time and place, yet their voices are strangely human and call out one's pity.

Our way is still along the Merced and Tuolumne divide, the streams on our right going to swell the songful Yosemite River, those on our left to the songful Tuolumne, slipping through sunny carex and lily meadows, and breaking into song down a thousand ravines almost as soon as they are born. A more tuneful set of streams surely nowhere exists, or more sparkling crystal pure, now gliding with tinkling whisper, now with merry dimpling rush, in and out through sunshine and shade, shimmering in pools, uniting their currents, bouncing, dancing from form to form over cliffs and inclines, ever more beautiful the farther they go until they pour into the main glacial rivers.

All day I have been gazing in growing admiration at the noble groups of the magnificent silver fir which more and more is taking the ground to itself. The woods above Crane Flat still continue comparatively open, letting in the sunshine on the brown needle-strewn ground. Not only are the individual trees admirable in symmetry and superb in foliage and port, but half a dozen or more often form temple groves in which the trees are so nicely graded in size and position as to seem one. Here, indeed, is the tree-lover's paradise. The dullest eye in the world must surely be quickened by such trees as these.

Fortunately the sheep need little attention, as they are driven slowly and allowed to nip and nibble as they like. Since leaving Hazel Green we have been following the Yosemite trail; visitors to the famous valley coming by way of Coulterville and Chinese Camp pass this way—the two trails uniting at Crane Flat—and enter the valley on the north side. Another trail enters on the south side by way of Mariposa. The tourists we saw were in parties of from three or four to fifteen or twenty, mounted on mules or small mustang ponies. A strange show they made, winding single file through the solemn woods in gaudy attire, scaring the wild creatures, and one might fancy that even the great pines would be disturbed and groan aghast. But what may we say of ourselves and the flock?

We are now camped at Tamarack Flat, within four or five miles of the lower end of Yosemite. Here is another fine meadow embosomed in the woods, with a deep, clear stream gliding through it, its banks rounded and beveled with a thatch of dipping sedges. The flat is named after the two-leaved pine (*Pinus contorta,* var. *Murrayana*), common here, especially around the cool margin of the meadow. On rocky ground it is a rough, thickset tree, about forty to sixty feet high and one to three feet in diameter, bark thin and gummy, branches rather naked, tassels, leaves, and cones small. But in damp, rich soil it grows close and slender, and reaches a height at times of nearly a hundred feet. Specimens only six inches in diameter at the ground are often fifty or sixty feet in height, as slender and sharp in outline as arrows, like the true tamarack (larch) of the Eastern States; hence the name, though it is a pine.

July 11. The Don has gone ahead on one of the pack animals to spy out the land to the north of Yosemite in search of the best point for a central camp. Much higher than this we cannot now go, for the upper pastures, said to be better than any hereabouts, are still buried in heavy winter snow. Glad I am that camp is to be fixed in the Yosemite region, for many a glorious ramble I'll have along the top of the walls, and then what landscapes I shall find with their new mountains and cañons, forests and gardens, lakes and streams and falls.

We are now about seven thousand feet above the sea, and the nights are so cool we have to pile coats and extra clothing on top of our blankets. Tamarack Creek is icy cold, delicious, exhilarating champagne water. It is flowing bank-full in the meadow with silent speed, but only a few hundred yards below our camp the ground is bare gray granite strewn with boulders, large spaces being without a single tree or only a small one here and there anchored in narrow seams and cracks. The boulders, many of them very large, are not in piles or scattered like rubbish among loose crumbling débris as if weathered out of the solid as boulders of disintegration; they mostly occur singly, and are lying on a clean pavement on which the sunshine falls in a glare that contrasts with the shimmer of light and shade we have been accustomed to in the leafy woods. And, strange to say, these boulders lying so still and deserted, with no moving force near them, no boulder carrier anywhere in sight, were nevertheless brought from a distance, as difference in color and composition shows, quarried and carried and laid down here each in its place; nor have they stirred, most of them, through calm and storm since first they arrived. They look lonely here, strangers in a strange land,—huge blocks, angular mountain chips, the largest twenty or thirty feet in diameter, the chips that Nature has made in modeling her landscapes, fashioning the forms of her mountains and valleys. And with what tool were they quarried and carried? On the pavement we find its marks. The most resisting unweathered portion of the surface is scored and striated in a rigidly parallel way, indicating that the region has been overswept by a glacier from the northeastward, grinding down the general mass of the mountains, scoring and polishing, producing a strange, raw, wiped appearance, and dropping whatever boulders it chanced to be carrying at the time it was melted at the close of the Glacial Period. A fine discovery this. As for the forests we have been passing through, they are probably growing on deposits of soil most of which has been laid down by this same ice agent in the form of moraines of different sorts, now in great part disintegrated and outspread by post-glacial weathering.

Out of the grassy meadow and down over this ice-planed granite runs the glad young Tamarack Creek, rejoicing, exulting, chanting, dancing in white, glowing, irised falls and cascades on its way to the Merced Cañon, a few miles below Yosemite, falling more than three thousand feet in a distance of about two miles.

All the Merced streams are wonderful singers, and Yosemite is the centre where the main tributaries meet. From a point about half a mile from our camp we can see into the lower end of the famous valley, with its wonderful cliffs and groves, a grand page of mountain manuscript that I would gladly give my life to be able to read. How vast it seems, how short human life when we happen to think of it, and how little we may learn, however hard we try! Yet why bewail our poor inevitable ignorance? Some of the external beauty is always in sight, enough to keep every fibre of us tingling, and this we are able to gloriously enjoy though the methods of its creation may lie beyond our ken. Sing on, brave Tamarack Creek, fresh from your snowy fountains, plash and swirl and dance to your fate in the sea; bathing, cheering every living thing along your way.

Have greatly enjoyed all this huge day, sauntering and seeing, steeping in the mountain influences, sketching, noting, pressing flowers, drinking ozone and Tamarack water. Found the white fragrant Washington lily, the finest of all the Sierra lilies. Its bulbs are buried in shaggy chaparral tangles, I suppose for safety from pawing bears; and its magnificent panicles sway and rock over the top of the rough snow-pressed bushes, while big, bold, blunt-nosed bees drone and mumble in its polleny bells. A lovely flower, worth going hungry and footsore endless miles to see. The whole world seems richer now that I have found this plant in so noble a landscape.

A log house serves to mark a claim to the Tamarack meadow, which may become valuable as a station in case travel to Yosemite should greatly increase. Belated parties occasionally stop here. A white man with an Indian woman is holding possession of the place.

Sauntered up the meadow about sundown, out of sight of camp and sheep and all human mark, into the deep peace of the solemn old woods, everything glowing with Heaven's unquenchable enthusiasm.

July 12. The Don has returned, and again we go on pilgrimage. "Looking over the Yosemite Creek country," he said, "from the tops of the hills you see nothing but rocks and patches of trees; but when you go down into the rocky desert you find no end of small grassy banks and meadows, and so the country is not half so lean as it looks. There we'll go and stay until the snow is melted from the upper country."

I was glad to hear that the high snow made a stay in the Yosemite region necessary, for I am anxious to see as much of it as possible. What fine times I shall have sketching, studying plants and rocks, and scrambling about the brink of the great valley alone, out of sight and sound of camp!

We saw another party of Yosemite tourists to-day. Somehow most of these travelers seem to care but little for the glorious objects about them, though enough to spend time and money and endure long rides to see the famous valley. And when they are fairly within the mighty walls of the temple and hear the psalms of the falls, they will forget themselves and become devout. Blessed, indeed, should be every pilgrim in these holy mountains!

We moved slowly eastward along the Mono Trail, and early in the afternoon unpacked and camped on the bank of Cascade Creek. The Mono Trail crosses the range by the Bloody Cañon Pass to gold mines near the north end of Mono Lake. These mines were reported to be rich when first discovered, and a grand rush took place, making a trail necessary. A few small bridges were built over streams where fording was not practicable on account of the softness of the bottom, sections of fallen trees cut out, and lanes made through thickets wide enough to allow the passage of bulky packs; but over the greater part of the way scarce a stone or shovelful of earth has been moved.

The woods we passed through are composed almost wholly of *Abies magnifica*, the companion species, *concolor*, being mostly left behind on account of altitude, while the increasing elevation seems grateful to the charming *magnifica*. No words can do anything like justice to this noble tree. At one place many had fallen during some heavy wind-storm, owing to the loose sandy character of the soil, which offered no secure anchorage. The soil is mostly decomposed and disintegrated moraine material.

The sheep are lying down on a bare rocky spot such as they like, chewing the cud in grassy peace. Cooking is going on, appetites growing keener every day. No lowlander can appreciate the mountain appetite, and the facility with which heavy food called "grub" is disposed of. Eating, walking, resting, seem alike delightful, and one feels inclined to shout lustily on rising in the morning like a crowing cock. Sleep and digestion as clear as the air. Fine spicy plush boughs for bedding we shall have to-night, and a glorious lullaby from this cascading creek. Never was stream more fittingly named, for as far as I have traced it above and below our camp it is one continuous bouncing, dancing, white bloom of cascades. And at the very last unwearied it finishes its wild course in a grand leap of three hundred feet or more to the bottom of the main Yosemite cañon near the fall of Tamarack Creek, a few miles below the foot of the valley. These falls almost rival some of the far-famed Yosemite falls. Never shall I forget these glad cascade songs, the low booming, the roaring, the keen, silvery clashing of the cool water rushing exulting from form to form beneath irised spray; or in the deep still night seen white in the darkness, and its multitude of voices sounding still more impressively sublime. Here I find the little water ouzel as much at home as any linnet in a leafy grove, seeming to take the greater delight the more boisterous the stream. The dizzy precipices, the swift dashing energy displayed, and the thunder tones of the sheer falls are awe-inspiring, but there is nothing awful about this little bird. Its song is sweet and low, and all its gestures, as it flits about amid the loud uproar, bespeak strength and peace and joy. Contemplating these darlings of Nature coming forth from spray-sprinkled nests on the brink of savage streams, Samson's riddle comes to mind, "Out of the strong cometh forth sweetness." A yet finer bloom is this little bird than the foam-bells in eddying pools. Gentle bird, a precious message you bring me. We may miss the meaning of the torrent, but thy sweet voice, only love is in it.

July 13. Our course all day has been eastward over the rim of Yosemite Creek basin and down about halfway to the bottom, where we have encamped on a sheet of glacier-polished granite, a firm foundation for beds. Saw the tracks of a very large bear on the trail, and the Don talked of bears in general. I said I should like to see the maker of these immense tracks as he marched along, and follow him for days, without disturbing him, to learn something of the life of this master beast of the wilderness. Lambs, the Don told me, born in the lowland, that never saw or heard a bear, snort and run in terror when they catch the scent, showing how fully they have inherited a knowledge of their enemy. Hogs, mules, horses, and cattle are afraid of bears, and are seized with ungovernable terror when they approach, particularly hogs and mules. Hogs are frequently driven to pastures in the foothills of the Coast Range and Sierra where acorns are abundant, and are herded in droves of hundreds like sheep. When a bear comes to the range they promptly leave it, emigrating in a body, usually in the night time, the keepers being powerless to prevent; they thus show more sense than sheep, that simply scatter in the rocks and brush and await their fate. Mules flee like the wind with or without riders when they see a bear, and, if picketed, sometimes break their necks in trying to break their ropes, though I have not heard of bears killing mules or horses. Of hogs they are said to be particularly fond, bolting small ones, bones and all, without choice of parts. In particular, Mr. Delaney assured me that all kinds of bears in the Sierra are very shy, and that hunters found far greater difficulty in getting within gunshot of them than of deer or indeed any other animal in the Sierra, and if I was anxious to see much of them I should have to wait and watch with endless Indian patience and pay no attention to anything else.

Night is coming on, the gray rock waves are growing dim in the twilight. How raw and young this region appears! Had the ice sheet that swept over it vanished but yesterday, its traces on the more resisting portions about our camp could hardly be more distinct than they now are. The horses and sheep and all of us, indeed, slipped on the smoothest places.

July 14. How deathlike is sleep in this mountain air, and quick the awakening into newness of life! A calm dawn, yellow and purple, then floods of sun-gold, making everything tingle and glow.

In an hour or two we came to Yosemite Creek, the stream that makes the greatest of all the Yosemite falls. It is about forty feet wide at the Mono Trail crossing, and now about four feet in average depth, flowing about three miles an hour. The distance to the verge of the Yosemite wall, where it makes its tremendous plunge, is only about two miles from here. Calm, beautiful, and nearly silent, it glides with stately gestures, a dense growth of the slender two-leaved pine along its banks, and a fringe of willow, purple spirea, sedges, daisies, lilies, and columbines. Some of the sedges and willow boughs dip into the current, and just outside of the close ranks of trees there is a sunny flat of washed gravelly sand which seems to have been deposited by some ancient flood. It is covered with millions of erethrea, eriogonum, and oxytheca, with more flowers than leaves, forming an even growth, slightly dimpled and ruffled here and there by rosettes of *Spraguea umbellata*. Back of this flowery strip there is a wavy upsloping plain of solid granite, so smoothly ice-polished in many places that it glistens in the sun like glass. In shallow hollows there are patches of trees, mostly the rough form of the two-leaved pine, rather scrawny looking where there is little or no soil. Also a few junipers (*Juniperus occidentalis*), short and stout, with bright cinnamon-colored bark and gray foliage, standing alone mostly, on the sun-beaten pavement, safe from fire, clinging by slight joints,—a sturdy storm-enduring mountaineer of a tree, living on sunshine and snow, maintaining tough health on this diet for perhaps more than a thousand years.

Up towards the head of the basin I see groups of domes rising above the wavelike ridges, and some picturesque castellated masses, and dark strips and patches of silver fir, indicating deposits of fertile soil. Would that I could command the time to study them! What rich excursions one could make in this well-defined basin! Its glacial inscriptions and sculptures, how marvelous they seem, how noble the studies they offer! I tremble with excitement in the dawn of these glorious mountain sublimities, but I can only gaze and wonder, and, like a child, gather here and there a lily, half hoping I may be able to study and learn in years to come.

The drivers and dogs had a lively, laborious time getting the sheep across the creek, the second large stream thus far that they have been compelled to cross without a bridge; the first being the North Fork of the Merced near Bower Cave. Men and dogs, shouting and barking, drove the timid, water-fearing creatures in a close crowd against the bank, but not one of the flock would launch away. While thus jammed, the Don and the shepherd rushed through the frightened crowd to stampede those in front, but this would only cause a break backward, and away they would scamper through the stream-bank trees and scatter over the rocky pavement. Then with the aid of the dogs the runaways would again be gathered and made to face the stream, and again the compacted mass would break away, amid wild shouting and barking that might well have disturbed the stream itself and marred the music of its falls, to which visitors no doubt from all quarters of the globe were listening. "Hold them there! Now hold them there!" shouted the Don; "the front ranks will soon tire of the pressure, and be glad to take to the water, then all will jump in and cross in a hurry." But they did nothing of the kind; they only avoided the pressure by breaking back in scores and hundreds, leaving the beauty of the banks sadly trampled.

If only one could be got to cross over, all would make haste to follow; but that one could not be found. A lamb was caught, carried across, and tied to a bush on the opposite bank, where it cried piteously for its mother. But though greatly concerned, the mother only called it back. That play on maternal affection failed, and we began to fear that we should be forced to make a long roundabout drive and cross the wide-spread tributaries of the creek in succession. This would require several days, but it had its advantages, for I was eager to see the sources of so famous a stream. Don Quixote, however, determined that they must ford just here, and immediately began a sort of siege by cutting down slender pines on the bank and building a corral barely large enough to hold the flock when well pressed together. And as the stream would form one side of the corral he believed that they could easily be forced into the water.

In a few hours the inclosure was completed, and the silly animals were driven in and rammed hard against the brink of the ford. Then the Don, forcing a way through the compacted mass, pitched a few of the terrified unfortunates into the stream by main strength; but instead of crossing over, they swam about close to the bank, making desperate attempts to get back into the flock. Then a dozen or more were shoved off, and the Don, tall like a crane and a good natural wader, jumped in after them, seized a struggling wether, and dragged it to the opposite shore. But no sooner did he let it go than it jumped into the stream and swam back to its frightened companions in the corral, thus manifesting sheep-nature as unchangeable as gravitation. Pan with his pipes would have had no better luck, I fear. We were now pretty well baffled. The silly creatures would suffer any sort of death rather than cross that stream. Calling a council, the dripping Don declared that starvation was now the only likely scheme to try, and that we might as well camp here in comfort and let the besieged flock grow hungry and cool, and come to their senses, if they had any. In a few minutes after being thus let alone, an adventurer in the foremost rank plunged in and swam bravely to the farther shore. Then suddenly all rushed in pell-mell together, trampling one another under water, while we vainly tried to hold them back. The Don jumped into the thickest of the gasping, gurgling, drowning mass, and shoved them right and left as if each sheep was a piece of floating timber. The current also served to drift them apart; a long bent column was soon formed, and in a few minutes all were over and began baaing and feeding as if nothing out of the common had happened. That none were drowned seems wonderful. I fully expected that hundreds would gain the romantic fate of being swept into Yosemite over the highest waterfall in the world.

As the day was far spent, we camped a little way back from the ford, and let the dripping flock scatter and feed until sundown. The wool is dry now, and calm, cud-chewing peace has fallen on all the comfortable band, leaving no trace of the watery battle. I have seen fish driven out of the water with less ado than was made in driving these animals into it. Sheep brain must surely be poor stuff. Compare to-day's exhibition with the performances of deer swimming quietly across broad and rapid rivers, and from island to island in seas and lakes;

or with dogs, or even with the squirrels that, as the story goes, cross the Mississippi River on selected chips, with tails for sails comfortably trimmed to the breeze. A sheep can hardly be called an animal; an entire flock is required to make one foolish individual.

Chapter V

THE YOSEMITE

JULY 15. Followed the Mono Trail up the eastern rim of the basin nearly to its summit, then turned off southward to a small shallow valley that extends to the edge of the Yosemite, which we reached about noon, and encamped. After luncheon I made haste to high ground, and from the top of the ridge on the west side of Indian Cañon gained the noblest view of the summit peaks I have ever yet enjoyed. Nearly all the upper basin of the Merced was displayed, with its sublime domes and cañons, dark upsweeping forests, and glorious array of white peaks deep in the sky, every feature glowing, radiating beauty that pours into our flesh and bones like heat rays from fire. Sunshine over all; no breath of wind to stir the brooding calm. Never before had I seen so glorious a landscape, so boundless an affluence of sublime mountain beauty. The most extravagant description I might give of this view to any one who has not seen similar landscapes with his own eyes would not so much as hint its grandeur and the spiritual glow that covered it. I shouted and gesticulated in a wild burst of ecstasy, much to the astonishment of St. Bernard Carlo, who came running up to me, manifesting in his intelligent eyes a puzzled concern that was very ludicrous, which had the effect of bringing me to my senses. A brown bear, too, it would seem, had been a spectator of the show I had made of myself, for I had gone but a few yards when I started one from a thicket of brush. He evidently considered me dangerous, for he ran away very fast, tumbling over the tops of the tangled manzanita bushes in his haste. Carlo drew back, with his ears depressed as if afraid, and kept looking me in the face, as if expecting me to pursue and shoot, for he had seen many a bear battle in his day.

Following the ridge, which made a gradual descent to the south, I came at length to the brow of that massive cliff that stands between Indian Cañon and Yosemite Falls, and here the far-famed valley came suddenly into view throughout almost its whole extent. The noble walls—sculptured into endless variety of domes and gables, spires and battlements and plain mural precipices—all a-tremble with the thunder tones of the falling water. The level bottom seemed to be dressed like a garden—sunny meadows here and there, and groves of pine and oak; the river of Mercy sweeping in majesty through the midst of them and flashing back the sunbeams. The great Tissiack, or Half-Dome, rising at the upper end of the valley to a height of nearly a mile, is nobly proportioned and life-like, the most impressive of all the rocks, holding the eye in devout admiration, calling it back again and again from falls or meadows, or even the mountains beyond,—marvelous cliffs, marvelous in sheer dizzy depth and sculpture, types of endurance. Thousands of years have they stood in the sky ex-posed to rain, snow, frost, earthquake and avalanche, yet they still wear the bloom of youth.

I rambled along the valley rim to the westward; most of it is rounded off on the very brink, so that it is not easy to find places where one may look clear down the face of the wall to the bottom. When such places were found, and I had cau-tiously set my feet and drawn my body erect, I could not help fearing a little that the rock might split off and let me down, and what a down!—more than three thousand feet. Still my limbs did not tremble, nor did I feel the least uncertainty as to the reliance to be placed on them. My only fear was that a flake of the granite, which in some places showed joints more or less open and running parallel with the face of the cliff, might give way. After withdrawing from such places, ex-cited with the view I had got, I would say to myself, "Now don't go out on the verge again." But in the face of Yosemite scenery cautious remonstrance is vain; under its spell one's body seems to go where it likes with a will over which we seem to have scarce any control.

After a mile or so of this memorable cliff work I approached Yosemite Creek, admiring its easy, graceful, confident gestures as it comes bravely forward in its narrow channel, singing the last of its mountain songs on its way to its fate—a few rods more over the shining granite, then down half a mile in showy foam to another world, to be lost in the Merced, where cli-mate, vegetation, inhabitants, all are different. Emerging from its last gorge, it glides in wide lace-like rapids down a smooth incline into a pool where it seems to rest and compose its gray, agitated waters before taking the grand plunge, then slowly slipping over the lip of the pool basin, it descends another glossy slope with rapidly accelerated speed to the brink of the tremendous cliff, and with sublime, fateful confidence springs out free in the air.

I took off my shoes and stockings and worked my way cautiously down alongside the rushing flood, keeping my feet and hands pressed firmly on the polished rock. The booming, roaring water, rushing past close to my head, was very exciting. I had expected that the sloping apron would terminate with the perpendicular wall of the valley, and that from the foot of it, where it is less steeply inclined, I should be able to lean far enough out to see the forms and behavior of the fall all the way down to the bottom. But I found that there was yet another small brow over which I could not see, and which appeared to be too steep for mortal feet. Scanning it keenly, I discovered a narrow shelf about three inches wide on the very brink, just wide enough for a rest for one's heels. But there seemed to be no way of reaching it over so steep a brow. At length, after careful scrutiny of the surface, I found an irregular edge of a flake of the rock some distance back from the margin of the torrent. If I was to get down to the brink at all that rough edge, which might offer slight finger-holds, was the only way. But the slope beside it looked dangerously smooth and steep, and the swift roaring flood beneath, overhead, and beside me was very nerve-trying. I therefore concluded not to venture farther, but did nevertheless. Tufts of artemisia were growing in clefts of the rock near by, and I filled my mouth with the bitter leaves, hoping they might help to prevent giddiness. Then, with a caution not known in ordinary circumstances, I crept down safely to the little ledge, got my heels well planted on it, then shuffled in a horizontal direction twenty or thirty feet until close to the outplunging current, which, by the time it had descended thus far, was already white. Here I obtained a perfectly free view down into the heart of the snowy, chanting throng of comet-like streamers, into which the body of the fall soon separates.

While perched on that narrow niche I was not distinctly conscious of danger. The tremendous grandeur of the fall in form and sound and motion, acting at close range, smothered the sense of fear, and in such places one's body takes keen care for safety on its own account. How long I remained down there, or how I returned, I can hardly tell. Anyhow I had a glorious time, and got back to camp about dark, enjoying triumphant exhilaration soon followed by dull weariness. Hereafter I'll try to keep from such extravagant, nerve-straining places. Yet such a day is well worth venturing for. My first view of the High Sierra, first view looking down into Yosemite, the death song of Yosemite Creek, and its flight over the vast cliff, each one of these is of itself enough for a great life-long landscape fortune—a most memorable day of days—enjoyment enough to kill if that were possible.

July 16. My enjoyments yesterday afternoon, especially at the head of the fall, were too great for good sleep. Kept starting up last night in a nervous tremor, half awake, fancying that the foundation of the mountain we were camped on had given way and was falling into Yosemite Valley. In vain I roused myself to make a new beginning for sound sleep. The nerve strain had been too great, and again and again I dreamed I was rushing through the air above a glorious avalanche of water and rocks. One time, springing to my feet, I said, "This time it is real—all must die, and where could mountaineer find a more glorious death!"

Left camp soon after sunrise for an all-day ramble eastward. Crossed the head of Indian Basin, forested with *Abies magnifica*, underbrush mostly *Ceanothus cordulatus* and manzanita, a mixture not easily trampled over or penetrated, for the ceanothus is thorny and grows in dense snow-pressed masses, and the manzanita has exceedingly crooked, stubborn branches. From the head of the cañon continued on past North Dome into the basin of Dome or Porcupine Creek. Here are many fine meadows imbedded in the woods, gay with *Lilium parvum* and its companions; the elevation, about eight thousand feet, seems to be best suited for it—saw specimens that were a foot or two higher than my head. Had more magnificent views of the upper mountains, and of the great South Dome, said to be the grandest rock in the world. Well it may be, since it is of such noble dimensions and sculpture. A wonderfully impressive monument, its lines exquisite in fineness, and though sublime in size, is finished like the finest work of art, and seems to be alive.

July 17. A new camp was made to-day in a magnificent silver fir grove at the head of a small stream that flows into Yosemite by way of Indian Cañon. Here we intend to stay several weeks,—a fine location from which to make excursions about the great valley and its fountains. Glorious days I'll have sketching, pressing plants, studying the wonderful topography and the wild animals, our happy fellow mortals and neighbors. But the vast mountains in the distance, shall I ever know them, shall I be allowed to enter into their midst and dwell with them?

We were pelted about noon by a short, heavy rainstorm, sublime thunder reverberating among the mountains and cañons,—some strokes near, crashing, ringing in the tense crisp air with startling keenness, while the distant peaks loomed gloriously through the cloud fringes and sheets of rain. Now the storm is past, and the fresh washed air is full of the essences of the flower gardens and groves. Winter storms in Yosemite must be glorious. May I see them!

Have got my bed made in our new camp,—plushy, sumptuous, and deliciously fragrant, most of it *magnifica* fir plumes, of course, with a variety of sweet flowers in the pillow. Hope to sleep to-night without tottering nerve-dreams. Watched a deer eating ceanothus leaves and twigs.

July 18. Slept pretty well; the valley walls did not seem to fall, though I still fancied myself at the brink, alongside the white, plunging flood, especially when half asleep. Strange the danger of that adventure should be more troublesome now that I am in the bosom of the peaceful woods, a mile or more from the fall, than it was while I was on the brink of it.

Bears seem to be common here, judging by their tracks. About noon we had another rainstorm with keen startling thunder, the metallic, ringing, clashing, clanging notes gradually fading into low bass rolling and muttering in the distance. For a few minutes the rain came in a grand torrent like a waterfall, then hail; some of the hailstones an inch in diameter, hard, icy, and irregular in form, like those oftentimes seen in Wisconsin. Carlo watched them with intelligent astonishment as they came pelting and thrashing through the quivering branches of the trees. The cloud scenery sublime. Afternoon calm, sunful, and clear, with delicious freshness and fragrance from the firs and flowers and steaming ground.

July 19. Watching the daybreak and sunrise. The pale rose and purple sky changing softly to daffodil yellow and white, sunbeams pouring through the passes between the peaks and over the Yosemite domes, making their edges burn; the silver firs in the middle ground catching the glow on their spiry tops, and our camp grove fills and thrills with the glorious light. Everything awakening alert and joyful; the birds begin to stir and innumerable insect people. Deer quietly withdraw into leafy hiding-places in the chaparral; the dew vanishes, flowers spread their petals, every pulse beats high, every life cell rejoices, the very rocks seem to thrill with life. The whole landscape glows like a human face in a glory of enthusiasm, and the blue sky, pale around the horizon, bends peacefully down over all like one vast flower.

About noon, as usual, big bossy cumuli began to grow above the forest, and the rainstorm pouring from them is the most imposing I have yet seen. The silvery zigzag lightning lances are longer than usual, and the thunder gloriously impressive, keen, crashing, intensely concentrated, speaking with such tremendous energy it would seem that an entire mountain is being shattered at every stroke, but probably only a few trees are being shattered, many of which I have seen on my walks hereabouts strewing the ground. At last the clear ringing strokes are succeeded by deep low tones that grow gradually fainter as they roll afar into the recesses of the echoing mountains, where they seem to be welcomed home. Then another and another peal, or rather crashing, splintering stroke, follows in quick succession, perchance splitting some giant pine or fir from top to bottom into long rails and slivers, and scattering them to all points of the compass. Now comes the rain, with corresponding extravagant grandeur, covering the ground high and low with a sheet of flowing water, a transparent film fitted like a skin upon the rugged anatomy of the landscape, making the rocks glitter and glow, gathering in the ravines, flooding the streams, and making them shout and boom in reply to the thunder.

How interesting to trace the history of a single raindrop! It is not long, geologically speaking, as we have seen, since the first raindrops fell on the newborn leafless Sierra landscapes. How different the lot of these falling now! Happy the showers that fall on so fair a wilderness,—scarce a single drop can fail to find a beautiful spot,—on the tops of the peaks, on the shining glacier pavements, on the great smooth domes, on forests and gardens and brushy moraines, plashing, glinting, pattering, laving. Some go to the high snowy fountains to swell their well-saved stores; some into the lakes, washing the mountain windows, patting their smooth glassy levels, making dimples and bubbles and spray; some into the waterfalls and cascades, as if eager to join in their dance and song and beat their foam yet finer; good luck and good work for the happy mountain raindrops, each one of them a high waterfall in it-self, descending from the cliffs and hollows of the clouds to the cliffs and hollows of the rocks, out of the sky-thunder into the thunder of the falling rivers. Some, falling on meadows and bogs, creep silently out of sight to the grass roots, hiding softly as in a nest, slipping, oozing hither, thither, seeking and finding their appointed work. Some, descending through the spires of the woods, sift spray through the shining needles, whispering peace and good cheer to each one of them. Some drops with happy aim glint on the sides of crystals,—quartz, hornblende, garnet, zircon, tourmaline, feldspar,—patter on grains of gold and heavy way-worn nuggets; some, with blunt plap-plap and low bass drumming, fall on the broad leaves of veratrum, saxifrage, cypripedium. Some happy drops fall straight into the cups of flowers, kissing the lips of lilies. How far they have to go, how many cups to fill, great and small, cells too small to be seen, cups holding half a drop as well as lake basins between the hills, each replenished with equal care, every drop in all the blessed throng a silvery newborn star with lake and river, garden and grove, valley and mountain, all that the landscape holds reflected in its crystal depths, God's messenger, angel of love sent on its way with majesty and pomp and display of power that make man's greatest shows ridiculous.

Now the storm is over, the sky is clear, the last rolling thun-der-wave is spent on the peaks, and where are the raindrops now—what has become of all the shining throng? In winged vapor rising some are already hastening back to the sky, some have gone into the plants, creeping through invisible doors into the round rooms of cells, some are locked in crystals of ice, some in rock crystals, some in porous moraines to keep their small springs flowing, some have gone journeying on in the rivers to join the larger raindrop of the ocean. From form to form, beauty to beauty, ever changing, never resting, all are speeding on with love's enthusiasm, singing with the stars the eternal song of creation.

July 20. Fine calm morning; air tense and clear; not the slightest breeze astir; everything shining, the rocks with wet crystals, the plants with dew, each receiving its portion of irised dewdrops and sunshine like living creatures getting their breakfast, their dew manna coming down from the starry sky like swarms of smaller stars. How wondrous fine are the particles in showers of dew, thousands required for a single drop, growing in the dark as silently as the grass! What pains are taken to keep this wilderness in health,—showers of snow, showers of rain, showers of dew, floods of light, floods of invisible vapor, clouds, winds, all sorts of weather, interaction of plant on plant, animal on animal, etc., beyond thought! How fine Nature's methods! How deeply with beauty is beauty overlaid! the ground covered with crystals, the crystals with mosses and lichens and low-spreading grasses and flowers, these with larger plants leaf over leaf with ever-changing color and form, the broad palms of the firs outspread over these, the azure dome over all like a bell-flower, and star above star.

Yonder stands the South Dome, its crown high above our camp, though its base is four thousand feet below us; a most noble rock, it seems full of thought, clothed with living light, no sense of dead stone about it, all spiritualized, neither heavy looking nor light, steadfast in serene strength like a god.

Our shepherd is a queer character and hard to place in this wilderness. His bed is a hollow made in red dry-rot punky dust beside a log which forms a portion of the south wall of the corral. Here he lies with his wonderful everlasting clothing on, wrapped in a red blanket, breathing not only the dust of the decayed wood but also that of the corral, as if determined to take ammoniacal snuff all night after chewing tobacco all day. Following the sheep he carries a heavy six-shooter swung from his belt on one side and his luncheon on the other. The ancient cloth in which the meat, fresh from the frying-pan, is tied serves as a filter through which the clear fat and gravy juices drip down on his right hip and leg in clustering stalactites. This oleaginous formation is soon broken up, however, and diffused and rubbed evenly into his scanty apparel, by sitting down, rolling over, crossing his legs while resting on logs, etc., making shirt and trousers water-tight and shiny. His trousers, in particular, have become so adhesive with the mixed fat and resin that pine needles, thin flakes and fibres of bark, hair, mica scales and minute grains of quartz, hornblende, etc., feathers, seed wings, moth and butterfly wings, legs and antennæ of innumerable insects, or even whole insects such as the small beetles, moths and mosquitoes, with flower petals, pollen dust and indeed bits of all plants, animals, and minerals of the region adhere to them and are safely imbedded, so that though far from being a naturalist he collects fragmentary specimens of everything and becomes richer than he knows. His specimens are kept passably fresh, too, by the purity of the air and the resiny bituminous beds into which they are pressed. Man is a microcosm, at least our shepherd is, or rather his trousers. These precious overalls are never taken off, and nobody knows how old they are, though one may guess by their thickness and concentric structure. Instead of wearing thin they wear thick, and in their stratification have no small geological significance.

Besides herding the sheep, Billy is the butcher, while I have agreed to wash the few iron and tin utensils and make the bread. Then, these small duties done, by the time the sun is fairly above the mountain-tops I am beyond the flock, free to rove and revel in the wilderness all the big immortal days.

Sketching on the North Dome. It commands views of nearly all the valley besides a few of the high mountains. I would fain draw everything in sight—rock, tree, and leaf. But little can I do beyond mere outlines,—marks with meanings like words, readable only to myself,—yet I sharpen my pencils and work on as if others might possibly be benefited. Whether these picture-sheets are to vanish like fallen leaves or go to friends like letters, matters not much; for little can they tell to those who have not themselves seen similar wildness, and like a language have learned it. No pain here, no dull empty hours, no fear of the past, no fear of the future. These blessed mountains are so compactly filled with God's beauty, no petty personal hope or experience has room to be. Drinking this champagne water is pure pleasure, so is breathing the living air, and every movement of limbs is pleasure, while the whole body seems to feel beauty when exposed to it as it feels the camp-fire or sunshine, entering not by the eyes alone, but equally through all one's flesh like radiant heat, making a passionate ecstatic pleasure-glow not explainable. One's body then seems homogeneous throughout, sound as a crystal.

Perched like a fly on this Yosemite dome, I gaze and sketch and bask, oftentimes settling down into dumb admiration without definite hope of ever learning much, yet with the longing, unresting effort that lies at the door of hope, humbly prostrate before the vast display of God's power, and eager to offer self-denial and renunciation with eternal toil to learn any lesson in the divine manuscript.

It is easier to feel than to realize, or in any way explain, Yosemite grandeur. The magnitudes of the rocks and trees and streams are so delicately harmonized they are mostly hidden. Sheer precipices three thousand feet high are fringed with tall trees growing close like grass on the brow of a lowland hill, and extending along the feet of these precipices a ribbon of meadow a mile wide and seven or eight long, that seems like a strip a farmer might mow in less than a day. Waterfalls, five hundred to one or two thousand feet high, are so subordinated to the mighty cliffs over which they pour that they seem like wisps of smoke, gentle as floating clouds, though their voices fill the valley and make the rocks tremble. The mountains, too, along the eastern sky, and the domes in front of them, and the succession of smooth rounded waves between, swelling higher, higher, with dark woods in their hollows, serene in massive exuberant bulk and beauty, tend yet more to hide the grandeur of the Yosemite temple and make it appear as a subdued subordinate feature of the vast harmonious landscape. Thus every attempt to appreciate any one feature is beaten down by the overwhelming influence of all the others. And, as if this were not enough, lo! in the sky arises another mountain range with topography as rugged and substantial-looking as the one beneath it—snowy peaks and domes and shadowy Yosemite valleys—another version of the snowy Sierra, a new creation heralded by a thunder-storm. How fiercely, devoutly wild is Nature in the midst of her beauty-loving tenderness!—painting lilies, watering them, caressing them with gentle hand, going from flower to flower like a gardener while building rock mountains and cloud mountains full of lightning and rain. Gladly we run for shelter beneath an overhanging cliff and examine the reassuring ferns and mosses, gentle love tokens growing in cracks and chinks. Daisies, too, and ivesias, confiding wild children of light, too small to fear. To these one's heart goes home, and the voices of the storm become gentle. Now the sun breaks forth and fragrant steam arises. The birds are out singing on the edges of the groves. The west is flaming in gold and purple, ready for the ceremony of the sunset, and back I go to camp with my notes and pictures, the best of them printed in my mind as dreams. A fruitful day, without measured beginning or ending. A terrestrial eternity. A gift of good God.

Wrote to my mother and a few friends, mountain hints to each. They seem as near as if within voice-reach or touch. The deeper the solitude the less the sense of loneliness, and the nearer our friends. Now bread and tea, fir bed and good-night to Carlo, a look at the sky lilies, and death sleep until the dawn of another Sierra to-morrow.

July 21. Sketching on the Dome—no rain; clouds at noon about quarter filled the sky, casting shadows with fine effect on the white mountains at the heads of the streams, and a soothing cover over the gardens during the warm hours.

Saw a common house-fly and a grasshopper and a brown bear. The fly and grasshopper paid me a merry visit on the top of the Dome, and I paid a visit to the bear in the middle of a small garden meadow between the Dome and the camp where he was standing alert among the flowers as if willing to be seen to advantage. I had not gone more than half a mile from camp this morning, when Carlo, who was trotting on a few yards ahead of me, came to a sudden, cautious standstill. Down went tail and ears, and forward went his knowing nose, while he seemed to be saying, "Ha, what's this? A bear, I guess." Then a cautious advance of a few steps, setting his feet down softly like a hunting cat, and questioning the air as to the scent he had caught until all doubt vanished. Then he came back to me, looked me in the face, and with his speaking eyes reported a bear near by; then led on softly, careful, like an experienced hunter, not to make the slightest noise, and frequently looking back as if whispering, "Yes, it's a bear; come and I'll show you." Presently we came to where the sunbeams were streaming through between the purple shafts of the firs, which showed that we were nearing an open spot, and here Carlo came behind me, evidently sure that the bear was very near. So I crept to a low ridge of moraine boulders on the edge of a narrow garden meadow, and in this meadow I felt pretty sure the bear must be. I was anxious to get a good look at the sturdy mountaineer without alarming him; so drawing myself up noiselessly back of one of the largest of the trees I peered past its bulging buttresses, exposing only a part of my head, and there stood neighbor Bruin within a stone's throw, his hips covered by tall grass and flowers, and his front feet on the trunk of a fir that had fallen out into the meadow, which raised his head so high that he seemed to be standing erect. He had not yet seen me, but was looking and listening attentively, showing that in some way he was aware of our approach. I watched his gestures and tried to make the most of my opportunity to learn what I could about him, fearing he would catch sight of me and run away. For I had been told that this sort of bear, the cinnamon, always ran from his bad brother man, never showing fight unless wounded or in defense of young. He made a telling picture standing alert in the sunny forest garden. How well he played his part, harmonizing in bulk and color and shaggy hair with the trunks of the trees and lush vegetation, as natural a feature as any other in the landscape. After examining at leisure, noting the sharp muzzle thrust inquiringly forward, the long shaggy hair on his broad chest, the stiff, erect ears nearly buried in hair, and the slow, heavy way he moved his head, I thought I should like to see his gait in running, so I made a sudden rush at him, shouting and swinging my hat to frighten him, expecting to see him make haste to get away. But to my dismay he did not run or show any sign of running. On the contrary, he stood his ground ready to fight and defend himself, lowered his head, thrust it forward, and looked sharply and fiercely at me. Then I suddenly began to fear that upon me would fall the work of running; but I was afraid to run, and therefore, like the bear, held my ground. We stood staring at each other in solemn silence within a dozen yards or thereabouts, while I fervently hoped that the power of the human eye over wild beasts would prove as great as it is said to be. How long our awfully strenuous interview lasted, I don't know; but at length in the slow fullness of time he pulled his huge paws down off the log, and with magnificent deliberation turned and walked leisurely up the meadow, stopping frequently to look back over his shoulder to see whether I was pursuing him, then moving on again, evidently neither fearing me very much nor trusting me. He was probably about five hundred pounds in weight, a broad, rusty bundle of ungovernable wildness, a happy fellow whose lines have fallen in pleasant places. The flowery glade in which I saw him so well, framed like a picture, is one of the best of all I have yet discovered, a conservatory of Nature's precious plant people. Tall lilies were swinging their bells over that bear's back, with geraniums, larkspurs, columbines, and daisies brushing against his sides. A place for angels, one would say, instead of bears.

In the great cañons Bruin reigns supreme. Happy fellow, whom no famine can reach while one of his thousand kinds of food is spared him. His bread is sure at all seasons, ranged on the mountain shelves like stores in a pantry. From one to the other, up or down he climbs, tasting and enjoying each in turn in different climates, as if he had journeyed thousands of miles to other countries north or south to enjoy their varied productions. I should like to know my hairy brothers better—though after this particular Yosemite bear, my very neighbor, had sauntered out of sight this morning, I reluctantly went back to camp for the Don's rifle to shoot him, if necessary, in defense of the flock. Fortunately I couldn't find him, and after tracking him a mile or two towards Mount Hoffman I bade him Godspeed and gladly returned to my work on the Yosemite Dome.

The house-fly also seemed at home and buzzed about me as I sat sketching, and enjoying my bear interview now it was over. I wonder what draws house-flies so far up the mountains, heavy gross feeders as they are, sensitive to cold, and fond of domestic ease. How have they been distributed from continent to continent, across seas and deserts and mountain chains, usually so influential in determining boundaries of species both of plants and animals. Beetles and butterflies are sometimes restricted to small areas. Each mountain in a range, and even the different zones of a mountain, may have its own peculiar species. But the house-fly seems to be everywhere. I wonder if any island in mid-ocean is flyless. The bluebottle is abundant in these Yosemite woods, ever ready with his marvelous store of eggs to make all dead flesh fly. Bumblebees are here, and are well fed on boundless stores of nectar and pollen. The honeybee, though abundant in the foothills, has not yet got so high. It is only a few years since the first swarm was brought to California.

A queer fellow and a jolly fellow is the grasshopper. Up the mountains he comes on excursions, how high I don't know, but at least as far and high as Yosemite tourists. I was much interested with the hearty enjoyment of the one that danced and sang for me on the Dome this afternoon. He seemed brimful of glad, hilarious energy, manifested by springing into the air to a height of twenty or thirty feet, then diving and springing up again and making a sharp musical rattle just as the lowest point in the descent was reached. Up and down a dozen times or so he danced and sang, then alighted to rest, then up and at it again. The curves he described in the air in diving and rattling resembled those made by cords hanging loosely and attached at the same height at the ends, the loops nearly covering each other. Braver, heartier, keener, care-free enjoyment of life I have never seen or heard in any creature, great or small. The life of this comic red-legs, the mountain's merriest child, seems to be made up of pure, condensed gayety. The Douglas squirrel is the only living creature that I can compare him with in exuberant, rollicking, irrepressible jollity. Wonderful that these sublime mountains are so loudly cheered and brightened by a creature so queer. Nature in him seems to be snapping her fingers in the face of all earthly dejection and melancholy with a boyish hip-hip-hurrah. How the sound is made I do not understand. When he was on the ground he

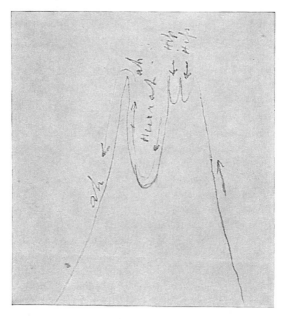

Track of singing dancing grasshopper in the air over North Dome

made not the slightest noise, nor when he was simply flying
from place to place, but only when diving in curves, the motion seeming to be required for the sound; for the more vigorous the diving the more energetic the corresponding
outbursts of jolly rattling. I tried to observe him closely while
he was resting in the intervals of his performances; but he
would not allow a near approach, always getting his jumping
legs ready to spring for immediate flight, and keeping his eyes
on me. A fine sermon the little fellow danced for me on the
Dome, a likely place to look for sermons in stones, but not
for grasshopper sermons. A large and imposing pulpit for so
small a preacher. No danger of weakness in the knees of the
world while Nature can spring such a rattle as this. Even the
bear did not express for me the mountain's wild health and
strength and happiness so tellingly as did this comical little
hopper. No cloud of care in his day, no winter of discontent
in sight. To him every day is a holiday; and when at length

his sun sets, I fancy he will cuddle down on the forest floor and die like the leaves and flowers, and like them leave no unsightly remains calling for burial.

Sundown, and I must to camp. Good-night, friends three,—brown bear, rugged boulder of energy in groves and gardens fair as Eden; restless, fussy fly with gauzy wings stirring the air around all the world; and grasshopper, crisp, electric spark of joy enlivening the massy sublimity of the mountains like the laugh of a child. Thank you, thank you all three for your quickening company. Heaven guide every wing and leg. Good-night friends three, good-night.

July 22. A fine specimen of the black-tailed deer went bounding past camp this morning. A buck with wide spread of antlers, showing admirable vigor and grace. Wonderful the beauty, strength, and graceful movements of animals in wildernesses, cared for by Nature only, when our experience with domestic animals would lead us to fear that all the so-called neglected wild beasts would degenerate. Yet the upshot of Nature's method of breeding and teaching seems to lead to excellence of every sort. Deer, like all wild animals, are as clean as plants. The beauties of their gestures and attitudes, alert or in repose, surprise yet more than their bounding exuberant strength. Every movement and posture is graceful, the very poetry of manners and motion. Mother Nature is too often spoken of as in reality no mother at all. Yet how wisely, sternly, tenderly she loves and looks after her children in all sorts of weather and wildernesses. The more I see of deer the more I admire them as mountaineers. They make their way into the heart of the roughest solitudes with smooth reserve of strength, through dense belts of brush and forest encumbered with fallen trees and boulder piles, across cañons, roaring streams, and snow-fields, ever showing forth beauty and courage. Over nearly all the continent the deer find homes. In the Florida savannas and hummocks, in the Canada woods, in the far north, roaming over mossy tundras, swimming lakes and rivers and arms of the sea from island to island washed with waves, or climbing rocky mountains, everywhere healthy and able, adding beauty to every landscape,—a truly admirable creature and great credit to Nature.

Have been sketching a silver fir that stands on a granite

ridge a few hundred yards to the eastward of camp—a fine tree with a particular snow-storm story to tell. It is about one hundred feet high, growing on bare rock, thrusting its roots into a weathered joint less than an inch wide, and bulging out to form a base to bear its weight. The storm came from the north while it was young and broke it down nearly to the ground, as is shown by the old, dead, weather-beaten top leaning out from the living trunk built up from a new shoot below the break. The annual rings of the trunk that have overgrown the dead sapling tell the year of the storm. Wonderful

Mt. Clark   Mt. Starr King

Top of S. Dome

Abies magnifica

that a side branch forming a portion of one of the level collars that encircle the trunk of this species (*Abies magnifica*) should bend upward, grow erect, and take the place of the lost axis to form a new tree.

Many others, pines as well as firs, bear testimony to the crushing severity of this particular storm. Trees, some of them fifty to seventy-five feet high, were bent to the ground and buried like grass, whole groves vanishing as if the forest had been cleared away, leaving not a branch or needle visible until the spring thaw. Then the more elastic undamaged saplings

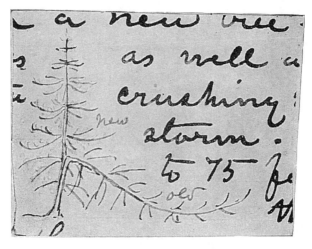

Illustrating growth of new pine from branch below the break of axis of snow-crushed tree

rose again, aided by the wind, some reaching a nearly erect attitude, others remaining more or less bent, while those with broken backs endeavored to specialize a side branch below the break and make a leader of it to form a new axis of development. It is as if a man, whose back was broken or nearly so and who was compelled to go bent, should find a branch backbone sprouting straight up from below the break and should gradually develop new arms and shoulders and head, while the old damaged portion of his body died.

Grand white cloud mountains and domes created about

noon as usual, ridges and ranges of endless variety, as if Nature
dearly loved this sort of work, doing it again and again nearly
every day with infinite industry, and producing beauty that
never palls. A few zigzags of lightning, five minutes' shower,
then a gradual wilting and clearing.

July 23. Another midday cloudland, displaying power and
beauty that one never wearies in beholding, but hopelessly
unsketchable and untellable. What can poor mortals say about
clouds? While a description of their huge glowing domes and
ridges, shadowy gulfs and cañons, and feather-edged ravines
is being tried, they vanish, leaving no visible ruins. Nevertheless, these fleeting sky mountains are as substantial and significant as the more lasting upheavals of granite beneath them.
Both alike are built up and die, and in God's calendar difference of duration is nothing. We can only dream about them
in wondering, worshiping admiration, happier than we dare
tell even to friends who see farthest in sympathy, glad to know
that not a crystal or vapor particle of them, hard or soft, is
lost; that they sink and vanish only to rise again and again in
higher and higher beauty. As to our own work, duty, influence, etc., concerning which so much fussy pother is made, it
will not fail of its due effect, though, like a lichen on a stone,
we keep silent.

July 24. Clouds at noon occupying about half the sky gave
half an hour of heavy rain to wash one of the cleanest landscapes in the world. How well it is washed! The sea is hardly
less dusty than the ice-burnished pavements and ridges, domes
and cañons, and summit peaks plashed with snow like waves
with foam. How fresh the woods are and calm after the last
films of clouds have been wiped from the sky! A few minutes
ago every tree was excited, bowing to the roaring storm, waving, swirling, tossing their branches in glorious enthusiasm
like worship. But though to the outer ear these trees are now
silent, their songs never cease. Every hidden cell is throbbing
with music and life, every fibre thrilling like harp strings, while
incense is ever flowing from the balsam bells and leaves. No
wonder the hills and groves were God's first temples, and the
more they are cut down and hewn into cathedrals and
churches, the farther off and dimmer seems the Lord himself.
The same may be said of stone temples. Yonder, to the east-

ward of our camp grove, stands one of Nature's cathedrals, hewn from the living rock, almost conventional in form, about two thousand feet high, nobly adorned with spires and pinnacles, thrilling under floods of sunshine as if alive like a grove-temple, and well named "Cathedral Peak." Even Shepherd Billy turns at times to this wonderful mountain building, though apparently deaf to all stone sermons. Snow that refused to melt in fire would hardly be more wonderful than unchanging dullness in the rays of God's beauty. I have been trying to get him to walk to the brink of Yosemite for a view, offering to watch the sheep for a day, while he should enjoy what tourists come from all over the world to see. But though within a mile of the famous valley, he will not go to it even out of mere curiosity. "What," says he, "is Yosemite but a cañon—a lot of rocks—a hole in the ground—a place dangerous about falling into—a d—d good place to keep away from." "But think of the waterfalls, Billy—just think of that big stream we crossed the other day, falling half a mile through the air—think of that, and the sound it makes. You can hear it now like the roar of the sea." Thus I pressed Yosemite upon him like a missionary offering the gospel, but he would have none of it. "I should be afraid to look over so high a wall," he said. "It would make my head swim. There is nothing worth seeing anywhere, only rocks, and I see plenty of them here. Tourists that spend their money to see rocks and falls are fools, that's all. You can't humbug me. I've been in this country too long for that." Such souls, I suppose, are asleep, or smothered and befogged beneath mean pleasures and cares.

July 25. Another cloudland. Some clouds have an over-ripe decaying look, watery and bedraggled and drawn out into wind-torn shreds and patches, giving the sky a littered appearance; not so these Sierra summer midday clouds. All are beautiful with smooth definite outlines and curves like those of glacier-polished domes. They begin to grow about eleven o'clock, and seem so wonderfully near and clear from this high camp one is tempted to try to climb them and trace the streams that pour like cataracts from their shadowy fountains. The rain to which they give birth is often very heavy, a sort of waterfall as imposing as if pouring from rock mountains.

Never in all my travels have I found anything more truly novel and interesting than these midday mountains of the sky, their fine tones of color, majestic visible growth, and ever-changing scenery and general effects, though mostly as well let alone as far as description goes. I oftentimes think of Shelley's cloud poem, "I sift the snow on the mountains below."

Chapter VI

MOUNT HOFFMAN AND LAKE TENAYA

J ULY 26. Ramble to the summit of Mount Hoffman, eleven thousand feet high, the highest point in life's journey my feet have yet touched. And what glorious landscapes are about me, new plants, new animals, new crystals, and multitudes of new mountains far higher than Hoffman, towering in glorious array along the axis of the range, serene, majestic, snow-laden, sun-drenched, vast domes and ridges shining below them, forests, lakes, and meadows in the hollows, the pure blue bell-flower sky brooding them all,—a glory day of admission into a new realm of wonders as if Nature had wooingly whispered, "Come higher." What questions I asked, and how little I know of all the vast show, and how eagerly, tremulously hopeful of some day knowing more, learning the meaning of these divine symbols crowded together on this wondrous page.

Mount Hoffman is the highest part of a ridge or spur about fourteen miles from the axis of the main range, perhaps a remnant brought into relief and isolated by unequal denudation. The southern slopes shed their waters into Yosemite Valley by Tenaya and Dome Creeks, the northern in part into the Tuolumne River, but mostly into the Merced by Yosemite Creek. The rock is mostly granite, with some small piles and crests rising here and there in picturesque pillared and castellated remnants of red metamorphic slates. Both the granite and slates are divided by joints, making them separable into blocks like the stones of artificial masonry, suggesting the Scripture "He hath built the mountains." Great banks of snow and ice are piled in hollows on the cool precipitous north side forming the highest perennial sources of Yosemite Creek. The southern slopes are much more gradual and accessible. Narrow slot-like gorges extend across the summit at right angles, which look like lanes, formed evidently by the erosion of less resisting beds. They are usually called "devil's slides," though they lie far above the region usually haunted by the devil; for though we read that he once climbed an exceeding high mountain, he cannot be much of a mountain-eer, for his tracks are seldom seen above the timber-line.

The broad gray summit is barren and desolate-looking in general views, wasted by ages of gnawing storms; but looking at the surface in detail, one finds it covered by thousands and millions of charming plants with leaves and flowers so small they form no mass of color visible at a distance of a few hundred yards. Beds of azure daisies smile confidingly in moist hollows, and along the banks of small rills, with several species of eriogonum, silky-leaved ivesia, pentstemon, orthocarpus,

Approach of Dome Creek to Yosemite

and patches of *Primula suffruticosa*, a beautiful shrubby species. Here also I found bryanthus, a charming heathwort covered with purple flowers and dark green foliage like heather, and three trees new to me—a hemlock and two pines. The hemlock (*Tsuga Mertensiana*) is the most beautiful conifer I have ever seen; the branches and also the main axis droop in a singularly graceful way, and the dense foliage covers the delicate, sensitive, swaying branchlets all around. It is now in full bloom, and the flowers, together with thousands of last season's cones still clinging to the drooping sprays, display wonderful wealth of color, brown and purple and blue. Gladly I climbed the first tree I found to revel in the midst of it. How the touch of the flowers makes one's flesh tingle! The pistillate are dark, rich purple, and almost translucent, the staminate blue,—a vivid, pure tone of blue like the mountain sky,—the most uncommonly beautiful of all the Sierra tree flowers I have seen. How wonderful that, with all its delicate feminine grace and beauty of form and dress and behavior, this lovely tree up here, exposed to the wildest blasts, has already endured the storms of centuries of winters!

The two pines also are brave storm-enduring trees, the mountain pine (*Pinus monticola*) and the dwarf pine (*Pinus albicaulis*). The mountain pine is closely related to the sugar pine, though the cones are only about four to six inches long. The largest trees are from five to six feet in diameter at four feet above the ground, the bark rich brown. Only a few storm-beaten adventurers approach the summit of the mountain. The dwarf or white-bark pine is the species that forms the timber-line, where it is so completely dwarfed that one may walk over the top of a bed of it as over snow-pressed chaparral.

How boundless the day seems as we revel in these storm-beaten sky gardens amid so vast a congregation of onlooking mountains! Strange and admirable it is that the more savage and chilly and storm-chafed the mountains, the finer the glow on their faces and the finer the plants they bear. The myriads of flowers tingeing the mountain-top do not seem to have grown out of the dry, rough gravel of disintegration, but rather they appear as visitors, a cloud of witnesses to Nature's love in what we in our timid ignorance and unbelief call howling desert. The surface of the ground, so dull and forbidding at first sight, besides being rich in plants, shines and sparkles with crystals: mica, hornblende, feldspar, quartz, tourmaline. The radiance in some places is so great as to be fairly dazzling, keen lance rays of every color flashing, sparkling in glorious abundance, joining the plants in their fine, brave beauty-work—every crystal, every flower a window opening into heaven, a mirror reflecting the Creator.

From garden to garden, ridge to ridge, I drifted enchanted, now on my knees gazing into the face of a daisy, now climbing again and again among the purple and azure flowers of the hemlocks, now down into the treasuries of the snow, or gazing afar over domes and peaks, lakes and woods, and the billowy glaciated fields of the upper Tuolumne, and trying to sketch them. In the midst of such beauty, pierced with its rays, one's body is all one tingling palate. Who wouldn't be a mountaineer! Up here all the world's prizes seem nothing.

The largest of the many glacier lakes in sight, and the one with the finest shore scenery, is Tenaya, about a mile long, with an imposing mountain dipping its feet into it on the south side, Cathedral Peak a few miles above its head, many smooth swelling rock-waves and domes on the north, and in the distance southward a multitude of snowy peaks, the fountain-heads of rivers. Lake Hoffman lies shimmering beneath my feet, mountain pines around its shining rim. To the northward the picturesque basin of Yosemite Creek glitters with lakelets and pools; but the eye is soon drawn away from these bright mirror wells, however attractive, to revel in the glorious congregation of peaks on the axis of the range in their robes of snow and light.

Carlo caught an unfortunate woodchuck when it was running from a grassy spot to its boulder-pile home—one of the hardiest of the mountain animals. I tried hard to save him, but in vain. After telling Carlo that he must be careful not to kill anything, I caught sight, for the first time, of the curious pika, or little chief hare, that cuts large quantities of lupines and other plants and lays them out to dry in the sun for hay, which it stores in underground barns to last through the long, snowy winter. Coming upon these plants freshly cut and lying in handfuls here and there on the rocks has a startling effect of busy life on the lonely mountain-top. These little hay-makers, endowed with brain stuff something like our own,—God up here looking after them,—what lessons they teach, how they widen our sympathy!

An eagle soaring above a sheer cliff, where I suppose its nest is, makes another striking show of life, and helps to bring to mind the other people of the so-called solitude—deer in the forest caring for their young; the strong, well-clad, well-fed bears; the lively throng of squirrels; the blessed birds, great and small, stirring and sweetening the groves; and the clouds of happy insects filling the sky with joyous hum as part and parcel of the down-pouring sunshine. All these come to mind, as well as the plant people, and the glad streams singing their way to the sea. But most impressive of all is the vast glowing countenance of the wilderness in awful, infinite repose.

Toward sunset, enjoyed a fine run to camp, down the long south slopes, across ridges and ravines, gardens and avalanche gaps, through the firs and chaparral, enjoying wild excitement and excess of strength, and so ends a day that will never end.

July 27. Up and away to Lake Tenaya,—another big day, enough for a lifetime. The rocks, the air, everything speaking with audible voice or silent; joyful, wonderful, enchanting, banishing weariness and sense of time. No longing for anything now or hereafter as we go home into the mountain's heart. The level sunbeams are touching the fir-tops, every leaf shining with dew. Am holding an easterly course, the deep cañon of Tenaya Creek on the right hand, Mount Hoffman on the left, and the lake straight ahead about ten miles distant, the summit of Mount Hoffman about three thousand feet above me, Tenaya Creek four thousand feet below and separated from the shallow, irregular valley, along which most of the way lies, by smooth domes and wave-ridges. Many mossy emerald bogs, meadows, and gardens in rocky hollows to wade and saunter through—and what fine plants they give me, what joyful streams I have to cross, and how many views are displayed of the Hoffman and Cathedral Peak masonry, and what a wondrous breadth of shining granite pavement to walk over for the first time about the shores of the lake! On I sauntered in freedom complete; body without weight as far as I was aware; now wading through starry parnassia bogs, now through gardens shoulder deep in larkspur and lilies, grasses and rushes, shaking off showers of dew; crossing piles of crystalline moraine boulders, bright mirror pavements, and cool, cheery streams going to Yosemite; crossing bryanthus carpets and the scoured pathways of avalanches, and thickets of snow-pressed ceanothus; then down a broad, majestic stairway into the ice-sculptured lake-basin.

The snow on the high mountains is melting fast, and the streams are singing bank-full, swaying softly through the level meadows and bogs, quivering with sun-spangles, swirling in pot-holes, resting in deep pools, leaping, shouting in wild, exulting energy over rough boulder dams, joyful, beautiful in all their forms. No Sierra landscape that I have seen holds anything truly dead or dull, or any trace of what in manufactories is called rubbish or waste; everything is perfectly clean and pure and full of divine lessons. This quick, inevitable interest attaching to everything seems marvelous until the hand of God becomes visible; then it seems reasonable that what interests Him may well interest us. When we try to pick out anything by itself, we find it hitched to everything else in the universe. One fancies a heart like our own must be beating in every crystal and cell, and we feel like stopping to speak to the plants and animals as friendly fellow mountaineers. Nature as a poet, an enthusiastic workingman, becomes more and more visible the farther and higher we go; for the mountains are fountains—beginning places, however related to sources beyond mortal ken.

I found three kinds of meadows: (1) Those contained in basins not yet filled with earth enough to make a dry surface. They are planted with several species of carex, and have their margins diversified with robust flowering plants such as veratrum, larkspur, lupine, etc. (2) Those contained in the same sort of basins, once lakes like the first, but so situated in relation to the streams that flow through them and beds of transportable sand, gravel, etc., that they are now high and dry and well drained. This dry condition and corresponding difference in their vegetation may be caused by no superiority of position, or power of transporting filling material in the streams that belong to them, but simply by the basin being shallow and therefore sooner filled. They are planted with grasses, mostly fine, silky, and rather short-leaved, *Calama-*

grostis and *Agrostis* being the principal genera. They form delightfully smooth, level sods in which one finds two or three species of gentian and as many of purple and yellow orthocarpus, violet, vaccinium, kalmia, bryanthus, and lonicera. (3) Meadows hanging on ridge and mountain slopes, not in basins at all, but made and held in place by masses of boulders and fallen trees, which, forming dams one above another in close succession on small, outspread, channelless streams, have collected soil enough for the growth of grasses, carices, and many flowering plants, and being kept well watered, without being subject to currents sufficiently strong to carry them away, a hanging or sloping meadow is the result. Their surfaces are seldom so smooth as the others, being roughened more or less by the projecting tops of the dam rocks or logs; but at a little distance this roughness is not noticed, and the effect is very striking—bright green, fluent, down-sweeping flowery ribbons on gray slopes. The broad shallow streams these meadows belong to are mostly derived from banks of snow and because the soil is well drained in some places, while in others the dam rocks are packed close and caulked with bits of wood and leaves, making boggy patches; the vegetation, of course, is correspondingly varied. I saw patches of willow, bryanthus, and a fine show of lilies on some of them, not forming a margin, but scattered about among the carex and grass. Most of these meadows are now in their prime. How wonderful must be the temper of the elastic leaves of grasses and sedges to make curves so perfect and fine. Tempered a little harder, they would stand erect, stiff and bristly, like strips of metal; a little softer, and every leaf would lie flat. And what fine painting and tinting there is on the glumes and pales, stamens and feathery pistils. Butterflies colored like the flowers waver above them in wonderful profusion, and many other beautiful winged people, numbered and known and loved only by the Lord, are waltzing together high over head, seemingly in pure play and hilarious enjoyment of their little sparks of life. How wonderful they are! How do they get a living, and endure the weather? How are their little bodies, with muscles, nerves, organs, kept warm and jolly in such admirable exuberant health? Regarded only as mechanical inventions, how wonderful they are! Compared with these, Godlike man's greatest machines are as nothing.

Most of the sandy gardens on moraines are in prime beauty like the meadows, though some on the north sides of rocks and beneath groves of sapling pines have not yet bloomed. On sunny sheets of crystal soil along the slopes of the Hoffman Mountains, I saw extensive patches of ivesia and purple gilia with scarce a green leaf, making fine clouds of color. Ribes bushes, vaccinium, and kalmia, now in flower, make beautiful rugs and borders along the banks of the streams. Shaggy beds of dwarf oak (*Quercus chrysolepis,* var. *vaccinifolia*) over which one may walk are common on rocky moraines, yet this is the same species as the large live oak seen near Brown's Flat. The most beautiful of the shrubs is the purple-flowered bryanthus, here making glorious carpets at an elevation of nine thousand feet.

The principal tree for the first mile or two from camp is the magnificent silver fir, which reaches perfection here both in size and form of individual trees, and in the mode of grouping in groves with open spaces between. So trim and tasteful are these silvery, spiry groves one would fancy they must have been placed in position by some master landscape gardener, their regularity seeming almost conventional. But Nature is the only gardener able to do work so fine. A few noble specimens two hundred feet high occupy central positions in the groups with younger trees around them; and outside of these another circle of yet smaller ones, the whole arranged like tastefully symmetrical bouquets, every tree fitting nicely the place assigned to it as if made especially for it; small roses and eriogonums are usually found blooming on the open spaces about the groves, forming charming pleasure grounds. Higher, the firs gradually become smaller and less perfect, many showing double summits, indicating storm stress. Still, where good moraine soil is found, even on the rim of the lake-basin, specimens one hundred and fifty feet in height and five feet in diameter occur nearly nine thousand feet above the sea. The saplings, I find, are mostly bent with the crushing weight of the winter snow, which at this elevation must be at least eight or ten feet deep, judging by marks on the trees;

and this depth of compacted snow is heavy enough to bend and bury young trees twenty or thirty feet in height and hold them down for four or five months. Some are broken; the others spring up when the snow melts and at length attain a size that enables them to withstand the snow pressure. Yet even in trees five feet thick the traces of this early discipline are still plainly to be seen in their curved insteps, and frequently in old dried saplings protruding from the trunk, partially overgrown by the new axis developed from a branch below the break. Yet through all this stress the forest is maintained in marvelous beauty.

Beyond the silver firs I find the two-leaved pine (*Pinus contorta,* var. *Murrayana*) forms the bulk of the forest up to an elevation of ten thousand feet or more—the highest timberbelt of the Sierra. I saw a specimen nearly five feet in diameter growing on deep, well-watered soil at an elevation of about nine thousand feet. The form of this species varies very much with position, exposure, soil, etc. On stream-banks, where it is closely planted, it is very slender; some specimens seventy-five feet high do not exceed five inches in diameter at the ground, but the ordinary form, as far as I have seen, is well proportioned. The average diameter when full grown at this elevation is about twelve or fourteen inches, height forty or fifty feet, the straggling branches bent up at the end, the bark thin and bedraggled with amber-colored resin. The pistillate flowers form little crimson rosettes a fourth of an inch in diameter on the ends of the branchlets, mostly hidden in the leaf-tassels; the staminate are about three eighths of an inch in diameter, sulphur-yellow, in showy clusters, giving a remarkably rich effect—a brave, hardy mountaineer pine, growing cheerily on rough beds of avalanche boulders and joints of rock pavements, as well as in fertile hollows, standing up to the waist in snow every winter for centuries, facing a thousand storms and blooming every year in colors as bright as those worn by the sun-drenched trees of the tropics.

A still hardier mountaineer is the Sierra juniper (*Juniperus occidentalis*), growing mostly on domes and ridges and glacier pavements. A thickset, sturdy, picturesque highlander, seemingly content to live for more than a score of centuries on sunshine and snow; a truly wonderful fellow, dogged endur-

Junipers in Tenaya Cañon

ance expressed in every feature, lasting about as long as the granite he stands on. Some are nearly as broad as high. I saw one on the shore of the lake nearly ten feet in diameter, and many six to eight feet. The bark, cinnamon-colored, flakes off in long ribbon-like strips with a satiny luster. Surely the most enduring of all tree mountaineers, it never seems to die a natural death, or even to fall after it has been killed. If protected from accidents, it would perhaps be immortal. I saw some that had withstood an avalanche from snowy Mount Hoffman cheerily putting out new branches, as if repeating, like Grip, "Never say die." Some were simply standing on the pavement where no fissure more than half an inch wide offered a hold for its roots. The common height for these rock-dwellers is from ten to twenty feet; most of the old ones have broken tops, and are mere stumps, with a few tufted branches, forming picturesque brown pillars on bare pavements, with plenty of elbow-room and a clear view in every direction. On good moraine soil it reaches a height of from forty to sixty feet, with dense gray foliage. The rings of the trunk are very thin, eighty to an inch of diameter in some specimens I examined. Those ten feet in diameter must be very old—thousands of years. Wish I could live, like these junipers, on sunshine and snow, and stand beside them on the shore of Lake Tenaya for a thousand years. How much I should see, and how delightful it would be! Everything in the mountains would find me and come to me, and everything from the heavens like light.

The lake was named for one of the chiefs of the Yosemite tribe. Old Tenaya is said to have been a good Indian to his tribe. When a company of soldiers followed his band into Yosemite to punish them for cattle-stealing and other crimes, they fled to this lake by a trail that leads out of the upper end of the valley, early in the spring, while the snow was still deep; but being pursued, they lost heart and surrendered. A fine monument the old man has in this bright lake, and likely to last a long time, though lakes die as well as Indians, being gradually filled with detritus carried in by the feeding streams, and to some extent also by snow avalanches and rain and wind. A considerable portion of the Tenaya basin is already changed into a forested flat and meadow at the upper end, where the main tributary enters from Cathedral Peak. Two other tributaries come from the Hoffman Range. The outlet flows westward through Tenaya Cañon to join the Merced River in Yosemite. Scarce a handful of loose soil is to be seen on the north shore. All is bare, shining granite, suggesting the Indian name of the lake, Pywiack, meaning shining rock. The basin seems to have been slowly excavated by the ancient glaciers, a marvelous work requiring countless thousands of years. On the south side an imposing mountain rises from the water's edge to a height of three thousand feet or more, feathered with hemlock and pine; and huge shining domes on the east, over the tops of which the grinding, wasting, molding glacier must have swept as the wind does to-day.

July 28. No cloud mountains, only curly cirrus wisps scarce perceptible, and the want of thunder to strike the noon hour seems strange, as if the Sierra clock had stopped. Have been studying the *magnifica* fir—measured one near two hundred and forty feet high, the tallest I have yet seen. This species is the most symmetrical of all conifers, but though gigantic in size it seldom lives more than four or five hundred years. Most of the trees die from the attacks of a fungus at the age of two or three centuries. This dry-rot fungus perhaps enters the trunk by way of the stumps of limbs broken off by the snow that loads the broad palmate branches. The younger specimens are marvels of symmetry, straight and erect as a plumbline, their branches in regular level whorls of five mostly, each branch as exact in its divisions as a fern frond, and thickly covered by the leaves, making a rich plush over all the tree, excepting only the trunk and a small portion of the main limbs. The leaves turn upward, especially on the branchlets, and are stiff and sharp, pointed on all the upper portion of the tree. They remain on the tree about eight or ten years, and as the growth is rapid it is not rare to find the leaves still in place on the upper part of the axis where it is three to four inches in diameter, wide apart of course, and their spiral arrangement beautifully displayed. The leaf-scars are conspicuous for twenty years or more, but there is a good deal of variation in different trees as to the thickness and sharpness of the leaves.

After the excursion to Mount Hoffman I had seen a complete cross-section of the Sierra forest, and I find that *Abies magnifica* is the most symmetrical tree of all the noble coniferous company. The cones are grand affairs, superb in form, size, and color, cylindrical, stand erect on the upper branches like casks, and are from five to eight inches in length by three or four in diameter, greenish gray, and covered with fine down which has a silvery luster in the sunshine, and their brilliance is augmented by beads of transparent balsam which seems to have been poured over each cone, bringing to mind the old ceremonies of anointing with oil. If possible, the inside of the cone is more beautiful than the outside; the scales, bracts, and seed wings are tinted with the loveliest rosy purple with a bright lustrous iridescence; the seeds, three fourths of an inch long, are dark brown. When the cones are ripe the scales and bracts fall off, setting the seeds free to fly to their predestined places, while the dead spike-like axes are left on the branches for many years to mark the positions of the vanished cones, excepting those cut off when green by the Douglas squirrel. How he gets his teeth under the broad bases of the sessile cones, I don't know. Climbing these trees on a sunny day to visit the growing cones and to gaze over the tops of the forest is one of my best enjoyments.

July 29. Bright, cool, exhilarating. Clouds about .05. Another glorious day of rambling, sketching, and universal enjoyment.

July 30. Clouds .20, but the regular shower did not reach us, though thunder was heard a few miles off striking the noon hour. Ants, flies, and mosquitoes seem to enjoy this fine climate. A few house-flies have discovered our camp. The Sierra mosquitoes are courageous and of good size, some of them measuring nearly an inch from tip of sting to tip of folded wings. Though less abundant than in most wildernesses, they occasionally make quite a hum and stir, and pay but little attention to time or place. They sting anywhere, any time of day, wherever they can find anything worth while, until they are themselves stung by frost. The large, jet-black ants are only ticklish and troublesome when one is lying down under the trees. Noticed a borer drilling a silver fir. Ovipositor about an inch and a half in length, polished and straight like a needle. When not in use, it is folded back in a sheath, which extends straight behind like the legs of a crane in flying. This drilling, I suppose, is to save nest building, and the after care of feeding the young. Who would guess that in the brain of a fly so much knowledge could find lodgment? How do they know that their eggs will hatch in such holes, or, after they hatch, that the soft, helpless grubs will find the right sort of nourishment in silver fir sap? This domestic arrangement calls to mind the curious family of gallflies. Each species seems to know what kind of plant will respond to the irritation or stimulus of the puncture it makes and the eggs it lays, in forming a growth that not only answers for a nest and home but also provides food for the young. Probably these gallflies make mistakes at times, like anybody else; but when they do, there is simply a failure of that particular brood, while enough to perpetuate the species do find the proper plants and nourishment. Many mistakes of this kind might be made without being discovered by us. Once a pair of wrens made the mistake of building a nest in the sleeve of a workman's coat, which was called for at sundown, much to the consternation and discomfiture of the birds. Still the marvel remains that any of the children of such small people as gnats and mosquitoes should escape their own and their parents' mistakes, as well as the vicissitudes of the weather and hosts of enemies, and come forth in full vigor and perfection to enjoy the sunny world. When we think of the small creatures that are visible, we are led to think of many that are smaller still and lead us on and on into infinite mystery.

July 31. Another glorious day, the air as delicious to the lungs as nectar to the tongue; indeed the body seems one palate, and tingles equally throughout. Cloudiness about .05, but our ordinary shower has not yet reached us, though I hear thunder in the distance.

The cheery little chipmunk, so common about Brown's Flat, is common here also, and perhaps other species. In their light, airy habits they recall the familiar species of the Eastern States, which we admired in the oak openings of Wisconsin as they skimmed along the zigzag rail fences. These Sierra chipmunks are more arboreal and squirrel-like. I first noticed them on the lower edge of the coniferous belt, where the Sabine and yellow pines meet,—exceedingly interesting little fellows, full of odd, funny ways, and without being true squirrels, have most of their acomplishments without their aggressive quarrelsomeness. I never weary watching them as they frisk about in the bushes gathering seeds and berries, like song sparrows poising daintily on slender twigs, and making even less stir than most birds of the same size. Few of the Sierra animals interest me more; they are so able, gentle, confiding, and beautiful, they take one's heart, and get themselves adopted as darlings. Though weighing hardly more than field mice, they are laborious collectors of seeds, nuts, and cones, and are therefore well fed, but never in the least swollen with fat or lazily full. On the contrary, of their frisky, birdlike liveliness there is no end. They have a great variety of notes corresponding with their movements, some sweet and liquid, like water dripping with tinkling sounds into pools. They seem dearly to love teasing a dog, coming frequently almost within reach, then frisking away with lively chipping, like sparrows, beating time to their music with their tails, which at each chip describe half circles from side to side. Not even the Douglas squirrel is surer-footed or more fearless. I have seen them running about on sheer precipices of the Yosemite walls seemingly holding on with as little effort as flies, and as unconscious of danger, where, if the slightest slip were made, they would have fallen two or three thousand feet. How fine it would be could we mountaineers climb these tremendous cliffs with the same sure grip! The venture I made the other day for a view of the Yosemite Fall, and which tried my nerves so sorely, this little Tamias would have made for an ear of grass.

The woodchuck (*Arctomys monax*) of the bleak mountaintops is a very different sort of mountaineer—the most bovine of rodents, a heavy eater, fat, aldermanic in bulk and fairly bloated, in his high pastures, like a cow in a clover field. One woodchuck would outweigh a hundred chipmunks, and yet he is by no means a dull animal. In the midst of what we regard as storm-beaten desolation he pipes and whistles right cheerily, and enjoys long life in his skyland homes. His burrow is made in disintegrated rocks or beneath large boulders. Coming out of his den in the cold hoarfrost mornings, he takes a sun-bath on some favorite flat-topped rock, then goes to breakfast in garden hollows, eats grass and flowers until comfortably swollen, then goes a-visiting to fight and play. How long a woodchuck lives in this bracing air I don't know, but some of them are rusty and gray like lichen-covered boulders.

August 1. A grand cloudland and five-minute shower, refreshing the blessed wilderness, already so fragrant and fresh, steeping the black meadow mold and dead leaves like tea.

The waycup, or flicker, so familiar to every boy in the old Middle West States, is one of the most common of the woodpeckers hereabouts, and makes one feel at home. I can see no difference in plumage or habits from the Eastern species, though the climate here is so different,—a fine, brave, confiding, beautiful bird. The robin, too, is here, with all his familiar notes and gestures, tripping daintily on open garden spots and high meadows. Over all America he seems to be at home, moving from the plains to the mountains and from north to south, back and forth, up and down, with the march of the seasons and food supply. How admirable the constitution and temper of this brave singer, keeping in cheery health over so vast and varied a range! Oftentimes, as I wander through these solemn woods, awe-stricken and silent, I hear the reassuring voice of this fellow wanderer ringing out, sweet and clear, "Fear not! fear not!"

The mountain quail (*Oreortyx ricta*) I often meet in my walks—a small brown partridge with a very long, slender, ornamental crest worn jauntily like a feather in a boy's cap, giving it a very marked appearance. This species is considerably larger than the valley quail, so common on the hot foothills. They seldom alight in trees, but love to wander in flocks of from five or six to twenty through the ceanothus and manzanita thickets and over open, dry meadows and rocks of the ridges where the forest is less dense or wanting, uttering a low clucking sound to enable them to keep together. When disturbed they rise with a strong birr of wing-beats, and scatter as if exploded to a distance of a quarter of a mile or so. After the danger is past they call one another together with a loud piping note—Nature's beautiful mountain chickens. I have not yet found their nests. The young of this season are already hatched and away—new broods of happy wanderers half as large as their parents. I wonder how they live through the long winters, when the ground is snow-covered ten feet deep. They must go down towards the lower edge of the forest, like the deer, though I have not heard of them there.

The blue, or dusky, grouse is also common here. They like the deepest and closest fir woods, and when disturbed, burst from the branches of the trees with a strong, loud whir of wing-beats, and vanish in a wavering, silent slide, without moving a feather—a stout, beautiful bird about the size of the prairie chicken of the old west, spending most of the time in the trees, excepting the breeding season, when it keeps to the ground. The young are now able to fly. When scattered by man or dog, they keep still until the danger is supposed to be passed, then the mother calls them together. The chicks can hear the call a distance of several hundred yards, though it is not loud. Should the young be unable to fly, the mother feigns desperate lameness or death to draw one away, throwing herself at one's feet within two or three yards, rolling over on her back, kicking and gasping, so as to deceive man or beast. They are said to stay all the year in the woods hereabouts, taking shelter in dense tufted branches of fir and yellow pine during snowstorms, and feeding on the young buds of these trees. Their legs are feathered down to their toes, and I have never heard of their suffering in any sort of weather. Able to live on pine and fir buds, they are forever independent in the matter of food, which troubles so many of us and controls our movements. Gladly, if I could, I would live forever on pine buds, however full of turpentine and pitch, for the sake of this grand independence. Just to think of our sufferings last month merely for grist-mill flour. Man seems to have more difficulty in gaining food than any other of the Lord's creatures. For many in towns it is a consuming, lifelong struggle; for others, the danger of coming to want is so great, the deadly habit of endless hoarding for the future is formed, which smothers all real life, and is continued long after every reasonable need has been over-supplied.

On Mount Hoffman I saw a curious dove-colored bird that seemed half woodpecker, half magpie, or crow. It screams something like a crow, but flies like a woodpecker, and has a long, straight bill, with which I saw it opening the cones of the mountain and white-barked pines. It seems to keep to the heights, though no doubt it comes down for shelter during winter, if not for food. So far as food is concerned, these bird-mountaineers, I guess, can glean nuts enough, even in winter, from the different kinds of conifers; for always there are a few that have been unable to fly out of the cones and remain for hungry winter gleaners.

Chapter VII

A STRANGE EXPERIENCE

AUGUST 2. Clouds and showers, about the same as yesterday. Sketching all day on the North Dome until four or five o'clock in the afternoon, when, as I was busily employed thinking only of the glorious Yosemite landscape, trying to draw every tree and every line and feature of the rocks, I was suddenly, and without warning, possessed with the notion that my friend, Professor J. D. Butler, of the State University of Wisconsin, was below me in the valley, and I jumped up full of the idea of meeting him, with almost as much startling excitement as if he had suddenly touched me to make me look up. Leaving my work without the slightest deliberation, I ran down the western slope of the Dome and along the brink of the valley wall, looking for a way to the bottom, until I came to a side cañon, which, judging by its apparently continuous growth of trees and bushes, I thought might afford a practical way into the valley, and immediately began to make the descent, late as it was, as if drawn irresistibly. But after a little, common sense stopped me and explained that it would be long after dark ere I could possibly reach the hotel, that the visitors would be asleep, that nobody would know me, that I had no money in my pockets, and moreover was without a coat. I therefore compelled myself to stop, and finally succeeded in reasoning myself out of the notion of seeking my friend in the dark, whose presence I only felt in a strange, telepathic way. I succeeded in dragging myself back through the woods to camp, never for a moment wavering, however, in my determination to go down to him next morning. This I think is the most unexplainable notion that ever struck me. Had some one whispered in my ear while I sat on the Dome, where I had spent so many days, that Professor Butler was in the valley, I could not have been more surprised and startled. When I was leaving the university, he said, "Now, John, I want to hold you in sight and watch your career. Promise to write me at least once a year." I received a letter from him in July, at our first camp in the Hollow, written in May, in which he

said that he might possibly visit California some time this summer, and therefore hoped to meet me. But inasmuch as he
named no meeting-place, and gave no directions as to the
course he would probably follow, and as I should be in the
wilderness all summer, I had not the slightest hope of seeing
him, and all thought of the matter had vanished from my
mind until this afternoon, when he seemed to be wafted bodily almost against my face. Well, to-morrow I shall see; for,
reasonable or unreasonable, I feel I must go.

August 3. Had a wonderful day. Found Professor Butler as
the compass-needle finds the pole. So last evening's telepathy,
transcendental revelation, or whatever else it may be called,
was true; for, strange to say, he had just entered the valley by
way of the Coulterville Trail and was coming up the valley
past El Capitan when his presence struck me. Had he then
looked toward the North Dome with a good glass when it
first came in sight, he might have seen me jump up from my
work and run toward him. This seems the one well-defined
marvel of my life of the kind called supernatural; for, absorbed
in glad Nature, spirit-rappings, second sight, ghost stories,
etc., have never interested me since boyhood, seeming comparatively useless and infinitely less wonderful than Nature's
open, harmonious, songful, sunny, everyday beauty.

This morning, when I thought of having to appear among
tourists at a hotel, I was troubled because I had no suitable
clothes, and at best am desperately bashful and shy. I was determined to go, however, to see my old friend after two years
among strangers; got on a clean pair of overalls, a cashmere
shirt, and a sort of jacket,—the best my camp wardrobe afforded,—tied my notebook on my belt, and strode away on
my strange journey, followed by Carlo. I made my way through
the gap discovered last evening, which proved to be Indian
Cañon. There was no trail in it, and the rocks and brush were
so rough that Carlo frequently called me back to help him
down precipitous places. Emerging from the cañon shadows,
I found a man making hay on one of the meadows, and asked
him whether Professor Butler was in the valley. "I don't
know," he replied; "but you can easily find out at the hotel.
There are but few visitors in the valley just now. A small party

came in yesterday afternoon, and I heard some one called Professor Butler, or Butterfield, or some name like that."

In front of the gloomy hotel I found a tourist party adjusting their fishing tackle. They all stared at me in silent wonderment, as if I had been seen dropping down through the trees from the clouds, mostly, I suppose, on account of my strange garb. Inquiring for the office, I was told it was locked, and that the landlord was away, but I might find the landlady, Mrs. Hutchings, in the parlor. I entered in a sad state of embarrassment, and after I had waited in the big, empty room and knocked at several doors the landlady at length appeared, and in reply to my question said she rather thought Professor Butler *was* in the valley, but to make sure, she would bring the register from the office. Among the names of the last arrivals I soon discovered the Professor's familiar handwriting, at the sight of which bashfulness vanished; and having learned that his party had gone up the valley,—probably to the Vernal and Nevada Falls,—I pushed on in glad pursuit, my heart now sure of its prey. In less than an hour I reached the head of the Nevada Cañon at the Vernal Fall, and just outside of the spray discovered a distinguished-looking gentleman, who, like everybody else I have seen to-day, regarded me curiously as I approached. When I made bold to inquire if he knew where Professor Butler was, he seemed yet more curious to know what could possibly have happened that required a messenger for the Professor, and instead of answering my question he asked with military sharpness, "Who wants him?" "I want him," I replied with equal sharpness. "Why? Do *you* know him?" "Yes," I said. "Do *you* know him?" Astonished that any one in the mountains could possibly know Professor Butler and find him as soon as he had reached the valley, he came down to meet the strange mountaineer on equal terms, and courteously replied, "Yes, I know Professor Butler very well. I am General Alvord, and we were fellow students in Rutland, Vermont, long ago, when we were both young." "But where is he now?" I persisted, cutting short his story. "He has gone beyond the falls with a companion, to try to climb that big rock, the top of which you see from here." His guide now volunteered the information that it was the Liberty Cap Professor Butler and his companion had gone to climb, and that if I waited at the head of the fall I should be sure to find them on their way down. I therefore climbed the ladders alongside the Vernal Fall, and was pushing forward, determined to go to the top of Liberty Cap rock in my hurry, rather than wait, if I should not meet my friend sooner. So heart-hungry at times may one be to see a friend in the flesh, however happily full and care-free one's life may be. I had gone but a short distance, however, above the brow of the Vernal Fall when I caught sight of him in the brush and rocks, half erect, groping his way, his sleeves rolled up, vest open, hat in his hand, evidently very hot and tired. When he saw me coming he sat down on a boulder to wipe the perspiration from his brow and neck, and taking me for one of the valley guides, he inquired the way to the fall ladders. I pointed out the path marked with little piles of stones, on seeing which he called his companion, saying that the way was found; but he did not yet recognize me. Then I stood directly in front of him, looked him in the face, and held out my hand. He thought I was offering to assist him in rising. "Never mind," he said. Then I said, "Professor Butler, don't you know me?" "I think not," he replied; but catching my eye, sudden recognition followed, and astonishment that I should have found him just when he was lost in the brush and did not know that I was within hundreds of miles of him. "John Muir, John Muir, where have you come from?" Then I told him the story of my feeling his presence when he entered the valley last evening, when he was four or five miles distant, as I sat sketching on the North Dome. This, of course, only made him wonder the more. Below the foot of the Vernal Fall the guide was waiting with his saddle-horse, and I walked along the trail, chatting all the way back to the hotel, talking of school days, friends in Madison, of the students, how each had prospered, etc., ever and anon gazing at the stupendous rocks about us, now growing indistinct in the gloaming, and again quoting from the poets—a rare ramble.

It was late ere we reached the hotel, and General Alvord was waiting the Professor's arrival for dinner. When I was introduced he seemed yet more astonished than the Professor at my descent from cloudland and going straight to my friend without knowing in any ordinary way that he was even in California. They had come on direct from the East, had not yet visited any of their friends in the state, and considered themselves undiscoverable. As we sat at dinner, the General leaned back in his chair, and looking down the table, thus introduced me to the dozen guests or so, including the staring fisherman mentioned above: "This man, you know, came down out of these huge, trackless mountains, you know, to find his friend Professor Butler here, the very day he arrived; and how did he know he was here? He just felt him, he says. This is the queerest case of Scotch farsightedness I ever heard of," etc., etc. While my friend quoted Shakespeare: "More things in heaven and earth, Horatio, than are dreamt of in your philosophy," "As the sun, ere he has risen, sometimes paints his image in the firmament, e'en so the shadows of events precede the events, and in to-day already walks to-morrow."

Had a long conversation, after dinner, over Madison days. The Professor wants me to promise to go with him, sometime, on a camping trip in the Hawaiian Islands, while I tried to get him to go back with me to camp in the high Sierra. But he says, "Not now." He must not leave the General; and I was surprised to learn they are to leave the valley to-morrow or next day. I'm glad I'm not great enough to be missed in the busy world.

August 4. It seemed strange to sleep in a paltry hotel chamber after the spacious magnificence and luxury of the starry sky and silver fir grove. Bade farewell to my friend and the General. The old soldier was very kind, and an interesting talker. He told me long stories of the Florida Seminole war, in which he took part, and invited me to visit him in Omaha. Calling Carlo, I scrambled home through the Indian Cañon gate, rejoicing, pitying the poor Professor and General, bound by clocks, almanacs, orders, duties, etc., and compelled to dwell with lowland care and dust and din, where Nature is covered and her voice smothered, while the poor, insignificant wanderer enjoys the freedom and glory of God's wilderness.

Apart from the human interest of my visit to-day, I greatly enjoyed Yosemite, which I had visited only once before, having spent eight days last spring in rambling amid its rocks and waters. Wherever we go in the mountains, or indeed in any of God's wild fields, we find more than we seek. Descending four thousand feet in a few hours, we enter a new world—climate, plants, sounds, inhabitants, and scenery all new or changed. Near camp the goldcup oak forms sheets of chaparral, on top of which we may make our beds. Going down the Indian Cañon we observe this little bush changing by regular gradations to a large bush, to a small tree, and then larger, until on the rocky taluses near the bottom of the valley we find it developed into a broad, wide-spreading, gnarled, picturesque tree from four to eight feet in diameter, and forty or fifty feet high. Innumerable are the forms of water displayed. Every gliding reach, cascade, and fall has characters of its own. Had a good view of the Vernal and Nevada, two of the main falls of the valley, less than a mile apart, and offering striking differences in voice, form, color, etc. The Vernal, four hundred feet high and about seventy-five or eighty feet wide, drops smoothly over a round-lipped precipice and forms a superb apron of embroidery, green and white, slightly folded and fluted, maintaining this form nearly to the bottom, where it is suddenly veiled in quick-flying billows of spray and mist, in which the afternoon sunbeams play with ravishing beauty of rainbow colors. The Nevada is white from its first appearance as it leaps out into the freedom of the air. At the head it presents a twisted appearance, by an overfolding of the current from striking on the side of its channel just before the first free outbounding leap is made. About two thirds of the way down, the hurrying throng of comet-shaped masses glance on an inclined part of the face of the precipice and are beaten into yet whiter foam, greatly expanded, and sent bounding outward, making an indescribably glorious show, especially when the afternoon sunshine is pouring into it. In this fall—one of the most wonderful in the world—the water does not seem to be under the dominion of ordinary laws, but rather as if it were a living creature, full of the strength of the mountains and their huge, wild joy.

From beneath heavy throbbing blasts of spray the broken river is seen emerging in ragged boulder-chafed strips. These are speedily gathered into a roaring torrent, showing that the young river is still gloriously alive. On it goes, shouting, roaring, exulting in its strength, passes through a gorge with sublime display of energy, then suddenly expands on a gently inclined pavement, down which it rushes in thin sheets and folds of lace-work into a quiet pool,—"Emerald Pool," as it is called,—a stopping-place, a period separating two grand sentences. Resting here long enough to part with its foam-bells and gray mixtures of air, it glides quietly to the verge of the Vernal precipice in a broad sheet and makes its new display in the Vernal Fall; then more rapids and rock tossings down the cañon, shaded by live oak, Douglas spruce, fir, maple, and dogwood. It receives the Illilouette tributary, and makes a long sweep out into the level, sun-filled valley to join the other streams which, like itself, have danced and sung their way down from snowy heights to form the main Merced—the river of Mercy. But of this there is no end, and life, when one thinks of it, is so short. Never mind, one day in the midst of these divine glories is well worth living and toiling and starving for.

Before parting with Professor Butler he gave me a book, and I gave him one of my pencil sketches for his little son Henry, who is a favorite of mine. He used to make many visits to my room when I was a student. Never shall I forget his patriotic speeches for the Union, mounted on a tall stool, when he was only six years old.

It seems strange that visitors to Yosemite should be so little influenced by its novel grandeur, as if their eyes were bandaged and their ears stopped. Most of those I saw yesterday were looking down as if wholly unconscious of anything going on about them, while the sublime rocks were trembling with the tones of the mighty chanting congregation of waters gathered from all the mountains round about, making music that might draw angels out of heaven. Yet respectable-looking, even wise-looking people were fixing bits of worms on bent pieces of wire to catch trout. Sport they called it. Should church-goers try to pass the time fishing in baptismal fonts while dull sermons were being preached, the so-called sport might not be so bad; but to play in the Yosemite temple, seeking pleasure in the pain of fishes struggling for their lives, while God himself is preaching his sublimest water and stone sermons!

Now I'm back at the camp-fire, and cannot help thinking about my recognition of my friend's presence in the valley while he was four or five miles away, and while I had no means of knowing that he was not thousands of miles away. It seems supernatural, but only because it is not understood. Anyhow, it seems silly to make so much of it, while the natural and common is more truly marvelous and mysterious than the so-called supernatural. Indeed most of the miracles we hear of are infinitely less wonderful than the commonest of natural phenomena, when fairly seen. Perhaps the invisible rays that struck me while I sat at work on the Dome are something like those which attract and repel people at first sight, concerning which so much nonsense has been written. The worst apparent effect of these mysterious odd things is blindness to all that is divinely common. Hawthorne, I fancy, could weave one of his weird romances out of this little telepathic episode, the one strange marvel of my life, probably replacing my good old Professor by an attractive woman.

August 5. We were awakened this morning before daybreak by the furious barking of Carlo and Jack and the sound of stampeding sheep. Billy fled from his punk bed to the fire, and refused to stir into the darkness to try to gather the scattered flock, or ascertain the nature of the disturbance. It was a bear attack, as we afterward learned, and I suppose little was gained by attempting to do anything before daylight. Nevertheless, being anxious to know what was up, Carlo and I groped our way through the woods, guided by the rustling sound made by fragments of the flock, not fearing the bear, for I knew that the runaways would go from their enemy as far as possible and Carlo's nose was also to be depended upon. About half a mile east of the corral we overtook twenty or thirty of the flock and succeeded in driving them back; then turning to the westward, we traced another band of fugitives and got them back to the flock. After daybreak I discovered the remains of a sheep carcass, still warm, showing that Bruin must have been enjoying his early mutton breakfast while I was seeking the runaways. He had eaten about half of it. Six dead sheep lay in the corral, evidently smothered by the crowding and piling up of the flock against the side of the corral wall when the bear entered. Making a wide circuit of the camp, Carlo and I discovered a third band of fugitives and drove them back to camp. We also discovered another dead sheep half eaten, showing there had been two of the shaggy freebooters at this early breakfast. They were easily traced. They had each caught a sheep, jumped over the corral fence with them, carrying them as a cat carries a mouse, laid them at the foot of fir trees a hundred yards or so back from the corral, and eaten their fill. After breakfast I set out to seek more of the lost, and found seventy-five at a considerable distance from camp. In the afternoon I succeeded, with Carlo's help, in getting them back to the flock. I don't know whether all are together again or not. I shall make a big fire this evening and keep watch.

When I asked Billy why he made his bed against the corral in rotten wood, when so many better places offered, he replied that he "wished to be as near the sheep as possible in case bears should attack them." Now that the bears have come, he has moved his bed to the far side of the camp, and seems afraid that he may be mistaken for a sheep.

This has been mostly a sheep day, and of course studies have been interrupted. Nevertheless, the walk through the gloom of the woods before the dawn was worth while, and I have learned something about these noble bears. Their tracks are very telling, and so are their breakfasts. Scarce a trace of clouds to-day, and of course our ordinary midday thunder is wanting.

August 6. Enjoyed the grand illumination of the camp grove, last night, from the fire we made to frighten the bears—compensation for loss of sleep and sheep. The noble pillars of verdure, vividly aglow, seemed to shoot into the sky like the flames that lighted them. Nevertheless, one of the bears paid us another visit, as if more attracted than repelled by the fire, climbed into the corral, killed a sheep and made off with it without being seen, while still another was lost by trampling and suffocation against the side of the corral. Now that our mutton has been tasted, I suppose it will be difficult to put a stop to the ravages of these freebooters.

The Don arrived to-day from the lowlands with provisions and a letter. On learning the losses he had sustained, he determined to move the flock at once to the Upper Tuolumne region, saying that the bears would be sure to visit the camp every night as long as we stayed, and that no fire or noise we might make would avail to frighten them. No clouds save a few thin, lustrous touches on the eastern horizon. Thunder heard in the distance.

Chapter VIII

AUGUST 7. Early this morning bade good-bye to the bears and blessed silver fir camp, and moved slowly eastward along the Mono Trail. At sundown camped for the night on one of the many small flowery meadows so greatly enjoyed on my excursion to Lake Tenaya. The dusty, noisy flock seems outrageously foreign and out of place in these nature gardens, more so than bears among sheep. The harm they do goes to the heart, but glorious hope lifts above all the dust and din and bids me look forward to a good time coming, when money enough will be earned to enable me to go walking where I like in pure wildness, with what I can carry on my back, and when the bread-sack is empty, run down to the nearest point on the bread-line for more. Nor will these run-downs be blanks, for, whether up or down, every step and jump on these blessed mountains is full of fine lessons.

August 8. Camp at the west end of Lake Tenaya. Arriving early, I took a walk on the glacier-polished pavements along the north shore, and climbed the magnificent mountain rock at the east end of the lake, now shining in the late afternoon light. Almost every yard of its surface shows the scoring and polishing action of a great glacier that enveloped it and swept heavily over its summit, though it is about two thousand feet high above the lake and ten thousand above sea-level. This majestic, ancient ice-flood came from the eastward, as the scoring and crushing of the surface shows. Even below the waters of the lake the rock in some places is still grooved and polished; the lapping of the waves and their disintegrating action have not as yet obliterated even the superficial marks of glaciation. In climbing the steepest polished places I had to take off shoes and stockings. A fine region this for study of glacial action in mountain-making. I found many charming plants: arctic daisies, phlox, white spiræa, bryanthus, and rock-ferns,—pellæa, cheilanthes, allosorus,—fringing weathered seams all the way up to the summit; and sturdy junipers, grand old gray and brown monuments, stood bravely erect on

View of Tenaya Lake showing Cathedral Peak

One of the tributary fountains of the Tuolumne Cañon waters,
on the north side of the Hoffman Range

fissured spots here and there, telling storm and avalanche stories of hundreds of winters. The view of the lake from the top
is, I think, the best of all. There is another rock, more striking
in form than this, standing isolated at the head of the lake,
but it is not more than half as high. It is a knob or knot of
burnished granite, perhaps about a thousand feet high, apparently as flawless and strong in structure as a wave-worn
pebble, and probably owes its existence to the superior resistance it offered to the action of the overflowing ice-flood.

Made sketch of the lake, and sauntered back to camp, my
iron-shod shoes clanking on the pavements disturbing the
chipmunks and birds. After dark went out to the shore,—not
a breath of air astir, the lake a perfect mirror reflecting the sky
and mountains with their stars and trees and wonderful sculpture, all their grandeur refined and doubled,—a marvelously
impressive picture, that seemed to belong more to heaven
than earth.

August 9. I went ahead of the flock, and crossed over the
divide between the Merced and Tuolumne Basins. The gap
between the east end of the Hoffman spur and the mass of
mountain rocks about Cathedral Peak, though roughened by
ridges and waving folds, seems to be one of the channels of a
broad ancient glacier that came from the mountains on the
summit of the range. In crossing this divide the ice-river made
an ascent of about five hundred feet from the Tuolumne
meadows. This entire region must have been overswept by ice.

From the top of the divide, and also from the big Tuolumne
Meadows, the wonderful mountain called Cathedral Peak is
in sight. From every point of view it shows marked individuality. It is a majestic temple of one stone, hewn from the
living rock, and adorned with spires and pinnacles in regular
cathedral style. The dwarf pines on the roof look like mosses.
I hope some time to climb to it to say my prayers and hear
the stone sermons.

The big Tuolumne Meadows are flowery lawns, lying along
the south fork of the Tuolumne River at a height of about
eighty-five hundred to nine thousand feet above the sea, partially separated by forests and bars of glaciated granite. Here
the mountains seem to have been cleared away or set back, so
that wide-open views may be had in every direction. The

upper end of the series lies at the base of Mount Lyell, the lower below the east end of the Hoffman Range, so the length must be about ten or twelve miles. They vary in width from a quarter of a mile to perhaps three quarters, and a good many branch meadows put out along the banks of the tributary streams. This is the most spacious and delightful high plea-sure-ground I have yet seen. The air is keen and bracing, yet warm during the day; and though lying high in the sky, the surrounding mountains are so much higher, one feels pro-tected as if in a grand hall. Mounts Dana and Gibbs, massive red mountains, perhaps thirteen thousand feet high or more, bound the view on the east, the Cathedral and Unicorn Peaks, with many nameless peaks, on the south, the Hoffman Range on the west, and a number of peaks unnamed, as far as I know, on the north. One of these last is much like the Cathedral. The grass of the meadows is mostly fine and silky, with ex-ceedingly slender leaves, making a close sod, above which the panicles of minute purple flowers seem to float in airy, misty lightness, while the sod is enriched with at least three species of gentian and as many or more of orthocarpus, potentilla, ivesia, solidago, pentstemon, with their gay colors,—purple, blue, yellow, and red,—all of which I may know better ere long. A central camp will probably be made in this region, from which I hope to make long excursions into the sur-rounding mountains.

On the return trip I met the flock about three miles east of Lake Tenaya. Here we camped for the night near a small lake lying on top of the divide in a clump of the two-leaved pine. We are now about nine thousand feet above the sea. Small lakes abound in all sorts of situations,—on ridges, along mountain sides, and in piles of moraine boulders, most of them mere pools. Only in those cañons of the larger streams at the foot of declivities, where the down thrust of the glaciers was heaviest, do we find lakes of considerable size and depth. How grateful a task it would be to trace them all and study them! How pure their waters are, clear as crystal in polished stone basins! None of them, so far as I have seen, have fishes, I suppose on account of falls making them inaccessible. Yet one would think their eggs might get into these lakes by some chance or other; on ducks' feet, for example, or in their mouths, or in their crops, as some plant seeds are distributed. Nature has so many ways of doing such things. How did the frogs, found in all the bogs and pools and lakes, however high, manage to get up these mountains? Surely not by jumping. Such excursions through miles of dry brush and boulders would be very hard on frogs. Perhaps their stringy gelatinous spawn is occasionally entangled or glued on the feet of water birds. Anyhow, they are here and in hearty health and voice. I like their cheery tronk and crink. They take the place of song-birds at a pinch.

August 10. Another of those charming exhilarating days that make the blood dance and excite nerve currents that render one unweariable and well-nigh immortal. Had another view of the broad ice-ploughed divide, and gazed again and again at the Sierra temple and the great red mountains east of the meadows.

We are camped near the Soda Springs on the north side of the river. A hard time we had getting the sheep across. They were driven into a horseshoe bend and fairly crowded off the bank. They seemed willing to suffer death rather than risk getting wet, though they swim well enough when they have to. Why sheep should be so unreasonably afraid of water, I don't know, but they do fear it as soon as they are born and perhaps before. I once saw a lamb only a few hours old approach a shallow stream about two feet wide and an inch deep, after it had walked only about a hundred yards on its life journey. All the flock to which it belonged had crossed this inch-deep stream, and as the mother and her lamb were the last to cross, I had a good opportunity to observe them. As soon as the flock was out of the way, the anxious mother crossed over and called the youngster. It walked cautiously to the brink, gazed at the water, bleated piteously, and refused to venture. The patient mother went back to it again and again to encourage it, but long without avail. Like the pilgrim on Jordan's stormy bank it feared to launch away. At length, gathering its trembling inexperienced legs for the mighty effort, throwing up its head as if it knew all about drowning, and was anxious to keep its nose above water, it made the tremendous leap, and landed in the middle of the inch-deep stream. It seemed astonished to find that, instead of sinking over head and ears, only its toes were wet, gazed at the shining water a few seconds, and then sprang to the shore safe and dry through the dreadful adventure. All kinds of wild sheep are mountain animals, and their descendants' dread of water is not easily accounted for.

August 11. Fine shining weather, with a ten minutes' noon thunderstorm and rain. Rambling all day getting acquainted with the region north of the river. Found a small lake and many charming glacier meadows embosomed in an extensive forest of the two-leaved pine. The forest is growing on broad, almost continuous deposits of moraine material, is remarkably even in its growth, and the trees are much closer together than in any of the fir or pine woods farther down the range. The evenness of the growth would seem to indicate that the trees are all of the same age or nearly so. This regularity has probably been in great part the result of fire. I saw several large patches and strips of dead bleached spars, the ground beneath them covered with a young even growth. Fire can run in these woods, not only because the thin bark of the trees is dripping with resin, but because the growth is close, and the comparatively rich soil produces good crops of tall broad-leaved grasses on which fire can travel, even when the weather is calm. Besides these fire-killed patches there are a good many fallen uprooted trees here and there, some with the bark and needles still on, as if they had lately been blown down in some thunderstorm blast. Saw a large black-tailed deer, a buck with antlers like the upturned roots of a fallen pine.

After a long ramble through the dense encumbered woods I emerged upon a smooth meadow full of sunshine like a lake of light, about a mile and a half long, a quarter to half a mile wide, and bounded by tall arrowy pines. The sod, like that of all the glacier meadows hereabouts, is made of silky agrostis and calamagrostis chiefly; their panicles of purple flowers and purple stems, exceedingly light and airy, seem to float above the green plush of leaves like a thin misty cloud, while the sod is brightened by several species of gentian, potentilla, ivesia, orthocarpus, and their corresponding bees and butterflies. All the glacier meadows are beautiful, but few are so perfect as this one. Compared with it the most carefully leveled, licked, snipped artificial lawns of pleasure-grounds are coarse things. I should like to live here always. It is so calm and withdrawn while open to the universe in full communion with everything good. To the north of this glorious meadow I discovered the camp of some Indian hunters. Their fire was still burning, but they had not yet returned from the chase.

Glacier meadow, on the headwaters of the Tuolumne,
9500 feet above the sea

From meadow to meadow, every one beautiful beyond telling, and from lake to lake through groves and belts of arrowy trees, I held my way northward toward Mount Conness, finding telling beauty everywhere, while the encompassing mountains were calling "Come." Hope I may climb them all.

August 12. The sky-scenery has changed but little so far with the change in elevation. Clouds about .05. Glorious pearly cumuli tinted with purple of ineffable fineness of tone. Moved camp to the side of the glacier meadow mentioned above. To let sheep trample so divinely fine a place seems barbarous. Fortunately they prefer the succulent broad-leaved triticum and other woodland grasses to the silky species of the meadows, and therefore seldom bite them or set foot on them.

The shepherd and the Don cannot agree about methods of

herding. Billy sets his dog Jack on the sheep far too often, so the Don thinks; and after some dispute to-day, in which the shepherd loudly claimed the right to dog the sheep as often as he pleased, he started for the plains. Now I suppose the care of the sheep will fall on me, though Mr. Delaney promises to do the herding himself for a while, then return to the low-lands and bring another shepherd, so as to leave me free to rove as I like.

Had another rich ramble. Pushed northward beyond the forests to the head of the general basin, where traces of glacial action are strikingly clear and interesting. The recesses among the peaks look like quarries, so raw and fresh are the moraine chips and boulders that strew the ground in Nature's glacial workshops.

Soon after my return to camp we received a visit from an Indian, probably one of the hunters whose camp I had dis-covered. He came from Mono, he said, with others of his tribe, to hunt deer. One that he had killed a short distance from here he was carrying on his back, its legs tied together in an ornamental bunch on his forehead. Throwing down his burden, he gazed stolidly for a few minutes in silent Indian fashion, then cut off eight or ten pounds of venison for us, and begged a "lill" (little) of everything he saw or could think of—flour, bread, sugar, tobacco, whiskey, needles, etc. We gave a fair price for the meat in flour and sugar and added a few needles. A strangely dirty and irregular life these dark-eyed, dark-haired, half-happy savages lead in this clean wilderness,—starvation and abundance, deathlike calm, indo-lence, and admirable, indefatigable action succeeding each other in stormy rhythm like winter and summer. Two things they have that civilized toilers might well envy them—pure air and pure water. These go far to cover and cure the grossness of their lives. Their food is mostly good berries, pine nuts, clover, lily bulbs, wild sheep, antelope, deer, grouse, sage hens, and the larvæ of ants, wasps, bees, and other insects.

August 13. Day all sunshine, dawn and evening purple, noon gold, no clouds, air motionless. Mr. Delaney arrived with two shepherds, one of them an Indian. On his way up from the plains he left some provisions at the Portuguese camp on Por-cupine Creek near our old Yosemite camp, and I set out this morning with one of the pack animals to fetch them. Arrived at the Porcupine camp at noon, and might have returned to the Tuolumne late in the evening, but concluded to stay over night with the Portuguese shepherds at their pressing invitation. They had sad stories to tell of losses from the Yosemite bears, and were so discouraged they seemed on the point of leaving the mountains; for the bears came every night and helped themselves to one or several of the flock in spite of all their efforts to keep them off.

I spent the afternoon in a grand ramble along the Yosemite walls. From the highest of the rocks called the Three Brothers, I enjoyed a magnificent view comprehending all the upper half of the floor of the valley and nearly all the rocks of the walls on both sides and at the head, with snowy peaks in the background. Saw also the Vernal and Nevada Falls, a truly glorious picture,—rocky strength and permanence combined with beauty of plants frail and fine and evanescent; water descending in thunder, and the same water gliding through meadows and groves in gentlest beauty. This standpoint is about eight thousand feet above the sea, or four thousand feet above the floor of the valley, and every tree, though looking small and feathery, stands in admirable clearness, and the shadows they cast are as distinct in outline as if seen at a distance of a few yards. They appeared even more so. No words will ever describe the exquisite beauty and charm of this mountain park— Nature's landscape garden at once tenderly beautiful and sublime. No wonder it draws nature-lovers from all over the world.

Glacial action even on this lofty summit is plainly displayed. Not only has all the lovely valley now smiling in sunshine been filled to the brim with ice, but it has been deeply overflowed.

I visited our old Yosemite camp-ground on the head of Indian Creek, and found it fairly patted and smoothed down with bear-tracks. The bears had eaten all the sheep that were smothered in the corral, and some of the grand animals must have died, for Mr. Delaney, before leaving camp, put a large quantity of poison in the carcasses. All sheep-men carry strychnine to kill coyotes, bears, and panthers, though neither coyotes nor panthers are at all numerous in the upper mountains. The little dog-like wolves are far more numerous in the

foothill region and on the plains, where they find a better
supply of food,—saw only one panther-track above eight
thousand feet.

On my return after sunset to the Portuguese camp I found
the shepherds greatly excited over the behavior of the bears
that have learned to like mutton. "They are getting worse and
worse," they lamented. Not willing to wait decently until after
dark for their suppers, they come and kill and eat their fill in
broad daylight. The evening before my arrival, when the two
shepherds were leisurely driving the flock toward camp half
an hour before sunset, a hungry bear came out of the chaparral within a few yards of them and shuffled deliberately toward the flock. "Portuguese Joe," who always carried a gun
loaded with buckshot, fired excitedly, threw down his gun,
fled to the nearest suitable tree, and climbed to a safe height
without waiting to see the effect of his shot. His companion
also ran, but said that he saw the bear rise on its hind legs
and throw out its arms as if feeling for somebody, and then
go into the brush as if wounded.

At another of their camps in this neighborhood, a bear with
two cubs attacked the flock before sunset, just as they were
approaching the corral. Joe promptly climbed a tree out of
danger, while Antone, rebuking his companion for cowardice
in abandoning his charge, said that he was not going to let
bears "eat up his sheeps" in daylight, and rushed towards the
bears, shouting and setting his dog on them. The frightened
cubs climbed a tree, but the mother ran to meet the shepherd
and seemed anxious to fight. Antone stood astonished for a
moment, eyeing the oncoming bear, then turned and fled,
closely pursued. Unable to reach a suitable tree for climbing,
he ran to the camp and scrambled up to the roof of the little
cabin; the bear followed, but did not climb to the roof,—only
stood glaring up at him for a few minutes, threatening him
and holding him in mortal terror, then went to her cubs,
called them down, went to the flock, caught a sheep for supper, and vanished in the brush. As soon as the bear left the
cabin, the trembling Antone begged Joe to show him a good
safe tree, up which he climbed like a sailor climbing a mast,
and remained as long as he could hold on, the tree being

almost branchless. After these disastrous experiences the two shepherds chopped and gathered large piles of dry wood and made a ring of fire around the corral every night, while one with a gun kept watch from a comfortable stage built on a neighboring pine that commanded a view of the corral. This evening the show made by the circle of fire was very fine, bringing out the surrounding trees in most impressive relief, and making the thousands of sheep eyes glow like a glorious bed of diamonds.

August 14. Up to the time I went to bed last night all was quiet, though we expected the shaggy freebooters every minute. They did not come till near midnight, when a pair walked boldly to the corral between two of the great fires, climbed in, killed two sheep and smothered ten, while the frightened watcher in the tree did not fire a single shot, saying that he was afraid he might kill some of the sheep, for the bears got into the corral before he got a good clear view of them. I told the shepherds they should at once move the flock to another camp. "Oh, no use, no use," they lamented; "where we go, the bears go too. See my poor dead sheeps—soon all dead. No use try another camp. We go down to the plains." And as I afterwards learned, they were driven out of the mountains a month before the usual time. Were bears much more numerous and destructive, the sheep would be kept away altogether.

It seems strange that bears, so fond of all sorts of flesh, running the risks of guns and fires and poison, should never attack men except in defense of their young. How easily and safely a bear could pick us up as we lie asleep! Only wolves and tigers seem to have learned to hunt man for food, and perhaps sharks and crocodiles. Mosquitoes and other insects would, I suppose, devour a helpless man in some parts of the world, and so might lions, leopards, wolves, hyenas, and panthers at times if pressed by hunger,—but under ordinary circumstances, perhaps, only the tiger among land animals may be said to be a man-eater,—unless we add man himself.

Clouds as usual about .05. Another glorious Sierra day, warm, crisp, fragrant, and clear. Many of the flowering plants have gone to seed, but many others are unfolding their petals every day, and the firs and pines are more fragrant than ever. Their seeds are nearly ripe, and will soon be flying in the merriest flocks that ever spread a wing.

On the way back to our Tuolumne camp, I enjoyed the scenery if possible more than when it first came to view. Every feature already seems familiar as if I had lived here always. I never weary gazing at the wonderful Cathedral. It has more individual character than any other rock or mountain I ever saw, excepting perhaps the Yosemite South Dome. The forests, too, seem kindly familiar, and the lakes and meadows and glad singing streams. I should like to dwell with them forever. Here with bread and water I should be content. Even if not allowed to roam and climb, tethered to a stake or tree in some meadow or grove, even then I should be content forever. Bathed in such beauty, watching the expressions ever varying on the faces of the mountains, watching the stars, which here have a glory that the lowlander never dreams of, watching the circling seasons, listening to the songs of the waters and winds and birds, would be endless pleasure. And what glorious cloudlands I should see, storms and calms,—a new heaven and a new earth every day, aye and new inhabitants. And how many visitors I should have. I feel sure I should not have one dull moment. And why should this appear extravagant? It is only common sense, a sign of health, genuine, natural, all-awake health. One would be at an endless Godful play, and what speeches and music and acting and scenery and lights!—sun, moon, stars, auroras. Creation just beginning, the morning stars "still singing together and all the sons of God shouting for joy."

Chapter IX

AUGUST 21. Have just returned from a fine wild excursion across the range to Mono Lake, by way of the Mono or Bloody Cañon Pass. Mr. Delaney has been good to me all summer, lending a helping, sympathizing hand at every opportunity, as if my wild notions and rambles and studies were his own. He is one of those remarkable California men who have been overflowed and denuded and remodeled by the excitements of the gold fields, like the Sierra landscapes by grinding ice, bringing the harder bosses and ridges of character into relief,—a tall, lean, big-boned, big-hearted Irishman, educated for a priest in Maynooth College,—lots of good in him, shining out now and then in this mountain light. Recognizing my love of wild places, he told me one evening that I ought to go through Bloody Cañon, for he was sure I should find it wild enough. He had not been there himself, he said, but had heard many of his mining friends speak of it as the wildest of all the Sierra passes. Of course I was glad to go. It lies just to the east of our camp and swoops down from the summit of the range to the edge of the Mono Desert, making a descent of about four thousand feet in a distance of about four miles. It was known and traveled as a pass by wild animals and the Indians long before its discovery by white men in the gold year of 1858, as is shown by old trails which come together at the head of it. The name may have been suggested by the red color of the metamorphic slates in which the cañon abounds, or by the blood stains on the rocks from the unfortunate animals that were compelled to slide and shuffle over the sharp-angled boulders.

Early in the morning I tied my notebook and some bread to my belt, and strode away full of eager hope, feeling that I was going to have a glorious revel. The glacier meadows that lay along my way served to soothe my morning speed, for the sod was full of blue gentians and daisies, kalmia and dwarf vaccinium, calling for recognition as old friends, and I had to stop many times to examine the shining rocks over which the ancient glacier had passed with tremendous pressure, polishing them so well that they reflected the sunlight like glass in some places, while fine striæ, seen clearly through a lens, indicated the direction in which the ice had flowed. On some of the sloping polished pavements abrupt steps occur, showing that occasionally large masses of the rock had given way before the glacial pressure, as well as small particles; moraines too, some scattered, others regular like long curving embankments and dams, occur here and there, giving the general surface of the region a young, new-made appearance. I watched the gradual dwarfing of the pines as I ascended, and the corresponding dwarfing of nearly all the rest of the vegetation. On the slopes of Mammoth Mountain, to the south of the pass, I saw many gaps in the woods reaching from the upper edge of the timber-line down to the level meadows, where avalanches of snow had descended, sweeping away every tree in their paths as well as the soil they were growing in, leaving the bed-rock bare. The trees are nearly all uprooted, but a few that had been extremely well anchored in clefts of the rock were broken off near the ground. It seems strange at first sight that trees that had been allowed to grow for a century or more undisturbed should in their old age be thus swished away at a stroke. Such avalanches can only occur under rare conditions of weather and snowfall. No doubt on some positions of the mountain slopes the inclination and smoothness of the surface is such that avalanches must occur every winter, or even after every heavy snowstorm, and of course no trees or even bushes can grow in their channels. I noticed a few clean-swept slopes of this kind. The uprooted trees that had grown in the pathway of what might be called "century avalanches" were piled in windrows, and tucked snugly against the wall-trees of the gaps, heads downward, excepting a few that were carried out into the open ground of the meadows, where the heads of the avalanches had stopped. Young pines, mostly the two-leaved and the white-barked, are already springing up in these cleared gaps. It would be interesting to ascertain the age of these saplings, for thus we should gain a fair approximation to the year that the great avalanches occurred. Perhaps most or all of them occurred the same winter. How glad I should be if free to pursue such studies!

Near the summit at the head of the pass I found a species
of dwarf willow lying perfectly flat on the ground, making a
nice, soft, silky gray carpet, not a single stem or branch more
than three inches high; but the catkins, which are now nearly
ripe, stand erect and make a close, nearly regular gray growth,
being larger than all the rest of the plants. Some of these
interesting dwarfs have only one catkin—willow bushes reduced to their lowest terms. I found patches of dwarf vaccinium also forming smooth carpets, closely pressed to the
ground or against the sides of stones, and covered with round
pink flowers in lavish abundance as if they had fallen from the
sky like hail. A little higher, almost at the very head of the
pass, I found the blue arctic daisy and purple-flowered bryanthus, the mountain's own darlings, gentle mountaineers face
to face with the sky, kept safe and warm by a thousand miracles, seeming always the finer and purer the wilder and
stormier their homes. The trees, tough and resiny, seem unable to go a step farther; but up and up, far above the tree-
line, these tender plants climb, cheerily spreading their gray
and pink carpets right up to the very edges of the snow-banks
in deep hollows and shadows. Here, too, is the familiar robin,
tripping on the flowery lawns, bravely singing the same cheery
song I first heard when a boy in Wisconsin newly arrived from
old Scotland. In this fine company sauntering enchanted, taking no heed of time, I at length entered the gate of the pass,
and the huge rocks began to close around me in all their
mysterious impressiveness. Just then I was startled by a lot of
queer, hairy, muffled creatures coming shuffling, shambling,
wallowing toward me as if they had no bones in their bodies.
Had I discovered them while they were yet a good way off, I
should have tried to avoid them. What a picture they made
contrasted with the others I had just been admiring. When I
came up to them, I found that they were only a band of Indians from Mono on their way to Yosemite for a load of
acorns. They were wrapped in blankets made of the skins of
sage-rabbits. The dirt on some of the faces seemed almost old
enough and thick enough to have a geological significance;
some were strangely blurred and divided into sections by
seams and wrinkles that looked like cleavage joints, and had
a worn abraded look as if they had lain exposed to the weather

for ages. I tried to pass them without stopping, but they wouldn't let me; forming a dismal circle about me, I was closely besieged while they begged whiskey or tobacco, and it was hard to convince them that I hadn't any. How glad I was to get away from the gray, grim crowd and see them vanish down the trail! Yet it seems sad to feel such desperate repulsion from one's fellow beings, however degraded. To prefer the society of squirrels and woodchucks to that of our own species must surely be unnatural. So with a fresh breeze and a hill or mountain between us I must wish them Godspeed and try to pray and sing with Burns, "It's coming yet, for a' that, that man to man, the warld o'er, shall brothers be for a' that."

How the day passed I hardly know. By the map I have come only about ten or twelve miles, though the sun is already low in the west, showing how long I must have lingered, observing, sketching, taking notes among the glaciated rocks and moraines and Alpine flower-beds.

At sundown the somber crags and peaks were inspired with the ineffable beauty of the alpenglow, and a solemn, awful stillness hushed everything in the landscape. Then I crept into a hollow by the side of a small lake near the head of the cañon, smoothed a sheltered spot, and gathered a few pine tassels for a bed. After the short twilight began to fade I kindled a sunny fire, made a tin cupful of tea, and lay down to watch the stars. Soon the night-wind began to flow from the snowy peaks overhead, at first only a gentle breathing, then gaining strength, in less than an hour rumbled in massive volume something like a boisterous stream in a boulder-choked channel, roaring and moaning down the cañon as if the work it had to do was tremendously important and fateful; and mingled with these storm tones were those of the waterfalls on the north side of the cañon, now sounding distinctly, now smothered by the heavier cataracts of air, making a glorious psalm of savage wildness. My fire squirmed and struggled as if ill at ease, for though in a sheltered nook, detached masses of icy wind often fell like icebergs on top of it, scattering sparks and coals, so that I had to keep well back to avoid being burned. But the big resiny roots and knots of the dwarf pine could neither be beaten out nor blown away, and the flames, now rushing up in long lances, now flattened and twisted on the rocky ground, roared as if trying to tell the storm stories of the trees they belonged to, as the light given out was telling the story of the sunshine they had gathered in centuries of summers.

The stars shone clear in the strip of sky between the huge dark cliffs; and as I lay recalling the lessons of the day, suddenly the full moon looked down over the cañon wall, her face apparently filled with eager concern, which had a startling effect, as if she had left her place in the sky and had come down to gaze on me alone, like a person entering one's bedroom. It was hard to realize that she was in her place in the sky, and was looking abroad on half the globe, land and sea, mountains, plains, lakes, rivers, oceans, ships, cities with their myriads of inhabitants sleeping and waking, sick and well. No, she seemed to be just on the rim of Bloody Cañon and looking only at me. This was indeed getting near to Nature. I remember watching the harvest moon rising above the oak trees in Wisconsin apparently as big as a cart-wheel and not farther than half a mile distant. With these exceptions I might say I never before had seen the moon, and this night she seemed so full of life and so near, the effect was marvelously impressive and made me forget the Indians, the great black rocks above me, and the wild uproar of the winds and waters making their way down the huge jagged gorge. Of course I slept but little and gladly welcomed the dawn over the Mono Desert. By the time I had made a cupful of tea the sunbeams were pouring through the cañon, and I set forth, gazing eagerly at the tremendous walls of red slates savagely hacked and scarred and apparently ready to fall in avalanches great enough to choke the pass and fill up the chain of lakelets. But soon its beauties came to view, and I bounded lightly from rock to rock, admiring the polished bosses shining in the slant sunshine with glorious effect in the general roughness of moraines and avalanche taluses, even toward the head of the cañon near the highest fountains of the ice. Here, too, are most of the lowly plant people seen yesterday on the other side of the divide now opening their beautiful eyes. None could fail to glory in Nature's tender care for them in so wild a place. The little ouzel is flitting from rock to rock along the rapid swirling Cañon Creek, diving for breakfast in icy pools, and merrily singing as if the huge rugged avalanche-swept gorge was the most delightful of all its mountain homes. Besides a high fall on the north wall of the cañon, apparently coming direct from the sky, there are many narrow cascades, bright silvery ribbons zigzagging down the red cliffs, tracing the diagonal cleavage joints of the metamorphic slates, now contracted and out of sight, now leaping from ledge to ledge in filmy sheets through which the sunbeams sift. And on the main Cañon Creek, to which all these are tributary, is a series of small falls, cascades, and rapids extending all the way down to the foot of the cañon, interrupted only by the lakes in which the tossed and beaten waters rest. One of the finest of the cascades is outspread on the face of a precipice, its waters separated into ribbon-like strips, and woven into a diamond-like pattern by tracing the cleavage joints of the rock, while tufts of bryanthus, grass, sedge, saxifrage form beautiful fringes. Who could imagine beauty so fine in so savage a place? Gardens are blooming in all sorts of nooks and hollows,—at the head alpine eriogonums, erigerons, saxifrages, gentians, cowania, bush primula; in the middle region larkspur, columbine, orthocarpus, castilleia, harebell, epilobium, violets, mints, yarrow; near the foot sunflowers, lilies, brier rose, iris, lonicera, clematis.

One of the smallest of the cascades, which I name the Bower Cascade, is in the lower region of the pass, where the vegetation is snowy and luxuriant. Wild rose and dogwood form dense masses overarching the stream, and out of this bower the creek, grown strong with many indashing tributaries, leaps forth into the light, and descends in a fluted curve thick-sown with crisp flashing spray. At the foot of the cañon there is a lake formed in part at least by the damming of the stream by a terminal moraine. The three other lakes in the cañon are in basins eroded from the solid rock, where the pressure of the glacier was greatest, and the most resisting portions of the basin rims are beautifully, tellingly polished. Below Moraine Lake at the foot of the cañon there are several old lake-basins lying between the large lateral moraines which extend out into the desert. These basins are now completely filled up by the material carried in by the streams, and changed to dry sandy flats covered mostly by grass and artemisia and sun-loving flowers. All these lower lake-basins were evidently formed by terminal moraine dams deposited where the receding glacier had lingered during short periods of less waste, or greater snowfall, or both.

Looking up the cañon from the warm sunny edge of the Mono plain my morning ramble seems a dream, so great is the change in the vegetation and climate. The lilies on the bank of Moraine Lake are higher than my head, and the sunshine is hot enough for palms. Yet the snow round the arctic gardens at the summit of the pass is plainly visible, only about four miles away, and between lie specimen zones of all the principal climates of the globe. In little more than an hour one may swoop down from winter to summer, from an Arctic to a torrid region, through as great changes of climate as one would encounter in traveling from Labrador to Florida.

The Indians I had met near the head of the cañon had camped at the foot of it the night before they made the ascent, and I found their fire still smoking on the side of a small tributary stream near Moraine Lake; and on the edge of what is called the Mono Desert, four or five miles from the lake, I came to a patch of elymus, or wild rye, growing in magnificent waving clumps six or eight feet high, bearing heads six to eight inches long. The crop was ripe, and Indian women were gathering the grain in baskets by bending down large handfuls, beating out the seed, and fanning it in the wind. The grains are about five eighths of an inch long, dark-colored and sweet. I fancy the bread made from it must be as good as wheat bread. A fine squirrelish employment this wild grain gathering seems, and the women were evidently enjoying it, laughing and chattering and looking almost natural, though most Indians I have seen are not a whit more natural in their lives than we civilized whites. Perhaps if I knew them better I should like them better. The worst thing about them is their uncleanliness. Nothing truly wild is unclean. Down on the shore of Mono Lake I saw a number of their flimsy huts on the banks of streams that dash swiftly into that dead sea,— mere brush tents where they lie and eat at their ease. Some of the men were feasting on buffalo berries, lying beneath the tall bushes now red with fruit. The berries are rather insipid, but they must needs be wholesome, since for days and weeks the Indians, it is said, eat nothing else. In the season they in like manner depend chiefly on the fat larvæ of a fly that breeds in the salt water of the lake, or on the big fat corrugated caterpillars of a species of silkworm that feeds on the leaves of the yellow pine. Occasionally a grand rabbit-drive is organized and hundreds are slain with clubs on the lake shore, chased and frightened into a dense crowd by dogs, boys, girls, men and women, and rings of sage brush fire, when of course they are quickly killed. The skins are made into blankets. In the autumn the more enterprising of the hunters bring in a good many deer, and rarely a wild sheep from the high peaks. Antelopes used to be abundant on the desert at the base of the interior mountain-ranges. Sage hens, grouse, and squirrels help to vary their wild diet of worms; pine nuts also from the small interesting *Pinus monophylla*, and good bread and good mush are made from acorns and wild rye. Strange to say, they seem to like the lake larvæ best of all. Long windrows are washed up on the shore, which they gather and dry like grain for winter use. It is said that wars, on account of encroachments on each other's worm-grounds, are of common occurrence among the various tribes and families. Each claims a certain marked portion of the shore. The pine nuts are delicious—large quantities are gathered every autumn. The tribes of the west flank of the range trade acorns for worms and pine nuts. The squaws carry immense loads on their backs across the rough passes and down the range, making journeys of about forty or fifty miles each way.

The desert around the lake is surprisingly flowery. In many places among the sage bushes I saw mentzelia, abronia, aster, bigelovia, and gilia, all of which seemed to enjoy the hot sunshine. The abronia, in particular, is a delicate, fragrant, and most charming plant.

Opposite the mouth of the cañon a range of volcanic cones extends southward from the lake, rising abruptly out of the desert like a chain of mountains. The largest of the cones are about twenty-five hundred feet high above the lake level, have well-formed craters, and all of them are evidently comparatively recent additions to the landscape. At a distance of a few miles they look like heaps of loose ashes that have never been

Mono Lake and volcanic cones, looking south

Highest Mono volcanic cones (near view)

blest by either rain or snow, but, for a' that and a' that, yellow pines are climbing their gray slopes, trying to clothe them and give beauty for ashes. A country of wonderful contrasts. Hot deserts bounded by snow-laden mountains,—cinders and ashes scattered on glacier-polished pavements,—frost and fire working together in the making of beauty. In the lake are several volcanic islands, which show that the waters were once mingled with fire.

Glad to get back to the green side of the mountains, though I have greatly enjoyed the gray east side and hope to see more of it. Reading these grand mountain manuscripts displayed through every vicissitude of heat and cold, calm and storm, upheaving volcanoes and down-grinding glaciers, we see that everything in Nature called destruction must be creation—a change from beauty to beauty.

Our glacier meadow camp north of the Soda Springs seems more beautiful every day. The grass covers all the ground though the leaves are thread-like in fineness, and in walking on the sod it seems like a plush carpet of marvelous richness and softness, and the purple panicles brushing against one's feet are not felt. This is a typical glacier meadow, occupying the basin of a vanished lake, very definitely bounded by walls of the arrowy two-leaved pines drawn up in a handsome orderly array like soldiers on parade. There are many other meadows of the same kind hereabouts imbedded in the woods. The main big meadows along the river are the same in general and extend with but little interruption for ten or twelve miles, but none I have seen are so finely finished and perfect as this one. It is richer in flowering plants than the prairies of Wisconsin and Illinois were when in all their wild glory. The showy flowers are mostly three species of gentian, a purple and yellow orthocarpus, a golden-rod or two, a small blue pentstemon almost like a gentian, potentilla, ivesia, pedicularis, white violet, kalmia, and bryanthus. There are no coarse weedy plants. Through this flowery lawn flows a stream silently gliding, swirling, slipping as if careful not to make the slightest noise. It is only about three feet wide in most places, widening here and there into pools six or eight feet in diameter with no apparent current, the banks bossily rounded by the down-curving mossy sod, grass panicles over-leaning like miniature pine trees, and rugs of bryanthus spreading here and there over sunken boulders. At the foot of the meadow the stream, rich with the juices of the plants it has refreshed, sings merrily down over shelving rock ledges on its way to the Tuolumne River. The sublime, massive Mount Dana and its companions, green, red, and white, loom impressively above the pines along the eastern horizon; a range or spur of gray rugged granite crags and mountains on the north; the curiously crested and battlemented Mount Hoffman on the west; and the Cathedral Range on the south with its grand Cathedral Peak, Cathedral Spires, Unicorn Peak, and several others, gray and pointed or massively rounded.

Chapter X

THE TUOLUMNE CAMP

AUGUST 22. Clouds none, cool west wind, slight hoarfrost on the meadows. Carlo is missing; have been seeking him all day. In the thick woods between camp and the river, among tall grass and fallen pines, I discovered a baby fawn. At first it seemed inclined to come to me; but when I tried to catch it, and got within a rod or two, it turned and walked softly away, choosing its steps like a cautious, stealthy, hunting cat. Then, as if suddenly called or alarmed, it began to buck and run like a grown deer, jumping high above the fallen trunks, and was soon out of sight. Possibly its mother may have called it, but I did not hear her. I don't think fawns ever leave the home thicket or follow their mothers until they are called or frightened. I am distressed about Carlo. There are several other camps and dogs not many miles from here, and I still hope to find him. He never left me before. Panthers are very rare here, and I don't think any of these cats would dare touch him. He knows bears too well to be caught by them, and as for Indians, they don't want him.

August 23. Cool, bright day, hinting Indian summer. Mr. Delaney has gone to the Smith Ranch, on the Tuolumne below Hetch-Hetchy Valley, thirty-five or forty miles from here, so I'll be alone for a week or more,—not really alone, for Carlo has come back. He was at a camp a few miles to the northwestward. He looked sheepish and ashamed when I asked him where he had been and why he had gone away without leave. He is now trying to get me to caress him and show signs of forgiveness. A wondrous wise dog. A great load is off my mind. I could not have left the mountains without him. He seems very glad to get back to me.

Rose and crimson sunset, and soon after the stars appeared the moon rose in most impressive majesty over the top of Mount Dana. I sauntered up the meadow in the white light. The jet-black tree-shadows were so wonderfully distinct and substantial looking, I often stepped high in crossing them, taking them for black charred logs.

August 24. Another charming day, warm and calm soon after sunrise, clouds only about .01,—faint, silky cirrus wisps, scarcely visible. Slight frost, Indian summerish, the mountains growing softer in outline and dreamy looking, their rough angles melted off, apparently. Sky at evening with fine, dark, subdued purple, almost like the evening purple of the San Joaquin plains in settled weather. The moon is now gazing over the summit of Dana. Glorious exhilarating air. I wonder if in all the world there is another mountain range of equal height blessed with weather so fine, and so openly kind and hospitable and approachable.

August 25. Cool as usual in the morning, quickly changing to the ordinary serene generous warmth and brightness. Toward evening the west wind was cool and sent us to the campfire. Of all Nature's flowery carpeted mountain halls none can be finer than this glacier meadow. Bees and butterflies seem as abundant as ever. The birds are still here, showing no sign of leaving for winter quarters though the frost must bring them to mind. For my part I should like to stay here all winter or all my life or even all eternity.

August 26. Frost this morning; all the meadow grass and some of the pine needles sparkling with irised crystals,—flowers of light. Large picturesque clouds, craggy like rocks, are piled on Mount Dana, reddish in color like the mountain itself; the sky for a few degrees around the horizon is pale purple, into which the pines dip their spires with fine effect. Spent the day as usual looking about me, watching the changing lights, the ripening autumn colors of the grass, seeds, late-blooming gentians, asters, goldenrods; parting the meadow grass here and there and looking down into the underworld of mosses and liverworts; watching the busy ants and beetles and other small people at work and play like squirrels and bears in a forest; studying the formation of lakes and meadows, moraines, mountain sculpture; making small beginnings in these directions, charmed by the serene beauty of everything.

The day has been extra cloudy, though bright on the whole, for the clouds were brighter than common. Clouds about .15, which in Switzerland would be considered extra clear. Probably more free sunshine falls on this majestic range than on

any other in the world I've ever seen or heard of. It has
the brightest weather, brightest glacier-polished rocks, the
greatest abundance of irised spray from its glorious waterfalls,
the brightest forests of silver firs and silver pines, more star-
shine, moonshine, and perhaps more crystal-shine than any
other mountain chain, and its countless mirror lakes, having
more light poured into them, glow and spangle most. And
how glorious the shining after the short summer showers and
after frosty nights when the morning sunbeams are pouring
through the crystals on the grass and pine needles, and how
ineffably spiritually fine is the morning-glow on the mountain-
tops and the alpenglow of evening. Well may the Sierra be
named, not the Snowy Range, but the Range of Light.

August 27. Clouds only .05,—mostly white and pink cumuli
over the Hoffman spur towards evening,—frosty morning.
Crystals grow in marvelous beauty and perfection of form
these still nights, every one built as carefully as the grandest
holiest temple, as if planned to endure forever.

Contemplating the lace-like fabric of streams outspread
over the mountains, we are reminded that everything is flowing—going somewhere, animals and so-called lifeless rocks as
well as water. Thus the snow flows fast or slow in grand
beauty-making glaciers and avalanches; the air in majestic
floods carrying minerals, plant leaves, seeds, spores, with
streams of music and fragrance; water streams carrying rocks
both in solution and in the form of mud particles, sand, pebbles, and boulders. Rocks flow from volcanoes like water from
springs, and animals flock together and flow in currents modified by stepping, leaping, gliding, flying, swimming, etc.
While the stars go streaming through space pulsed on and on
forever like blood globules in Nature's warm heart.

August 28. The dawn a glorious song of color. Sky absolutely cloudless. A fine crop of hoarfrost. Warm after ten
o'clock. The gentians don't mind the first frost though their
petals seem so delicate; they close every night as if going to
sleep, and awake fresh as ever in the morning sun-glory. The
grass is a shade browner since last week, but there are no
nipped wilted plants of any sort as far as I have seen. Butterflies and the grand host of smaller flies are benumbed every
night, but they hover and dance in the sunbeams over the

meadows before noon with no apparent lack of playful, joyful life. Soon they must all fall like petals in an orchard, dry and wrinkled, not a wing of all the mighty host left to tingle the air. Nevertheless new myriads will arise in the spring, rejoicing, exulting, as if laughing cold death to scorn.

August 29. Clouds about .05, slight frost. Bland serene Indian summer weather. Have been gazing all day at the mountains, watching the changing lights. More and more plainly are they clothed with light as a garment, white tinged with pale purple, palest during the midday hours, richest in the morning and evening. Everything seems consciously peaceful, thoughtful, faithfully waiting God's will.

August 30. This day just like yesterday. A few clouds motionless and apparently with no work to do beyond looking beautiful. Frost enough for crystal building,—glorious fields of ice-diamonds destined to last but a night. How lavish is Nature building, pulling down, creating, destroying, chasing every material particle from form to form, ever changing, ever beautiful.

Mr. Delaney arrived this morning. Felt not a trace of loneliness while he was gone. On the contrary, I never enjoyed grander company. The whole wilderness seems to be alive and familiar, full of humanity. The very stones seem talkative, sympathetic, brotherly. No wonder when we consider that we all have the same Father and Mother.

August 31. Clouds .05. Silky cirrus wisps and fringes so fine they almost escape notice. Frost enough for another crop of crystals on the meadows but none on the forests. The gentians, goldenrods, asters, etc., don't seem to feel it; neither petals nor leaves are touched though they seem so tender. Every day opens and closes like a flower, noiseless, effortless. Divine peace glows on all the majestic landscape like the silent enthusiastic joy that sometimes transfigures a noble human face.

September 1. Clouds .05—motionless, of no particular color—ornaments with no hint of rain or snow in them. Day all calm—another grand throb of Nature's heart, ripening late flowers and seeds for next summer, full of life and the thoughts and plans of life to come, and full of ripe and ready death beautiful as life, telling divine wisdom and goodness and immortality. Have been up Mount Dana, making haste to see as much as I can now that the time of departure is drawing nigh. The views from the summit reach far and wide, eastward over the Mono Lake and Desert; mountains beyond mountains looking strangely barren and gray and bare like heaps of ashes dumped from the sky. The lake, eight or ten miles in diameter, shines like a burnished disk of silver, no trees about its gray, ashy, cindery shores. Looking westward, the glorious forests are seen sweeping over countless ridges and hills, girdling domes and subordinate mountains, fringing in long curving lines the dividing ridges, and filling every hollow where the glaciers have spread soil-beds however rocky or smooth. Looking northward and southward along the axis of the range, you see the glorious array of high mountains, crags and peaks and snow, the fountain-heads of rivers that are flowing west to the sea through the famous Golden Gate, and east to hot salt lakes and deserts to evaporate and hurry back into the sky. Innumerable lakes are shining like eyes beneath heavy rock brows, bare or tree fringed, or imbedded in black forests.

One of the highest Mount Ritter fountains

Meadow openings in the woods seem as numerous as the lakes or perhaps more so. Far up the moraine-covered slopes and among crumbling rocks I found many delicate hardy plants, some of them still in flower. The best gains of this trip were the lessons of unity and interrelation of all the features of the landscape revealed in general views. The lakes and meadows are located just where the ancient glaciers bore heaviest at the foot of the steepest parts of their channels, and of course their longest diameters are approximately parallel with each other and with the belts of forests growing in long curving lines on the lateral and medial moraines, and in broad outspreading fields on the terminal beds deposited toward the end of the ice period when the glaciers were receding. The domes, ridges, and spurs also show the influence of glacial action in their forms, which approximately seem to be the forms of greatest strength with reference to the stress of oversweeping, past-sweeping, down-grinding ice-streams; survivals of the most resisting masses, or those most favorably situated. How interesting everything is! Every rock, mountain, stream, plant, lake, lawn, forest, garden, bird, beast, insect seems to call and invite us to come and learn something of its history and relationship. But shall the poor ignorant scholar be allowed to try the lessons they offer? It seems too great and good to be true. Soon I'll be going to the lowlands. The bread camp must soon be removed. If I had a few sacks of flour, an axe, and some matches, I would build a cabin of pine logs, pile up plenty of firewood about it and stay all winter to see the grand fertile snow-storms, watch the birds and animals that winter thus high, how they live, how the forests look snow-laden or buried, and how the avalanches look and sound on their way down the mountains. But now I'll have to go, for there is nothing to spare in the way of provisions. I'll surely be back, however, surely I'll be back. No other place has ever so overwhelmingly attracted me as this hospitable, Godful wilderness.

September 2. A grand, red, rosy, crimson day,—a perfect glory of a day. What it means I don't know. It is the first marked change from tranquil sunshine with purple mornings and evenings and still, white noons. There is nothing like a storm, however. The average cloudiness only about .08, and there is no sighing in the woods to betoken a big weather change. The sky was red in the morning and evening, the color not diffused like the ordinary purple glow, but loaded upon separate well-defined clouds that remained motionless, as if anchored around the jagged mountain-fenced horizon. A deep-red cap, bluffy around its sides, lingered a long time on Mount Dana and Mount Gibbs, drooping so low as to hide most of their bases, but leaving Dana's round summit free, which seemed to float separate and alone over the big crimson cloud. Mammoth Mountain, to the south of Gibbs and Bloody Cañon, striped and spotted with snow-banks and clumps of dwarf pine, was also favored with a glorious crimson cap, in the making of which there was no trace of economy— a huge bossy pile colored with a perfect passion of crimson that seemed important enough to be sent off to burn among the stars in majestic independence. One is constantly reminded of the infinite lavishness and fertility of Nature—inexhaustible abundance amid what seems enormous waste. And yet when we look into any of her operations that lie within reach of our minds, we learn that no particle of her material is wasted or worn out. It is eternally flowing from use to use, beauty to yet higher beauty; and we soon cease to lament waste and death, and rather rejoice and exult in the imperishable, unspendable wealth of the universe, and faithfully watch and wait the reappearance of everything that melts and fades and dies about us, feeling sure that its next appearance will be better and more beautiful than the last.

I watched the growth of these red-lands of the sky as eagerly as if new mountain ranges were being built. Soon the group of snowy peaks in whose recesses lie the highest fountains of the Tuolumne, Merced, and North Fork of the San Joaquin were decorated with majestic colored clouds like those already described, but more complicated, to correspond with the grand fountain-heads of the rivers they overshadowed. The Sierra Cathedral, to the south of camp, was overshadowed like Sinai. Never before noticed so fine a union of rock and cloud in form and color and substance, drawing earth and sky together as one; and so human is it, every feature and tint of color goes to one's heart, and we shout, exulting in wild enthusiasm as if all the divine show were our own. More and more, in a place like this, we feel ourselves part of wild Nature, kin to everything. Spent most of the day high up on the north rim of the valley, commanding views of the clouds in all their red glory spreading their wonderful light over all the basin, while the rocks and trees and small Alpine plants at my feet seemed hushed and thoughtful, as if they also were conscious spectators of the glorious new cloud-world.

Here and there, as I plodded farther and higher, I came to small garden-patches and ferneries just where one would naturally decide that no plant-creature could possibly live. But, as in the region about the head of Mono Pass and the top of Dana, it was in the wildest, highest places that the most beautiful and tender and enthusiastic plant-people were found. Again and again, as I lingered over these charming plants, I said, How came you here? How do you live through the winter? Our roots, they explained, reach far down the joints of the summer-warmed rocks, and beneath our fine snow mantle killing frosts cannot reach us, while we sleep away the dark half of the year dreaming of spring.

Ever since I was allowed entrance into these mountains I have been looking for cassiope, said to be the most beautiful and best loved of the heathworts, but, strange to say, I have not yet found it. On my high mountain walks I keep muttering, "Cassiope, cassiope." This name, as Calvinists say, is driven in upon me, notwithstanding the glorious host of plants that come about me uncalled as soon as I show myself. Cassiope seems the highest name of all the small mountain-heath people, and as if conscious of her worth, keeps out of my way. I must find her soon, if at all this year.

September 4. All the vast sky dome is clear, filled only with mellow Indian summer light. The pine and hemlock and fir cones are nearly ripe and are falling fast from morning to night, cut off and gathered by the busy squirrels. Almost all the plants have matured their seeds, their summer work done; and the summer crop of birds and deer will soon be able to follow their parents to the foothills and plains at the approach of winter, when the snow begins to fly.

September 5. No clouds. Weather cool, calm, bright as if no great thing was yet ready to be done. Have been sketching the North Tuolumne Church. The sunset gloriously colored.

September 6. Still another perfectly cloudless day, purple evening and morning, all the middle hours one mass of pure serene sunshine. Soon after sunrise the air grew warm, and there was no wind. One naturally halted to see what Nature intended to do. There is a suggestion of real Indian summer in the hushed brooding, faintly hazy weather. The yellow atmosphere, though thin, is still plainly of the same general character as that of eastern Indian summer. The peculiar mellowness is perhaps in part caused by myriads of ripe spores adrift in the sky.

Mr. Delaney now keeps up a solemn talk about the need of getting away from these high mountains, telling sad stories of flocks that perished in storms that broke suddenly into the midst of fine innocent weather like this we are now enjoying. "In no case," said he, "will I venture to stay so high and far back in the mountains as we now are later than the middle of this month, no matter how warm and sunny it may be." He would move the flock slowly at first, a few miles a day until the Yosemite Creek basin was reached and crossed, then while lingering in the heavy pine woods should the weather threaten he could hurry down to the foothills, where the snow never falls deep enough to smother a sheep. Of course I am anxious to see as much of the wilderness as possible in the few days left me, and I say again,—May the good time come when I can stay as long as I like with plenty of bread, far and free from trampling flocks, though I may well be thankful for this generous foodful inspiring summer. Anyhow we never know where we must go nor what guides we are to get,—men, storms, guardian angels, or sheep. Perhaps almost everybody in the least natural is guarded more than he is ever aware of. All the wilderness seems to be full of tricks and plans to drive and draw us up into God's Light.

Have been busy planning, and baking bread for at least one more good wild excursion among the high peaks, and surely none, however hopefully aiming at fortune or fame, ever felt so gloriously happily excited by the outlook.

September 7. Left camp at daybreak and made direct for Cathedral Peak, intending to strike eastward and southward from that point among the peaks and ridges at the heads of the Tuolumne, Merced, and San Joaquin Rivers. Down through the pine woods I made my way, across the Tuolumne River and meadows, and up the heavily timbered slope forming the south boundary of the upper Tuolumne basin, along the east side of Cathedral Peak, and up to its topmost spire, which I reached at noon, having loitered by the way to study the fine trees—two-leaved pine, mountain pine, albicaulis pine, silver fir, and the most charming, most graceful of all the evergreens, the mountain hemlock. High, cool, late-flowering meadows also detained me, and lakelets and avalanche tracks and huge quarries of moraine rocks above the forests.

All the way up from the Big Meadows to the base of the Cathedral the ground is covered with moraine material, the left lateral moraine of the great glacier that must have completely filled this upper Tuolumne basin. Higher there are several small terminal moraines of residual glaciers shoved forward at right angles against the grand simple lateral of the main Tuolumne Glacier. A fine place to study mountain sculpture and soil making. The view from the Cathedral Spires is very fine and telling in every direction. Innumerable peaks, ridges, domes, meadows, lakes, and woods; the forests extending in long curving lines and broad fields wherever the glaciers have left soil for them to grow on, while the sides of the highest mountains show a straggling dwarf growth clinging to rifts in the rocks apparently independent of soil. The dark heath-like growth on the Cathedral roof I found to be dwarf snow-pressed albicaulis pine, about three or four feet high, but very old looking. Many of them are bearing cones, and the noisy Clarke crow is eating the seeds, using his long bill like a woodpecker in digging them out of the cones. A good many flowers are still in bloom about the base of the peak, and even on the roof among the little pines, especially a woody yellow-flowered eriogonum and a handsome aster. The body of the Cathedral is nearly square, and the roof slopes are wonderfully regular and symmetrical, the ridge trending northeast and southwest. This direction has apparently been determined by structure joints in the granite. The gable on the northeast end is magnificent in size and simplicity, and at its base there is a big snow-bank protected by the shadow of the building. The front is adorned with many pinnacles and a tall spire of curious workmanship. Here too the

Glacier meadow strewn with moraine boulders, 10,000 feet above the sea (near Mount Dana)

Front of Cathedral Peak

joints in the rock are seen to have played an important part in determining their forms and size and general arrangement. The Cathedral is said to be about eleven thousand feet above the sea, but the height of the building itself above the level of the ridge it stands on is about fifteen hundred feet. A mile or so to the westward there is a handsome lake, and the glacier-polished granite about it is shining so brightly it is not easy in some places to trace the line between the rock and water, both shining alike. Of this lake with its silvery basin and bits of meadow and groves I have a fine view from the spires; also of Lake Tenaya, Cloud's Rest and the South Dome of Yosemite, Mount Starr King, Mount Hoffman, the Merced peaks, and the vast multitude of snowy fountain peaks extending far north and south along the axis of the range. No feature, however, of all the noble landscape as seen from here seems more wonderful than the Cathedral itself, a temple displaying Nature's best masonry and sermons in stones. How often I have gazed at it from the tops of hills and ridges, and through openings in the forests on my many short excursions, devoutly wondering, admiring, longing! This I may say is the first time I have been at church in California, led here at last, every door graciously opened for the poor lonely worshiper. In our best times everything turns into religion, all the world seems a church and the mountains altars. And lo, here at last in front of the Cathedral is blessed cassiope, ringing her thousands of sweet-toned bells, the sweetest church music I ever enjoyed. Listening, admiring, until late in the afternoon I compelled myself to hasten away eastward back of rough, sharp, spiry, splintery peaks, all of them granite like the Cathedral, sparkling with crystals—feldspar, quartz, hornblende, mica, tourmaline. Had a rather difficult walk and creep across an immense snow and ice cliff which gradually increased in steepness as I advanced until it was almost impassable. Slipped on a dangerous place, but managed to stop by digging my heels into the thawing surface just on the brink of a yawning ice gulf. Camped beside a little pool and a group of crinkled dwarf pines; and as I sit by the fire trying to write notes the shallow pool seems fathomless with the infinite starry heavens in it, while the onlooking rocks and trees, tiny shrubs and daisies and sedges, brought forward in the fire-glow, seem full of thought as if about to speak aloud and tell all their wild stories. A marvelously impressive meeting in which every one has something worth while to tell. And beyond the fire-beams out in the solemn darkness, how impressive is the music of a choir of rills singing their way down from the snow to the river! And when we call to mind that thousands of these rejoicing rills are assembled in each one of the main streams, we wonder the less that our Sierra rivers are songful all the way to the sea.

Mt   Ritter

View of Upper Tuolumne Valley

About sundown saw a flock of dun grayish sparrows going to roost in crevices of a crag above the big snow-field. Charming little mountaineers! Found a species of sedge in flower within eight or ten feet of a snow-bank. Judging by the looks of the ground, it can hardly have been out in the sunshine much longer than a week, and it is likely to be buried again in fresh snow in a month or so, thus making a winter about ten months long, while spring, summer, and autumn are crowded and hurried into two months. How delightful it is to be alone here! How wild everything is—wild as the sky and as pure! Never shall I forget this big, divine day—the Cathedral and its thousands of cassiope bells, and the landscapes around them, and this camp in the gray crags above the woods, with its stars and streams and snow.

September 8. Day of climbing, scrambling, sliding on the peaks around the highest source of the Tuolumne and Merced. Climbed three of the most commanding of the mountains, whose names I don't know; crossed streams and huge beds of ice and snow more than I could keep count of. Neither could I keep count of the lakes scattered on tablelands and in the cirques of the peaks, and in chains in the cañons, linked together by the streams—a tremendously wild gray wilderness of hacked, shattered crags, ridges, and peaks, a few clouds drifting over and through the midst of them as if looking for work. In general views all the immense round landscape seems raw and lifeless as a quarry, yet the most charming flowers were found rejoicing in countless nooks and garden-like patches everywhere. I must have done three or four days' climbing work in this one. Limbs perfectly tireless until near sundown, when I descended into the main upper Tuolumne valley at the foot of Mount Lyell, the camp still eight or ten miles distant. Going up through the pine woods past the Soda Springs Dome in the dark, where there is much fallen timber, and when all the excitement of seeing things was wanting, I was tired. Arrived at the main camp at nine o'clock, and soon was sleeping sound as death.

Chapter XI

SEPTEMBER 9. Weariness rested away and I feel eager and ready for another excursion a month or two long in the same wonderful wilderness. Now, however, I must turn toward the lowlands, praying and hoping Heaven will shove me back again.

The most telling thing learned in these mountain excursions is the influence of cleavage joints on the features sculptured from the general mass of the range. Evidently the denudation has been enormous, while the inevitable outcome is subtle balanced beauty. Comprehended in general views, the features of the wildest landscape seem to be as harmoniously related as the features of a human face. Indeed, they look human and radiate spiritual beauty, divine thought, however covered and concealed by rock and snow.

Mr. Delaney has hardly had time to ask me how I enjoyed my trip, though he has facilitated and encouraged my plans all summer, and declares I'll be famous some day, a kind guess that seems strange and incredible to a wandering wilderness-lover with never a thought or dream of fame while humbly trying to trace and learn and enjoy Nature's lessons.

The camp stuff is now packed on the horses, and the flock is headed for the home ranch. Away we go, down through the pines, leaving the lovely lawn where we have camped so long. I wonder if I'll ever see it again. The sod is so tough and close it is scarcely at all injured by the sheep. Fortunately they are not fond of silky glacier meadow grass. The day is perfectly clear, not a cloud or the faintest hint of a cloud is visible, and there is no wind. I wonder if in all the world, at a height of nine thousand feet, weather so steadily, faithfully calm and bright and hospitable may anywhere else be found. We are going away fearing destructive storms, though it is difficult to conceive weather changes so great.

Though the water is now low in the river, the usual difficulty occurred in getting the flock across it. Every sheep seemed to be invincibly determined to die any sort of dry death rather than wet its feet. Carlo has learned the sheep business as perfectly as the best shepherd, and it is interesting to watch his intelligent efforts to push or frighten the silly creatures into the water. They had to be fairly crowded and shoved over the bank; and when at last one crossed because it could not push its way back, the whole flock suddenly plunged in headlong together, as if the river was the only desirable part of the world. Aside from mere money profit one would rather herd wolves than sheep. As soon as they clambered up the opposite bank, they began baaing and feeding as if nothing unusual had happened. We crossed the meadows and drove slowly up the south rim of the valley through the same woods I had passed on my way to Cathedral Peak, and camped for the night by the side of a small pond on top of the big lateral moraine.

September 10. In the morning at daybreak not one of the two thousand sheep was in sight. Examining the tracks, we discovered that they had been scattered, perhaps by a bear. In a few hours all were found and gathered into one flock again. Had fine view of a deer. How graceful and perfect in every way it seemed as compared with the silly, dusty, tousled sheep! From the high ground hereabouts had another grand view to the northward—a heaving, swelling sea of domes and round-backed ridges fringed with pines, and bounded by innumerable sharp-pointed peaks, gray and barren-looking, though so full of beautiful life. Another day of the calm, cloudless kind, purple in the morning and evening. The evening glow has been very marked for the last two or three weeks. Perhaps the "zodiacal light."

September 11. Cloudless. Slight frost. Calm. Fairly started downhill, and now are camped at the west end meadows of Lake Tenaya—a charming place. Lake smooth as glass, mirroring its miles of glacier-polished pavements and bold mountain walls. Find aster still in flower. Here is about the upper limit of the dwarf form of the goldcup oak,—eight thousand feet above sea-level,—reaching about two thousand feet higher than the California black oak (*Quercus Californica*). Lovely evening, the lake reflections after dark marvelously impressive.

September 12. Cloudless day, all pure sun-gold. Among the

magnificent silver firs once more, within two miles of the brink of Yosemite, at the famous Portuguese bear camp. Chaparral of goldcup oak, manzanita, and ceanothus abundant hereabouts, wanting about the Tuolumne meadows, although the elevation is but little higher there. The two-leaved pine, though far more abundant about the Tuolumne meadow region, reaches its greatest size on stream-sides hereabouts and around meadows that are rather boggy. All the best dry ground is taken by the magnificent silver fir, which here reaches its greatest size and forms a well-defined belt. A glorious tree. Have fine bed of its boughs to-night.

September 13. Camp this evening at Yosemite Creek, close to the stream, on a little sand flat near our old camp-ground. The vegetation is already brown and yellow and dry; the creek almost dry also. The slender form of the two-leaved pine on its banks is, I think, the handsomest I have anywhere seen. It might easily pass at first sight for a distinct species, though surely only a variety (*Murrayana*), due to crowded and rapid growth on good soil. The yellow pine is as variable, or perhaps more so. The form here and a thousand feet higher, on crumbling rocks, is broad branching, with closely furrowed, reddish bark, large cones, and long leaves. It is one of the hardiest of pines, and has wonderful vitality. The tassels of long, stout needles shining silvery in the sun, when the wind is blowing them all in the same direction, is one of the most splendid spectacles these glorious Sierra forests have to show. This variety of *Pinus ponderosa* is regarded as a distinct species, *Pinus Jeffreyi*, by some botanists. The basin of this famous Yosemite stream is extremely rocky,—seems fairly to be paved with domes like a street with big cobblestones. I wonder if I shall ever be allowed to explore it. It draws me so strongly, I would make any sacrifice to try to read its lessons. I thank God for this glimpse of it. The charms of these mountains are beyond all common reason, unexplainable and mysterious as life itself.

September 14. Nearly all day in magnificent fir forest, the top branches laden with superb erect gray cones shining with beads of pure balsam. The squirrels are cutting them off at a great rate. Bump, bump, I hear them falling, soon to be gathered and stored for winter bread. Those that chance to be left by the industrious harvesters drop the scales and bracts when fully ripe, and it is fine to see the purple-winged seeds flying in swirling, merry-looking flocks seeking their fortunes. The bole and dead limbs of nearly every tree in the main forest-belt are ornamented by conspicuous tufts and strips of a yellow lichen.

Camped for the night at Cascade Creek, near the Mono Trail crossing. Manzanita berries now ripe. Cloudiness to-day about .10. The sunset very rich, flaming purple and crimson showing gloriously through the aisles of the woods.

September 15. The weather pure gold, cloudiness about .05, white cirrus flects and pencilings around the horizon. Move two or three miles and camp at Tamarack Flat. Wandering in the woods here back of the pines which bound the meadows, I found very noble specimens of the magnificent silver fir, the tallest about two hundred and forty feet high and five feet in diameter four feet from the ground.

September 16. Crawled slowly four or five miles to-day through the glorious forest to Crane Flat, where we are camped for the night. The forests we so admired in summer seem still more beautiful and sublime in this mellow autumn light. Lovely starry night, the tall, spiring tree-tops relieved in jet black against the sky. I linger by the fire, loath to go to bed.

September 17. Left camp early. Ran over the Tuolumne divide and down a few miles to a grove of sequoias that I had heard of, directed by the Don. They occupy an area of perhaps less than a hundred acres. Some of the trees are noble, colossal old giants, surrounded by magnificent sugar pines and Douglas spruces. The perfect specimens not burned or broken are singularly regular and symmetrical, though not at all conventional, showing infinite variety in general unity and harmony; the noble shafts with rich purplish brown fluted bark, free of limbs for one hundred and fifty feet or so, ornamented here and there with leafy rosettes; main branches of the oldest trees very large, crooked and rugged, zigzagging stiffly outward seemingly lawless, yet unexpectedly stooping just at the right distance from the trunk and dissolving in dense bossy masses of branchlets, thus making a regular though greatly varied outline,—a cylinder of leafy, outbulging spray masses, terminating in a noble dome, that may be recognized while yet far off upheaved against the sky above the dark bed of pines and firs and spruces, the king of all conifers, not only in size but in sublime majesty of behavior and port. I found a black, charred stump about thirty feet in diameter and eighty or ninety feet high—a venerable, impressive old monument of a tree that in its prime may have been the monarch of the grove; seedlings and saplings growing up here and there, thrifty and hopeful, giving no hint of the dying out of the species. Not any unfavorable change of climate, but only fire, threatens the existence of these noblest of God's trees. Sorry I was not able to get a count of the old monument's annual rings.

Camp this evening at Hazel Green, on the broad back of the dividing ridge near our old camp-ground when we were on the way up the mountains in the spring. This ridge has the finest sugar-pine groves and finest manzanita and ceanothus thickets I have yet found on all this wonderful summer journey.

September 18. Made a long descent on the south side of the divide to Brown's Flat, the grand forests now left above us, though the sugar pine still flourishes fairly well, and with the yellow pine, libocedrus, and Douglas spruce, makes forests that would be considered most wonderful in any other part of the world.

The Indians here, with great concern, pointed to an old garden patch on the flat and told us to keep away from it. Perhaps some of their tribe are buried here.

September 19. Camped this evening at Smith's Mill, on the first broad mountain bench or plateau reached in ascending the range, where pines grow large enough for good lumber. Here wheat, apples, peaches, and grapes grow, and we were treated to wine and apples. The wine I didn't like, but Mr. Delaney and the Indian driver and the shepherd seemed to think the stuff divine. Compared to sparkling Sierra water fresh from the heavens, it seemed a dull, muddy, stupid drink. But the apples, best of fruits, how delicious they were—fit for gods or men.

On the way down from Brown's Flat we stopped at Bower Cave, and I spent an hour in it—one of the most novel and interesting of all Nature's underground mansions. Plenty of sunlight pours into it through the leaves of the four maple trees growing in its mouth, illuminating its clear, calm pool and marble chambers,—a charming place, ravishingly beautiful, but the accessible parts of the walls sadly disfigured with names of vandals.

September 20. The weather still golden and calm, but hot. We are now in the foot-hills, and all the conifers are left behind except the gray Sabine pine. Camped at the Dutch Boy's Ranch, where there are extensive barley fields now showing nothing save dusty stubble.

September 21. A terribly hot, dusty, sun-burned day, and as nothing was to be gained by loitering where the flock could find nothing to eat save thorny twigs and chaparral, we made a long drive, and before sundown reached the home ranch on the yellow San Joaquin plain.

September 22. The sheep were let out of the corral one by one, this morning, and counted, and strange to say, after all their adventurous wanderings in bewildering rocks and brush and streams, scattered by bears, poisoned by azalea, kalmia, alkali, all are accounted for. Of the two thousand and fifty that left the corral in the spring lean and weak, two thousand and twenty-five have returned fat and strong. The losses are: ten killed by bears, one by a rattlesnake, one that had to be killed after it had broken its leg on a boulder slope, and one that ran away in blind terror on being accidentally separated from the flock,—thirteen all told. Of the other twelve doomed never to return, three were sold to ranchmen and nine were made camp mutton.

Here ends my forever memorable first High Sierra excursion. I have crossed the Range of Light, surely the brightest and best of all the Lord has built; and rejoicing in its glory, I gladly, gratefully, hopefully pray I may see it again.

THE MOUNTAINS
OF CALIFORNIA

Contents

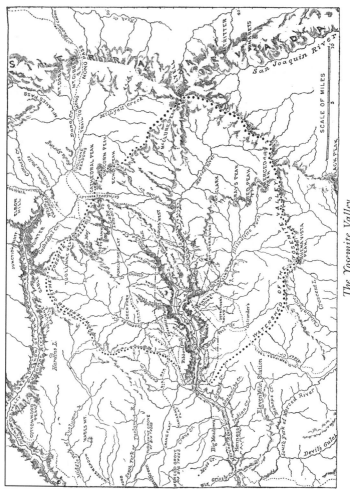

The Yosemite Valley

Chapter I

THE SIERRA NEVADA

Go where you may within the bounds of California, mountains are ever in sight, charming and glorifying every landscape. Yet so simple and massive is the topography of the State in general views, that the main central portion displays only one valley, and two chains of mountains which seem almost perfectly regular in trend and height: the Coast Range on the west side, the Sierra Nevada on the east. These two ranges coming together in curves on the north and south inclose a magnificent basin, with a level floor more than 400 miles long, and from 35 to 60 miles wide. This is the grand Central Valley of California, the waters of which have only one outlet to the sea through the Golden Gate. But with this general simplicity of features there is great complexity of hidden detail. The Coast Range, rising as a grand green barrier against the ocean, from 2000 to 8000 feet high, is composed of innumerable forest-crowned spurs, ridges, and rolling hill-waves which inclose a multitude of smaller valleys; some looking out through long, forest-lined vistas to the sea; others, with but few trees, to the Central Valley; while a thousand others yet smaller are embosomed and concealed in mild, round-browed hills, each with its own climate, soil, and productions.

Making your way through the mazes of the Coast Range to the summit of any of the inner peaks or passes opposite San Francisco, in the clear springtime, the grandest and most telling of all California landscapes is outspread before you. At your feet lies the great Central Valley glowing golden in the sunshine, extending north and south farther than the eye can reach, one smooth, flowery, lake-like bed of fertile soil. Along its eastern margin rises the mighty Sierra, miles in height, reposing like a smooth, cumulous cloud in the sunny sky, and so gloriously colored, and so luminous, it seems to be not clothed with light, but wholly composed of it, like the wall of some celestial city. Along the top, and extending a good way down, you see a pale, pearl-gray belt of snow; and below it a

315

belt of blue and dark purple, marking the extension of the forests; and along the base of the range a broad belt of rose-purple and yellow, where lie the miner's goldfields and the foot-hill gardens. All these colored belts blending smoothly make a wall of light ineffably fine, and as beautiful as a rain-bow, yet firm as adamant.

When I first enjoyed this superb view, one glowing April day, from the summit of the Pacheco Pass, the Central Valley, but little trampled or plowed as yet, was one furred, rich sheet of golden compositæ, and the luminous wall of the mountains shone in all its glory. Then it seemed to me the Sierra should be called not the Nevada, or Snowy Range, but the Range of Light. And after ten years spent in the heart of it, rejoicing and wondering, bathing in its glorious floods of light, seeing the sunbursts of morning among the icy peaks, the noonday radiance on the trees and rocks and snow, the flush of the alpenglow, and a thousand dashing waterfalls with their mar-velous abundance of irised spray, it still seems to me above all others the Range of Light, the most divinely beautiful of all the mountain-chains I have ever seen.

The Sierra is about 500 miles long, 70 miles wide, and from 7000 to nearly 15,000 feet high. In general views no mark of man is visible on it, nor anything to suggest the richness of the life it cherishes, or the depth and grandeur of its sculpture. None of its magnificent forest-crowned ridges rises much above the general level to publish its wealth. No great valley or lake is seen, or river, or group of well-marked features of any kind, standing out in distinct pictures. Even the summit-peaks, so clear and high in the sky, seem comparatively smooth and featureless. Nevertheless, glaciers are still at work in the shadows of the peaks, and thousands of lakes and meadows shine and bloom beneath them, and the whole range is fur-rowed with cañons to a depth of from 2000 to 5000 feet, in which once flowed majestic glaciers, and in which now flow and sing a band of beautiful rivers.

Though of such stupendous depth, these famous cañons are not raw, gloomy, jagged-walled gorges, savage and inacces-sible. With rough passages here and there they still make de-lightful pathways for the mountaineer, conducting from the fertile lowlands to the highest icy fountains, as a kind of mountain streets full of charming life and light, graded and sculptured by the ancient glaciers, and presenting, throughout all their courses, a rich variety of novel and attractive scenery, the most attractive that has yet been discovered in the mountain-ranges of the world.

In many places, especially in the middle region of the western flank of the range, the main cañons widen into spacious valleys or parks, diversified like artificial landscape-gardens, with charming groves and meadows, and thickets of blooming bushes, while the lofty, retiring walls, infinitely varied in form and sculpture, are fringed with ferns, flowering-plants of many species, oaks, and evergreens, which find anchorage on a thousand narrow steps and benches; while the whole is enlivened and made glorious with rejoicing streams that come dancing and foaming over the sunny brows of the cliffs to join the shining river that flows in tranquil beauty down the middle of each one of them.

The walls of these park valleys of the Yosemite kind are made up of rocks mountains in size, partly separated from each other by narrow gorges and side-cañons; and they are so sheer in front, and so compactly built together on a level floor, that, comprehensively seen, the parks they inclose look like immense halls or temples lighted from above. Every rock seems to glow with life. Some lean back in majestic repose; others, absolutely sheer, or nearly so, for thousands of feet, advance their brows in thoughtful attitudes beyond their companions, giving welcome to storms and calms alike, seemingly conscious yet heedless of everything going on about them, awful in stern majesty, types of permanence, yet associated with beauty of the frailest and most fleeting forms; their feet set in pine-groves and gay emerald meadows, their brows in the sky; bathed in light, bathed in floods of singing water, while snow-clouds, avalanches, and the winds shine and surge and wreathe about them as the years go by, as if into these mountain mansions Nature had taken pains to gather her choicest treasures to draw her lovers into close and confiding communion with her.

Here, too, in the middle region of deepest cañons are the grandest forest-trees, the Sequoia, king of conifers, the noble Sugar and Yellow Pines, Douglas Spruce, Libocedrus, and the

Silver Firs, each a giant of its kind, assembled together in one and the same forest, surpassing all other coniferous forests in the world, both in the number of its species and in the size and beauty of its trees. The winds flow in melody through their colossal spires, and they are vocal everywhere with the songs of birds and running water. Miles of fragrant ceanothus and manzanita bushes bloom beneath them, and lily gardens and meadows, and damp, ferny glens in endless variety of fragrance and color, compelling the admiration of every observer. Sweeping on over ridge and valley, these noble trees extend a continuous belt from end to end of the range, only slightly interrupted by sheer-walled cañons at intervals of about fifteen and twenty miles. Here the great burly brown bears delight to roam, harmonizing with the brown boles of the trees beneath which they feed. Deer, also, dwell here, and find food and shelter in the ceanothus tangles, with a multitude of smaller people. Above this region of giants, the trees grow smaller until the utmost limit of the timber line is reached on the stormy mountain-slopes at a height of from ten to twelve thousand feet above the sea, where the Dwarf Pine is so lowly and hard beset by storms and heavy snow, it is pressed into flat tangles, over the tops of which we may easily walk. Below the main forest belt the trees likewise diminish in size, frost and burning drouth repressing and blasting alike.

The rose-purple zone along the base of the range comprehends nearly all the famous gold region of California. And here it was that miners from every country under the sun assembled in a wild, torrent-like rush to seek their fortunes. On the banks of every river, ravine, and gully they have left their marks. Every gravel- and boulder-bed has been desperately riddled over and over again. But in this region the pick and shovel, once wielded with savage enthusiasm, have been laid away, and only quartz-mining is now being carried on to any considerable extent. The zone in general is made up of low, tawny, waving foot-hills, roughened here and there with brush and trees, and outcropping masses of slate, colored gray and red with lichens. The smaller masses of slate, rising abruptly from the dry, grassy sod in leaning slabs, look like ancient tombstones in a deserted burying-ground. In early spring, say from February to April, the whole of this foot-hill belt is a paradise of bees and flowers. Refreshing rains then fall freely, birds are busy building their nests, and the sunshine is balmy and delightful. But by the end of May the soil, plants, and sky seem to have been baked in an oven. Most of the plants crumble to dust beneath the foot, and the ground is full of cracks; while the thirsty traveler gazes with eager longing through the burning glare to the snowy summits looming like hazy clouds in the distance.

The trees, mostly *Quercus Douglasii* and *Pinus Sabiniana*, thirty to forty feet high, with thin, pale-green foliage, stand far apart and cast but little shade. Lizards glide about on the rocks enjoying a constitution that no drouth can dry, and ants in amazing numbers, whose tiny sparks of life seem to burn the brighter with the increasing heat, ramble industriously in long trains in search of food. Crows, ravens, magpies—friends in distress—gather on the ground beneath the best shade-trees, panting with drooping wings and bills wide open, scarce a note from any of them during the midday hours. Quails, too, seek the shade during the heat of the day about tepid pools in the channels of the larger mid-river streams. Rabbits scurry from thicket to thicket among the ceanothus bushes, and occasionally a long-eared hare is seen cantering gracefully across the wider openings. The nights are calm and dewless during the summer, and a thousand voices proclaim the abundance of life, notwithstanding the desolating effect of dry sunshine on the plants and larger animals. The hylas make a delightfully pure and tranquil music after sunset; and coyotes, the little, despised dogs of the wilderness, brave, hardy fellows, looking like withered wisps of hay, bark in chorus for hours. Mining-towns, most of them dead, and a few living ones with bright bits of cultivation about them, occur at long intervals along the belt, and cottages covered with climbing roses, in the midst of orange and peach orchards, and sweet-scented hay-fields in fertile flats where water for irrigation may be had. But they are mostly far apart, and make scarce any mark in general views.

Every winter the High Sierra and the middle forest region get snow in glorious abundance, and even the foot-hills are at times whitened. Then all the range looks like a vast beveled wall of purest marble. The rough places are then made smooth, the death and decay of the year is covered gently and kindly, and the ground seems as clean as the sky. And though silent in its flight from the clouds, and when it is taking its place on rock, or tree, or grassy meadow, how soon the gentle snow finds a voice! Slipping from the heights, gathering in avalanches, it booms and roars like thunder, and makes a glorious show as it sweeps down the mountain-side, arrayed in long, silken streamers and wreathing, swirling films of crystal dust.

The north half of the range is mostly covered with floods of lava, and dotted with volcanoes and craters, some of them recent and perfect in form, others in various stages of decay. The south half is composed of granite nearly from base to summit, while a considerable number of peaks, in the middle of the range, are capped with metamorphic slates, among which are Mounts Dana and Gibbs to the east of Yosemite Valley. Mount Whitney, the culminating point of the range near its southern extremity, lifts its helmet-shaped crest to a height of nearly 14,700 feet. Mount Shasta, a colossal volcanic cone, rises to a height of 14,440 feet at the northern extremity, and forms a noble landmark for all the surrounding region within a radius of a hundred miles. Residual masses of volcanic rocks occur throughout most of the granitic southern portion also, and a considerable number of old volcanoes on the flanks, especially along the eastern base of the range near Mono Lake and southward. But it is only to the northward that the entire range, from base to summit, is covered with lava.

From the summit of Mount Whitney only granite is seen. Innumerable peaks and spires but little lower than its own storm-beaten crags rise in groups like forest-trees, in full view, segregated by cañons of tremendous depth and ruggedness. On Shasta nearly every feature in the vast view speaks of the old volcanic fires. Far to the northward, in Oregon, the icy volcanoes of Mount Pitt and the Three Sisters rise above the dark evergreen woods. Southward innumerable smaller craters and cones are distributed along the axis of the range and on each flank. Of these, Lassen's Butte is the highest, being nearly 11,000 feet above sea-level. Miles of its flanks are reeking and bubbling with hot springs, many of them so boisterous and sulphurous they seem ever ready to become spouting geysers like those of the Yellowstone.

The Cinder Cone near marks the most recent volcanic eruption in the Sierra. It is a symmetrical truncated cone about 700 feet high, covered with gray cinders and ashes, and has a regular unchanged crater on its summit, in which a few small Two-leaved Pines are growing. These show that the age of the cone is not less than eighty years. It stands between two lakes, which a short time ago were one. Before the cone was built, a flood of rough vesicular lava was poured into the lake, cutting it in two, and, overflowing its banks, the fiery flood advanced into the pine-woods, overwhelming the trees in its way, the charred ends of some of which may still be seen projecting from beneath the snout of the lava-stream where it came to rest. Later still there was an eruption of ashes and loose obsidian cinders, probably from the same vent, which, besides forming the Cinder Cone, scattered a heavy shower over the surrounding woods for miles to a depth of from six inches to several feet.

The history of this last Sierra eruption is also preserved in the traditions of the Pitt River Indians. They tell of a fearful time of darkness, when the sky was black with ashes and smoke that threatened every living thing with death, and that when at length the sun appeared once more it was red like blood.

Less recent craters in great numbers roughen the adjacent region; some of them with lakes in their throats, others overgrown with trees and flowers, Nature in these old hearths and firesides having literally given beauty for ashes. On the northwest side of Mount Shasta there is a subordinate cone about 3000 feet below the summit, which has been active subsequent to the breaking up of the main ice-cap that once covered the mountain, as is shown by its comparatively unwasted crater and the streams of unglaciated lava radiating from it. The main summit is about a mile and a half in diameter, bounded by small crumbling peaks and ridges, among which we seek in vain for the outlines of the ancient crater.

These ruinous masses, and the deep glacial grooves that flute the sides of the mountain, show that it has been considerably lowered and wasted by ice; how much we have no sure means of knowing. Just below the extreme summit hot sulphurous gases and vapor issue from irregular fissures, mixed with spray derived from melting snow, the last feeble expression of the mighty force that built the mountain. Not in one great convulsion was Shasta given birth. The crags of the summit and the sections exposed by the glaciers down the sides display enough of its internal framework to prove that comparatively long periods of quiescence intervened between many distinct eruptions, during which the cooling lavas ceased to flow, and became permanent additions to the bulk of the growing mountain. With alternate haste and deliberation eruption succeeded eruption till the old volcano surpassed even its present sublime height.

Standing on the icy top of this, the grandest of all the fire-mountains of the Sierra, we can hardly fail to look forward to its next eruption. Gardens, vineyards, homes have been planted confidingly on the flanks of volcanoes which, after remaining steadfast for ages, have suddenly blazed into violent action, and poured forth overwhelming floods of fire. It is known that more than a thousand years of cool calm have intervened between violent eruptions. Like gigantic geysers spouting molten rock instead of water, volcanoes work and rest, and we have no sure means of knowing whether they are dead when still, or only sleeping.

Along the western base of the range a telling series of sedimentary rocks containing the early history of the Sierra are now being studied. But leaving for the present these first chapters, we see that only a very short geological time ago, just before the coming on of that winter of winters called the glacial period, a vast deluge of molten rocks poured from many a chasm and crater on the flanks and summit of the range, filling lake basins and river channels, and obliterating nearly every existing feature on the northern portion. At length these all-destroying floods ceased to flow. But while the great volcanic cones built up along the axis still burned and smoked, the whole Sierra passed under the domain of ice and snow. Then over the bald, featureless, fire-blackened mountains, glaciers began to crawl, covering them from the summits to the sea with a mantle of ice; and then with infinite deliberation the work went on of sculpturing the range anew. These mighty agents of erosion, halting never through un-numbered centuries, crushed and ground the flinty lavas and granites beneath their crystal folds, wasting and building until in the fullness of time the Sierra was born again, brought to light nearly as we behold it to-day, with glaciers and snow-crushed pines at the top of the range, wheat-fields and orange-groves at the foot of it.

This change from icy darkness and death to life and beauty was slow, as we count time, and is still going on, north and south, over all the world wherever glaciers exist, whether in the form of distinct rivers, as in Switzerland, Norway, the mountains of Asia, and the Pacific Coast; or in continuous mantling folds, as in portions of Alaska, Greenland, Franz-Joseph-Land, Nova Zembla, Spitzbergen, and the lands about the South Pole. But in no country, as far as I know, may these majestic changes be studied to better advantage than in the plains and mountains of California.

Toward the close of the glacial period, when the snow-clouds became less fertile and the melting waste of sunshine became greater, the lower folds of the ice-sheet in California, discharging fleets of icebergs into the sea, began to shallow and recede from the lowlands, and then move slowly up the flanks of the Sierra in compliance with the changes of climate. The great white mantle on the mountains broke up into a series of glaciers more or less distinct and river-like, with many tributaries, and these again were melted and divided into still smaller glaciers, until now only a few of the smallest residual topmost branches of the grand system exist on the cool slopes of the summit peaks.

Plants and animals, biding their time, closely followed the retiring ice, bestowing quick and joyous animation on the new-born landscapes. Pine-trees marched up the sun-warmed moraines in long, hopeful files, taking the ground and establishing themselves as soon as it was ready for them; brown-spiked sedges fringed the shores of the new-born lakes; young rivers roared in the abandoned channels of the glaciers; flowers bloomed around the feet of the great burnished domes,—while with quick fertility mellow beds of soil, settling and warming, offered food to multitudes of Nature's waiting children, great and small, animals as well as plants; mice, squirrels, marmots, deer, bears, elephants, etc. The ground burst into bloom with magical rapidity, and the young forests into bird-song: life in every form warming and sweetening and growing richer as the years passed away over the mighty Sierra so lately suggestive of death and consummate desolation only.

It is hard without long and loving study to realize the magnitude of the work done on these mountains during the last glacial period by glaciers, which are only streams of closely compacted snow-crystals. Careful study of the phenomena presented goes to show that the pre-glacial condition of the range was comparatively simple: one vast wave of stone in which a thousand mountains, domes, cañons, ridges, etc., lay concealed. And in the development of these Nature chose for a tool not the earthquake or lightning to rend and split asunder, not the stormy torrent or eroding rain, but the tender snow-flowers noiselessly falling through unnumbered centuries, the offspring of the sun and sea. Laboring harmoniously in united strength they crushed and ground and wore away the rocks in their march, making vast beds of soil, and at the same time developed and fashioned the landscapes into the delightful variety of hill and dale and lordly mountain that mortals call beauty. Perhaps more than a mile in average depth has the range been thus degraded during the last glacial period,—a quantity of mechanical work almost inconceivably great. And our admiration must be excited again and again as we toil and study and learn that this vast job of rockwork, so far-reaching in its influences, was done by agents so fragile and small as are these flowers of the mountain clouds. Strong only by force of numbers, they carried away entire mountains, particle by particle, block by block, and cast them into the sea; sculptured, fashioned, modeled all the range, and developed its predestined beauty. All these new Sierra landscapes were evidently predestined, for the physical structure of the rocks on which the features of the scenery depend was acquired while they lay at least a mile deep below the pre-glacial surface. And it was while these features were taking form in the depths of the range, the particles of the rocks marching to their appointed places in the dark with reference to the coming beauty, that the particles of icy vapor in the sky marching to the same music assembled to bring them to the light. Then, after their grand task was done, these bands of snow-flowers, these mighty glaciers, were melted and removed as if of no more importance than dew destined to last but an hour. Few, however, of Nature's agents have left monuments so noble and enduring as they. The great granite domes a mile high, the cañons as deep, the noble peaks, the Yosemite valleys, these, and indeed nearly all other features of the Sierra scenery, are glacier monuments.

Contemplating the works of these flowers of the sky, one may easily fancy them endowed with life: messengers sent down to work in the mountain mines on errands of divine love. Silently flying through the darkened air, swirling, glinting, to their appointed places, they seem to have taken counsel together, saying, "Come, we are feeble; let us help one another. We are many, and together we will be strong. Marching in close, deep ranks, let us roll away the stones from these mountain sepulchers, and set the landscapes free. Let us uncover these clustering domes. Here let us carve a lake basin; there, a Yosemite Valley; here, a channel for a river with fluted steps and brows for the plunge of songful cataracts. Yonder let us spread broad sheets of soil, that man and beast may be fed; and here pile trains of boulders for pines and giant Sequoias. Here make ground for a meadow; there, for a garden and grove, making it smooth and fine for small daisies and violets and beds of heathy bryanthus, spicing it well with crystals, garnet feldspar, and zircon." Thus and so on it has oftentimes seemed to me sang and planned and labored the hearty snow-flower crusaders; and nothing that I can write can possibly exaggerate the grandeur and beauty of their work. Like morning mist they have vanished in sunshine, all save the few small companies that still linger on the coolest mountain-sides, and, as residual glaciers, are still busily at work completing the last of the lake basins, the last beds of soil, and the sculpture of some of the highest peaks.

Chapter II

THE GLACIERS

OF the small residual glaciers mentioned in the preceding chapter, I have found sixty-five in that portion of the range lying between latitude 36° 30′ and 39°. They occur singly or in small groups on the north sides of the peaks of the High Sierra, sheltered beneath broad frosty shadows, in amphitheaters of their own making, where the snow, shooting down from the surrounding heights in avalanches, is most abundant. Over two thirds of the entire number lie between latitude 37° and 38°, and form the highest fountains of the San Joaquin, Merced, Tuolumne, and Owen's rivers.

The glaciers of Switzerland, like those of the Sierra, are mere wasting remnants of mighty ice-floods that once filled the great valleys and poured into the sea. So, also, are those of Norway, Asia, and South America. Even the grand continuous mantles of ice that still cover Greenland, Spitzbergen, Nova Zembla, Franz-Joseph-Land, parts of Alaska, and the south polar region are shallowing and shrinking. Every glacier in the world is smaller than it once was. All the world is growing warmer, or the crop of snow-flowers is diminishing. But in contemplating the condition of the glaciers of the world, we must bear in mind while trying to account for the changes going on that the same sunshine that wastes them builds them. Every glacier records the expenditure of an enormous amount of sun-heat in lifting the vapor for the snow of which it is made from the ocean to the mountains, as Tyndall strikingly shows.

The number of glaciers in the Alps, according to the Schlagintweit brothers, is 1100, of which 100 may be regarded as primary, and the total area of ice, snow, and *névé* is estimated at 1177 square miles, or an average for each glacier of little more than one square mile. On the same authority, the average height above sea-level at which they melt is about 7414 feet. The Grindelwald glacier descends below 4000 feet, and one of the Mont Blanc glaciers reaches nearly as low a point. One of the largest of the Himalaya glaciers on the head waters of the Ganges does not, according to Captain Hodgson, descend below 12,914 feet. The largest of the Sierra glaciers on Mount Shasta descends to within 9500 feet of the level of the sea, which, as far as I have observed, is the lowest point reached by any glacier within the bounds of California, the average height of all being not far from 11,000 feet.

The changes that have taken place in the glacial conditions of the Sierra from the time of greatest extension is well illustrated by the series of glaciers of every size and form extending along the mountains of the coast to Alaska. A general exploration of this instructive region shows that to the north of California, through Oregon and Washington, groups of active glaciers still exist on all the high volcanic cones of the Cascade Range,—Mount Pitt, the Three Sisters, Mounts Jefferson, Hood, St. Helens, Adams, Rainier, Baker, and others,—some of them of considerable size, though none of them approach the sea. Of these mountains Rainier, in Washington, is the highest and iciest. Its dome-like summit, between 14,000 and 15,000 feet high, is capped with ice, and eight glaciers, seven to twelve miles long, radiate from it as a center, and form the sources of the principal streams of the State. The lowest-descending of this fine group flows through beautiful forests to within 3500 feet of the sea-level, and sends forth a river laden with glacier mud and sand. On through British Columbia and southeastern Alaska the broad, sustained mountain-chain, extending along the coast, is generally glacier-bearing. The upper branches of nearly all the main cañons and fiords are occupied by glaciers, which gradually increase in size, and descend lower until the high region between Mount Fairweather and Mount St. Elias is reached, where a considerable number discharge into the waters of the ocean. This is preëminently the ice-land of Alaska and of the entire Pacific Coast.

Northward from here the glaciers gradually diminish in size and thickness, and melt at higher levels. In Prince William Sound and Cook's Inlet many fine glaciers are displayed, pouring from the surrounding mountains; but to the north of latitude 62° few, if any, glaciers remain, the ground being mostly low and the snowfall light. Between latitude 56° and 60° there are probably more than 5000 glaciers, not counting the smallest. Hundreds of the largest size descend through the forests to the level of the sea, or near it, though as far as my own observations have reached, after a pretty thorough examination of the region, not more than twenty-five discharge icebergs into the sea. All the long high-walled fiords into which these great glaciers of the first class flow are of course crowded with icebergs of every conceivable form, which are detached with thundering noise at intervals of a few minutes from an imposing ice-wall that is thrust forward into deep water. But these Pacific Coast icebergs are small as compared with those of Greenland and the Antarctic region, and only a few of them escape from the intricate system of channels, with which this portion of the coast is fringed, into the open sea. Nearly all of them are swashed and drifted by wind and tide back and forth in the fiords until finally melted by the ocean water, the sunshine, the warm winds, and the copious rains of summer. Only one glacier on the coast, observed by Prof. Russell, discharges its bergs directly into the open sea, at Icy Cape, opposite Mount St. Elias. The southernmost of the glaciers that reach the sea occupies a narrow, picturesque fiord about twenty miles to the northwest of the mouth of the Stikeen River, in latitude 56° 50'. The fiord is called by the natives "Hutli," or Thunder Bay, from the noise made by the discharge of the icebergs. About one degree farther north there are four of these complete glaciers, discharging at the heads of the long arms of Holkam Bay. At the head of the Tahkoo Inlet, still farther north, there is one; and at the head and around the sides of Glacier Bay, trending in a general northerly direction from Cross Sound in latitude 58° to 59°, there are seven of these complete glaciers pouring bergs into the bay and its branches, and keeping up an eternal thundering. The largest of this group, the Muir, has upward of 200 tributaries, and a width below the confluence of the main tributaries of about twenty-five miles. Between the west side of this icy bay and the ocean all the ground, high and low, excepting the peaks of the Fairweather Range, is covered with a mantle of ice from 1000 to probably 3000 feet thick, which discharges by many distinct mouths.

This fragmentary ice-sheet, and the immense glaciers about Mount St. Elias, together with the multitude of separate river-like glaciers that load the slopes of the coast mountains, evidently once formed part of a continuous ice-sheet that flowed over all the region hereabouts, and only a comparatively short time ago extended as far southward as the mouth of the Strait of Juan de Fuca, probably farther. All the islands of the Alexander Archipelago, as well as the headlands and promontories of the mainland, display telling traces of this great mantle that are still fresh and unmistakable. They all have the forms of the greatest strength with reference to the action of a vast rigid press of oversweeping ice from the north and northwest, and their surfaces have a smooth, rounded, over-rubbed appearance, generally free from angles. The intricate labyrinth of canals, channels, straits, passages, sounds, narrows, etc., between the islands, and extending into the mainland, of course manifest in their forms and trends and general characteristics the same subordination to the grinding action of universal glaciation as to their origin, and differ from the islands and banks of the fiords only in being portions of the pre-glacial margin of the continent more deeply eroded, and therefore covered by the ocean waters which flowed into them as the ice was melted out of them. The formation and extension of fiords in this manner is still going on, and may be witnessed in many places in Glacier Bay, Yakutat Bay, and adjacent regions. That the domain of the sea is being extended over the land by the wearing away of its shores, is well known, but in these icy regions of Alaska, and even as far south as Vancouver Island, the coast rocks have been so short a time exposed to wave-action they are but little wasted as yet. In these regions the extension of the sea effected by its own action in post-glacial time is scarcely appreciable as compared with that effected by ice-action.

Traces of the vanished glaciers made during the period of greater extension abound on the Sierra as far south as latitude 36°. Even the polished rock surfaces, the most evanescent of glacial records, are still found in a wonderfully perfect state of preservation on the upper half of the middle portion of the range, and form the most striking of all the glacial phenomena. They occur in large irregular patches in the summit and middle regions, and though they have been subjected to the action of the weather with its corroding storms for thousands of years, their mechanical excellence is such that they still reflect the sunbeams like glass, and attract the attention of every observer. The attention of the mountaineer is seldom arrested by moraines, however regular and high they may be, or by cañons, however deep, or by rocks, however noble in form and sculpture; but he stoops and rubs his hands admiringly on the shining surfaces and tries hard to account for their mysterious smoothness. He has seen the snow descending in avalanches, but concludes this cannot be the work of snow, for he finds it where no avalanches occur. Nor can water have done it, for he sees this smoothness glowing on the sides and tops of the highest domes. Only the winds of all the agents he knows seem capable of flowing in the directions indicated by the scoring. Indians, usually so little curious about geological phenomena, have come to me occasionally and asked me, "What makeum the ground so smooth at Lake Tenaya?" Even horses and dogs gaze wonderingly at the strange brightness of the ground, and smell the polished spaces and place their feet cautiously on them when they come to them for the first time, as if afraid of sinking. The most perfect of the polished pavements and walls lie at an elevation of from 7000 to 9000 feet above the sea, where the rock is compact silicious granite. Small dim patches may be found as low as 3000 feet on the driest and most enduring portions of sheer walls with a southern exposure, and on compact swelling bosses partially protected from rain by a covering of large boulders. On the north half of the range the striated and polished surfaces are less common, not only because this part of the chain is lower, but because the surface rocks are chiefly porous lavas subject to comparatively rapid waste. The ancient moraines also, though well preserved on most of the south half of the range, are nearly obliterated to the northward, but their material is found scattered and disintegrated.

A similar blurred condition of the superficial records of glacial action obtains throughout most of Oregon, Washington, British Columbia, and Alaska, due in great part to the action of excessive moisture. Even in southeastern Alaska, where the most extensive glaciers on the continent are, the more evanescent of the traces of their former greater extension, though comparatively recent, are more obscure than those of the ancient California glaciers where the climate is drier and the rocks more resisting.

These general views of the glaciers of the Pacific Coast will enable my readers to see something of the changes that have taken place in California, and will throw light on the residual glaciers of the High Sierra.

Prior to the autumn of 1871 the glaciers of the Sierra were unknown. In October of that year I discovered the Black Mountain Glacier in a shadowy amphitheater between Black and Red Mountains, two of the peaks of the Merced group. This group is the highest portion of a spur that straggles out from the main axis of the range in the direction of Yosemite Valley. At the time of this interesting discovery I was exploring the *névé* amphitheaters of the group, and tracing the courses of the ancient glaciers that once poured from its ample fountains through the Illilouette Basin and the Yosemite Valley, not expecting to find any active glaciers so far south in the land of sunshine.

Beginning on the northwestern extremity of the group, I explored the chief tributary basins in succession, their moraines, roches moutonnées, and splendid glacier pavements, taking them in regular succession without any reference to the time consumed in their study. The monuments of the tributary that poured its ice from between Red and Black Mountains I found to be the most interesting of them all; and when I saw its magnificent moraines extending in majestic curves from the spacious amphitheater between the mountains, I was exhilarated with the work that lay before me. It was one of the golden days of the Sierra Indian summer, when the rich sunshine glorifies every landscape however rocky and cold, and suggests anything rather than glaciers. The path of the vanished glacier was warm now, and shone in many places as if washed with silver. The tall pines growing on the moraines stood transfigured in the glowing light, the poplar groves on the levels of the basin were masses of orange-yellow, and the late-blooming goldenrods added gold to gold. Pushing on over my rosy glacial highway, I passed lake after lake set in solid basins of granite, and many a thicket and meadow watered by a stream that issues from the amphitheater and links the lakes together; now wading through plushy bogs knee-deep in yellow and purple sphagnum; now passing over bare rock. The main lateral moraines that bounded the view on either hand are from 100 to nearly 200 feet high, and about as regular as artificial embankments, and covered with a superb growth of Silver Fir and Pine. But this garden and forest luxuriance was speedily left behind. The trees were dwarfed as I ascended; patches of the alpine bryanthus and cassiope began to appear, and arctic willows pressed into flat carpets by the winter snow. The lakelets, which a few miles down the valley were so richly embroidered with flowery meadows, had here, at an elevation of 10,000 feet, only small brown mats of carex, leaving bare rocks around more than half their shores. Yet amid this alpine suppression the Mountain Pine bravely tossed his storm-beaten branches on the ledges and buttresses of Red Mountain, some specimens being over 100 feet high, and 24 feet in circumference, seemingly as fresh and vigorous as the giants of the lower zones.

Evening came on just as I got fairly within the portal of the main amphitheater. It is about a mile wide, and a little less than two miles long. The crumbling spurs and battlements of Red Mountain bound it on the north, the somber, rudely sculptured precipices of Black Mountain on the south, and a hacked, splintery *col*, curving around from mountain to mountain, shuts it in on the east.

I chose a camping-ground on the brink of one of the lakes where a thicket of Hemlock Spruce sheltered me from the night wind. Then, after making a tin-cupful of tea, I sat by my camp-fire reflecting on the grandeur and significance of the glacial records I had seen. As the night advanced the mighty rock walls of my mountain mansion seemed to come nearer, while the starry sky in glorious brightness stretched across like a ceiling from wall to wall, and fitted closely down into all the spiky irregularities of the summits. Then, after a long fireside rest and a glance at my note-book, I cut a few leafy branches for a bed, and fell into the clear, death-like sleep of the tired mountaineer.

Early next morning I set out to trace the grand old glacier that had done so much for the beauty of the Yosemite region back to its farthest fountains, enjoying the charm that every explorer feels in Nature's untrodden wildernesses. The voices of the mountains were still asleep. The wind scarce stirred the pine-needles. The sun was up, but it was yet too cold for the birds and the few burrowing animals that dwell here. Only the stream, cascading from pool to pool, seemed to be wholly awake. Yet the spirit of the opening day called to action. The sunbeams came streaming gloriously through the jagged openings of the *col*, glancing on the burnished pavements and lighting the silvery lakes, while every sun-touched rock burned white on its edges like melting iron in a furnace. Passing round the north shore of my camp lake I followed the central stream past many cascades from lakelet to lakelet. The scenery became more rigidly arctic, the Dwarf Pines and Hemlocks disappeared, and the stream was bordered with icicles. As the sun rose higher rocks were loosened on shattered portions of the cliffs, and came down in rattling avalanches, echoing wildly from crag to crag.

The main lateral moraines that extend from the jaws of the amphitheater into the Illilouette Basin are continued in straggling masses along the walls of the amphitheater, while separate boulders, hundreds of tons in weight, are left stranded here and there out in the middle of the channel. Here, also, I observed a series of small terminal moraines ranged along the south wall of the amphitheater, corresponding in size and form with the shadows cast by the highest portions. The meaning of this correspondence between moraines and shadows was afterward made plain. Tracing the stream back to the last of its chain of lakelets, I noticed a deposit of fine gray mud on the bottom except where the force of the entering current had prevented its settling. It looked like the mud worn from a grindstone, and I at once suspected its glacial origin, for the stream that was carrying it came gurgling out of the base of a raw moraine that seemed in process of formation. Not a plant or weather-stain was visible on its rough, unsettled surface. It is from 60 to over 100 feet high, and plunges forward at an angle of 38°. Cautiously picking my way, I gained the top of the moraine and was delighted to see a small but well characterized glacier swooping down from the gloomy precipices of Black Mountain in a finely graduated curve to the moraine on which I stood. The compact ice appeared on all the lower portions of the glacier, though gray with dirt and stones embedded in it. Farther up the ice disappeared beneath coarse granulated snow. The surface of the glacier was further characterized by dirt bands and the outcropping edges of the blue veins, showing the laminated structure of the ice. The uppermost crevasse, or "bergschrund," where the *névé* was attached to the mountain, was from 12 to 14 feet wide, and was bridged in a few places by the remains of snow avalanches. Creeping along the edge of the schrund, holding on with be-numbed fingers, I discovered clear sections where the bedded structure was beautifully revealed. The surface snow, though sprinkled with stones shot down from the cliffs, was in some places almost pure, gradually becoming crystalline and chang-ing to whitish porous ice of different shades of color, and this again changing at a depth of 20 or 30 feet to blue ice, some of the ribbon-like bands of which were nearly pure, and blended with the paler bands in the most gradual and delicate manner imaginable. A series of rugged zigzags enabled me to make my way down into the weird under-world of the cre-vasse. Its chambered hollows were hung with a multitude of clustered icicles, amid which pale, subdued light pulsed and shimmered with indescribable loveliness. Water dripped and tinkled overhead, and from far below came strange, solemn murmurings from currents that were feeling their way through veins and fissures in the dark. The chambers of a glacier are perfectly enchanting, notwithstanding one feels out of place in their frosty beauty. I was soon cold in my shirt-sleeves, and the leaning wall threatened to engulf me; yet it was hard to leave the delicious music of the water and the lovely light. Coming again to the surface, I noticed boulders of every size on their journeys to the terminal moraine—jour-neys of more than a hundred years, without a single stop, night or day, winter or summer.

The sun gave birth to a network of sweet-voiced rills that ran gracefully down the glacier, curling and swirling in their shining channels, and cutting clear sections through the po-rous surface-ice into the solid blue, where the structure of the glacier was beautifully illustrated.

The series of small terminal moraines which I had observed in the morning, along the south wall of the amphitheater, correspond in every way with the moraine of this glacier, and their distribution with reference to shadows was now understood. When the climatic changes came on that caused the melting and retreat of the main glacier that filled the amphitheater, a series of residual glaciers were left in the cliff shadows, under the protection of which they lingered, until they formed the moraines we are studying. Then, as the snow became still less abundant, all of them vanished in succession, except the one just described; and the cause of its longer life is sufficiently apparent in the greater area of snow-basin it drains, and its more perfect protection from wasting sunshine. How much longer this little glacier will last depends, of course, on the amount of snow it receives from year to year, as compared with melting waste.

After this discovery, I made excursions over all the High Sierra, pushing my explorations summer after summer, and discovered that what at first sight in the distance looked like extensive snow-fields, were in great part glaciers, busily at work completing the sculpture of the summit-peaks so grandly blocked out by their giant predecessors.

On August 21, I set a series of stakes in the Maclure Glacier, near Mount Lyell, and found its rate of motion to be little more than an inch a day in the middle, showing a great contrast to the Muir Glacier in Alaska, which, near the front, flows at a rate of from five to ten feet in twenty-four hours.

Mount Shasta has three glaciers, but Mount Whitney, although it is the highest mountain in the range, does not now cherish a single glacier. Small patches of lasting snow and ice occur on its northern slopes, but they are shallow, and present no well marked evidence of glacial motion. Its sides, however, are scored and polished in many places by the action of its ancient glaciers that flowed east and west as tributaries of the great glaciers that once filled the valleys of the Kern and Owen's rivers.

Chapter III

THE SNOW

T HE first snow that whitens the Sierra, usually falls about the end of October or early in November, to a depth of a few inches, after months of the most charming Indian summer weather imaginable. But in a few days, this light covering mostly melts from the slopes exposed to the sun and causes but little apprehension on the part of mountaineers who may be lingering among the high peaks at this time. The first general winter storm that yields snow that is to form a lasting portion of the season's supply, seldom breaks on the mountains before the end of November. Then, warned by the sky, cautious mountaineers, together with the wild sheep, deer, and most of the birds and bears, make haste to the lowlands or foot-hills; and burrowing marmots, mountain beavers, wood-rats, and such people go into winter quarters, some of them not again to see the light of day until the general awakening and resurrection of the spring in June or July. The first heavy fall is usually from about two to four feet in depth. Then, with intervals of splendid sunshine, storm succeeds storm, heaping snow on snow, until thirty to fifty feet has fallen. But on account of its settling and compacting, and the almost constant waste from melting and evaporation, the average depth actually found at any time seldom exceeds ten feet in the forest region, or fifteen feet along the slopes of the summit peaks.

Even during the coldest weather evaporation never wholly ceases, and the sunshine that abounds between the storms is sufficiently powerful to melt the surface more or less through all the winter months. Waste from melting also goes on to some extent on the bottom from heat stored up in the rocks, and given off slowly to the snow in contact with them, as is shown by the rising of the streams on all the higher regions after the first snowfall, and their steady sustained flow all winter.

The greater portion of the snow deposited around the lofty summits of the range falls in small crisp flakes and broken crystals, or, when accompanied by strong winds and low temperature, the crystals, instead of being locked together in their fall to form tufted flakes, are beaten and broken into meal and fine dust. But down in the forest region the greater portion comes gently to the ground, light and feathery, some of the flakes in mild weather being nearly an inch in diameter, and it is evenly distributed and kept from drifting to any great extent by the shelter afforded by the large trees. Every tree during the progress of gentle storms is loaded with fairy bloom at the coldest and darkest time of year, bending the branches, and hushing every singing needle. But as soon as the storm is over, and the sun shines, the snow at once begins to shift and settle and fall from the branches in miniature avalanches, and the white forest soon becomes green again. The snow on the ground also settles and thaws every bright day, and freezes at night, until it becomes coarsely granulated, and loses every trace of its rayed crystalline structure, and then a man may walk firmly over its frozen surface as if on ice. The forest region up to an elevation of 7000 feet is usually in great part free from snow in June, but at this time the higher regions are still heavy-laden, and are not touched by spring weather to any considerable extent before the middle or end of July.

One of the most striking effects of the snow on the mountains is the burial of the rivers and small lakes.

> As the snaw fa's in the river
> A moment white, then lost forever,

sang Burns, in illustrating the fleeting character of human pleasure. The first snowflakes that fall into the Sierra rivers vanish thus suddenly; but in great storms, when the temperature is low, the abundance of the snow at length chills the water nearly to the freezing-point, and then, of course, it ceases to melt and consume the snow so suddenly. The falling flakes and crystals form cloud-like masses of blue sludge, which are swept forward with the current and carried down to warmer climates many miles distant, while some are lodged against logs and rocks and projecting points of the banks, and last for days, piled high above the level of the water, and show white again, instead of being at once "lost forever," while the rivers themselves are at length lost for months during the snowy period. The snow is first built out from the banks in bossy, over-curling drifts, compacting and cementing until the streams are spanned. They then flow in the dark beneath a continuous covering across the snowy zone, which is about thirty miles wide. All the Sierra rivers and their tributaries in these high regions are thus lost every winter, as if another glacial period had come on. Not a drop of running water is to be seen excepting at a few points where large falls occur, though the rush and rumble of the heavier currents may still be heard. Toward spring, when the weather is warm during the day and frosty at night, repeated thawing and freezing and new layers of snow render the bridging-masses dense and firm, so that one may safely walk across the streams, or even lead a horse across them without danger of falling through. In June the thinnest parts of the winter ceiling, and those most ex-posed to sunshine, begin to give way, forming dark, rugged-edged, pit-like sinks, at the bottom of which the rushing water may be seen. At the end of June only here and there may the mountaineer find a secure snow-bridge. The most lasting of the winter bridges, thawing from below as well as from above, because of warm currents of air passing through the tunnels, are strikingly arched and sculptured; and by the occasional freezing of the oozing, dripping water of the ceiling they be-come brightly and picturesquely icy. In some of the reaches, where there is a free margin, we may walk through them. Small skylights appearing here and there, these tunnels are not very dark. The roaring river fills all the arching way with im-pressively loud reverberating music, which is sweetened at times by the ouzel, a bird that is not afraid to go wherever a stream may go, and to sing wherever a stream sings.

All the small alpine pools and lakelets are in like manner obliterated from the winter landscapes, either by being first frozen and then covered by snow, or by being filled in by avalanches. The first avalanche of the season shot into a lake basin may perhaps find the surface frozen. Then there is a grand crashing of breaking ice and dashing of waves mingled with the low, deep booming of the avalanche. Detached masses of the invading snow, mixed with fragments of ice, drift about in sludgy, island-like heaps, while the main body of it

forms a talus with its base wholly or in part resting on the
bottom of the basin, as controlled by its depth and the size
of the avalanche. The next avalanche, of course, encroaches
still farther, and so on with each in succession until the entire
basin may be filled and its water sponged up or displaced. This
huge mass of sludge, more or less mixed with sand, stones,
and perhaps timber, is frozen to a considerable depth, and
much sun-heat is required to thaw it. Some of these unfortunate lakelets are not clear of ice and snow until near the end
of summer. Others are never quite free, opening only on the
side opposite the entrance of the avalanches. Some show only
a narrow crescent of water lying between the shore and sheer
bluffs of icy compacted snow, masses of which breaking off
float in front like icebergs in a miniature Arctic Ocean, while
the avalanche heaps leaning back against the mountains look
like small glaciers. The frontal cliffs are in some instances quite
picturesque, and with the berg-dotted waters in front of them
lighted with sunshine are exceedingly beautiful. It often happens that while one side of a lake basin is hopelessly snow-
buried and frozen, the other, enjoying sunshine, is adorned
with beautiful flower-gardens. Some of the smaller lakes are
extinguished in an instant by a heavy avalanche either of rocks
or snow. The rolling, sliding, ponderous mass entering on one
side sweeps across the bottom and up the opposite side, dis-
placing the water and even scraping the basin clean, and shoving the accumulated rocks and sediments up the farther bank
and taking full possession. The dislodged water is in part absorbed, but most of it is sent around the front of the avalanche
and down the channel of the outlet, roaring and hurrying as
if frightened and glad to escape.

SNOW-BANNERS

The most magnificent storm phenomenon I ever saw, surpassing in showy grandeur the most imposing effects of
clouds, floods, or avalanches, was the peaks of the High Sierra,
back of Yosemite Valley, decorated with snow-banners. Many
of the starry snow-flowers, out of which these banners are
made, fall before they are ripe, while most of those that do

attain perfect development as six-rayed crystals glint and chafe against one another in their fall through the frosty air, and are broken into fragments. This dry fragmentary snow is still further prepared for the formation of banners by the action of the wind. For, instead of finding rest at once, like the snow which falls into the tranquil depths of the forests, it is rolled over and over, beaten against rock-ridges, and swirled in pits and hollows, like boulders, pebbles, and sand in the pot-holes of a river, until finally the delicate angles of the crystals are worn off, and the whole mass is reduced to dust. And whenever storm-winds find this prepared snow-dust in a loose condition on exposed slopes, where there is a free upward sweep to leeward, it is tossed back into the sky, and borne onward from peak to peak in the form of banners or cloudy drifts, according to the velocity of the wind and the conformation of the slopes up or around which it is driven. While thus flying through the air, a small portion makes good its escape, and remains in the sky as vapor. But far the greater part, after being driven into the sky again and again, is at length locked fast in bossy drifts, or in the wombs of glaciers, some of it to remain silent and rigid for centuries before it is finally melted and sent singing down the mountain-sides to the sea.

Yet, notwithstanding the abundance of winter snow-dust in the mountains, and the frequency of high winds, and the length of time the dust remains loose and exposed to their action, the occurrence of well-formed banners is, for causes we shall hereafter note, comparatively rare. I have seen only one display of this kind that seemed in every way perfect. This was in the winter of 1873, when the snow-laden summits were swept by a wild "norther." I happened at the time to be wintering in Yosemite Valley, that sublime Sierra temple where every day one may see the grandest sights. Yet even here the wild gala-day of the north wind seemed surpassingly glorious. I was awakened in the morning by the rocking of my cabin and the beating of pine-burs on the roof. Detached torrents and avalanches from the main wind-flood overhead were rushing wildly down the narrow side cañons, and over the precipitous walls, with loud resounding roar, rousing the pines to enthusiastic action, and making the whole valley vibrate as though it were an instrument being played.

But afar on the lofty exposed peaks of the range standing so high in the sky, the storm was expressing itself in still grander characters, which I was soon to see in all their glory. I had long been anxious to study some points in the structure of the ice-cone that is formed every winter at the foot of the upper Yosemite fall, but the blinding spray by which it is invested had hitherto prevented me from making a sufficiently near approach. This morning the entire body of the fall was torn into gauzy shreds, and blown horizontally along the face of the cliff, leaving the cone dry; and while making my way to the top of an overlooking ledge to seize so favorable an opportunity to examine the interior of the cone, the peaks of the Merced group came in sight over the shoulder of the South Dome, each waving a resplendent banner against the blue sky, as regular in form, and as firm in texture, as if woven of fine silk. So rare and splendid a phenomenon, of course, overbore all other considerations, and I at once let the ice-cone go, and began to force my way out of the valley to some dome or ridge sufficiently lofty to command a general view of the main summits, feeling assured that I should find them bannered still more gloriously; nor was I in the least disappointed. Indian Cañon, through which I climbed, was choked with snow that had been shot down in avalanches from the high cliffs on either side, rendering the ascent difficult; but inspired by the roaring storm, the tedious wallowing brought no fatigue, and in four hours I gained the top of a ridge above the valley, 8000 feet high. And there in bold relief, like a clear painting, appeared a most imposing scene. Innumerable peaks, black and sharp, rose grandly into the dark blue sky, their bases set in solid white, their sides streaked and splashed with snow, like ocean rocks with foam; and from every summit, all free and unconfused, was streaming a beautiful silky silvery banner, from half a mile to a mile in length, slender at the point of attachment, then widening gradually as it extended from the peak until it was about 1000 or 1500 feet in breadth, as near as I could estimate. The cluster of peaks called the "Crown of the Sierra," at the head of the Merced and Tuolumne rivers,—Mounts Dana, Gibbs, Conness, Lyell, Maclure, Ritter, with their nameless compeers,—each had its own refulgent banner, waving with a clearly visible motion in the sunglow, and there was not a single cloud in the sky to mar their simple grandeur. Fancy yourself standing on this Yosemite ridge looking eastward. You notice a strange garish glitter in the air. The gale drives wildly overhead with a fierce, tempestuous roar, but its violence is not felt, for you are looking through a sheltered opening in the woods as through a window. There, in the immediate foreground of your picture, rises a majestic forest of Silver Fir blooming in eternal freshness, the foliage yellow-green, and the snow beneath the trees strewn with their beautiful plumes, plucked off by the wind. Beyond, and extending over all the middle ground, are somber swaths of pine, interrupted by huge swelling ridges and domes; and just beyond the dark forest you see the monarchs of the High Sierra waving their magnificent banners. They are twenty miles away, but you would not wish them nearer, for every feature is distinct, and the whole glorious show is seen in its right proportions. After this general view, mark how sharply the dark snowless ribs and buttresses and summits of the peaks are defined, excepting the portions veiled by the banners, and how delicately their sides are streaked with snow, where it has come to rest in narrow flutings and gorges. Mark, too, how grandly the banners wave as the wind is deflected against their sides, and how trimly each is attached to the very summit of its peak, like a streamer at a masthead; how smooth and silky they are in texture, and how finely their fading fringes are penciled on the azure sky. See how dense and opaque they are at the point of attachment, and how filmy and translucent toward the end, so that the peaks back of them are seen dimly, as though you were looking through ground glass. Yet again observe how some of the longest, belonging to the loftiest summits, stream perfectly free all the way across intervening notches and passes from peak to peak, while others overlap and partly hide each other. And consider how keenly every particle of this wondrous cloth of snow is flashing out jets of light. These are the main features of the beautiful and terrible picture as seen from the forest window; and it would still be surpassingly glorious were the fore- and middle-grounds obliterated altogether, leaving only the black peaks, the white banners, and the blue sky.

Glancing now in a general way at the formation of snow-banners, we find that the main causes of the wondrous beauty and perfection of those we have been contemplating were the favorable direction and great force of the wind, the abundance of snow-dust, and the peculiar conformation of the slopes of the peaks. It is essential not only that the wind should move with great velocity and steadiness to supply a sufficiently copious and continuous stream of snow-dust, but that it should come from the north. No perfect banner is ever hung on the Sierra peaks by a south wind. Had the gale that day blown from the south, leaving other conditions unchanged, only a dull, confused, fog-like drift would have been produced; for the snow, instead of being spouted up over the tops of the peaks in concentrated currents to be drawn out as streamers, would have been shed off around the sides, and piled down into the glacier wombs. The cause of the concentrated action of the north wind is found in the peculiar form of the north sides of the peaks, where the amphitheaters of the residual glaciers are. In general the south sides are convex and irregular, while the north sides are concave both in their vertical and horizontal sections; the wind in ascending these curves converges toward the summits, carrying the snow in concentrating currents with it, shooting it almost straight up into the air above the peaks, from which it is then carried away in a horizontal direction.

This difference in form between the north and south sides of the peaks was almost wholly produced by the difference in the kind and quantity of the glaciation to which they have been subjected, the north sides having been hollowed by residual shadow-glaciers of a form that never existed on the sun-beaten sides.

It appears, therefore, that shadows in great part determine not only the forms of lofty icy mountains, but also those of the snow-banners that the wild winds hang on them.

Chapter IV

A NEAR VIEW OF THE HIGH SIERRA

EARLY one bright morning in the middle of Indian summer, while the glacier meadows were still crisp with frost crystals, I set out from the foot of Mount Lyell, on my way down to Yosemite Valley, to replenish my exhausted store of bread and tea. I had spent the past summer, as many preceding ones, exploring the glaciers that lie on the head waters of the San Joaquin, Tuolumne, Merced, and Owen's rivers; measuring and studying their movements, trends, crevasses, moraines, etc., and the part they had played during the period of their greater extension in the creation and development of the landscapes of this alpine wonderland. The time for this kind of work was nearly over for the year, and I began to look forward with delight to the approaching winter with its wondrous storms, when I would be warmly snow-bound in my Yosemite cabin with plenty of bread and books; but a tinge of regret came on when I considered that possibly I might not see this favorite region again until the next summer, excepting distant views from the heights about the Yosemite walls.

To artists, few portions of the High Sierra are, strictly speaking, picturesque. The whole massive uplift of the range is one great picture, not clearly divisible into smaller ones; differing much in this respect from the older, and what may be called, riper mountains of the Coast Range. All the landscapes of the Sierra, as we have seen, were born again, remodeled from base to summit by the developing ice-floods of the last glacial winter. But all these new landscapes were not brought forth simultaneously; some of the highest, where the ice lingered longest, are tens of centuries younger than those of the warmer regions below them. In general, the younger the mountain-landscapes,—younger, I mean, with reference to the time of their emergence from the ice of the glacial period,—the less separable are they into artistic bits capable of being made into warm, sympathetic, lovable pictures with appreciable humanity in them.

Here, however, on the head waters of the Tuolumne, is a group of wild peaks on which the geologist may say that the sun has but just begun to shine, which is yet in a high degree picturesque, and in its main features so regular and evenly balanced as almost to appear conventional—one somber cluster of snow-laden peaks with gray pine-fringed granite bosses braided around its base, the whole surging free into the sky from the head of a magnificent valley, whose lofty walls are beveled away on both sides so as to embrace it all without admitting anything not strictly belonging to it. The foreground was now aflame with autumn colors, brown and purple and gold, ripe in the mellow sunshine; contrasting brightly with the deep, cobalt blue of the sky, and the black and gray, and pure, spiritual white of the rocks and glaciers. Down through the midst, the young Tuolumne was seen pouring from its crystal fountains, now resting in glassy pools as if changing back again into ice, now leaping in white cascades as if turning to snow; gliding right and left between granite bosses, then sweeping on through the smooth, meadowy levels of the valley, swaying pensively from side to side with calm, stately gestures past dipping willows and sedges, and around groves of arrowy pine; and throughout its whole eventful course, whether flowing fast or slow, singing loud or low, ever filling the landscape with spiritual animation, and manifesting the grandeur of its sources in every movement and tone.

Pursuing my lonely way down the valley, I turned again and again to gaze on the glorious picture, throwing up my arms to inclose it as in a frame. After long ages of growth in the darkness beneath the glaciers, through sunshine and storms, it seemed now to be ready and waiting for the elected artist, like yellow wheat for the reaper; and I could not help wishing that I might carry colors and brushes with me on my travels, and learn to paint. In the mean time I had to be content with photographs on my mind and sketches in my note-books. At length, after I had rounded a precipitous headland that puts out from the west wall of the valley, every peak vanished from sight, and I pushed rapidly along the frozen meadows, over the divide between the waters of the Merced and Tuolumne, and down through the forests that clothe the slopes of Cloud's Rest, arriving in Yosemite in due time—which, with me, is *any* time. And, strange to say, among the first people I met here were two artists who, with letters of introduction, were awaiting my return. They inquired whether in the course of my explorations in the adjacent mountains I had ever come upon a landscape suitable for a large painting; whereupon I began a description of the one that had so lately excited my admiration. Then, as I went on further and further into details, their faces began to glow, and I offered to guide them to it, while they declared that they would gladly follow, far or near, whithersoever I could spare the time to lead them.

Since storms might come breaking down through the fine weather at any time, burying the colors in snow, and cutting off the artists' retreat, I advised getting ready at once.

I led them out of the valley by the Vernal and Nevada Falls, thence over the main dividing ridge to the Big Tuolumne Meadows, by the old Mono trail, and thence along the upper Tuolumne River to its head. This was my companions' first excursion into the High Sierra, and as I was almost always alone in my mountaineering, the way that the fresh beauty was reflected in their faces made for me a novel and interesting study. They naturally were affected most of all by the colors— the intense azure of the sky, the purplish grays of the granite, the red and browns of dry meadows, and the translucent purple and crimson of huckleberry bogs; the flaming yellow of aspen groves, the silvery flashing of the streams, and the bright green and blue of the glacier lakes. But the general expression of the scenery—rocky and savage—seemed sadly disappointing; and as they threaded the forest from ridge to ridge, eagerly scanning the landscapes as they were unfolded, they said: "All this is huge and sublime, but we see nothing as yet at all available for effective pictures. Art is long, and art is limited, you know; and here are foregrounds, middle-grounds, backgrounds, all alike; bare rock-waves, woods, groves, diminutive flecks of meadow, and strips of glittering water." "Never mind," I replied, "only bide a wee, and I will show you something you will like."

At length, toward the end of the second day, the Sierra Crown began to come into view, and when we had fairly rounded the projecting headland before mentioned, the whole picture stood revealed in the flush of the alpenglow. Their enthusiasm was excited beyond bounds, and the more impulsive of the two, a young Scotchman, dashed ahead, shouting and gesticulating and tossing his arms in the air like a madman. Here, at last, was a typical alpine landscape.

After feasting awhile on the view, I proceeded to make camp in a sheltered grove a little way back from the meadow, where pine-boughs could be obtained for beds, and where there was plenty of dry wood for fires, while the artists ran here and there, along the river-bends and up the sides of the cañon, choosing foregrounds for sketches. After dark, when our tea was made and a rousing fire had been built, we began to make our plans. They decided to remain several days, at the least, while I concluded to make an excursion in the mean time to the untouched summit of Ritter.

It was now about the middle of October, the springtime of snow-flowers. The first winter-clouds had already bloomed, and the peaks were strewn with fresh crystals, without, however, affecting the climbing to any dangerous extent. And as the weather was still profoundly calm, and the distance to the foot of the mountain only a little more than a day, I felt that I was running no great risk of being storm-bound.

Mount Ritter is king of the mountains of the middle portion of the High Sierra, as Shasta of the north and Whitney of the south sections. Moreover, as far as I know, it had never been climbed. I had explored the adjacent wilderness summer after summer, but my studies thus far had never drawn me to the top of it. Its height above sea-level is about 13,300 feet, and it is fenced round by steeply inclined glaciers, and cañons of tremendous depth and ruggedness, which render it almost inaccessible. But difficulties of this kind only exhilarate the mountaineer.

Next morning, the artists went heartily to their work and I to mine. Former experiences had given good reason to know that passionate storms, invisible as yet, might be brooding in the calm sun-gold; therefore, before bidding farewell, I warned the artists not to be alarmed should I fail to appear before a week or ten days, and advised them, in case a snow-storm should set in, to keep up big fires and shelter themselves as best they could, and on no account to become frightened and attempt to seek their way back to Yosemite alone through the drifts.

My general plan was simply this: to scale the cañon wall, cross over to the eastern flank of the range, and then make my way southward to the northern spurs of Mount Ritter in compliance with the intervening topography; for to push on directly southward from camp through the innumerable peaks and pinnacles that adorn this portion of the axis of the range, however interesting, would take too much time, besides being extremely difficult and dangerous at this time of year.

All my first day was pure pleasure; simply mountaineering indulgence, crossing the dry pathways of the ancient glaciers, tracing happy streams, and learning the habits of the birds and marmots in the groves and rocks. Before I had gone a mile from camp, I came to the foot of a white cascade that beats its way down a rugged gorge in the cañon wall, from a height of about nine hundred feet, and pours its throbbing waters into the Tuolumne. I was acquainted with its fountains, which, fortunately, lay in my course. What a fine traveling companion it proved to be, what songs it sang, and how passionately it told the mountain's own joy! Gladly I climbed along its dashing border, absorbing its divine music, and bathing from time to time in waftings of irised spray. Climbing higher, higher, new beauty came streaming on the sight: painted meadows, late-blooming gardens, peaks of rare architecture, lakes here and there, shining like silver, and glimpses of the forested middle region and the yellow lowlands far in the west. Beyond the range I saw the so-called Mono Desert, lying dreamily silent in thick purple light—a desert of heavy sun-glare beheld from a desert of ice-burnished granite. Here the waters divide, shouting in glorious enthusiasm, and falling eastward to vanish in the volcanic sands and dry sky of the Great Basin, or westward to the Great Valley of California, and thence through the Bay of San Francisco and the Golden Gate to the sea.

Passing a little way down over the summit until I had reached an elevation of about 10,000 feet, I pushed on southward toward a group of savage peaks that stand guard about Ritter on the north and west, groping my way, and dealing instinctively with every obstacle as it presented itself. Here a huge gorge would be found cutting across my path, along the dizzy edge of which I scrambled until some less precipitous point was discovered where I might safely venture to the bottom and then, selecting some feasible portion of the opposite wall, reascend with the same slow caution. Massive, flat-topped spurs alternate with the gorges, plunging abruptly from the shoulders of the snowy peaks, and planting their feet in the warm desert. These were everywhere marked and adorned with characteristic sculptures of the ancient glaciers that swept over this entire region like one vast ice-wind, and the polished surfaces produced by the ponderous flood are still so perfectly preserved that in many places the sunlight reflected from them is about as trying to the eyes as sheets of snow.

God's glacial-mills grind slowly, but they have been kept in motion long enough in California to grind sufficient soil for a glorious abundance of life, though most of the grist has been carried to the lowlands, leaving these high regions comparatively lean and bare; while the post-glacial agents of erosion have not yet furnished sufficient available food over the general surface for more than a few tufts of the hardiest plants, chiefly carices and eriogonæ. And it is interesting to learn in this connection that the sparseness and repressed character of the vegetation at this height is caused more by want of soil than by harshness of climate; for, here and there, in sheltered hollows (countersunk beneath the general surface) into which a few rods of well-ground moraine chips have been dumped, we find groves of spruce and pine thirty to forty feet high, trimmed around the edges with willow and huckleberry bushes, and oftentimes still further by an outer ring of tall grasses, bright with lupines, larkspurs, and showy columbines, suggesting a climate by no means repressingly severe. All the streams, too, and the pools at this elevation are furnished with little gardens wherever soil can be made to lie, which, though making scarce any show at a distance, constitute charming surprises to the appreciative observer. In these bits of leafiness a few birds find grateful homes. Having no acquaintance with man, they fear no ill, and flock curiously about the stranger, almost allowing themselves to be taken in the hand. In so wild and so beautiful a region was spent my first day, every sight and sound inspiring, leading one far out of himself, yet feeding and building up his individuality.

Now came the solemn, silent evening. Long, blue, spiky shadows crept out across the snow-fields, while a rosy glow, at first scarce discernible, gradually deepened and suffused every mountain-top, flushing the glaciers and the harsh crags above them. This was the alpenglow, to me one of the most impressive of all the terrestrial manifestations of God. At the touch of this divine light, the mountains seemed to kindle to a rapt, religious consciousness, and stood hushed and waiting like devout worshipers. Just before the alpenglow began to fade, two crimson clouds came streaming across the summit like wings of flame, rendering the sublime scene yet more impressive; then came darkness and the stars.

Icy Ritter was still miles away, but I could proceed no farther that night. I found a good campground on the rim of a glacier basin about 11,000 feet above the sea. A small lake nestles in the bottom of it, from which I got water for my tea, and a stormbeaten thicket near by furnished abundance of resiny fire-wood. Somber peaks, hacked and shattered, circled half-way around the horizon, wearing a savage aspect in the gloaming, and a waterfall chanted solemnly across the lake on its way down from the foot of a glacier. The fall and the lake and the glacier were almost equally bare; while the scraggy pines anchored in the rock-fissures were so dwarfed and shorn by storm-winds that you might walk over their tops. In tone and aspect the scene was one of the most desolate I ever beheld. But the darkest scriptures of the mountains are illumined with bright passages of love that never fail to make themselves felt when one is alone.

I made my bed in a nook of the pine-thicket, where the branches were pressed and crinkled overhead like a roof, and bent down around the sides. These are the best bedchambers the high mountains afford—snug as squirrel-nests, well ventilated, full of spicy odors, and with plenty of wind-played needles to sing one asleep. I little expected company, but, creeping in through a low side-door, I found five or six birds nestling among the tassels. The night-wind began to blow soon after dark; at first only a gentle breathing, but increasing toward midnight to a rough gale that fell upon my leafy roof in ragged surges like a cascade, bearing wild sounds from the crags overhead. The waterfall sang in chorus, filling the old ice-fountain with its solemn roar, and seeming to increase in power as the night advanced—fit voice for such a landscape. I had to creep out many times to the fire during the night, for it was biting cold and I had no blankets. Gladly I welcomed the morning star.

The dawn in the dry, wavering air of the desert was glorious. Everything encouraged my undertaking and betokened success. There was no cloud in the sky, no storm-tone in the wind. Breakfast of bread and tea was soon made. I fastened a hard, durable crust to my belt by way of provision, in case I should be compelled to pass a night on the mountain-top; then, securing the remainder of my little stock against wolves and wood-rats, I set forth free and hopeful.

How glorious a greeting the sun gives the mountains! To behold this alone is worth the pains of any excursion a thousand times over. The highest peaks burned like islands in a sea of liquid shade. Then the lower peaks and spires caught the glow, and long lances of light, streaming through many a notch and pass, fell thick on the frozen meadows. The majestic form of Ritter was full in sight, and I pushed rapidly on over rounded rock-bosses and pavements, my iron-shod shoes making a clanking sound, suddenly hushed now and then in rugs of bryanthus, and sedgy lake-margins soft as moss. Here, too, in this so-called "land of desolation," I met cassiope, growing in fringes among the battered rocks. Her blossoms had faded long ago, but they were still clinging with happy memories to the evergreen sprays, and still so beautiful as to thrill every fiber of one's being. Winter and summer, you may hear her voice, the low, sweet melody of her purple bells. No evangel among all the mountain plants speaks Nature's love more plainly than cassiope. Where she dwells, the redemption of the coldest solitude is complete. The very rocks and glaciers seem to feel her presence, and become imbued with her own fountain sweetness. All things were warming and awakening. Frozen rills began to flow, the marmots came out of their nests in boulder-piles and climbed sunny rocks to bask, and the dun-headed sparrows were flitting about seeking their breakfasts. The lakes seen from every ridge-top were brilliantly rippled and spangled, shimmering like the thickets of the low Dwarf Pines. The rocks, too, seemed responsive to the vital heat—rock-crystals and snow-crystals thrilling alike. I strode on exhilarated, as if never more to feel fatigue, limbs moving of themselves, every sense unfolding like the thawing flowers, to take part in the new day harmony.

All along my course thus far, excepting when down in the cañons, the landscapes were mostly open to me, and expansive, at least on one side. On the left were the purple plains of Mono, reposing dreamily and warm; on the right, the near peaks springing keenly into the thin sky with more and more impressive sublimity. But these larger views were at length lost. Rugged spurs, and moraines, and huge, projecting buttresses began to shut me in. Every feature became more rigidly alpine, without, however, producing any chilling effect; for going to the mountains is like going home. We always find that the strangest objects in these fountain wilds are in some degree familiar, and we look upon them with a vague sense of having seen them before.

On the southern shore of a frozen lake, I encountered an extensive field of hard, granular snow, up which I scampered in fine tone, intending to follow it to its head, and cross the rocky spur against which it leans, hoping thus to come direct upon the base of the main Ritter peak. The surface was pitted with oval hollows, made by stones and drifted pine-needles that had melted themselves into the mass by the radiation of absorbed sun-heat. These afforded good footholds, but the surface curved more and more steeply at the head, and the pits became shallower and less abundant, until I found myself in danger of being shed off like avalanching snow. I persisted, however, creeping on all fours, and shuffling up the smoothest places on my back, as I had often done on burnished granite, until, after slipping several times, I was compelled to retrace my course to the bottom, and make my way around the west end of the lake, and thence up to the summit of the divide between the head waters of Rush Creek and the northernmost tributaries of the San Joaquin.

Arriving on the summit of this dividing crest, one of the most exciting pieces of pure wilderness was disclosed that I ever discovered in all my mountaineering. There, immediately in front, loomed the majestic mass of Mount Ritter, with a glacier swooping down its face nearly to my feet, then curving westward and pouring its frozen flood into a dark blue lake, whose shores were bound with precipices of crystalline snow; while a deep chasm drawn between the divide and the glacier separated the massive picture from everything else. I could see only the one sublime mountain, the one glacier, the one lake; the whole veiled with one blue shadow—rock, ice, and water close together without a single leaf or sign of life. After gazing spellbound, I began instinctively to scrutinize every notch and gorge and weathered buttress of the mountain, with reference to making the ascent. The entire front above the glacier appeared as one tremendous precipice, slightly receding at the top, and bristling with spires and pinnacles set above one another in formidable array. Massive lichen-stained battlements stood forward here and there, hacked at the top with angular notches, and separated by frosty gullies and recesses that have been veiled in shadow ever since their creation; while to right and left, as far as I could see, were huge, crumbling buttresses, offering no hope to the climber. The head of the glacier sends up a few finger-like branches through narrow *couloirs*; but these seemed too steep and short to be available, especially as I had no ax with which to cut steps, and the numerous narrow-throated gullies down which stones and snow are avalanched seemed hopelessly steep, besides being interrupted by vertical cliffs; while the whole front was rendered still more terribly forbidding by the chill shadow and the gloomy blackness of the rocks.

Descending the divide in a hesitating mood, I picked my way across the yawning chasm at the foot, and climbed out upon the glacier. There were no meadows now to cheer with their brave colors, nor could I hear the dun-headed sparrows, whose cheery notes so often relieve the silence of our highest mountains. The only sounds were the gurgling of small rills down in the veins and crevasses of the glacier, and now and then the rattling report of falling stones, with the echoes they shot out into the crisp air.

I could not distinctly hope to reach the summit from this side, yet I moved on across the glacier as if driven by fate.

Contending with myself, the season is too far spent, I said, and even should I be successful, I might be storm-bound on the mountain; and in the cloud-darkness, with the cliffs and crevasses covered with snow, how could I escape? No; I must wait till next summer. I would only approach the mountain now, and inspect it, creep about its flanks, learn what I could of its history, holding myself ready to flee on the approach of the first storm-cloud. But we little know until tried how much of the uncontrollable there is in us, urging across glaciers and torrents, and up dangerous heights, let the judgment forbid as it may.

I succeeded in gaining the foot of the cliff on the eastern extremity of the glacier, and there discovered the mouth of a narrow avalanche gully, through which I began to climb, intending to follow it as far as possible, and at least obtain some fine wild views for my pains. Its general course is oblique to the plane of the mountain-face, and the metamorphic slates of which the mountain is built are cut by cleavage planes in such a way that they weather off in angular blocks, giving rise to irregular steps that greatly facilitate climbing on the sheer places. I thus made my way into a wilderness of crumbling spires and battlements, built together in bewildering combinations, and glazed in many places with a thin coating of ice, which I had to hammer off with stones. The situation was becoming gradually more perilous; but, having passed several dangerous spots, I dared not think of descending; for, so steep was the entire ascent, one would inevitably fall to the glacier in case a single misstep were made. Knowing, therefore, the tried danger beneath, I became all the more anxious concerning the developments to be made above, and began to be conscious of a vague foreboding of what actually befell; not that I was given to fear, but rather because my instincts, usually so positive and true, seemed vitiated in some way, and were leading me astray. At length, after attaining an elevation of about 12,800 feet, I found myself at the foot of a sheer drop in the bed of the avalanche channel I was tracing, which seemed absolutely to bar further progress. It was only about forty-five or fifty feet high, and somewhat roughened by fissures and projections; but these seemed so slight and insecure, as footholds, that I tried hard to avoid the precipice altogether, by scaling the wall of the channel on either side. But, though less steep, the walls were smoother than the obstructing rock, and repeated efforts only showed that I must either go right ahead or turn back. The tried dangers beneath seemed even greater than that of the cliff in front; therefore, after scanning its face again and again, I began to scale it, picking my holds with intense caution. After gaining a point about half-way to the top, I was suddenly brought to a dead stop, with arms outspread, clinging close to the face of the rock, unable to move hand or foot either up or down. My doom appeared fixed. I *must* fall. There would be a moment of bewilderment, and then a lifeless rumble down the one general precipice to the glacier below.

When this final danger flashed upon me, I became nerve-shaken for the first time since setting foot on the mountains, and my mind seemed to fill with a stifling smoke. But this terrible eclipse lasted only a moment, when life blazed forth again with preternatural clearness. I seemed suddenly to become possessed of a new sense. The other self, bygone experiences, Instinct, or Guardian Angel,—call it what you will, —came forward and assumed control. Then my trembling muscles became firm again, every rift and flaw in the rock was seen as through a microscope, and my limbs moved with a positiveness and precision with which I seemed to have nothing at all to do. Had I been borne aloft upon wings, my deliverance could not have been more complete.

Above this memorable spot, the face of the mountain is still more savagely hacked and torn. It is a maze of yawning chasms and gullies, in the angles of which rise beetling crags and piles of detached boulders that seem to have been gotten ready to be launched below. But the strange influx of strength I had received seemed inexhaustible. I found a way without effort, and soon stood upon the topmost crag in the blessed light.

How truly glorious the landscape circled around this noble summit!—giant mountains, valleys innumerable, glaciers and meadows, rivers and lakes, with the wide blue sky bent tenderly over them all. But in my first hour of freedom from that terrible shadow, the sunlight in which I was laving seemed all in all.

Looking southward along the axis of the range, the eye is first caught by a row of exceedingly sharp and slender spires, which rise openly to a height of about a thousand feet, above a series of short, residual glaciers that lean back against their bases; their fantastic sculpture and the unrelieved sharpness with which they spring out of the ice rendering them peculiarly wild and striking. These are "The Minarets." Beyond them you behold a sublime wilderness of mountains, their snowy summits towering together in crowded abundance, peak beyond peak, swelling higher, higher as they sweep on southward, until the culminating point of the range is reached on Mount Whitney, near the head of the Kern River, at an elevation of nearly 14,700 feet above the level of the sea.

Westward, the general flank of the range is seen flowing sublimely away from the sharp summits, in smooth undulations; a sea of huge gray granite waves dotted with lakes and meadows, and fluted with stupendous cañons that grow steadily deeper as they recede in the distance. Below this gray region lies the dark forest zone, broken here and there by upswelling ridges and domes; and yet beyond lies a yellow, hazy belt, marking the broad plain of the San Joaquin, bounded on its farther side by the blue mountains of the coast.

Turning now to the northward, there in the immediate foreground is the glorious Sierra Crown, with Cathedral Peak, a temple of marvelous architecture, a few degrees to the left of it; the gray, massive form of Mammoth Mountain to the right; while Mounts Ord, Gibbs, Dana, Conness, Tower Peak, Castle Peak, Silver Mountain, and a host of noble companions, as yet nameless, make a sublime show along the axis of the range.

Eastward, the whole region seems a land of desolation covered with beautiful light. The torrid volcanic basin of Mono, with its one bare lake fourteen miles long; Owen's Valley and the broad lava table-land at its head, dotted with craters, and the massive Inyo Range, rivaling even the Sierra in height; these are spread, map-like, beneath you, with countless ranges beyond, passing and overlapping one another and fading on the glowing horizon.

At a distance of less than 3,000 feet below the summit of Mount Ritter you may find tributaries of the San Joaquin and

Owen's rivers, bursting forth from the ice and snow of the glaciers that load its flanks; while a little to the north of here are found the highest affluents of the Tuolumne and Merced. Thus, the fountains of four of the principal rivers of California are within a radius of four or five miles.

Lakes are seen gleaming in all sorts of places,—round, or oval, or square, like very mirrors; others narrow and sinuous, drawn close around the peaks like silver zones, the highest reflecting only rocks, snow, and the sky. But neither these nor the glaciers, nor the bits of brown meadow and moorland that occur here and there, are large enough to make any marked impression upon the mighty wilderness of mountains. The eye, rejoicing in its freedom, roves about the vast expanse, yet returns again and again to the fountain peaks. Perhaps some one of the multitude excites special attention, some gigantic castle with turret and battlement, or some Gothic cathedral more abundantly spired than Milan's. But, generally, when looking for the first time from an all-embracing standpoint like this, the inexperienced observer is oppressed by the incomprehensible grandeur, variety, and abundance of the mountains rising shoulder to shoulder beyond the reach of vision; and it is only after they have been studied one by one, long and lovingly, that their far-reaching harmonies become manifest. Then, penetrate the wilderness where you may, the main telling features, to which all the surrounding topography is subordinate, are quickly perceived, and the most complicated clusters of peaks stand revealed harmoniously correlated and fashioned like works of art—eloquent monuments of the ancient ice-rivers that brought them into relief from the general mass of the range. The cañons, too, some of them a mile deep, mazing wildly through the mighty host of mountains, however lawless and ungovernable at first sight they appear, are at length recognized as the necessary effects of causes which followed each other in harmonious sequence—Nature's poems carved on tables of stone—the simplest and most emphatic of her glacial compositions.

Could we have been here to observe during the glacial period, we should have overlooked a wrinkled ocean of ice as continuous as that now covering the landscapes of Greenland; filling every valley and cañon with only the tops of the fountain peaks rising darkly above the rock-encumbered ice-waves like islets in a stormy sea—those islets the only hints of the glorious landscapes now smiling in the sun. Standing here in the deep, brooding silence all the wilderness seems motionless, as if the work of creation were done. But in the midst of this outer steadfastness we know there is incessant motion and change. Ever and anon, avalanches are falling from yonder peaks. These cliff-bound glaciers, seemingly wedged and immovable, are flowing like water and grinding the rocks beneath them. The lakes are lapping their granite shores and wearing them away, and every one of these rills and young rivers is fretting the air into music, and carrying the mountains to the plains. Here are the roots of all the life of the valleys, and here more simply than elsewhere is the eternal flux of nature manifested. Ice changing to water, lakes to meadows, and mountains to plains. And while we thus contemplate Nature's methods of landscape creation, and, reading the records she has carved on the rocks, reconstruct, however imperfectly, the landscapes of the past, we also learn that as these we now behold have succeeded those of the pre-glacial age, so they in turn are withering and vanishing to be succeeded by others yet unborn.

But in the midst of these fine lessons and landscapes, I had to remember that the sun was wheeling far to the west, while a new way down the mountain had to be discovered to some point on the timber line where I could have a fire; for I had not even burdened myself with a coat. I first scanned the western spurs, hoping some way might appear through which I might reach the northern glacier, and cross its snout; or pass around the lake into which it flows, and thus strike my morning track. This route was soon sufficiently unfolded to show that, if practicable at all, it would require so much time that reaching camp that night would be out of the question. I therefore scrambled back eastward, descending the southern slopes obliquely at the same time. Here the crags seemed less formidable, and the head of a glacier that flows northeast came in sight, which I determined to follow as far as possible, hoping thus to make my way to the foot of the peak on the east side, and thence across the intervening cañons and ridges to camp.

The inclination of the glacier is quite moderate at the head, and, as the sun had softened the *névé*, I made safe and rapid progress, running and sliding, and keeping up a sharp outlook for crevasses. About half a mile from the head, there is an ice-cascade, where the glacier pours over a sharp declivity and is shattered into massive blocks separated by deep, blue fissures. To thread my way through the slippery mazes of this crevassed portion seemed impossible, and I endeavored to avoid it by climbing off to the shoulder of the mountain. But the slopes rapidly steepened and at length fell away in sheer precipices, compelling a return to the ice. Fortunately, the day had been warm enough to loosen the ice-crystals so as to admit of hollows being dug in the rotten portions of the blocks, thus enabling me to pick my way with far less difficulty than I had anticipated. Continuing down over the snout, and along the left lateral moraine, was only a confident saunter, showing that the ascent of the mountain by way of this glacier is easy, provided one is armed with an ax to cut steps here and there.

The lower end of the glacier was beautifully waved and barred by the outcropping edges of the bedded ice-layers which represent the annual snowfalls, and to some extent the irregularities of structure caused by the weathering of the walls of crevasses, and by separate snowfalls which have been followed by rain, hail, thawing and freezing, etc. Small rills were gliding and swirling over the melting surface with a smooth, oily appearance, in channels of pure ice—their quick, compliant movements contrasting most impressively with the rigid, invisible flow of the glacier itself, on whose back they all were riding.

Night drew near before I reached the eastern base of the mountain, and my camp lay many a rugged mile to the north; but ultimate success was assured. It was now only a matter of endurance and ordinary mountain-craft. The sunset was, if possible, yet more beautiful than that of the day before. The Mono landscape seemed to be fairly saturated with warm, purple light. The peaks marshaled along the summit were in shadow, but through every notch and pass streamed vivid sun-fire, soothing and irradiating their rough, black angles, while companies of small, luminous clouds hovered above them like very angels of light.

Darkness came on, but I found my way by the trends of the cañons and the peaks projected against the sky. All excitement died with the light, and then I was weary. But the joyful sound of the waterfall across the lake was heard at last, and soon the stars were seen reflected in the lake itself. Taking my bearings from these, I discovered the little pine thicket in which my nest was, and then I had a rest such as only a tired mountaineer may enjoy. After lying loose and lost for awhile, I made a sunrise fire, went down to the lake, dashed water on my head, and dipped a cupful for tea. The revival brought about by bread and tea was as complete as the exhaustion from excessive enjoyment and toil. Then I crept beneath the pine-tassels to bed. The wind was frosty and the fire burned low, but my sleep was none the less sound, and the evening constellations had swept far to the west before I awoke.

After thawing and resting in the morning sunshine, I sauntered home,—that is, back to the Tuolumne camp,—bearing away toward a cluster of peaks that hold the fountain snows of one of the north tributaries of Rush Creek. Here I discovered a group of beautiful glacier lakes, nestled together in a grand amphitheater. Toward evening, I crossed the divide separating the Mono waters from those of the Tuolumne, and entered the glacier basin that now holds the fountain snows of the stream that forms the upper Tuolumne cascades. This stream I traced down through its many dells and gorges, meadows and bogs, reaching the brink of the main Tuolumne at dusk.

A loud whoop for the artists was answered again and again. Their camp-fire came in sight, and half an hour afterward I was with them. They seemed unreasonably glad to see me. I had been absent only three days; nevertheless, though the weather was fine, they had already been weighing chances as to whether I would ever return, and trying to decide whether they should wait longer or begin to seek their way back to the lowlands. Now their curious troubles were over. They packed their precious sketches, and next morning we set out homeward bound, and in two days entered the Yosemite Valley from the north by way of Indian Cañon.

Chapter V

THE PASSES

THE sustained grandeur of the High Sierra is strikingly illustrated by the great height of the passes. Between latitude 36° 20′ and 38° the lowest pass, gap, gorge, or notch of any kind cutting across the axis of the range, as far as I have discovered, exceeds 9000 feet in height above the level of the sea; while the average height of all that are in use, either by Indians or whites, is perhaps not less than 11,000 feet, and not one of these is a carriage-pass.

Farther north a carriage-road has been constructed through what is known as the Sonora Pass, on the head waters of the Stanislaus and Walker's rivers, the summit of which is about 10,000 feet above the sea. Substantial wagon-roads have also been built through the Carson and Johnson passes, near the head of Lake Tahoe, over which immense quantities of freight were hauled from California to the mining regions of Nevada, before the construction of the Central Pacific Railroad.

Still farther north a considerable number of comparatively low passes occur, some of which are accessible to wheeled vehicles, and through these rugged defiles during the exciting years of the gold period long emigrant-trains with foot-sore cattle wearily toiled. After the toil-worn adventurers had escaped a thousand dangers and had crawled thousands of miles across the plains the snowy Sierra at last loomed in sight, the eastern wall of the land of gold. And as with shaded eyes they gazed through the tremulous haze of the desert, with what joy must they have descried the pass through which they were to enter the better land of their hopes and dreams!

Between the Sonora Pass and the southern extremity of the High Sierra, a distance of nearly 160 miles, there are only five passes through which trails conduct from one side of the range to the other. These are barely practicable for animals; a pass in these regions meaning simply any notch or cañon through which one may, by the exercise of unlimited patience, make out to lead a mule, or a sure-footed mustang; animals that can slide or jump as well as walk. Only three of the five passes may be said to be in use, viz.: the Kearsarge, Mono, and Virginia Creek; the tracks leading through the others being only obscure Indian trails, not graded in the least, and scarcely traceable by white men; for much of the way is over solid rock and earthquake avalanche taluses, where the unshod ponies of the Indians leave no appreciable sign. Only skilled mountaineers are able to detect the marks that serve to guide the Indians, such as slight abrasions of the looser rocks, the displacement of stones here and there, and bent bushes and weeds. A general knowledge of the topography is, then, the main guide, enabling one to determine where the trail ought to go—*must* go. One of these Indian trails crosses the range by a nameless pass between the head waters of the south and middle forks of the San Joaquin, the other between the north and middle forks of the same river, just to the south of "The Minarets"; this last being about 9000 feet high, is the lowest of the five. The Kearsarge is the highest, crossing the summit near the head of the south fork of King's River, about eight miles to the north of Mount Tyndall, through the midst of the most stupendous rock-scenery. The summit of this pass is over 12,000 feet above sea-level; nevertheless, it is one of the safest of the five, and is used every summer, from July to October or November, by hunters, prospectors, and stock-owners, and to some extent by enterprising pleasure-seekers also. For, besides the surpassing grandeur of the scenery about the summit, the trail, in ascending the western flank of the range, conducts through a grove of the giant Sequoias, and through the magnificent Yosemite Valley of the south fork of King's River. This is, perhaps, the highest traveled pass on the North American continent.

The Mono Pass lies to the east of Yosemite Valley, at the head of one of the tributaries of the south fork of the Tuolumne. This is the best known and most extensively traveled of all that exist in the High Sierra. A trail was made through it about the time of the Mono gold excitement, in the year 1858, by adventurous miners and prospectors—men who would build a trail down the throat of darkest Erebus on the way to gold. Though more than a thousand feet lower than the Kearsarge, it is scarcely less sublime in rock-scenery, while in snowy, falling water it far surpasses it. Being so favorably situated for the stream of Yosemite travel, the more adventurous tourists cross over through this glorious gateway to the volcanic region around Mono Lake. It has therefore gained a name and fame above every other pass in the range. According to the few barometrical observations made upon it, its highest point is 10,765 feet above the sea. The other pass of the five we have been considering is somewhat lower, and crosses the axis of the range a few miles to the north of the Mono Pass, at the head of the southernmost tributary of Walker's River. It is used chiefly by roaming bands of the Pah Ute Indians and "sheepmen."

But, leaving wheels and animals out of the question, the free mountaineer with a sack of bread on his shoulders and an ax to cut steps in ice and frozen snow can make his way across the range almost everywhere, and at any time of year when the weather is calm. To him nearly every notch between the peaks is a pass, though much patient step-cutting is at times required up and down steeply inclined glaciers, with cautious climbing over precipices that at first sight would seem hopelessly inaccessible.

In pursuing my studies, I have crossed from side to side of the range at intervals of a few miles all along the highest portion of the chain, with far less real danger than one would naturally count on. And what fine wildness was thus revealed—storms and avalanches, lakes and waterfalls, gardens and meadows, and interesting animals—only those will ever know who give the freest and most buoyant portion of their lives to climbing and seeing for themselves.

To the timid traveler, fresh from the sedimentary levels of the lowlands, these highways, however picturesque and grand, seem terribly forbidding—cold, dead, gloomy gashes in the bones of the mountains, and of all Nature's ways the ones to be most cautiously avoided. Yet they are full of the finest and most telling examples of Nature's love; and though hard to travel, none are safer. For they lead through regions that lie far above the ordinary haunts of the devil, and of the pestilence that walks in darkness. True, there are innumerable places where the careless step will be the last step; and a rock falling from the cliffs may crush without warning like lightning from the sky; but what then? Accidents in the mountains are less common than in the lowlands, and these mountain mansions are decent, delightful, even divine, places to die in, compared with the doleful chambers of civilization. Few places in this world are more dangerous than home. Fear not, therefore, to try the mountain-passes. They will kill care, save you from deadly apathy, set you free, and call forth every faculty into vigorous, enthusiastic action. Even the sick should try these so-called dangerous passes, because for every unfortunate they kill, they cure a thousand.

All the passes make their steepest ascents on the eastern flank. On this side the average rise is not far from a thousand feet to the mile, while on the west it is about two hundred feet. Another marked difference between the eastern and western portions of the passes is that the former begin at the very foot of the range, while the latter can hardly be said to begin lower than an elevation of from seven to ten thousand feet. Approaching the range from the gray levels of Mono and Owen's Valley on the east, the traveler sees before him the steep, short passes in full view, fenced in by rugged spurs that come plunging down from the shoulders of the peaks on either side, the courses of the more direct being disclosed from top to bottom without interruption. But from the west one sees nothing of the way he may be seeking until near the summit, after days have been spent in threading the forests growing on the main dividing ridges between the river cañons.

It is interesting to observe how surely the alp-crossing animals of every kind fall into the same trails. The more rugged and inaccessible the general character of the topography of any particular region, the more surely will the trails of white men, Indians, bears, wild sheep, etc., be found converging into the best passes. The Indians of the western slope venture cautiously over the passes in settled weather to attend dances, and obtain loads of pine-nuts and the larvæ of a small fly that breeds in Mono and Owen's lakes, which, when dried, forms an important article of food; while the Pah Utes cross over from the east to hunt the deer and obtain supplies of acorns; and it is truly astonishing to see what immense loads the haggard old squaws make out to carry barefooted through these rough passes, oftentimes for a distance of sixty or seventy miles. They are always accompanied by the men, who stride on, unburdened and erect, a little in advance, kindly stooping at difficult places to pile stepping-stones for their patient, pack-animal wives, just as they would prepare the way for their ponies.

Bears evince great sagacity as mountaineers, but although they are tireless and enterprising travelers they seldom cross the range. I have several times tracked them through the Mono Pass, but only in late years, after cattle and sheep had passed that way, when they doubtless were following to feed on the stragglers and on those that had been killed by falling over the rocks. Even the wild sheep, the best mountaineers of all, choose regular passes in making journeys across the summits. Deer seldom cross the range in either direction. I have never yet observed a single specimen of the mule-deer of the Great Basin west of the summit, and rarely one of the black-tailed species on the eastern slope, notwithstanding many of the latter ascend the range nearly to the summit every summer, to feed in the wild gardens and bring forth their young.

The glaciers are the pass-makers, and it is by them that the courses of all mountaineers are predestined. Without exception every pass in the Sierra was created by them without the slightest aid or predetermining guidance from any of the cataclysmic agents. I have seen elaborate statements of the amount of drilling and blasting accomplished in the construction of the railroad across the Sierra, above Donner Lake; but for every pound of rock moved in this way, the glaciers which descended east and west through this same pass, crushed and carried away more than a hundred tons.

The so-called practicable road-passes are simply those portions of the range more degraded by glacial action than the adjacent portions, and degraded in such a way as to leave the summits rounded, instead of sharp; while the peaks, from the superior strength and hardness of their rocks, or from more favorable position, having suffered less degradation, are left towering above the passes as if they had been heaved into the sky by some force acting from beneath.

The scenery of all the passes, especially at the head, is of the wildest and grandest description,—lofty peaks massed together and laden around their bases with ice and snow; chains of glacier lakes; cascading streams in endless variety, with glorious views, westward over a sea of rocks and woods, and eastward over strange ashy plains, volcanoes, and the dry, dead-looking ranges of the Great Basin. Every pass, however, possesses treasures of beauty all its own.

Having thus in a general way indicated the height, leading features, and distribution of the principal passes, I will now endeavor to describe the Mono Pass in particular, which may, I think, be regarded as a fair example of the higher alpine passes in general.

The main portion of the Mono Pass is formed by Bloody Cañon, which begins at the summit of the range, and runs in a general east-northeasterly direction to the edge of the Mono Plain.

The first white men who forced a way through its somber depths were, as we have seen, eager gold-seekers. But the cañon was known and traveled as a pass by the Indians and mountain animals long before its discovery by white men, as is shown by the numerous tributary trails which come into it from every direction. Its name accords well with the character of the "early times" in California, and may perhaps have been suggested by the predominant color of the metamorphic slates in which it is in great part eroded; or more probably by blood-stains made by the unfortunate animals which were compelled to slip and shuffle awkwardly over its rough, cutting rocks. I have never known an animal, either mule or horse, to make its way through the cañon, either in going up or down, without losing more or less blood from wounds on the legs. Occasionally one is killed outright—falling headlong and rolling over precipices like a boulder. But such accidents are rarer than from the terrible appearance of the trail one would be led to expect; the more experienced when driven loose find their way over the dangerous places with a caution and sagacity that is truly wonderful. During the gold excitement it was at times a matter of considerable pecuniary importance to force a way through the cañon with pack-trains early in the spring while it was yet heavily blocked with snow; and then the mules with their loads had sometimes to be let down over the steepest drifts and avalanche beds by means of ropes.

A good bridle-path leads from Yosemite through many a grove and meadow up to the head of the cañon, a distance of about thirty miles. Here the scenery undergoes a sudden and startling condensation. Mountains, red, gray, and black, rise close at hand on the right, whitened around their bases with banks of enduring snow; on the left swells the huge red mass of Mount Gibbs, while in front the eye wanders down the shadowy cañon, and out on the warm plain of Mono, where the lake is seen gleaming like a burnished metallic disk, with clusters of lofty volcanic cones to the south of it.

When at length we enter the mountain gateway, the somber rocks seem aware of our presence, and seem to come thronging closer about us. Happily the ouzel and the old familiar robin are here to sing us welcome, and azure daisies beam with trustfulness and sympathy, enabling us to feel something of Nature's love even here, beneath the gaze of her coldest rocks.

The effect of this expressive outspokenness on the part of the cañon-rocks is greatly enhanced by the quiet aspect of the alpine meadows through which we pass just before entering the narrow gateway. The forests in which they lie, and the mountain-tops rising beyond them, seem quiet and tranquil. We catch their restful spirit, yield to the soothing influences of the sunshine, and saunter dreamily on through flowers and bees, scarce touched by a definite thought; then suddenly we find ourselves in the shadowy cañon, closeted with Nature in one of her wildest strongholds.

After the first bewildering impression begins to wear off, we perceive that it is not altogether terrible; for besides the reassuring birds and flowers we discover a chain of shining lakelets hanging down from the very summit of the pass, and linked together by a silvery stream. The highest are set in bleak, rough bowls, scantily fringed with brown and yellow sedges. Winter storms blow snow through the cañon in blinding drifts, and avalanches shoot from the heights. Then are these sparkling tarns filled and buried, leaving not a hint of their existence. In June and July they begin to blink and thaw out like sleepy eyes, the carices thrust up their short brown spikes, the daisies bloom in turn, and the most profoundly buried of them all is at length warmed and summered as if winter were only a dream.

Red Lake is the lowest of the chain, and also the largest. It seems rather dull and forbidding at first sight, lying motionless in its deep, dark bed. The cañon wall rises sheer from the water's edge on the south, but on the opposite side there is sufficient space and sunshine for a sedgy daisy garden, the center of which is brilliantly lighted with lilies, castilleias, larkspurs, and columbines, sheltered from the wind by leafy willows, and forming a most joyful outburst of plant-life keenly emphasized by the chill baldness of the onlooking cliffs.

After indulging here in a dozing, shimmering lake-rest, the happy stream sets forth again, warbling and trilling like an ouzel, ever delightfully confiding, no matter how dark the way; leaping, gliding, hither, thither, clear or foaming: manifesting the beauty of its wildness in every sound and gesture.

One of its most beautiful developments is the Diamond Cascade, situated a short distance below Red Lake. Here the tense, crystalline water is first dashed into coarse, granular spray mixed with dusty foam, and then divided into a diamond pattern by following the diagonal cleavage-joints that intersect the face of the precipice over which it pours. Viewed in front, it resembles a strip of embroidery of definite pattern, varying through the seasons with the temperature and the volume of water. Scarce a flower may be seen along its snowy border. A few bent pines look on from a distance, and small fringes of cassiope and rock-ferns are growing in fissures near the head, but these are so lowly and undemonstrative that only the attentive observer will be likely to notice them.

On the north wall of the cañon, a little below the Diamond Cascade, a glittering side stream makes its appearance, seeming to leap directly out of the sky. It first resembles a crinkled ribbon of silver hanging loosely down the wall, but grows wider as it descends, and dashes the dull rock with foam. A long rough talus curves up against this part of the cliff, overgrown with snow-pressed willows, in which the fall disappears with many an eager surge and swirl and plashing leap, finally beating its way down to its confluence with the main cañon stream.

Below this point the climate is no longer arctic. Butterflies become larger and more abundant, grasses with imposing spread of panicle wave above your shoulders, and the summery drone of the bumblebee thickens the air. The Dwarf Pine, the tree-mountaineer that climbs highest and braves the coldest blasts, is found scattered in stormbeaten clumps from the summit of the pass about half-way down the cañon. Here it is succeeded by the hardy Two-leaved Pine, which is speedily joined by the taller Yellow and Mountain Pines. These, with the burly juniper, and shimmering aspen, rapidly grow larger as the sunshine becomes richer, forming groves that block the view; or they stand more apart here and there in picturesque groups, that make beautiful and obvious harmony with the rocks and with one another. Blooming underbrush becomes abundant,—azalea, spiræa, and the brier-rose weaving fringes for the streams, and shaggy rugs to relieve the stern, unflinching rock-bosses.

Through this delightful wilderness, Cañon Creek roves without any constraining channel, throbbing and wavering; now in sunshine, now in thoughtful shade; falling, swirling, flashing from side to side in weariless exuberance of energy. A glorious milky way of cascades is thus developed, of which Bower Cascade, though one of the smallest, is perhaps the most beautiful of them all. It is situated in the lower region of the pass, just where the sunshine begins to mellow between the cold and warm climates. Here the glad creek, grown strong with tribute gathered from many a snowy fountain on the heights, sings richer strains, and becomes more human and lovable at every step. Now you may by its side find the rose and homely yarrow, and small meadows full of bees and clover. At the head of a low-browed rock, luxuriant dogwood bushes and willows arch over from bank to bank, embowering the stream with their leafy branches; and drooping plumes, kept in motion by the current, fringe the brow of the cascade in front. From this leafy covert the stream leaps out into the light in a fluted curve thick sown with sparkling crystals, and falls into a pool filled with brown boulders, out of which it creeps gray with foam-bells and disappears in a tangle of verdure like that from which it came.

Hence, to the foot of the cañon, the metamorphic slates give place to granite, whose nobler sculpture calls forth expressions of corresponding beauty from the stream in passing over it,—bright trills of rapids, booming notes of falls, solemn hushes of smooth-gliding sheets, all chanting and blending in glorious harmony. When, at length, its impetuous alpine life is done, it slips through a meadow with scarce an audible whisper, and falls asleep in Moraine Lake.

This water-bed is one of the finest I ever saw. Evergreens wave soothingly about it, and the breath of flowers floats over it like incense. Here our blessed stream rests from its rocky wanderings, all its mountaineering done,—no more foaming rock-leaping, no more wild, exulting song. It falls into a smooth, glassy sleep, stirred only by the night-wind, which, coming down the cañon, makes it croon and mutter in ripples along its broidered shores.

Leaving the lake, it glides quietly through the rushes, destined never more to touch the living rock. Henceforth its path lies through ancient moraines and reaches of ashy sage-plain, which nowhere afford rocks suitable for the development of cascades or sheer falls. Yet this beauty of maturity, though less striking, is of a still higher order, enticing us lovingly on through gentian meadows and groves of rustling aspen to Lake Mono, where, spirit-like, our happy stream vanishes in vapor, and floats free again in the sky.

Bloody Cañon, like every other in the Sierra, was recently occupied by a glacier, which derived its fountain snows from the adjacent summits, and descended into Mono Lake, at a time when its waters stood at a much higher level than now. The principal characters in which the history of the ancient glaciers is preserved are displayed here in marvelous freshness and simplicity, furnishing the student with extraordinary advantages for the acquisition of knowledge of this sort. The most striking passages are polished and striated surfaces, which in many places reflect the rays of the sun like smooth water. The dam of Red Lake is an elegantly modeled rib of metamorphic slate, brought into relief because of its superior strength, and because of the greater intensity of the glacial erosion of the rock immediately above it, caused by a steeply inclined tributary glacier, which entered the main trunk with a heavy down-thrust at the head of the lake.

Moraine Lake furnishes an equally interesting example of a basin formed wholly, or in part, by a terminal moraine dam curved across the path of a stream between two lateral moraines.

At Moraine Lake the cañon proper terminates, although

apparently continued by the two lateral moraines of the vanished glacier. These moraines are about 300 feet high, and extend unbrokenly from the sides of the cañon into the plain, a distance of about five miles, curving and tapering in beautiful lines. Their sunward sides are gardens, their shady sides are groves; the former devoted chiefly to eriogonæ, compositæ, and graminæ; a square rod containing five or six profusely flowered eriogonums of several species, about the same number of bahia and linosyris, and a few grass tufts; each species being planted trimly apart, with bare gravel between, as if cultivated artificially.

My first visit to Bloody Cañon was made in the summer of 1869, under circumstances well calculated to heighten the impressions that are the peculiar offspring of mountains. I came from the blooming tangles of Florida, and waded out into the plant-gold of the great valley of California, when its flora was as yet untrodden. Never before had I beheld congregations of social flowers half so extensive or half so glorious. Golden compositæ covered all the ground from the Coast Range to the Sierra like a stratum of curdled sunshine, in which I reveled for weeks, watching the rising and setting of their innumerable suns; then I gave myself up to be borne forward on the crest of the summer wave that sweeps annually up the Sierra and spends itself on the snowy summits.

At the Big Tuolumne Meadows I remained more than a month, sketching, botanizing, and climbing among the surrounding mountains. The mountaineer with whom I then happened to be camping was one of those remarkable men one so frequently meets in California, the hard angles and bosses of whose characters have been brought into relief by the grinding excitements of the gold period, until they resemble glacial landscapes. But at this late day, my friend's activities had subsided, and his craving for rest caused him to become a gentle shepherd and literally to lie down with the lamb.

Recognizing the unsatisfiable longings of my Scotch Highland instincts, he threw out some hints concerning Bloody Cañon, and advised me to explore it. "I have never seen it myself," he said, "for I never was so unfortunate as to pass that way. But I have heard many a strange story about it, and I warrant you will at least find it wild enough."

Then of course I made haste to see it. Early next morning I made up a bundle of bread, tied my note-book to my belt, and strode away in the bracing air, full of eager, indefinite hope. The plushy lawns that lay in my path served to soothe my morning haste. The sod in many places was starred with daisies and blue gentians, over which I lingered. I traced the paths of the ancient glaciers over many a shining pavement, and marked the gaps in the upper forests that told the power of the winter avalanches. Climbing higher, I saw for the first time the gradual dwarfing of the pines in compliance with climate, and on the summit discovered creeping mats of the arctic willow overgrown with silky catkins, and patches of the dwarf vaccinium with its round flowers sprinkled in the grass like purple hail; while in every direction the landscape stretched sublimely away in fresh wildness—a manuscript written by the hand of Nature alone.

At length, as I entered the pass, the huge rocks began to close around in all their wild, mysterious impressiveness, when suddenly, as I was gazing eagerly about me, a drove of gray hairy beings came in sight, lumbering toward me with a kind of boneless, wallowing motion like bears.

I never turn back, though often so inclined, and in this particular instance, amid such surroundings, everything seemed singularly unfavorable for the calm acceptance of so grim a company. Suppressing my fears, I soon discovered that although as hairy as bears and as crooked as summit pines, the strange creatures were sufficiently erect to belong to our own species. They proved to be nothing more formidable than Mono Indians dressed in the skins of sage-rabbits. Both the men and the women begged persistently for whisky and tobacco, and seemed so accustomed to denials that I found it impossible to convince them that I had none to give. Excepting the names of these two products of civilization, they seemed to understand not a word of English; but I afterward learned that they were on their way to Yosemite Valley to feast awhile on trout and procure a load of acorns to carry back through the pass to their huts on the shore of Mono Lake.

Occasionally a good countenance may be seen among the Mono Indians, but these, the first specimens I had seen, were mostly ugly, and some of them altogether hideous. The dirt on their faces was fairly stratified, and seemed so ancient and so undisturbed it might almost possess a geological significance. The older faces were, moreover, strangely blurred and divided into sections by furrows that looked like the cleavage-joints of rocks, suggesting exposure on the mountains in a cast-away condition for ages. Somehow they seemed to have no right place in the landscape, and I was glad to see them fading out of sight down the pass.

Then came evening, and the somber cliffs were inspired with the ineffable beauty of the alpenglow. A solemn calm fell upon everything. All the lower portion of the cañon was in gloaming shadow, and I crept into a hollow near one of the upper lakelets to smooth the ground in a sheltered nook for a bed. When the short twilight faded, I kindled a sunny fire, made a cup of tea, and lay down to rest and look at the stars. Soon the night-wind began to flow and pour in torrents among the jagged peaks, mingling strange tones with those of the waterfalls sounding far below; and as I drifted toward sleep I began to experience an uncomfortable feeling of nearness to the furred Monos. Then the full moon looked down over the edge of the cañon wall, her countenance seemingly filled with intense concern, and apparently so near as to produce a startling effect as if she had entered my bedroom, forgetting all the world, to gaze on me alone.

The night was full of strange sounds, and I gladly welcomed the morning. Breakfast was soon done, and I set forth in the exhilarating freshness of the new day, rejoicing in the abundance of pure wildness so close about me. The stupendous rocks, hacked and scarred with centuries of storms, stood sharply out in the thin early light, while down in the bottom of the cañon grooved and polished bosses heaved and glistened like swelling sea-waves, telling a grand old story of the ancient glacier that poured its crushing floods above them.

Here for the first time I met the arctic daisies in all their perfection of purity and spirituality,—gentle mountaineers face to face with the stormy sky, kept safe and warm by a thousand miracles. I leaped lightly from rock to rock, glorying in the eternal freshness and sufficiency of Nature, and in the ineffable tenderness with which she nurtures her mountain darlings in the very fountains of storms. Fresh beauty appeared at every step, delicate rock-ferns, and groups of the fairest flowers. Now another lake came to view, now a water-fall. Never fell light in brighter spangles, never fell water in whiter foam. I seemed to float through the cañon enchanted, feeling nothing of its roughness, and was out in the Mono levels before I was aware.

Looking back from the shore of Moraine Lake, my morning ramble seemed all a dream. There curved Bloody Cañon, a mere glacial furrow 2000 feet deep, with smooth rocks projecting from the sides and braided together in the middle, like bulging, swelling muscles. Here the lilies were higher than my head, and the sunshine was warm enough for palms. Yet the snow around the arctic willows was plainly visible only four miles away, and between were narrow specimen zones of all the principal climates of the globe.

On the bank of a small brook that comes gurgling down the side of the left lateral moraine, I found a camp-fire still burning, which no doubt belonged to the gray Indians I had met on the summit, and I listened instinctively and moved cautiously forward, half expecting to see some of their grim faces peering out of the bushes.

Passing on toward the open plain, I noticed three well-defined terminal moraines curved gracefully across the cañon stream, and joined by long splices to the two noble laterals. These mark the halting-places of the vanished glacier when it was retreating into its summit shadows on the breaking-up of the glacial winter.

Five miles below the foot of Moraine Lake, just where the lateral moraines lose themselves in the plain, there was a field of wild rye, growing in magnificent waving bunches six to eight feet high, bearing heads from six to twelve inches long. Rubbing out some of the grains, I found them about five eighths of an inch long, dark-colored, and sweet. Indian women were gathering it in baskets, bending down large handfuls, beating it out, and fanning it in the wind. They were quite picturesque, coming through the rye, as one caught glimpses of them here and there, in winding lanes and openings, with splendid tufts arching above their heads, while their incessant chat and laughter showed their heedless joy.

Like the rye-field, I found the so-called desert of Mono

blooming in a high state of natural cultivation with the wild rose, cherry, aster, and the delicate abronia; also innumerable gilias, phloxes, poppies, and bush-compositæ. I observed their gestures and the various expressions of their corollas, inquiring how they could be so fresh and beautiful out in this volcanic desert. They told as happy a life as any plant-company I ever met, and seemed to enjoy even the hot sand and the wind.

But the vegetation of the pass has been in great part destroyed, and the same may be said of all the more accessible passes throughout the range. Immense numbers of starving sheep and cattle have been driven through them into Nevada, trampling the wild gardens and meadows almost out of existence. The lofty walls are untouched by any foot, and the falls sing on unchanged; but the sight of crushed flowers and stripped, bitten bushes goes far toward destroying the charm of wildness.

The cañon should be seen in winter. A good, strong traveler, who knows the way and the weather, might easily make a safe excursion through it from Yosemite Valley on snowshoes during some tranquil time, when the storms are hushed. The lakes and falls would be buried then; but so, also, would be the traces of destructive feet, while the views of the mountains in their winter garb, and the ride at lightning speed down the pass between the snowy walls, would be truly glorious.

Chapter VI

AMONG the many unlooked-for treasures that are bound up
and hidden away in the depths of Sierra solitudes, none
more surely charm and surprise all kinds of travelers than the
glacier lakes. The forests and the glaciers and the snowy fountains of the streams advertise their wealth in a more or less
telling manner even in the distance, but nothing is seen of the
lakes until we have climbed above them. All the upper
branches of the rivers are fairly laden with lakes, like orchard
trees with fruit. They lie embosomed in the deep woods,
down in the grovy bottoms of cañons, high on bald table-
lands, and around the feet of the icy peaks, mirroring back
their wild beauty over and over again. Some conception of
their lavish abundance may be made from the fact that, from
one standpoint on the summit of Red Mountain, a day's journey to the east of Yosemite Valley, no fewer than forty-two
are displayed within a radius of ten miles. The whole number
in the Sierra can hardly be less than fifteen hundred, not
counting the smaller pools and tarns, which are innumerable.
Perhaps two thirds or more lie on the western flank of the
range, and all are restricted to the alpine and subalpine
regions. At the close of the last glacial period, the middle and
foot-hill regions also abounded in lakes, all of which have long
since vanished as completely as the magnificent ancient glaciers that brought them into existence.

Though the eastern flank of the range is excessively steep,
we find lakes pretty regularly distributed throughout even the
most precipitous portions. They are mostly found in the upper
branches of the cañons, and in the glacial amphitheaters
around the peaks.

Occasionally long, narrow specimens occur upon the steep
sides of dividing ridges, their basins swung lengthwise like
hammocks, and very rarely one is found lying so exactly on
the summit of the range at the head of some pass that its
waters are discharged down both flanks when the snow is
melting fast. But, however situated, they soon cease to form

surprises to the studious mountaineer; for, like all the love-work of Nature, they are harmoniously related to one another, and to all the other features of the mountains. It is easy, therefore, to find the bright lake-eyes in the roughest and most ungovernable-looking topography of any landscape countenance. Even in the lower regions, where they have been closed for many a century, their rocky orbits are still discernible, filled in with the detritus of flood and avalanche. A beautiful system of grouping in correspondence with the glacial fountains is soon perceived; also their extension in the direction of the trends of the ancient glaciers; and in general their dependence as to form, size, and position upon the character of the rocks in which their basins have been eroded, and the quantity and direction of application of the glacial force expended upon each basin.

In the upper cañons we usually find them in pretty regular succession, strung together like beads on the bright ribbons of their feeding-streams, which pour, white and gray with foam and spray, from one to the other, their perfect mirror stillness making impressive contrasts with the grand blare and glare of the connecting cataracts. In Lake Hollow, on the north side of the Hoffman spur, immediately above the great Tuolumne cañon, there are ten lovely lakelets lying near together in one general hollow, like eggs in a nest. Seen from above, in a general view, feathered with Hemlock Spruce, and fringed with sedge, they seem to me the most singularly beautiful and interestingly located lake-cluster I have ever yet discovered.

Lake Tahoe, 22 miles long by about 10 wide, and from 500 to over 1600 feet in depth, is the largest of all the Sierra lakes. It lies just beyond the northern limit of the higher portion of the range between the main axis and a spur that puts out on the east side from near the head of the Carson River. Its forested shores go curving in and out around many an emerald bay and pine-crowned promontory, and its waters are everywhere as keenly pure as any to be found among the highest mountains.

Donner Lake, rendered memorable by the terrible fate of the Donner party, is about three miles long, and lies about ten miles to the north of Tahoe, at the head of one of the tributaries of the Truckee. A few miles farther north lies Lake

Independence, about the same size as Donner. But far the greater number of the lakes lie much higher and are quite small, few of them exceeding a mile in length, most of them less than half a mile.

Along the lower edge of the lake-belt, the smallest have disappeared by the filling-in of their basins, leaving only those of considerable size. But all along the upper freshly glaciated margin of the lake-bearing zone, every hollow, however small, lying within reach of any portion of the close network of streams, contains a bright, brimming pool; so that the landscape viewed from the mountain-tops seems to be sown broadcast with them. Many of the larger lakes are encircled with smaller ones like central gems girdled with sparkling brilliants. In general, however, there is no marked dividing line as to size. In order, therefore, to prevent confusion, I would state here that in giving numbers, I include none less than 500 yards in circumference.

In the basin of the Merced River, I counted 131, of which 111 are upon the tributaries that fall so grandly into Yosemite Valley. Pohono Creek, which forms the fall of that name, takes its rise in a beautiful lake, lying beneath the shadow of a lofty granite spur that puts out from Buena Vista peak. This is now the only lake left in the whole Pohono Basin. The Illilouette has sixteen, the Nevada no fewer than sixty-seven, the Tenaya eight, Hoffmann Creek five, and Yosemite Creek fourteen. There are but two other lake-bearing affluents of the Merced, viz., the South Fork with fifteen, and Cascade Creek with five, both of which unite with the main trunk below Yosemite.

The Merced River, as a whole, is remarkably like an elm-tree, and it requires but little effort on the part of the imagination to picture it standing upright, with all its lakes hanging upon its spreading branches, the topmost eighty miles in height. Now add all the other lake-bearing rivers of the Sierra, each in its place, and you will have a truly glorious spectacle,— an avenue the length and width of the range; the long, slender, gray shafts of the main trunks, the milky way of arching branches, and the silvery lakes, all clearly defined and shining on the sky. How excitedly such an addition to the scenery would be gazed at! Yet these lakeful rivers are still more excitingly beautiful and impressive in their natural positions to those who have the eyes to see them as they lie imbedded in their meadows and forests and glacier-sculptured rocks.

When a mountain lake is born,—when, like a young eye, it first opens to the light,—it is an irregular, expressionless crescent, inclosed in banks of rock and ice,—bare, glaciated rock on the lower side, the rugged snout of a glacier on the upper. In this condition it remains for many a year, until at length, toward the end of some auspicious cluster of seasons, the glacier recedes beyond the upper margin of the basin, leaving it open from shore to shore for the first time, thousands of years after its conception beneath the glacier that excavated its basin. The landscape, cold and bare, is reflected in its pure depths; the winds ruffle its glassy surface, and the sun fills it with throbbing spangles, while its waves begin to lap and murmur around its leafless shores,—sun-spangles during the day and reflected stars at night its only flowers, the winds and the snow its only visitors. Meanwhile, the glacier continues to recede, and numerous rills, still younger than the lake itself, bring down glacier-mud, sand-grains, and pebbles, giving rise to margin-rings and plats of soil. To these fresh soil-beds come many a waiting plant. First, a hardy carex with arching leaves and a spike of brown flowers; then, as the seasons grow warmer, and the soil-beds deeper and wider, other sedges take their appointed places, and these are joined by blue gentians, daisies, dodecatheons, violets, honeyworts, and many a lowly moss. Shrubs also hasten in time to the new gardens,—kalmia with its glossy leaves and purple flowers, the arctic willow, making soft woven carpets, together with the heathy bryanthus and cassiope, the fairest and dearest of them all. Insects now enrich the air, frogs pipe cheerily in the shallows, soon followed by the ouzel, which is the first bird to visit a glacier lake, as the sedge is the first of plants.

So the young lake grows in beauty, becoming more and more humanly lovable from century to century. Groves of aspen spring up, and hardy pines, and the Hemlock Spruce, until it is richly overshadowed and embowered. But while its shores are being enriched, the soil-beds creep out with incessant growth, contracting its area, while the lighter mud-particles deposited on the bottom cause it to grow constantly shallower, until at length the last remnant of the lake vanishes,

—closed forever in ripe and natural old age. And now its feeding-stream goes winding on without halting through the new gardens and groves that have taken its place.

The length of the life of any lake depends ordinarily upon the capacity of its basin, as compared with the carrying power of the streams that flow into it, the character of the rocks over which these streams flow, and the relative position of the lake toward other lakes. In a series whose basins lie in the same cañon, and are fed by one and the same main stream, the uppermost will, of course, vanish first unless some other lake-filling agent comes in to modify the result; because at first it receives nearly all of the sediments that the stream brings down, only the finest of the mud-particles being carried through the highest of the series to the next below. Then the next higher, and the next would be successively filled, and the lowest would be the last to vanish. But this simplicity as to duration is broken in upon in various ways, chiefly through the action of side-streams that enter the lower lakes direct. For, notwithstanding many of these side tributaries are quite short, and, during late summer, feeble, they all become powerful torrents in springtime when the snow is melting, and carry not only sand and pine-needles, but large trunks and boulders tons in weight, sweeping them down their steeply inclined channels and into the lake basins with astounding energy. Many of these side affluents also have the advantage of access to the main lateral moraines of the vanished glacier that occupied the cañon, and upon these they draw for lake-filling material, while the main trunk stream flows mostly over clean glacier pavements, where but little moraine matter is ever left for them to carry. Thus a small rapid stream with abundance of loose transportable material within its reach may fill up an extensive basin in a few centuries, while a large perennial trunk stream, flowing over clean, enduring pavements, though ordinarily a hundred times larger, may not fill a smaller basin in thousands of years.

The comparative influence of great and small streams as lake-fillers is strikingly illustrated in Yosemite Valley, through which the Merced flows. The bottom of the valley is now composed of level meadow-lands and dry, sloping soil-beds planted with oak and pine, but it was once a lake stretching from wall to wall and nearly from one end of the valley to the other, forming one of the most beautiful cliff-bound sheets of water that ever existed in the Sierra. And though never per-haps seen by human eye, it was but yesterday, geologically speaking, since it disappeared, and the traces of its existence are still so fresh, it may easily be restored to the eye of imag-ination and viewed in all its grandeur, about as truly and viv-idly as if actually before us. Now we find that the detritus which fills this magnificent basin was not brought down from the distant mountains by the main streams that converge here to form the river, however powerful and available for the pur-pose at first sight they appear; but almost wholly by the small local tributaries, such as those of Indian Cañon, the Sentinel, and the Three Brothers, and by a few small residual glaciers which lingered in the shadows of the walls long after the main trunk glacier had receded beyond the head of the valley.

Had the glaciers that once covered the range been melted at once, leaving the entire surface bare from top to bottom simultaneously, then of course all the lakes would have come into existence at the same time, and the highest, other cir-cumstances being equal, would, as we have seen, be the first to vanish. But because they melted gradually from the foot of the range upward, the lower lakes were the first to see the light and the first to be obliterated. Therefore, instead of finding the lakes of the present day at the foot of the range, we find them at the top. Most of the lower lakes vanished thousands of years before those now brightening the alpine landscapes were born. And in general, owing to the deliber-ation of the upward retreat of the glaciers, the lowest of the existing lakes are also the oldest, a gradual transition being apparent throughout the entire belt, from the older, forested, meadow-rimmed and contracted forms all the way up to those that are new born, lying bare and meadowless among the highest peaks.

A few small lakes unfortunately situated are extinguished suddenly by a single swoop of an avalanche, carrying down immense numbers of trees, together with the soil they were growing upon. Others are obliterated by land-slips, earth-quake taluses, etc., but these lake-deaths compared with those resulting from the deliberate and incessant deposition of sediments, may be termed accidental. Their fate is like that of trees struck by lightning.

The lake-line is of course still rising, its present elevation being about 8000 feet above sea-level; somewhat higher than this toward the southern extremity of the range, lower toward the northern, on account of the difference in time of the withdrawal of the glaciers, due to difference in climate. Specimens occur here and there considerably below this limit, in basins specially protected from inwashing detritus, or exceptional in size. These, however, are not sufficiently numerous to make any marked irregularity in the line. The highest I have yet found lies at an elevation of about 12,000 feet, in a glacier womb, at the foot of one of the highest of the summit peaks, a few miles to the north of Mount Ritter. The basins of perhaps twenty-five or thirty are still in process of formation beneath the few lingering glaciers, but by the time they are born, an equal or greater number will probably have died. Since the beginning of the close of the ice-period the whole number in the range has perhaps never been greater than at present.

A rough approximation to the average duration of these mountain lakes may be made from data already suggested, but I cannot stop here to present the subject in detail. I must also forego, in the mean time, the pleasure of a full discussion of the interesting question of lake-basin formation, for which fine, clear, demonstrative material abounds in these mountains. In addition to what has been already given on the subject, I will only make this one statement. Every lake in the Sierra is a glacier lake. Their basins were not merely remodeled and scoured out by this mighty agent, but in the first place were eroded from the solid.

I must now make haste to give some nearer views of representative specimens lying at different elevations on the main lake-belt, confining myself to descriptions of the features most characteristic of each.

SHADOW LAKE

This is a fine specimen of the oldest and lowest of the existing lakes. It lies about eight miles above Yosemite Valley,

on the main branch of the Merced, at an elevation of about
7350 feet above the sea; and is everywhere so securely cliff-
bound that without artificial trails only wild animals can get
down to its rocky shores from any direction. Its original
length was about a mile and a half; now it is only half a mile
in length by about a fourth of a mile in width, and over the
lowest portion of the basin ninety-eight feet deep. Its crystal
waters are clasped around on the north and south by majestic
granite walls sculptured in true Yosemitic style into domes,
gables, and battlemented headlands, which on the south come
plunging down sheer into deep water, from a height of from
1500 to 2000 feet. The South Lyell glacier eroded this magnificent basin out of solid porphyritic granite while forcing its
way westward from the summit fountains toward Yosemite,
and the exposed rocks around the shores, and the projecting
bosses of the walls, ground and burnished beneath the vast
ice-flood, still glow with silvery radiance, notwithstanding the
innumerable corroding storms that have fallen upon them.
The general conformation of the basin, as well as the moraines
laid along the top of the walls, and the grooves and scratches
on the bottom and sides, indicate in the most unmistakable
manner the direction pursued by this mighty ice-river, its great
depth, and the tremendous energy it exerted in thrusting itself
into and out of the basin; bearing down with superior pressure
upon this portion of its channel, because of the greater declivity, consequently eroding it deeper than the other portions
about it, and producing the lake-bowl as the necessary result.

With these magnificent ice-characters so vividly before us it
is not easy to realize that the old glacier that made them vanished tens of centuries ago; for, excepting the vegetation that
has sprung up, and the changes effected by an earthquake that
hurled rock-avalanches from the weaker headlands, the basin
as a whole presents the same appearance that it did when first
brought to light. The lake itself, however, has undergone
marked changes; one sees at a glance that it is growing old.
More than two thirds of its original area is now dry land,
covered with meadow-grasses and groves of pine and fir, and
the level bed of alluvium stretching across from wall to wall
at the head is evidently growing out all along its lakeward
margin, and will at length close the lake forever.

Every lover of fine wildness would delight to saunter on a summer day through the flowery groves now occupying the filled-up portion of the basin. The curving shore is clearly traced by a ribbon of white sand upon which the ripples play; then comes a belt of broad-leafed sedges, interrupted here and there by impenetrable tangles of willows; beyond this there are groves of trembling aspen; then a dark, shadowy belt of Two-leaved Pine, with here and there a round carex meadow ensconced nest-like in its midst; and lastly, a narrow outer margin of majestic Silver Fir 200 feet high. The ground beneath the trees is covered with a luxuriant crop of grasses, chiefly triticum, bromus, and calamagrostis, with purple spikes and panicles arching to one's shoulders; while the open meadow patches glow throughout the summer with showy flowers,—heleniums, goldenrods, erigerons, lupines, castilleias, and lilies, and form favorite hiding- and feeding-grounds for bears and deer.

The rugged south wall is feathered darkly along the top with an imposing array of spirey Silver Firs, while the rifted precipices all the way down to the water's edge are adorned with picturesque old junipers, their cinnamon-colored bark showing finely upon the neutral gray of the granite. These, with a few venturesome Dwarf Pines and Spruces, lean out over fissured ribs and tablets, or stand erect back in shadowy niches, in an indescribably wild and fearless manner. Moreover, the white-flowered Douglas spiræa and dwarf evergreen oak form graceful fringes along the narrower seams, wherever the slightest hold can be effected. Rock-ferns, too, are here, such as allosorus, pellæa, and cheilanthes, making handsome rosettes on the drier fissures; and the delicate maidenhair, cistoperis, and woodsia hide back in mossy grottoes, moistened by some trickling rill; and then the orange wall-flower holds up its showy panicles here and there in the sunshine, and bahia makes bosses of gold. But, notwithstanding all this plant beauty, the general impression in looking across the lake is of stern, unflinching rockiness; the ferns and flowers are scarcely seen, and not one fiftieth of the whole surface is screened with plant life.

The sunnier north wall is more varied in sculpture, but the general tone is the same. A few head-lands, flat-topped and soil-covered, support clumps of cedar and pine; and up-curving tangles of chinquapin and live-oak, growing on rough earthquake taluses, girdle their bases. Small streams come cascading down between them, their foaming margins brightened with gay primulas, gilias, and mimuluses. And close along the shore on this side there is a strip of rocky meadow enameled with buttercups, daisies, and white violets, and the purple-topped grasses out on its beveled border dip their leaves into the water.

The lower edge of the basin is a dam-like swell of solid granite, heavily abraded by the old glacier, but scarce at all cut into as yet by the outflowing stream, though it has flowed on unceasingly since the lake came into existence.

As soon as the stream is fairly over the lake-lip it breaks into cascades, never for a moment halting, and scarce abating one jot of its glad energy, until it reaches the next filled-up basin, a mile below. Then swirling and curving drowsily through meadow and grove, it breaks forth anew into gray rapids and falls, leaping and gliding in glorious exuberance of wild bound and dance down into another and yet another filled-up lake basin. Then, after a long rest in the levels of Little Yosemite, it makes its grandest display in the famous Nevada Fall. Out of the clouds of spray at the foot of the fall the battered, roaring river gropes its way, makes another mile of cascades and rapids, rests a moment in Emerald Pool, then plunges over the grand cliff of the Vernal Fall, and goes thundering and chafing down a boulder-choked gorge of tremendous depth and wildness into the tranquil reaches of the old Yosemite lake basin.

The color-beauty about Shadow Lake during the Indian summer is much richer than one could hope to find in so young and so glacial a wilderness. Almost every leaf is tinted then, and the goldenrods are in bloom; but most of the color is given by the ripe grasses, willows, and aspens. At the foot of the lake you stand in a trembling aspen grove, every leaf painted like a butterfly, and away to right and left round the shores sweeps a curving ribbon of meadow, red and brown dotted with pale yellow, shading off here and there into hazy purple. The walls, too, are dashed with bits of bright color that gleam out on the neutral granite gray. But neither the walls, nor the margin meadow, nor yet the gay, fluttering grove in which you stand, nor the lake itself, flashing with spangles, can long hold your attention; for at the head of the lake there is a gorgeous mass of orange-yellow, belonging to the main aspen belt of the basin, which seems the very fountain whence all the color below it had flowed, and here your eye is filled and fixed. This glorious mass is about thirty feet high, and extends across the basin nearly from wall to wall. Rich bosses of willow flame in front of it, and from the base of these the brown meadow comes forward to the water's edge, the whole being relieved against the unyielding green of the coniferæ, while thick sun-gold is poured over all.

During these blessed color-days no cloud darkens the sky, the winds are gentle, and the landscape rests, hushed everywhere, and indescribably impressive. A few ducks are usually seen sailing on the lake, apparently more for pleasure than anything else, and the ouzels at the head of the rapids sing always; while robins, grosbeaks, and the Douglas squirrels are busy in the groves, making delightful company, and intensifying the feeling of grateful sequestration without ruffling the deep, hushed calm and peace.

This autumnal mellowness usually lasts until the end of November. Then come days of quite another kind. The winter clouds grow, and bloom, and shed their starry crystals on every leaf and rock, and all the colors vanish like a sunset. The deer gather and hasten down their well-known trails, fearful of being snow-bound. Storm succeeds storm, heaping snow on the cliffs and meadows, and bending the slender pines to the ground in wide arches, one over the other, clustering and interlacing like lodged wheat. Avalanches rush and boom from the shelving heights, piling immense heaps upon the frozen lake, and all the summer glory is buried and lost. Yet in the midst of this hearty winter the sun shines warm at times, calling the Douglas squirrel to frisk in the snowy pines and seek out his hidden stores; and the weather is never so severe as to drive away the grouse and little nut-hatches and chickadees.

Toward May, the lake begins to open. The hot sun sends down innumerable streams over the cliffs, streaking them round and round with foam. The snow slowly vanishes, and the meadows show tintings of green. Then spring comes on apace; flowers and flies enrich the air and the sod, and the deer come back to the upper groves like birds to an old nest.

I first discovered this charming lake in the autumn of 1872, while on my way to the glaciers at the head of the river. It was rejoicing then in its gayest colors, untrodden, hidden in the glorious wildness like unmined gold. Year after year I walked its shores without discovering any other trace of humanity than the remains of an Indian camp-fire, and the thigh-bones of a deer that had been broken to get at the marrow. It lies out of the regular ways of Indians, who love to hunt in more accessible fields adjacent to trails. Their knowledge of deer-haunts had probably enticed them here some hunger-time when they wished to make sure of a feast; for hunting in this lake-hollow is like hunting in a fenced park. I had told the beauty of Shadow Lake only to a few friends, fearing it might come to be trampled and "improved" like Yosemite. On my last visit, as I was sauntering along the shore on the strip of sand between the water and sod, reading the tracks of the wild animals that live here, I was startled by a human track, which I at once saw belonged to some shepherd; for each step was turned out 35° or 40° from the general course pursued, and was also run over in an uncertain sprawling fashion at the heel, while a row of round dots on the right indicated the staff that shepherds carry. None but a shepherd could make such a track, and after tracing it a few minutes I began to fear that he might be seeking pasturage; for what else could he be seeking? Returning from the glaciers shortly afterward, my worst fears were realized. A trail had been made down the mountain-side from the north, and all the gardens and meadows were destroyed by a horde of hoofed locusts, as if swept by a fire. The money-changers were in the temple.

ORANGE LAKE

Besides these larger cañon lakes, fed by the main cañon streams, there are many smaller ones lying aloft on the top of rock benches, entirely independent of the general drainage channels, and of course drawing their supplies from a very limited area. Notwithstanding they are mostly small and shallow, owing to their immunity from avalanche detritus and the inwashings of powerful streams, they often endure longer than others many times larger but less favorably situated. When very shallow they become dry toward the end of summer; but because their basins are ground out of seamless stone they suffer no loss save from evaporation alone; and the great depth of snow that falls, lasting into June, makes their dry season short in any case.

Orange Lake is a fair illustration of this bench form. It lies in the middle of a beautiful glacial pavement near the lower margin of the lake-line, about a mile and a half to the northwest of Shadow Lake. It is only about 100 yards in circumference. Next the water there is a girdle of carices with wide overarching leaves, then in regular order a shaggy ruff of huckleberry bushes, a zone of willows with here and there a bush of the Mountain Ash, then a zone of aspens with a few pines around the outside. These zones are of course concentric, and together form a wall beyond which the naked ice-burnished granite stretches away in every direction, leaving it conspicuously relieved, like a bunch of palms in a desert.

In autumn, when the colors are ripe, the whole circular grove, at a little distance, looks like a big handful of flowers set in a cup to be kept fresh—a tuft of goldenrods. Its feeding-streams are exceedingly beautiful, notwithstanding their inconstancy and extreme shallowness. They have no channel whatever, and consequently are left free to spread in thin sheets upon the shining granite and wander at will. In many places the current is less than a fourth of an inch deep, and flows with so little friction it is scarcely visible. Sometimes there is not a single foam-bell, or drifting pine-needle, or irregularity of any sort to manifest its motion. Yet when observed narrowly it is seen to form a web of gliding lacework exquisitely woven, giving beautiful reflections from its minute curving ripples and eddies, and differing from the water-laces of large cascades in being everywhere transparent. In spring, when the snow is melting, the lake-bowl is brimming full, and sends forth quite a large stream that slips glassily for 200 yards or so, until it comes to an almost vertical precipice 800 feet high, down which it plunges in a fine cataract; then it gathers its scattered waters and goes smoothly over folds of gently dipping granite to its confluence with the main cañon stream. During the greater portion of the year, however, not a single water sound will you hear either at head or foot of the lake, not even the whispered lappings of ripple-waves along the shore; for the winds are fenced out. But the deep mountain silence is sweetened now and then by birds that stop here to rest and drink on their way across the cañon.

LAKE STARR KING

A beautiful variety of the bench-top lakes occurs just where the great lateral moraines of the main glaciers have been shoved forward in outswelling concentric rings by small residual tributary glaciers. Instead of being encompassed by a narrow ring of trees like Orange Lake, these lie embosomed in dense moraine woods, so dense that in seeking them you may pass them by again and again, although you may know nearly where they lie concealed.

Lake Starr King, lying to the north of the cone of that name, above the Little Yosemite Valley, is a fine specimen of this variety. The ouzels pass it by, and so do the ducks; they could hardly get into it if they would, without plumping straight down inside the circling trees.

Yet these isolated gems, lying like fallen fruit detached from the branches, are not altogether without inhabitants and joyous, animating visitors. Of course fishes cannot get into them, and this is generally true of nearly every glacier lake in the range, but they are all well stocked with happy frogs. How did the frogs get into them in the first place? Perhaps their sticky spawn was carried in on the feet of ducks or other birds, else their progenitors must have made some exciting excursions through the woods and up the sides of the cañons. Down in the still, pure depths of these hidden lakelets you may also find the larvæ of innumerable insects and a great variety of beetles, while the air above them is thick with humming wings, through the midst of which fly-catchers are constantly darting. And in autumn, when the huckleberries are ripe, bands of robins and grosbeaks come to feast, forming altogether delightful little byworlds for the naturalist.

Pushing our way upward toward the axis of the range, we find lakes in greater and greater abundance, and more youthful in aspect. At an elevation of about 9000 feet above sea-level they seem to have arrived at middle age,—that is, their basins seem to be about half filled with alluvium. Broad sheets of meadow-land are seen extending into them, imperfect and boggy in many places and more nearly level than those of the older lakes below them, and the vegetation of their shores is of course more alpine. Kalmia, ledum, and cassiope fringe the meadow rocks, while the luxuriant, waving groves, so characteristic of the lower lakes, are represented only by clumps of the Dwarf Pine and Hemlock Spruce. These, however, are oftentimes very picturesquely grouped on rocky headlands around the outer rim of the meadows, or with still more striking effect crown some rocky islet.

Moreover, from causes that we cannot stop here to explain, the cliffs about these middle-aged lakes are seldom of the massive Yosemite type, but are more broken, and less sheer, and they usually stand back, leaving the shores comparatively free; while the few precipitous rocks that do come forward and plunge directly into deep water are seldom more than three or four hundred feet high.

I have never yet met ducks in any of the lakes of this kind, but the ouzel is never wanting where the feeding-streams are perennial. Wild sheep and deer may occasionally be seen on the meadows, and very rarely a bear. One might camp on the rugged shores of these bright fountains for weeks, without meeting any animal larger than the marmots that burrow beneath glacier boulders along the edges of the meadows.

The highest and youngest of all the lakes lie nestled in glacier wombs. At first sight, they seem pictures of pure bloodless desolation, miniature arctic seas, bound in perpetual ice and snow, and overshadowed by harsh, gloomy, crumbling precipices. Their waters are keen ultramarine blue in the deepest parts, lively grass-green toward the shore shallows and around the edges of the small bergs usually floating about in them. A few hardy sedges, frost-pinched every night, are occasionally found making soft sods along the sun-touched portions of their shores, and when their northern banks slope openly to the south, and are soil-covered, no matter how coarsely, they

are sure to be brightened with flowers. One lake in particular
now comes to mind which illustrates the floweriness of the
sun-touched banks of these icy gems. Close up under the
shadow of the Sierra Matterhorn, on the eastern slope of the
range, lies one of the iciest of these glacier lakes at an elevation
of about 12,000 feet. A short, ragged-edged glacier crawls into
it from the south, and on the opposite side it is embanked
and dammed by a series of concentric terminal moraines,
made by the glacier when it entirely filled the basin. Half a
mile below lies a second lake, at a height of 11,500 feet, about
as cold and as pure as a snow-crystal. The waters of the first
come gurgling down into it over and through the moraine
dam, while a second stream pours into it direct from a glacier
that lies to the southeast. Sheer precipices of crystalline snow
rise out of deep water on the south, keeping perpetual winter
on that side, but there is a fine summery spot on the other,
notwithstanding the lake is only about 300 yards wide. Here,
on August 25, 1873, I found a charming company of flowers,
not pinched, crouching dwarfs, scarce able to look up, but
warm and juicy, standing erect in rich cheery color and bloom.
On a narrow strip of shingle, close to the water's edge, there
were a few tufts of carex gone to seed; and a little way back
up the rocky bank at the foot of a crumbling wall so inclined
as to absorb and radiate as well as reflect a considerable quantity of sun-heat, was the garden, containing a thrifty thicket
of Cowania covered with large yellow flowers; several bushes
of the alpine ribes with berries nearly ripe and wildly acid; a
few handsome grasses belonging to two distinct species, and
one goldenrod; a few hairy lupines and radiant spragueas,
whose blue and rose-colored flowers were set off to fine advantage amid green carices; and along a narrow seam in the
very warmest angle of the wall a perfectly gorgeous fringe of
Epilobium obcordatum with flowers an inch wide, crowded together in lavish profusion, and colored as royal a purple as
ever was worn by any high-bred plant of the tropics; and best
of all, and greatest of all, a noble thistle in full bloom, standing
erect, head and shoulders above his companions, and thrusting out his lances in sturdy vigor as if growing on a Scottish
brae. All this brave warm bloom among the raw stones, right
in the face of the onlooking glaciers.

As far as I have been able to find out, these upper lakes are snow-buried in winter to a depth of about thirty-five or forty feet, and those most exposed to avalanches, to a depth of even a hundred feet or more. These last are, of course, nearly lost to the landscape. Some remain buried for years, when the snowfall is exceptionally great, and many open only on one side late in the season. The snow of the closed side is composed of coarse granules compacted and frozen into a firm, faintly stratified mass, like the *névé* of a glacier. The lapping waves of the open portion gradually undermine and cause it to break off in large masses like icebergs, which gives rise to a precipitous front like the discharging wall of a glacier entering the sea. The play of the lights among the crystal angles of these snow-cliffs, the pearly white of the outswelling bosses, the bergs drifting in front, aglow in the sun and edged with green water, and the deep blue disk of the lake itself extending to your feet,—this forms a picture that enriches all your after-life, and is never forgotten. But however perfect the season and the day, the cold incompleteness of these young lakes is always keenly felt. We approach them with a kind of mean caution, and steal unconfidingly around their crystal shores, dashed and ill at ease, as if expecting to hear some forbidding voice. But the love-songs of the ouzels and the love-looks of the daisies gradually reassure us, and manifest the warm fountain humanity that pervades the coldest and most solitary of them all.

Chapter VII

AFTER the lakes on the High Sierra come the glacier meadows. They are smooth, level, silky lawns, lying embedded in the upper forests, on the floors of the valleys, and along
the broad backs of the main dividing ridges, at a height of
about 8000 to 9500 feet above the sea.

They are nearly as level as the lakes whose places they have
taken, and present a dry, even surface free from rock-heaps,
mossy bogginess, and the frowsy roughness of rank, coarse-
leaved, weedy, and shrubby vegetation. The sod is close and
fine, and so complete that you cannot see the ground; and at
the same time so brightly enameled with flowers and butterflies that it may well be called a garden-meadow, or meadow-
garden; for the plushy sod is in many places so crowded with
gentians, daisies, ivesias, and various species of orthocarpus
that the grass is scarcely noticeable, while in others the flowers
are only pricked in here and there singly, or in small ornamental rosettes.

The most influential of the grasses composing the sod is a
delicate calamagrostis with fine filiform leaves, and loose, airy
panicles that seem to float above the flowery lawn like a purple
mist. But, write as I may, I cannot give anything like an adequate idea of the exquisite beauty of these mountain carpets
as they lie smoothly outspread in the savage wilderness. What
words are fine enough to picture them? to what shall we liken
them? The flowery levels of the prairies of the old West, the
luxuriant savannahs of the South, and the finest of cultivated
meadows are coarse in comparison. One may at first sight
compare them with the carefully tended lawns of pleasure-
grounds; for they are as free from weeds as they, and as
smooth, but here the likeness ends; for these wild lawns, with
all their exquisite fineness, have no trace of that painful, licked,
snipped, repressed appearance that pleasure-ground lawns are
apt to have even when viewed at a distance. And, not to mention the flowers with which they are brightened, their grasses
are very much finer both in color and texture, and instead of

lying flat and motionless, matted together like a dead green cloth, they respond to the touches of every breeze, rejoicing in pure wildness, blooming and fruiting in the vital light.

Glacier meadows abound throughout all the alpine and sub-alpine regions of the Sierra in still greater numbers than the lakes. Probably from 2500 to 3000 exist between latitude 36° 30′ and 39°, distributed, of course, like the lakes, in concordance with all the other glacial features of the landscape.

On the head waters of the rivers there are what are called "Big Meadows," usually about from five to ten miles long. These occupy the basins of the ancient ice-seas, where many tributary glaciers came together to form the grand trunks. Most, however, are quite small, averaging perhaps but little more than three fourths of a mile in length.

One of the very finest of the thousands I have enjoyed lies hidden in an extensive forest of the Two-leaved Pine, on the edge of the basin of the ancient Tuolumne Mer de Glace, about eight miles to the west of Mount Dana.

Imagine yourself at the Tuolumne Soda Springs on the bank of the river, a day's journey above Yosemite Valley. You set off northward through a forest that stretches away indefinitely before you, seemingly unbroken by openings of any kind. As soon as you are fairly into the woods, the gray mountain-peaks, with their snowy gorges and hollows, are lost to view. The ground is littered with fallen trunks that lie crossed and recrossed like storm-lodged wheat; and besides this close forest of pines, the rich moraine soil supports a luxuriant growth of ribbon-leaved grasses—bromus, triticum, calama-grostis, agrostis, etc., which rear their handsome spikes and panicles above your waist. Making your way through the fertile wilderness,—finding lively bits of interest now and then in the squirrels and Clark crows, and perchance in a deer or bear,—after the lapse of an hour or two vertical bars of sunshine are seen ahead between the brown shafts of the pines, showing that you are approaching an open space, and then you suddenly emerge from the forest shadows upon a delightful purple lawn lying smooth and free in the light like a lake. This is a glacier meadow. It is about a mile and a half long by a quarter of a mile wide. The trees come pressing forward all around in close serried ranks, planting their feet exactly on its margin, and holding themselves erect, strict and orderly like soldiers on parade; thus bounding the meadow with exquisite precision, yet with free curving lines such as Nature alone can draw. With inexpressible delight you wade out into the grassy sun-lake, feeling yourself contained in one of Nature's most sacred chambers, withdrawn from the sterner influences of the mountains, secure from all intrusion, secure from yourself, free in the universal beauty. And notwithstanding the scene is so impressively spiritual, and you seem dissolved in it, yet everything about you is beating with warm, terrestrial, human love and life delightfully substantial and familiar. The resiny pines are types of health and steadfastness; the robins feeding on the sod belong to the same species you have known since childhood; and surely these daisies, larkspurs, and goldenrods are the very friend-flowers of the old home garden. Bees hum as in a harvest noon, butterflies waver above the flowers, and like them you lave in the vital sunshine, too richly and homogeneously joy-filled to be capable of partial thought. You are all eye, sifted through and through with light and beauty. Sauntering along the brook that meanders silently through the meadow from the east, special flowers call you back to discriminating consciousness. The sod comes curving down to the water's edge, forming bossy outswelling banks, and in some places overlapping countersunk boulders and forming bridges. Here you find mats of the curious dwarf willow scarce an inch high, yet sending up a multitude of gray silky catkins, illumined here and there with the purple cups and bells of bryanthus and vaccinium.

Go where you may, you everywhere find the lawn divinely beautiful, as if Nature had fingered and adjusted every plant this very day. The floating grass panicles are scarcely felt in brushing through their midst, so fine are they, and none of the flowers have tall or rigid stalks. In the brightest places you find three species of gentians with different shades of blue, daisies pure as the sky, silky leaved ivesias with warm yellow flowers, several species of orthocarpus with blunt, bossy spikes, red and purple and yellow; the alpine goldenrod, pentstemon, and clover, fragrant and honeyful, with their colors massed and blended. Parting the grasses and looking more closely you may trace the branching of their shining stems, and note the marvelous beauty of their mist of flowers, the glumes and pales exquisitely penciled, the yellow dangling stamens, and feathery pistils. Beneath the lowest leaves you discover a fairy realm of mosses,—hypnum, dicranum, polytrichum, and many others,—their precious spore-cups poised daintily on polished shafts, curiously hooded, or open, showing the richly ornate peristomas worn like royal crowns. Creeping liverworts are here also in abundance, and several rare species of fungi, exceedingly small, and frail, and delicate, as if made only for beauty. Caterpillars, black beetles, and ants roam the wilds of this lower world, making their way through miniature groves and thickets like bears in a thick wood.

And how rich, too, is the life of the sunny air! Every leaf and flower seems to have its winged representative overhead. Dragon-flies shoot in vigorous zigzags through the dancing swarms, and a rich profusion of butterflies—the leguminosæ of insects—make a fine addition to the general show. Many of these last are comparatively small at this elevation, and as yet almost unknown to science; but every now and then a familiar vanessa or papilio comes sailing past. Humming-birds, too, are quite common here, and the robin is always found along the margin of the stream, or out in the shallowest portions of the sod, and sometimes the grouse and mountain quail, with their broods of precious fluffy chickens. Swallows skim the grassy lake from end to end, fly-catchers come and go in fitful flights from the tops of dead spars, while woodpeckers swing across from side to side in graceful festoon curves,—birds, insects, and flowers all in their own way telling a deep summer joy.

The influences of pure nature seem to be so little known as yet, that it is generally supposed that complete pleasure of this kind, permeating one's very flesh and bones, unfits the student for scientific pursuits in which cool judgment and observation are required. But the effect is just the opposite. Instead of producing a dissipated condition, the mind is fertilized and stimulated and developed like sun-fed plants. All that we have seen here enables us to see with surer vision the fountains among the summit-peaks to the east whence flowed the glaciers that ground soil for the surrounding forest; and down at the foot of the meadow the moraine which formed the dam which gave rise to the lake that occupied this basin before the meadow was made; and around the margin the stones that were shoved back and piled up into a rude wall by the expansion of the lake ice during long bygone winters; and along the sides of the streams the slight hollows of the meadow which mark those portions of the old lake that were the last to vanish.

I would fain ask my readers to linger awhile in this fertile wilderness, to trace its history from its earliest glacial beginnings, and learn what we may of its wild inhabitants and visitors. How happy the birds are all summer and some of them all winter; how the pouched marmots drive tunnels under the snow, and how fine and brave a life the slandered coyote lives here, and the deer and bears! But, knowing well the difference between reading and seeing, I will only ask attention to some brief sketches of its varying aspects as they are presented throughout the more marked seasons of the year.

The summer life we have been depicting lasts with but little abatement until October, when the night frosts begin to sting, bronzing the grasses, and ripening the leaves of the creeping heathworts along the banks of the stream to reddish purple and crimson; while the flowers disappear, all save the goldenrods and a few daisies, that continue to bloom on unscathed until the beginning of snowy winter. In still nights the grass panicles and every leaf and stalk are laden with frost crystals, through which the morning sunbeams sift in ravishing splendor, transforming each to a precious diamond radiating the colors of the rainbow. The brook shallows are plaited across and across with slender lances of ice, but both these and the grass crystals are melted before midday, and, notwithstanding the great elevation of the meadow, the afternoons are still warm enough to revive the chilled butterflies and call them out to enjoy the late-flowering goldenrods. The divine alpenglow flushes the surrounding forest every evening, followed by a crystal night with hosts of lily stars, whose size and brilliancy cannot be conceived by those who have never risen above the lowlands.

Thus come and go the bright sun-days of autumn, not a cloud in the sky, week after week until near December. Then comes a sudden change. Clouds of a peculiar aspect with a slow, crawling gait gather and grow in the azure, throwing out satiny fringes, and becoming gradually darker until every lake-like rift and opening is closed and the whole bent firmament is obscured in equal structureless gloom. Then comes the snow, for the clouds are ripe, the meadows of the sky are in bloom, and shed their radiant blossoms like an orchard in the spring. Lightly, lightly they lodge in the brown grasses and in the tasseled needles of the pines, falling hour after hour, day after day, silently, lovingly,—all the winds hushed,—glancing and circling hither, thither, glinting against one another, rays interlocking in flakes as large as daisies; and then the dry grasses, and the trees, and the stones are all equally abloom again. Thunder-showers occur here during the summer months, and impressive it is to watch the coming of the big transparent drops, each a small world in itself,—one unbroken ocean without islands hurling free through the air like planets through space. But still more impressive to me is the coming of the snow-flowers,—falling stars, winter daisies,—giving bloom to all the ground alike. Raindrops blossom brilliantly in the rainbow, and change to flowers in the sod, but snow comes in full flower direct from the dark, frozen sky.

The later snow-storms are oftentimes accompanied by winds that break up the crystals, when the temperature is low, into single petals and irregular dusty fragments; but there is comparatively little drifting on the meadow, so securely is it embosomed in the woods. From December to May, storm succeeds storm, until the snow is about fifteen or twenty feet deep, but the surface is always as smooth as the breast of a bird.

Hushed now is the life that so late was beating warmly. Most of the birds have gone down below the snow-line, the plants sleep, and all the fly-wings are folded. Yet the sun beams gloriously many a cloudless day in midwinter, casting long lance shadows athwart the dazzling expanse. In June small flecks of the dead, decaying sod begin to appear, gradually widening and uniting with one another, covered with creeping rags of water during the day, and ice by night, looking as hopeless and unvital as crushed rocks just emerging from the darkness of the glacial period. Walk the meadow now! Scarce the memory of a flower will you find. The ground seems twice dead. Nevertheless, the annual resurrection is drawing near. The life-giving sun pours his floods, the last snow-wreath melts, myriads of growing points push eagerly through the steaming mold, the birds come back, new wings fill the air, and fervid summer life comes surging on, seemingly yet more glorious than before.

This is a perfect meadow, and under favorable circumstances exists without manifesting any marked changes for centuries. Nevertheless, soon or late it must inevitably grow old and vanish. During the calm Indian summer, scarce a sand-grain moves around its banks, but in flood-times and storm-times, soil is washed forward upon it and laid in successive sheets around its gently sloping rim, and is gradually extended to the center, making it dryer. Through a considerable period the meadow vegetation is not greatly affected thereby, for it gradually rises with the rising ground, keeping on the surface like water-plants rising on the swell of waves. But at length the elevation of the meadow-land goes on so far as to produce too dry a soil for the specific meadow-plants, when, of course, they have to give up their places to others fitted for the new conditions. The most characteristic of the new-comers at this elevation above the sea are principally sun-loving gilias, eriogonæ, and compositæ, and finally forest-trees. Henceforward the obscuring changes are so manifold that the original lake-meadow can be unveiled and seen only by the geologist.

Generally speaking, glacier lakes vanish more slowly than the meadows that succeed them, because, unless very shallow, a greater quantity of material is required to fill up their basins and obliterate them than is required to render the surface of the meadow too high and dry for meadow vegetation. Furthermore, owing to the weathering to which the adjacent rocks are subjected, material of the finer sort, susceptible of transportation by rains and ordinary floods, is more abundant during the meadow period than during the lake period. Yet doubtless many a fine meadow favorably situated exists in almost prime beauty for thousands of years, the process of extinction being exceedingly slow, as we reckon time. This is especially the case with meadows circumstanced like the one we have described—embosomed in deep woods, with the ground rising gently away from it all around, the network of tree-roots in which all the ground is clasped preventing any rapid torrential washing. But, in exceptional cases, beautiful lawns formed with great deliberation are overwhelmed and obliterated at once by the action of land-slips, earthquake avalanches, or extraordinary floods, just as lakes are.

In those glacier meadows that take the places of shallow lakes which have been fed by feeble streams, glacier mud and fine vegetable humus enter largely into the composition of the soil; and on account of the shallowness of this soil, and the seamless, water-tight, undrained condition of the rock-basins, they are usually wet, and therefore occupied by tall grasses and sedges, whose coarse appearance offers a striking contrast to that of the delicate lawn-making kind described above. These shallow-soiled meadows are oftentimes still further roughened and diversified by partially buried moraines and swelling bosses of the bed-rock, which, with the trees and shrubs growing upon them, produce a striking effect as they stand in relief like islands in the grassy level, or sweep across in rugged curves from one forest wall to the other.

Throughout the upper meadow region, wherever water is sufficiently abundant and low in temperature, in basins secure from flood-washing, handsome bogs are formed with a deep growth of brown and yellow sphagnum picturesquely ruffled with patches of kalmia and ledum which ripen masses of beautiful color in the autumn. Between these cool, spongy bogs and the dry, flowery meadows there are many interesting varieties which are graduated into one another by the varied conditions already alluded to, forming a series of delightful studies.

HANGING MEADOWS

Another very well-marked and interesting kind of meadow, differing greatly both in origin and appearance from the lake-meadows, is found lying aslant upon moraine-covered hillsides trending in the direction of greatest declivity, waving up and down over rock heaps and ledges, like rich green ribbons brilliantly illumined with tall flowers. They occur both in the alpine and subalpine regions in considerable numbers, and never fail to make telling features in the landscape. They are often a mile or more in length, but never very wide—usually from thirty to fifty yards. When the mountain or cañon side on which they lie dips at the required angle, and other conditions are at the same time favorable, they extend from above the timber line to the bottom of a cañon or lake basin, descending in fine, fluent lines like cascades, breaking here and there into a kind of spray on large boulders, or dividing and flowing around on either side of some projecting islet. Sometimes a noisy stream goes brawling down through them, and again, scarcely a drop of water is in sight. They owe their existence, however, to streams, whether visible or invisible, the wildest specimens being found where some perennial fountain, as a glacier or snowbank or moraine spring sends down its waters across a rough sheet of soil in a dissipated web of feeble, oozing rivulets. These conditions give rise to a meadowy vegetation, whose extending roots still more obstruct the free flow of the waters, and tend to dissipate them out over a yet wider area. Thus the moraine soil and the necessary moisture requisite for the better class of meadow plants are at times combined about as perfectly as if smoothly outspread on a level surface. Where the soil happens to be composed of the finer qualities of glacial detritus and the water is not in excess, the nearest approach is made by the vegetation to that of the lake-meadow. But where, as is more commonly the case, the soil is coarse and bouldery, the vegetation is correspondingly rank. Tall, wide-leaved grasses take their places along the sides, and rushes and nodding carices in the wetter portions, mingled with the most beautiful and imposing flowers,—orange lilies and larkspurs seven or eight feet high, lupines, senecios, aliums, painted-cups, many species of mimulus and pentstemon, the ample boat-leaved *veratrum alba*, and the magnificent alpine columbine, with spurs an inch and a half long. At an elevation of from seven to nine thousand feet showy flowers frequently form the bulk of the vegetation; then the hanging meadows become hanging gardens.

In rare instances we find an alpine basin the bottom of which is a perfect meadow, and the sides nearly all the way round, rising in gentle curves, are covered with moraine soil, which, being saturated with melting snow from encircling fountains, gives rise to an almost continuous girdle of down-curving meadow vegetation that blends gracefully into the level meadow at the bottom, thus forming a grand, smooth, soft, meadow-lined mountain nest. It is in meadows of this sort that the mountain beaver (*Haplodon*) loves to make his home, excavating snug chambers beneath the sod, digging canals, turning the underground waters from channel to channel to suit his convenience, and feeding the vegetation.

Another kind of meadow or bog occurs on densely timbered hillsides where small perennial streams have been dammed at short intervals by fallen trees. Still another kind is found hanging down smooth, flat precipices, while corresponding leaning meadows rise to meet them.

There are also three kinds of small pot-hole meadows one of which is found along the banks of the main streams, another on the summits of rocky ridges, and the third on glacier pavements, all of them interesting in origin and brimful of plant beauty.

Chapter VIII

THE FORESTS

THE coniferous forests of the Sierra are the grandest and most beautiful in the world, and grow in a delightful climate on the most interesting and accessible of mountain-ranges, yet strange to say they are not well known. More than sixty years ago David Douglas, an enthusiastic botanist and tree lover, wandered alone through fine sections of the Sugar Pine and Silver Fir woods wild with delight. A few years later, other botanists made short journeys from the coast into the lower woods. Then came the wonderful multitude of miners into the foot-hill zone, mostly blind with gold-dust, soon followed by "sheepmen," who, with wool over their eyes, chased their flocks through all the forest belts from one end of the range to the other. Then the Yosemite Valley was discovered, and thousands of admiring tourists passed through sections of the lower and middle zones on their way to that wonderful park, and gained fine glimpses of the Sugar Pines and Silver Firs along the edges of dusty trails and roads. But few indeed, strong and free with eyes undimmed with care, have gone far enough and lived long enough with the trees to gain anything like a loving conception of their grandeur and significance as manifested in the harmonies of their distribution and varying aspects throughout the seasons, as they stand arrayed in their winter garb rejoicing in storms, putting forth their fresh leaves in the spring while steaming with resiny fragrance, receiving the thunder-showers of summer, or reposing heavy-laden with ripe cones in the rich sungold of autumn. For knowledge of this kind one must dwell with the trees and grow with them, without any reference to time in the almanac sense.

The distribution of the general forest in belts is readily perceived. These, as we have seen, extend in regular order from one extremity of the range to the other; and however dense and somber they may appear in general views, neither on the rocky heights nor down in the leafiest hollows will you find anything to remind you of the dank, malarial selvas of the Amazon and Orinoco, with their "boundless contiguity of shade," the monotonous uniformity of the Deodar forests of the Himalaya, the Black Forest of Europe, or the dense dark woods of Douglas Spruce where rolls the Oregon. The giant pines, and firs, and Sequoias hold their arms open to the sunlight, rising above one another on the mountain benches, marshaled in glorious array, giving forth the utmost expression of grandeur and beauty with inexhaustible variety and harmony.

The inviting openness of the Sierra woods is one of their most distinguishing characteristics. The trees of all the species stand more or less apart in groves, or in small, irregular groups, enabling one to find a way nearly everywhere, along sunny colonnades and through openings that have a smooth, park-like surface, strewn with brown needles and burs. Now you cross a wild garden, now a meadow, now a ferny, willowy stream; and ever and anon you emerge from all the groves and flowers upon some granite pavement or high, bare ridge commanding superb views above the waving sea of evergreens far and near.

One would experience but little difficulty in riding on horseback through the successive belts all the way up to the storm-beaten fringes of the icy peaks. The deep cañons, however, that extend from the axis of the range, cut the belts more or less completely into sections, and prevent the mounted traveler from tracing them lengthwise.

This simple arrangement in zones and sections brings the forest, as a whole, within the comprehension of every observer. The different species are ever found occupying the same relative positions to one another, as controlled by soil, climate, and the comparative vigor of each species in taking and holding the ground; and so appreciable are these relations, one need never be at a loss in determining, within a few hundred feet, the elevation above sea-level by the trees alone; for, notwithstanding some of the species range upward for several thousand feet, and all pass one another more or less, yet even those possessing the greatest vertical range are available in this connection, in as much as they take on new forms corresponding with the variations in altitude.

Crossing the treeless plains of the Sacramento and San Joaquin from the west and reaching the Sierra foot-hills, you enter the lower fringe of the forest, composed of small oaks and pines, growing so far apart that not one twentieth of the surface of the ground is in shade at clear noonday. After advancing fifteen or twenty miles, and making an ascent of from two to three thousand feet, you reach the lower margin of the main pine belt, composed of the gigantic Sugar Pine, Yellow Pine, Incense Cedar, and Sequoia. Next you come to the magnificent Silver Fir belt, and lastly to the upper pine belt, which sweeps up the rocky acclivities of the summit peaks in a dwarfed, wavering fringe to a height of from ten to twelve thousand feet.

This general order of distribution, with reference to climate dependent on elevation, is perceived at once, but there are other harmonies, as far-reaching in this connection, that become manifest only after patient observation and study. Perhaps the most interesting of these is the arrangement of the forests in long, curving bands, braided together into lace-like patterns, and outspread in charming variety. The key to this beautiful harmony is the ancient glaciers; where they flowed the trees followed, tracing their wavering courses along cañons, over ridges, and over high, rolling plateaus. The Cedars of Lebanon, says Hooker, are growing upon one of the moraines of an ancient glacier. All the forests of the Sierra are growing upon moraines. But moraines vanish like the glaciers that make them. Every storm that falls upon them wastes them, cutting gaps, disintegrating boulders, and carrying away their decaying material into new formations, until at length they are no longer recognizable by any save students, who trace their transitional forms down from the fresh moraines still in process of formation, through those that are more and more ancient, and more and more obscured by vegetation and all kinds of post-glacial weathering.

Had the ice-sheet that once covered all the range been melted simultaneously from the foot-hills to the summits, the flanks would, of course, have been left almost bare of soil, and these noble forests would be wanting. Many groves and thickets would undoubtedly have grown up on lake and avalanche beds, and many a fair flower and shrub would have found food and a dwelling-place in weathered nooks and crevices, but the Sierra as a whole would have been a bare, rocky desert.

It appears, therefore, that the Sierra forests in general indicate the extent and positions of the ancient moraines as well as they do lines of climate. For forests, properly speaking, cannot exist without soil; and, since the moraines have been deposited upon the solid rock, and only upon elected places, leaving a considerable portion of the old glacial surface bare, we find luxuriant forests of pine and fir abruptly terminated by scored and polished pavements on which not even a moss is growing, though soil alone is required to fit them for the growth of trees 200 feet in height.

THE NUT PINE
(Pinus Sabiniana)

The Nut Pine, the first conifer met in ascending the range from the west, grows only on the torrid foot-hills, seeming to delight in the most ardent sun-heat, like a palm; springing up here and there singly, or in scattered groups of five or six, among scrubby White Oaks and thickets of ceanothus and manzanita; its extreme upper limit being about 4000 feet above the sea, its lower about from 500 to 800 feet.

This tree is remarkable for its airy, widespread, tropical appearance, which suggests a region of palms, rather than cool, resiny pine woods. No one would take it at first sight to be a conifer of any kind, it is so loose in habit and so widely branched, and its foliage is so thin and gray. Full-grown specimens are from forty to fifty feet in height, and from two to three feet in diameter. The trunk usually divides into three or four main branches, about fifteen and twenty feet from the ground, which, after bearing away from one another, shoot straight up and form separate summits; while the crooked subordinate branches aspire, and radiate, and droop in ornamental sprays. The slender, grayish-green needles are from eight to twelve inches long, loosely tasseled, and inclined to droop in handsome curves, contrasting with the stiff, dark-colored trunk and branches in a very striking manner. No other tree of my acquaintance, so substantial in body, is in its foliage so thin and so pervious to the light. The sunbeams sift through even the leafiest trees with scarcely any interruption, and the weary, heated traveler finds but little protection in their shade.

The generous crop of nutritious nuts which the Nut Pine yields makes it a favorite with Indians, bears, and squirrels. The cones are most beautiful, measuring from five to eight inches in length, and not much less in thickness, rich chocolate-brown in color, and protected by strong, down-curving hooks which terminate the scales. Nevertheless, the little Douglas squirrel can open them. Indians gathering the ripe nuts make a striking picture. The men climb the trees like bears and beat off the cones with sticks, or recklessly cut off the more fruitful branches with hatchets, while the squaws gather the big, generous cones, and roast them until the scales open sufficiently to allow the hard-shelled seeds to be beaten out. Then, in the cool evenings, men, women, and children, with their capacity for dirt greatly increased by the soft resin with which they are all bedraggled, form circles around camp-fires, on the bank of the nearest stream, and lie in easy independence cracking nuts and laughing and chattering, as heedless of the future as the squirrels.

Pinus tuberculata

This curious little pine is found at an elevation of from 1500 to 3000 feet, growing in close, willowy groves. It is exceedingly slender and graceful in habit, although trees that chance to stand alone outside the groves sweep forth long, curved branches, producing a striking contrast to the ordinary grove form. The foliage is of the same peculiar gray-green color as that of the Nut Pine, and is worn about as loosely, so that the body of the tree is scarcely obscured by it.

At the age of seven or eight years it begins to bear cones, not on branches, but on the main axis, and, as they never fall off, the trunk is soon picturesquely dotted with them. The branches also become fruitful after they attain sufficient size. The average size of the older trees is about thirty or forty feet in height, and twelve to fourteen inches in diameter. The cones are about four inches long, exceedingly hard, and covered with a sort of silicious varnish and gum, rendering them impervious to moisture, evidently with a view to the careful preservation of the seeds.

No other conifer in the range is so closely restricted to special localities. It is usually found apart, standing deep in chaparral on sunny hill- and cañon-sides where there is but little depth of soil, and, where found at all, it is quite plentiful; but the ordinary traveler, following carriage-roads and trails, may ascend the range many times without meeting it.

While exploring the lower portion of the Merced Cañon I found a lonely miner seeking his fortune in a quartz vein on a wild mountain-side planted with this singular tree. He told me that he called it the Hickory Pine, because of the whiteness and toughness of the wood. It is so little known, however, that it can hardly be said to have a common name. Most mountaineers refer to it as "that queer little pine-tree covered all over with burs." In my studies of this species I found a very interesting and significant group of facts, whose relations will be seen almost as soon as stated:

1st. All the trees in the groves I examined, however unequal in size, are of the same age.

2d. Those groves are all planted on dry hillsides covered with chaparral, and therefore are liable to be swept by fire.

3d. There are no seedlings or saplings in or about the living groves, but there is always a fine, hopeful crop springing up on the ground once occupied by any grove that has been destroyed by the burning of the chaparral.

4th. The cones never fall off and never discharge their seeds until the tree or branch to which they belong dies.

A full discussion of the bearing of these facts upon one another would perhaps be out of place here, but I may at least call attention to the admirable adaptation of the tree to the fire-swept regions where alone it is found. After a grove has been destroyed, the ground is at once sown lavishly with all the seeds ripened during its whole life, which seem to have been carefully held in store with reference to such a calamity. Then a young grove immediately springs up, giving beauty for ashes.

SUGAR PINE
(Pinus Lambertiana)

This is the noblest pine yet discovered, surpassing all others not merely in size but also in kingly beauty and majesty.

It towers sublimely from every ridge and cañon of the range, at an elevation of from three to seven thousand feet above the sea, attaining most perfect development at a height of about 5000 feet.

Full-grown specimens are commonly about 220 feet high, and from six to eight feet in diameter near the ground, though some grand old patriarch is occasionally met that has enjoyed five or six centuries of storms, and attained a thickness of ten or even twelve feet, living on undecayed, sweet and fresh in every fiber.

In southern Oregon, where it was first discovered by David Douglas, on the head waters of the Umpqua, it attains still grander dimensions, one specimen having been measured that was 245 feet high, and over eighteen feet in diameter three feet from the ground. The discoverer was the Douglas for whom the noble Douglas Spruce is named, and many other plants which will keep his memory sweet and fresh as long as trees and flowers are loved. His first visit to the Pacific Coast was made in the year 1825. The Oregon Indians watched him with curiosity as he wandered in the woods collecting specimens, and, unlike the fur-gathering strangers they had hitherto known, caring nothing about trade. And when at length they came to know him better, and saw that from year to year the growing things of the woods and prairies were his only objects of pursuit, they called him "The Man of Grass," a title of which he was proud. During his first summer on the waters of the Columbia he made Fort Vancouver his headquarters, making excursions from this Hudson Bay post in every direction. On one of his long trips he saw in an Indian's pouch some of the seeds of a new species of pine which he learned were obtained from a very large tree far to the southward of the Columbia. At the end of the next summer, returning to Fort Vancouver after the setting in of the winter rains, bearing in mind the big pine he had heard of, he set out on an excursion up the Willamette Valley in search of it; and how he fared, and what dangers and hardships he endured, are best told in his own journal, from which I quote as follows:

October 26, 1826. Weather dull. Cold and cloudy. When my friends in England are made acquainted with my travels I fear they will think I have told them nothing but my miseries. . . . I quitted my camp early in the morning to survey the neighboring country, leaving my guide to take charge of the horses until my return in the evening. About an hour's walk from the camp I met an Indian, who on perceiving me instantly strung his bow, placed on his left arm a sleeve of raccoon skin and stood on the defensive. Being quite sure that conduct was prompted by fear and not by hostile intentions, the poor fellow having probably never seen such a being as myself before, I laid my gun at my feet on the ground and waved my hand for him to come to me, which he did slowly and with great caution. I then made him place his bow and quiver of arrows beside my gun, and striking a light gave him a smoke out of my own pipe and a present of a few beads. With my pencil I made a rough sketch of the cone and pine tree which I wanted to obtain, and drew his attention to it, when he instantly pointed with his hand to the hills fifteen or twenty miles distant towards the south; and when I expressed my intention of going thither, cheerfully set out to accompany me. At midday I reached my long-wished-for pines, and lost no time in examining them and endeavoring to collect specimens and seeds. New and strange things seldom fail to make strong impressions, and are therefore frequently over-rated; so that, lest I should never see my friends in England to inform them verbally of this most beautiful and immensely grand tree, I shall here state the dimensions of the largest I could find among several that had been blown down by the wind. At 3 feet from the ground its circumference is 57 feet 9 inches; at 134 feet, 17 feet 5 inches; the extreme length 245 feet. . . . As it was impossible either to climb the tree or hew it down, I endeavored to knock off the cones by firing at them with ball, when the report of my gun brought eight Indians, all of them painted with red earth, armed with bows, arrows, bone-tipped spears, and flint-knives. They appeared anything but friendly. I explained to them what I wanted, and they seemed satisfied and sat down to smoke; but presently I saw one of them string his bow, and another sharpen his flint knife with a pair of wooden pincers and suspend it on the wrist of his right hand. Further testimony of their intentions was unnecessary. To save myself by flight was impossible, so without hesitation I stepped back about five paces, cocked my gun, drew one of the pistols out of my belt, and holding it in my left hand and the gun in my right, showed myself determined to fight for my life. As much as possible I en-

deavored to preserve my coolness, and thus we stood looking at one
another without making any movement or uttering a word for perhaps ten minutes, when one at last, who seemed to be the leader,
gave a sign that they wished for some tobacco; this I signified that
they should have if they fetched a quantity of cones. They went off
immediately in search of them, and no sooner were they all out of
sight than I picked up my three cones and some twigs of the trees
and made the quickest possible retreat, hurrying back to the camp,
which I reached before dusk. . . . I now write lying on the grass
with my gun cocked beside me, and penning these lines by the light
of my Columbian candle, namely, an ignited piece of rosin-wood.

This grand pine discovered under such exciting circumstances Douglas named in honor of his friend Dr. Lambert of
London.

The trunk is a smooth, round, delicately tapered shaft,
mostly without limbs, and colored rich purplish-brown, usually enlivened with tufts of yellow lichen. At the top of this
magnificent bole, long, curving branches sweep gracefully
outward and downward, sometimes forming a palm-like
crown, but far more nobly impressive than any palm crown I
ever beheld. The needles are about three inches long, finely
tempered and arranged in rather close tassels at the ends of
slender branchlets that clothe the long, outsweeping limbs.
How well they sing in the wind, and how strikingly harmonious an effect is made by the immense cylindrical cones that
depend loosely from the ends of the main branches! No one
knows what Nature can do in the way of pine-burs until he
has seen those of the Sugar Pine. They are commonly from
fifteen to eighteen inches long, and three in diameter; green,
shaded with dark purple on their sunward sides. They are ripe
in September and October. Then the flat scales open and the
seeds take wing, but the empty cones become still more beautiful and effective, for their diameter is nearly doubled by the
spreading of the scales, and their color changes to a warm
yellowish-brown; while they remain swinging on the tree all
the following winter and summer, and continue effectively
beautiful even on the ground many years after they fall. The
wood is deliciously fragrant, and fine in grain and texture; it
is of a rich cream-yellow, as if formed of condensed sunbeams.
Retinospora obtusa, Siebold, the glory of Eastern forests, is

called "Fu-si-no-ki" (tree of the sun) by the Japanese; the Sugar Pine is the sun-tree of the Sierra. Unfortunately it is greatly prized by the lumbermen, and in accessible places is always the first tree in the woods to feel their steel. But the regular lumbermen, with their saw-mills, have been less generally destructive thus far than the shingle-makers. The wood splits freely, and there is a constant demand for the shingles. And because an ax, and saw, and frow are all the capital required for the business, many of that drifting, unsteady class of men so large in California engage in it for a few months in the year. When prospectors, hunters, ranch hands, etc., touch their "bottom dollar" and find themselves out of employment, they say, "Well, I can at least go to the Sugar Pines and make shingles." A few posts are set in the ground, and a single length cut from the first tree felled produces boards enough for the walls and roof of a cabin; all the rest the lumberman makes is for sale, and he is speedily independent. No gardener or hay-maker is more sweetly perfumed than these rough mountaineers while engaged in this business, but the havoc they make is most deplorable.

The sugar, from which the common name is derived, is to my taste the best of sweets—better than maple sugar. It exudes from the heartwood, where wounds have been made, either by forest fires, or the ax, in the shape of irregular, crisp, candy-like kernels, which are crowded together in masses of considerable size, like clusters of resin-beads. When fresh, it is perfectly white and delicious, but, because most of the wounds on which it is found have been made by fire, the exuding sap is stained on the charred surface, and the hardened sugar becomes brown. Indians are fond of it, but on account of its laxative properties only small quantities may be eaten. Bears, so fond of sweet things in general, seem never to taste it; at least I have failed to find any trace of their teeth in this connection.

No lover of trees will ever forget his first meeting with the Sugar Pine, nor will he afterward need a poet to call him to "listen what the pine-tree saith." In most pine-trees there is a sameness of expression, which, to most people, is apt to become monotonous; for the typical spiry form, however beautiful, affords but little scope for appreciable individual character. The Sugar Pine is as free from conventionalities of form and motion as any oak. No two are alike, even to the most inattentive observer; and, notwithstanding they are ever tossing out their immense arms in what might seem most extravagant gestures, there is a majesty and repose about them that precludes all possibility of the grotesque, or even picturesque, in their general expression. They are the priests of pines, and seem ever to be addressing the surrounding forest. The Yellow Pine is found growing with them on warm hillsides, and the White Silver Fir on cool northern slopes; but, noble as these are, the Sugar Pine is easily king, and spreads his arms above them in blessing while they rock and wave in sign of recognition. The main branches are sometimes found to be forty feet in length, yet persistently simple, seldom dividing at all, excepting near the end; but anything like a bare cable appearance is prevented by the small, tasseled branchlets that extend all around them; and when these superb limbs sweep out symmetrically on all sides, a crown sixty or seventy feet wide is formed, which, gracefully poised on the summit of the noble shaft, and filled with sunshine, is one of the most glorious forest objects conceivable. Commonly, however, there is a great preponderance of limbs toward the east, away from the direction of the prevailing winds.

No other pine seems to me so unfamiliar and self-contained. In approaching it, we feel as if in the presence of a superior being, and begin to walk with a light step, holding our breath. Then, perchance, while we gaze awe-stricken, along comes a merry squirrel, chattering and laughing, to break the spell, running up the trunk with no ceremony, and gnawing off the cones as if they were made only for him; while the carpenter-woodpecker hammers away at the bark, drilling holes in which to store his winter supply of acorns.

Although so wild and unconventional when full-grown, the Sugar Pine is a remarkably proper tree in youth. The old is the most original and independent in appearance of all the Sierra evergreens; the young is the most regular,—a strict follower of coniferous fashions,—slim, erect, with leafy, supple branches kept exactly in place, each tapering in outline and terminating in a spiry point. The successive transitional forms presented between the cautious neatness of youth and bold freedom of maturity offer a delightful study. At the age of fifty or sixty years, the shy, fashionable form begins to be broken up. Specialized branches push out in the most unthought-of places, and bend with the great cones, at once marking individual character, and this being constantly augmented from year to year by the varying action of the sunlight, winds, snow-storms, etc., the individuality of the tree is never again lost in the general forest.

The most constant companion of this species is the Yellow Pine, and a worthy companion it is. The Douglas Spruce, Libocedrus, Sequoia, and the White Silver Fir are also more or less associated with it; but on many deep-soiled mountain-sides, at an elevation of about 5000 feet above the sea, it forms the bulk of the forest, filling every swell and hollow and down-plunging ravine. The majestic crowns, approaching each other in bold curves, make a glorious canopy through which the tempered sunbeams pour, silvering the needles, and gilding the massive boles, and flowery, park-like ground, into a scene of enchantment.

On the most sunny slopes the white-flowered fragrant chamoebatia is spread like a carpet, brightened during early summer with the crimson Sarcodes, the wild rose, and innumerable violets and gilias. Not even in the shadiest nooks will you find any rank, untidy weeds or unwholesome darkness. On the north sides of ridges the boles are more slender, and the ground is mostly occupied by an underbrush of hazel, ceanothus, and flowering dogwood, but never so densely as to prevent the traveler from sauntering where he will; while the crowning branches are never impenetrable to the rays of the sun, and never so interblended as to lose their individuality.

View the forest from beneath or from some commanding ridge-top; each tree presents a study in itself, and proclaims the surpassing grandeur of the species.

YELLOW, OR SILVER PINE
(Pinus ponderosa)

The Silver, or Yellow, Pine, as it is commonly called, ranks second among the pines of the Sierra as a lumber tree, and almost rivals the Sugar Pine in stature and nobleness of port. Because of its superior powers of enduring variations of climate and soil, it has a more extensive range than any other conifer growing on the Sierra. On the western slope it is first met at an elevation of about 2000 feet, and extends nearly to the upper limit of the timber line. Thence, crossing the range by the lowest passes, it descends to the eastern base, and pushes out for a considerable distance into the hot volcanic plains, growing bravely upon well-watered moraines, gravelly lake basins, arctic ridges, and torrid lava-beds; planting itself upon the lips of craters, flourishing vigorously even there, and tossing ripe cones among the ashes and cinders of Nature's hearths.

The average size of full-grown trees on the western slope, where it is associated with the Sugar Pine, is a little less than 200 feet in height and from five to six feet in diameter, though specimens may easily be found that are considerably larger. I measured one, growing at an elevation of 4000 feet in the valley of the Merced, that is a few inches over eight feet in diameter, and 220 feet high.

Where there is plenty of free sunshine and other conditions are favorable, it presents a striking contrast in form to the Sugar Pine, being a symmetrical spire, formed of a straight round trunk, clad with innumerable branches that are divided over and over again. About one half of the trunk is commonly branchless, but where it grows at all close, three fourths or more become naked; the tree presenting then a more slender and elegant shaft than any other tree in the woods. The bark is mostly arranged in massive plates, some of them measuring four or five feet in length by eighteen inches in width, with a thickness of three or four inches, forming a quite marked and distinguishing feature. The needles are of a fine, warm, yellow-green color, six to eight inches long, firm and elastic, and crowded in handsome, radiant tassels on the upturning ends of the branches. The cones are about three or four inches long, and two and a half wide, growing in close, sessile clusters among the leaves.

The species attains its noblest form in filled-up lake basins, especially in those of the older yosemites, and so prominent a part does it form of their groves that it may well be called

the Yosemite Pine. Ripe specimens favorably situated are almost always 200 feet or more in height, and the branches
clothe the trunk nearly to the ground, as seen in the illustration.

The Jeffrey variety attains its finest development in the
northern portion of the range, in the wide basins of the
McCloud and Pitt rivers, where it forms magnificent forests
scarcely invaded by any other tree. It differs from the ordinary
form in size, being only about half as tall, and in its redder
and more closely furrowed bark, grayish-green foliage, less
divided branches, and larger cones; but intermediate forms
come in which make a clear separation impossible, although
some botanists regard it as a distinct species. It is this variety
that climbs storm-swept ridges, and wanders out among the
volcanoes of the Great Basin. Whether exposed to extremes
of heat or cold, it is dwarfed like every other tree, and becomes all knots and angles, wholly unlike the majestic forms
we have been sketching. Old specimens, bearing cones about
as big as pine-apples, may sometimes be found clinging to
rifted rocks at an elevation of seven or eight thousand feet,
whose highest branches scarce reach above one's shoulders.

I have oftentimes feasted on the beauty of these noble trees
when they were towering in all their winter grandeur, laden
with snow—one mass of bloom; in summer, too, when the
brown, staminate clusters hang thick among the shimmering
needles, and the big purple burs are ripening in the mellow
light; but it is during cloudless wind-storms that these colossal
pines are most impressively beautiful. Then they bow like willows, their leaves streaming forward all in one direction, and,
when the sun shines upon them at the required angle, entire
groves glow as if every leaf were burnished silver. The fall of
tropic light on the royal crown of a palm is a truly glorious
spectacle, the fervid sun-flood breaking upon the glossy leaves
in long lance-rays, like mountain water among boulders. But
to me there is something more impressive in the fall of light
upon these Silver Pines. It seems beaten to the finest dust,
and is shed off in myriads of minute sparkles that seem to
come from the very heart of the trees, as if, like rain falling
upon fertile soil, it had been absorbed, to reappear in flowers
of light.

This species also gives forth the finest music to the wind. After listening to it in all kinds of winds, night and day, season after season, I think I could approximate to my position on the mountains by this pine-music alone. If you would catch the tones of separate needles, climb a tree. They are well tempered, and give forth no uncertain sound, each standing out, with no interference excepting during heavy gales; then you may detect the click of one needle upon another, readily distinguishable from their free, wing-like hum. Some idea of their temper may be drawn from the fact that, notwithstanding they are so long, the vibrations that give rise to the peculiar shimmering of the light are made at the rate of about two hundred and fifty per minute.

When a Sugar Pine and one of this species equal in size are observed together, the latter is seen to be far more simple in manners, more lithely graceful, and its beauty is of a kind more easily appreciated; but then, it is, on the other hand, much less dignified and original in demeanor. The Silver Pine seems eager to shoot aloft. Even while it is drowsing in autumn sun-gold, you may still detect a skyward aspiration. But the Sugar Pine seems too unconsciously noble, and too complete in every way, to leave room for even a heavenward care.

DOUGLAS SPRUCE
(Pseudotsuga Douglasii)

This tree is the king of the spruces, as the Sugar Pine is king of pines. It is by far the most majestic spruce I ever beheld in any forest, and one of the largest and longest lived of the giants that flourish throughout the main pine belt, often attaining a height of nearly 200 feet, and a diameter of six or seven. Where the growth is not too close, the strong, spreading branches come more than halfway down the trunk, and these are hung with innumerable slender, swaying sprays, that are handsomely feathered with the short leaves which radiate at right angles all around them. This vigorous spruce is ever beautiful, welcoming the mountain winds and the snow as well as the mellow summer light, and maintaining its youthful freshness undiminished from century to century through a thousand storms.

It makes its finest appearance in the months of June and July. The rich brown buds with which its sprays are tipped swell and break about this time, revealing the young leaves, which at first are bright yellow, making the tree appear as if covered with gay blossoms; while the pendulous bracted cones with their shell-like scales are a constant adornment.

The young trees are mostly gathered into beautiful family groups, each sapling exquisitely symmetrical. The primary branches are whorled regularly around the axis, generally in fives, while each is draped with long, feathery sprays, that descend in curves as free and as finely drawn as those of falling water.

In Oregon and Washington it grows in dense forests, growing tall and mast-like to a height of 300 feet, and is greatly prized as a lumber tree. But in the Sierra it is scattered among other trees, or forms small groves, seldom ascending higher than 5500 feet, and never making what would be called a forest. It is not particular in its choice of soil—wet or dry, smooth or rocky, it makes out to live well on them all. Two of the largest specimens I have measured are in Yosemite Valley, one of which is more than eight feet in diameter, and is growing upon the terminal moraine of the residual glacier that occupied the South Fork Cañon; the other is nearly as large, growing upon angular blocks of granite that have been shaken from the precipitous front of the Liberty Cap near the Nevada Fall. No other tree seems so capable of adapting itself to earthquake taluses, and many of these rough boulder-slopes are occupied by it almost exclusively, especially in yosemite gorges moistened by the spray of waterfalls.

INCENSE CEDAR
(Libocedrus decurrens)

The Incense Cedar is another of the giants quite generally distributed throughout this portion of the forest, without exclusively occupying any considerable area, or even making extensive groves. It ascends to about 5000 feet on the warmer hillsides, and reaches the climate most congenial to it at about from 3000 to 4000 feet, growing vigorously at this elevation on all kinds of soil, and in particular it is capable of enduring more moisture about its roots than any of its companions, excepting only the Sequoia.

The largest specimens are about 150 feet high, and seven feet in diameter. The bark is brown, of a singularly rich tone very attractive to artists, and the foliage is tinted with a warmer yellow than that of any other evergreen in the woods. Casting your eye over the general forest from some ridge-top, the color alone of its spiry summits is sufficient to identify it in any company.

In youth, say up to the age of seventy or eighty years, no other tree forms so strictly tapered a cone from top to bottom. The branches swoop outward and downward in bold curves, excepting the younger ones near the top, which aspire, while the lowest droop to the ground, and all spread out in flat, ferny plumes, beautifully fronded, and imbricated upon one another. As it becomes older, it grows strikingly irregular and picturesque. Large special branches put out at right angles from the trunk, form big, stubborn elbows, and then shoot up parallel with the axis. Very old trees are usually dead at the top, the main axis protruding above ample masses of green plumes, gray and lichen-covered, and drilled full of acorn holes by the woodpeckers. The plumes are exceedingly beautiful; no waving fern-frond in shady dell is more unreservedly beautiful in form and texture, or half so inspiring in color and spicy fragrance. In its prime, the whole tree is thatched with them, so that they shed off rain and snow like a roof, making fine mansions for storm-bound birds and mountaineers. But if you would see the *Libocedrus* in all its glory, you must go to the woods in winter. Then it is laden with myriads of four-sided staminate cones about the size of wheat grains,—winter wheat,—producing a golden tinge, and forming a noble illustration of Nature's immortal vigor and virility. The fertile cones are about three fourths of an inch long, borne on the outside of the plumy branchlets, where they serve to enrich still more the surpassing beauty of this grand winter-blooming goldenrod.

WHITE SILVER FIR
(Abies concolor)

We come now to the most regularly planted of all the main forest belts, composed almost exclusively of two noble firs— *A. concolor* and *A. magnifica*. It extends with no marked interruption for 450 miles, at an elevation of from 5000 to nearly 9000 feet above the sea. In its youth *A. concolor* is a charmingly symmetrical tree with branches regularly whorled in level collars around its whitish-gray axis, which terminates in a strong, hopeful shoot. The leaves are in two horizontal rows, along branchlets that commonly are less than eight years old, forming handsome plumes, pinnated like the fronds of ferns. The cones are grayish-green when ripe, cylindrical, about from three to four inches long by one and a half to two inches wide, and stand upright on the upper branches.

Full-grown trees, favorably situated as to soil and exposure, are about 200 feet high, and five or six feet in diameter near the ground, though larger specimens are by no means rare.

As old age creeps on, the bark becomes rougher and grayer, the branches lose their exact regularity, many are snow-bent or broken off, and the main axis often becomes double or otherwise irregular from accidents to the terminal bud or shoot; but throughout all the vicissitudes of its life on the mountains, come what may, the noble grandeur of the species is patent to every eye.

MAGNIFICENT SILVER FIR, OR RED FIR
(Abies magnifica)

This is the most charmingly symmetrical of all the giants of the Sierra woods, far surpassing its companion species in this respect, and easily distinguished from it by the purplish-red bark, which is also more closely furrowed than that of the white, and by its larger cones, more regularly whorled and fronded branches, and by its leaves, which are shorter, and grow all around the branchlets and point upward.

In size, these two Silver Firs are about equal, the *magnifica* perhaps a little the taller. Specimens from 200 to 250 feet high are not rare on well-ground moraine soil, at an elevation of from 7500 to 8500 feet above sea-level. The largest that I measured stands back three miles from the brink of the north wall of Yosemite Valley. Fifteen years ago it was 240 feet high, with a diameter of a little more than five feet.

Happy the man with the freedom and the love to climb one of these superb trees in full flower and fruit. How admirable the forest-work of Nature is then seen to be, as one makes his way up through the midst of the broad, fronded branches, all arranged in exquisite order around the trunk, like the whorled leaves of lilies, and each branch and branchlet about as strictly pinnate as the most symmetrical fern-frond. The staminate cones are seen growing straight downward from the under side of the young branches in lavish profusion, making fine purple clusters amid the grayish-green foliage. On the topmost branches the fertile cones are set firmly on end like small casks. They are about six inches long, three wide, covered with a fine gray down, and streaked with crystal balsam that seems to have been poured upon each cone from above.

Both the Silver Firs live 250 years or more when the conditions about them are at all favorable. Some venerable patriarch may often be seen, heavily storm-marked, towering in severe majesty above the rising generation, with a protecting grove of saplings pressing close around his feet, each dressed with such loving care that not a leaf seems wanting. Other companies are made up of trees near the prime of life, exquisitely harmonized to one another in form and gesture, as if Nature had culled them one by one with nice discrimination from all the rest of the woods.

It is from this tree, called Red Fir by the lumberman, that mountaineers always cut boughs to sleep on when they are so fortunate as to be within its limits. Two rows of the plushy branches overlapping along the middle, and a crescent of smaller plumes mixed with ferns and flowers for a pillow, form the very best bed imaginable. The essences of the pressed leaves seem to fill every pore of one's body, the sounds of falling water make a soothing hush, while the spaces between the grand spires afford noble openings through which to gaze dreamily into the starry sky. Even in the matter of sensuous ease, any combination of cloth, steel springs, and feathers seems vulgar in comparison.

The fir woods are delightful sauntering-grounds at any time of year, but most so in autumn. Then the noble trees are hushed in the hazy light, and drip with balsam; the cones are ripe, and the seeds, with their ample purple wings, mottle the air like flocks of butterflies; while deer feeding in the flowery openings between the groves, and birds and squirrels in the branches, make a pleasant stir which enriches the deep, brooding calm of the wilderness, and gives a peculiar impressiveness to every tree. No wonder the enthusiastic Douglas went wild with joy when he first discovered this species. Even in the Sierra, where so many noble evergreens challenge admiration, we linger among these colossal firs with fresh love, and extol their beauty again and again, as if no other in the world could henceforth claim our regard.

It is in these woods the great granite domes rise that are so striking and characteristic a feature of the Sierra. And here too we find the best of the garden meadows. They lie level on the tops of the dividing ridges, or sloping on the sides of them, embedded in the magnificent forest. Some of these meadows are in great part occupied by *Veratrum alba*, which here grows rank and tall, with boat-shaped leaves thirteen inches long and twelve inches wide, ribbed like those of cypripedium. Columbine grows on the drier margins with tall larkspurs and lupines waist-deep in grasses and sedges; several species of castilleia also make a bright show in beds of blue and white violets and daisies. But the glory of these forest meadows is a lily—*L. parvum*. The flowers are orange-colored and quite small, the smallest I ever saw of the true lilies; but it is showy nevertheless, for it is seven to eight feet high and waves magnificent racemes of ten to twenty flowers or more over one's head, while it stands out in the open ground with just enough of grass and other plants about it to make a fringe for its feet and show it off to best advantage.

A dry spot a little way back from the margin of a Silver Fir lily garden makes a glorious camp-ground, especially where the slope is toward the east and opens a view of the distant peaks along the summit of the range. The tall lilies are brought forward in all their glory by the light of your blazing camp-fire, relieved against the outer darkness, and the nearest of the trees with their whorled branches tower above you like larger lilies, and the sky seen through the garden opening seems one vast meadow of white lily stars.

In the morning everything is joyous and bright, the delicious purple of the dawn changes softly to daffodil yellow and white; while the sunbeams pouring through the passes between the peaks give a margin of gold to each of them. Then the spires of the firs in the hollows of the middle region catch the glow, and your camp grove is filled with light. The birds begin to stir, seeking sunny branches on the edge of the meadow for sun-baths after the cold night, and looking for their breakfasts, every one of them as fresh as a lily and as charmingly arrayed. Innumerable insects begin to dance, the deer withdraw from the open glades and ridge-tops to their leafy hiding-places in the chaparral, the flowers open and straighten their petals as the dew vanishes, every pulse beats high, every life-cell rejoices, the very rocks seem to tingle with life, and God is felt brooding over everything great and small.

BIG TREE
(Sequoia gigantea)

Between the heavy pine and Silver Fir belts we find the Big Tree, the king of all the conifers in the world, "the noblest of a noble race." It extends in a widely interrupted belt from a small grove on the middle fork of the American River to the head of Deer Creek, a distance of about 260 miles, the northern limit being near the thirty-ninth parallel, the southern a little below the thirty-sixth, and the elevation of the belt above the sea varies from about 5000 to 8000 feet. From the American River grove to the forest on King's River the species occurs only in small isolated groups so sparsely distributed along the belt that three of the gaps in it are from forty to sixty miles wide. But from King's River southward the Sequoia is not restricted to mere groves, but extends across the broad rugged basins of the Kaweah and Tule rivers in noble forests, a distance of nearly seventy miles, the continuity of this part of the belt being broken only by deep cañons. The Fresno, the largest of the northern groves, occupies an area of three or four square miles, a short distance to the southward of the famous Mariposa Grove. Along the beveled rim of the cañon of the south fork of King's River there is a majestic forest of Sequoia about six miles long by two wide. This is the northernmost assemblage of Big Trees that may fairly be called a forest. Descending the precipitous divide between the King's River and Kaweah you enter the grand forests that form the main continuous portion of the belt. Advancing southward the giants become more and more irrepressibly exuberant, heaving their massive crowns into the sky from every ridge and slope, and waving onward in graceful compliance with the complicated topography of the region. The finest of the Kaweah section of the belt is on the broad ridge between Marble Creek and the middle fork, and extends from the granite head-lands overlooking the hot plains to within a few miles of the cool glacial fountains of the summit peaks. The extreme upper limit of the belt is reached between the middle and south forks of the Kaweah at an elevation of 8400 feet. But the finest block of Big Tree forest in the entire belt is on the north fork of Tule River. In the northern groves there are comparatively few young trees or saplings. But here for every old, storm-stricken giant there are many in all the glory of prime vigor, and for each of these a crowd of eager, hopeful young trees and saplings growing heartily on moraines, rocky ledges, along watercourses, and in the moist alluvium of meadows, seemingly in hot pursuit of eternal life.

But though the area occupied by the species increases so much from north to south there is no marked increase in the size of the trees. A height of 275 feet and a diameter near the ground of about 20 feet is perhaps about the average size of full-grown trees favorably situated; specimens 25 feet in diameter are not very rare, and a few are nearly 300 feet high. In the Calaveras Grove there are four trees over 300 feet in height, the tallest of which by careful measurement is 325 feet. The largest I have yet met in the course of my explorations is a majestic old scarred monument in the King's River forest. It is 35 feet 8 inches in diameter inside the bark four feet from the ground. Under the most favorable conditions these giants probably live 5000 years or more, though few of even the

larger trees are more than half as old. I never saw a Big Tree
that had died a natural death; barring accidents they seem to
be immortal, being exempt from all the diseases that afflict
and kill other trees. Unless destroyed by man, they live on
indefinitely until burned, smashed by lightning, or cast down
by storms, or by the giving way of the ground on which they
stand. The age of one that was felled in the Calaveras Grove,
for the sake of having its stump for a dancing-floor, was about
1300 years, and its diameter, measured across the stump, 24
feet inside the bark. Another that was cut down in the King's
River forest was about the same size, but nearly a thousand
years older (2200 years), though not a very old-looking tree.
It was felled to procure a section for exhibition, and thus an
opportunity was given to count its annual rings of growth.
The colossal scarred monument in the King's River forest
mentioned above is burned half through, and I spent a day in
making an estimate of its age, clearing away the charred surface with an ax and carefully counting the annual rings with
the aid of a pocket-lens. The wood-rings in the section I laid
bare were so involved and contorted in some places that I was
not able to determine its age exactly, but I counted over 4000
rings, which showed that this tree was in its prime, swaying
in the Sierra winds, when Christ walked the earth. No other
tree in the world, as far as I know, has looked down on so
many centuries as the Sequoia, or opens such impressive and
suggestive views into history.

So exquisitely harmonious and finely balanced are even the
very mightiest of these monarchs of the woods in all their
proportions and circumstances there never is anything overgrown or monstrous-looking about them. On coming in sight
of them for the first time, you are likely to say, "Oh, see what
beautiful, noble-looking trees are towering there among the
firs and pines!"—their grandeur being in the mean time in
great part invisible, but to the living eye it will be manifested
sooner or later, stealing slowly on the senses, like the grandeur
of Niagara, or the lofty Yosemite domes. Their great size is
hidden from the inexperienced observer as long as they are
seen at a distance in one harmonious view. When, however,
you approach them and walk round them, you begin to wonder at their colossal size and seek a measuring-rod. These

giants bulge considerably at the base, but not more than is required for beauty and safety; and the only reason that this bulging seems in some cases excessive is that only a comparatively small section of the shaft is seen at once in near views. One that I measured in the King's River forest was 25 feet in diameter at the ground, and 10 feet in diameter 200 feet above the ground, showing that the taper of the trunk as a whole is charmingly fine. And when you stand back far enough to see the massive columns from the swelling instep to the lofty summit dissolving in a dome of verdure, you rejoice in the unrivaled display of combined grandeur and beauty. About a hundred feet or more of the trunk is usually branchless, but its massive simplicity is relieved by the bark furrows, which instead of making an irregular network run evenly parallel, like the fluting of an architectural column, and to some extent by tufts of slender sprays that wave lightly in the winds and cast flecks of shade, seeming to have been pinned on here and there for the sake of beauty only. The young trees have slender simple branches down to the ground, put on with strict regularity, sharply aspiring at the top, horizontal about half-way down, and drooping in handsome curves at the base. By the time the sapling is five or six hundred years old this spiry, feathery, juvenile habit merges into the firm, rounded dome form of middle age, which in turn takes on the eccentric picturesqueness of old age. No other tree in the Sierra forest has foliage so densely massed or presents outlines so firmly drawn and so steadily subordinate to a special type. A knotty ungovernable-looking branch five to eight feet thick may be seen pushing out abruptly from the smooth trunk, as if sure to throw the regular curve into confusion, but as soon as the general outline is reached it stops short and dissolves in spreading bosses of law-abiding sprays, just as if every tree were growing beneath some huge, invisible bell-glass, against whose sides every branch was being pressed and molded, yet somehow indulging in so many small departures from the regular form that there is still an appearance of freedom.

The foliage of the saplings is dark bluish-green in color, while the older trees ripen to a warm brownish-yellow tint like Libocedrus. The bark is rich cinnamon-brown, purplish in young trees and in shady portions of the old, while the ground is covered with brown leaves and burs forming color-masses of extraordinary richness, not to mention the flowers and underbrush that rejoice about them in their seasons. Walk the Sequoia woods at any time of year and you will say they are the most beautiful and majestic on earth. Beautiful and impressive contrasts meet you everywhere: the colors of tree and flower, rock and sky, light and shade, strength and frailty, endurance and evanescence, tangles of supple hazel-bushes, tree-pillars about as rigid as granite domes, roses and violets, the smallest of their kind, blooming around the feet of the giants, and rugs of the lowly chamæbatia where the sunbeams fall. Then in winter the trees themselves break forth in bloom, myriads of small four-sided staminate cones crowd the ends of the slender sprays, coloring the whole tree, and when ripe dusting the air and the ground with golden pollen. The fertile cones are bright grass-green, measuring about two inches in length by one and a half in thickness, and are made up of about forty firm rhomboidal scales densely packed, with from five to eight seeds at the base of each. A single cone, therefore, contains from two to three hundred seeds, which are about a fourth of an inch long by three sixteenths wide, including a thin, flat margin that makes them go glancing and wavering in their fall like a boy's kite. The fruitfulness of Sequoia may be illustrated by two specimen branches one and a half and two inches in diameter on which I counted 480 cones. No other Sierra conifer produces nearly so many seeds. Millions are ripened annually by a single tree, and in a fruitful year the product of one of the northern groves would be enough to plant all the mountain-ranges of the world. Nature takes care, however, that not one seed in a million shall germinate at all, and of those that do perhaps not one in ten thousand is suffered to live through the many vicissitudes of storm, drought, fire, and snow-crushing that beset their youth.

The Douglas squirrel is the happy harvester of most of the Sequoia cones. Out of every hundred perhaps ninety fall to his share, and unless cut off by his ivory sickle they shake out their seeds and remain on the tree for many years. Watching the squirrels at their harvest work in the Indian summer is one of the most delightful diversions imaginable. The woods are calm and the ripe colors are blazing in all their glory; the cone-laden trees stand motionless in the warm, hazy air, and you may see the crimson-crested woodcock, the prince of Sierra woodpeckers, drilling some dead limb or fallen trunk with his bill, and ever and anon filling the glens with his happy cackle. The humming-bird, too, dwells in these noble woods, and may oftentimes be seen glancing among the flowers or resting wing-weary on some leafless twig; here also are the familiar robin of the orchards, and the brown and grizzly bears so obviously fitted for these majestic solitudes; and the Douglas squirrel, making more hilarious, exuberant, vital stir than all the bears, birds, and humming wings together.

As soon as any accident happens to the crown of these Sequoias, such as being stricken off by lightning or broken by storms, then the branches beneath the wound, no matter how situated, seem to be excited like a colony of bees that have lost their queen, and become anxious to repair the damage. Limbs that have grown outward for centuries at right angles to the trunk begin to turn upward to assist in making a new crown, each speedily assuming the special form of true summits. Even in the case of mere stumps, burned half through, some mere ornamental tuft will try to go aloft and do its best as a leader in forming a new head.

Groups of two or three of these grand trees are often found standing close together, the seeds from which they sprang having probably grown on ground cleared for their reception by the fall of a large tree of a former generation. These patches of fresh, mellow soil beside the upturned roots of the fallen giant may be from forty to sixty feet wide, and they are speedily occupied by seedlings. Out of these seedling-thickets perhaps two or three may become trees, forming those close groups called "three graces," "loving couples," etc. For even supposing that the trees should stand twenty or thirty feet apart while young, by the time they are full-grown their trunks will touch and crowd against each other and even appear as one in some cases.

It is generally believed that this grand Sequoia was once far more widely distributed over the Sierra; but after long and careful study I have come to the conclusion that it never was, at least since the close of the glacial period, because a diligent search along the margins of the groves, and in the gaps between, fails to reveal a single trace of its previous existence beyond its present bounds. Notwithstanding, I feel confident that if every Sequoia in the range were to die to-day, numerous monuments of their existence would remain, of so imperishable a nature as to be available for the student more than ten thousand years hence.

In the first place we might notice that no species of coniferous tree in the range keeps its individuals so well together as Sequoia; a mile is perhaps the greatest distance of any straggler from the main body, and all of those stragglers that have come under my observation are young, instead of old monumental trees, relics of a more extended growth.

Again, Sequoia trunks frequently endure for centuries after they fall. I have a specimen block, cut from a fallen trunk, which is hardly distinguishable from specimens cut from living trees, although the old trunk-fragment from which it was derived has lain in the damp forest more than 380 years, probably thrice as long. The time measure in the case is simply this: when the ponderous trunk to which the old vestige belonged fell, it sunk itself into the ground, thus making a long, straight ditch, and in the middle of this ditch a Silver Fir is growing that is now four feet in diameter and 380 years old, as determined by cutting it half through and counting the rings, thus demonstrating that the remnant of the trunk that made the ditch has lain on the ground *more* than 380 years. For it is evident that to find the whole time, we must add to the 380 years the time that the vanished portion of the trunk lay in the ditch before being burned out of the way, plus the time that passed before the seed from which the monumental fir sprang fell into the prepared soil and took root. Now, because Sequoia trunks are never wholly consumed in one forest fire, and those fires recur only at considerable intervals, and because Sequoia ditches after being cleared are often left unplanted for centuries, it becomes evident that the trunk remnant in question may probably have lain a thousand years or more. And this instance is by no means a rare one.

But admitting that upon those areas supposed to have been once covered with Sequoia every tree may have fallen, and every trunk may have been burned or buried, leaving not a remnant, many of the ditches made by the fall of the ponderous trunks, and the bowls made by their upturning roots, would remain patent for thousands of years after the last vestige of the trunks that made them had vanished. Much of this ditch-writing would no doubt be quickly effaced by the flood-action of overflowing streams and rain-washing; but no inconsiderable portion would remain enduringly engraved on ridge-tops beyond such destructive action; for, where all the conditions are favorable, it is almost imperishable. *Now these historic ditches and root bowls occur in all the present Sequoia groves and forests, but as far as I have observed, not the faintest vestige of one presents itself outside of them.*

We therefore conclude that the area covered by Sequoia has not been diminished during the last eight or ten thousand years, and probably not at all in post-glacial times.

Is the species verging to extinction? What are its relations to climate, soil, and associated trees?

All the phenomena bearing on these questions also throw light, as we shall endeavor to show, upon the peculiar distribution of the species, and sustain the conclusion already arrived at on the question of extension.

In the northern groups, as we have seen, there are few young trees or saplings growing up around the failing old ones to perpetuate the race, and in as much as those aged Sequoias, so nearly childless, are the only ones commonly known, the species, to most observers, seems doomed to speedy extinction, as being nothing more than an expiring remnant, vanquished in the so-called struggle for life by pines and firs that have driven it into its last strongholds in moist glens where climate is exceptionally favorable. But the language of the majestic continuous forests of the south creates a very different impression. No tree of all the forest is more enduringly established in concordance with climate and soil. It grows heartily everywhere—on moraines, rocky ledges, along watercourses, and in the deep, moist alluvium of meadows, with a multitude of seedlings and saplings crowding up around the aged, seemingly abundantly able to maintain the forest in prime vigor. For every old storm-stricken tree, there is one or more in all the glory of prime; and for each of these many young trees and crowds of exuberant saplings. So that if all the trees of any section of the main Sequoia forest were ranged together according to age, a very promising curve would be presented, all the way up from last year's seedlings to giants, and with the young and middle-aged portion of the curve many times longer than the old portion. Even as far north as the Fresno, I counted 536 saplings and seedlings growing promisingly upon a piece of rough avalanche soil not exceeding two acres in area. This soil bed is about seven years old, and has been seeded almost simultaneously by pines, firs, Libocedrus, and Sequoia, presenting a simple and instructive illustration of the struggle for life among the rival species; and it was interesting to note that the conditions thus far affecting them have enabled the young Sequoias to gain a marked advantage.

In every instance like the above I have observed that the seedling Sequoia is capable of growing on both drier and wetter soil than its rivals, but requires more sunshine than they; the latter fact being clearly shown wherever a Sugar Pine or fir is growing in close contact with a Sequoia of about equal age and size, and equally exposed to the sun; the branches of the latter in such cases are always less leafy. Toward the south, however, where the Sequoia becomes *more* exuberant and numerous, the rival trees become *less* so; and where they mix with Sequoias, they mostly grow up beneath them, like slender grasses among stalks of Indian corn. Upon a bed of sandy flood-soil I counted ninety-four Sequoias, from one to twelve feet high, on a patch of ground once occupied by four large Sugar Pines which lay crumbling beneath them,—an instance of conditions which have enabled Sequoias to crowd out the pines.

I also noted eighty-six vigorous saplings upon a piece of fresh ground prepared for their reception by fire. Thus fire, the great destroyer of Sequoia, also furnishes bare virgin ground, one of the conditions essential for its growth from the seed. Fresh ground is, however, furnished in sufficient quantities for the constant renewal of the forests without fire, viz., by the fall of old trees. The soil is thus upturned and mellowed, and many trees are planted for every one that falls. Land-slips and floods also give rise to bare virgin ground; and a tree now and then owes its existence to a burrowing wolf or squirrel, but the most regular supply of fresh soil is furnished by the fall of aged trees.

The climatic changes in progress in the Sierra, bearing on the tenure of tree life, are entirely misapprehended, especially as to the time and the means employed by Nature in effecting them. It is constantly asserted in a vague way that the Sierra was vastly wetter than now, and that the increasing drought will of itself extinguish Sequoia, leaving its ground to other trees supposed capable of flourishing in a drier climate. But that Sequoia can and does grow on as dry ground as any of its present rivals, is manifest in a thousand places. "Why, then," it will be asked, "are Sequoias always found in greatest abundance in well-watered places where streams are exceptionally abundant?" Simply because a growth of Sequoias creates those streams. The thirsty mountaineer knows well that in every Sequoia grove he will find running water, but it is a mistake to suppose that the water is the cause of the grove being there; on the contrary, the grove is the cause of the water being there. Drain off the water and the trees will remain, but cut off the trees, and the streams will vanish. Never was cause more completely mistaken for effect than in the case of these related phenomena of Sequoia woods and perennial streams, and I confess that at first I shared in the blunder.

When attention is called to the method of Sequoia stream-making, it will be apprehended at once. The roots of this immense tree fill the ground, forming a thick sponge that absorbs and holds back the rains and melting snows, only allowing them to ooze and flow gently. Indeed, every fallen leaf and rootlet, as well as long clasping root, and prostrate trunk, may be regarded as a dam hoarding the bounty of storm-clouds, and dispensing it as blessings all through the summer, instead of allowing it to go headlong in short-lived floods. Evaporation is also checked by the dense foliage to a greater extent than by any other Sierra tree, and the air is entangled in masses and broad sheets that are quickly saturated; while thirsty winds are not allowed to go sponging and licking along the ground.

So great is the retention of water in many places in the main belt, that bogs and meadows are created by the killing of the trees. A single trunk falling across a stream in the woods forms a dam 200 feet long, and from ten to thirty feet high, giving rise to a pond which kills the trees within its reach. These dead trees fall in turn, thus making a clearing, while sediments gradually accumulate changing the pond into a bog, or meadow, for a growth of carices and sphagnum. In some instances a series of small bogs or meadows rise above one another on a hillside, which are gradually merged into one another, forming sloping bogs, or meadows, which make striking features of Sequoia woods, and since all the trees that have fallen into them have been preserved, they contain records of the generations that have passed since they began to form.

Since, then, it is a fact that thousands of Sequoias are growing thriftily on what is termed dry ground, and even clinging like mountain pines to rifts in granite precipices; and since it has also been shown that the extra moisture found in connection with the denser growths is an effect of their presence, instead of a cause of their presence, then the notions as to the former extension of the species and its near approach to extinction, based upon its supposed dependence on greater moisture, are seen to be erroneous.

The decrease in the rain- and snowfall since the close of the glacial period in the Sierra is much less than is commonly guessed. The highest post-glacial watermarks are well preserved in all the upper river channels, and they are not greatly higher than the spring floodmarks of the present; showing conclusively that no extraordinary decrease has taken place in the volume of the upper tributaries of post-glacial Sierra streams since they came into existence. But in the mean time, eliminating all this complicated question of climatic change, the plain fact remains that *the present rain- and snowfall is abundantly sufficient for the luxuriant growth of Sequoia forests.* Indeed, all my observations tend to show that in a prolonged drought the Sugar Pines and firs would perish before the Sequoia, not alone because of the greater longevity of individual trees, but because the species can endure more drought, and make the most of whatever moisture falls.

Again, if the restriction and irregular distribution of the species be interpreted as a result of the desiccation of the range, then instead of increasing as it does in individuals toward the south where the rainfall is less, it should diminish.

If, then, the peculiar distribution of Sequoia has not been governed by superior conditions of soil as to fertility or moisture, by what has it been governed?

In the course of my studies I observed that the northern groves, the only ones I was at first acquainted with, were located on just those portions of the general forest soil-belt that were first laid bare toward the close of the glacial period when the ice-sheet began to break up into individual glaciers. And while searching the wide basin of the San Joaquin, and trying to account for the absence of Sequoia where every condition seemed favorable for its growth, it occurred to me that this remarkable gap in the Sequoia belt is located exactly in the basin of the vast ancient *mer de glace* of the San Joaquin and King's River basins, which poured its frozen floods to the plain, fed by the snows that fell on more than fifty miles of the summit. I then perceived that the next great gap in the belt to the northward, forty miles wide, extending between the Calaveras and Tuolumne groves, occurs in the basin of the great ancient *mer de glace* of the Tuolumne and Stanislaus basins, and that the smaller gap between the Merced and Mariposa groves occurs in the basin of the smaller glacier of the Merced. *The wider the ancient glacier, the wider the corresponding gap in the Sequoia belt.*

Finally, pursuing my investigations across the basins of the Kaweah and Tule, I discovered that the Sequoia belt attained its greatest development just where, owing to the topographical peculiarities of the region, the ground had been most perfectly protected from the main ice-rivers that continued to pour past from the summit fountains long after the smaller local glaciers had been melted.

Taking now a general view of the belt, beginning at the south, we see that the majestic ancient glaciers were shed off right and left down the valleys of Kern and King's rivers by the lofty protective spurs outspread embracingly above the warm Sequoia-filled basins of the Kaweah and Tule. Then, next northward, occurs the wide Sequoia-less channel, or basin, of the ancient San Joaquin and King's River *mer de glace*; then the warm, protected spots of Fresno and Mariposa groves; then the Sequoia-less channel of the ancient Merced glacier; next the warm, sheltered ground of the Merced and Tuolumne groves; then the Sequoia-less channel of the grand ancient *mer de glace* of the Tuolumne and Stanislaus; then the warm old ground of the Calaveras and Stanislaus groves. It appears, therefore, that just where, at a certain period in the history of the Sierra, the glaciers were not, there the Sequoia is, and just where the glaciers were, there the Sequoia is not.

What the other conditions may have been that enabled Sequoia to establish itself upon these oldest and warmest portions of the main glacial soil-belt, I cannot say. I might venture to state, however, in this connection, that since the Sequoia forests present a more and more ancient aspect as they extend southward, I am inclined to think that the species was distributed from the south, while the Sugar Pine, its great rival in the northern groves, seems to have come around the head of the Sacramento valley and down the Sierra from the north; consequently, when the Sierra soil-beds were first thrown open to preëmption on the melting of the ice-sheet, the Sequoia may have established itself along the available portions of the south half of the range prior to the arrival of the Sugar Pine, while the Sugar Pine took possession of the north half prior to the arrival of Sequoia.

But however much uncertainty may attach to this branch of the question, there are no obscuring shadows upon the grand general relationship we have pointed out between the present distribution of Sequoia and the ancient glaciers of the Sierra. And when we bear in mind that all the present forests of the Sierra are young, growing on moraine soil recently deposited, and that the flank of the range itself, with all its landscapes, is new-born, recently sculptured, and brought to the light of day from beneath the ice mantle of the glacial winter, then a thousand lawless mysteries disappear, and broad harmonies take their places.

But although all the observed phenomena bearing on the post-glacial history of this colossal tree point to the conclusion that it never was more widely distributed on the Sierra since the close of the glacial epoch; that its present forests are scarcely past prime, if, indeed, they have reached prime; that the post-glacial day of the species is probably not half done;

yet, when from a wider outlook the vast antiquity of the genus is considered, and its ancient richness in species and individuals; comparing our Sierra Giant and *Sequoia sempervirens* of the Coast Range, the only other living species of Sequoia, with the twelve fossil species already discovered and described by Heer and Lesquereux, some of which seem to have flourished over vast areas in the Arctic regions and in Europe and our own territories, during tertiary and cretaceous times,—then indeed it becomes plain that our two surviving species, restricted to narrow belts within the limits of California, are mere remnants of the genus, both as to species and individuals, and that they probably are verging to extinction. But the verge of a period beginning in cretaceous times may have a breadth of tens of thousands of years, not to mention the possible existence of conditions calculated to multiply and reëxtend both species and individuals. This, however, is a branch of the question into which I do not now purpose to enter.

In studying the fate of our forest king, we have thus far considered the action of purely natural causes only; but, unfortunately, *man* is in the woods, and waste and pure destruction are making rapid headway. If the importance of forests were at all understood, even from an economic standpoint, their preservation would call forth the most watchful attention of government. Only of late years by means of forest reservations has the simplest groundwork for available legislation been laid, while in many of the finest groves every species of destruction is still moving on with accelerated speed.

In the course of my explorations I found no fewer than five mills located on or near the lower edge of the Sequoia belt, all of which were cutting considerable quantities of Big Tree lumber. Most of the Fresno group are doomed to feed the mills recently erected near them, and a company of lumbermen are now cutting the magnificent forest on King's River. In these milling operations waste far exceeds use, for after the choice young manageable trees on any given spot have been felled, the woods are fired to clear the ground of limbs and refuse with reference to further operations, and, of course, most of the seedlings and saplings are destroyed.

These mill ravages, however, are small as compared with the

comprehensive destruction caused by "sheepmen." Incredible
numbers of sheep are driven to the mountain pastures every
summer, and their course is ever marked by desolation. Every
wild garden is trodden down, the shrubs are stripped of leaves
as if devoured by locusts, and the woods are burned. Running
fires are set everywhere, with a view to clearing the ground of
prostrate trunks, to facilitate the movements of the flocks and
improve the pastures. The entire forest belt is thus swept and
devastated from one extremity of the range to the other, and,
with the exception of the resinous *Pinus contorta*, Sequoia
suffers most of all. Indians burn off the underbrush in certain
localities to facilitate deer-hunting, mountaineers and lumbermen carelessly allow their camp-fires to run; but the fires of
the sheepmen, or *muttoneers*, form more than ninety per cent.
of all destructive fires that range the Sierra forests.

It appears, therefore, that notwithstanding our forest king
might live on gloriously in Nature's keeping, it is rapidly vanishing before the fire and steel of man; and unless protective
measures be speedily invented and applied, in a few decades,
at the farthest, all that will be left of *Sequoia gigantea* will be
a few hacked and scarred monuments.

TWO-LEAVED, OR TAMARACK, PINE
(*Pinus contorta*, var. *Murrayana*)

This species forms the bulk of the alpine forests, extending
along the range, above the fir zone, up to a height of from
8000 to 9500 feet above the sea, growing in beautiful order
upon moraines that are scarcely changed as yet by post-glacial
weathering. Compared with the giants of the lower zones, this
is a small tree, seldom attaining a height of a hundred feet.
The largest specimen I ever measured was ninety feet in
height, and a little over six in diameter four feet from the
ground. The average height of mature trees throughout the
entire belt is probably not far from fifty or sixty feet, with a
diameter of two feet. It is a well-proportioned, rather handsome little pine, with grayish-brown bark, and crooked,
much-divided branches, which cover the greater portion of
the trunk, not so densely, however, as to prevent its being

seen. The lower limbs curve downward, gradually take a horizontal position about half-way up the trunk, then aspire more
and more toward the summit, thus forming a sharp, conical
top. The foliage is short and rigid, two leaves in a fascicle,
arranged in comparatively long, cylindrical tassels at the ends
of the tough, up-curving branchlets. The cones are about two
inches long, growing in stiff clusters among the needles, without making any striking effect, except while very young, when
they are of a vivid crimson color, and the whole tree appears
to be dotted with brilliant flowers. The sterile cones are still
more showy, on account of their great abundance, often giving a reddish-yellow tinge to the whole mass of the foliage,
and filling the air with pollen.

No other pine on the range is so regularly planted as this
one. Moraine forests sweep along the sides of the high, rocky
valleys for miles without interruption; still, strictly speaking,
they are not dense, for flecks of sunshine and flowers find their
way into the darkest places, where the trees grow tallest and
thickest. Tall, nutritious grasses are specially abundant beneath
them, growing over all the ground, in sunshine and shade,
over extensive areas like a farmer's crop, and serving as pasture
for the multitude of sheep that are driven from the arid plains
every summer as soon as the snow is melted.

The Two-leaved Pine, more than any other, is subject to
destruction by fire. The thin bark is streaked and sprinkled
with resin, as though it had been showered down upon it like
rain, so that even the green trees catch fire readily, and during
strong winds whole forests are destroyed, the flames leaping
from tree to tree, forming one continuous belt of roaring fire
that goes surging and racing onward above the bending
woods, like the grass-fires of a prairie. During the calm, dry
season of Indian summer, the fire creeps quietly along the
ground, feeding on the dry needles and burs; then, arriving
at the foot of a tree, the resiny bark is ignited, and the heated
air ascends in a powerful current, increasing in velocity, and
dragging the flames swiftly upward; then the leaves catch fire,
and an immense column of flame, beautifully spired on the
edges, and tinted a rose-purple hue, rushes aloft thirty or forty
feet above the top of the tree, forming a grand spectacle, especially on a dark night. It lasts, however, only a few seconds,

vanishing with magical rapidity, to be succeeded by others along the fire-line at irregular intervals for weeks at a time— tree after tree flashing and darkening, leaving the trunks and branches hardly scarred. The heat, however, is sufficient to kill the trees, and in a few years the bark shrivels and falls off. Belts miles in extent are thus killed and left standing with the branches on, peeled and rigid, appearing gray in the distance, like misty clouds. Later the branches drop off, leaving a forest of bleached spars. At length the roots decay, and the forlorn trunks are blown down during some storm, and piled one upon another encumbering the ground until they are consumed by the next fire, and leave it ready for a fresh crop.

The endurance of the species is shown by its wandering occasionally out over the lava plains with the Yellow Pine, and climbing moraineless mountain-sides with the Dwarf Pine, clinging to any chance support in rifts and crevices of storm-beaten rocks—always, however, showing the effects of such hardships in every feature.

Down in sheltered lake hollows, on beds of rich alluvium, it varies so far from the common form as frequently to be taken for a distinct species. Here it grows in dense sods, like grasses, from forty to eighty feet high, bending all together to the breeze and whirling in eddying gusts more lithely than any other tree in the woods. I have frequently found specimens fifty feet high less than five inches in diameter. Being thus slender, and at the same time well clad with leafy boughs, it is oftentimes bent to the ground when laden with soft snow, forming beautiful arches in endless variety, some of which last until the melting of the snow in spring.

MOUNTAIN PINE
(Pinus monticola)

The Mountain Pine is king of the alpine woods, brave, hardy, and long-lived, towering grandly above its companions, and becoming stronger and more imposing just where other species begin to crouch and disappear. At its best it is usually about ninety feet high and five or six in diameter, though a specimen is often met considerably larger than this. The trunk is as massive and as suggestive of enduring strength as that of an oak. About two thirds of the trunk is commonly free of limbs, but close, fringy tufts of sprays occur all the way down, like those which adorn the colossal shafts of Sequoia. The bark is deep reddish-brown upon trees that occupy exposed situations near its upper limit, and furrowed rather deeply, the main furrows running nearly parallel with each other, and connected by conspicuous cross furrows, which, with one exception, are, as far as I have noticed, peculiar to this species.

The cones are from four to eight inches long, slender, cylindrical, and somewhat curved, resembling those of the common White Pine of the Atlantic coast. They grow in clusters of about from three to six or seven, becoming pendulous as they increase in weight, chiefly by the bending of the branches.

This species is nearly related to the Sugar Pine, and, though not half so tall, it constantly suggests its noble relative in the way that it extends its long arms and in general habit. The Mountain Pine is first met on the upper margin of the fir zone, growing singly in a subdued, inconspicuous form, in what appear as chance situations, without making much impression on the general forest. Continuing up through the Two-leaved Pines in the same scattered growth, it begins to show its character, and at an elevation of about 10,000 feet attains its noblest development near the middle of the range, tossing its tough arms in the frosty air, welcoming storms and feeding on them, and reaching the grand old age of 1000 years.

JUNIPER, OR RED CEDAR
(*Juniperus occidentalis*)

The Juniper is preëminently a rock tree, occupying the baldest domes and pavements, where there is scarcely a handful of soil, at a height of from 7000 to 9500 feet. In such situations the trunk is frequently over eight feet in diameter, and not much more in height. The top is almost always dead in old trees, and great stubborn limbs push out horizontally that are mostly broken and bare at the ends, but densely covered and embedded here and there with bossy mounds of gray foliage. Some are mere weathered stumps, as broad as long, decorated with a few leafy sprays, reminding one of the crumbling towers of some ancient castle scantily draped with ivy. Only upon the head waters of the Carson have I found this species established on good moraine soil. Here it flourishes with the Silver and Two-leaved Pines, in great beauty and luxuriance, attaining a height of from forty to sixty feet, and manifesting but little of that rocky angularity so characteristic a feature throughout the greater portion of its range. Two of the largest, growing at the head of Hope Valley, measured twenty-nine feet three inches and twenty-five feet six inches in circumference, respectively, four feet from the ground. The bark is of a bright cinnamon color, and, in thrifty trees, beautifully braided and reticulated, flaking off in thin, lustrous ribbons that are sometimes used by Indians for tent-matting. Its fine color and odd picturesqueness always catch an artist's eye, but to me the Juniper seems a singularly dull and taciturn tree, never speaking to one's heart. I have spent many a day and night in its company, in all kinds of weather, and have ever found it silent, cold, and rigid, like a column of ice. Its broad stumpiness, of course, precludes all possibility of waving, or even shaking; but it is not this rocky steadfastness that constitutes its silence. In calm, sun-days the Sugar Pine preaches the grandeur of the mountains like an apostle without moving a leaf.

On level rocks it dies standing, and wastes insensibly out of existence like granite, the wind exerting about as little control over it alive or dead as it does over a glacier boulder. Some are undoubtedly over 2000 years old. All the trees of the alpine woods suffer, more or less, from avalanches, the Two-leaved Pine most of all. Gaps two or three hundred yards wide, extending from the upper limit of the tree-line to the bottoms of valleys and lake basins, are of common occurrence in all the upper forests, resembling the clearings of settlers in the old backwoods. Scarcely a tree is spared, even the soil is scraped away, while the thousands of uprooted pines and spruces are piled upon one another heads downward, and tucked snugly in along the sides of the clearing in two wind-rows, like lateral moraines. The pines lie with branches wilted and drooping like weeds. Not so the burly junipers. After

braving in silence the storms of perhaps a dozen or twenty
centuries, they seem in this, their last calamity, to become
somewhat communicative, making sign of a very unwilling
acceptance of their fate, holding themselves well up from the
ground on knees and elbows, seemingly ill at ease, and anxious, like stubborn wrestlers, to rise again.

HEMLOCK SPRUCE
(Tsuga Pattoniana)

The Hemlock Spruce is the most singularly beautiful of all
the California coniferæ. So slender is its axis at the top, that
it bends over and droops like the stalk of a nodding lily. The
branches droop also, and divide into innumerable slender,
waving sprays, which are arranged in a varied, eloquent harmony that is wholly indescribable. Its cones are purple, and
hang free, in the form of little tassels two inches long from
all the sprays from top to bottom. Though exquisitely delicate
and feminine in expression, it grows best where the snow lies
deepest, far up in the region of storms, at an elevation of from
9000 to 9500 feet, on frosty northern slopes; but it is capable
of growing considerably higher, say 10,500 feet. The tallest
specimens, growing in sheltered hollows somewhat beneath
the heaviest wind-currents, are from eighty to a hundred feet
high, and from two to four feet in diameter. The very largest
specimen I ever found was nineteen feet seven inches in circumference four feet from the ground, growing on the edge
of Lake Hollow, at an elevation of 9250 feet above the level
of the sea. At the age of twenty or thirty years it becomes
fruitful, and hangs out its beautiful purple cones at the ends
of the slender sprays, where they swing free in the breeze, and
contrast delightfully with the cool green foliage. They are
translucent when young, and their beauty is delicious. After
they are fully ripe, they spread their shell-like scales and allow
the brown-winged seeds to fly in the mellow air, while the
empty cones remain to beautify the tree until the coming of
a fresh crop.

The staminate cones of all the coniferæ are beautiful, growing in bright clusters, yellow, and rose, and crimson. Those of

the Hemlock Spruce are the most beautiful of all, forming little conelets of blue flowers, each on a slender stem.

Under all conditions, sheltered or stormbeaten, well-fed or ill-fed, this tree is singularly graceful in habit. Even at its highest limit upon exposed ridge-tops, though compelled to crouch in dense thickets, huddled close together, as if for mutual protection, it still manages to throw out its sprays in irrepressible loveliness; while on well-ground moraine soil it develops a perfectly tropical luxuriance of foliage and fruit, and is the very loveliest tree in the forest; poised in thin white sunshine, clad with branches from head to foot, yet not in the faintest degree heavy or bunchy, it towers in unassuming majesty, drooping as if unaffected with the aspiring tendencies of its race, loving the ground while transparently conscious of heaven and joyously receptive of its blessings, reaching out its branches like sensitive tentacles, feeling the light and reveling in it. No other of our alpine conifers so finely veils its strength. Its delicate branches yield to the mountains' gentlest breath; yet is it strong to meet the wildest onsets of the gale,—strong not in resistance, but compliance, bowing, snow-laden, to the ground, gracefully accepting burial month after month in the darkness beneath the heavy mantle of winter.

When the first soft snow begins to fall, the flakes lodge in the leaves, weighing down the branches against the trunk. Then the axis bends yet lower and lower, until the slender top touches the ground, thus forming a fine ornamental arch. The snow still falls lavishly, and the whole tree is at length buried, to sleep and rest in its beautiful grave as though dead. Entire groves of young trees, from ten to forty feet high, are thus buried every winter like slender grasses. But, like the violets and daisies which the heaviest snows crush not, they are safe. It is as though this were only Nature's method of putting her darlings to sleep instead of leaving them exposed to the biting storms of winter.

Thus warmly wrapped they await the summer resurrection. The snow becomes soft in the sunshine, and freezes at night, making the mass hard and compact, like ice, so that during the months of April and May you can ride a horse over the prostrate groves without catching sight of a single leaf. At length the down-pouring sunshine sets them free. First the elastic tops of the arches begin to appear, then one branch after another, each springing loose with a gentle rustling sound, and at length the whole tree, with the assistance of the winds, gradually unbends and rises and settles back into its place in the warm air, as dry and feathery and fresh as young ferns just out of the coil.

Some of the finest groves I have yet found are on the southern slopes of Lassen's Butte. There are also many charming companies on the head waters of the Tuolumne, Merced, and San Joaquin, and, in general, the species is so far from being rare that you can scarcely fail to find groves of considerable extent in crossing the range, choose what pass you may. The Mountain Pine grows beside it, and more frequently the two-leaved species; but there are many beautiful groups, numbering 1000 individuals, or more, without a single intruder.

I wish I had space to write more of the surpassing beauty of this favorite spruce. Every tree-lover is sure to regard it with special admiration; apathetic mountaineers, even, seeking only game or gold, stop to gaze on first meeting it, and mutter to themselves: "That's a mighty pretty tree," some of them adding, "d——d pretty!" In autumn, when its cones are ripe, the little striped tamias, and the Douglas squirrel, and the Clark crow make a happy stir in its groves. The deer love to lie down beneath its spreading branches; bright streams from the snow that is always near ripple through its groves, and bryanthus spreads precious carpets in its shade. But the best words only hint its charms. Come to the mountains and see.

DWARF PINE
(Pinus albicaulis)

This species forms the extreme edge of the timber line throughout nearly the whole extent of the range on both flanks. It is first met growing in company with *Pinus contorta*, var. *Murrayana*, on the upper margin of the belt, as an erect tree from fifteen to thirty feet high and from one to two feet in thickness; thence it goes straggling up the flanks of the summit peaks, upon moraines or crumbling ledges, wherever it can obtain a foothold, to an elevation of from 10,000 to

12,000 feet, where it dwarfs to a mass of crumpled, prostrate branches, covered with slender, upright shoots, each tipped with a short, close-packed tassel of leaves. The bark is smooth and purplish, in some places almost white. The fertile cones grow in rigid clusters upon the upper branches, dark chocolate in color while young, and bear beautiful pearly seeds about the size of peas, most of which are eaten by two species of tamias and the notable Clark crow. The staminate cones occur in clusters, about an inch wide, down among the leaves, and, as they are colored bright rose-purple, they give rise to a lively, flowery appearance little looked for in such a tree.

Pines are commonly regarded as sky-loving trees that must necessarily aspire or die. This species forms a marked exception, creeping lowly, in compliance with the most rigorous demands of climate, yet enduring bravely to a more advanced age than many of its lofty relatives in the sun-lands below. Seen from a distance, it would never be taken for a tree of any kind. Yonder, for example, is Cathedral Peak, some three miles away, with a scattered growth of this pine creeping like mosses over the roof and around the beveled edges of the north gable, nowhere giving any hint of an ascending axis. When approached quite near it still appears matted and heathy, and is so low that one experiences no great difficulty in walking over the top of it. Yet it is seldom absolutely prostrate, at its lowest usually attaining a height of three or four feet, with a main trunk, and branches outspread and intertangled above it, as if in ascending they had been checked by a ceiling, against which they had grown and been compelled to spread horizontally. The winter snow is indeed such a ceiling, lasting half the year; while the pressed, shorn surface is made yet smoother by violent winds, armed with cutting sandgrains, that beat down any shoot that offers to rise much above the general level, and carve the dead trunks and branches in beautiful patterns.

During stormy nights I have often camped snugly beneath the interlacing arches of this little pine. The needles, which have accumulated for centuries, make fine beds, a fact well known to other mountaineers, such as deer and wild sheep, who paw out oval hollows and lie beneath the larger trees in safe and comfortable concealment.

The longevity of this lowly dwarf is far greater than would be guessed. Here, for example, is a specimen, growing at an elevation of 10,700 feet, which seems as though it might be plucked up by the roots, for it is only three and a half inches in diameter, and its topmost tassel is hardly three feet above the ground. Cutting it half through and counting the annual rings with the aid of a lens, we find its age to be no less than 255 years. Here is another telling specimen about the same height, 426 years old, whose trunk is only six inches in diameter; and one of its supple branchlets, hardly an eighth of an inch in diameter inside the bark, is seventy-five years old, and so filled with oily balsam, and so well seasoned by storms, that we may tie it in knots like a whip-cord.

WHITE PINE
(Pinus flexilis)

This species is widely distributed throughout the Rocky Mountains, and over all the higher of the many ranges of the Great Basin, between the Wahsatch Mountains and the Sierra, where it is known as White Pine. In the Sierra it is sparsely scattered along the eastern flank, from Bloody Cañon southward nearly to the extremity of the range, opposite the village of Lone Pine, nowhere forming any appreciable portion of the general forest. From its peculiar position, in loose, straggling parties, it seems to have been derived from the Basin ranges to the eastward, where it is abundant.

It is a larger tree than the Dwarf Pine. At an elevation of about 9000 feet above the sea, it often attains a height of forty or fifty feet, and a diameter of from three to five feet. The cones open freely when ripe, and are twice as large as those of the *albicaulis*, and the foliage and branches are more open, having a tendency to sweep out in free, wild curves, like those of the Mountain Pine, to which it is closely allied. It is seldom found lower than 9000 feet above sea-level, but from this elevation it pushes upward over the roughest ledges to the extreme limit of tree-growth, where, in its dwarfed, storm-crushed condition, it is more like the white-barked species.

Throughout Utah and Nevada it is one of the principal

timber-trees, great quantities being cut every year for the mines. The famous White Pine Mining District, White Pine City, and the White Pine Mountains have derived their names from it.

NEEDLE PINE
(Pinus aristata)

This species is restricted in the Sierra to the southern portion of the range, about the head waters of Kings and Kern rivers, where it forms extensive forests, and in some places accompanies the Dwarf Pine to the extreme limit of tree-growth.

It is first met at an elevation of between 9000 and 10,000 feet, and runs up to 11,000 without seeming to suffer greatly from the climate or the leanness of the soil. It is a much finer tree than the Dwarf Pine. Instead of growing in clumps and low, heathy mats, it manages in some way to maintain an erect position, and usually stands single. Wherever the young trees are at all sheltered, they grow up straight and arrowy, with delicately tapered bole, and ascending branches terminated with glossy, bottle-brush tassels. At middle age, certain limbs are specialized and pushed far out for the bearing of cones, after the manner of the Sugar Pine; and in old age these branches droop and cast about in every direction, giving rise to very picturesque effects. The trunk becomes deep brown and rough, like that of the Mountain Pine, while the young cones are of a strange, dull, blackish-blue color, clustered on the upper branches. When ripe they are from three to four inches long, yellowish brown, resembling in every way those of the Mountain Pine. Excepting the Sugar Pine, no tree on the mountains is so capable of individual expression, while in grace of form and movement it constantly reminds one of the Hemlock Spruce.

The largest specimen I measured was a little over five feet in diameter and ninety feet in height, but this is more than twice the ordinary size.

This species is common throughout the Rocky Mountains and most of the short ranges of the Great Basin, where it is called the Fox-tail Pine, from its long dense leaf-tassels. On the Hot Creek, White Pine, and Golden Gate ranges it is quite abundant. About a foot or eighteen inches of the ends of the branches is densely packed with stiff outstanding needles which radiate like an electric fox or squirrel's tail. The needles have a glossy polish, and the sunshine sifting through them makes them burn with silvery luster, while their number and elastic temper tell delightfully in the winds. This tree is here still more original and picturesque than in the Sierra, far surpassing not only its companion conifers in this respect, but also the most noted of the lowland oaks. Some stand firmly erect, feathered with radiant tassels down to the ground, forming slender tapering towers of shining verdure; others, with two or three specialized branches pushed out at right angles to the trunk and densely clad with tasseled sprays, take the form of beautiful ornamental crosses. Again in the same woods you find trees that are made up of several boles united near the ground, spreading at the sides in a plane parallel to the axis of the mountain, with the elegant tassels hung in charming order between them, making a harp held against the main wind lines where they are most effective in playing the grand storm harmonies. And besides these there are many variable arching forms, alone or in groups, with innumerable tassels drooping beneath the arches or radiant above them, and many lowly giants of no particular form that have braved the storms of a thousand years. But whether old or young, sheltered or exposed to the wildest gales, this tree is ever found irrepressibly and extravagantly picturesque, and offers a richer and more varied series of forms to the artist than any other conifer I know of.

NUT PINE
(Pinus monophylla)

The Nut Pine covers or rather dots the eastern flank of the Sierra, to which it is mostly restricted, in grayish, bush-like patches, from the margin of the sage-plains to an elevation of from 7000 to 8000 feet.

A more contentedly fruitful and unaspiring conifer could

not be conceived. All the species we have been sketching make departures more or less distant from the typical spire form, but none goes so far as this. Without any apparent exigency of climate or soil, it remains near the ground, throwing out crooked, divergent branches like an orchard apple-tree, and seldom pushes a single shoot higher than fifteen or twenty feet above the ground.

The average thickness of the trunk is, perhaps, about ten or twelve inches. The leaves are mostly undivided, like round awls, instead of being separated, like those of other pines, into twos and threes and fives. The cones are green while growing, and are usually found over all the tree, forming quite a marked feature as seen against the bluish-gray foliage. They are quite small, only about two inches in length, and give no promise of edible nuts; but when we come to open them, we find that about half the entire bulk of the cone is made up of sweet, nutritious seeds, the kernels of which are nearly as large as those of hazel-nuts.

This is undoubtedly the most important food-tree on the Sierra, and furnishes the Mono, Carson, and Walker River Indians with more and better nuts than all the other species taken together. It is the Indians' own tree, and many a white man have they killed for cutting it down.

In its development Nature seems to have aimed at the formation of as great a fruit-bearing surface as possible. Being so low and accessible, the cones are readily beaten off with poles, and the nuts procured by roasting them until the scales open. In bountiful seasons a single Indian will gather thirty or forty bushels of them—a fine squirrelish employment.

Of all the conifers along the eastern base of the Sierra, and on all the many mountain groups and short ranges of the Great Basin, this foodful little pine is the commonest tree, and the most important. Nearly every mountain is planted with it to a height of from 8000 to 9000 feet above the sea. Some are covered from base to summit by this one species, with only a sparse growth of juniper on the lower slopes to break the continuity of its curious woods, which, though dark-looking at a distance, are almost shadeless, and have none of the damp, leafy glens and hollows so characteristic of other pine woods. Tens of thousands of acres occur in continuous belts.

Indeed, viewed comprehensively the entire Basin seems to be pretty evenly divided into level plains dotted with sage-bushes and mountain-chains covered with Nut Pines. No slope is too rough, none too dry, for these bountiful orchards of the red man.

The value of this species to Nevada is not easily over-estimated. It furnishes charcoal and timber for the mines, and, with the juniper, supplies the ranches with fuel and rough fencing. In fruitful seasons the nut crop is perhaps greater than the California wheat crop, which exerts so much influence throughout the food markets of the world. When the crop is ripe, the Indians make ready the long beating-poles; bags, baskets, mats, and sacks are collected; the women out at service among the settlers, washing or drudging, assemble at the family huts; the men leave their ranch work; old and young, all are mounted on ponies and start in great glee to the nut-lands, forming curiously picturesque cavalcades; flaming scarfs and calico skirts stream loosely over the knotty ponies, two squaws usually astride of each, with baby midgets bandaged in baskets slung on their backs or balanced on the saddle-bow; while nut-baskets and water-jars project from each side, and the long beating-poles make angles in every direction. Arriving at some well-known central point where grass and water are found, the squaws with baskets, the men with poles ascend the ridges to the laden trees, followed by the children. Then the beating begins right merrily, the burs fly in every direction, rolling down the slopes, lodging here and there against rocks and sage-bushes, chased and gathered by the women and children with fine natural gladness. Smoke-columns speedily mark the joyful scene of their labors as the roasting-fires are kindled, and, at night, assembled in gay circles garrulous as jays, they begin the first nut feast of the season.

The nuts are about half an inch long and a quarter of an inch in diameter, pointed at the top, round at the base, light brown in general color, and, like many other pine seeds, handsomely dotted with purple, like birds' eggs. The shells are thin and may be crushed between the thumb and finger. The kernels are white, becoming brown by roasting, and are sweet to every palate, being eaten by birds, squirrels, dogs, horses, and men. Perhaps less than one bushel in a thousand of the whole crop is ever gathered. Still, besides supplying their own wants, in times of plenty the Indians bring large quantities to market; then they are eaten around nearly every fireside in the State, and are even fed to horses occasionally instead of barley.

Of other trees growing on the Sierra, but forming a very small part of the general forest, we may briefly notice the following:

Chamæcyparis Lawsoniana is a magnificent tree in the coast ranges, but small in the Sierra. It is found only well to the northward along the banks of cool streams on the upper Sacramento toward Mount Shasta. Only a few trees of this species, as far as I have seen, have as yet gained a place in the Sierra woods. It has evidently been derived from the coast range by way of the tangle of connecting mountains at the head of the Sacramento Valley.

In shady dells and on cool stream banks of the northern Sierra we also find the Yew (*Taxus brevifolia*).

The interesting Nutmeg Tree (*Torreya Californica*) is sparsely distributed along the western flank of the range at an elevation of about 4000 feet, mostly in gulches and cañons. It is a small, prickly leaved, glossy evergreen, like a conifer, from twenty to fifty feet high, and one to two feet in diameter. The fruit resembles a green-gage plum, and contains one seed, about the size of an acorn, and like a nutmeg, hence the common name. The wood is fine-grained and of a beautiful, creamy yellow color like box, sweet-scented when dry, though the green leaves emit a disagreeable odor.

Betula occidentalis, the only birch, is a small, slender tree restricted to the eastern flank of the range along stream-sides below the pine-belt, especially in Owen's Valley.

Alder, Maple, and Nuttall's Flowering Dogwood make beautiful bowers over swift, cool streams at an elevation of from 3000 to 5000 feet, mixed more or less with willows and cottonwood; and above these in lake basins the aspen forms fine ornamental groves, and lets its light shine gloriously in the autumn months.

The Chestnut Oak (*Quercus densiflora*) seems to have come from the coast range around the head of the Sacramento Valley, like the *Chamæcyparis*, but as it extends southward along the lower edge of the main pine-belt it grows smaller until it finally dwarfs to a mere chaparral bush. In the coast mountains it is a fine, tall, rather slender tree, about from sixty to seventy-five feet high, growing with the grand *Sequoia sempervirens*, or Redwood. But unfortunately it is too good to live, and is now being rapidly destroyed for tanbark.

Besides the common Douglas Oak and the grand *Quercus Wislizeni* of the foot-hills, and several small ones that make dense growths of chaparral, there are two mountain-oaks that grow with the pines up to an elevation of about 5000 feet above the sea, and greatly enhance the beauty of the yosemite parks. These are the Mountain Live Oak and the Kellogg Oak, named in honor of the admirable botanical pioneer of California. Kellogg's Oak (*Quercus Kelloggii*) is a firm, bright, beautiful tree, reaching a height of sixty feet, four to seven feet in diameter, with wide-spreading branches, and growing at an elevation of from 3000 to 5000 feet in sunny valleys and flats among the evergreens, and higher in a dwarfed state. In the cliff-bound parks about 4000 feet above the sea it is so abundant and effective it might fairly be called the Yosemite Oak. The leaves make beautiful masses of purple in the spring, and yellow in ripe autumn; while its acorns are eagerly gathered by Indians, squirrels, and woodpeckers. The Mountain Live Oak (*Q. Chrysolepis*) is a tough, rugged mountaineer of a tree, growing bravely and attaining noble dimensions on the roughest earthquake taluses in deep cañons and yosemite valleys. The trunk is usually short, dividing near the ground into great, wide-spreading limbs, and these again into a multitude of slender sprays, many of them cord-like and drooping to the ground, like those of the Great White Oak of the lowlands (*Q. lobata*). The top of the tree where there is plenty of space is broad and bossy, with a dense covering of shining leaves, making delightful canopies, the complicated system of gray, interlacing, arching branches as seen from beneath being exceedingly rich and picturesque. No other tree that I know dwarfs so regularly and completely as this under changes of climate due to changes in elevation. At the foot of a cañon 4000 feet above the sea you may find magnificent specimens of this oak fifty feet high, with craggy, bulging trunks, five to seven feet in diameter, and at the head of the cañon, 2500 feet higher, a dense, soft, low, shrubby growth of the same species, while all the way up the cañon between these extremes of size and habit a perfect gradation may be traced. The largest I have seen was fifty feet high, eight feet in diameter, and about seventy-five feet in spread. The trunk was all knots and buttresses, gray like granite, and about as angular and irregular as the boulders on which it was growing—a type of steadfast, unwedgeable strength.

Chapter IX

THE DOUGLAS SQUIRREL
(Sciurus Douglasii)

THE Douglas Squirrel is by far the most interesting and influential of the California sciuridæ, surpassing every other species in force of character, numbers, and extent of range, and in the amount of influence he brings to bear upon the health and distribution of the vast forests he inhabits.

Go where you will throughout the noble woods of the Sierra Nevada, among the giant pines and spruces of the lower zones, up through the towering Silver Firs to the storm-bent thickets of the summit peaks, you everywhere find this little squirrel the master-existence. Though only a few inches long, so intense is his fiery vigor and restlessness, he stirs every grove with wild life, and makes himself more important than even the huge bears that shuffle through the tangled underbrush beneath him. Every wind is fretted by his voice, almost every bole and branch feels the sting of his sharp feet. How much the growth of the trees is stimulated by this means it is not easy to learn, but his action in manipulating their seeds is more appreciable. Nature has made him master forester and committed most of her coniferous crops to his paws. Probably over fifty per cent. of all the cones ripened on the Sierra are cut off and handled by the Douglas alone, and of those of the Big Trees perhaps ninety per cent. pass through his hands: the greater portion is of course stored away for food to last during the winter and spring, but some of them are tucked separately into loosely covered holes, where some of the seeds germinate and become trees. But the Sierra is only one of the many provinces over which he holds sway, for his dominion extends over all the Redwood Belt of the Coast Mountains, and far northward throughout the majestic forests of Oregon, Washington, and British Columbia. I make haste to mention these facts, to show upon how substantial a foundation the importance I ascribe to him rests.

The Douglas is closely allied to the Red Squirrel or Chickaree of the eastern woods. Ours may be a lineal descendant

of this species, distributed westward to the Pacific by way of
the Great Lakes and the Rocky Mountains, and thence southward along our forested ranges. This view is suggested by the
fact that our species becomes redder and more Chickaree-
like in general, the farther it is traced back along the course
indicated above. But whatever their relationship, and the
evolutionary forces that have acted upon them, the Douglas
is now the larger and more beautiful animal.

From the nose to the root of the tail he measures about
eight inches; and his tail, which he so effectively uses in interpreting his feelings, is about six inches in length. He wears
dark bluish-gray over the back and half-way down the sides,
bright buff on the belly, with a stripe of dark gray, nearly
black, separating the upper and under colors; this dividing
stripe, however, is not very sharply defined. He has long black
whiskers, which gives him a rather fierce look when observed
closely, strong claws, sharp as fish-hooks, and the brightest of
bright eyes, full of telling speculation.

A King's River Indian told me that they call him "Pillil-
looeet," which, rapidly pronounced with the first syllable
heavily accented, is not unlike the lusty exclamation he utters
on his way up a tree when excited. Most mountaineers in
California call him the Pine Squirrel; and when I asked an old
trapper whether he knew our little forester, he replied with
brightening countenance: "Oh, yes, of course I know him;
everybody knows him. When I'm huntin' in the woods, I often find out where the deer are by his barkin' at 'em. I call
'em Lightnin' Squirrels, because they're so mighty quick and
peert."

All the true squirrels are more or less birdlike in speech and
movements; but the Douglas is preëminently so, possessing,
as he does, every attribute peculiarly squirrelish enthusiasti-
cally concentrated. He is the squirrel of squirrels, flashing
from branch to branch of his favorite evergreens crisp and
glossy and undiseased as a sunbeam. Give him wings and he
would outfly any bird in the woods. His big gray cousin is a
looser animal, seemingly light enough to float on the wind;
yet when leaping from limb to limb, or out of one tree-top
to another, he sometimes halts to gather strength, as if making
efforts concerning the upshot of which he does not always

feel exactly confident. But the Douglas, with his denser body, leaps and glides in hidden strength, seemingly as independent of common muscles as a mountain stream. He threads the tasseled branches of the pines, stirring their needles like a rustling breeze; now shooting across openings in arrowy lines; now launching in curves, glinting deftly from side to side in sudden zigzags, and swirling in giddy loops and spirals around the knotty trunks; getting into what seem to be the most impossible situations without sense of danger; now on his haunches, now on his head; yet ever graceful, and punctuating his most irrepressible outbursts of energy with little dots and dashes of perfect repose. He is, without exception, the wildest animal I ever saw,—a fiery, sputtering little bolt of life, luxuriating in quick oxygen and the woods' best juices. One can hardly think of such a creature being dependent, like the rest of us, on climate and food. But, after all, it requires no long acquaintance to learn he is human, for he works for a living. His busiest time is in the Indian summer. Then he gathers burs and hazel-nuts like a plodding farmer, working continuously every day for hours; saying not a word; cutting off the ripe cones at the top of his speed, as if employed by the job, and examining every branch in regular order, as if careful that not one should escape him; then, descending, he stores them away beneath logs and stumps, in anticipation of the pinching hunger days of winter. He seems himself a kind of coniferous fruit,—both fruit and flower. The resiny essences of the pines pervade every pore of his body, and eating his flesh is like chewing gum.

One never tires of this bright chip of nature,—this brave little voice crying in the wilderness,—of observing his many works and ways, and listening to his curious language. His musical, piny gossip is as savory to the ear as balsam to the palate; and, though he has not exactly the gift of song, some of his notes are as sweet as those of a linnet—almost flute-like in softness, while others prick and tingle like thistles. He is the mocking-bird of squirrels, pouring forth mixed chatter and song like a perennial fountain; barking like a dog, screaming like a hawk, chirping like a blackbird or a sparrow; while in bluff, audacious noisiness he is a very jay.

In descending the trunk of a tree with the intention of alighting on the ground, he preserves a cautious silence, mindful, perhaps, of foxes and wildcats; but while rocking safely at home in the pine-tops there is no end to his capers and noise; and woe to the gray squirrel or chipmunk that ventures to set foot on his favorite tree! No matter how slyly they trace the furrows of the bark, they are speedily discovered, and kicked down-stairs with comic vehemence, while a torrent of angry notes comes rushing from his whiskered lips that sounds remarkably like swearing. He will even attempt at times to drive away dogs and men, especially if he has had no previous knowledge of them. Seeing a man for the first time, he approaches nearer and nearer, until within a few feet; then, with an angry outburst, he makes a sudden rush, all teeth and eyes, as if about to eat you up. But, finding that the big, forked animal doesn't scare, he prudently beats a retreat, and sets himself up to reconnoiter on some overhanging branch, scrutinizing every movement you make with ludicrous solemnity. Gathering courage, he ventures down the trunk again, churring and chirping, and jerking nervously up and down in curious loops, eyeing you all the time, as if showing off and demanding your admiration. Finally, growing calmer, he settles down in a comfortable posture on some horizontal branch commanding a good view, and beats time with his tail to a steady "Chee-up! chee-up!" or, when somewhat less excited, "Pee-ah!" with the first syllable keenly accented, and the second drawn out like the scream of a hawk,—repeating this slowly and more emphatically at first, then gradually faster, until a rate of about 150 words a minute is reached; usually sitting all the time on his haunches, with paws resting on his breast, which pulses visibly with each word. It is remarkable, too, that, though articulating distinctly, he keeps his mouth shut most of the time, and speaks through his nose. I have occasionally observed him even eating Sequoia seeds and nibbling a troublesome flea, without ceasing or in any way confusing his "Pee-ah! pee-ah!" for a single moment.

While ascending trees all his claws come into play, but in descending the weight of his body is sustained chiefly by those of the hind feet; still in neither case do his movements suggest effort, though if you are near enough you may see the bulging strength of his short, bear-like arms, and note his sinewy fists clinched in the bark.

Whether going up or down, he carries his tail extended at full length in line with his body, unless it be required for gestures. But while running along horizontal limbs or fallen trunks, it is frequently folded forward over the back, with the airy tip daintily upcurled. In cool weather it keeps him warm. Then, after he has finished his meal, you may see him crouched close on some level limb with his tail-robe neatly spread and reaching forward to his ears, the electric, outstanding hairs quivering in the breeze like pine-needles. But in wet or very cold weather he stays in his nest, and while curled up there his comforter is long enough to come forward around his nose. It is seldom so cold, however, as to prevent his going out to his stores when hungry.

Once as I lay storm-bound on the upper edge of the timber line on Mount Shasta, the thermometer nearly at zero and the sky thick with driving snow, a Douglas came bravely out several times from one of the lower hollows of a Dwarf Pine near my camp, faced the wind without seeming to feel it much, frisked lightly about over the mealy snow, and dug his way down to some hidden seeds with wonderful precision, as if to his eyes the thick snow-covering were glass.

No other of the Sierra animals of my acquaintance is better fed, not even the deer, amid abundance of sweet herbs and shrubs, or the mountain sheep, or omnivorous bears. His food consists of grass-seeds, berries, hazel-nuts, chinquapins, and the nuts and seeds of all the coniferous trees without exception,—Pine, Fir, Spruce, Libocedrus, Juniper, and Sequoia,— he is fond of them all, and they all agree with him, green or ripe. No cone is too large for him to manage, none so small as to be beneath his notice. The smaller ones, such as those of the Hemlock, and the Douglas Spruce, and the Two-leaved Pine, he cuts off and eats on a branch of the tree, without allowing them to fall; beginning at the bottom of the cone and cutting away the scales to expose the seeds; not gnawing by guess, like a bear, but turning them round and round in regular order, in compliance with their spiral arrangement.

When thus employed, his location in the tree is betrayed by

a dribble of scales, shells, and seed-wings, and, every few minutes, by the fall of the stripped axis of the cone. Then of course he is ready for another, and if you are watching you may catch a glimpse of him as he glides silently out to the end of a branch and see him examining the cone-clusters until he finds one to his mind; then, leaning over, pull back the springy needles out of his way, grasp the cone with his paws to prevent its falling, snip it off in an incredibly short time, seize it with jaws grotesquely stretched, and return to his chosen seat near the trunk. But the immense size of the cones of the Sugar Pine—from fifteen to twenty inches in length—and those of the Jeffrey variety of the Yellow Pine compel him to adopt a quite different method. He cuts them off without attempting to hold them, then goes down and drags them from where they have chanced to fall up to the bare, swelling ground around the instep of the tree, where he demolishes them in the same methodical way, beginning at the bottom and following the scale-spirals to the top.

From a single Sugar Pine cone he gets from two to four hundred seeds about half the size of a hazel-nut, so that in a few minutes he can procure enough to last a week. He seems, however, to prefer those of the two Silver Firs above all others; perhaps because they are most easily obtained, as the scales drop off when ripe without needing to be cut. Both species are filled with an exceedingly pungent, aromatic oil, which spices all his flesh, and is of itself sufficient to account for his lightning energy.

You may easily know this little workman by his chips. On sunny hillsides around the principal trees they lie in big piles,—bushels and basketfuls of them, all fresh and clean, making the most beautiful kitchen-middens imaginable. The brown and yellow scales and nut-shells are as abundant and as delicately penciled and tinted as the shells along the sea-shore; while the beautiful red and purple seed-wings mingled with them would lead one to fancy that innumerable butterflies had there met their fate.

He feasts on all the species long before they are ripe, but is wise enough to wait until they are matured before he gathers them into his barns. This is in October and November, which with him are the two busiest months of the year. All

kinds of burs, big and little, are now cut off and showered
down alike, and the ground is speedily covered with them. A
constant thudding and bumping is kept up; some of the larger
cones chancing to fall on old logs make the forest reëcho with
the sound. Other nut-eaters less industrious know well what
is going on, and hasten to carry away the cones as they fall.
But however busy the harvester may be, he is not slow to
descry the pilferers below, and instantly leaves his work to
drive them away. The little striped tamias is a thorn in his flesh,
stealing persistently, punish him as he may. The large Gray
Squirrel gives trouble also, although the Douglas has been
accused of stealing from him. Generally, however, just the opposite is the case.

The excellence of the Sierra evergreens is well known to
nurserymen throughout the world, consequently there is considerable demand for the seeds. The greater portion of the
supply has hitherto been procured by chopping down the
trees in the more accessible sections of the forest alongside of
bridle-paths that cross the range. Sequoia seeds at first
brought from twenty to thirty dollars per pound, and therefore were eagerly sought after. Some of the smaller fruitful
trees were cut down in the groves not protected by government, especially those of Fresno and King's River. Most of the
Sequoias, however, are of so gigantic a size that the seedsmen
have to look for the greater portion of their supplies to the
Douglas, who soon learns he is no match for these freebooters. He is wise enough, however, to cease working the instant
he perceives them, and never fails to embrace every opportunity to recover his burs whenever they happen to be stored
in any place accessible to him, and the busy seedsman often
finds on returning to camp that the little Douglas has ex-
haustively spoiled the spoiler. I know one seed-gatherer who,
whenever he robs the squirrels, scatters wheat or barley beneath the trees as conscience-money.

The want of appreciable life remarked by so many travelers
in the Sierra forests is never felt at this time of year. Banish
all the humming insects and the birds and quadrupeds, leaving
only Sir Douglas, and the most solitary of our so-called solitudes would still throb with ardent life. But if you should go
impatiently even into the most populous of the groves on

purpose to meet him, and walk about looking up among the branches, you would see very little of him. But lie down at the foot of one of the trees and straightway he will come. For, in the midst of the ordinary forest sounds, the falling of burs, piping of quails, the screaming of the Clark Crow, and the rustling of deer and bears among the chaparral, he is quick to detect your strange footsteps, and will hasten to make a good, close inspection of you as soon as you are still. First, you may hear him sounding a few notes of curious inquiry, but more likely the first intimation of his approach will be the prickly sounds of his feet as he descends the tree overhead, just before he makes his savage onrush to frighten you and proclaim your presence to every squirrel and bird in the neighborhood. If you remain perfectly motionless, he will come nearer and nearer, and probably set your flesh a-tingle by frisking across your body. Once, while I was seated at the foot of a Hemlock Spruce in one of the most inaccessible of the San Joaquin yosemites engaged in sketching, a reckless fellow came up behind me, passed under my bended arm, and jumped on my paper. And one warm afternoon, while an old friend of mine was reading out in the shade of his cabin, one of his Douglas neighbors jumped from the gable upon his head, and then with admirable assurance ran down over his shoulder and on to the book he held in his hand.

Our Douglas enjoys a large social circle; for, besides his numerous relatives, *Sciurus fossor*, *Tamias quadrivitatus*, *T. Townsendii*, *Spermophilus Beecheyi*, *S. Douglasii*, he maintains intimate relations with the nut-eating birds, particularly the Clark Crow (*Picicorvus columbianus*) and the numerous woodpeckers and jays. The two spermophiles are astonishingly abundant in the lowlands and lower foot-hills, but more and more sparingly distributed up through the Douglas domains,—seldom venturing higher than six or seven thousand feet above the level of the sea. The gray sciurus ranges but little higher than this. The little striped tamias alone is associated with him everywhere. In the lower and middle zones, where they all meet, they are tolerably harmonious—a happy family, though very amusing skirmishes may occasionally be witnessed. Wherever the ancient glaciers have spread forest soil there you find our wee hero, most abundant where depth of soil and genial climate have given rise to a corresponding luxuriance in the trees, but following every kind of growth up the curving moraines to the highest glacial fountains.

Though I cannot of course expect all my readers to sympathize fully in my admiration of this little animal, few, I hope, will think this sketch of his life too long. I cannot begin to tell here how much he has cheered my lonely wanderings during all the years I have been pursuing my studies in these glorious wilds; or how much unmistakable humanity I have found in him. Take this for example: One calm, creamy Indian summer morning, when the nuts were ripe, I was camped in the upper pine-woods of the south fork of the San Joaquin, where the squirrels seemed to be about as plentiful as the ripe burs. They were taking an early breakfast before going to their regular harvest-work. While I was busy with my own breakfast I heard the thudding fall of two or three heavy cones from a Yellow Pine near me. I stole noiselessly forward within about twenty feet of the base of it to observe. In a few moments down came the Douglas. The breakfast-burs he had cut off had rolled on the gently sloping ground into a clump of ceanothus bushes, but he seemed to know exactly where they were, for he found them at once, apparently without searching for them. They were more than twice as heavy as himself, but after turning them into the right position for getting a good hold with his long sickle-teeth he managed to drag them up to the foot of the tree from which he had cut them, moving backward. Then seating himself comfortably, he held them on end, bottom up, and demolished them at his ease. A good deal of nibbling had to be done before he got anything to eat, because the lower scales are barren, but when he had patiently worked his way up to the fertile ones he found two sweet nuts at the base of each, shaped like trimmed hams, and spotted purple like birds' eggs. And notwithstanding these cones were dripping with soft balsam, and covered with prickles, and so strongly put together that a boy would be puzzled to cut them open with a jack-knife, he accomplished his meal with easy dignity and cleanliness, making less effort apparently than a man would in eating soft cookery from a plate.

Breakfast done, I whistled a tune for him before he went to work, curious to see how he would be affected by it. He had not seen me all this while; but the instant I began to whistle he darted up the tree nearest to him, and came out on a small dead limb opposite me, and composed himself to listen. I sang and whistled more than a dozen airs, and as the music changed his eyes sparkled, and he turned his head quickly from side to side, but made no other response. Other squirrels, hearing the strange sounds, came around on all sides, also chipmunks and birds. One of the birds, a handsome, speckle-breasted thrush, seemed even more interested than the squirrels. After listening for awhile on one of the lower dead sprays of a pine, he came swooping forward within a few feet of my face, and remained fluttering in the air for half a minute or so, sustaining himself with whirring wing-beats, like a humming-bird in front of a flower, while I could look into his eyes and see his innocent wonder.

By this time my performance must have lasted nearly half an hour. I sang or whistled "Bonnie Doon," "Lass o' Gowrie," "O'er the Water to Charlie," "Bonnie Woods o' Cragie Lee," etc., all of which seemed to be listened to with bright interest, my first Douglas sitting patiently through it all, with his telling eyes fixed upon me until I ventured to give the "Old Hundredth," when he screamed his Indian name, Pillil-looeet, turned tail, and darted with ludicrous haste up the tree out of sight, his voice and actions in the case leaving a somewhat profane impression, as if he had said, "I'll be hanged if you get me to hear anything so solemn and unpiny." This acted as a signal for the general dispersal of the whole hairy tribe, though the birds seemed willing to wait further developments, music being naturally more in their line.

What there can be in that grand old church-tune that is so offensive to birds and squirrels I can't imagine. A year or two after this High Sierra concert, I was sitting one fine day on a hill in the Coast Range where the common Ground Squirrels were abundant. They were very shy on account of being hunted so much; but after I had been silent and motionless for half an hour or so they began to venture out of their holes and to feed on the seeds of the grasses and thistles around me as if I were no more to be feared than a tree-stump. Then it occurred to me that this was a good opportunity to find out whether they also disliked "Old Hundredth." Therefore I began to whistle as nearly as I could remember the same familiar airs that had pleased the mountaineers of the Sierra. They at once stopped eating, stood erect, and listened patiently until I came to "Old Hundredth," when with ludicrous haste every one of them rushed to their holes and bolted in, their feet twinkling in the air for a moment as they vanished.

No one who makes the acquaintance of our forester will fail to admire him; but he is far too self-reliant and warlike ever to be taken for a darling.

How long the life of a Douglas Squirrel may be, I don't know. The young seem to sprout from knot-holes, perfect from the first, and as enduring as their own trees. It is difficult, indeed, to realize that so condensed a piece of sun-fire should ever become dim or die at all. He is seldom killed by hunters, for he is too small to encourage much of their attention, and when pursued in settled regions becomes excessively shy, and keeps close in the furrows of the highest trunks, many of which are of the same color as himself. Indian boys, however, lie in wait with unbounded patience to shoot them with arrows. In the lower and middle zones a few fall a prey to rattlesnakes. Occasionally he is pursued by hawks and wildcats, etc. But, upon the whole, he dwells safely in the deep bosom of the woods, the most highly favored of all his happy tribe. May his tribe increase!

Chapter X

T HE mountain winds, like the dew and rain, sunshine and snow, are measured and bestowed with love on the forests to develop their strength and beauty. However restricted the scope of other forest influences, that of the winds is universal. The snow bends and trims the upper forests every winter, the lightning strikes a single tree here and there, while avalanches mow down thousands at a swoop as a gardener trims out a bed of flowers. But the winds go to every tree, fingering every leaf and branch and furrowed bole; not one is forgotten; the Mountain Pine towering with outstretched arms on the rugged buttresses of the icy peaks, the lowliest and most retiring tenant of the dells; they seek and find them all, caressing them tenderly, bending them in lusty exercise, stimulating their growth, plucking off a leaf or limb as required, or removing an entire tree or grove, now whispering and cooing through the branches like a sleepy child, now roaring like the ocean; the winds blessing the forests, the forests the winds, with ineffable beauty and harmony as the sure result.

After one has seen pines six feet in diameter bending like grasses before a mountain gale, and ever and anon some giant falling with a crash that shakes the hills, it seems astonishing that any, save the lowest thickset trees, could ever have found a period sufficiently stormless to establish themselves; or, once established, that they should not, sooner or later, have been blown down. But when the storm is over, and we behold the same forests tranquil again, towering fresh and unscathed in erect majesty, and consider what centuries of storms have fallen upon them since they were first planted,—hail, to break the tender seedlings; lightning, to scorch and shatter; snow, winds, and avalanches, to crush and overwhelm,—while the manifest result of all this wild storm-culture is the glorious perfection we behold; then faith in Nature's forestry is established, and we cease to deplore the violence of her most destructive gales, or of any other storm-implement whatsoever.

There are two trees in the Sierra forests that are never

blown down, so long as they continue in sound health. These are the Juniper and the Dwarf Pine of the summit peaks. Their stiff, crooked roots grip the storm-beaten ledges like eagles' claws, while their lithe, cord-like branches bend round compliantly, offering but slight holds for winds, however violent. The other alpine conifers—the Needle Pine, Mountain Pine, Two-leaved Pine, and Hemlock Spruce—are never thinned out by this agent to any destructive extent, on account of their admirable toughness and the closeness of their growth. In general the same is true of the giants of the lower zones. The kingly Sugar Pine, towering aloft to a height of more than 200 feet, offers a fine mark to storm-winds; but it is not densely foliaged, and its long, horizontal arms swing round compliantly in the blast, like tresses of green, fluent algæ in a brook; while the Silver Firs in most places keep their ranks well together in united strength. The Yellow or Silver Pine is more frequently overturned than any other tree on the Sierra, because its leaves and branches form a larger mass in proportion to its height, while in many places it is planted sparsely, leaving open lanes through which storms may enter with full force. Furthermore, because it is distributed along the lower portion of the range, which was the first to be left bare on the breaking up of the ice-sheet at the close of the glacial winter, the soil it is growing upon has been longer exposed to post-glacial weathering, and consequently is in a more crumbling, decayed condition than the fresher soils farther up the range, and therefore offers a less secure anchorage for the roots.

While exploring the forest zones of Mount Shasta, I discovered the path of a hurricane strewn with thousands of pines of this species. Great and small had been uprooted or wrenched off by sheer force, making a clean gap, like that made by a snow avalanche. But hurricanes capable of doing this class of work are rare in the Sierra, and when we have explored the forests from one extremity of the range to the other, we are compelled to believe that they are the most beautiful on the face of the earth, however we may regard the agents that have made them so.

There is always something deeply exciting, not only in the sounds of winds in the woods, which exert more or less in-

fluence over every mind, but in their varied waterlike flow as
manifested by the movements of the trees, especially those of
the conifers. By no other trees are they rendered so extensively
and impressively visible, not even by the lordly tropic palms
or tree-ferns responsive to the gentlest breeze. The waving of
a forest of the giant Sequoias is indescribably impressive and
sublime, but the pines seem to me the best interpreters of
winds. They are mighty waving goldenrods, ever in tune, singing and writing wind-music all their long century lives. Little,
however, of this noble tree-waving and tree-music will you see
or hear in the strictly alpine portion of the forests. The burly
Juniper, whose girth sometimes more than equals its height,
is about as rigid as the rocks on which it grows. The slender
lash-like sprays of the Dwarf Pine stream out in wavering ripples, but the tallest and slenderest are far too unyielding to
wave even in the heaviest gales. They only shake in quick,
short vibrations. The Hemlock Spruce, however, and the
Mountain Pine, and some of the tallest thickets of the Two-
leaved species bow in storms with considerable scope and
gracefulness. But it is only in the lower and middle zones that
the meeting of winds and woods is to be seen in all its
grandeur.

One of the most beautiful and exhilarating storms I ever
enjoyed in the Sierra occurred in December, 1874, when I
happened to be exploring one of the tributary valleys of the
Yuba River. The sky and the ground and the trees had been
thoroughly rain-washed and were dry again. The day was intensely pure, one of those incomparable bits of California winter, warm and balmy and full of white sparkling sunshine,
redolent of all the purest influences of the spring, and at the
same time enlivened with one of the most bracing wind-
storms conceivable. Instead of camping out, as I usually do,
I then chanced to be stopping at the house of a friend. But
when the storm began to sound, I lost no time in pushing
out into the woods to enjoy it. For on such occasions Nature
has always something rare to show us, and the danger to life
and limb is hardly greater than one would experience crouching deprecatingly beneath a roof.

It was still early morning when I found myself fairly adrift.
Delicious sunshine came pouring over the hills, lighting the

tops of the pines, and setting free a steam of summery fragrance that contrasted strangely with the wild tones of the
storm. The air was mottled with pine-tassels and bright green
plumes, that went flashing past in the sunlight like birds pursued. But there was not the slightest dustiness, nothing less
pure than leaves, and ripe pollen, and flecks of withered
bracken and moss. I heard trees falling for hours at the rate
of one every two or three minutes; some uprooted, partly on
account of the loose, water-soaked condition of the ground;
others broken straight across, where some weakness caused by
fire had determined the spot. The gestures of the various trees
made a delightful study. Young Sugar Pines, light and feathery
as squirrel-tails, were bowing almost to the ground; while the
grand old patriarchs, whose massive boles had been tried in a
hundred storms, waved solemnly above them, their long,
arching branches streaming fluently on the gale, and every
needle thrilling and ringing and shedding off keen lances of
light like a diamond. The Douglas Spruces, with long sprays
drawn out in level tresses, and needles massed in a gray, shimmering glow, presented a most striking appearance as they
stood in bold relief along the hilltops. The madroños in the
dells, with their red bark and large glossy leaves tilted every
way, reflected the sunshine in throbbing spangles like those
one so often sees on the rippled surface of a glacier lake. But
the Silver Pines were now the most impressively beautiful of
all. Colossal spires 200 feet in height waved like supple goldenrods chanting and bowing low as if in worship, while the
whole mass of their long, tremulous foliage was kindled into
one continuous blaze of white sun-fire. The force of the gale
was such that the most steadfast monarch of them all rocked
down to its roots with a motion plainly perceptible when one
leaned against it. Nature was holding high festival, and every
fiber of the most rigid giants thrilled with glad excitement.

I drifted on through the midst of this passionate music and
motion, across many a glen, from ridge to ridge; often halting
in the lee of a rock for shelter, or to gaze and listen. Even
when the grand anthem had swelled to its highest pitch, I
could distinctly hear the varying tones of individual trees,—
Spruce, and Fir, and Pine, and leafless Oak,—and even the
infinitely gentle rustle of the withered grasses at my feet. Each

was expressing itself in its own way,—singing its own song, and making its own peculiar gestures,—manifesting a richness of variety to be found in no other forest I have yet seen. The coniferous woôds of Canada, and the Carolinas, and Florida, are made up of trees that resemble one another about as nearly as blades of grass, and grow close together in much the same way. Coniferous trees, in general, seldom possess individual character, such as is manifest among Oaks and Elms. But the California forests are made up of a greater number of distinct species than any other in the world. And in them we find, not only a marked differentiation into special groups, but also a marked individuality in almost every tree, giving rise to storm effects indescribably glorious.

Toward midday, after a long, tingling scramble through copses of hazel and ceanothus, I gained the summit of the highest ridge in the neighborhood; and then it occurred to me that it would be a fine thing to climb one of the trees to obtain a wider outlook and get my ear close to the Æolian music of its topmost needles. But under the circumstances the choice of a tree was a serious matter. One whose instep was not very strong seemed in danger of being blown down, or of being struck by others in case they should fall; another was branchless to a considerable height above the ground, and at the same time too large to be grasped with arms and legs in climbing; while others were not favorably situated for clear views. After cautiously casting about, I made choice of the tallest of a group of Douglas Spruces that were growing close together like a tuft of grass, no one of which seemed likely to fall unless all the rest fell with it. Though comparatively young, they were about 100 feet high, and their lithe, brushy tops were rocking and swirling in wild ecstasy. Being accustomed to climb trees in making botanical studies, I experienced no difficulty in reaching the top of this one, and never before did I enjoy so noble an exhilaration of motion. The slender tops fairly flapped and swished in the passionate torrent, bending and swirling backward and forward, round and round, tracing indescribable combinations of vertical and horizontal curves, while I clung with muscles firm braced, like a bobolink on a reed.

In its widest sweeps my tree-top described an arc of from

twenty to thirty degrees, but I felt sure of its elastic temper, having seen others of the same species still more severely tried—bent almost to the ground indeed, in heavy snows— without breaking a fiber. I was therefore safe, and free to take the wind into my pulses and enjoy the excited forest from my superb outlook. The view from here must be extremely beautiful in any weather. Now my eye roved over the piny hills and dales as over fields of waving grain, and felt the light running in ripples and broad swelling undulations across the valleys from ridge to ridge, as the shining foliage was stirred by corresponding waves of air. Oftentimes these waves of reflected light would break up suddenly into a kind of beaten foam, and again, after chasing one another in regular order, they would seem to bend forward in concentric curves, and disappear on some hillside, like sea-waves on a shelving shore. The quantity of light reflected from the bent needles was so great as to make whole groves appear as if covered with snow, while the black shadows beneath the trees greatly enhanced the effect of the silvery splendor.

Excepting only the shadows there was nothing somber in all this wild sea of pines. On the contrary, notwithstanding this was the winter season, the colors were remarkably beautiful. The shafts of the pine and libocedrus were brown and purple, and most of the foliage was well tinged with yellow; the laurel groves, with the pale undersides of their leaves turned upward, made masses of gray; and then there was many a dash of chocolate color from clumps of manzanita, and jet of vivid crimson from the bark of the madroños, while the ground on the hillsides, appearing here and there through openings between the groves, displayed masses of pale purple and brown.

The sounds of the storm corresponded gloriously with this wild exuberance of light and motion. The profound bass of the naked branches and boles booming like waterfalls; the quick, tense vibrations of the pine-needles, now rising to a shrill, whistling hiss, now falling to a silky murmur; the rustling of laurel groves in the dells, and the keen metallic click of leaf on leaf—all this was heard in easy analysis when the attention was calmly bent.

The varied gestures of the multitude were seen to fine advantage, so that one could recognize the different species at a distance of several miles by this means alone, as well as by their forms and colors, and the way they reflected the light. All seemed strong and comfortable, as if really enjoying the storm, while responding to its most enthusiastic greetings. We hear much nowadays concerning the universal struggle for existence, but no struggle in the common meaning of the word was manifest here; no recognition of danger by any tree; no deprecation; but rather an invincible gladness as remote from exultation as from fear.

I kept my lofty perch for hours, frequently closing my eyes to enjoy the music by itself, or to feast quietly on the delicious fragrance that was streaming past. The fragrance of the woods was less marked than that produced during warm rain, when so many balsamic buds and leaves are steeped like tea; but, from the chafing of resiny branches against each other, and the incessant attrition of myriads of needles, the gale was spiced to a very tonic degree. And besides the fragrance from these local sources there were traces of scents brought from afar. For this wind came first from the sea, rubbing against its fresh, briny waves, then distilled through the redwoods, threading rich ferny gulches, and spreading itself in broad undulating currents over many a flower-enameled ridge of the coast mountains, then across the golden plains, up the purple foot-hills, and into these piny woods with the varied incense gathered by the way.

Winds are advertisements of all they touch, however much or little we may be able to read them; telling their wanderings even by their scents alone. Mariners detect the flowery perfume of land-winds far at sea, and sea-winds carry the fragrance of dulse and tangle far inland, where it is quickly recognized, though mingled with the scents of a thousand land-flowers. As an illustration of this, I may tell here that I breathed sea-air on the Firth of Forth, in Scotland, while a boy; then was taken to Wisconsin, where I remained nineteen years; then, without in all this time having breathed one breath of the sea, I walked quietly, alone, from the middle of the Mississippi Valley to the Gulf of Mexico, on a botanical excursion, and while in Florida, far from the coast, my attention wholly bent on the splendid tropical vegetation about me, I suddenly recognized a sea-breeze, as it came sifting through the palmettos and blooming vine-tangles, which at once awakened and set free a thousand dormant associations, and made me a boy again in Scotland, as if all the intervening years had been annihilated.

Most people like to look at mountain rivers, and bear them in mind; but few care to look at the winds, though far more beautiful and sublime, and though they become at times about as visible as flowing water. When the north winds in winter are making upward sweeps over the curving summits of the High Sierra, the fact is sometimes published with flying snow-banners a mile long. Those portions of the winds thus embodied can scarce be wholly invisible, even to the darkest imagination. And when we look around over an agitated forest, we may see something of the wind that stirs it, by its effects upon the trees. Yonder it descends in a rush of water-like ripples, and sweeps over the bending pines from hill to hill. Nearer, we see detached plumes and leaves, now speeding by on level currents, now whirling in eddies, or, escaping over the edges of the whirls, soaring aloft on grand, upswelling domes of air, or tossing on flame-like crests. Smooth, deep currents, cascades, falls, and swirling eddies, sing around every tree and leaf, and over all the varied topography of the region with telling changes of form, like mountain rivers conforming to the features of their channels.

After tracing the Sierra streams from their fountains to the plains, marking where they bloom white in falls, glide in crystal plumes, surge gray and foam-filled in boulder-choked gorges, and slip through the woods in long, tranquil reaches—after thus learning their language and forms in detail, we may at length hear them chanting all together in one grand anthem, and comprehend them all in clear inner vision, covering the range like lace. But even this spectacle is far less sublime and not a whit more substantial than what we may behold of these storm-streams of air in the mountain woods.

We all travel the milky way together, trees and men; but it never occurred to me until this storm-day, while swinging in the wind, that trees are travelers, in the ordinary sense. They make many journeys, not extensive ones, it is true; but our own little journeys, away and back again, are only little more than tree-wavings—many of them not so much.

When the storm began to abate, I dismounted and sauntered down through the calming woods. The storm-tones died away, and, turning toward the east, I beheld the countless hosts of the forests hushed and tranquil, towering above one another on the slopes of the hills like a devout audience. The setting sun filled them with amber light, and seemed to say, while they listened, "My peace I give unto you."

As I gazed on the impressive scene, all the so-called ruin of the storm was forgotten, and never before did these noble woods appear so fresh, so joyous, so immortal.

Chapter XI

THE RIVER FLOODS

THE Sierra rivers are flooded every spring by the melting of the snow as regularly as the famous old Nile. They begin to rise in May, and in June high-water mark is reached. But because the melting does not go on rapidly over all the fountains, high and low, simultaneously, and the melted snow is not reinforced at this time of year by rain, the spring floods are seldom very violent or destructive. The thousand falls, however, and the cascades in the cañons are then in full bloom, and sing songs from one end of the range to the other. Of course the snow on the lower tributaries of the rivers is first melted, then that on the higher fountains most exposed to sunshine, and about a month later the cooler, shadowy fountains send down their treasures, thus allowing the main trunk streams nearly six weeks to get their waters hurried through the foot-hills and across the lowlands to the sea. Therefore very violent spring floods are avoided, and will be as long as the shading, restraining forests last. The rivers of the north half of the range are still less subject to sudden floods, because their upper fountains in great part lie protected from the changes of the weather beneath thick folds of lava, just as many of the rivers of Alaska lie beneath folds of ice, coming to the light farther down the range in large springs, while those of the high Sierra lie on the surface of solid granite, exposed to every change of temperature. More than ninety per cent. of the water derived from the snow and ice of Mount Shasta is at once absorbed and drained away beneath the porous lava folds of the mountain, where mumbling and groping in the dark they at length find larger fissures and tunnel-like caves from which they emerge, filtered and cool, in the form of large springs, some of them so large they give birth to rivers that set out on their journeys beneath the sun without any visible intermediate period of childhood. Thus the Shasta River issues from a large lake-like spring in Shasta Valley, and about two thirds of the volume of the

McCloud River gushes forth suddenly from the face of a lava bluff in a roaring spring seventy-five yards wide.

These spring rivers of the north are of course shorter than those of the south whose tributaries extend up to the tops of the mountains. Fall River, an important tributary of the Pitt or Upper Sacramento, is only about ten miles long, and is all falls, cascades, and springs from its head to its confluence with the Pitt. Bountiful springs, charmingly embowered, issue from the rocks at one end of it, a snowy fall a hundred and eighty feet high thunders at the other, and a rush of crystal rapids sing and dance between. Of course such streams are but little affected by the weather. Sheltered from evaporation their flow is nearly as full in the autumn as in the time of general spring floods. While those of the high Sierra diminish to less than the hundredth part of their springtime prime, shallowing in autumn to a series of silent pools among the rocks and hollows of their channels, connected by feeble, creeping threads of water, like the sluggish sentences of a tired writer, connected by a drizzle of "ands" and "buts." Strange to say, the greatest floods occur in winter, when one would suppose all the wild waters would be muffled and chained in frost and snow. The same long, all-day storms of the so-called Rainy Season in California, that give rain to the lowlands, give dry frosty snow to the mountains. But at rare intervals warm rains and warm winds invade the mountains and push back the snow line from 2000 feet to 8000, or even higher, and then come the big floods.

I was usually driven down out of the High Sierra about the end of November, but the winter of 1874 and 1875 was so warm and calm that I was tempted to seek general views of the geology and topography of the basin of Feather River in January. And I had just completed a hasty survey of the region, and made my way down to winter quarters, when one of the grandest flood-storms that I ever saw broke on the mountains. I was then in the edge of the main forest belt at a small foot-hill town called Knoxville, on the divide between the waters of the Feather and Yuba rivers. The cause of this notable flood was simply a sudden and copious fall of warm wind and rain on the basins of these rivers at a time when they contained a considerable quantity of snow. The rain was so heavy and long-sustained that it was, of itself, sufficient to make a good wild flood, while the snow which the warm wind and rain melted on the upper and middle regions of the basins was sufficient to make another flood equal to that of the rain. Now these two distinct harvests of flood waters were gathered simultaneously and poured out on the plain in one magnificent avalanche. The basins of the Yuba and Feather, like many others of the Sierra, are admirably adapted to the growth of floods of this kind. Their many tributaries radiate far and wide, comprehending extensive areas, and the tributaries are steeply inclined, while the trunks are comparatively level. While the flood-storm was in progress the thermometer at Knoxville ranged between 44° and 50°; and when warm wind and warm rain fall simultaneously on snow contained in basins like these, both the rain and that portion of the snow which the rain and wind melt are at first sponged up and held back until the combined mass becomes sludge, which at length, suddenly dissolving, slips and descends all together to the trunk channel; and since the deeper the stream the faster it flows, the flooded portion of the current above overtakes the slower foot-hill portion below it, and all sweeping forward together with a high, overcurling front, debouches on the open plain with a violence and suddenness that at first seem wholly unaccountable. The destructiveness of the lower portion of this particular flood was somewhat augmented by mining gravel in the river channels, and by levees which gave way after having at first restrained and held back the accumulating waters. These exaggerating conditions did not, however, greatly influence the general result, the main effect having been caused by the rare combination of flood factors indicated above. It is a pity that but few people meet and enjoy storms so noble as this in their homes in the mountains, for, spending themselves in the open levels of the plains, they are likely to be remembered more by the bridges and houses they carry away than by their beauty or the thousand blessings they bring to the fields and gardens of Nature.

On the morning of the flood, January 19th, all the Feather and Yuba landscapes were covered with running water, muddy torrents filled every gulch and ravine, and the sky was thick with rain. The pines had long been sleeping in sunshine; they were now awake, roaring and waving with the beating storm, and the winds sweeping along the curves of hill and dale, streaming through the woods, surging and gurgling on the tops of rocky ridges, made the wildest of wild storm melody.

It was easy to see that only a small part of the rain reached the ground in the form of drops. Most of it was thrashed into dusty spray like that into which small waterfalls are divided when they dash on shelving rocks. Never have I seen water coming from the sky in denser or more passionate streams. The wind chased the spray forward in choking drifts, and compelled me again and again to seek shelter in the dell copses and back of large trees to rest and catch my breath. Wherever I went, on ridges or in hollows, enthusiastic water still flashed and gurgled about my ankles, recalling a wild winter flood in Yosemite when a hundred waterfalls came booming and chanting together and filled the grand valley with a sea-like roar.

After drifting an hour or two in the lower woods, I set out for the summit of a hill 900 feet high, with a view to getting as near the heart of the storm as possible. In order to reach it I had to cross Dry Creek, a tributary of the Yuba that goes crawling along the base of the hill on the northwest. It was now a booming river as large as the Tuolumne at ordinary stages, its current brown with mining-mud washed down from many a "claim," and mottled with sluice-boxes, fence-rails, and logs that had long lain above its reach. A slim foot-bridge stretched across it, now scarcely above the swollen current. Here I was glad to linger, gazing and listening, while the storm was in its richest mood—the gray rain-flood above, the brown river-flood beneath. The language of the river was scarcely less enchanting than that of the wind and rain; the sublime overboom of the main bouncing, exulting current, the swash and gurgle of the eddies, the keen dash and clash of heavy waves breaking against rocks, and the smooth, downy hush of shallow currents feeling their way through the willow thickets of the margin. And amid all this varied throng of sounds I heard the smothered bumping and rumbling of boulders on the bottom as they were shoving and rolling forward against one another in a wild rush, after having lain still for probably 100 years or more.

The glad creek rose high above its banks and wandered from its channel out over many a briery sand-flat and meadow. Alders and willows waist-deep were bearing up against the current with nervous trembling gestures, as if afraid of being carried away, while supple branches bending confidingly, dipped lightly and rose again, as if stroking the wild waters in play. Leaving the bridge and passing on through the storm-thrashed woods, all the ground seemed to be moving. Pine-tassels, flakes of bark, soil, leaves, and broken branches were being swept forward, and many a rock-fragment, weathered from exposed ledges, was now receiving its first rounding and polishing in the wild streams of the storm. On they rushed through every gulch and hollow, leaping, gliding, working with a will, and rejoicing like living creatures.

Nor was the flood confined to the ground. Every tree had a water system of its own spreading far and wide like miniature Amazons and Mississippis.

Toward midday, cloud, wind, and rain reached their highest development. The storm was in full bloom, and formed, from my commanding outlook on the hilltop, one of the most glorious views I ever beheld. As far as the eye could reach, above, beneath, around, wind-driven rain filled the air like one vast waterfall. Detached clouds swept imposingly up the valley, as if they were endowed with independent motion and had special work to do in replenishing the mountain wells, now rising above the pine-tops, now descending into their midst, fondling their arrowy spires and soothing every branch and leaf with gentleness in the midst of all the savage sound and motion. Others keeping near the ground glided behind separate groves, and brought them forward into relief with admirable distinctness; or, passing in front, eclipsed whole groves in succession, pine after pine melting in their gray fringes and bursting forth again seemingly clearer than before.

The forms of storms are in great part measured, and controlled by the topography of the regions where they rise and over which they pass. When, therefore, we attempt to study them from the valleys, or from gaps and openings of the forest, we are confounded by a multitude of separate and apparently antagonistic impressions. The bottom of the storm is broken up into innumerable waves and currents that surge against the hillsides like sea-waves against a shore, and these, reacting on the nether surface of the storm, erode immense cavernous hollows and cañons, and sweep forward the resulting detritus in long trains, like the moraines of glaciers. But, as we ascend, these partial, confusing effects disappear and the phenomena are beheld united and harmonious.

The longer I gazed into the storm, the more plainly visible it became. The drifting cloud detritus gave it a kind of visible body, which explained many perplexing phenomena, and published its movements in plain terms, while the texture of the falling mass of rain rounded it out and rendered it more complete. Because raindrops differ in size they fall at different velocities and overtake and clash against one another, producing mist and spray. They also, of course, yield unequal compliance to the force of the wind, which gives rise to a still greater degree of interference, and passionate gusts sweep off clouds of spray from the groves like that torn from wave-tops in a gale. All these factors of irregularity in density, color, and texture of the general rain mass tend to make it the more appreciable and telling. It is then seen as one grand flood rushing over bank and brae, bending the pines like weeds, curving this way and that, whirling in huge eddies in hollows and dells, while the main current pours grandly over all, like ocean currents over the landscapes that lie hidden at the bottom of the sea.

I watched the gestures of the pines while the storm was at its height, and it was easy to see that they were not distressed. Several large Sugar Pines stood near the thicket in which I was sheltered, bowing solemnly and tossing their long arms as if interpreting the very words of the storm while accepting its wildest onsets with passionate exhilaration. The lions were feeding. Those who have observed sunflowers feasting on sunshine during the golden days of Indian summer know that none of their gestures express thankfulness. Their celestial food is too heartily given, too heartily taken to leave room for thanks. The pines were evidently accepting the benefactions of the storm in the same whole-souled manner; and when I looked down among the budding hazels, and still lower to the young violets and fern-tufts on the rocks, I noticed the same divine methods of giving and taking, and the same exquisite adaptations of what seems an outbreak of violent and uncontrollable force to the purposes of beautiful and delicate life. Calms like sleep come upon landscapes, just as they do on people and trees, and storms awaken them in the same way. In the dry midsummer of the lower portion of the range the withered hills and valleys seem to lie as empty and expressionless as dead shells on a shore. Even the highest mountains may be found occasionally dull and uncommunicative as if in some way they had lost countenance and shrunk to less than half their real stature. But when the lightnings crash and echo in the cañons, and the clouds come down wreathing and crowning their bald snowy heads, every feature beams with expression and they rise again in all their imposing majesty.

Storms are fine speakers, and tell all they know, but their voices of lightning, torrent, and rushing wind are much less numerous than the nameless still, small voices too low for human ears; and because we are poor listeners we fail to catch much that is fairly within reach. Our best rains are heard mostly on roofs, and winds in chimneys; and when by choice or compulsion we are pushed into the heart of a storm, the confusion made by cumbersome equipments and nervous haste and mean fear, prevent our hearing any other than the loudest expressions. Yet we may draw enjoyment from storm sounds that are beyond hearing, and storm movements we cannot see. The sublime whirl of planets around their suns is as silent as raindrops oozing in the dark among the roots of plants. In this great storm, as in every other, there were tones and gestures inexpressibly gentle manifested in the midst of what is called violence and fury, but easily recognized by all who look and listen for them. The rain brought out the colors of the woods with delightful freshness, the rich brown of the bark of the trees and the fallen burs and leaves and dead ferns; the grays of rocks and lichens; the light purple of swelling buds, and the warm yellow greens of the libocedrus and mosses. The air was steaming with delightful fragrance, not rising and wafting past in separate masses, but diffused through all the atmosphere. Pine woods are always fragrant, but most so in spring when the young tassels are opening and in warm weather when the various gums and balsams are softened by the sun. The wind was now chafing their innumerable needles and the warm rain was steeping them. Monardella grows here in large beds in the openings, and there is plenty of laurel in dells and manzanita on the hillsides, and the rosy, fragrant chamœbatia carpets the ground almost everywhere. These, with the gums and balsams of the woods, form the main local fragrance-fountains of the storm. The ascending clouds of aroma wind-rolled and rain-washed became pure like light and traveled with the wind as part of it. Toward the middle of the afternoon the main flood cloud lifted along its western border revealing a beautiful section of the Sacramento Valley some twenty or thirty miles away, brilliantly sun-lighted and glistering with rain-sheets as if paved with silver. Soon afterward a jagged bluff-like cloud with a sheer face appeared over the valley of the Yuba, dark-colored and roughened with numerous furrows like some huge lava-table. The blue Coast Range was seen stretching along the sky like a beveled wall, and the somber, craggy Marysville Buttes rose impressively out of the flooded plain like islands out of the sea. Then the rain began to abate and I sauntered down through the dripping bushes reveling in the universal vigor and freshness that inspired all the life about me. How clean and unworn and immortal the woods seemed to be!—the lofty cedars in full bloom laden with golden pollen and their washed plumes shining; the pines rocking gently and settling back into rest, and the evening sunbeams spangling on the broad leaves of the madroños, their tracery of yellow boughs relieved against dusky thickets of Chestnut Oak; liverworts, lycopodiums, ferns were exulting in glorious revival, and every moss that had ever lived seemed to be coming crowding back from the dead to clothe each trunk and stone in living green. The steaming ground seemed fairly to throb and tingle with life; smilax, fritillaria, saxifrage, and young violets were pushing up as if already conscious of the summer glory, and innumerable green and yellow buds were peeping and smiling everywhere.

As for the birds and squirrels, not a wing or tail of them was to be seen while the storm was blowing. Squirrels dislike wet weather more than cats do; therefore they were at home rocking in their dry nests. The birds were hiding in the dells out of the wind, some of the strongest of them pecking at acorns and manzanita berries, but most were perched on low twigs, their breast feathers puffed out and keeping one another company through the hard time as best they could.

When I arrived at the village about sundown, the good people bestirred themselves, pitying my bedraggled condition as if I were some benumbed castaway snatched from the sea, while I, in turn, warm with excitement and reeking like the ground, pitied them for being dry and defrauded of all the glory that Nature had spread round about them that day.

Chapter XII

T HE weather of spring and summer in the middle region of the Sierra is usually well flecked with rains and light dustings of snow, most of which are far too obviously joyful and life-giving to be regarded as storms; and in the picturesque beauty and clearness of outlines of their clouds they offer striking contrasts to those boundless, all-embracing cloud-mantles of the storms of winter. The smallest and most perfectly individualized specimens present a richly modeled cumulous cloud rising above the dark woods, about 11 A. M., swelling with a visible motion straight up into the calm, sunny sky to a height of 12,000 to 14,000 feet above the sea, its white, pearly bosses relieved by gray and pale purple shadows in the hollows, and showing outlines as keenly defined as those of the glacier-polished domes. In less than an hour it attains full development and stands poised in the blazing sunshine like some colossal mountain, as beautiful in form and finish as if it were to become a permanent addition to the landscape. Presently a thunderbolt crashes through the crisp air, ringing like steel on steel, sharp and clear, its startling detonation breaking into a spray of echoes against the cliffs and cañon walls. Then down comes a cataract of rain. The big drops sift through the pine-needles, plash and patter on the granite pavements, and pour down the sides of ridges and domes in a network of gray, bubbling rills. In a few minutes the cloud withers to a mesh of dim filaments and disappears, leaving the sky perfectly clear and bright, every dust-particle wiped and washed out of it. Everything is refreshed and invigorated, a steam of fragrance rises, and the storm is finished—one cloud, one lightning-stroke, and one dash of rain. This is the Sierra midsummer thunder-storm reduced to its lowest terms. But some of them attain much larger proportions, and assume a grandeur and energy of expression hardly surpassed by those bred in the depths of winter, producing those sudden floods called "cloud-bursts," which are local, and to a considerable extent periodical, for they appear nearly every day about the same time for weeks, usually about eleven o'clock, and lasting from five minutes to an hour or two. One soon becomes so accustomed to see them that the noon sky seems empty and abandoned without them, as if Nature were forgetting something. When the glorious pearl and alabaster clouds of these noonday storms are being built I never give attention to anything else. No mountain or mountain-range, however divinely clothed with light, has a more enduring charm than those fleeting mountains of the sky—floating fountains bearing water for every well, the angels of the streams and lakes; brooding in the deep azure, or sweeping softly along the ground over ridge and dome, over meadow, over forest, over garden and grove; lingering with cooling shadows, refreshing every flower, and soothing rugged rock-brows with a gentleness of touch and gesture wholly divine.

The most beautiful and imposing of the summer storms rise just above the upper edge of the Silver Fir zone, and all are so beautiful that it is not easy to choose any one for particular description. The one that I remember best fell on the mountains near Yosemite Valley, July 19, 1869, while I was encamped in the Silver Fir woods. A range of bossy cumuli took possession of the sky, huge domes and peaks rising one beyond another with deep cañons between them, bending this way and that in long curves and reaches, interrupted here and there with white upboiling masses that looked like the spray of waterfalls. Zigzag lances of lightning followed each other in quick succession, and the thunder was so gloriously loud and massive it seemed as if surely an entire mountain was being shattered at every stroke. Only the trees were touched, however, so far as I could see,—a few firs 200 feet high, perhaps, and five to six feet in diameter, were split into long rails and slivers from top to bottom and scattered to all points of the compass. Then came the rain in a hearty flood, covering the ground and making it shine with a continuous sheet of water that, like a transparent film or skin, fitted closely down over all the rugged anatomy of the landscape.

It is not long, geologically speaking, since the first raindrop fell on the present landscapes of the Sierra; and in the few tens of thousands of years of stormy cultivation they have been blest with, how beautiful they have become! The first rains fell on raw, crumbling moraines and rocks without a plant. Now scarcely a drop can fail to find a beautiful mark: on the tops of the peaks, on the smooth glacier pavements, on the curves of the domes, on moraines full of crystals, on the thousand forms of yosemitic sculpture with their tender beauty of balmy, flowery vegetation, laving, plashing, glinting, pattering; some falling softly on meadows, creeping out of sight, seeking and finding every thirsty rootlet, some through the spires of the woods, sifting in dust through the needles, and whispering good cheer to each of them; some falling with blunt tapping sounds, drumming on the broad leaves of veratrum, cypripedium, saxifrage; some falling straight into fragrant corollas, kissing the lips of lilies, glinting on the sides of crystals, on shining grains of gold; some falling into the fountains of snow to swell their well-saved stores; some into the lakes and rivers, patting the smooth glassy levels, making dimples and bells and spray, washing the mountain windows, washing the wandering winds; some plashing into the heart of snowy falls and cascades as if eager to join in the dance and the song and beat the foam yet finer. Good work and happy work for the merry mountain raindrops, each one of them a brave fall in itself, rushing from the cliffs and hollows of the clouds into the cliffs and hollows of the mountains; away from the thunder of the sky into the thunder of the roaring rivers. And how far they have to go, and how many cups to fill— cassiope-cups, holding half a drop, and lake basins between the hills, each replenished with equal care—every drop God's messenger sent on its way with glorious pomp and display of power—silvery new-born stars with lake and river, mountain and valley—all that the landscape holds—reflected in their crystal depths.

Chapter XIII

THE WATER-OUZEL

T HE waterfalls of the Sierra are frequented by only one bird,—the Ouzel or Water Thrush (*Cinclus Mexicanus,* Sw.). He is a singularly joyous and lovable little fellow, about the size of a robin, clad in a plain waterproof suit of bluish gray, with a tinge of chocolate on the head and shoulders. In form he is about as smoothly plump and compact as a pebble that has been whirled in a pot-hole, the flowing contour of his body being interrupted only by his strong feet and bill, the crisp wing-tips, and the up-slanted wren-like tail.

Among all the countless waterfalls I have met in the course of ten years' exploration in the Sierra, whether among the icy peaks, or warm foot-hills, or in the profound yosemitic cañons of the middle region, not one was found without its Ouzel. No cañon is too cold for this little bird, none too lonely, provided it be rich in falling water. Find a fall, or cascade, or rushing rapid, anywhere upon a clear stream, and there you will surely find its complementary Ouzel, flitting about in the spray, diving in foaming eddies, whirling like a leaf among beaten foam-bells; ever vigorous and enthusiastic, yet self-contained, and neither seeking nor shunning your company.

If disturbed while dipping about in the margin shallows, he either sets off with a rapid whir to some other feeding-ground up or down the stream, or alights on some half-submerged rock or snag out in the current, and immediately begins to nod and courtesy like a wren, turning his head from side to side with many other odd dainty movements that never fail to fix the attention of the observer.

He is the mountain streams' own darling, the hummingbird of blooming waters, loving rocky ripple-slopes and sheets of foam as a bee loves flowers, as a lark loves sunshine and meadows. Among all the mountain birds, none has cheered me so much in my lonely wanderings,—none so unfailingly. For both in winter and summer he sings, sweetly, cheerily, independent alike of sunshine and of love, requiring no other inspiration than the stream on which he dwells. While water sings, so must he, in heat or cold, calm or storm, ever attuning his voice in sure accord; low in the drought of summer and the drought of winter, but never silent.

During the golden days of Indian summer, after most of the snow has been melted, and the mountain streams have become feeble,—a succession of silent pools, linked together by shallow, transparent currents and strips of silvery lace-work,—then the song of the Ouzel is at its lowest ebb. But as soon as the winter clouds have bloomed, and the mountain treasuries are once more replenished with snow, the voices of the streams and ouzels increase in strength and richness until the flood season of early summer. Then the torrents chant their noblest anthems, and then is the flood-time of our song-ster's melody. As for weather, dark days and sun days are the same to him. The voices of most song-birds, however joyous, suffer a long winter eclipse; but the Ouzel sings on through all the seasons and every kind of storm. Indeed no storm can be more violent than those of the waterfalls in the midst of which he delights to dwell. However dark and boisterous the weather, snowing, blowing, or cloudy, all the same he sings, and with never a note of sadness. No need of spring sunshine to thaw *his* song, for it never freezes. Never shall you hear anything wintry from *his* warm breast; no pinched cheeping, no wavering notes between sorrow and joy; his mellow, fluty voice is ever tuned to downright gladness, as free from dejection as cock-crowing.

It is pitiful to see wee frost-pinched sparrows on cold mornings in the mountain groves shaking the snow from their feathers, and hopping about as if anxious to be cheery, then hastening back to their hidings out of the wind, puffing out their breast-feathers over their toes, and subsiding among the leaves, cold and breakfastless, while the snow continues to fall, and there is no sign of clearing. But the Ouzel never calls forth a single touch of pity; not because he is strong to en-dure, but rather because he seems to live a charmed life be-yond the reach of every influence that makes endurance necessary.

One wild winter morning, when Yosemite Valley was swept its length from west to east by a cordial snow-storm, I sallied forth to see what I might learn and enjoy. A sort of gray, gloaming-like darkness filled the valley, the huge walls were out of sight, all ordinary sounds were smothered, and even the loudest booming of the falls was at times buried beneath the roar of the heavy-laden blast. The loose snow was already over five feet deep on the meadows, making extended walks impossible without the aid of snow-shoes. I found no great difficulty, however, in making my way to a certain ripple on the river where one of my ouzels lived. He was at home, busily gleaning his breakfast among the pebbles of a shallow portion of the margin, apparently unaware of anything extraordinary in the weather. Presently he flew out to a stone against which the icy current was beating, and turning his back to the wind, sang as delightfully as a lark in springtime.

After spending an hour or two with my favorite, I made my way across the valley, boring and wallowing through the drifts, to learn as definitely as possible how the other birds were spending their time. The Yosemite birds are easily found during the winter because all of them excepting the Ouzel are restricted to the sunny north side of the valley, the south side being constantly eclipsed by the great frosty shadow of the wall. And because the Indian Cañon groves, from their peculiar exposure, are the warmest, the birds congregate there, more especially in severe weather.

I found most of the robins cowering on the lee side of the larger branches where the snow could not fall upon them, while two or three of the more enterprising were making desperate efforts to reach the mistletoe berries by clinging nervously to the under side of the snow-crowned masses, back downward, like woodpeckers. Every now and then they would dislodge some of the loose fringes of the snow-crown, which would come sifting down on them and send them screaming back to camp, where they would subside among their companions with a shiver, muttering in low, querulous chatter like hungry children.

Some of the sparrows were busy at the feet of the larger trees gleaning seeds and benumbed insects, joined now and then by a robin weary of his unsuccessful attempts upon the snow-covered berries. The brave woodpeckers were clinging to the snowless sides of the larger boles and overarching branches of the camp trees, making short flights from side to side of the grove, pecking now and then at the acorns they had stored in the bark, and chattering aimlessly as if unable to keep still, yet evidently putting in the time in a very dull way, like storm-bound travelers at a country tavern. The hardy nut-hatches were threading the open furrows of the trunks in their usual industrious manner, and uttering their quaint notes, evidently less distressed than their neighbors. The Steller jays were of course making more noisy stir than all the other birds combined; ever coming and going with loud bluster, screaming as if each had a lump of melting sludge in his throat, and taking good care to improve the favorable opportunity afforded by the storm to steal from the acorn stores of the woodpeckers. I also noticed one solitary gray eagle braving the storm on the top of a tall pine-stump just outside the main grove. He was standing bolt upright with his back to the wind, a tuft of snow piled on his square shoulders, a monument of passive endurance. Thus every snow-bound bird seemed more or less uncomfortable if not in positive distress. The storm was reflected in every gesture, and not one cheerful note, not to say song, came from a single bill; their cowering, joyless endurance offering a striking contrast to the spontaneous, irrepressible gladness of the Ouzel, who could no more help exhaling sweet song than a rose sweet fragrance. He *must* sing though the heavens fall. I remember noticing the distress of a pair of robins during the violent earthquake of the year 1872, when the pines of the Valley, with strange movements, flapped and waved their branches, and beetling rock-brows came thundering down to the meadows in tremendous avalanches. It did not occur to me in the midst of the excitement of other observations to look for the ouzels, but I doubt not they were singing straight on through it all, regarding the terrible rock-thunder as fearlessly as they do the booming of the waterfalls.

What may be regarded as the separate songs of the Ouzel are exceedingly difficult of description, because they are so variable and at the same time so confluent. Though I have been acquainted with my favorite ten years, and during most of this time have heard him sing nearly every day, I still detect notes and strains that seem new to me. Nearly all of his music is sweet and tender, lapsing from his round breast like water over the smooth lip of a pool, then breaking farther on into a sparkling foam of melodious notes, which glow with subdued enthusiasm, yet without expressing much of the strong, gushing ecstasy of the bobolink or skylark.

The more striking strains are perfect arabesques of melody, composed of a few full, round, mellow notes, embroidered with delicate trills which fade and melt in long slender cadences. In a general way his music is that of the streams refined and spiritualized. The deep booming notes of the falls are in it, the trills of rapids, the gurgling of margin eddies, the low whispering of level reaches, and the sweet tinkle of separate drops oozing from the ends of mosses and falling into tranquil pools.

The Ouzel never sings in chorus with other birds, nor with his kind, but only with the streams. And like flowers that bloom beneath the surface of the ground, some of our favorite's best song-blossoms never rise above the surface of the heavier music of the water. I have often observed him singing in the midst of beaten spray, his music completely buried beneath the water's roar; yet I knew he was surely singing by his gestures and the movements of his bill.

His food, as far as I have noticed, consists of all kinds of water insects, which in summer are chiefly procured along shallow margins. Here he wades about ducking his head under water and deftly turning over pebbles and fallen leaves with his bill, seldom choosing to go into deep water where he has to use his wings in diving.

He seems to be especially fond of the larvæ of mosquitos, found in abundance attached to the bottom of smooth rock channels where the current is shallow. When feeding in such places he wades up-stream, and often while his head is under water the swift current is deflected upward along the glossy curves of his neck and shoulders, in the form of a clear, crystalline shell, which fairly incloses him like a bell-glass, the shell being broken and re-formed as he lifts and dips his head; while ever and anon he sidles out to where the too powerful current carries him off his feet; then he dexterously rises on the wing and goes gleaning again in shallower places.

But during the winter, when the stream-banks are embossed in snow, and the streams themselves are chilled nearly to the freezing-point, so that the snow falling into them in stormy weather is not wholly dissolved, but forms a thin, blue sludge, thus rendering the current opaque—then he seeks the deeper portions of the main rivers, where he may dive to clear water beneath the sludge. Or he repairs to some open lake or mill-pond, at the bottom of which he feeds in safety.

When thus compelled to betake himself to a lake, he does not plunge into it at once like a duck, but always alights in the first place upon some rock or fallen pine along the shore. Then flying out thirty or forty yards, more or less, according to the character of the bottom, he alights with a dainty glint on the surface, swims about, looks down, finally makes up his mind, and disappears with a sharp stroke of his wings. After feeding for two or three minutes he suddenly reappears, showers the water from his wings with one vigorous shake, and rises abruptly into the air as if pushed up from beneath, comes back to his perch, sings a few minutes, and goes out to dive again; thus coming and going, singing and diving at the same place for hours.

The Ouzel is usually found singly; rarely in pairs, excepting during the breeding season, and *very* rarely in threes or fours. I once observed three thus spending a winter morning in company, upon a small glacier lake, on the Upper Merced, about 7500 feet above the level of the sea. A storm had occurred during the night, but the morning sun shone unclouded, and the shadowy lake, gleaming darkly in its setting of fresh snow, lay smooth and motionless as a mirror. My camp chanced to be within a few feet of the water's edge, opposite a fallen pine, some of the branches of which leaned out over the lake. Here my three dearly welcome visitors took up their station, and at once began to embroider the frosty air with their delicious melody, doubly delightful to me that particular morning, as I had been somewhat apprehensive of danger in breaking my way down through the snow-choked cañons to the lowlands.

The portion of the lake bottom selected for a feeding-ground lies at a depth of fifteen or twenty feet below the surface, and is covered with a short growth of algæ and other aquatic plants,—facts I had previously determined while sailing over it on a raft. After alighting on the glassy surface, they occasionally indulged in a little play, chasing one another round about in small circles; then all three would suddenly dive together, and then come ashore and sing.

The Ouzel seldom swims more than a few yards on the surface, for, not being web-footed, he makes rather slow progress, but by means of his strong, crisp wings he swims, or rather flies, with celerity under the surface, often to considerable distances. But it is in withstanding the force of heavy rapids that his strength of wing in this respect is most strikingly manifested. The following may be regarded as a fair illustration of his power of sub-aquatic flight. One stormy morning in winter when the Merced River was blue and green with unmelted snow, I observed one of my ouzels perched on a snag out in the midst of a swift-rushing rapid, singing cheerily, as if everything was just to his mind; and while I stood on the bank admiring him, he suddenly plunged into the sludgy current, leaving his song abruptly broken off. After feeding a minute or two at the bottom, and when one would suppose that he must inevitably be swept far down-stream, he emerged just where he went down, alighted on the same snag, showered the water-beads from his feathers, and continued his unfinished song, seemingly in tranquil ease as if it had suffered no interruption.

The Ouzel alone of all birds dares to enter a white torrent. And though strictly terrestrial in structure, no other is so inseparably related to water, not even the duck, or the bold ocean albatross, or the stormy-petrel. For ducks go ashore as soon as they finish feeding in undisturbed places, and very often make long flights overland from lake to lake or field to field. The same is true of most other aquatic birds. But the Ouzel, born on the brink of a stream, or on a snag or boulder in the midst of it, seldom leaves it for a single moment. For, notwithstanding he is often on the wing, he never flies overland, but whirs with rapid, quail-like beat above the stream, tracing all its windings. Even when the stream is quite small, say from five to ten feet wide, he seldom shortens his flight by crossing a bend, however abrupt it may be; and even when disturbed by meeting some one on the bank, he prefers to fly over one's head, to dodging out over the ground. When, therefore, his flight along a crooked stream is viewed endwise, it appears most strikingly wavered—a description on the air of every curve with lightning-like rapidity.

The vertical curves and angles of the most precipitous torrents he traces with the same rigid fidelity, swooping down the inclines of cascades, dropping sheer over dizzy falls amid the spray, and ascending with the same fearlessness and ease, seldom seeking to lessen the steepness of the acclivity by beginning to ascend before reaching the base of the fall. No matter though it may be several hundred feet in height he holds straight on, as if about to dash headlong into the throng of booming rockets, then darts abruptly upward, and, after alighting at the top of the precipice to rest a moment, proceeds to feed and sing. His flight is solid and impetuous, without any intermission of wing-beats,—one homogeneous buzz like that of a laden bee on its way home. And while thus buzzing freely from fall to fall, he is frequently heard giving utterance to a long outdrawn train of unmodulated notes, in no way connected with his song, but corresponding closely with his flight in sustained vigor.

Were the flights of all the ouzels in the Sierra traced on a chart, they would indicate the direction of the flow of the entire system of ancient glaciers, from about the period of the breaking up of the ice-sheet until near the close of the glacial winter; because the streams which the ouzels so rigidly follow are, with the unimportant exceptions of a few side tributaries, all flowing in channels eroded for them out of the solid flank of the range by the vanished glaciers,—the streams tracing the ancient glaciers, the ouzels tracing the streams. Nor do we find so complete compliance to glacial conditions in the life of any other mountain bird, or animal of any kind. Bears frequently accept the pathways laid down by glaciers as the easiest to travel; but they often leave them and cross over from cañon to cañon. So also, most of the birds trace the moraines to some extent, because the forests are growing on them. But they wander far, crossing the cañons from grove to grove, and draw exceedingly angular and complicated courses.

The Ouzel's nest is one of the most extraordinary pieces of bird architecture I ever saw, odd and novel in design, perfectly fresh and beautiful, and in every way worthy of the genius of the little builder. It is about a foot in diameter, round and bossy in outline, with a neatly arched opening near the bottom, somewhat like an old-fashioned brick oven, or Hottentot's hut. It is built almost exclusively of green and yellow mosses, chiefly the beautiful fronded hypnum that covers the rocks and old drift-logs in the vicinity of waterfalls. These are deftly interwoven, and felted together into a charming little hut; and so situated that many of the outer mosses continue to flourish as if they had not been plucked. A few fine, silky-stemmed grasses are occasionally found interwoven with the mosses, but, with the exception of a thin layer lining the floor, their presence seems accidental, as they are of a species found growing with the mosses and are probably plucked with them. The site chosen for this curious mansion is usually some little rock-shelf within reach of the lighter particles of the spray of a waterfall, so that its walls are kept green and growing, at least during the time of high water.

No harsh lines are presented by any portion of the nest as seen in place, but when removed from its shelf, the back and bottom, and sometimes a portion of the top, is found quite sharply angular, because it is made to conform to the surface of the rock upon which and against which it is built, the little architect always taking advantage of slight crevices and protuberances that may chance to offer, to render his structure stable by means of a kind of gripping and dovetailing.

In choosing a building-spot, concealment does not seem to be taken into consideration; yet notwithstanding the nest is large and guilelessly exposed to view, it is far from being easily detected, chiefly because it swells forward like any other bulging moss-cushion growing naturally in such situations. This is more especially the case where the nest is kept fresh by being well sprinkled. Sometimes these romantic little huts have their beauty enhanced by rock-ferns and grasses that spring up around the mossy walls, or in front of the door-sill, dripping with crystal beads.

Furthermore, at certain hours of the day, when the sunshine is poured down at the required angle, the whole mass of the spray enveloping the fairy establishment is brilliantly irised; and it is through so glorious a rainbow atmosphere as this that some of our blessed ouzels obtain their first peep at the world.

Ouzels seem so completely part and parcel of the streams

they inhabit, they scarce suggest any other origin than the streams themselves; and one might almost be pardoned in fancying they come direct from the living waters, like flowers from the ground. At least, from whatever cause, it never occurred to me to look for their nests until more than a year after I had made the acquaintance of the birds themselves, although I found one the very day on which I began the search. In making my way from Yosemite to the glaciers at the heads of the Merced and Tuolumne rivers, I camped in a particularly wild and romantic portion of the Nevada cañon where in previous excursions I had never failed to enjoy the company of my favorites, who were attracted here, no doubt, by the safe nesting-places in the shelving rocks, and by the abundance of food and falling water. The river, for miles above and below, consists of a succession of small falls from ten to sixty feet in height, connected by flat, plume-like cascades that go flashing from fall to fall, free and almost channelless, over waving folds of glacier-polished granite.

On the south side of one of the falls, that portion of the precipice which is bathed by the spray presents a series of little shelves and tablets caused by the development of planes of cleavage in the granite, and by the consequent fall of masses through the action of the water. "Now here," said I, "of all places, is the most charming spot for an Ouzel's nest." Then carefully scanning the fretted face of the precipice through the spray, I at length noticed a yellowish moss-cushion, growing on the edge of a level tablet within five or six feet of the outer folds of the fall. But apart from the fact of its being situated where one acquainted with the lives of ouzels would fancy an Ouzel's nest ought to be, there was nothing in its appearance visible at first sight, to distinguish it from other bosses of rock-moss similarly situated with reference to perennial spray; and it was not until I had scrutinized it again and again, and had removed my shoes and stockings and crept along the face of the rock within eight or ten feet of it, that I could decide certainly whether it was a nest or a natural growth.

In these moss huts three or four eggs are laid, white like foam-bubbles; and well may the little birds hatched from them sing water songs, for they hear them all their lives, and even before they are born.

I have often observed the young just out of the nest making their odd gestures, and seeming in every way as much at home as their experienced parents, like young bees on their first excursions to the flower fields. No amount of familiarity with people and their ways seems to change them in the least. To all appearance their behavior is just the same on seeing a man for the first time, as when they have seen him frequently.

On the lower reaches of the rivers where mills are built, they sing on through the din of the machinery, and all the noisy confusion of dogs, cattle, and workmen. On one occasion, while a wood-chopper was at work on the river-bank, I observed one cheerily singing within reach of the flying chips. Nor does any kind of unwonted disturbance put him in bad humor, or frighten him out of calm self-possession. In passing through a narrow gorge, I once drove one ahead of me from rapid to rapid, disturbing him four times in quick succession where he could not very well fly past me on account of the narrowness of the channel. Most birds under similar circumstances fancy themselves pursued, and become suspiciously uneasy; but, instead of growing nervous about it, he made his usual dippings, and sang one of his most tranquil strains. When observed within a few yards their eyes are seen to express remarkable gentleness and intelligence; but they seldom allow so near a view unless one wears clothing of about the same color as the rocks and trees, and knows how to sit still. On one occasion, while rambling along the shore of a mountain lake, where the birds, at least those born that season, had never seen a man, I sat down to rest on a large stone close to the water's edge, upon which it seemed the ouzels and sandpipers were in the habit of alighting when they came to feed on that part of the shore, and some of the other birds also, when they came down to wash or drink. In a few minutes, along came a whirring Ouzel and alighted on the stone beside me, within reach of my hand. Then suddenly observing me, he stooped nervously as if about to fly on the instant, but as I remained as motionless as the stone, he gained confidence, and looked me steadily in the face for about a minute, then flew quietly to the outlet and began to sing. Next came a sandpiper and gazed at me with much the same guileless expression of eye as the Ouzel. Lastly, down with a swoop came a Steller's jay out of a fir-tree, probably with the intention of moistening his noisy throat. But instead of sitting confidingly as my other visitors had done, he rushed off at once, nearly tumbling heels over head into the lake in his suspicious confusion, and with loud screams roused the neighborhood.

Love for song-birds, with their sweet human voices, appears to be more common and unfailing than love for flowers. Every one loves flowers to some extent, at least in life's fresh morning, attracted by them as instinctively as humming-birds and bees. Even the young Digger Indians have sufficient love for the brightest of those found growing on the mountains to gather them and braid them as decorations for the hair. And I was glad to discover, through the few Indians that could be induced to talk on the subject, that they have names for the wild rose and the lily, and other conspicuous flowers, whether available as food or otherwise. Most men, however, whether savage or civilized, become apathetic toward all plants that have no other apparent use than the use of beauty. But fortunately one's first instinctive love of song-birds is never wholly obliterated, no matter what the influences upon our lives may be. I have often been delighted to see a pure, spiritual glow come into the countenances of hard business-men and old miners, when a song-bird chanced to alight near them. Nevertheless, the little mouthful of meat that swells out the breasts of some song-birds is too often the cause of their death. Larks and robins in particular are brought to market in hundreds. But fortunately the Ouzel has no enemy so eager to eat his little body as to follow him into the mountain solitudes. I never knew him to be chased even by hawks.

An acquaintance of mine, a sort of foot-hill mountaineer, had a pet cat, a great, dozy, overgrown creature, about as broad-shouldered as a lynx. During the winter, while the snow lay deep, the mountaineer sat in his lonely cabin among the pines smoking his pipe and wearing the dull time away. Tom was his sole companion, sharing his bed, and sitting beside him on a stool with much the same drowsy expression of eye as his master. The good-natured bachelor was content with his hard fare of soda-bread and bacon, but Tom, the only creature in the world acknowledging dependence on him, must needs be provided with fresh meat. Accordingly he bestirred himself to contrive squirrel-traps, and waded the snowy woods with his gun, making sad havoc among the few winter birds, sparing neither robin, sparrow, nor tiny nut-hatch, and the pleasure of seeing Tom eat and grow fat was his great reward.

One cold afternoon, while hunting along the river-bank, he noticed a plain-feathered little bird skipping about in the shallows, and immediately raised his gun. But just then the confiding songster began to sing, and after listening to his summery melody the charmed hunter turned away, saying, "Bless your little heart, I can't shoot you, not even for Tom."

Even so far north as icy Alaska, I have found my glad singer. When I was exploring the glaciers between Mount Fairweather and the Stikeen River, one cold day in November, after trying in vain to force a way through the innumerable icebergs of Sum Dum Bay to the great glaciers at the head of it, I was weary and baffled and sat resting in my canoe convinced at last that I would have to leave this part of my work for another year. Then I began to plan my escape to open water before the young ice which was beginning to form should shut me in. While I thus lingered drifting with the bergs, in the midst of these gloomy forebodings and all the terrible glacial desolation and grandeur, I suddenly heard the well-known whir of an Ouzel's wings, and, looking up, saw my little comforter coming straight across the ice from the shore. In a second or two he was with me, flying three times round my head with a happy salute, as if saying, "Cheer up, old friend; you see I'm here, and all's well." Then he flew back to the shore, alighted on the topmost jag of a stranded iceberg, and began to nod and bow as though he were on one of his favorite boulders in the midst of a sunny Sierra cascade.

The species is distributed all along the mountain-ranges of the Pacific Coast from Alaska to Mexico, and east to the Rocky Mountains. Nevertheless, it is as yet comparatively little known. Audubon and Wilson did not meet it. Swainson was, I believe, the first naturalist to describe a specimen from Mexico. Specimens were shortly afterward procured by Drummond near the sources of the Athabasca River, between the fifty-fourth and fifty-sixth parallels; and it has been collected by nearly all of the numerous exploring expeditions undertaken of late through our Western States and Territories; for it never fails to engage the attention of naturalists in a very particular manner.

Such, then, is our little cinclus, beloved of every one who is so fortunate as to know him. Tracing on strong wing every curve of the most precipitous torrents from one extremity of the Sierra to the other; not fearing to follow them through their darkest gorges and coldest snow-tunnels; acquainted with every waterfall, echoing their divine music; and throughout the whole of their beautiful lives interpreting all that we in our unbelief call terrible in the utterances of torrents and storms, as only varied expressions of God's eternal love.

Chapter XIV

THE WILD SHEEP
(Ovis montana)

THE wild sheep ranks highest among the animal mountaineers of the Sierra. Possessed of keen sight and scent,
and strong limbs, he dwells secure amid the loftiest summits,
leaping unscathed from crag to crag, up and down the fronts
of giddy precipices, crossing foaming torrents and slopes of
frozen snow, exposed to the wildest storms, yet maintaining
a brave, warm life, and developing from generation to generation in perfect strength and beauty.

Nearly all the lofty mountain-chains of the globe are inhabited by wild sheep, most of which, on account of the remote
and all but inaccessible regions where they dwell, are imperfectly known as yet. They are classified by different naturalists
under from five to ten distinct species or varieties, the best
known being the burrhel of the Himalaya (*Ovis burrhel*,
Blyth); the argali, the large wild sheep of central and northeastern Asia (*O. ammon*, Linn., or *Caprovis argali*); the
Corsican mouflon (*O. musimon*, Pal.); the aoudad of the
mountains of northern Africa (*Ammotragus tragelaphus*); and
the Rocky Mountain bighorn (*O. montana*, Cuv.). To this
last-named species belongs the wild sheep of the Sierra. Its
range, according to the late Professor Baird of the Smithson-
ian Institution, extends "from the region of the upper Missouri and Yellowstone to the Rocky Mountains and the high
grounds adjacent to them on the eastern slope, and as far
south as the Rio Grande. Westward it extends to the coast
ranges of Washington, Oregon, and California, and follows
the highlands some distance into Mexico."* Throughout the
vast region bounded on the east by the Wahsatch Mountains
and on the west by the Sierra there are more than a hundred
subordinate ranges and mountain groups, trending north and
south, range beyond range, with summits rising from eight to
twelve thousand feet above the level of the sea, probably all

*Pacific Railroad Survey, Vol. VIII, page 678.

of which, according to my own observations, is, or has been, inhabited by this species.

Compared with the argali, which, considering its size and the vast extent of its range, is probably the most important of all the wild sheep, our species is about the same size, but the horns are less twisted and less divergent. The more important characteristics are, however, essentially the same, some of the best naturalists maintaining that the two are only varied forms of one species. In accordance with this view, Cuvier conjectures that since central Asia seems to be the region where the sheep first appeared, and from which it has been distributed, the argali may have been distributed over this continent from Asia by crossing Bering Strait on ice. This conjecture is not so ill founded as at first sight would appear; for the Strait is only about fifty miles wide, is interrupted by three islands, and is jammed with ice nearly every winter. Furthermore the argali is abundant on the mountains adjacent to the Strait at East Cape, where it is well known to the Tschuckchi hunters and where I have seen many of their horns.

On account of the extreme variability of the sheep under culture, it is generally supposed that the innumerable domestic breeds have all been derived from the few wild species; but the whole question is involved in obscurity. According to Darwin, sheep have been domesticated from a very ancient period, the remains of a small breed, differing from any now known, having been found in the famous Swiss lake-dwellings.

Compared with the best-known domestic breeds, we find that our wild species is much larger, and, instead of an all-wool garment, wears a thick overcoat of hair like that of the deer, and an undercovering of fine wool. The hair, though rather coarse, is comfortably soft and spongy, and lies smooth, as if carefully tended with comb and brush. The predominant color during most of the year is brownish-gray, varying to bluish-gray in the autumn; the belly and a large, conspicuous patch on the buttocks are white; and the tail, which is very short, like that of a deer, is black, with a yellowish border. The wool is white, and grows in beautiful spirals down out of sight among the shining hair, like delicate climbing vines among stalks of corn.

The horns of the male are of immense size, measuring in

their greater diameter from five to six and a half inches, and from two and a half to three feet in length around the curve. They are yellowish-white in color, and ridged transversely, like those of the domestic ram. Their cross-section near the base is somewhat triangular in outline, and flattened toward the tip. Rising boldly from the top of the head, they curve gently backward and outward, then forward and outward, until about three fourths of a circle is described, and until the flattened, blunt tips are about two feet or two and a half feet apart. Those of the female are flattened throughout their entire length, are less curved than those of the male, and much smaller, measuring less than a foot along the curve.

A ram and ewe that I obtained near the Modoc lava-beds, to the northeast of Mount Shasta, measured as follows:

	Ram.		Ewe.	
	ft.	in.	ft.	in.
Height at shoulders	3	6	3	0
Girth around shoulders	3	11	3	$3\frac{3}{4}$
Length from nose to root of tail	5	$10\frac{1}{4}$	4	$3\frac{1}{2}$
Length of ears	0	$4\frac{3}{4}$	0	5
Length of tail	0	$4\frac{1}{2}$	0	$4\frac{1}{2}$
Length of horns around curve	2	9	0	$11\frac{1}{2}$
Distance across from tip to tip of horns .	2	$5\frac{1}{2}$		
Circumference of horns at base	1	4	0	6

The measurements of a male obtained in the Rocky Mountains by Audubon vary but little as compared with the above. The weight of his specimen was 344 pounds,* which is, perhaps, about an average for full-grown males. The females are about a third lighter.

Besides these differences in size, color, hair, etc., as noted above, we may observe that the domestic sheep, in a general way, is expressionless, like a dull bundle of something only half alive, while the wild is as elegant and graceful as a deer, every movement manifesting admirable strength and character. The tame is timid; the wild is bold. The tame is always more or less ruffled and dirty; while the wild is as smooth and clean as the flowers of his mountain pastures.

The earliest mention that I have been able to find of the

*Audubon and Bachman's "Quadrupeds of North America."

wild sheep in America is by Father Picolo, a Catholic missionary at Monterey, in the year 1797, who, after describing it,
oddly enough, as "a kind of deer with a sheep-like head, and
about as large as a calf one or two years old," naturally hurries
on to remark: "I have eaten of these beasts; their flesh is very
tender and delicious." Mackenzie, in his northern travels,
heard the species spoken of by the Indians as "white buffaloes." And Lewis and Clark tell us that, in a time of great
scarcity on the head waters of the Missouri, they saw plenty
of wild sheep, but they were "too shy to be shot."

A few of the more energetic of the Pah Ute Indians hunt
the wild sheep every season among the more accessible
sections of the High Sierra, in the neighborhood of passes,
where, from having been pursued, they have become extremely
wary; but in the rugged wilderness of peaks and cañons, where
the foaming tributaries of the San Joaquin and King's rivers
take their rise, they fear no hunter save the wolf, and are more
guileless and approachable than their tame kindred.

While engaged in the work of exploring high regions where
they delight to roam I have been greatly interested in studying
their habits. In the months of November and December, and
probably during a considerable portion of midwinter, they all
flock together, male and female, old and young. I once found
a complete band of this kind numbering upward of fifty,
which, on being alarmed, went bounding away across a jagged
lava-bed at admirable speed, led by a majestic old ram, with
the lambs safe in the middle of the flock.

In spring and summer, the full-grown rams form separate
bands of from three to twenty, and are usually found feeding
along the edges of glacier meadows, or resting among the
castle-like crags of the high summits; and whether quietly
feeding, or scaling the wild cliffs, their noble forms and the
power and beauty of their movements never fail to strike the
beholder with lively admiration.

Their resting-places seem to be chosen with reference to
sunshine and a wide outlook, and most of all to safety. Their
feeding-grounds are among the most beautiful of the wild
gardens, bright with daisies and gentians and mats of purple
bryanthus, lying hidden away on rocky headlands and cañon
sides, where sunshine is abundant, or down in the shady

glacier valleys, along the banks of the streams and lakes, where the plushy sod is greenest. Here they feast all summer, the happy wanderers, perhaps relishing the beauty as well as the taste of the lovely flora on which they feed.

When the winter storms set in, loading their highland pastures with snow, then, like the birds, they gather and go to lower climates, usually descending the eastern flank of the range to the rough, volcanic table-lands and treeless ranges of the Great Basin adjacent to the Sierra. They never make haste, however, and seem to have no dread of storms, many of the strongest only going down leisurely to bare, wind-swept ridges, to feed on bushes and dry bunch-grass, and then returning up into the snow. Once I was snow-bound on Mount Shasta for three days, a little below the timber line. It was a dark and stormy time, well calculated to test the skill and endurance of mountaineers. The snow-laden gale drove on night and day in hissing, blinding floods, and when at length it began to abate, I found that a small band of wild sheep had weathered the storm in the lee of a clump of Dwarf Pines a few yards above my storm-nest, where the snow was eight or ten feet deep. I was warm back of a rock, with blankets, bread, and fire. My brave companions lay in the snow, without food, and with only the partial shelter of the short trees, yet they made no sign of suffering or faintheartedness.

In the months of May and June, the wild sheep bring forth their young in solitary and almost inaccessible crags, far above the nesting-rocks of the eagle. I have frequently come upon the beds of the ewes and lambs at an elevation of from 12,000 to 13,000 feet above sea-level. These beds are simply oval-shaped hollows, pawed out among loose, disintegrating rock-chips and sand, upon some sunny spot commanding a good outlook, and partially sheltered from the winds that sweep those lofty peaks almost without intermission. Such is the cradle of the little mountaineer, aloft in the very sky; rocked in storms, curtained in clouds, sleeping in thin, icy air; but, wrapped in his hairy coat, and nourished by a strong, warm mother, defended from the talons of the eagle and the teeth of the sly coyote, the bonny lamb grows apace. He soon learns to nibble the tufted rock-grasses and leaves of the white spiræa; his horns begin to shoot, and before summer is done he is strong and agile, and goes forth with the flock, watched by the same divine love that tends the more helpless human lamb in its cradle by the fireside.

Nothing is more commonly remarked by noisy, dusty trail-travelers in the Sierra than the want of animal life—no song-birds, no deer, no squirrels, no game of any kind, they say. But if such could only go away quietly into the wilderness, sauntering afoot and alone with natural deliberation, they would soon learn that these mountain mansions are not without inhabitants, many of whom, confiding and gentle, would not try to shun their acquaintance.

In the fall of 1873 I was tracing the South Fork of the San Joaquin up its wild cañon to its farthest glacier fountains. It was the season of alpine Indian summer. The sun beamed lovingly; the squirrels were nutting in the pine-trees, butterflies hovered about the last of the goldenrods, the willow and maple thickets were yellow, the meadows brown, and the whole sunny, mellow landscape glowed like a countenance in the deepest and sweetest repose. On my way over the glacier-polished rocks along the river, I came to an expanded portion of the cañon, about two miles long and half a mile wide, which formed a level park inclosed with picturesque granite walls like those of Yosemite Valley. Down through the middle of it poured the beautiful river shining and spangling in the golden light, yellow groves on its banks, and strips of brown meadow; while the whole park was astir with wild life, some of which even the noisiest and least observing of travelers must have seen had they been with me. Deer, with their supple, well-grown fawns, bounded from thicket to thicket as I advanced; grouse kept rising from the brown grass with a great whirring of wings, and, alighting on the lower branches of the pines and poplars, allowed a near approach, as if curious to see me. Farther on, a broad-shouldered wildcat showed himself, coming out of a grove, and crossing the river on a flood-jamb of logs, halting for a moment to look back. The bird-like tamias frisked about my feet everywhere among the pine-needles and seedy grass-tufts; cranes waded the shallows of the river-bends, the kingfisher rattled from perch to perch, and the blessed ouzel sang amid the spray of every cascade.

Where may lonely wanderer find a more interesting family of mountain-dwellers, earth-born companions and fellow-mortals? It was afternoon when I joined them, and the glorious landscape began to fade in the gloaming before I awoke from their enchantment. Then I sought a camp-ground on the river-bank, made a cupful of tea, and lay down to sleep on a smooth place among the yellow leaves of an aspen grove. Next day I discovered yet grander landscapes and grander life. Following the river over huge, swelling rock-bosses through a majestic cañon, and past innumerable cascades, the scenery in general became gradually wilder and more alpine. The Sugar Pine and Silver Firs gave place to the hardier Cedar and Hemlock Spruce. The cañon walls became more rugged and bare, and gentians and arctic daisies became more abundant in the gardens and strips of meadow along the streams. Toward the middle of the afternoon I came to another valley, strikingly wild and original in all its features, and perhaps never before touched by human foot. As regards area of level bottom-land, it is one of the very smallest of the Yosemite type, but its walls are sublime, rising to a height of from 2000 to 4000 feet above the river. At the head of the valley the main cañon forks, as is found to be the case in all yosemites. The formation of this one is due chiefly to the action of two great glaciers, whose fountains lay to the eastward, on the flanks of Mounts Humphrey and Emerson and a cluster of nameless peaks farther south.

The gray, boulder-chafed river was singing loudly through the valley, but above its massy roar I heard the booming of a waterfall, which drew me eagerly on; and just as I emerged from the tangled groves and brier-thickets at the head of the valley, the main fork of the river came in sight, falling fresh from its glacier fountains in a snowy cascade, between granite walls 2000 feet high. The steep incline down which the glad waters thundered seemed to bar all farther progress. It was not long, however, before I discovered a crooked seam in the rock, by which I was enabled to climb to the edge of a terrace that crosses the cañon, and divides the cataract nearly in the middle. Here I sat down to take breath and make some entries in my note-book, taking advantage, at the same time, of my elevated position above the trees to gaze back over the valley into the heart of the noble landscape, little knowing the while what neighbors were near.

After spending a few minutes in this way, I chanced to look across the fall, and there stood three sheep quietly observing me. Never did the sudden appearance of a mountain, or fall, or human friend more forcibly seize and rivet my attention. Anxiety to observe accurately held me perfectly still. Eagerly I marked the flowing undulations of their firm, braided muscles, their strong legs, ears, eyes, heads, their graceful rounded necks, the color of their hair, and the bold, upsweeping curves of their noble horns. When they moved I watched every gesture, while they, in no wise disconcerted either by my attention or by the tumultuous roar of the water, advanced deliberately alongside the rapids, between the two divisions of the cataract, turning now and then to look at me. Presently they came to a steep, ice-burnished acclivity, which they ascended by a succession of quick, short, stiff-legged leaps, reaching the top without a struggle. This was the most startling feat of mountaineering I had ever witnessed, and, considering only the mechanics of the thing, my astonishment could hardly have been greater had they displayed wings and taken to flight. "Sure-footed" mules on such ground would have fallen and rolled like loosened boulders. Many a time, where the slopes are far lower, I have been compelled to take off my shoes and stockings, tie them to my belt, and creep barefooted, with the utmost caution. No wonder then, that I watched the progress of these animal mountaineers with keen sympathy, and exulted in the boundless sufficiency of wild nature displayed in their invention, construction, and keeping. A few minutes later I caught sight of a dozen more in one band, near the foot of the upper fall. They were standing on the same side of the river with me, only twenty-five or thirty yards away, looking as unworn and perfect as if created on the spot. It appeared by their tracks, which I had seen in the Little Yosemite, and by their present position, that when I came up the cañon they were all feeding together down in the valley, and in their haste to reach high ground, where they could look about them to ascertain the nature of the strange disturbance, they were divided, three ascending on one side the river, the rest on the other.

The main band, headed by an experienced chief, now began to cross the wild rapids between the two divisions of the cascade. This was another exciting feat; for, among all the varied experiences of mountaineers, the crossing of boisterous, rock-dashed torrents is found to be one of the most trying to the nerves. Yet these fine fellows walked fearlessly to the brink, and jumped from boulder to boulder, holding themselves in easy poise above the whirling, confusing current, as if they were doing nothing extraordinary.

In the immediate foreground of this rare picture there was a fold of ice-burnished granite, traversed by a few bold lines in which rock-ferns and tufts of bryanthus were growing, the gray cañon walls on the sides, nobly sculptured and adorned with brown cedars and pines; lofty peaks in the distance, and in the middle ground the snowy fall, the voice and soul of the landscape; fringing bushes beating time to its thunder-tones, the brave sheep in front of it, their gray forms slightly obscured in the spray, yet standing out in good, heavy relief against the close white water, with their huge horns rising like the upturned roots of dead pine-trees, while the evening sunbeams streaming up the cañon colored all the picture a rosy purple and made it glorious. After crossing the river, the dauntless climbers, led by their chief, at once began to scale the cañon wall, turning now right, now left, in long, single file, keeping well apart out of one another's way, and leaping in regular succession from crag to crag, now ascending slippery dome-curves, now walking leisurely along the edges of precipices, stopping at times to gaze down at me from some flat-topped rock, with heads held aslant, as if curious to learn what I thought about it, or whether I was likely to follow them. After reaching the top of the wall, which, at this place, is somewhere between 1500 and 2000 feet high, they were still visible against the sky as they lingered, looking down in groups of twos or threes.

Throughout the entire ascent they did not make a single awkward step, or an unsuccessful effort of any kind. I have frequently seen tame sheep in mountains jump upon a sloping rock-surface, hold on tremulously a few seconds, and fall back baffled and irresolute. But in the most trying situations, where the slightest want or inaccuracy would have been fatal, these always seemed to move in comfortable reliance on their strength and skill, the limits of which they never appeared to know. Moreover, each one of the flock, while following the guidance of the most experienced, yet climbed with intelligent independence as a perfect individual, capable of separate existence whenever it should wish or be compelled to withdraw from the little clan. The domestic sheep, on the contrary, is only a fraction of an animal, a whole flock being required to form an individual, just as numerous flowerets are required to make one complete sunflower.

Those shepherds who, in summer, drive their flocks to the mountain pastures, and, while watching them night and day, have seen them frightened by bears and storms, and scattered like wind-driven chaff, will, in some measure, be able to appreciate the self-reliance and strength and noble individuality of Nature's sheep.

Like the Alp-climbing ibex of Europe, our mountaineer is said to plunge headlong down the faces of sheer precipices, and alight on his big horns. I know only two hunters who claim to have actually witnessed this feat; I never was so fortunate. They describe the act as a diving head-foremost. The horns are so large at the base that they cover the upper portion of the head down nearly to a level with the eyes, and the skull is exceedingly strong. I struck an old, bleached specimen on Mount Ritter a dozen blows with my ice-ax without breaking it. Such skulls would not fracture very readily by the wildest rock-diving, but other bones could hardly be expected to hold together in such a performance; and the mechanical difficulties in the way of controlling their movements, after striking upon an irregular surface, are, in themselves, sufficient to show this boulder-like method of progression to be impossible, even in the absence of all other evidence on the subject; moreover, the ewes follow wherever the rams may lead, although their horns are mere spikes. I have found many pairs of the horns of the old rams considerably battered, doubtless a result of fighting. I was particularly interested in the question, after witnessing the performances of this San Joaquin band upon the glaciated rocks at the foot of the falls; and as soon as I procured specimens and examined their feet, all the mystery disappeared. The secret, considered in connection

with exceptionally strong muscles, is simply this: the wide pos-
terior portion of the bottom of the foot, instead of wearing
down and becoming flat and hard, like the feet of tame sheep
and horses, bulges out in a soft, rubber-like pad or cushion,
which not only grips and holds well on smooth rocks, but fits
into small cavities, and down upon or against slight protuberances. Even the hardest portions of the edge of the hoof
are comparatively soft and elastic; furthermore, the toes admit
of an extraordinary amount of both lateral and vertical movement, allowing the foot to accommodate itself still more perfectly to the irregularities of rock surfaces, while at the same
time increasing the gripping power.

At the base of Sheep Rock, one of the winter strongholds
of the Shasta flocks, there lives a stock-raiser who has had the
advantage of observing the movements of wild sheep every
winter; and, in the course of a conversation with him on the
subject of their diving habits, he pointed to the front of a lava
headland about 150 feet high, which is only eight or ten degrees out of the perpendicular. "There," said he, "I followed
a band of them fellows to the back of that rock yonder, and
expected to capture them all, for I thought I had a dead thing
on them. I got behind them on a narrow bench that runs
along the face of the wall near the top and comes to an end
where they couldn't get away without falling and being killed;
but they jumped off, and landed all right, as if that were the
regular thing with them."

"What!" said I, "jumped 150 feet perpendicular! Did you
see them do it?"

"No," he replied, "I didn't see them going down, for I was
behind them; but I saw them go off over the brink, and then
I went below and found their tracks where they struck on the
loose rubbish at the bottom. They just *sailed right off*, and
landed on their feet right side up. That is the kind of animal
they is—beats anything else that goes on four legs."

On another occasion, a flock that was pursued by hunters
retreated to another portion of this same cliff where it is still
higher, and, on being followed, they were seen jumping down
in perfect order, one behind another, by two men who happened to be chopping where they had a fair view of them and
could watch their progress from top to bottom of the preci-

pice. Both ewes and rams made the frightful descent without evincing any extraordinary concern, hugging the rock closely, and controlling the velocity of their half falling, half leaping movements by striking at short intervals and holding back with their cushioned, rubber feet upon small ledges and roughened inclines until near the bottom, when they "sailed off" into the free air and alighted on their feet, but with their bodies so nearly in a vertical position that they appeared to be diving.

It appears, therefore, that the methods of this wild mountaineering become clearly comprehensible as soon as we make ourselves acquainted with the rocks, and the kind of feet and muscles brought to bear upon them.

The Modoc and Pah Ute Indians are, or rather have been, the most successful hunters of the wild sheep in the regions that have come under my own observation. I have seen large numbers of heads and horns in the caves of Mount Shasta and the Modoc lava-beds, where the Indians had been feasting in stormy weather; also in the cañons of the Sierra opposite Owen's Valley; while the heavy obsidian arrow-heads found on some of the highest peaks show that this warfare has long been going on.

In the more accessible ranges that stretch across the desert regions of western Utah and Nevada, considerable numbers of Indians used to hunt in company like packs of wolves, and being perfectly acquainted with the topography of their hunting-grounds, and with the habits and instincts of the game, they were pretty successful. On the tops of nearly every one of the Nevada mountains that I have visited, I found small, nest-like inclosures built of stones, in which, as I afterward learned, one or more Indians would lie in wait while their companions scoured the ridges below, knowing that the alarmed sheep would surely run to the summit, and when they could be made to approach with the wind they were shot at short range.

Still larger bands of Indians used to make extensive hunts upon some dominant mountain much frequented by the sheep, such as Mount Grant on the Wassuck Range to the west of Walker Lake. On some particular spot, favorably situated with reference to the well-known trails of the sheep, they built a high-walled corral, with long guiding wings diverging from the gateway; and into this inclosure they sometimes succeeded in driving the noble game. Great numbers of Indians were of course required, more, indeed, than they could usually muster, counting in squaws, children, and all; they were compelled, therefore, to build rows of dummy hunters out of stones, along the ridge-tops which they wished to prevent the sheep from crossing. And, without discrediting the sagacity of the game, these dummies were found effective; for, with a few live Indians moving about excitedly among them, they could hardly be distinguished at a little distance from men, by any one not in the secret. The whole ridge-top then seemed to be alive with hunters.

The only animal that may fairly be regarded as a companion or rival of the sheep is the so-called Rocky Mountain goat (*Aplocerus montana*, Rich.), which, as its name indicates, is more antelope than goat. He, too, is a brave and hardy climber, fearlessly crossing the wildest summits, and braving the severest storms, but he is shaggy, short-legged, and much less dignified in demeanor than the sheep. His jet-black horns are only about five or six inches in length, and the long, white hair with which he is covered obscures the expression of his limbs. I have never yet seen a single specimen in the Sierra, though possibly a few flocks may have lived on Mount Shasta a comparatively short time ago.

The ranges of these two mountaineers are pretty distinct, and they see but little of each other; the sheep being restricted mostly to the dry, inland mountains; the goat or chamois to the wet, snowy glacier-laden mountains of the northwest coast of the continent in Oregon, Washington, British Columbia, and Alaska. Probably more than 200 dwell on the icy, volcanic cone of Mount Rainier; and while I was exploring the glaciers of Alaska I saw flocks of these admirable mountaineers nearly every day, and often followed their trails through the mazes of bewildering crevasses, in which they are excellent guides.

Three species of deer are found in California,—the blacktailed, white-tailed, and mule deer. The first mentioned (*Cervus Columbianus*) is by far the most abundant, and occasionally meets the sheep during the summer on high glacier meadows, and along the edge of the timber line; but being a forest animal, seeking shelter and rearing its young in dense thickets, it seldom visits the wild sheep in its higher homes. The antelope, though not a mountaineer, is occasionally met in winter by the sheep while feeding along the edges of the sage-plains and bare volcanic hills to the east of the Sierra. So also is the mule deer, which is almost restricted in its range to this eastern region. The white-tailed species belongs to the coast ranges.

Perhaps no wild animal in the world is without enemies, but highlanders, as a class, have fewer than lowlanders. The wily panther, slipping and crouching among long grass and bushes, pounces upon the antelope and deer, but seldom crosses the bald, craggy thresholds of the sheep. Neither can the bears be regarded as enemies; for, though they seek to vary their every-day diet of nuts and berries by an occasional meal of mutton, they prefer to hunt tame and helpless flocks. Eagles and coyotes, no doubt, capture an unprotected lamb at times, or some unfortunate beset in deep, soft snow, but these cases are little more than accidents. So, also, a few perish in long-continued snow-storms, though, in all my mountaineering, I have not found more than five or six that seemed to have met their fate in this way. A little band of three were discovered snow-bound in Bloody Cañon a few years ago, and were killed with an ax by mountaineers, who chanced to be crossing the range in winter.

Man is the most dangerous enemy of all, but even from him our brave mountain-dweller has little to fear in the remote solitudes of the High Sierra. The golden plains of the Sacramento and San Joaquin were lately thronged with bands of elk and antelope, but, being fertile and accessible, they were required for human pastures. So, also, are many of the feeding-grounds of the deer—hill, valley, forest, and meadow—but it will be long before man will care to take the highland castles of the sheep. And when we consider here how rapidly entire species of noble animals, such as the elk, moose, and buffalo, are being pushed to the very verge of extinction, all lovers of wildness will rejoice with me in the rocky security of *Ovis montana*, the bravest of all the Sierra mountaineers.

Chapter XV

Murphy's Camp is a curious old mining-town in Calaveras County, at an elevation of 2400 feet above the
sea, situated like a nest in the center of a rough, gravelly region, rich in gold. Granites, slates, lavas, limestone, iron ores,
quartz veins, auriferous gravels, remnants of dead fire-rivers
and dead water-rivers are developed here side by side within
a radius of a few miles, and placed invitingly open before the
student like a book, while the people and the region beyond
the camp furnish mines of study of never-failing interest and
variety.

When I discovered this curious place, I was tracing the
channels of the ancient pre-glacial rivers, instructive sections
of which have been laid bare here and in the adjacent regions
by the miners. Rivers, according to the poets, "go on forever";
but those of the Sierra are young as yet and have scarcely
learned the way down to the sea; while at least one generation
of them have died and vanished together with most of the
basins they drained. All that remains of them to tell their history is a series of interrupted fragments of channels, mostly
choked with gravel, and buried beneath broad, thick sheets of
lava. These are known as the "Dead Rivers of California," and
the gravel deposited in them is comprehensively called the
"Blue Lead." In some places the channels of the present rivers
trend in the same direction, or nearly so, as those of the ancient rivers; but, in general, there is little correspondence between them, the entire drainage having been changed, or,
rather, made new. Many of the hills of the ancient landscapes
have become hollows, and the old hollows have become hills.
Therefore the fragmentary channels, with their loads of auriferous gravel, occur in all kinds of unthought-of places, trending obliquely, or even at right angles to the present drainage,
across the tops of lofty ridges or far beneath them, presenting
impressive illustrations of the magnitude of the changes accomplished since those ancient streams were annihilated. The
last volcanic period preceding the regeneration of the Sierra

landscapes seems to have come on over all the range almost simultaneously, like the glacial period, notwithstanding lavas of different age occur together in many places, indicating numerous periods of activity in the Sierra fire-fountains. The most important of the ancient river-channels in this region is a section that extends from the south side of the town beneath Coyote Creek and the ridge beyond it to the Cañon of the Stanislaus; but on account of its depth below the general surface of the present valleys the rich gold gravels it is known to contain cannot be easily worked on a large scale. Their extraordinary richness may be inferred from the fact that many claims were profitably worked in them by sinking shafts to a depth of 200 feet or more, and hoisting the dirt by a windlass. Should the dip of this ancient channel be such as to make the Stanislaus Cañon available as a dump, then the grand deposit might be worked by the hydraulic method, and although a long, expensive tunnel would be required, the scheme might still prove profitable, for there is "millions in it."

The importance of these ancient gravels as gold fountains is well known to miners. Even the superficial placers of the present streams have derived much of their gold from them. According to all accounts, the Murphy placers have been very rich—"terrific rich," as they say here. The hills have been cut and scalped, and every gorge and gulch and valley torn to pieces and disemboweled, expressing a fierce and desperate energy hard to understand. Still, any kind of effort-making is better than inaction, and there is something sublime in seeing men working in dead earnest at anything, pursuing an object with glacier-like energy and persistence. Many a brave fellow has recorded a most eventful chapter of life on these Calaveras rocks. But most of the pioneer miners are sleeping now, their wild day done, while the few survivors linger languidly in the washed-out gulches or sleepy village like harried bees around the ruins of their hive. "We have no industry left *now*," they told me, "and no men; everybody and everything hereabouts has gone to decay. We are only bummers—out of the game, a thin scatterin' of poor, dilapidated cusses, compared with what we used to be in the grand old gold-days. We were giants then, and you can look around here and see our tracks." But although these lingering pioneers are perhaps more exhausted than the mines, and about as dead as the dead rivers, they are yet a rare and interesting set of men, with much gold mixed with the rough, rocky gravel of their characters; and they manifest a breeding and intelligence little looked for in such surroundings as theirs. As the heavy, long-continued grinding of the glaciers brought out the features of the Sierra, so the intense experiences of the gold period have brought out the features of these old miners, forming a richness and variety of character little known as yet. The sketches of Bret Harte, Hayes, and Miller have not exhausted this field by any means. It is interesting to note the extremes possible in one and the same character: harshness and gentleness, manliness and childishness, apathy and fierce endeavor. Men who, twenty years ago, would not cease their shoveling to save their lives, now play in the streets with children. Their long, Micawber-like waiting after the exhaustion of the placers has brought on an exaggerated form of dotage. I heard a group of brawny pioneers in the street eagerly discussing the quantity of tail required for a boy's kite; and one graybeard undertook the sport of flying it, volunteering the information that he was a boy, "always was a boy, and d—n a man who was not a boy inside, however ancient outside!" Mines, morals, politics, the immortality of the soul, etc., were discussed beneath shade-trees and in saloons, the time for each being governed apparently by the temperature. Contact with Nature, and the habits of observation acquired in gold-seeking, had made them all, to some extent, collectors, and, like wood-rats, they had gathered all kinds of odd specimens into their cabins, and now required me to examine them. They were themselves the oddest and most interesting specimens. One of them offered to show me around the old diggings, giving me fair warning before setting out that I might not like him, "because," said he, "people say I'm eccentric. I notice everything, and gather beetles and snakes and anything that's queer; and so some don't like me, and call me eccentric. I'm always trying to find out things. Now, there's a weed; the Indians eat it for greens. What do you call those long-bodied flies with big heads?" "Dragon-flies," I suggested. "Well, their jaws work sidewise, instead of up and down, and grasshoppers' jaws work the same way, and therefore I think they are the same species. I always notice everything like that, and just because I do, they say I'm eccentric," etc.

Anxious that I should miss none of the wonders of their old gold-field, the good people had much to say about the marvelous beauty of Cave City Cave, and advised me to explore it. This I was very glad to do, and finding a guide who knew the way to the mouth of it, I set out from Murphy the next morning.

The most beautiful and extensive of the mountain caves of California occur in a belt of metamorphic limestone that is pretty generally developed along the western flank of the Sierra from the McCloud River on the north to the Kaweah on the south, a distance of over 400 miles, at an elevation of from 2000 to 7000 feet above the sea. Besides this regular belt of caves, the California landscapes are diversified by long imposing ranks of sea-caves, rugged and variable in architecture, carved in the coast headlands and precipices by centuries of wave-dashing; and innumerable lava-caves, great and small, originating in the unequal flowing and hardening of the lava sheets in which they occur, fine illustrations of which are presented in the famous Modoc Lava Beds, and around the base of icy Shasta. In this comprehensive glance we may also notice the shallow wind-worn caves in stratified sandstones along the margins of the plains; and the cave-like recesses in the Sierra slates and granites, where bears and other mountaineers find shelter during the fall of sudden storms. In general, however, the grand massive uplift of the Sierra, as far as it has been laid bare to observation, is about as solid and caveless as a boulder.

Fresh beauty opens one's eyes wherever it is really seen, but the very abundance and completeness of the common beauty that besets our steps prevents its being absorbed and appreciated. It is a good thing, therefore, to make short excursions now and then to the bottom of the sea among dulse and coral, or up among the clouds on mountain-tops, or in balloons, or even to creep like worms into dark holes and caverns underground, not only to learn something of what is going on in those out-of-the-way places, but to see better what the sun sees on our return to common every-day beauty.

Our way from Murphy's to the cave lay across a series of picturesque, moory ridges in the chaparral region between the brown foot-hills and the forests, a flowery stretch of rolling hill-waves breaking here and there into a kind of rocky foam on the higher summits, and sinking into delightful bosky hollows embowered with vines. The day was a fine specimen of California summer, pure sunshine, unshaded most of the time by a single cloud. As the sun rose higher, the heated air began to flow in tremulous waves from every southern slope. The sea-breeze that usually comes up the foot-hills at this season, with cooling on its wings, was scarcely perceptible. The birds were assembled beneath leafy shade, or made short, languid flights in search of food, all save the majestic buzzard; with broad wings outspread he sailed the warm air unwearily from ridge to ridge, seeming to enjoy the fervid sunshine like a butterfly. Squirrels, too, whose spicy ardor no heat or cold may abate, were nutting among the pines, and the innumerable hosts of the insect kingdom were throbbing and wavering unwearied as sunbeams.

This brushy, berry-bearing region used to be a deer and bear pasture, but since the disturbances of the gold period these fine animals have almost wholly disappeared. Here, also, once roamed the mastodon and elephant, whose bones are found entombed in the river gravels and beneath thick folds of lava. Toward noon, as we were riding slowly over bank and brae, basking in the unfeverish sun-heat, we witnessed the upheaval of a new mountain-range, a Sierra of clouds abounding in landscapes as truly sublime and beautiful—if only we have a mind to think so and eyes to see—as the more ancient rocky Sierra beneath it, with its forests and waterfalls; reminding us that, as there is a lower world of caves, so, also, there is an upper world of clouds. Huge, bossy cumuli developed with astonishing rapidity from mere buds, swelling with visible motion into colossal mountains, and piling higher, higher, in long massive ranges, peak beyond peak, dome over dome, with many a picturesque valley and shadowy cave between; while the dark firs and pines of the upper benches of the Sierra were projected against their pearl bosses with exquisite clearness of outline. These cloud mountains vanished in the azure as quickly as they were developed, leaving no detritus; but they were not a whit less real or interesting on this account. The more enduring hills over which we rode were vanishing as surely as they, only not so fast, a difference which is great or small according to the standpoint from which it is contemplated.

At the bottom of every dell we found little homesteads embosomed in wild brush and vines wherever the recession of the hills left patches of arable ground. These secluded flats are settled mostly by Italians and Germans, who plant a few vegetables and grape-vines at odd times, while their main business is mining and prospecting. In spite of all the natural beauty of these dell cabins, they can hardly be called homes. They are only a better kind of camp, gladly abandoned whenever the hoped-for gold harvest has been gathered. There is an air of profound unrest and melancholy about the best of them. Their beauty is thrust upon them by exuberant Nature, apart from which they are only a few logs and boards rudely jointed and without either ceiling or floor, a rough fireplace with corresponding cooking utensils, a shelf-bed, and stool. The ground about them is strewn with battered prospecting-pans, picks, sluice-boxes, and quartz specimens from many a ledge, indicating the trend of their owners' hard lives.

The ride from Murphy's to the cave is scarcely two hours long, but we lingered among quartz-ledges and banks of dead river gravel until long after noon. At length emerging from a narrow-throated gorge, a small house came in sight set in a thicket of fig-trees at the base of a limestone hill. "That," said my guide, pointing to the house, "is Cave City, and the cave is in that gray hill." Arriving at the one house of this one-house city, we were boisterously welcomed by three drunken men who had come to town to hold a spree. The mistress of the house tried to keep order, and in reply to our inquiries told us that the cave guide was then in the cave with a party of ladies. "And must we wait until he returns?" we asked. No, that was unnecessary; we might take candles and go into the cave alone, provided we shouted from time to time so as to be found by the guide, and were careful not to fall over the rocks or into the dark pools. Accordingly taking a trail from the house, we were led around the base of the hill to the mouth of the cave, a small inconspicuous archway, mossy around the edges and shaped like the door of a water-ouzel's nest, with no appreciable hint or advertisement of the grandeur of the many crystal chambers within. Lighting our candles, which seemed to have no illuminating power in the thick darkness, we groped our way onward as best we could along narrow lanes and alleys, from chamber to chamber, around rustic columns and heaps of fallen rocks, stopping to rest now and then in particularly beautiful places—fairy alcoves furnished with admirable variety of shelves and tables, and round bossy stools covered with sparkling crystals. Some of the corridors were muddy, and in plodding along these we seemed to be in the streets of some prairie village in springtime. Then we would come to handsome marble stairways conducting right and left into upper chambers ranged above one another three or four stories high, floors, ceilings, and walls lavishly decorated with innumerable crystalline forms. After thus wandering exploringly, and alone for a mile or so, fairly enchanted, a murmur of voices and a gleam of light betrayed the approach of the guide and his party, from whom, when they came up, we received a most hearty and natural stare, as we stood half concealed in a side recess among stalagmites. I ventured to ask the dripping, crouching company how they had enjoyed their saunter, anxious to learn how the strange sunless scenery of the underworld had impressed them. "Ah, it's nice! It's splendid!" they all replied and echoed. "The Bridal Chamber back here is just glorious! This morning we came down from the Calaveras Big Tree Grove, and the trees are nothing to it." After making this curious comparison they hastened sunward, the guide promising to join us shortly on the bank of a deep pool, where we were to wait for him. This is a charming little lakelet of unknown depth, never yet stirred by a breeze, and its eternal calm excites the imagination even more profoundly than the silvery lakes of the glaciers rimmed with meadows and snow and reflecting sublime mountains.

Our guide, a jolly, rollicking Italian, led us into the heart of the hill, up and down, right and left, from chamber to chamber more and more magnificent, all a-glitter like a glacier cave with icicle-like stalactites and stalagmites combined in forms of indescribable beauty. We were shown one large room that was occasionally used as a dancing-hall; another that was used as a chapel, with natural pulpit and crosses and pews, sermons in every stone, where a priest had said mass. Mass-saying is not so generally developed in connection with natural wonders as dancing. One of the first conceits excited by the giant Sequoias was to cut one of them down and dance on its stump. We have also seen dancing in the spray of Niagara; dancing in the famous Bower Cave above Coulterville; and nowhere have I seen so much dancing as in Yosemite. A dance on the inaccessible South Dome would likely follow the making of an easy way to the top of it.

It was delightful to witness here the infinite deliberation of Nature, and the simplicity of her methods in the production of such mighty results, such perfect repose combined with restless enthusiastic energy. Though cold and bloodless as a landscape of polar ice, building was going on in the dark with incessant activity. The archways and ceilings were everywhere hung with down-growing crystals, like inverted groves of leafless saplings, some of them large, others delicately attenuated, each tipped with a single drop of water, like the terminal bud of a pine-tree. The only appreciable sounds were the dripping and tinkling of water falling into pools or faintly plashing on the crystal floors.

In some places the crystal decorations are arranged in graceful flowing folds deeply plicated like stiff silken drapery. In others straight lines of the ordinary stalactite forms are combined with reference to size and tone in a regularly graduated system like the strings of a harp with musical tones corresponding thereto; and on these stone harps we played by striking the crystal strings with a stick. The delicious liquid tones they gave forth seemed perfectly divine as they sweetly whispered and wavered through the majestic halls and died away in faintest cadence,—the music of fairy-land. Here we lingered and reveled, rejoicing to find so much music in stony silence, so much splendor in darkness, so many mansions in the depths of the mountains, buildings ever in process of construction, yet ever finished, developing from perfection to perfection, profusion without overabundance; every particle visible or invisible in glorious motion, marching to the music of the spheres in a region regarded as the abode of eternal stillness and death.

The outer chambers of mountain caves are frequently selected as homes by wild beasts. In the Sierra, however, they seem to prefer homes and hiding-places in chaparral and beneath shelving precipices, as I have never seen their tracks in any of the caves. This is the more remarkable because notwithstanding the darkness and oozing water there is nothing uncomfortably cellar-like or sepulchral about them.

When we emerged into the bright landscapes of the sun everything looked brighter, and we felt our faith in Nature's beauty strengthened, and saw more clearly that beauty is universal and immortal, above, beneath, on land and sea, mountain and plain, in heat and cold, light and darkness.

Chapter XVI

THE BEE-PASTURES

W HEN California was wild, it was one sweet bee-garden throughout its entire length, north and south, and all the way across from the snowy Sierra to the ocean.

Wherever a bee might fly within the bounds of this virgin wilderness—through the redwood forests, along the banks of the rivers, along the bluffs and headlands fronting the sea, over valley and plain, park and grove, and deep, leafy glen, or far up the piny slopes of the mountains—throughout every belt and section of climate up to the timber line, bee-flowers bloomed in lavish abundance. Here they grew more or less apart in special sheets and patches of no great size, there in broad, flowing folds hundreds of miles in length—zones of polleny forests, zones of flowery chaparral, stream-tangles of rubus and wild rose, sheets of golden compositæ, beds of violets, beds of mint, beds of bryanthus and clover, and so on, certain species blooming somewhere all the year round.

But of late years plows and sheep have made sad havoc in these glorious pastures, destroying tens of thousands of the flowery acres like a fire, and banishing many species of the best honey-plants to rocky cliffs and fence-corners, while, on the other hand, cultivation thus far has given no adequate compensation, at least in kind; only acres of alfalfa for miles of the richest wild pasture, ornamental roses and honeysuckles around cottage doors for cascades of wild roses in the dells, and small, square orchards and orange-groves for broad mountain-belts of chaparral.

The Great Central Plain of California, during the months of March, April, and May, was one smooth, continuous bed of honey-bloom, so marvelously rich that, in walking from one end of it to the other, a distance of more than 400 miles, your foot would press about a hundred flowers at every step. Mints, gilias, nemophilas, castilleias, and innumerable compositæ were so crowded together that, had ninety-nine per cent. of them been taken away, the plain would still have seemed to any but Californians extravagantly flowery. The radiant, honeyful corollas, touching and overlapping, and rising above one another, glowed in the living light like a sunset sky—one sheet of purple and gold, with the bright Sacramento pouring through the midst of it from the north, the San Joaquin from the south, and their many tributaries sweeping in at right angles from the mountains, dividing the plain into sections fringed with trees.

Along the rivers there is a strip of bottom-land, countersunk beneath the general level, and wider toward the foot-hills, where magnificent oaks, from three to eight feet in diameter, cast grateful masses of shade over the open, prairie-like levels. And close along the water's edge there was a fine jungle of tropical luxuriance, composed of wild-rose and bramble bushes and a great variety of climbing vines, wreathing and interlacing the branches and trunks of willows and alders, and swinging across from summit to summit in heavy festoons. Here the wild bees reveled in fresh bloom long after the flowers of the drier plain had withered and gone to seed. And in midsummer, when the "blackberries" were ripe, the Indians came from the mountains to feast—men, women, and babies in long, noisy trains, often joined by the farmers of the neighborhood, who gathered this wild fruit with commendable appreciation of its superior flavor, while their home orchards were full of ripe peaches, apricots, nectarines, and figs, and their vineyards were laden with grapes. But, though these luxuriant, shaggy river-beds were thus distinct from the smooth, treeless plain, they made no heavy dividing lines in general views. The whole appeared as one continuous sheet of bloom bounded only by the mountains.

When I first saw this central garden, the most extensive and regular of all the bee-pastures of the State, it seemed all one sheet of plant gold, hazy and vanishing in the distance, distinct as a new map along the foot-hills at my feet.

Descending the eastern slopes of the Coast Range through beds of gilias and lupines, and around many a breezy hillock and bush-crowned headland, I at length waded out into the midst of it. All the ground was covered, not with grass and green leaves, but with radiant corollas, about ankle-deep next the foot-hills, knee-deep or more five or six miles out. Here were bahia, madia, madaria, burrielia, chrysopsis, corethrogyne, grindelia, etc., growing in close social congregations of various shades of yellow, blending finely with the purples of clarkia, orthocarpus, and œnothera, whose delicate petals were drinking the vital sunbeams without giving back any sparkling glow.

Because so long a period of extreme drought succeeds the rainy season, most of the vegetation is composed of annuals, which spring up simultaneously, and bloom together at about the same height above the ground, the general surface being but slightly ruffled by the taller phacelias, pentstemons, and groups of *Salvia carduacea*, the king of the mints.

Sauntering in any direction, hundreds of these happy sun-plants brushed against my feet at every step, and closed over them as if I were wading in liquid gold. The air was sweet with fragrance, the larks sang their blessed songs, rising on the wing as I advanced, then sinking out of sight in the polleny sod, while myriads of wild bees stirred the lower air with their monotonous hum—monotonous, yet forever fresh and sweet as every-day sunshine. Hares and spermophiles showed themselves in considerable numbers in shallow places, and small bands of antelopes were almost constantly in sight, gazing curiously from some slight elevation, and then bounding swiftly away with unrivaled grace of motion. Yet I could discover no crushed flowers to mark their track, nor, indeed, any destructive action of any wild foot or tooth whatever.

The great yellow days circled by uncounted, while I drifted toward the north, observing the countless forms of life thronging about me, lying down almost anywhere on the approach of night. And what glorious botanical beds I had! Oftentimes on awaking I would find several new species leaning over me and looking me full in the face, so that my studies would begin before rising.

About the first of May I turned eastward, crossing the San Joaquin River between the mouths of the Tuolumne and Merced, and by the time I had reached the Sierra foot-hills most of the vegetation had gone to seed and become as dry as hay.

All the seasons of the great plain are warm or temperate, and bee-flowers are never wholly wanting; but the grand springtime—the annual resurrection—is governed by the rains, which usually set in about the middle of November or the beginning of December. Then the seeds, that for six months have lain on the ground dry and fresh as if they had been gathered into barns, at once unfold their treasured life. The general brown and purple of the ground, and the dead vegetation of the preceding year, give place to the green of mosses and liverworts and myriads of young leaves. Then one species after another comes into flower, gradually overspreading the green with yellow and purple, which lasts until May.

The "rainy season" is by no means a gloomy, soggy period of constant cloudiness and rain. Perhaps nowhere else in North America, perhaps in the world, are the months of December, January, February, and March so full of bland, plant-building sunshine. Referring to my notes of the winter and spring of 1868–69, every day of which I spent out of doors, on that section of the plain lying between the Tuolumne and Merced rivers, I find that the first rain of the season fell on December 18th. January had only six rainy days—that is, days on which rain fell; February three, March five, April three, and May three, completing the so-called rainy season, which was about an average one. The ordinary rain-storm of this region is seldom very cold or violent. The winds, which in settled weather come from the northwest, veer round into the opposite direction, the sky fills gradually and evenly with one general cloud, from which the rain falls steadily, often for days in succession, at a temperature of about 45° or 50°.

More than seventy-five per cent. of all the rain of this season came from the northwest, down the coast over southeastern Alaska, British Columbia, Washington, and Oregon, though the local winds of these circular storms blow from the southeast. One magnificent local storm from the northwest fell on March 21. A massive, round-browed cloud came swelling and thundering over the flowery plain in most imposing majesty, its bossy front burning white and purple in the full blaze of the sun, while warm rain poured from its ample fountains like a cataract, beating down flowers and bees, and flooding the dry watercourses as suddenly as those of Nevada are flooded by the so-called "cloud-bursts." But in less than half an hour not a trace of the heavy, mountain-like cloud-structure was left in the sky, and the bees were on the wing, as if nothing more gratefully refreshing could have been sent them.

By the end of January four species of plants were in flower, and five or six mosses had already adjusted their hoods and were in the prime of life; but the flowers were not sufficiently numerous as yet to affect greatly the general green of the young leaves. Violets made their appearance in the first week of February, and toward the end of this month the warmer portions of the plain were already golden with myriads of the flowers of rayed compositæ.

This was the full springtime. The sunshine grew warmer and richer, new plants bloomed every day; the air became more tuneful with humming wings, and sweeter with the fragrance of the opening flowers. Ants and ground squirrels were getting ready for their summer work, rubbing their benumbed limbs, and sunning themselves on the husk-piles before their doors, and spiders were busy mending their old webs, or weaving new ones.

In March, the vegetation was more than doubled in depth and color; claytonia, calandrinia, a large white gilia, and two nemophilas were in bloom, together with a host of yellow compositæ, tall enough now to bend in the wind and show wavering ripples of shade.

In April, plant-life, as a whole, reached its greatest height, and the plain, over all its varied surface, was mantled with a close, furred plush of purple and golden corollas. By the end of this month, most of the species had ripened their seeds, but undecayed, still seemed to be in bloom from the numerous corolla-like involucres and whorls of chaffy scales of the compositæ. In May, the bees found in flower only a few deep-set liliaceous plants and eriogonums.

June, July, August, and September is the season of rest and sleep,—a winter of dry heat,—followed in October by a second outburst of bloom at the very driest time of the year. Then, after the shrunken mass of leaves and stalks of the dead vegetation crinkle and turn to dust beneath the foot, as if it had been baked in an oven, *Hemizonia virgata*, a slender, unobtrusive little plant, from six inches to three feet high, suddenly makes its appearance in patches miles in extent, like a resurrection of the bloom of April. I have counted upward of 3000 flowers, five eighths of an inch in diameter, on a single plant. Both its leaves and stems are so slender as to be nearly invisible, at a distance of a few yards, amid so showy a multitude of flowers. The ray and disk flowers are both yellow, the stamens purple, and the texture of the rays is rich and velvety, like the petals of garden pansies. The prevailing wind turns all the heads round to the southeast, so that in facing northwestward we have the flowers looking us in the face. In my estimation, this little plant, the last born of the brilliant host of compositæ that glorify the plain, is the most interesting of all. It remains in flower until November, uniting with two or three species of wiry eriogonums, which continue the floral chain around December to the spring flowers of January. Thus, although the main bloom and honey season is only about three months long, the floral circle, however thin around some of the hot, rainless months, is never completely broken.

How long the various species of wild bees have lived in this honey-garden, nobody knows; probably ever since the main body of the present flora gained possession of the land, toward the close of the glacial period. The first brown honey-bees brought to California are said to have arrived in San Francisco in March, 1853. A bee-keeper by the name of Shelton purchased a lot, consisting of twelve swarms, from some one at Aspinwall, who had brought them from New York. When landed at San Francisco, all the hives contained live bees, but they finally dwindled to one hive, which was taken to San José. The little immigrants flourished and multiplied in the bountiful pastures of the Santa Clara Valley, sending off three swarms the first season. The owner was killed shortly afterward, and in settling up his estate, two of the swarms were sold at auction for $105 and $110 respectively. Other importations were made, from time to time, by way of the Isthmus, and, though great pains were taken to insure success, about one half usually died on the way. Four swarms were brought safely across the plains in 1859, the hives being placed in the rear end of a wagon, which was stopped in the afternoon to allow the bees to fly and feed in the floweriest places that were within reach until dark, when the hives were closed.

In 1855, two years after the time of the first arrivals from New York, a single swarm was brought over from San José, and let fly in the Great Central Plain. Bee-culture, however, has never gained much attention here, notwithstanding the extraordinary abundance of honey-bloom, and the high price of honey during the early years. A few hives are found here and there among settlers who chanced to have learned something about the business before coming to the State. But sheep, cattle, grain, and fruit raising are the chief industries, as they require less skill and care, while the profits thus far have been greater. In 1856 honey sold here at from one and a half to two dollars per pound. Twelve years later the price had fallen to twelve and a half cents. In 1868 I sat down to dinner with a band of ravenous sheep-shearers at a ranch on the San Joaquin, where fifteen or twenty hives were kept, and our host advised us not to spare the large pan of honey he had placed on the table, as it was the cheapest article he had to offer. In all my walks, however, I have never come upon a regular bee-ranch in the Central Valley like those so common and so skilfully managed in the southern counties of the State. The few pounds of honey and wax produced are consumed at home, and are scarcely taken into account among the coarser products of the farm. The swarms that escape from their careless owners have a weary, perplexing time of it in seeking suitable homes. Most of them make their way to the foot-hills of the mountains, or to the trees that line the banks of the rivers, where some hollow log or trunk may be found. A friend of mine, while out hunting on the San Joaquin, came upon an old coon trap, hidden among some tall grass, near the edge of the river, upon which he sat down to rest. Shortly afterward his attention was attracted to a crowd of angry bees that were flying excitedly about his head, when he discovered that he was sitting upon their hive, which was found to contain more than 200 pounds of honey. Out in the broad, swampy delta of the Sacramento and San Joaquin rivers, the little wanderers have been known to build their combs in a bunch of rushes, or stiff, wiry grass, only slightly protected from the weather, and in danger every spring of being carried away by floods. They have the advantage, however, of a vast extent of fresh pasture, accessible only to themselves.

The present condition of the Grand Central Garden is very different from that we have sketched. About twenty years ago, when the gold placers had been pretty thoroughly exhausted, the attention of fortune-seekers—not home-seekers—was, in great part, turned away from the mines to the fertile plains, and many began experiments in a kind of restless, wild agriculture. A load of lumber would be hauled to some spot on the free wilderness, where water could be easily found, and a rude box-cabin built. Then a gang-plow was procured, and a dozen mustang ponies, worth ten or fifteen dollars apiece, and with these hundreds of acres were stirred as easily as if the land had been under cultivation for years, tough, perennial roots being almost wholly absent. Thus a ranch was established, and from these bare wooden huts, as centers of desolation, the wild flora vanished in ever-widening circles. But the arch destroyers are the shepherds, with their flocks of hoofed locusts, sweeping over the ground like a fire, and trampling down every rod that escapes the plow as completely as if the whole plain were a cottage garden-plot without a fence. But notwithstanding these destroyers, a thousand swarms of bees may be pastured here for every one now gathering honey. The greater portion is still covered every season with a repressed growth of bee-flowers, for most of the species are annuals, and many of them are not relished by sheep or cattle, while the rapidity of their growth enables them to develop and mature their seeds before any foot has time to crush them. The ground is, therefore, kept sweet, and the race is perpetuated, though only as a suggestive shadow of the magnificence of its wildness.

The time will undoubtedly come when the entire area of this noble valley will be tilled like a garden, when the fertilizing waters of the mountains, now flowing to the sea, will be distributed to every acre, giving rise to prosperous towns, wealth, arts, etc. Then, I suppose, there will be few left, even among botanists, to deplore the vanished primeval flora. In the mean time, the pure waste going on—the wanton destruction of the innocents—is a sad sight to see, and the sun may well be pitied in being compelled to look on.

The bee-pastures of the Coast Ranges last longer and are more varied than those of the great plain, on account of differences of soil and climate, moisture, and shade, etc. Some of the mountains are upward of 4000 feet in height, and small streams, springs, oozy bogs, etc., occur in great abundance and variety in the wooded regions, while open parks, flooded with sunshine, and hill-girt valleys lying at different elevations, each with its own peculiar climate and exposure, possess the required conditions for the development of species and families of plants widely varied.

Next the plain there is, first, a series of smooth hills, planted with a rich and showy vegetation that differs but little from that of the plain itself—as if the edge of the plain had been lifted and bent into flowing folds, with all its flowers in place, only toned down a little as to their luxuriance, and a few new species introduced, such as the hill lupines, mints, and gilias. The colors show finely when thus held to view on the slopes; patches of red, purple, blue, yellow, and white, blending around the edges, the whole appearing at a little distance like a map colored in sections.

Above this lies the park and chaparral region, with oaks, mostly evergreen, planted wide apart, and blooming shrubs from three to ten feet high; manzanita and ceanothus of several species, mixed with rhamnus, cercis, pickeringia, cherry, amelanchier, and adenostoma, in shaggy, interlocking thickets, and many species of hosackia, clover, monardella, castilleia, etc., in the openings.

The main ranges send out spurs somewhat parallel to their axes, inclosing level valleys, many of them quite extensive, and containing a great profusion of sun-loving bee-flowers in their wild state; but these are, in great part, already lost to the bees by cultivation.

Nearer the coast are the giant forests of the redwoods, extending from near the Oregon line to Santa Cruz. Beneath the cool, deep shade of these majestic trees the ground is occupied by ferns, chiefly woodwardia and aspidiums, with only a few flowering plants—oxalis, trientalis, erythronium, fritillaria, smilax, and other shade-lovers. But all along the redwood belt there are sunny openings on hill-slopes looking to the south, where the giant trees stand back, and give the ground to the small sunflowers and the bees. Around the lofty redwood walls of these little bee-acres there is usually a fringe of Chestnut Oak, Laurel, and Madroño, the last of which is a surpassingly beautiful tree, and a great favorite with the bees. The trunks of the largest specimens are seven or eight feet thick, and about fifty feet high; the bark red and chocolate colored, the leaves plain, large, and glossy, like those of *Magnolia grandiflora*, while the flowers are yellowish-white, and urn-shaped, in well-proportioned panicles, from five to ten inches long. When in full bloom, a single tree seems to be visited at times by a whole hive of bees at once, and the deep hum of such a multitude makes the listener guess that more than the ordinary work of honey-winning must be going on.

How perfectly enchanting and care-obliterating are these withdrawn gardens of the woods—long vistas opening to the sea—sunshine sifting and pouring upon the flowery ground in a tremulous, shifting mosaic, as the light-ways in the leafy wall open and close with the swaying breeze—shining leaves and flowers, birds and bees, mingling together in springtime harmony, and soothing fragrance exhaling from a thousand thousand fountains! In these balmy, dissolving days, when the deep heart-beats of Nature are felt thrilling rocks and trees and everything alike, common business and friends are happily forgotten, and even the natural honey-work of bees, and the care of birds for their young, and mothers for their children, seem slightly out of place.

To the northward, in Humboldt and the adjacent counties, whole hillsides are covered with rhododendron, making a glorious melody of bee-bloom in the spring. And the Western azalea, hardly less flowery, grows in massy thickets three to eight feet high around the edges of groves and woods as far south as San Luis Obispo, usually accompanied by manzanita; while the valleys, with their varying moisture and shade, yield a rich variety of the smaller honey-flowers, such as mentha, lycopus, micromeria, audibertia, trichostema, and other mints; with vaccinium, wild strawberry, geranium, calais, and goldenrod; and in the cool glens along the stream-banks, where the shade of trees is not too deep, spiræa, dog-wood, heteromeles, and calycanthus, and many species of rubus form interlacing tangles, some portion of which continues in bloom for months.

Though the coast region was the first to be invaded and settled by white men, it has suffered less from a bee point of view than either of the other main divisions, chiefly, no doubt, because of the unevenness of the surface, and because it is owned and protected instead of lying exposed to the flocks of the wandering "sheepmen." These remarks apply more particularly to the north half of the coast. Farther south there is less moisture, less forest shade, and the honey flora is less varied.

The Sierra region is the largest of the three main divisions of the bee-lands of the State, and the most regularly varied in its subdivisions, owing to their gradual rise from the level of the Central Plain to the alpine summits. The foot-hill region is about as dry and sunful, from the end of May until the setting in of the winter rains, as the plain. There are no shady forests, no damp glens, at all like those lying at the same elevations in the Coast Mountains. The social compositæ of the plain, with a few added species, form the bulk of the herbaceous portion of the vegetation up to a height of 1500 feet or more, shaded lightly here and there with oaks and Sabine Pines, and interrupted by patches of ceanothus and buckeye. Above this, and just below the forest region, there is a dark, heath-like belt of chaparral, composed almost exclusively of *Adenostoma fasciculata*, a bush belonging to the rose family, from five to eight feet high, with small, round leaves in fascicles, and bearing a multitude of small white flowers in panicles on the ends of the upper branches. Where it occurs at all, it usually covers all the ground with a close, impenetrable growth, scarcely broken for miles.

Up through the forest region, to a height of about 9000 feet above sea-level, there are ragged patches of manzanita, and five or six species of ceanothus, called deer-brush or California lilac. These are the most important of all the honey-bearing bushes of the Sierra. *Chamæbatia foliolosa*, a little shrub about a foot high, with flowers like the strawberry, makes handsome carpets beneath the pines, and seems to be a favorite with the bees; while pines themselves furnish unlimited quantities of pollen and honey-dew. The product of a single tree, ripening its pollen at the right time of year, would be sufficient for the wants of a whole hive. Along the streams there is a rich growth of lilies, larkspurs, pedicularis, castilleias, and clover. The alpine region contains the flowery glacier meadows, and countless small gardens in all sorts of places full of potentilla of several species, spraguea, ivesia, epilobium, and goldenrod, with beds of bryanthus and the charming cassiope covered with sweet bells. Even the tops of the mountains are blessed with flowers,—dwarf phlox, polemonium, ribes, hulsea, etc. I have seen wild bees and butterflies feeding at a height of 13,000 feet above the sea. Many, however, that go up these dangerous heights never come down again. Some, undoubtedly, perish in storms, and I have found thousands lying dead or benumbed on the surface of the glaciers, to which they had perhaps been attracted by the white glare, taking them for beds of bloom.

From swarms that escaped their owners in the lowlands, the honey-bee is now generally distributed throughout the whole length of the Sierra, up to an elevation of 8000 feet above sea-level. At this height they flourish without care, though the snow every winter is deep. Even higher than this several bee-trees have been cut which contained over 200 pounds of honey.

The destructive action of sheep has not been so general on the mountain pastures as on those of the great plain, but in many places it has been more complete, owing to the more friable character of the soil, and its sloping position. The slant digging and down-raking action of hoofs on the steeper slopes of moraines has uprooted and buried many of the tender plants from year to year, without allowing them time to mature their seeds. The shrubs, too, are badly bitten, especially the various species of ceanothus. Fortunately, neither sheep nor cattle care to feed on the manzanita, spiræa, or adenostoma; and these fine honey-bushes are too stiff and tall, or grow in places too rough and inaccessible, to be trodden under foot. Also the cañon walls and gorges, which form so considerable a part of the area of the range, while inaccessible to domestic sheep, are well fringed with honey-shrubs, and contain thousands of lovely bee-gardens, lying hid in narrow side-cañons and recesses fenced with avalanche taluses, and on the top of flat, projecting headlands, where only bees would think to look for them.

But, on the other hand, a great portion of the woody plants that escape the feet and teeth of the sheep are destroyed by the shepherds by means of running fires, which are set everywhere during the dry autumn for the purpose of burning off the old fallen trunks and underbrush, with a view to improving the pastures, and making more open ways for the flocks. These destructive sheep-fires sweep through nearly the entire forest belt of the range, from one extremity to the other, consuming not only the underbrush, but the young trees and seedlings on which the permanence of the forests depends; thus setting in motion a long train of evils which will certainly reach far beyond bees and bee-keepers.

The plow has not yet invaded the forest region to any appreciable extent, neither has it accomplished much in the foot-hills. Thousands of bee-ranches might be established along the margin of the plain, and up to a height of 4000 feet, wherever water could be obtained. The climate at this elevation admits of the making of permanent homes, and by moving the hives to higher pastures as the lower pass out of bloom, the annual yield of honey would be nearly doubled. The foot-hill pastures, as we have seen, fail about the end of May, those of the chaparral belt and lower forests are in full bloom in June, those of the upper and alpine region in July, August, and September. In Scotland, after the best of the Lowland bloom is past, the bees are carried in carts to the Highlands, and set free on the heather hills. In France, too, and in Poland, they are carried from pasture to pasture among orchards and fields in the same way, and along the rivers in barges to collect the honey of the delightful vegetation of the banks. In Egypt they are taken far up the Nile, and floated slowly home again, gathering the honey-harvest of the various fields on the way, timing their movements in accord with the seasons. Were similar methods pursued in California the productive season would last nearly all the year.

The average elevation of the north half of the Sierra is, as we have seen, considerably less than that of the south half, and small streams, with the bank and meadow gardens dependent upon them, are less abundant. Around the head waters of the Yuba, Feather, and Pitt rivers, the extensive table-lands of lava are sparsely planted with pines, through which the sunshine reaches the ground with little interruption. Here flourishes a scattered, tufted growth of golden applopappus, linosyris, bahia, wyetheia, arnica, artemisia, and similar plants; with manzanita, cherry, plum, and thorn in ragged patches on the cooler hill-slopes. At the extremities of the Great Central Plain, the Sierra and Coast Ranges curve around and lock together in a labyrinth of mountains and valleys, throughout which their floras are mingled, making at the north, with its temperate climate and copious rainfall, a perfect paradise for bees, though, strange to say, scarcely a single regular bee-ranch has yet been established in it.

Of all the upper flower fields of the Sierra, Shasta is the most honeyful, and may yet surpass in fame the celebrated honey hills of Hybla and hearthy Hymettus. Regarding this noble mountain from a bee point of view, encircled by its many climates, and sweeping aloft from the torrid plain into the frosty azure, we find the first 5000 feet from the summit generally snow-clad, and therefore about as honeyless as the sea. The base of this arctic region is girdled by a belt of crumbling lava measuring about 1000 feet in vertical breadth, and is mostly free from snow in summer. Beautiful lichens enliven the faces of the cliffs with their bright colors, and in some of the warmer nooks there are a few tufts of alpine daisies, wallflowers and pentstemons; but, notwithstanding these bloom freely in the late summer, the zone as a whole is almost as honeyless as the icy summit, and its lower edge may be taken as the honey-line. Immediately below this comes the forest zone, covered with a rich growth of conifers, chiefly Silver Firs, rich in pollen and honey-dew, and diversified with countless garden openings, many of them less than a hundred yards across. Next, in orderly succession, comes the great bee zone. Its area far surpasses that of the icy summit and both the other zones combined, for it goes sweeping majestically around the entire mountain, with a breadth of six or seven miles and a circumference of nearly a hundred miles.

Shasta, as we have already seen, is a fire-mountain created by a succession of eruptions of ashes and molten lava, which, flowing over the lips of its several craters, grew outward and upward like the trunk of a knotty exogenous tree. Then followed a strange contrast. The glacial winter came on, loading the cooling mountain with ice, which flowed slowly outward in every direction, radiating from the summit in the form of one vast conical glacier—a down-crawling mantle of ice upon a fountain of smoldering fire, crushing and grinding for centuries its brown, flinty lavas with incessant activity, and thus degrading and remodeling the entire mountain. When, at length, the glacial period began to draw near its close, the ice-mantle was gradually melted off around the bottom, and, in receding and breaking into its present fragmentary condition, irregular rings and heaps of moraine matter were stored upon its flanks. The glacial erosion of most of the Shasta lavas produces detritus, composed of rough, sub-angular boulders of moderate size and of porous gravel and sand, which yields freely to the transporting power of running water. Magnificent floods from the ample fountains of ice and snow working with sublime energy upon this prepared glacial detritus, sorted it out and carried down immense quantities from the higher slopes, and reformed it in smooth, delta-like beds around the base; and it is these flood-beds joined together that now form the main honey-zone of the old volcano.

Thus, by forces seemingly antagonistic and destructive, has Mother Nature accomplished her beneficent designs—now a flood of fire, now a flood of ice, now a flood of water; and at length an outburst of organic life, a milky way of snowy petals and wings, girdling the rugged mountain like a cloud, as if the vivifying sunbeams beating against its sides had broken into a foam of plant-bloom and bees, as sea-waves break and bloom on a rock shore.

In this flowery wilderness the bees rove and revel, rejoicing in the bounty of the sun, clambering eagerly through bramble and hucklebloom, ringing the myriad bells of the manzanita, now humming aloft among polleny willows and firs, now down on the ashy ground among gilias and buttercups, and anon plunging deep into snowy banks of cherry and buckthorn. They consider the lilies and roll into them, and, like lilies, they toil not, for they are impelled by sun-power, as water-wheels by water-power; and when the one has plenty of high-pressure water, the other plenty of sunshine, they hum and quiver alike. Sauntering in the Shasta bee-lands in the sun-days of summer, one may readily infer the time of day from the comparative energy of bee-movements alone—drowsy and moderate in the cool of the morning, increasing in energy with the ascending sun, and, at high noon, thrilling and quivering in wild ecstasy, then gradually declining again to the stillness of night. In my excursions among the glaciers I occasionally meet bees that are hungry, like mountaineers who venture too far and remain too long above the bread-line; then they droop and wither like autumn leaves. The Shasta bees are perhaps better fed than any others in the Sierra. Their field-work is one perpetual feast; but, however exhilarating the sunshine or bountiful the supply of flowers, they are always dainty feeders. Humming-moths and humming-birds seldom set foot upon a flower, but poise on the wing in front of it, and reach forward as if they were sucking through straws. But bees, though as dainty as they, hug their favorite flowers with profound cordiality, and push their blunt, polleny faces against them, like babies on their mother's bosom. And fondly, too, with eternal love, does Mother Nature clasp her small bee-babies, and suckle them, multitudes at once, on her warm Shasta breast.

Besides the common honey-bee there are many other species here—fine mossy, burly fellows, who were nourished on the mountains thousands of sunny seasons before the advent of the domestic species. Among these are the bumblebees, mason-bees, carpenter-bees, and leaf-cutters. Butterflies, too, and moths of every size and pattern; some broad-winged like bats, flapping slowly, and sailing in easy curves; others like small, flying violets, shaking about loosely in short, crooked flights close to the flowers, feasting luxuriously night and day. Great numbers of deer also delight to dwell in the brushy portions of the bee-pastures.

Bears, too, roam the sweet wilderness, their blunt, shaggy forms harmonizing well with the trees and tangled bushes, and with the bees, also, notwithstanding the disparity in size. They are fond of all good things, and enjoy them to the utmost, with but little troublesome discrimination—flowers and leaves as well as berries, and the bees themselves as well as their honey. Though the California bears have as yet had but little experience with honey-bees, they often succeed in reaching their bountiful stores, and it seems doubtful whether bees themselves enjoy honey with so great a relish. By means of their powerful teeth and claws they can gnaw and tear open almost any hive conveniently accessible. Most honey-bees, however, in search of a home are wise enough to make choice of a hollow in a living tree, a considerable distance above the ground, when such places are to be had; then they are pretty secure, for though the smaller black and brown bears climb well, they are unable to break into strong hives while compelled to exert themselves to keep from falling, and at the same time to endure the stings of the fighting bees without having their paws free to rub them off. But woe to the black bumblebees discovered in their mossy nests in the ground! With a few strokes of their huge paws the bears uncover the entire establishment, and, before time is given for a general buzz, bees old and young, larvæ, honey, stings, nest, and all are taken in one ravishing mouthful.

Not the least influential of the agents concerned in the superior sweetness of the Shasta flora are its storms—storms I mean that are strictly local, bred and born on the mountain. The magical rapidity with which they are grown on the mountain-top, and bestow their charity in rain and snow, never fails to astonish the inexperienced lowlander. Often in calm, glowing days, while the bees are still on the wing, a storm-cloud may be seen far above in the pure ether, swelling its pearl bosses, and growing silently, like a plant. Presently a clear, ringing discharge of thunder is heard, followed by a rush of wind that comes sounding over the bending woods like the roar of the ocean, mingling raindrops, snow-flowers, honey-flowers, and bees in wild storm harmony.

Still more impressive are the warm, reviving days of spring in the mountain pastures. The blood of the plants throbbing beneath the life-giving sunshine seems to be heard and felt. Plant growth goes on before our eyes, and every tree in the woods, and every bush and flower is seen as a hive of restless industry. The deeps of the sky are mottled with singing wings of every tone and color; clouds of brilliant chrysididæ dancing and swirling in exquisite rhythm, golden-barred vespidæ, dragon-flies, butterflies, grating cicadas, and jolly, rattling grasshoppers, fairly enameling the light.

On bright, crisp mornings a striking optical effect may frequently be observed from the shadows of the higher mountains while the sunbeams are pouring past overhead. Then every insect, no matter what may be its own proper color, burns white in the light. Gauzy-winged hymenoptera, moths, jet-black beetles, all are transfigured alike in pure, spiritual white, like snowflakes.

In Southern California, where bee-culture has had so much skilful attention of late years, the pasturage is not more abundant, or more advantageously varied as to the number of its honey-plants and their distribution over mountain and plain, than that of many other portions of the State where the industrial currents flow in other channels. The famous White Sage (*Audibertia*), belonging to the mint family, flourishes here in all its glory, blooming in May, and yielding great quantities of clear, pale honey, which is greatly prized in every market it has yet reached. This species grows chiefly in the valleys and low hills. The Black Sage on the mountains is part of a dense, thorny chaparral, which is composed chiefly of adenostoma, ceanothus, manzanita, and cherry—not differing greatly from that of the southern portion of the Sierra, but more dense and continuous, and taller, and remaining longer in bloom. Stream-side gardens, so charming a feature of both the Sierra and Coast Mountains, are less numerous in Southern California, but they are exceedingly rich in honey-flowers, wherever found,—melilotus, columbine, collinsia, verbena, zauschneria, wild rose, honeysuckle, philadelphus, and lilies rising from the warm, moist dells in a very storm of exuberance. Wild buckwheat of many species is developed in abundance over the dry, sandy valleys and lower slopes of the mountains, toward the end of summer, and is, at this time, the main dependence of the bees, reinforced here and there by orange groves, alfalfa fields, and small home gardens.

The main honey months, in ordinary seasons, are April, May, June, July, and August; while the other months are usually flowery enough to yield sufficient for the bees.

According to Mr. J. T. Gordon, President of the Los Angeles County Bee-keepers' Association, the first bees introduced into the county were a single hive, which cost $150 in San Francisco, and arrived in September, 1854.* In April, of the following year, this hive sent out two swarms, which were sold for $100 each. From this small beginning the bees grad-

*Fifteen hives of Italian bees were introduced into Los Angeles County in 1855, and in 1876 they had increased to 500. The marked superiority claimed for them over the common species is now attracting considerable attention.

ually multiplied to about 3000 swarms in the year 1873. In 1876 it was estimated that there were between 15,000 and 20,000 hives in the county, producing an annual yield of about 100 pounds to the hive—in some exceptional cases, a much greater yield.

In San Diego County, at the beginning of the season of 1878, there were about 24,000 hives, and the shipments from the one port of San Diego for the same year, from July 17 to November 10, were 1071 barrels, 15,544 cases, and nearly 90 tons. The largest bee-ranches have about a thousand hives, and are carefully and skilfully managed, every scientific appliance of merit being brought into use. There are few bee-keepers, however, who own half as many as this, or who give their undivided attention to the business. Orange culture, at present, is heavily overshadowing every other business.

A good many of the so-called bee-ranches of Los Angeles and San Diego counties are still of the rudest pioneer kind imaginable. A man unsuccessful in everything else hears the interesting story of the profits and comforts of bee-keeping, and concludes to try it; he buys a few colonies, or gets them from some overstocked ranch on shares, takes them back to the foot of some cañon, where the pasturage is fresh, squats on the land, with, or without, the permission of the owner, sets up his hives, makes a box-cabin for himself, scarcely bigger than a bee-hive, and awaits his fortune.

Bees suffer sadly from famine during the dry years which occasionally occur in the southern and middle portions of the State. If the rainfall amounts only to three or four inches, instead of from twelve to twenty, as in ordinary seasons, then sheep and cattle die in thousands, and so do these small, winged cattle, unless they are carefully fed, or removed to other pastures. The year 1877 will long be remembered as exceptionally rainless and distressing. Scarcely a flower bloomed on the dry valleys away from the stream-sides, and not a single grain-field depending upon rain was reaped. The seed only sprouted, came up a little way, and withered. Horses, cattle, and sheep grew thinner day by day, nibbling at bushes and weeds, along the shallowing edges of streams, many of which were dried up altogether, for the first time since the settlement of the country.

In the course of a trip I made during the summer of that year through Monterey, San Luis Obispo, Santa Barbara, Ventura, and Los Angeles counties, the deplorable effects of the drought were everywhere visible—leafless fields, dead and dying cattle, dead bees, and half-dead people with dusty, doleful faces. Even the birds and squirrels were in distress, though their suffering was less painfully apparent than that of the poor cattle. These were falling one by one in slow, sure starvation along the banks of the hot, sluggish streams, while thousands of buzzards correspondingly fat were sailing above them, or standing gorged on the ground beneath the trees, waiting with easy faith for fresh carcasses. The quails, prudently considering the hard times, abandoned all thought of pairing. They were too poor to marry, and so continued in flocks all through the year without attempting to rear young. The ground-squirrels, though an exceptionally industrious and enterprising race, as every farmer knows, were hard pushed for a living; not a fresh leaf or seed was to be found save in the trees, whose bossy masses of dark green foliage presented a striking contrast to the ashen baldness of the ground beneath them. The squirrels, leaving their accustomed feeding-grounds, betook themselves to the leafy oaks to gnaw out the acorn stores of the provident woodpeckers, but the latter kept up a vigilant watch upon their movements. I noticed four woodpeckers in league against one squirrel, driving the poor fellow out of an oak that they claimed. He dodged round the knotty trunk from side to side, as nimbly as he could in his famished condition, only to find a sharp bill everywhere. But the fate of the bees that year seemed the saddest of all. In different portions of Los Angeles and San Diego counties, from one half to three fourths of them died of sheer starvation. Not less than 18,000 colonies perished in these two counties alone, while in the adjacent counties the death-rate was hardly less.

Even the colonies nearest to the mountains suffered this year, for the smaller vegetation on the foot-hills was affected by the drought almost as severely as that of the valleys and plains, and even the hardy, deep-rooted chaparral, the surest dependence of the bees, bloomed sparingly, while much of it was beyond reach. Every swarm could have been saved, how-

ever, by promptly supplying them with food when their own
stores began to fail, and before they became enfeebled and
discouraged; or by cutting roads back into the mountains, and
taking them into the heart of the flowery chaparral. The Santa
Lucia, San Rafael, San Gabriel, San Jacinto, and San Bernardino ranges are almost untouched as yet save by the wild bees.
Some idea of their resources, and of the advantages and disadvantages they offer to bee-keepers, may be formed from an
excursion that I made into the San Gabriel Range about the
beginning of August of "the dry year." This range, containing
most of the characteristic features of the other ranges just
mentioned, overlooks the Los Angeles vineyards and orange
groves from the north, and is more rigidly inaccessible in the
ordinary meaning of the word than any other that I ever attempted to penetrate. The slopes are exceptionally steep and
insecure to the foot, and they are covered with thorny bushes
from five to ten feet high. With the exception of little spots
not visible in general views, the entire surface is covered with
them, massed in close hedge growth, sweeping gracefully
down into every gorge and hollow, and swelling over every
ridge and summit in shaggy, ungovernable exuberance, offering more honey to the acre for half the year than the most
crowded cloverfield. But when beheld from the open San Gabriel Valley, beaten with dry sunshine, all that was seen of the
range seemed to wear a forbidding aspect. From base to summit all seemed gray, barren, silent, its glorious chaparral appearing like dry moss creeping over its dull, wrinkled ridges
and hollows.

Setting out from Pasadena, I reached the foot of the range
about sundown; and being weary and heated with my walk
across the shadeless valley, concluded to camp for the night.
After resting a few moments, I began to look about among
the flood-boulders of Eaton Creek for a camp-ground, when
I came upon a strange, dark-looking man who had been chopping cord-wood. He seemed surprised at seeing me, so I sat
down with him on the live-oak log he had been cutting, and
made haste to give a reason for my appearance in his solitude,
explaining that I was anxious to find out something about the
mountains, and meant to make my way up Eaton Creek next
morning. Then he kindly invited me to camp with him, and

led me to his little cabin, situated at the foot of the mountains, where a small spring oozes out of a bank overgrown with wild-rose bushes. After supper, when the daylight was gone, he explained that he was out of candles; so we sat in the dark, while he gave me a sketch of his life in a mixture of Spanish and English. He was born in Mexico, his father Irish, his mother Spanish. He had been a miner, rancher, prospector, hunter, etc., rambling always, and wearing his life away in mere waste; but now he was going to settle down. His past life, he said, was of "no account," but the future was promising. He was going to "make money and marry a Spanish woman." People mine here for water as for gold. He had been running a tunnel into a spur of the mountain back of his cabin. "My prospect is good," he said, "and if I chance to strike a good, strong flow, I'll soon be worth $5000 or $10,000. For that flat out there," referring to a small, irregular patch of bouldery detritus, two or three acres in size, that had been deposited by Eaton Creek during some flood season,— "that flat is large enough for a nice orange-grove, and the bank behind the cabin will do for a vineyard, and after watering my own trees and vines I will have some water left to sell to my neighbors below me, down the valley. And then," he continued, "I can keep bees, and make money that way, too, for the mountains above here are just full of honey in the summer-time, and one of my neighbors down here says that he will let me have a whole lot of hives, on shares, to start with. You see I've a good thing; I'm all right now." All this prospective affluence in the sunken, boulder-choked flood-bed of a mountain-stream! Leaving the bees out of the count, most fortune-seekers would as soon think of settling on the summit of Mount Shasta. Next morning, wishing my hopeful entertainer good luck, I set out on my shaggy excursion.

About half an hour's walk above the cabin, I came to "The Fall," famous throughout the valley settlements as the finest yet discovered in the San Gabriel Mountains. It is a charming little thing, with a low, sweet voice, singing like a bird, as it pours from a notch in a short ledge, some thirty-five or forty feet into a round mirror-pool. The face of the cliff back of it, and on both sides, is smoothly covered and embossed with mosses, against which the white water shines out in showy relief, like a silver instrument in a velvet case. Hither come the San Gabriel lads and lassies, to gather ferns and dabble away their hot holidays in the cool water, glad to escape from their commonplace palm-gardens and orange-groves. The delicate maidenhair grows on fissured rocks within reach of the spray, while broad-leaved maples and sycamores cast soft, mellow shade over a rich profusion of bee-flowers, growing among boulders in front of the pool—the fall, the flowers, the bees, the ferny rocks, and leafy shade forming a charming little poem of wildness, the last of a series extending down the flowery slopes of Mount San Antonio through the rugged, foam-beaten bosses of the main Eaton Cañon.

From the base of the fall I followed the ridge that forms the western rim of the Eaton basin to the summit of one of the principal peaks, which is about 5000 feet above sea-level. Then, turning eastward, I crossed the middle of the basin, forcing a way over its many subordinate ridges and across its eastern rim, having to contend almost everywhere with the floweriest and most impenetrable growth of honey-bushes I had ever encountered since first my mountaineering began. Most of the Shasta chaparral is leafy nearly to the ground; here the main stems are naked for three or four feet, and interspiked with dead twigs, forming a stiff *chevaux de frise* through which even the bears make their way with difficulty. I was compelled to creep for miles on all fours, and in following the bear-trails often found tufts of hair on the bushes where they had forced themselves through.

For 100 feet or so above the fall the ascent was made possible only by tough cushions of club-moss that clung to the rock. Above this the ridge weathers away to a thin knife-blade for a few hundred yards, and thence to the summit of the range it carries a bristly mane of chaparral. Here and there small openings occur on rocky places, commanding fine views across the cultivated valley to the ocean. These I found by the tracks were favorite outlooks and resting-places for the wild animals—bears, wolves, foxes, wildcats, etc.—which abound here, and would have to be taken into account in the establishment of bee-ranches. In the deepest thickets I found wood-rat villages—groups of huts four to six feet high, built of sticks and leaves in rough, tapering piles, like musk-rat cabins. I noticed a good many bees, too, most of them wild. The tame honey-bees seemed languid and wing-weary, as if they had come all the way up from the flowerless valley.

After reaching the summit I had time to make only a hasty survey of the basin, now glowing in the sunset gold, before hastening down into one of the tributary cañons in search of water. Emerging from a particularly tedious breadth of chaparral, I found myself free and erect in a beautiful park-like grove of Mountain Live Oak, where the ground was planted with aspidiums and brier-roses, while the glossy foliage made a close canopy overhead, leaving the gray dividing trunks bare to show the beauty of their interlacing arches. The bottom of the cañon was dry where I first reached it, but a bunch of scarlet mimulus indicated water at no great distance, and I soon discovered about a bucketful in a hollow of the rock. This, however, was full of dead bees, wasps, beetles, and leaves, well steeped and simmered, and would, therefore, require boiling and filtering through fresh charcoal before it could be made available. Tracing the dry channel about a mile farther down to its junction with a larger tributary cañon, I at length discovered a lot of boulder pools, clear as crystal, brimming full, and linked together by glistening streamlets just strong enough to sing audibly. Flowers in full bloom adorned their margins, lilies ten feet high, larkspur, columbines, and luxuriant ferns, leaning and overarching in lavish abundance, while a noble old Live Oak spread its rugged arms over all. Here I camped, making my bed on smooth cobblestones.

Next day, in the channel of a tributary that heads on Mount San Antonio, I passed about fifteen or twenty gardens like the one in which I slept—lilies in every one of them, in the full pomp of bloom. My third camp was made near the middle of the general basin, at the head of a long system of cascades from ten to 200 feet high, one following the other in close succession down a rocky, inaccessible cañon, making a total descent of nearly 1700 feet. Above the cascades the main stream passes through a series of open, sunny levels, the largest of which are about an acre in size, where the wild bees and their companions were feasting on a showy growth of zauschneria, painted cups, and monardella; and gray squirrels were busy harvesting the burs of the Douglas Spruce, the only conifer I met in the basin.

The eastern slopes of the basin are in every way similar to those we have described, and the same may be said of other portions of the range. From the highest summit, far as the eye could reach, the landscape was one vast bee-pasture, a rolling wilderness of honey-bloom, scarcely broken by bits of forest or the rocky outcrops of hilltops and ridges.

Behind the San Bernardino Range lies the wild "sage-brush country," bounded on the east by the Colorado River, and extending in a general northerly direction to Nevada and along the eastern base of the Sierra beyond Mono Lake.

The greater portion of this immense region, including Owen's Valley, Death Valley, and the Sink of the Mohave, the area of which is nearly one fifth that of the entire State, is usually regarded as a desert, not because of any lack in the soil, but for want of rain, and rivers available for irrigation. Very little of it, however, is desert in the eyes of a bee.

Looking now over all the available pastures of California, it appears that the business of bee-keeping is still in its infancy. Even in the more enterprising of the southern counties, where so vigorous a beginning has been made, less than a tenth of their honey resources have as yet been developed; while in the Great Plain, the Coast Ranges, the Sierra Nevada, and the northern region about Mount Shasta, the business can hardly be said to exist at all. What the limits of its developments in the future may be, with the advantages of cheaper transportation and the invention of better methods in general, it is not easy to guess. Nor, on the other hand, are we able to measure the influence on bee interests likely to follow the destruction of the forests, now rapidly falling before fire and the ax. As to the sheep evil, that can hardly become greater than it is at the present day. In short, notwithstanding the wide-spread deterioration and destruction of every kind already effected, California, with her incomparable climate and flora, is still, as far as I know, the best of all the bee-lands of the world.

STICKEEN

TO MY DOG BLANCO

BY J. G. HOLLAND

My dear dumb friend, low lying there,
    A willing vassal at my feet;
Glad partner of my home and fare,
    My shadow in the street;

I look into your great brown eyes,
    Where love and loyal homage shine,
And wonder where the difference lies
    Between your soul and mine!
        . . . .
I scan the whole broad earth around
    For that one heart which, leal and true,
Bears friendship without end or bound,
    And find the prize in you.
        . . . .
Ah, Blanco! did I worship God
    As truly as you worship me,
Or follow where my Master trod
    With your humility:

Did I sit fondly at His feet
    As you, dear Blanco, sit at mine,
And watch Him with a love as sweet,
    My life would grow divine!

Stickeen

In the summer of 1880 I set out from Fort Wrangel in a canoe to continue the exploration of the icy region of southeastern Alaska, begun in the fall of 1879. After the necessary provisions, blankets, etc., had been collected and stowed away, and my Indian crew were in their places ready to start, while a crowd of their relatives and friends on the wharf were bidding them good-by and good-luck, my companion, the Rev. S. H. Young, for whom we were waiting, at last came aboard, followed by a little black dog, that immediately made himself at home by curling up in a hollow among the baggage. I like dogs, but this one seemed so small and worthless that I objected to his going, and asked the missionary why he was taking him.

"Such a little helpless creature will only be in the way," I said; "you had better pass him up to the Indian boys on the wharf, to be taken home to play with the children. This trip is not likely to be good for toy-dogs. The poor silly thing will be in rain and snow for weeks or months, and will require care like a baby."

But his master assured me that he would be no trouble at all; that he was a perfect wonder of a dog, could endure cold and hunger like a bear, swim like a seal, and was wondrous wise and cunning, etc., making out a list of virtues to show he might be the most interesting member of the party.

Nobody could hope to unravel the lines of his ancestry. In all the wonderfully mixed and varied dog-tribe I never saw any creature very much like him, though in some of his sly, soft, gliding motions and gestures he brought the fox to mind. He was short-legged and bunchy-bodied, and his hair, though smooth, was long and silky and slightly waved, so that when the wind was at his back it ruffled, making him look shaggy. At first sight his only noticeable feature was his fine tail, which was about as airy and shady as a squirrel's, and was carried curling forward almost to his nose. On closer inspection you might notice his thin sensitive ears, and sharp eyes with cunning tan-spots above them. Mr. Young told me that when the little fellow was a pup about the size of a woodrat he was presented to his wife by an Irish prospector at Sitka, and that on his arrival at Fort Wrangel he was adopted with enthusiasm by the Stickeen Indians as a sort of new good-luck totem, was named "Stickeen" for the tribe, and became a universal favorite; petted, protected, and admired wherever he went, and regarded as a mysterious fountain of wisdom.

On our trip he soon proved himself a queer character—odd, concealed, independent, keeping invincibly quiet, and doing many little puzzling things that piqued my curiosity. As we sailed week after week through the long intricate channels and inlets among the innumerable islands and mountains of the coast, he spent most of the dull days in sluggish ease, motionless, and apparently as unobserving as if in deep sleep. But I discovered that somehow he always knew what was going on. When the Indians were about to shoot at ducks or seals, or when anything along the shore was exciting our attention, he would rest his chin on the edge of the canoe and calmly look out like a dreamy-eyed tourist. And when he heard us talking about making a landing, he immediately roused himself to see what sort of a place we were coming to, and made ready to jump overboard and swim ashore as soon as the canoe neared the beach. Then, with a vigorous shake to get rid of the brine in his hair, he ran into the woods to hunt small game. But though always the first out of the canoe, he was always the last to get into it. When we were ready to start he could never be found, and refused to come to our call. We soon found out, however, that though we could not see him at such times, he saw us, and from the cover of the briers and huckleberry bushes in the fringe of the woods was watching the canoe with wary eye. For as soon as we were fairly off he came trotting down the beach, plunged into the surf, and swam after us, knowing well that we would cease rowing and take him in. When the contrary little vagabond came alongside, he was lifted by the neck, held at arm's length a moment to drip, and dropped aboard. We tried to cure him of this trick by compelling him to swim a long way, as if we had a mind to abandon him; but this did no good: the longer the swim the better he seemed to like it.

Though capable of great idleness, he never failed to be

ready for all sorts of adventures and excursions. One pitch-dark rainy night we landed about ten o'clock at the mouth of a salmon stream when the water was phosphorescent. The salmon were running, and the myriad fins of the onrushing multitude were churning all the stream into a silvery glow, wonderfully beautiful and impressive in the ebon darkness. To get a good view of the show I set out with one of the Indians and sailed up through the midst of it to the foot of a rapid about half a mile from camp, where the swift current dashing over rocks made the luminous glow most glorious. Happening to look back down the stream, while the Indian was catching a few of the struggling fish, I saw a long spreading fan of light like the tail of a comet, which we thought must be made by some big strange animal that was pursuing us. On it came with its magnificent train, until we imagined we could see the monster's head and eyes; but it was only Stickeen, who, finding I had left the camp, came swimming after me to see what was up.

When we camped early, the best hunter of the crew usually went to the woods for a deer, and Stickeen was sure to be at his heels, provided I had not gone out. For, strange to say, though I never carried a gun, he always followed me, forsaking the hunter and even his master to share my wanderings. The days that were too stormy for sailing I spent in the woods, or on the adjacent mountains, wherever my studies called me; and Stickeen always insisted on going with me, however wild the weather, gliding like a fox through dripping huckleberry bushes and thorny tangles of panax and rubus, scarce stirring their rain-laden leaves; wading and wallowing through snow, swimming icy streams, skipping over logs and rocks and the crevasses of glaciers with the patience and endurance of a de-termined mountaineer, never tiring or getting discouraged. Once he followed me over a glacier the surface of which was so crusty and rough that it cut his feet until every step was marked with blood; but he trotted on with Indian fortitude until I noticed his red track, and, taking pity on him, made him a set of moccasins out of a handkerchief. However great his troubles he never asked help or made any complaint, as if, like a philosopher, he had learned that without hard work and suffering there could be no pleasure worth having.

Yet none of us was able to make out what Stickeen was really good for. He seemed to meet danger and hardships without anything like reason, insisted on having his own way, never obeyed an order, and the hunter could never set him on anything, or make him fetch the birds he shot. His equanimity was so steady it seemed due to want of feeling; ordinary storms were pleasures to him, and as for mere rain, he flourished in it like a vegetable. No matter what advances you might make, scarce a glance or a tail-wag would you get for your pains. But though he was apparently as cold as a glacier and about as impervious to fun, I tried hard to make his acquaintance, guessing there must be something worth while hidden beneath so much courage, endurance, and love of wild-weathery adventure. No superannuated mastiff or bulldog grown old in office surpassed this fluffy midget in stoic dignity. He sometimes reminded me of a small, squat, unshakable desert cactus. For he never displayed a single trace of the merry, tricksy, elfish fun of the terriers and collies that we all know, nor of their touching affection and devotion. Like children, most small dogs beg to be loved and allowed to love; but Stickeen seemed a very Diogenes, asking only to be let alone: a true child of the wilderness, holding the even tenor of his hidden life with the silence and serenity of nature. His strength of character lay in his eyes. They looked as old as the hills, and as young, and as wild. I never tired of looking into them: it was like looking into a landscape; but they were small and rather deep-set, and had no explaining lines around them to give out particulars. I was accustomed to look into the faces of plants and animals, and I watched the little sphinx more and more keenly as an interesting study. But there is no estimating the wit and wisdom concealed and latent in our lower fellow mortals until made manifest by profound experiences; for it is through suffering that dogs as well as saints are developed and made perfect.

After we had explored the Sundum and Tahkoo fiords and their glaciers, we sailed through Stephen's Passage into Lynn Canal and thence through Icy Strait into Cross Sound, searching for unexplored inlets leading toward the great fountain ice-fields of the Fairweather Range. Here, while the tide was in our favor, we were accompanied by a fleet of icebergs drifting out to the ocean from Glacier Bay. Slowly we paddled around Vancouver's Point, Wimbleton, our frail canoe tossed like a feather on the massive heaving swells coming in past Cape Spenser. For miles the sound is bounded by precipitous mural cliffs, which, lashed with wave-spray and their heads hidden in clouds, looked terribly threatening and stern. Had our canoe been crushed or upset we could have made no landing here, for the cliffs, as high as those of Yosemite, sink sheer into deep water. Eagerly we scanned the wall on the north side for the first sign of an opening fiord or harbor, all of us anxious except Stickeen, who dozed in peace or gazed dreamily at the tremendous precipices when he heard us talking about them. At length we made the joyful discovery of the mouth of the inlet now called "Taylor Bay," and about five o'clock reached the head of it and encamped in a spruce grove near the front of a large glacier.

While camp was being made, Joe the hunter climbed the mountain wall on the east side of the fiord in pursuit of wild goats, while Mr. Young and I went to the glacier. We found that it is separated from the waters of the inlet by a tide-washed moraine, and extends, an abrupt barrier, all the way across from wall to wall of the inlet, a distance of about three miles. But our most interesting discovery was that it had recently advanced, though again slightly receding. A portion of the terminal moraine had been plowed up and shoved forward, uprooting and overwhelming the woods on the east side. Many of the trees were down and buried, or nearly so, others were leaning away from the ice-cliffs, ready to fall, and some stood erect, with the bottom of the ice-plow still beneath their roots and its lofty crystal spires towering high above their tops. The spectacle presented by these century-old trees standing close beside a spiry wall of ice, with their branches almost touching it, was most novel and striking. And when I climbed around the front, and a little way up the west side of the glacier, I found that it had swelled and increased in height and width in accordance with its advance, and carried away the outer ranks of trees on its bank.

On our way back to camp after these first observations I planned a far-and-wide excursion for the morrow. I awoke early, called not only by the glacier, which had been on my mind all night, but by a grand flood-storm. The wind was blowing a gale from the north and the rain was flying with the clouds in a wide passionate horizontal flood, as if it were all passing over the country instead of falling on it. The main perennial streams were booming high above their banks, and hundreds of new ones, roaring like the sea, almost covered the lofty gray walls of the inlet with white cascades and falls. I had intended making a cup of coffee and getting something like a breakfast before starting, but when I heard the storm and looked out I made haste to join it; for many of Nature's finest lessons are to be found in her storms, and if careful to keep in right relations with them, we may go safely abroad with them, rejoicing in the grandeur and beauty of their works and ways, and chanting with the old Norsemen, "The blast of the tempest aids our oars, the hurricane is our servant and drives us whither we wish to go." So, omitting breakfast, I put a piece of bread in my pocket and hurried away.

Mr. Young and the Indians were asleep, and so, I hoped, was Stickeen; but I had not gone a dozen rods before he left his bed in the tent and came boring through the blast after me. That a man should welcome storms for their exhilarating music and motion, and go forth to see God making land-scapes, is reasonable enough; but what fascination could there be in such tremendous weather for a dog? Surely nothing akin to human enthusiasm for scenery or geology. Anyhow, on he came, breakfastless, through the choking blast. I stopped and did my best to turn him back. "Now don't," I said, shouting to make myself heard in the storm, "now don't, Stickeen. What has got into your queer noddle now? You must be daft. This wild day has nothing for you. There is no game abroad, nothing but weather. Go back to camp and keep warm, get a good breakfast with your master, and be sensible for once. I can't carry you all day or feed you, and this storm will kill you."

But Nature, it seems, was at the bottom of the affair, and she gains her ends with dogs as well as with men, making us do as she likes, shoving and pulling us along her ways, how-ever rough, all but killing us at times in getting her lessons driven hard home. After I had stopped again and again, shout-ing good warning advice, I saw that he was not to be shaken off; as well might the earth try to shake off the moon. I had once led his master into trouble, when he fell on one of the topmost jags of a mountain and dislocated his arm; now the turn of his humble companion was coming. The pitiful little wanderer just stood there in the wind, drenched and blinking, saying doggedly, "Where thou goest I will go." So at last I told him to come on if he must, and gave him a piece of the bread I had in my pocket; then we struggled on together, and thus began the most memorable of all my wild days.

The level flood, driving hard in our faces, thrashed and washed us wildly until we got into the shelter of a grove on the east side of the glacier near the front, where we stopped awhile for breath and to listen and look out. The exploration of the glacier was my main object, but the wind was too high to allow excursions over its open surface, where one might be dangerously shoved while balancing for a jump on the brink of a crevasse. In the mean time the storm was a fine study. Here the end of the glacier, descending an abrupt swell of resisting rock about five hundred feet high, leans forward and falls in ice cascades. And as the storm came down the glacier from the North, Stickeen and I were beneath the main current of the blast, while favorably located to see and hear it. What a psalm the storm was singing, and how fresh the smell of the washed earth and leaves, and how sweet the still small voices of the storm! Detached wafts and swirls were coming through the woods, with music from the leaves and branches and furrowed boles, and even from the splintered rocks and ice-crags overhead, many of the tones soft and low and flute-like, as if each leaf and tree, crag and spire were a tuned reed. A broad torrent, draining the side of the glacier, now swollen by scores of new streams from the mountains, was rolling boulders along its rocky channel, with thudding, bumping, muffled sounds, rushing towards the bay with tremendous energy, as if in haste to get out of the mountains; the waters above and beneath calling to each other, and all to the ocean, their home.

Looking southward from our shelter, we had this great torrent and the forested mountain wall above it on our left, the spiry ice-crags on our right, and smooth gray gloom ahead. I tried to draw the marvelous scene in my note-book, but the rain blurred the page in spite of all my pains to shelter it, and the sketch was almost worthless. When the wind began to abate, I traced the east side of the glacier. All the trees standing on the edge of the woods were barked and bruised, showing high-ice mark in a very telling way, while tens of thousands of those that had stood for centuries on the bank of the glacier farther out lay crushed and being crushed. In many places I could see down fifty feet or so beneath the margin of the glacier-mill, where trunks from one to two feet in diameter were being ground to pulp against outstanding rock-ribs and bosses of the bank.

About three miles above the front of the glacier I climbed to the surface of it by means of axe-steps made easy for Stickeen. As far as the eye could reach, the level, or nearly level, glacier stretched away indefinitely beneath the gray sky, a seemingly boundless prairie of ice. The rain continued, and grew colder, which I did not mind, but a dim snowy look in the drooping clouds made me hesitate about venturing far from land. No trace of the west shore was visible, and in case the clouds should settle and give snow, or the wind again become violent, I feared getting caught in a tangle of crevasses. Snow-crystals, the flowers of the mountain clouds, are frail, beautiful things, but terrible when flying on storm-winds in darkening, benumbing swarms, or, when welded together into glaciers full of deadly crevasses. Watching the weather, I sauntered about on the crystal sea. For a mile or two out I found the ice remarkably safe. The marginal crevasses were mostly narrow, while the few wider ones were easily avoided by passing around them, and the clouds began to open here and there.

Thus encouraged, I at last pushed out for the other side; for Nature can make us do anything she likes. At first we made rapid progress, and the sky was not very threatening, while I took bearings occasionally with a pocket compass to enable me to find my way back more surely in case the storm should become blinding; but the structure lines of the glacier were my main guide. Toward the west side we came to a closely crevassed section in which we had to make long, narrow tacks and doublings, tracing the edges of tremendous transverse and longitudinal crevasses, many of which were from twenty to thirty feet wide, and perhaps a thousand feet deep—beautiful and awful. In working a way through them I was severely cautious, but Stickeen came on as unhesitating as the flying clouds. The widest crevasse that I could jump he would leap without so much as halting to take a look at it. The weather was now making quick changes, scattering bits of dazzling brightness through the wintry gloom; at rare intervals, when the sun broke forth wholly free, the glacier was seen from shore to shore with a bright array of encompassing mountains partly revealed, wearing the clouds as garments, while the prairie bloomed and sparkled with irised light from myriads of washed crystals. Then suddenly all the glorious show would be darkened and blotted out.

Stickeen seemed to care for none of these things, bright or dark, nor for the crevasses, wells, moulins, or swift flashing streams into which he might fall. The little adventurer was only about two years old, yet nothing seemed novel to him, nothing daunted him. He showed neither caution nor curiosity, wonder nor fear, but bravely trotted on as if glaciers were playgrounds. His stout, muffled body seemed all one skipping muscle, and it was truly wonderful to see how swiftly and to all appearance heedlessly he flashed across nerve-trying chasms six or eight feet wide. His courage was so unwavering that it seemed to be due to dullness of perception, as if he were only blindly bold; and I kept warning him to be careful. For we had been close companions on so many wilderness trips that I had formed the habit of talking to him as if he were a boy and understood every word.

We gained the west shore in about three hours; the width of the glacier here being about seven miles. Then I pushed northward in order to see as far back as possible into the fountains of the Fairweather Mountains, in case the clouds should rise. The walking was easy along the margin of the forest, which, of course, like that on the other side, had been invaded and crushed by the swollen, overflowing glacier. In an hour or so, after passing a massive headland, we came suddenly on a branch of the glacier, which, in the form of a magnificent ice-cascade two miles wide, was pouring over the rim of the main basin in a westerly direction, its surface broken into wave-shaped blades and shattered blocks, suggesting the wildest updashing, heaving, plunging motion of a great river cataract. Tracing it down three or four miles, I found that it discharged into a lake, filling it with icebergs.

I would gladly have followed the lake outlet to tide-water, but the day was already far spent, and the threatening sky called for haste on the return trip to get off the ice before dark. I decided therefore to go no farther, and, after taking a general view of the wonderful region, turned back, hoping to see it again under more favorable auspices. We made good speed up the cañon of the great ice-torrent, and out on the main glacier until we had left the west shore about two miles behind us. Here we got into a difficult network of crevasses, the gathering clouds began to drop misty fringes, and soon the dreaded snow came flying thick and fast. I now began to feel anxious about finding a way in the blurring storm. Stickeen showed no trace of fear. He was still the same silent, able little hero. I noticed, however, that after the storm-darkness came on he kept close up behind me. The snow urged us to make still greater haste, but at the same time hid our way. I pushed on as best I could, jumping innumerable crevasses, and for every hundred rods or so of direct advance traveling a mile in doubling up and down in the turmoil of chasms and dislocated ice-blocks. After an hour or two of this work we came to a series of longitudinal crevasses of appalling width, and almost straight and regular in trend, like immense furrows. These I traced with firm nerve, excited and strengthened by the danger, making wide jumps, poising cautiously on their dizzy edges after cutting hollows for my feet before making the spring, to avoid possible slipping or any uncertainty on the farther sides, where only one trial is granted—exercise at once frightful and inspiring. Stickeen followed seemingly without effort.

Many a mile we thus traveled, mostly up and down, making but little real headway in crossing, running instead of walking most of the time as the danger of being compelled to spend the night on the glacier became threatening. Stickeen seemed able for anything. Doubtless we could have weathered the storm for one night, dancing on a flat spot to keep from freezing, and I faced the threat without feeling anything like despair; but we were hungry and wet, and the wind from the

mountains was still thick with snow and bitterly cold, so of
course that night would have seemed a very long one. I could
not see far enough through the blurring snow to judge in
which general direction the least dangerous route lay, while
the few dim, momentary glimpses I caught of mountains
through rifts in the flying clouds were far from encouraging
either as weather signs or as guides. I had simply to grope my
way from crevasse to crevasse, holding a general direction by
the ice-structure, which was not to be seen everywhere, and
partly by the wind. Again and again I was put to my mettle,
but Stickeen followed easily, his nerve apparently growing
more unflinching as the danger increased. So it always is with
mountaineers when hard beset. Running hard and jumping,
holding every minute of the remaining daylight, poor as it
was, precious, we doggedly persevered and tried to hope that
every difficult crevasse we overcame would prove to be the
last of its kind. But on the contrary, as we advanced they
became more deadly trying.

At length our way was barred by a very wide and straight
crevasse, which I traced rapidly northward a mile or so without finding a crossing or hope of one; then down the glacier
about as far, to where it united with another uncrossable crevasse. In all this distance of perhaps two miles there was only
one place where I could possibly jump it, but the width of
this jump was the utmost I dared attempt, while the danger
of slipping on the farther side was so great that I was loath
to try it. Furthermore, the side I was on was about a foot
higher than the other, and even with this advantage the crevasse seemed dangerously wide. One is liable to underestimate
the width of crevasses where the magnitudes in general are
great. I therefore stared at this one mighty keenly, estimating
its width and the shape of the edge on the farther side, until
I thought that I could jump it if necessary, but that in case I
should be compelled to jump back from the lower side I
might fail. Now, a cautious mountaineer seldom takes a step
on unknown ground which seems at all dangerous that he
cannot retrace in case he should be stopped by unseen ob-
stacles ahead. This is the rule of mountaineers who live long,
and, though in haste, I compelled myself to sit down and
calmly deliberate before I broke it.

Retracing my devious path in imagination as if it were drawn on a chart, I saw that I was recrossing the glacier a mile or two farther up stream than the course pursued in the morning, and that I was now entangled in a section I had not before seen. Should I risk this dangerous jump, or try to regain the woods on the west shore, make a fire, and have only hunger to endure while waiting for a new day? I had already crossed so broad a stretch of dangerous ice that I saw it would be difficult to get back to the woods through the storm, before dark, and the attempt would most likely result in a dismal night-dance on the glacier; while just beyond the present barrier the surface seemed more promising, and the east shore was now perhaps about as near as the west. I was therefore eager to go on. But this wide jump was a dreadful obstacle.

At length, because of the dangers already behind me, I determined to venture against those that might be ahead, jumped and landed well, but with so little to spare that I more than ever dreaded being compelled to take that jump back from the lower side. Stickeen followed, making nothing of it, and we ran eagerly forward, hoping we were leaving all our troubles behind. But within the distance of a few hundred yards we were stopped by the widest crevasse yet encountered. Of course I made haste to explore it, hoping all might yet be remedied by finding a bridge or a way around either end. About three-fourths of a mile upstream I found that it united with the one we had just crossed, as I feared it would. Then, tracing it down, I found it joined the same crevasse at the lower end also, maintaining throughout its whole course a width of forty to fifty feet. Thus to my dismay I discovered that we were on a narrow island about two miles long, with two barely possible ways of escape: one back by the way we came, the other ahead by an almost inaccessible sliver-bridge that crossed the great crevasse from near the middle of it!

After this nerve-trying discovery I ran back to the sliver-bridge and cautiously examined it. Crevasses, caused by strains from variations in the rate of motion of different parts of the glacier and convexities in the channel, are mere cracks when they first open, so narrow as hardly to admit the blade of a pocket-knife, and gradually widen according to the extent of the strain and the depth of the glacier. Now some of these cracks are interrupted, like the cracks in wood, and in opening, the strip of ice between overlapping ends is dragged out, and may maintain a continuous connection between the sides, just as the two sides of a slivered crack in wood that is being split are connected. Some crevasses remain open for months or even years, and by the melting of their sides continue to increase in width long after the opening strain has ceased; while the sliver-bridges, level on top at first and perfectly safe, are at length melted to thin, vertical, knife-edged blades, the upper portion being most exposed to the weather; and since the exposure is greatest in the middle, they at length curve downward like the cables of suspension bridges. This one was evidently very old, for it had been weathered and wasted until it was the most dangerous and inaccessible that ever lay in my way. The width of the crevasse was here about fifty feet, and the sliver crossing diagonally was about seventy feet long; its thin knife-edge near the middle was depressed twenty-five or thirty feet below the level of the glacier, and the upcurving ends were attached to the sides eight or ten feet below the brink. Getting down the nearly vertical wall to the end of the sliver and up the other side were the main difficulties, and they seemed all but insurmountable. Of the many perils encountered in my years of wandering on mountains and glaciers none seemed so plain and stern and merciless as this. And it was presented when we were wet to the skin and hungry, the sky dark with quick driving snow, and the night near. But we were forced to face it. It was a tremendous necessity.

Beginning, not immediately above the sunken end of the bridge, but a little to one side, I cut a deep hollow on the brink for my knees to rest in. Then, leaning over, with my short-handled axe I cut a step sixteen or eighteen inches below, which on account of the sheerness of the wall was necessarily shallow. That step, however, was well made; its floor sloped slightly inward and formed a good hold for my heels. Then, slipping cautiously upon it, and crouching as low as possible, with my left side toward the wall, I steadied myself against the wind with my left hand in a slight notch, while with the right I cut other similar steps and notches in succession, guarding against losing balance by glinting of the axe, or by wind-gusts, for life and death were in every stroke and in the niceness of finish of every foothold.

After the end of the bridge was reached I chipped it down until I had made a level platform six or eight inches wide, and it was a trying thing to poise on this little slippery platform while bending over to get safely astride of the sliver. Crossing was then comparatively easy by chipping off the sharp edge with short, careful strokes, and hitching forward an inch or two at a time, keeping my balance with my knees pressed against the sides. The tremendous abyss on either hand I studiously ignored. To me the edge of that blue sliver was then all the world. But the most trying part of the adventure, after working my way across inch by inch and chipping another small platform, was to rise from the safe position astride and to cut a step-ladder in the nearly vertical face of the wall,— chipping, climbing, holding on with feet and fingers in mere notches. At such times one's whole body is eye, and common skill and fortitude are replaced by power beyond our call or knowledge. Never before had I been so long under deadly strain. How I got up that cliff I never could tell. The thing seemed to have been done by somebody else. I never have held death in contempt, though in the course of my explorations I have oftentimes felt that to meet one's fate on a noble mountain, or in the heart of a glacier, would be blessed as compared with death from disease, or from some shabby lowland accident. But the best death, quick and crystal-pure, set so glaringly open before us, is hard enough to face, even though we feel gratefully sure that we have already had happiness enough for a dozen lives.

But poor Stickeen, the wee, hairy, sleekit beastie, think of him! When I had decided to dare the bridge, and while I was on my knees chipping a hollow on the rounded brow above it, he came behind me, pushed his head past my shoulder, looked down and across, scanned the sliver and its approaches with his mysterious eyes, then looked me in the face with a startled air of surprise and concern, and began to mutter and whine; saying as plainly as if speaking with words, "Surely, you are not going into that awful place." This was the first time I had seen him gaze deliberately into a crevasse, or into my face with an eager, speaking, troubled look. That he should have recognized and appreciated the danger at the first glance showed wonderful sagacity. Never before had the daring midget seemed to know that ice was slippery or that there was any such thing as danger anywhere. His looks and tones of voice when he began to complain and speak his fears were so human that I unconsciously talked to him in sympathy as I would to a frightened boy, and in trying to calm his fears perhaps in some measure moderated my own. "Hush your fears, my boy," I said, "we will get across safe, though it is not going to be easy. No right way is easy in this rough world. We must risk our lives to save them. At the worst we can only slip, and then how grand a grave we will have, and by and by our nice bones will do good in the terminal moraine."

But my sermon was far from reassuring him: he began to cry, and after taking another piercing look at the tremendous gulf, ran away in desperate excitement, seeking some other crossing. By the time he got back, baffled of course, I had made a step or two. I dared not look back, but he made himself heard; and when he saw that I was certainly bent on crossing he cried aloud in despair. The danger was enough to daunt anybody, but it seems wonderful that he should have been able to weigh and appreciate it so justly. No mountaineer could have seen it more quickly or judged it more wisely, discriminating between real and apparent peril.

When I gained the other side, he screamed louder than ever, and after running back and forth in vain search for a way of escape, he would return to the brink of the crevasse above the bridge, moaning and wailing as if in the bitterness of death. Could this be the silent, philosophic Stickeen? I shouted encouragement, telling him the bridge was not so bad as it looked, that I had left it flat and safe for his feet, and he could walk it easily. But he was afraid to try. Strange so small an animal should be capable of such big, wise fears. I called again and again in a reassuring tone to come on and fear nothing; that he could come if he would only try. He would hush for a moment, look down again at the bridge, and shout his unshakable conviction that he could never, never come that way; then lie back in despair, as if howling, "O-o-oh! what a place! No-o-o, I can never go-o-o down there!" His natural com-

posure and courage had vanished utterly in a tumultuous
storm of fear. Had the danger been less, his distress would
have seemed ridiculous. But in this dismal, merciless abyss lay
the shadow of death, and his heartrending cries might well
have called Heaven to his help. Perhaps they did. So hidden
before, he was now transparent, and one could see the work-
ings of his heart and mind like the movements of a clock out
of its case. His voice and gestures, hopes and fears, were so
perfectly human that none could mistake them; while he
seemed to understand every word of mine. I was troubled at
the thought of having to leave him out all night, and of the
danger of not finding him in the morning. It seemed impossible to get him to venture. To compel him to try through
fear of being abandoned, I started off as if leaving him to his
fate, and disappeared back of a hummock; but this did no
good; he only lay down and moaned in utter hopeless misery.
So, after hiding a few minutes, I went back to the brink of
the crevasse and in a severe tone of voice shouted across to
him that now I must certainly leave him, I could wait no
longer, and that, if he would not come, all I could promise
was that I would return to seek him next day. I warned him
that if he went back to the woods the wolves would kill him,
and finished by urging him once more by words and gestures
to come on, come on.

He knew very well what I meant, and at last, with the courage of despair, hushed and breathless, he crouched down on
the brink in the hollow I had made for my knees, pressed his
body against the ice as if trying to get the advantage of the
friction of every hair, gazed into the first step, put his little
feet together and slid them slowly, slowly over the edge and
down into it, bunching all four in it and almost standing on
his head. Then, without lifting his feet, as well as I could see
through the snow, he slowly worked them over the edge of
the step and down into the next and the next in succession in
the same way, and gained the end of the bridge. Then, lifting
his feet with the regularity and slowness of the vibrations of
a seconds pendulum, as if counting and measuring *one-two-
three*, holding himself steady against the gusty wind, and giving separate attention to each little step, he gained the foot
of the cliff, while I was on my knees leaning over to give him

a lift should he succeed in getting within reach of my arm.
Here he halted in dead silence, and it was here I feared he
might fail, for dogs are poor climbers. I had no cord. If I had
had one, I would have dropped a noose over his head and
hauled him up. But while I was thinking whether an available
cord might be made out of clothing, he was looking keenly
into the series of notched steps and finger-holds I had made,
as if counting them, and fixing the position of each one of
them in his mind. Then suddenly up he came in a springy
rush, hooking his paws into the steps and notches so quickly
that I could not see how it was done, and whizzed past my
head, safe at last!

And now came a scene! "Well done, well done, little boy!
Brave boy!" I cried, trying to catch and caress him; but he
would not be caught. Never before or since have I seen anything like so passionate a revulsion from the depths of despair
to exultant, triumphant, uncontrollable joy. He flashed and
darted hither and thither as if fairly demented, screaming and
shouting, swirling round and round in giddy loops and circles
like a leaf in a whirlwind, lying down, and rolling over and
over, sidewise and heels over head, and pouring forth a tumultuous flood of hysterical cries and sobs and gasping mut-
terings. When I ran up to him to shake him, fearing he might
die of joy, he flashed off two or three hundred yards, his feet
in a mist of motion; then, turning suddenly, came back in a
wild rush and launched himself at my face, almost knocking
me down, all the time screeching and screaming and shouting
as if saying, "Saved! saved! saved!" Then away again, dropping
suddenly at times with his feet in the air, trembling and fairly
sobbing. Such passionate emotion was enough to kill him.
Moses' stately song of triumph after escaping the Egyptians
and the Red Sea was nothing to it. Who could have guessed
the capacity of the dull, enduring little fellow for all that most
stirs this mortal frame? Nobody could have helped crying with
him!

But there is nothing like work for toning down excessive
fear or joy. So I ran ahead, calling him in as gruff a voice as
I could command to come on and stop his nonsense, for we
had far to go and it would soon be dark. Neither of us feared
another trial like this. Heaven would surely count one enough

for a lifetime. The ice ahead was gashed by thousands of crevasses, but they were common ones. The joy of deliverance burned in us like fire, and we ran without fatigue, every muscle with immense rebound glorying in its strength. Stickeen flew across everything in his way, and not till dark did he settle into his normal fox-like trot. At last the cloudy mountains came in sight, and we soon felt the solid rock beneath our feet, and were safe. Then came weakness. Danger had vanished, and so had our strength. We tottered down the lateral moraine in the dark, over boulders and tree trunks, through the bushes and devil-club thickets of the grove where we had sheltered ourselves in the morning, and across the level mudslope of the terminal moraine. We reached camp about ten o'clock, and found a big fire and a big supper. A party of Hoona Indians had visited Mr. Young, bringing a gift of porpoise meat and wild strawberries, and Hunter Joe had brought in a wild goat. But we lay down, too tired to eat much, and soon fell into a troubled sleep. The man who said, "The harder the toil, the sweeter the rest," never was profoundly tired. Stickeen kept springing up and muttering in his sleep, no doubt dreaming that he was still on the brink of the crevasse; and so did I, that night and many others long afterward, when I was overtired.

Thereafter Stickeen was a changed dog. During the rest of the trip, instead of holding aloof, he always lay by my side, tried to keep me constantly in sight, and would hardly accept a morsel of food, however tempting, from any hand but mine. At night, when all was quiet about the camp-fire, he would come to me and rest his head on my knee with a look of devotion as if I were his god. And often as he caught my eye he seemed to be trying to say, "Wasn't that an awful time we had together on the glacier?"

Nothing in after years has dimmed that Alaska storm-day. As I write it all comes rushing and roaring to mind as if I were again in the heart of it. Again I see the gray flying clouds with their rain-floods and snow, the ice-cliffs towering above the shrinking forest, the majestic ice-cascade, the vast glacier outspread before its white mountain fountains, and in the heart of it the tremendous crevasse,—emblem of the valley of the shadow of death,—low clouds trailing over it, the snow falling into it; and on its brink I see little Stickeen, and I hear his cries for help and his shouts of joy. I have known many dogs, and many a story I could tell of their wisdom and devotion; but to none do I owe so much as to Stickeen. At first the least promising and least known of my dog-friends, he suddenly became the best known of them all. Our storm-battle for life brought him to light, and through him as through a window I have ever since been looking with deeper sympathy into all my fellow mortals.

None of Stickeen's friends knows what finally became of him. After my work for the season was done I departed for California, and I never saw the dear little fellow again. In reply to anxious inquiries his master wrote me that in the summer of 1883 he was stolen by a tourist at Fort Wrangel and taken away on a steamer. His fate is wrapped in mystery. Doubtless he has left this world—crossed the last crevasse—and gone to another. But he will not be forgotten. To me Stickeen is immortal.

SELECTED ESSAYS

Contents

Yosemite Glaciers

YOSEMITE VALLEY, Cal., Sept. 28.—Two years ago, when picking flowers in the mountains back of Yosemite Valley, I found a book. It was blotted and storm-beaten; all of its outer pages were mealy and crumbly, the paper seeming to dissolve like the snow beneath which it had been buried; but many of the inner pages were well preserved, and though all were more or less stained and torn, whole chapters were easily readable. In just this condition is the great open book of Yosemite glaciers to-day; its granite pages have been torn and blurred by the same storms that wasted the castaway book. The grand central chapters of the Hoffman, and Tenaya, and Nevada glaciers are stained and corroded by the frosts and rains, yet, nevertheless, they contain scarce one unreadable page; but the outer chapters of the Pohono, and the Illilouette, and the Yosemite Creek, and Ribbon, and Cascade glaciers, are all dimmed and eaten away on the bottom, though the tops of their pages have not been so long exposed, and still proclaim in splendid characters the glorious actions of their departed ice. The glacier which filled the basin of Yosemite Creek was the fourth ice-stream that flowed to Yosemite Valley. It was about fifteen miles in length by five in breadth at the middle of the main stream, and in many places was not less than 1,000 feet in depth. It united with the central glaciers in the valley by a mouth reaching from the east side of El Capitan to Yosemite Point, east of the falls. Its western rim was rayed with short tributaries, and on the north its divide from the Tuolumne glacier was deeply grooved; but few if any of its ridges were here high enough to separate the descending ice into distinct tributaries. The main central trunk flowed nearly south, and, at a distance of about 10 miles, separated into three nearly equal branches, which were turned abruptly to the east.

BRANCH BASINS.

Those branch basins are laid among the highest spurs of the Hoffman range, and abound in small, bright lakes, set in the

solid granite without the usual terminal moraine dam. The
structure of those dividing spurs is exactly similar, all three
appearing as if ruins of one mountain, or rather as perfect
units hewn from one mountain rock during long ages of glacial activity. As their north sides are precipitous, and as they
extend east and west, they were enabled to shelter and keep
alive their hiding glaciers long after the death of the main
trunk. Their basins are still dazzling bright, and their lakes
have as yet accumulated but narrow rings of border meadow,
because their feeding streams have had but little time to carry
the sand of which they are made. The east bank of the main
stream, all the way from the three forks to the mouth, is a
continuous, regular wall, which also forms the west bank of
Indian Cañon glacier-basin. The tributaries of the west side
of the main basin touched the east tributaries of the cascade,
and the great Tuolumne glacier from Mount Dana, the mightiest ice-river of this whole region, flowed past on the north.
The declivity of the tributaries was great, especially those
which flowed from the spurs of the Hoffman on the Tuolumne divide, but the main stream was rather level, and in
approaching Yosemite was compelled to make a considerable
ascent back of Eagle Cliff. To the concentrated currents of the
central glaciers, and to the levelness and width of mouth of
this one, we in a great measure owe the present height of the
Yosemite Falls. Yosemite Creek lives the most tranquil life of
all the large streams that leap into the valley, the others occupying the cañons of narrower and, consequently, of deeper
glaciers, while yet far from the valley, abound in loud falls and
snowy cascades, but Yosemite Creek flows straight on through
smooth meadows and hollows, with only two or three gentle
cascades, and now and then a row of soothing, rumbling
rapids, biding its time, and hoarding up the best music and
poetry of its life for the one anthem at Yosemite, as planned
by the ice.

YOSEMITE BASIN.

When a birdseye view of Yosemite Basin is obtained from
any of its upper domes, it is seen to possess a great number
of dense patches of black forest, planted in abrupt contact
with bare gray rocks. Those forest plots mark the number and

the size of all the entire and fragmentary moraines of the basin, as the later eroding agents have not yet had sufficient time to form a soil fit for the vigorous life of large trees.

Wherever a deep-wombed tributary was laid against a narrow ridge, and was also shielded from the sun by compassing rock-shadows, there we invariably find one or more small terminal moraines, because when such tributaries were melted off from the trunk they retired to those upper strongholds of shade, and lived and worked in full independence, and the moraines which they built are left entire because the water-collecting basins behind them are too small to make streams large enough to wash them away; but in the basins of exposed tributaries there are no terminal moraines, because their glaciers died *with* the trunk. Medial and lateral moraines are common upon all the outside slopes, some of them nearly perfect in form; but down in the main basin there is not left one unaltered moraine of any kind, immense floods having washed down and leveled them into border meadows for the present stream, and into sandy flower-beds and fields for forests.

GLACIER HISTORY.

Such was Yosemite glacier, and such is its basin, the magnificent work of its hands. There is sublimity in the life of a glacier. Water rivers work openly, and so do the rains and the gentle dews, and the great sea also grasping all the world; and even this universal ocean of breath, though invisible, yet speaks aloud in a thousand voices, and proclaims its modes of working and its power; but glaciers work apart from men, exerting their tremendous energies in silence and darkness, outspread, spirit-like, brooding above predestined rocks unknown to light, unborn, working on unwearied through unmeasured times, unhalting as the stars, until at length, their creations complete, their mountains brought forth, homes made for the meadows and the lakes, moraine banks for chosen flowers, and fields for waiting forests, earnest, calm as when they came in crystals from the sky, they depart.

The great valley itself, together with all of its various domes and walls, was brought forth and fashioned by a grand combination of glaciers, acting in certain directions against granite of peculiar physical structure. All of the rocks and mountains and lakes and meadows of the whole upper Merced basin received their specific forms and carvings almost entirely from this same agency of ice.

I have been drifting about among the rocks of this region for several years, anxious to spell out some of the mountain truths which are written here; and since the number, and magnitude, and significance of these ice rivers began to appear, I have become anxious for more exact knowledge regarding them; with this object, supplying myself with blankets and bread, I climbed out of Yosemite by Indian Cañon, and am now searching the upper rocks and moraines for readable glacier manuscript.

I meant to begin by exploring the main trunk glacier of Yosemite Creek, together with all of its rim tributaries one by one, gathering what data I could find regarding their depth, direction of flow, the kind and amount of work which each had done, etc., but when I was upon the El Capitan Mountain, seeking for the western shore of the main stream, I discovered that the Yosemite Creek glacier was not the lowest ice stream which flowed to the valley, but that the Ribbon Stream basin west of El Capitan had also been occupied by a glacier, which flowed nearly south, and united with the main central glaciers of the summits in the valley below El Capitan.

RIBBON STREAM BASIN.

I spent two days in this new basin. It must have been one of the smallest ice streams that entered the valley being only about four miles in length by three in width. It received some small tributaries from the slopes of El Capitan ridge, which flowed south 35° west; but most of its ice was derived from a spur of the Hoffman group, running nearly south-west. The slope of its bed is steep and pretty regular, and it must have flowed with considerable velocity. I have not thus far discovered any of the original striated surfaces, though possibly some patches may still exist somewhere in the basin upon hard plates of quartz, or where a bowlder of protecting form has settled upon a rounded surface. I found many such patches in the basin of Yosemite Glacier; one within half a mile of the top of the falls—about two feet square in extent of surface, very perfect in polish, and its striæ distinct, although the surrounding unprotected rock is disintegrated to a depth of at least four inches. As this small glacier sloped fully with unsheltered bosom to the sun, it was one of the first to die, and of course its tablets have been longer exposed to blurring rains and dews, and all eroding agents; but notwithstanding the countless blotting, crumbling storms which have fallen upon the historic lithographs of its surface, the great truth of its former existence printed in characters of moraine and meadow and valley groove, is still as clear as when every one of its pebbles and new-born rocks gleamed forth the full unshadowed poetry of its whole life. With the exception of a few castled piles and broken domes upon its east banks, its basin is rather smooth and lake-like, but it has charming meadows, most interesting in their present flora and glacier history, and noble forests of the two silver firs (Picea Amabilis and P. grandis) planted upon moraines spread out and leveled by overflowing waters.

These researches in the basin of the Ribbon Creek recalled some observations made by me some time ago in the lower portions of the basins of the Cascade and Tamarac streams, and I now thought it probable that careful search would discover abundant traces of glacial action in those basins also. Accordingly, on reaching the highest northern slope of the Ribbon, I obtained comprehensive views of both the Cascade and Tamarac basins, and amid their countless adornments could note many forms of lake and rock which appeared as genuine glacier characters unmarred and unaltered. Running down the bare slope of an icy-looking cañon, in less than half an hour I came upon a large patch of the old glacier bed, polished and striated, with the direction of the flow of the long dead stream clearly written—South 40° West. This proved to be the lowest, easternmost tributary of the Cascade glacier. I proceeded westward as far as the Cascade meadows on the Mono trail, then turning to the right, entered the mouth of the tributary at the head of the meadows. Here there is a well-defined terminal moraine, and the ends of both ridges which formed the banks of the ice are broken and precipitous, giving evidence of great pressure. I followed up this tributary to its source on the west bank of the Yosemite glacier about two miles north of the Mono trail, and throughout its entire length there is abundance of polished tablets with moraines, rock sculpture, etc., giving glacier testimony as clear and indisputable as can be found in the most recent glacier pathways of the Alps.

VANISHED GLACIERS.

I would gladly have explored the main trunk of this beautiful basin, from its highest snows upon the divide of the Tuolumne, to its mouth in the Merced Cañon below Yosemite, but alas! I had not sufficient bread, besides I felt sure that I should also have to explore the Tamarac basin, and, following westward among the fainter, most changed, and covered glacier pathways, I might probably be called as far as the end of the Pilot Peak Ridge. Therefore, I concluded to leave those lower chapters for future lessons, and go on with the easier Yosemite pages which I had already begun.

But before taking leave of those lower streams let me distinctly state, that in my opinion future investigation will discover proofs of the existence in the earlier ages of Sierra Nevada ice, of vast glaciers which flowed to the very foot of the range. Already it is clear that all of the upper basins were filled with ice so deep and universal, that but few of the highest crests and ridges were sufficiently great to separate it into individual glaciers, many of the highest mountains having been flowed over and rounded like the bowlders in a river. Glaciers poured into Yosemite by every one of its cañons; and at a comparatively recent period of its history its northern wall, with perhaps the single exception of the crest of Eagle Cliff, was covered by one unbroken flow of ice, the several glaciers having united before they reached the wall.

SEPTEMBER 30.—Last evening I was camped in a small round glacier meadow, at the head of the easternmost tributary of the cascade. The meadow was velvet with grass, and circled with the most beautiful of all the coniferæ, the Williamson spruce. I built a great fire, and the daisies of the sod rayed as if conscious of a sun. As I lay on my back, feeling the presence of the trees—gleaming upon the dark, and gushing with life—coming closer and closer about me, and saw the small round sky coming down with its stars to dome my trees, I said, "Never was mountain mansion more beautiful, more

spiritual; never was mortal wanderer more blessedly homed."
When the sun rose, my charmed walls were taken down, the
trees returned to the common fund of the forest, and my little
sky fused back into the measureless blue, I was left upon common ground to follow my glacial labor.

YOSEMITE RIVER BASINS.

I followed the main Yosemite River northward, passing
round the head of the second Yosemite tributary, which
flowed about north-east until bent southward by the main
current. About noon I came to the basin of the third ice tributary of the west rim, a place of domes which had long engaged my attention, and as I was anxious to study their
structure, and the various moraines, &c., of the little glacier
which had issued from their midst, I camped here close to the
foot of two of the most beautiful of the domes, in a sheltered
hollow, the womb of the glacier. At the foot of these two
domes are two lakes exactly alike in size and history, beautiful
as any I ever beheld; first there is the crystal water center, then
a yellowish fringe of Carex, which has long arching leaves that
dip to the water; then a beveled bossy border of yellow Sphagnum moss, exactly marking the limits of the lake; further back
is a narrow zone of dryer meadow, smooth and purple with
grasses which grow in soft plushy sods, interrupted here and
there by clumpy gatherings of blue berry bushes. The purple
Kalmia grows here also, and the splendidly flowered Phyllo-
doce; but these are small, and weave into the sod, spreading
low in the grasses and glowing with them. Beside these flowering shrubs, the meadow is lightly sprinkled with daisies, and
dodecatheons and white violets, most lovely meadows divinely
adjusted to most lovely lakes.

In the afternoon I followed down the bed of the tributary
to its junction with the main glacier; then, turning to the
right, crossed the mouths of the first two tributaries which I
had passed in the morning; then, bearing east, examined a
cross section of the main trunk, and reached camp by following up the north bank of the tributary. Between the three
tributaries above-mentioned are well-defined medial moraines,
having been preserved from leveling floods by their position
on the higher slopes, with but small water-collecting basins

behind them. Down at their junctions, where they were swept round by the main stream, is a large, level field of moraine matter, which, like all the drift-fields of this basin, is planted with heavy forests, composed mainly of a pine and fir (Pinus contarta, and Picea amabilis). This forest is now on fire. I wanted to pass through it, but feared the falling trees. As I stood watching the flapping flames and estimating chances, a tall blazing pine crashed across the gap which I wished to pass, and in a few minutes two more fell. This stirred a broken thought about special providences, and caused me to go around out of danger. Pinus contorta is very susceptible of fire, as it grows very close, in grovy thickets, and usually every tree is trickled and beaded with gum. The summit forests are almost entirely composed of this pine.

DEER IN THE VALLEY.

Emerging from this wooded moraine I found a great quantity of loose separate bowlders upon a polished hilltop, which had formed a part of the bottom of the main ice stream. They were of extraordinary size, some large as houses, and I started northward to seek the mountain from which they had been torn. I had gone but a little way when I discovered a deer quietly feeding upon a narrow strip of green meadow about sixty or seventy yards ahead of me. As the wind blew gently toward it, I thought the opportunity good for testing the truth of hunters' accounts of the deer's wonderful keenness of scent, and stood quite still, and as the deer continued to feed tranquilly, only casting round his head upon his shoulder occasionally to drive away the flies. I began to think that his nose was no better than my own, when suddenly, as if pierced by a bullet, he sprang up into the air and galloped confusedly off without turning to look; but in a few seconds, as if doubtful of the direction of the danger, he came bounding back, caught a glimpse of me, and ran off a second time in a settled direction.

The Yosemite basin is a favorite Summer home of the deer. The leguminous vines and juicy grasses of the great moraines supply savory food, while the many high hidings of the Hoffman Mountains, accessible by narrow passes, afford favorite shelter. Grizzly and brown bears also love Yosemite Creek.

Berries of the dwarf manzanita, and acorns of the dwarf live-
oak are abundant upon the dry hilltops; and these with some
plants, and the larvæ of black ants, are the favorite food of
bears, if varied occasionally by a stolen sheep or a shepherd.
The gorges of the Tuolumne Cañon, on the north end of the
basin, are their principal hiding places in this region. Higher
in the range their food is not plentiful, and lower they are
molested by man.

On returning to camp I passed three of the domes of the
north bank, and was struck with the exact similarity of their
structure, the same concentric layers, with a perpendicular
cleavage also, but less perfectly developed and more irregular.
This little dome tributary, about 2½ miles long by 1½ wide,
must have been one of the most beautiful of the basin; all of
its upper circling rim is adorned with domes, some half-born,
sunk in the parent rock; some broken and torn upon the sides
by the ice, and a few nearly perfect, from their greater strength
of structure or more favorable position. The two lakes above
described are the only ones of the tributary basin, both domes
and lakes handiwork of the glacier.

A GLACIER'S DEATH.

In the waning days of this mountain ice, when the main
river began to shallow and break like a Summer cloud, its
crests and domes rising higher and higher, and island rocks
coming to light far out in the main current, then many a
tributary died, and this one, cut off from its trunk, moved
slowly back amid the gurgling and gushing of its bleeding rills,
until, crouching in the shadows of this half-mile hollow, it
lived a feeble separate life. Here its days come and go, and
the hiding glacier lives and works. It brings bowlders and sand
and fine dust polishings from its sheltering domes and cañons,
building up a terminal moraine, which forms a dam for the
waters which issue from it; and beneath, working in the dark,
it scoops a shallow lake basin. Again the glacier retires,
crouching under cooler shadows, and a cluster of steady years
enables the dying glacier to make yet another moraine dam
like the first; and, where the granite begins to rise in curves
to form the upper dam, it scoops another lake. Its last work
is done, and it dies. The twin lakes are full of pure green water,

and floating masses of snow and broken ice. The domes, perfect in sculpture, gleam in new-born purity, lakes and domes reflecting each other bright as the ice which made them. God's seasons circle on, glad brooks born of the snow and the rain sing in the rocks, and carry sand to the naked lakes, and, in the fullness of time comes many a chosen plant; first a lowly carex with dark brown spikes, then taller sedges and rushes, fixing a shallow soil, and now come many grasses, and daisies, and blooming shrubs, until lake and meadow growing throughout the season like a flower in Summer, develop to the perfect beauty of to-day.

How softly comes night to the mountains. Shadows grow upon all the landscape; only the Hoffman Peaks are open to the sun. Down in this hollow it is twilight, and my two domes, more impressive than in broad day, seem to approach me. They are not vast and over-spiritual, like Yosemite Tissiack, but comprehensible and companionable, and susceptible of human affinities. The darkness grows, and all of their finer sculpture dims. Now the great arches and deep curves sink also, and the whole structure is massed in black against the starry sky.

I have set fire to two pine logs, and the neighboring trees are coming to my charmed circle of light. The two-leaved pine, with sprays and tassels innumerable, the silver fir, with magnificent frouded whorls of shining boughs, and the graceful nodding spruce, dripping with cones, and seeming yet more spiritual in this camp-fire light. Grandly do my logs give back their light, slow gleaned from suns of a hundred Summers, garnered beautifully away in dotted cells and in beads of amber gum; and, together with this outgush of light, seems to flow all the other riches of their life, and their living companions are looking down as if to witness their perfect and beautiful death. But I am weary and must rest. Good-night to my two logs and two lakes, and to my two domes high and black on the sky, with a cluster of stars between.

New-York Tribune, December 5, 1871

Yosemite Valley in Flood

MANY a joyful stream is born in the Sierras, but not one can sing like the Merced. In childhood, high on the mountains, her silver thread is a moving melody; of sublime Yosemite she is the voice; the blooming *chaparral* or the flowery plains owe to her fullness their plant-wealth of purple and gold, and to the loose dipping willows and broad green oaks she is bounteous in blessing. I think she is the most absorbing and readable of rivers. I have lived with her for three years, sharing all her life and fortunes, dreaming that I appreciated her; but I never have so much as imagined the sublimity, the majesty of her music, until seeing and listening at every pore I stood in her temple to-day.

December brought to Yosemite, first of all, a cluster of ripe, golden days and silvery nights—a radiant company of the sweetest winter children of the sun. The blue sky had Sabbath and slept in its high dome, and down in its many mansions of *cañon* and cave, crystals grew in the calm nights, and fringed the rocks like mosses. The November torrents were soothed, and settled tranquillity beamed from every feature of rock and sky.

In the afternoon of December 16th, 1871, an immense crimson cloud grew up in solitary grandeur above Cathedral Rocks. It resembled a fungus, with a bulging base like a sequoia, a smooth, tapering stalk, and a round, bossy, down-curled head like a mushroom—stalk, head, and root, in equal, glowing, half-transparent crimson: one of the most gorgeous and symmetrical clouds I ever beheld. Next morning, I looked eagerly at the weather, but all seemed tranquil; and whatever was being done in the deep places of the sky, little stir was visible below. An ill-defined dimness consumed the best of the sunbeams, and toward noon well-developed grayish clouds appeared, having a close, curly grain, like bird's-eye maple. Late in the night some rain fell, which changed to snow, and, in the morning, about ten inches remained unmelted on the meadows, and was still falling—a fine, cordial snow-storm; but the end was not yet.

On the night of the 18th rain fell in torrents, but, as it had
a temperature of 34° Fahrenheit, the snow-line was only a few
feet above the meadows, and there was no promise of flood;
yet sometime after eleven o'clock the temperature was suddenly raised by a south wind to 42°, carrying the snow-line to
the top of the wall and far beyond—out on the upper basins,
perhaps, to the very summit of the range—and morning saw
Yosemite in the glory of flood. Torrents of warm rain were
washing the valley walls, and melting the upper snows of the
surrounding mountains; and the liberated waters held jubilee.
On both sides the Sentinel foamed a splendid cascade, and
across the valley by the Three Brothers, down through the
pine grove, I could see fragments of an unaccountable outgush of snowy cascades. I ran for the open meadow, that I
might hear and see the whole glowing circumference at once,
but the tinkling brook was an unfordable torrent, bearing
down snow and bowlders like a giant. Farther up on the *débris*
I discovered a place where the stream was broken up into
three or four strips among the bowlders, where I crossed
easily, and ran for the meadows. But, on emerging from the
bordering bushes, I found them filled with green lakes, edged
and islanded with floating snow. I had to keep along the *débris*
as far as Hutchings', where I crossed the river, and reached a
wadable meadow in the midst of the most glorious congregation of water-falls ever laid bare to mortal eyes. Between
Black's and Hutchings' there were ten snowy, majestic, loud-
voiced cascades and falls; in the neighborhood of Glacier
Point, six; from Three Brothers to Yosemite Falls, nine; between Yosemite and Arch Falls, ten; between Washington Column and Mount Watkins, ten; on the slopes of South Dome,
facing Mirror Lake, eight; on the shoulder of South Dome,
facing the main valley, three. Fifty-six new-born falls occupying
this upper end of the valley; besides a countless host of silvery-
netted arteries gleaming everywhere! I did not go down to
the Ribbon or Pohono; but in the whole valley there must
have been upward of a hundred. As if inspired with some great
water purpose, cascades and falls had come thronging, in Yosemite costume, from every grove and *cañon* of the mountains; and be it remembered, that these falls and cascades were
not small, dainty, momentary gushes, but broad, noble-

mannered water creations; sublime in all their attributes, and well worthy Yosemite rocks, shooting in arrowy foam from a height of near three thousand feet; the very smallest of which could be heard several miles away: a perfect storm of water-falls throbbing out their lives in one stupendous song. I have criticised Hill's painting for having two large falls between the Sentinel and Cathedral rocks; now I would not be unbelieving against fifty. From my first stand-point on the meadow toward Lamon's only one fall is usually seen; now there are forty. A most glorious convention this of vocal waters—not remote and dim, as only half present, but with forms and voices wholly seen and felt, each throbbing out rays of beauty warm and palpable as those of the sun.

All who have seen Yosemite in summer will remember the comet forms of upper Yosemite Falls, and the laces of Nevada. In these waters of the jubilee, the lace tissue predominates; but there is also a plentiful mingling of arrowy comets. A cascade back of Black's is composed of two white shafts set against the dark wall about thirty feet apart, and filled in with chained and beaded gauze of splendid pattern, among the living meshes of which the dark, purple granite is dimly seen. A little above Glacier Point there is a half-woven, half-divided web of cascades, with warp and woof so similar in song and in ges-tures, that they appear as one existence: living and rejoicing by the pulsings of one heart. The row of cascades between Washington Column and the Arch Falls are so closely side by side that they form an almost continuous sheet; and those about Indian Cañon and the Brothers are not a whit less noble. Tissiack is crowned with surpassing glory. Her sculp-tured walls and bosses and her great dome are nobly adorned with clouds and waters, and her thirteen cascades give her voice of song.

The upper Yosemite is queen of all these mountain waters; nevertheless, in the first half-day of jubilee, her voice was scarce heard. Ever since the coming of the first November storms, Yosemite has flowed with a constant stream, although far from being equal to the high water in May and June. About three o'clock this afternoon I heard a sudden crash and booming, mixed with heavy gaspings and rocky, angular ex-plosions, and I ran out, sure that a rock-avalanche had started near the top of the wall, and hoping to see some of the huge blocks journeying down; but I quickly discovered that these craggy, sharp-angled notes belonged to the flood-wave of the upper fall. The great wave, gathered from many a glacier-*cañon* of the Hoffman spurs, had just arrived, sweeping logs and ice before it, and, plunging over the tremendous verge, was blended with the storm-notes of crowning grandeur.

During the whole two days of storm no idle, unconscious water appeared, and the clouds, and winds, and rocks were inspired with corresponding activity and life. Clouds rose hastily, upon some errand, to the very summit of the walls, with a single effort, and as suddenly returned; or, sweeping horizontally, near the ground, draggled long-bent streamers through the pine-tops; while others traveled up and down Indian Cañon, and overtopped the highest brows, then suddenly drooped and condensed, or, thinning to gauze, veiled half the valley, leaving here and there a summit looming alone. These clouds, and the crooked cascades, raised the valley-rocks to double their usual height, for the eye, mounting from cloud to cloud, and from angle to angle upon the cascades, obtained a truer measure of their sublime stature.

The warm wind still poured in from the south, melting the snows far out on the highest mountains. Thermometer, at noon, 45°. The smaller streams of the valley edge are waning, by the slackening of the rain; but the far-reaching streams, coming in by the Tenaya, Nevada, and Illilouette *cañons*, are still increasing. The Merced, in some places, overflows its banks, having risen at once from a shallow, prattling, ill-proportioned stream, to a deep, majestic river. The upper Yosemite is in full, gushing, throbbing glory of prime; still louder spring its shafts of song; still deeper grows the intense whiteness of its mingled meteors; fearlessly blow the winds among its dark, shadowy chambers, now softly bearing away the outside sprays, now swaying and bending the whole massive column. So sings Yosemite, with her hundred fellow-falls, to the trembling bushes, and solemn-waving pines, and winds, and clouds, and living, pulsing rocks—one stupendous unit of mountain power—one harmonious storm of mountain love.

On the third day the storm ceased. Frost killed the new falls; the clouds are withered and empty; a score of light is drawn across the sky, and our chapter of flood is finished. Visions like these do not remain with us as mere maps and pictures—flat shadows cast upon our minds, to brighten, at times, when touched by association or will, and fade again from our view, like landscapes in the gloaming. They saturate every fibre of the body and soul, dwelling in us and with us, like holy spirits, through all of our after-deaths and after-lives.

The Overland Monthly, April 1872

A Geologist's Winter Walk

AFTER reaching Turlock, I sped afoot over the stubble-fields, and through miles of brown *Hemizonia* and purple *Erigeron*, to Hopeton, conscious of little more than that the town was behind and beneath me, and the mountains above and before me; on through the oaks and *chaparral* of the foothills to Coulterville, and then ascended the first great mountain step upon which grows the sugar-pine. Here I slackened pace, for I drank the spicy, resiny wind, and was at home—never did pine-trees seem so dear. How sweet their breath and their song, and how grandly they winnowed the sky. I tingled my fingers among their tassels, and rustled my feet among their brown needles and burrs.

When I reached the valley, all the rocks seemed talkative, and more lovable than ever. They are dear friends, and have warm blood gushing through their granite flesh; and I love them with a love intensified by long and close companionship. After I had bathed in the bright river, sauntered over the meadows, conversed with the domes, and played with the pines, I still felt muddy, and weary, and tainted with the sticky sky of your streets; I determined, therefore, to run out to the higher temples. "The days are sunful," I said, "and though now winter, no great danger need be encountered, and a sudden storm will not block my return, if I am watchful."

The morning after this decision, I started up the Cañon of Tenaya, caring little about the quantity of bread I carried; for, I thought, a fast and a storm and a difficult cañon are just the medicine I require. When I passed Mirror Lake, I scarcely noticed it, for I was absorbed in the great Tissiack—her crown a mile away in the hushed azure; her purple drapery flowing in soft and graceful folds low as my feet, embroidered gloriously around with deep, shadowy forest. I have gazed on Tissiack a thousand times—in days of solemn storms, and when her form shone divine with jewels of winter, or was veiled in living clouds; I have heard her voice of winds, or snowy, tuneful waters; yet never did her soul reveal itself more impressively than now. I hung about her skirts, lingering timidly, till the glaciers compelled me to push up the cañon. This cañon is accessible only to determined mountaineers, and I was anxious to carry my barometer and chronometer through it, to obtain sections and altitudes. After I had passed the tall groves that stretch a mile above Mirror Lake, and scrambled around the Tenaya Fall, which is just at the head of the lake groves, and crept through the dense and spiny *chaparral* that plushes the roots of all the mountains here for miles, in warm, unbroken green, and was ascending a precipitous rock-front, where the foot-holds were good, when I suddenly stumbled, for the first time since I touched foot to Sierra rocks. After several involuntary somersaults, I became insensible, and when consciousness returned, I found myself wedged among short, stiff bushes, not injured in the slightest. Judging by the sun, I could not have been insensible very long; probably not a minute, possibly an hour; and I could not remember what made me fall, or where I had fallen from; but I saw that if I had rolled a little further, my mountain-climbing would have been finished. "There," said I, addressing my feet, to whose separate skill I had learned to trust night and day on any mountain, "that is what you get by intercourse with stupid town stairs, and dead pavements." I felt angry and worthless. I had not reached yet the difficult portion of the cañon, but I determined to guide my humbled body over the highest practicable precipices, in the most intricate and nerve-trying places I could find; for I was now fairly awake, and felt confident that the last town-fog had been shaken from both head and feet.

I camped at the mouth of a narrow gorge, which is cut into the bottom of the main cañon, determined to take earnest exercise next day. No plush boughs did my ill-behaved bones receive that night, nor did my bumped head get any spicy cedar-plumes for pillow. I slept on a naked bowlder, and when I awoke all my nervous trembling was gone.

The gorged portion of the cañon, in which I spent all the next day, is about a mile and a half in length; and I passed the time very profitably in tracing the action of the forces that determined this peculiar bottom gorge, which is an abrupt, ragged-walled, narrow-throated cañon, formed in the bottom of a wide-mouthed, smooth, and beveled cañon. I will not stop now to tell you more; some day you may see it, like a shadowy line, from Cloud's Rest. In high water, the stream occupies all the bottom of the gorge, surging and chafing in glorious power from wall to wall, but the sound of the grinding was low as I entered the gorge, scarcely hoping to be able to pass through its entire length. By cool efforts, along glassy, ice-worn slopes, I reached the upper end in a little over a day, but was compelled to pass the second night in the gorge, and in the moonlight I wrote you this short pencil-letter in my note-book:

"The moon is looking down into the cañon, and how marvelously the great rocks kindle to her light—every dome, and brow, and swelling boss touched by her white rays, glows, as if lighted with snow. I am now only a mile from last night's camp; and have been climbing and sketching all day in this difficult but instructive gorge. It is formed in the bottom of the main cañon, among the roots of Cloud's Rest. It begins at the dead lake where I camped last night, and ends a few hundred yards above, in another dead lake. The walls everywhere are craggy and vertical, and in some places they overlean. It is only from twenty to sixty feet wide, and not, though black and broken enough, the thin, crooked mouth of some mysterious abyss; for in many places I saw the solid, seamless floor. I am sitting on a big stone, against which the stream divides, and goes brawling by in rapids on both sides; half my rock is white in the light, half in shadow. Looking from the opening jaws of this shadowy gorge, South Dome is immediately in front—high in the stars, her face turned from the moon, with the rest of her body gloriously muffled in waved folds of granite. On the left, cut from Cloud's Rest, by the lip of the gorge, are three magnificent rocks, sisters of the great South Dome. On the right is the massive, moonlit front of Mount Watkins, and between, low down in the furthest distance, is Sentinel Dome, girdled and darkened with forest. In the near foreground is the joyous creek, Tenaya, singing against bowlders that are white with the snow. Now, look back twenty yards, and you will see a water-fall, fair as a spirit; the moonlight just touches it, bringing it in relief against the deepest, dark background. A little to the left, and a dozen steps this side of the fall, a flickering light marks my camp—

and a precious camp it is. A huge, glacier-polished slab, in falling from the glassy flank of Cloud's Rest, happened to settle on edge against the wall of the gorge. I did not know that this slab was glacier-polished, until I lighted my fire. Judge of my delight. I think it was sent here by an earthquake. I wish I could take it down to the valley. It is about twelve feet square. Beneath this slab is the only place in this torrent-swept gorge where I have seen sand sufficient for a bed. I expected to sleep on the bowlders, for I spent most of the afternoon on the slippery wall of the cañon, endeavoring to get around this difficult part of the gorge, and was compelled to hasten down here for water before dark. I will sleep soundly on this sand; half of it is mica. Here, wonderful to behold, are a few green stems of prickly *Rubus*, and a tiny grass. They are here to meet us. Ay, even here, in this darksome gorge, 'frightful and tormented' with raging torrents and choking avalanches of snow. Can it be? As if the *Rubus* and the grass-leaf were not enough of God's tender prattle-words of love, which we so much need in these mighty temples of power, yonder in the 'benmost bore' are two blessed *Adiantums*. Listen to them. How wholly infused with God is this one big word of love that we call the world! Good-night. Do you see the fireglow on my ice-smoothed slab, and on my two ferns? And do you hear how sweet a sleep-song the fall and cascades are singing?"

The water-ground chips and knots that I found fastened between rocks, kept my fire alive all through the night, and I rose nerved and ready for another day of sketching and noting, and any form of climbing. I escaped from the gorge about noon, after accomplishing some of the most delicate feats of mountaineering I ever attempted; and here the cañon is all broadly open again—a dead lake, luxuriantly forested with pine, and spruce, and silver fir, and brown-trunked *Librocedrus*. The walls rise in Yosemite forms, and the stream comes down 700 feet, in a smooth brush of foam. This is a genuine Yosemite valley. It is about 2,000 feet above the level of Yosemite, and about 2,400 below Lake Tenaya. Lake Tenaya was frozen, and the ice was so clear and unruffled, that the mountains and the groves that looked upon it were reflected almost as perfectly as I ever beheld them in the calm evening mirrors of summer. At a little distance, it was difficult to believe the lake frozen at all; and when I walked out on it, cautiously stamping at short intervals to test the strength of the ice, I seemed to walk mysteriously, without any adequate faith, on the surface of the water. The ice was so transparent, that I could see the beautifully wave-rippled, sandy bottom, and the scales of mica glinting back the down-pouring light. When I knelt down with my face close to the ice, through which clear sunshine was pouring, I was delighted to discover myriads of Tyndall's six-sided ice-flowers, magnificently colored. A grand old mountain mansion is this Tenaya region. In the glacier period, it was a *mer de glace*, far grander than the *mer de glace* of Switzerland, which is only about half a mile broad. The Tenaya *mer de glace* was not less than two miles broad, late in the glacier epoch, when all the principal dividing crests were bare; and its depth was not less than fifteen hundred feet. Ice-streams from Mounts Lyell and Dana, and all the mountains between, and from the nearer Cathedral Peak, flowed hither, welded into one, and worked together. After accomplishing this Tenaya Lake basin, and all the splendidly-sculptured rocks and mountains that surround and adorn it, and the great Tenaya Cañon, with its wealth of all that makes mountains sublime, they were welded with the vast South Lyell and Illilouette glaciers on one side, and with those of Hoffman on the other—thus forming a portion of a yet grander *mer de glace*.

Now your finger is raised admonishingly, and you say, "This letter-writing will not do." Therefore, I will not try to register my homeward ramblings; but since this letter is already so long, you must allow me to tell you of Cloud's Rest and Tissiack; then will I cast away my letter pen, and begin "Articles," rigid as granite and slow as glaciers.

I reached the Tenaya Cañon, on my way home, by coming in from the northeast, rambling down over the shoulders of Mount Watkins, touching bottom a mile above Mirror Lake. From thence home was but a saunter in the moonlight. After resting one day, and the weather continuing calm, I ran up over the east shoulder of the South Dome, and down in front of its grand split face, to make some measurements; completed my work, climbed to the shoulder again, and struck off along the ridge for Cloud's Rest, and reached the topmost sprays of her sunny wave in ample time for sunset. Cloud's Rest is a thousand feet higher than Tissiack. It is a wave-like crest upon a ridge, which begins at Yosemite with Tissiack, and runs continuously eastward to the thicket of peaks and crests around Tenaya. This lofty granite wall is bent this way and that by the restless and weariless action of glaciers, just as if it had been made of dough—semi-plastic, as Prof. Whitney would say. But the grand circumference of mountains and forests are coming from far and near, densing into one close assemblage; for the sun, their god and father, with love ineffable, is glowing a sunset farewell. Not one of all the assembled rocks or trees seemed remote. How impressively their faces shone with responsive love!

I ran home in the moonlight, with long, firm strides; for the sun-love made me strong. Down through the junipers—down through the firs; now in jet-shadows, now in white light; over sandy moraines and bare, clanking rock; past the huge ghost of South Dome, rising weird through the firs—past glorious Nevada—past the groves of Illilouette—through the pines of the valley; frost-crystals flashing all the sky beneath, as star-crystals on all the sky above. All of this big mountain-bread for one day! One of the rich, ripe days that enlarge one's life—so much of sun upon one side of it, so much of moon on the other.

The Overland Monthly, April 1873

Wild Wool

Moral improvers have calls to preach. I have a friend who has a call to plow, and woe to the daisy sod or azalea thicket that falls under the savage redemption of his keen steel shares. Not content with the so-called subjugation of every terrestrial bog, rock, and moor-land, he would fain discover some method of reclamation applicable to the ocean and the sky, that in due calendar time they might be made to bud and blossom as the rose. Our efforts are of no avail when we seek to turn his attention to wild roses, or to the fact that both ocean and sky are already about as rosy as possible—the one with stars, the other with dulse, and foam, and wild light. The practical developments of his culture are orchards and clover-fields that wear a smiling, benevolent aspect, and are very excellent in their way, though a near view discloses something barbarous in them all. Wildness charms not my friend, charm it never so wisely; and whatsoever may be the character of his heaven, his earth seems only a chaos of agricultural possibilities calling for grubbing-hoes and manures.

Sometimes I venture to approach him with a plea for wildness, when he good-naturedly shakes a big mellow apple in my face, and reiterates his favorite aphorism: "Culture is an orchard apple; nature is a crab." All culture, however, is not equally destructive and inappreciative. Azure skies and crystal waters find loving recognition, and few there be who would welcome the axe among mountain pines, or would care to apply any correction to the tones and costumes of mountain water-falls. Nevertheless, the barbarous notion is almost universally entertained by civilized men, that there is in all the manufactures of nature something essentially coarse which can and must be eradicated by human culture. I was, therefore, delighted in finding that the wild wool growing upon mountain sheep in the neighborhood of Mount Shasta was much finer than the average grades of cultivated wool. This *fine* discovery was made some three months ago, while hunting between Shasta and Lower Klamath Lake. Three fleeces were obtained—one that belonged to a large ram about four years old, another to a ewe about the same age, and another to a yearling lamb. After parting their beautiful wool on the side and many places along the back, shoulders, and hips, and examining it closely with my lens, I shouted:

"Well done for wildness! Wild wool is finer than tame!"

My companions stooped down and examined the fleeces for themselves, pulling out tufts and ringlets, spinning them between their fingers, and measuring the length of the staple, each in turn paying tribute to wildness. It *was* finer, and no mistake; finer than Spanish Merino. Wild wool *is* finer than tame.

"Here," said I, "is an argument for fine wildness that needs no explanation. Not that such arguments are by any means rare, for all wildness is finer than tameness, but because fine wool is appreciable by everybody alike—from the most speculative president of national wool-growers' associations all the way down to the humblest gude-wife spinning by her ingleside."

Nature is a good mother, and sees well to the clothing of her many bairns—birds with smoothly imbricated feathers, beetles with shining jackets, and bears with shaggy furs. In the tropical south, where the sun warms like a fire, they are allowed to go thinly clad; but in the snowy north-land she takes care to clothe warmly. The squirrel has socks and mittens, and a tail broad enough for a blanket; the grouse is densely feathered down to the ends of his toes; and the wild sheep, besides his under-garment of fine wool, has a thick overcoat of hair that sheds off both the snow and the rain. Other provisions and adaptations in the dresses of animals, relating less to climate than to the more mechanical circumstances of life, are made with the same consummate skill that characterizes all the love-work of nature. Land, water, and air, jagged rocks, muddy ground, sand-beds, forests, underbrush, grassy plains, etc., are considered in all their possible combinations while the clothing of her beautiful wildlings is preparing. No matter what the circumstances of their lives may be, she never allows them to go dirty or ragged. The mole, living always in the dark and in the dirt, is yet as clean as the otter or the wave-washed seal; and our wild sheep, wading in snow, roaming through bushes, and leaping among jagged storm-beaten cliffs, wears a dress so exquisitely adapted to its mountain life that it is always found as unruffled and stainless as a bird.

On leaving the Shasta hunting-grounds I selected a few specimen tufts, and brought them away with a view to making more leisurely examinations; but, owing to the imperfectness of the instruments at my command, the results thus far obtained must be regarded only as rough approximations.

As already stated, the clothing of our wild sheep is composed of fine wool and coarse hair. The hairs are from about two to four inches long, mostly of a dull bluish-gray color, though varying somewhat with the seasons. In general characteristics they are closely related to the hairs of the deer and antelope, being light, spongy, and elastic, with a highly polished surface, and though somewhat ridged and spiraled, like wool, they do not manifest the slightest tendency to felt or become taggy. A hair two and a half inches long, which is perhaps near the average length, will stretch about one-fourth of an inch before breaking. The diameter decreases rapidly both at the top and bottom, but is maintained throughout the greater portion of the length with a fair degree of regularity. The slender tapering point in which the hairs terminate is nearly black; but, owing to its fineness as compared with the main trunk, the quantity of blackness is not sufficient to greatly affect the general color. The number of hairs growing upon a square inch is about 10,000; the number of wool fibres is about 25,000, or two and a half times that of the hairs. The wool fibres are white and glossy, and beautifully spiraled into ringlets. The average length of the staple is about an inch and a half. A fibre of this length, when growing undisturbed down among the hairs, measures about an inch; hence the degree of curliness may easily be inferred. I regret exceedingly that my instruments do not enable me to measure the diameter of the fibres, in order that their degrees of fineness might be definitely compared with each other and with the finest of the domestic breeds; but that the three wild fleeces under consideration are considerably finer than the average grades of Merino shipped from San Francisco is, I think, unquestionable.

When the fleece is parted and looked into with a good lens, the skin appears of a beautiful pale-yellow color, and the delicate wool fibres are seen growing up among the strong hairs, like grass among stalks of corn, every individual fibre being protected about as specially and effectively as if inclosed in a separate husk. Wild wool is too fine to stand by itself, the fibres being about as frail and invisible as the floating threads of spiders, while the hairs against which they lean stand erect like hazel wands; but, notwithstanding their great dissimilarity in size and appearance, the wool and hair are forms of the same thing, modified in just that way and to just that degree that renders them most perfectly subservient to the well-being of the sheep. Furthermore, it will be observed that these wild modifications are entirely distinct from those which are brought chancingly into existence through the accidents and caprices of culture; the former being inventions of God for the attainment of definite ends. Like the modifications of limbs—the fin for swimming, the wing for flying, the foot for walking—so the fine wool for warmth, the hair for additional warmth and to protect the wool, and both together for a fabric to wear well in mountain roughness and wash well in mountain storms.

The effects of human culture upon wild wool are analogous to those produced upon wild roses. In the one case there is an abnormal development of petals at the expense of the stamens, in the other an abnormal development of wool at the expense of the hair. Garden roses frequently exhibit stamens in which the transmutation to petals may be observed in various stages of accomplishment, and analogously the fleeces of tame sheep occasionally contain a few wild hairs that are undergoing transmutation to wool. Even wild wool presents here and there a fibre that appears to be in a state of change. In the course of my examinations of the wild fleeces mentioned above, three fibres were found that were wool at one end and hair at the other. This, however, does not necessarily imply imperfection, or any process of change similar to that caused by human culture. Water-lilies contain parts variously developed into stamens at one end, petals at the other, as the constant and normal condition. These half-wool half-hair fibres may therefore subserve some fixed requirement essential to the perfection of the whole, or they may simply be the fine boundary lines where an exact balance between the wool and hair is attained.

I have been offering samples of mountain wool to my friends, demanding in return that the fineness of wildness be fairly recognized and confessed, but the returns are deplorably tame. The first question asked is, "Wild sheep, wild sheep, have you any wool?" while they peer curiously down among the hairs through lenses and spectacles. "Yes, wild sheep, you *have* wool; but Mary's lamb had more. In the name of use, how many wild sheep think you would be required to furnish wool sufficient for a pair of socks?" I endeavor to point out the irrelevancy of the latter question, arguing that wild wool was not made for men but for sheep, and that, however deficient as clothing for other animals, it is just the thing for the brave mountain-dweller that wears it. Plain, however, as all this appears, the quantity question rises again and again in all its commonplace tameness. To obtain a hearing on behalf of nature from any other stand-point than that of human use is almost impossible. Domestic flocks yield more flannel per sheep than the wild, therefore it is claimed that culture has improved upon wildness; and so it has as far as flannel is concerned, but all to the contrary as far as a sheep's dress is concerned. If every wild sheep inhabiting the Sierra were to put on tame wool, probably only a few would survive the dangers of a single season. With their fine limbs muffled and buried beneath a tangle of hairless wool, they would become short-winded, and fall an easy prey to the strong mountain wolves. In descending precipices they would be thrown out of balance and killed, by their taggy wool catching upon sharp points of rocks. Disease would also be brought on by the dirt which always finds a lodgment in tame wool, and by the draggled and water-soaked condition into which it falls during stormy weather.

No dogma taught by the present civilization seems to form so insuperable an obstacle in the way of a right understanding of the relations which culture sustains to wildness, as that which declares that the world was made especially for the uses of men. Every animal, plant, and crystal controverts it in the plainest terms. Yet it is taught from century to century as something ever new and precious, and in the resulting darkness the enormous conceit is allowed to go unchallenged.

I have never yet happened upon a trace of evidence that

seemed to show that any one animal was ever made for another as much as it was made for itself. Not that nature manifests any such thing as selfish isolation. In the making of every animal the presence of every other animal has been recognized. Indeed, every atom in creation may be said to be acquainted with and married to every other, but with universal union there is a division sufficient in degree for the purposes of the most intense individuality; and no matter what may be the note which any creature forms in the song of existence, it is made first for itself, then more and more remotely for all the world and worlds.

Were it not for the exercise of individualizing cares on the part of nature, the universe would be felted together like a fleece of tame wool. We are governed more than we know, and most when we are wildest. Plants, animals, and stars are all kept in place, bridled along appointed ways, *with* one another, and *through the midst* of one another—killing and being killed, eating and being eaten, in harmonious proportions and quantities. And it is right that we should thus reciprocally make use of one another, rob, cook, and consume, to the utmost of our healthy abilities and desires. Stars attract each other as they are able, and harmony results. Wild lambs eat as many wild flowers as they can find or desire, and men and wolves eat the lambs to just the same extent. This consumption of one another in its various modifications is a kind of culture varying with the degree of directness with which it is carried out, but we should be careful not to ascribe to such culture any improving qualities upon those on whom it is brought to bear. The water-ousel plucks moss from the riverbank to build its nest, but it does not improve the moss by plucking it. We pluck feathers from birds, and less directly wool from wild sheep, for the manufacture of clothing and cradle-nests, without improving the wool for the sheep, or the feathers for the bird that wore them. When a hawk pounces upon a linnet and proceeds to pull out its feathers, preparatory to making a meal, the hawk may be said to be cultivating the linnet, and he certainly does effect an improvement as far as hawk-food is concerned; but what of the songster? He ceases to be a linnet as soon as he is snatched from the woodland choir; and when, hawk-like, we snatch the wild sheep from its native rock, and, instead of eating and wearing it at once, carry it home, and breed the hair out of its wool and the bones out of its body, it ceases to be a sheep. These breeding and plucking processes are similarly improving as regards the secondary uses aimed at; and, although the one requires but a few minutes for its accomplishment, the other many years or centuries, they are essentially alike. We eat wild oysters alive with great directness, waiting for no cultivation, and leaving scarce a second of distance between the shell and the lip; but we take wild sheep home and subject them to the many extended processes of husbandry, and finish by cooking them—a process which completes all sheep improvements as far as man is concerned. It will be seen, therefore, that wild wool and tame wool—wild sheep and tame sheep—are not properly comparable, nor are they in any correct sense to be considered as bearing any antagonism toward each other; they are different things, planned and accomplished for wholly different purposes.

Illustrative examples bearing upon this interesting subject may be multiplied indefinitely, for they abound everywhere in the plant and animal kingdoms wherever culture has reached. Recurring for a moment to apples. The beauty and completeness of a wild apple-tree living its own life in the woods is heartily acknowledged by all those who have been so happy as to form its acquaintance. The fine wildly piquancy of its fruit is unrivaled, but in the great question of quantity as human food wild apples are found wanting. Man, therefore, takes the tree from the woods, manures and prunes and grafts, plans and guesses, adds a little of this and that, until apples of every conceivable size and pulpiness are produced, like nutgalls in response to the irritating punctures of insects. Orchard apples are to me the most eloquent words that culture has ever spoken, but they reflect no imperfection upon nature's spicy crab. Every cultivated apple is a crab, not improved, *but cooked*, variously softened and swelled out in the process, mellowed, sweetened, spiced, and rendered good for food, but as utterly unfit for the uses of nature as a meadow lark killed and plucked and roasted. Give to nature every apple—codling, pippin, russet—and every sheep so laboriously compounded—muffled Southdowns, hairy Cotswolds, wrinkled Merinoes—

and she would throw the one to her caterpillars, the other to her wolves.

It is now some 3,600 years since Jacob kissed his mother and set out across the plains of Padan-aram to begin his experiments upon the flocks of his uncle, Laban; and, notwithstanding the high degree of excellence he attained as a wool-grower, and the innumerable painstaking efforts subsequently made by individuals and associations in all kinds of pastures and climates, we still seem to be as far from definite and satisfactory results as we ever were. In one breed the wool is apt to wither and crinkle like hay on a sun-beaten hill-side. In another, it is lodged and matted together like the lush tangled grass of a manured meadow. In one the staple is deficient in length, in another in fineness; while in all there is a constant tendency toward disease, rendering various washings and dippings indispensable to prevent its falling out. The problem of the quality and quantity of the carcass seems to be as doubtful and as far removed from a satisfactory solution as that of the wool. Desirable breeds blundered upon by long series of groping experiments are often found to be unstable and subject to disease—bots, foot-rot, blind-staggers, etc.—causing infinite trouble, both among breeders and manufacturers. Would it not be well, therefore, for some one to go back as far as possible and take a fresh start?

The source or sources whence the various breeds were derived is not positively known, but there can be hardly any doubt of their being descendants of the four or five wild species so generally distributed throughout the mountainous portions of the globe, the marked differences between the wild and domestic species being readily accounted for by the known variability of the animal. No other animal seems to yield so submissively to the manipulations of culture. Jacob controlled the color of his flocks merely by causing them to stare at objects of the desired hue; and possibly Merinoes may have caught their wrinkles from the perplexed brows of their breeders. The California species (*Ovis montana*) is a noble animal, weighing when full grown some 350 pounds, and is well worthy the attention of wool-growers as a point from which to make a new departure. That it will breed with the domestic sheep I have not the slightest doubt, and I cordially recommend the experiment to the various wool-growers' associations as one of great national importance. From my knowledge of the homes and habits of our wild sheep I feel confident that several hundred could be obtained for breeding purposes from the Sierra alone, and I am ready to undertake their capture. A little pure wildness is the one great present want, both of men and sheep.

The Overland Monthly, April 1875

Flood-Storm in the Sierra

BEARS, wild sheep, and other denizens of the mountains are usually driven down out of the high Sierra about the beginning of winter, and are seldom allowed to return before late spring. But the extraordinary sunfulness of last winter, and my eagerness to obtain general views of the geology and topography of the Feather River basin, caused me to make a reconnoissance of its upper tributary valleys in the month of January. I had just completed this hasty survey and pushed my way down to comfortable winter quarters, when that fine storm broke upon the mountains which gave rise to the Marysville flood. I was then at Knoxville, a small village on the divide between the waters of the Yuba and Feather, some twenty miles back from the edge of the plains, and about 2,000 feet above the level of the sea. The cause of this notable flood was simply a sudden and copious fall of warm rain and warm wind upon the basins of the Yuba and Feather rivers at a time when these contained a considerable quantity of snow. The rain was of itself sufficient to produce a vigorous flood, while the snow which was so suddenly melted on the upper and middle regions of the basins may have been sufficiently abundant for the production of another flood equal in size to that of the rain. Now, these two distinct harvests of flood-waters were gathered simultaneously and poured down upon the plain in one magnificent avalanche. In the pursuit of clear conceptions concerning the formation of floods upon mountain rivers, we soon perceive that it is essential, not only that the water delivered by the tributaries be sufficient in quantity, but that it be delivered so rapidly that the trunk will not be able to discharge it without becoming choked and overflowed.

The basins of the Feather and Yuba are admirably adapted for the growth of floods. Their numerous tributary valleys radiate far and wide, comprehending large areas, and the tributaries are steeply inclined, while the trunks are comparatively level. While the storm under consideration was in progress, the thermometer at Knoxville ranged between 44 and 50°, and when warm wind and warm rain fall simultaneously upon snow contained in basins like those of the Yuba and Feather, both the rain and that portion of the snow which the rain and wind melt are sponged up and held back until the combined mass becomes sludge, which at length, suddenly dissolving, descends all together to the trunk, where, heaping and swelling, flood over flood, they debouch upon the plain with a violence and suddenness that at first seem wholly unaccountable. The destructiveness of the Marysville portion of the flood was augmented somewhat by mining-gravel occupying the river channels, and by levees which gave way after having first restrained and accumulated a portion of the waters. These exaggerating conditions did not, however, greatly influence the general result, the main effect having been caused by the rare combination of flood-factors indicated above.

It is a pity that so few people were fortunate enough to fairly meet with and enjoy this noble storm in its own home among the mountains; for, dying as it did so little known, it will doubtless be remembered far more for the drifted bridges and houses that chanced to lie in its way than for its own beauty, or for the thousand thousand blessings it brought to the fields and gardens of nature. The impressions which storms excite in the minds of different individuals vary with the degree of development to which they have attained, and with the ever-changing accidents of health, business position, and so on. Nevertheless, there seemed to be much in the voices and aspects of the Marysville storm which was in every way proper to arouse universal admiration. I will, therefore, offer a few of the more characteristic outlines.

On the morning of the flood (January 19th of this year) all the Knoxville landscapes were covered with running water, muddy torrents descended every gulch and ravine, and the sky was thick with rain. The pines had long slept in sunshine; they were now awake, and with one accord waved time to the beatings of the storm. The winds swept along the music curves of many a hill and dale, streaming through the pines, cascading over rocks, and blending all their tones and chords in one grand harmony. After fairly going out into and joining the storm, it was easy to see that only a small portion of the rain reached the ground in the form of drops; most of it seemed to have been dashed and beaten into a kind of coarse spray, like that into which small water-falls are broken when they strike glancingly on rough rock-shelves. Never have I beheld water falling from the sky in denser or more passionate streams. The heavy wind beat forward the spray in suffocating drifts, often compelling me to shelter in the copse or behind big pines. Go where I would, on ridges or in hollows, water still flashed and gurgled around my ankles, vividly recalling a wild storm morning in Yosemite, when a hundred water-falls from 1,000 to 3,000 feet in height came and sung together, filling all the valley with their sea-like roar.

After drifting compliantly an hour or two, I set out for the summit of a hill some 900 feet high, with a view to getting as far up into the storm as possible. This hill, which is the highest in the neighborhood, lies immediately to the south of Knoxville, and in order to reach it, I had to cross Dry Creek, a small tributary of the Yuba, that goes brawling along its base on the north-west. The creek was now a booming river as large as the Tuolumne, its current brown with mining-mud washed down from many a "claim," and mottled with sluice-boxes, fence-rails, and many a ponderous log that had long lain above its reach. A little distance below the village a slim foot-bridge stretches across from bank to bank, scarcely above the current. Here I was glad to linger, gazing and listening, while the storm was in its finest mood—the gray driving rain-stream above, the brown savage flood-river beneath. The storm-language of the river was hardly less enchanting than that of the forest wind; the sublime overboom of the main current, the swash and gurgle of eddies, the keen clash of firm wave-masses breaking against rocks, and the smooth hush of shallow currentlets feeling their way through the willows of the margin: and amid all this throng of sounds I could hear the smothered bumping and rumbling of bowlders down on the bottom, as they were shoving or rolling forward against one another. The glad strong creek rose high above its banks and wandered from its channel out over many a briery sand-flat and sedgy meadow. Alders and willows were standing waist-deep, bearing up against the current with nervous gestures, as if fearful of being carried away, while supple branches bending over the flood dipped lightly and rose again as if stroking the wild waters in play. Leaving the bridge and pushing on through the storm-swept forest, all the ground seemed in motion. Pine-tassels, flakes of bark, soil, leaves, and broken branches were being borne down; and many a rock-fragment weathered from exposed ledges was now receiving its first rounding and polishing at the hands of the strong enthusiastic storm-streams. On they rushed through every gulch and hollow, leaping, gliding, working with a will, and rejoicing like living creatures.

Nor were the phenomena confined to the ground. Every tree possessed a water system of its own; streams of every species were pouring down the grooves of each trunk, organized as regularly as Amazons and Mississippis; their tributaries widely branched and distributed over the valleys and table-lands of the bark; their currents in flood-time choked with moss-pedicels and muddy with spores and pollen, spreading over shallows, deepening in gorges, dividing, conflowing, and leaping from ledge to ledge. When patiently explored, these tree-rivers are found to possess much the same scenery as the rivers of the ground. Their valleys abound in fine miniature landscapes, moss-bogs enliven their banks like meadows, and thickets of fruited hypnæ rise here and there like forests. And though nearly vertical, these minute tree-rivers are not all fall. They flow in most places with smooth currents that mirror the banks and break into a bloom of foam only in a few special places.

Toward midday, cloud, wind, and rain seemed to have reached their highest pitch of grandeur. The storm was wholly developed; it was in full bloom, and formed, from my commanding outlook on the hill-top, one of the most glorious spectacles I ever beheld. As far as the eye could reach—above, beneath, around—the dusty wind-beaten rain filled the air like one vast water-fall. Detached cloud-masses swept imposingly up the valley as if endowed with independent motion—now rising high above the pine-tops, now descending into their midst, fondling their dark arrowy spires, and soothing every leaf and branch with infinite gentleness. Others, keeping near the ground, glided behind separate groves and brought them forward into relief with admirable distinctness; or passing in front, eclipsed whole groves in succession, pine after pine gradually melting in their gray fringes and emerging again seemingly clearer than before.

The topography of storms is in great measure controlled by the topography of the regions where they rise, or over which they pass. When, therefore, we attempt to study storms from the valleys or from the gaps and openings of the forest, we are confounded by a multitude of separate and apparently antagonistic impressions. The bottom of the main wind-stream is broken up into innumerable waves and currents that surge against the hill-sides like sea-waves against a shore, and these wind irregularities react in turn upon the nether surface of the main storm-cloud, eroding immense cavernous hollows and rugged cañons, and sweeping forward the resulting *detritus* in long curving trains like the moraines of glaciers. But in proportion as we ascend, these partial and confusing effects disappear, we escape above the region of dashing wind-waves and broken clouds, and the phenomena are beheld altogether united and harmonious.

The longer I gazed out into the storm, the more visible it became. The numerous trains and heaps of cloud-*detritus* gave it a kind of visible body, which explained many perplexing phenomena and published its motions in plain terms. This cloud-body was rounded out and rendered more visible and complete by the texture of the falling rain-mass. Rain-drops differ in shape and size; therefore, they fall at different velocities, and overtake and clash against one another, producing white mist and spray. They, of course, yield unequal compliance to the force of the wind, which gives rise to a still greater degree of interference and clashing; strong passionate gusts also sweep off clouds of spray from the groves like that torn from wave-tops in a gale. And all these factors of irregularity in the density, color, and general texture of the rain-mass, tend to make the visible body of the storm with all its motions more complete and telling. It is then seen definitely as a river, rushing over bank and brae, bending the pines like weeds, curving this way and that, whirling in immense eddies in hollows and dells, while the main body pours grandly over all like an ocean current above the landscapes that lie hidden at the bottom of the sea.

I watched the gestures of the pines while the storm was at its height, and it was easy to see that they were not at all distressed. Several large sugar-pines stood near the thicket in which I was sheltered, bowing solemnly and tossing their giant arms as if interpreting the very words of the storm while accepting its wildest onsets with a passionate exhilaration. The lions were feeding. Those who have observed sunflowers eating light during any of the golden days of autumn know that none of their gestures express thankfulness. Their divine food is too heartily given, too heartily taken, to leave room for thanks. The sugar-pines were evidently accepting the benefactions of the storm in the same whole-souled manner; and when I looked down among the budding hazels, and still lower to the young violets and fern-tufts on the rocks, I noticed the same divine methods of giving and taking, and the same exquisite adaptations of what seems an outbreak of violent and uncontrollable force to the purposes of beautiful and delicate life.

Calms resembling deep sleep come upon whole landscapes just as they do upon individual pines, and storms awaken them in the same way. All through the dry midsummer of the lower portion of the range the withered hills and valleys seem to lie as empty and expressionless as dead shells on a shore. Even the loftiest alps may occasionally be found dull and uncommunicative, as if in some way they had lost countenance and shrunk to less than half their real stature. But when the lightnings crash and echo among these cañons, and the clouds come down and wreathe and crown their jagged summits, every feature beams with expression, and they rise again and hold themselves erect in all their imposing nobleness.

Storms are fine speakers and tell all they know, but their voices of lightning, torrent, and rushing wind are infinitely less numerous than their nameless still small voices too low for human ears; and because we are poor listeners we fail to catch much that is even fairly within reach. Our best rains are heard mostly on roofs, and winds in chimneys; and when, by choice or compulsion, we are fairly stormed upon, the confusion made by cumbersome equipments, and our nervous haste, and the noise of hail or rain on hard-brimmed hats, prevent our hearing any other than the loudest expressions.

Yet we may draw intense enjoyment from a knowledge of storm-sounds that we can not hear, and of storm-movements that we can not see. The sublime rush of planets around their suns is not heard any more than the oozing of rain-drops among the roots of plants.

How interesting would be the history of a single rain-drop followed back from the ground to its farthest fountains. It is hard to obtain clear general views of storms so extensive and seemingly so shapeless as the one under consideration, notwithstanding the aid derived from a thousand observers furnished with the best instruments. The smallest and most comprehensible species of Sierra storm is found growing in the middle region of the range, some specimens being so local and small that we can go round their bases and see them from all sides like a mountain. Like the rains of the greater portion of equatorial regions, they seem to obey a kind of rhythm, appearing day after day a little before noon, sometimes for weeks in succession, and forming one of the most imposing and characteristic features of the midday scenery. Their periods are well known and taken into account by Indians and mountaineers. It is not long, geologically speaking, since the first rain-drop fell upon the present landscapes of the Sierra; for, however old the range may be, regarded as a whole, its features are young. They date back only to the glacial period. Yet in the few tens of thousands of years that have elapsed since these foot-hill landscapes were left bare by the melting ice-sheet, great superficial changes have taken place. The first post-glacial rains fell upon bare rocks and plantless moraines, but under nature's stormy cultivation these cold fields became fruitful. The ridged soils were spread out and mellowed, the seasons became warmer, and vegetation came gradually on— sedge and rush and waving grass, pine and fir, flower after flower—to make the lavish beauty that fills them to-day.

In the present storm, as in every other, there were tones and gestures inexpressibly gentle manifested in the midst of what is called violence and fury, and easily recognized by all who look and listen for them. The rain brought out all the colors of the woods with the most delightful freshness—the rich browns of bark, and burs, and fallen leaves, and dead ferns; the grays of rocks and lichens; the light purple of swelling buds, and the fine warm yellow greens of mosses and libocedrus. The air was steaming with fragrance, not rising and wafting past in separate masses, but equally diffused throughout all the wind. Pine woods are at all times fragrant, but most in spring when putting out their tassels, and in warm weather when their gums and balsams are softened by the sun. The wind was now chafing their needles, and the warm rain was steeping them. Monardella grows here in large beds, in sunny openings among the pines; and there is plenty of bog in the dells, and manzanita on the hill-sides; and the rosy fragrant-leaved *chamæbatia* carpets the ground almost everywhere. These with the gums and balsams of the evergreens formed the chief local fragrance-fountains within reach of the wind. Sailors tell that the flowery woods of Colombia scent the breeze a hundred miles to sea. Our Sierra wind seemed so perfectly filled, it could hardly lose its wealth go where it would; for the ascending clouds of aroma when first set free were wind-rolled and washed and parted from all their heaviness, and they became pure, like light, and were diffused and fairly lodged in the body of the air, and worked with it in close accord as an essential part of it.

Toward the middle of the afternoon the main flood-cloud lifted along its western border, revealing a beautiful section of the Sacramento Valley lying some twenty or thirty miles away, brilliantly sunlighted and glistening with rain-pools as if it were paved with burnished silver. Soon afterward a remarkably jagged bluff-like cloud with a sheer face appeared over the valley of the Yuba, dark colored and roughened with numerous furrows like some huge lava table. The blue Coast Range was seen stretching along the sky like a beveled wall, and the sombre and craggy Marysville Buttes rose imposingly out of the flooded plain like an island out of the sea. The rain began to abate, and the whole body of the storm was evidently withering and going to pieces.

I sauntered down through the dripping bushes, reveling in the universal vigor and freshness with which all the life about me was inspired. The woods were born again. How clean and unworn and immortal the world seemed to be!—the lofty cedars in full bloom, laden with golden pollen, and their washed plumes tipped with glowing rain-beads; the pines rocking gently and settling back into rest; light spangling on the broad mirror-leaves of the magnolia, and its tracery of yellow boughs relieved against dusky thickets of chestnut oak; liverworts, lycopodiums, ferns, all exulting in their glorious revival, and every moss that had ever lived seemed to have come crowding back from the dead to clothe each trunk and stone in living green. Young violets, smilax, frutillaria, saxifrage, were pushing up through the steaming ground as if conscious of all their coming glory; and innumerable green and yellow buds, scarce visible before the storm, were smiling everywhere, making the whole ground throb and tingle with glad life. As for the birds and squirrels, not a wing or tail was to be seen. Squirrels are dainty fellows, and dislike wetness more than cats. They were, therefore, snug at home, rocking in their dry nests. The birds were down in the sheltered dells, out of the wind, some of the strongest pecking at acorns or madroña berries, but most sitting in low copses with breast-feathers puffed out and keeping each other company.

Arriving at the Knox House, the good people bestirred themselves, pitying my bedraggled condition as if I were some benumbed castaway snatched from the sea; while I, in turn, pitied them, and for pity proclaimed but half the exalted beauty and riches of the storm. A fire, dry clothing, and special food were provided, all of which attentions were, I suppose, sufficiently commonplace to many, but truly novel to me.

How terribly downright must seem the utterances of storms and earthquakes to those accustomed to the soft hypocrisies of society. Man's control is being steadily extended over the forces of nature, but it is well, at least for the present, that storms can still make themselves heard through our thickest walls. On the night of the Marysville flood the easy-going apathy of many persons was broken up, and some were made to think, and the stars were seen, and the earnest roar of a flood-torrent was heard for the first time—a fine lesson. True, some goods were destroyed, and a few rats and people were drowned, and some took cold on the house-tops and died, but the total loss was less than the gain.

The Knoxville I have spoken of—sometimes called Brownsville—is a desirable place of resort, not so much for the regular tourist, as for tired town-dwellers seeking health and rest. It lies some thirty miles to the east of Marysville, and is easily reached from this point by stage. The elevation above sea-level (2,000 feet) gives a delightful spring and autumn climate, diversified with storms of the most gentle and picturesque species. The woods are everywhere open to saunterers, for the trees are grouped in groves, and the hazel-bushes and dog-woods and most species of *chapparal* are kept together in tidy thickets, allowing room to pass between. In the larger of these openings flower-lovers will find plenty of mint, smilax, lilies, and mariposa tulips, and beds of gilias, violets, and hosackias, laid out in sunny parterres with their various colors and ex-pressions in beautiful accord. The adjacent mountains, though not lofty, command an endless series of charming landscapes, and though the booming of strong Yosemitic falls is not heard, many a fine-voiced streamlet may be found in the leafy dells, singing like a bird as it leaps lightly from linn to linn beneath the cool shadows of alders and maples and broad plumy ferns.

Willow Glen lies a few miles to the west of the village, and contains a thousand objects of interest, picturesque rocks, cas-cades, ferny nooks, acres of polypodium and aspidium, wild gardens charmingly laid out, slopes of blooming shrubs, iris-beds, vine-tangles, birds, groves, and so on, among which the appreciative tourist might revel for weeks.

The Fox Den is another noteworthy point lying a little to the north-west of the village, and about 500 feet above it. It is a picturesque rock-pile resembling the ruins of some old feudal stronghold, where the red foxes of the neighborhood find shelter and sun themselves in the early morning, and where they watch and plan concerning the squirrels and quails that feed beneath the trees. In the spring-time the Den rocks are singularly rich in ferns, pellæa, polypodium, gymno-gramma, and cheilanthes. In autumn they are brightened with lavish bunches of scarlet photinia berries, which show finely among their own warm yellow leaves and the gray-lichened rock-fronts, and, besides its own especial attractions, it com-mands noble views of the Sacramento Valley, and of the surrounding pictures of hill and dale.

The operations of all kinds of gold-mining may be witnessed in the neighborhood within short walks, or drives, and one of the guides attached to the hotel is wise in plants, more especially in ferns, and knows well the hollows where woodwardias are tallest, and the rocks most rosetted with pellæa and cheilanthes.

The house itself is about as fresh as the woods after rain, and full of home-like sunshine. One of its rooms is a fine marvel, well deserving special mention. It is built entirely of plain sugar-pine, and filled with apples of every tint and taste, from the floor to the ceiling, all nicely assorted, rising regularly above one another in tiers, and shining as if the sunniest side of every apple were facing you.

Knoxville, though not containing above a dozen houses, is said to be noted for ministers. This apple-room is at any rate a kind of church, free to all, where one may enjoy capital sermons on color, fragrance, and sweetness, with very direct enforcements of their moral and religious correlations.

The world needs the woods, and is beginning to come to them; but it is not yet ready for the fine banks and braes of the lower Sierra, any more than for storms. Tourists make their way through the foot-hill landscapes as if blind to all their best beauty, and like children seek the emphasized mountains—the big alpine capitals whitened with glaciers and adorned with conspicuous spires. In like manner rivers are ascended hundreds of miles to see the water-falls at their heads, because they are as yet the only portions of river beauty plainly visible to all. Nevertheless the world moves onward, and "it is coming yet for a' that" that the beauty of storms will be as visible as that of calms, and that lowlands will be loved more than alps, and lakes and level rivers more than water-falls.

The Overland Monthly, June 1875

Living Glaciers of California

THE Sierra Nevada of California may be regarded as one grand wrinkled sheet of glacial records. For the scriptures of the ancient glaciers cover every rock, mountain, and valley of the range, and are in many places so well preserved, and are written in so plain a hand, they have long been recognized even by those who were not seeking for them, while the small living glaciers, lying hidden away among the dark recesses of the loftiest and most inaccessible summits, remain almost wholly unknown.

Looking from the summit of Mount Diablo across the San Joaquin Valley, after the atmosphere has been washed with winter rains, the Sierra is beheld stretching along the plain in simple grandeur, like some immense wall, two and a half miles high, and colored almost as bright as a rainbow, in four horizontal bands—the lowest rose purple, the next higher dark purple, the next blue, and the topmost pearly white—all beautifully interblended, and varying in tone with the time of day and the advance of the seasons.

The rose purple band, rising out of the yellow plain, is the foot-hill region, sparsely planted with oak and pine, the color in great measure depending upon argillaceous soils exposed in extensive openings among the trees; the dark purple is the region of the yellow and sugar pines; the blue is the cool middle region of the silver-firs; and the pearly band of summits is the Sierra Alps, composed of a vast wilderness of peaks, variously grouped, and segregated by stupendous cañons and swept with torrents and avalanches. Here are the homes of all the glaciers left alive in the Sierra Nevada. During the last five years I have discovered no less than sixty-five in that portion of the range embraced between latitudes 36° 30′ and 39°. They occur scattered throughout this vast region singly or in small groups, on the north sides of the loftiest peaks, sheltered beneath broad, frosty shadows. Over two-thirds of the entire number are contained between latitudes 37° and 38°, and form the highest fountains of the San Joaquin, Tuolumne, and Owens rivers.

The first Sierra glacier was discovered in October, 1871, in a wide, shadowy amphitheatre, comprehended by the bases of Red and Black mountains, two of the dominating summits of the Merced group. This group consists of the highest portion of a long crooked spur that straggles out from the main axis of the range in the direction of Yosemite Valley. At the time of my discovery I was engaged in exploring its *névé* amphitheatres, and in tracing the channels of the ancient glaciers which they poured down into the basin of Illilouette. Beginning on the northwestern extremity of the group with Mount Clark, I examined the chief tributaries in succession, their moraines, *roches moutonnées*, and shining glacial pavements, taking them as they came in regular course without any reference to the time consumed in their study.

The monuments of the tributary that poured its ice from between Red and Black mountains I found to be far the grandest of them all; and when I beheld its magnificent moraines ascending in majestic curves to the dark, mysterious solitudes at its head, I was exhilarated with the work that lay before me, as if on the verge of some great discovery. It was one of the golden days of Indian summer, when the sun melts all the roughness from the rockiest alpine landscapes. The path of the dead glacier shone as if washed with silver, the pines stood transfigured in the living light, poplar groves were masses of orange and yellow, and solidagoes were in full bloom, adding gold to gold.

Pushing on over my glacial highway, I passed lake after lake set in solid basins of granite, and many a thicket and meadow watered by the stream; now clanking over naked rock where not a leaf tries to grow, now wading through plushy bogs knee-deep in yellow and purple sphagnum, or brushing through luxuriant garden patches among larkspurs eight feet high and lilies with thirty flowers on a single stalk. The main lateral moraines bounded the view on either side like artificial embankments, covered with a superb growth of silver-fir and pine, many specimens attaining a height of two hundred feet or more. But all this garden and forest luxuriance was speedily left behind. The trees were dwarfed. The gardens became exclusively alpine. Patches of the heathy bryanthus and cassiope began to appear, and arctic willows, pressed into flat close carpets with the weight of winter snow. The lakelets, which a few miles down the valley were so richly broidered with meadows, had here, at an elevation of about 10,000 feet above the sea, only small mats of carex, leaving bare glaciated rocks around more than half their shores. Yet amidst all this alpine suppression the sturdy brown-barked mountain pine tossed his storm-beaten branches on ledges and buttresses of Red Mountain; some specimens over a hundred feet high and twenty-four feet in circumference, seemingly as fresh and vigorous as if made wholly of sunlight and snow.

Evening came on just as I got fairly within the portal of the grand fountain amphitheatre. I found it to be about a mile wide in the middle, and a little less than two miles long. Crumbling spurs and battlements of Red Mountain inclose it on the north, the sombre, rudely sculptured precipices of Black Mountain on the south, and a hacked and splintery *col* curves around from mountain to mountain at the head, shutting it in on the east.

I chose a camping ground for the night down on the brink of a glacier lake, where a thicket of Williamson spruce sheltered me from the night wind. After making a tin-cupful of tea, I sat by my camp fire, reflecting on the grandeur and significance of the glacial records I had seen, and speculating on the developments of the morrow. As the night advanced, the mighty rocks of my mountain mansion seemed to come nearer. The starry sky stretched across from wall to wall like a ceiling, and fitted closely down into all the spiky irregularities of the summits. After a long fireside rest and a glance at my field-notes, I cut a few pine tassels for a bed, and fell into the clear death-like sleep that always comes to the tired mountaineer.

Early next morning I set out to trace the ancient ice current back to its farthest recesses, filled with that inexpressible joy experienced by every explorer in nature's untrodden wilds. The mountain voices were still as in the hush of evening; the wind scarce stirred the branches of the mountain pine; the sun was up, but it was yet too cold for the birds and marmots—only the stream, cascading from pool to pool, seemed wholly awake and doing. Yet the spirit of the opening, blooming day called to action. The sunbeams came streaming gloriously through jagged openings of the *col*, glancing on ice-burnished pavements, and lighting the mirror surface of the lake, while every sunward rock and pinnacle burned white on the edges, like melting iron in a furnace. I passed round the north shore of the lake, and then followed the guidance of the stream back into the recesses of the amphitheatre. It led me past a chain of small lakelets set on bare granite benches, and connected by cascades and falls. The scenery became more rigidly arctic. The last dwarf pine was left far below, and the stream was bordered with icicles. As the sun advanced, rocks were loosened on shattered portions of the walls, and came bounding down gullies and *couloirs* in smoky, spattering avalanches, echoing wildly from crag to crag.

The main lateral moraines, that stretch so formally from the huge jaws of the amphitheatre out into the middle of the Illilouette basin, are continued upward in straggled masses along the amphitheatre walls, while separate stones, thousands of tons in weight, are left stranded here and there out in the middle of the main channel. Here, also, I observed a series of small, well-characterized, frontal moraines, ranged in regular order along the south wall of the amphitheatre, the shape and size of each moraine corresponding with the shapes and sizes of the daily shadows cast by different portions of the walls. This correspondence between moraines and shadows afterward became plain.

Tracing the stream back to the last of its chain of lakelets, I noticed a fine gray mud covering the stones on the bottom, excepting where the force of the entering and outflowing currents prevented its settling. On examination it proved to be wholly mineral in composition, and resembled the mud worn from a fine-grit grindstone. I at once suspected its glacial origin, for the stream which carried it came gurgling out of the base of a raw, fresh-looking moraine, which seemed to be in process of formation at that very moment. Not a plant, lichen, or weather-stain was any where visible upon its rough, unsettled surface. It is from sixty to over a hundred feet in height, and comes plunging down in front at an angle of thirty-eight degrees, which is the very steepest at which this moraine material will lie. Climbing the moraine in front was, therefore, no easy undertaking. The slightest touch loosened ponderous blocks, that went rumbling to the bottom, followed by a train of smaller stones and sand. Picking my way with the utmost caution, I at length gained the top, and beheld a small but well-characterized glacier swooping down from the sombre precipices of Black Mountain to the terminal moraine in a finely graduated curve. The solid ice appeared on all the lower portions of the glacier, though it was gray with dirt and stones imbedded in its surface. Farther up, the ice disappeared beneath coarsely granulated snow.

The surface of the glacier was still further characterized by dirt bands and the outcropping edges of blue veins that swept across from side to side in beautiful concentric curves, showing the laminated structure of the mass of the glacier ice. At the head of the glacier, where the *névé* joined the mountain, it was traversed by a huge yawning *Bergschrund*, in some places twelve or fourteen feet wide, and bridged at intervals by the remains of snow avalanches. Creeping along the edge of the *Schrund*, holding on with benumbed fingers, I discovered clear sections where the bedded and ribbon structure was beautifully illustrated. The surface snow, though every where sprinkled with stones shot down from the cliffs above, was in some places almost pure white, gradually becoming crystal-line, and changing to porous whitish ice of different shades, and this again changing at a depth of twenty or thirty feet to bluer ice, some of the ribbon-like bands of which were nearly pure and solid, and blended with the paler bands in the most gradual and exquisite manner imaginable, reminding one of the way that color bands come together in a rainbow.

A series of rugged zigzags enabled me to make my way down into the weird ice world of the *Schrund*. Its chambered hollows were hung with a multitude of clustered icicles, amidst which thin subdued light pulsed and shimmered with indescribable loveliness. Water dripped and tinkled overhead, and from far below there came strange solemn murmurs from currents that were feeling their way among veins and fissures on the bottom.

Ice creations of this kind are perfectly enchanting, notwith-standing one feels so entirely out of place in their pure fountain beauty. I was soon uncomfortably cold in my shirt sleeves, and the leaning wall of the *Schrund* seemed ready to ingulph me. Yet it was hard to leave the delicious music of the water, and still more the intense loveliness of the light.

Coming again to the surface of the glacier, I noticed blocks of every size setting out on their downward journey to be built into the terminal moraine.

The noon sun gave birth to a multitude of sweet-voiced rills that ran gracefully down the glacier, curling and swirling in their shining channels, and cutting clear sections in which the structure of the ice was beautifully revealed.

The series of frontal moraines I had observed in the morning extending along the base of the south wall of the amphitheatre corresponds in every particular with the moraines of this active glacier; and the causes of all that is special in their forms and order of distribution with reference to shadows now plainly unfolded themselves. When those climatic changes came on that broke up the main glacier that once filled the amphitheatre from wall to wall, a series of residual glaciers was left in the cliff shadows, under whose protection they lingered until they formed the frontal moraines we are studying. But as the seasons became warmer, or the snow supply became less abundant, they died in succession, all excepting the one we have just examined, and the causes of its longer life are sufficiently apparent in the greater extent of snow basin it drains and in its more perfect shelter from the sun. How much longer this little glacier will live will, of course, depend upon climate and the changes slowly effected in the form and exposure of its basin.

Soon after this discovery I made excursions to the ice wombs situated on the head cañons of the Tuolumne and San Joaquin, and discovered that what at first sight and from a distance resemble extensive snow-fields are really active glaciers, still grinding the rocks over which they flow, and thus completing the sculpture of the summits so grandly blocked out by their giant predecessors.

That these residual glaciers are wearing the rocks on which they flow is shown by the fact that all the streams rushing out from beneath them are turbid with finely ground rock mud. They all present solid ice snouts creeping out from beneath their fountain snows, and all are carrying down stones that have fallen upon them, to be at length deposited in moraines.

All the specific crevasses of glaciers are also exhibited by
them—marginal, transversal, and the jagged-edged *Bergschrund*. In some transversal crevasses, as, for example, near
the middle of the eastern branch of the Lyell Glacier, sections
of blue ice eighty to a hundred feet deep occur, while the
differential motion is manifested in the curves of the dirt
bands and of the blue veins and moraines, not a single glacial
attribute being either wanting or obscure. But notwithstanding the plainness and completeness of the proof, some of my
friends who never take much trouble to investigate for themselves continued to regard my observations and deductions
with distrust. I therefore determined to fix stakes in one of
the more accessible of the glaciers, and measure their displacement, with a view to making the ordinary demonstration of
true glacial movement, while subserving other desirable objects at the same time. The Maclure Glacier, situated on the
north side of the mountain of that name, seemed best fitted
for my purposes, and, with the assistance of my friend Galen
Clark, I planted five stakes in it on the 21st of August, 1872,
guarding against their being melted out by sinking them to a
depth of five feet. Four of them were extended across the
glacier in a straight line, beginning on the east side about
halfway between the head and foot of the glacier, and terminating near the middle of the current. Stake No. 1 was placed
about twenty-five yards from the side of the glacier; No. 2,
ninety-four yards; No. 3, one hundred and fifty-two yards;
No. 4, two hundred and twenty-five yards. No. 5 was placed
up the glacier about midway between the *Bergschrund* and
No. 4. On the 6th of October, or forty-six days after being
planted, I found the displacement of stake No. 1 to be eleven
inches, No. 2 to be eighteen inches, No. 3 to be thirty-four
inches, No. 4 to be forty-seven inches, and No. 5 to be forty-
six inches. As stake No. 4 was near the middle of the current,
it was probably not far from the point of maximum velocity—
forty-seven inches in forty-six days, or about one inch per
twenty-four hours.

On setting out from Yosemite Valley to fix stakes in the
Maclure Glacier, I invited Professor Joseph Leconte to accompany me. He had already given in his adhesion to my glacial
theory for the formation of Yosemite Valley, and I was anxious

to direct attention to other erosive effects of the ancient glaciers in the formation of mountains, ridges, lake basins, etc.,
as well as to point out some of the newly discovered glaciers.

Shortly after his return to Oakland he prepared a paper "On
some of the Ancient Glaciers of the Sierra," which was read
before the California Academy of Sciences, and afterward published in the *American Journal of Science and Arts*, in which
he says, "Here, then" (on Mount Lyell), "we have *now existing not a true glacier*, perhaps, *certainly not a typical glacier*
(since there is no true glacier ice *visible*, but only snow and
névé, and certainly *no protrusion of an icy tongue* beyond the
snow-field), yet nevertheless in some sense a glacier."

The above is an example of the rashness sometimes evinced
by scientific observers in allowing themselves to decide upon
imperfect data. Professor Leconte had never before seen a glacier of any kind, and did nothing more by way of investigation
of this one than to spend a few minutes on the terminal moraine. Yet this, it seems, was deemed sufficient to enable him
to decide "certainly" concerning it. Now the Lyell Glacier,
which Professor Leconte approached, but did not set foot
upon, was at the time of his visit (August 19) still covered with
winter snow. Had his visit been delayed a few weeks he would
have observed the required "icy tongue protruding from beneath the *névé*," because by this time the sun melted the covering of snow, and, according to his own chosen definition,
the glacier suddenly became changed to a typical one.

As to the statement, "there is no true glacier ice visible," it
is only necessary to observe that though there was none visible
from the moraine where he was seated, there were many fine
sections of "true glacier ice" visible in marginal and transversal
crevasses, had he taken the pains to reach them.

Great vagueness prevails concerning the essential characteristics of glaciers. The icy snout creeping down out of the *névé*
fountains is not available for all glaciers at all seasons, because
in years of extraordinary snow-fall the whole surface of some
slow-flowing glaciers remains covered during the whole year,
and would accordingly be classified as true glaciers one season,
névé fields another; and, as we have seen, the Lyell Glacier,
though not typical in August, became typical in September.

A glacier is a current of ice derived from snow. Complete

glaciers of the first order take their rise on the mountains, and descend into the sea, just as all complete rivers of the first order do. In North Greenland the snow supply and general climatic conditions are such that its glaciers pour directly into the ocean, and so undoubtedly did those of the Pacific slope during the flush times of the glacial epoch; but now the world is so warm and the snow crop so scanty, nearly all the glaciers left alive have melted to mere hints of their former selves. The Lyell Glacier is now less than a mile long; yet, setting out from the frontal moraine, we may trace its former course on grooved and polished surfaces and by immense cañons and moraines a distance of more than forty miles.

The glaciers of Switzerland are in a like decaying condition as compared with their former grandeur; so also are those of Norway, Asia, and South America. They have come to resemble the short rivers of the eastern slope of the Sierra that flow out into the hot plains and are dried up. According to the Schlagintweit brothers, the glaciers of Switzerland melt at an average elevation above the level of the sea of 7414 feet. The glacier of Grindelwald melts at less than 4000 feet; that of the Aar at about 6000. The Himalaya glacier, in which the Ganges takes its rise, does not, according to Captain Hodgson, descend below 12,914 feet. The average elevation at which the glaciers of the Sierra melt is not far from 11,000 feet above sea-level. The Whitney Glacier, discovered by Clarence King, is situated on the north side of Mount Shasta, and descends to 9500 feet above the sea, which is the lowest point reached by any glacier within the limits of California. Mount Shasta, however, is an isolated volcanic cone, and can not in any sense be regarded as a portion of the Sierra. Mount Whitney, situated near the southern extremity of the Sierra, although the highest mountain in the range (nearly 15,000 feet), does not give birth to a single glacier. Small patches of perpetual snow and ice occur on its northern slopes, but they are shallow, and give no evidence of glacial motion. Its sides, however, are still brilliantly polished by vanished glaciers that once descended into the main trunk glacier of Kern Valley on the west and to the Owens River on the east.

Mount Ritter, about 13,300 feet in height, still nourishes five glaciers, which, though small, are exceedingly well characterized, and differ in no particular from those of Switzerland excepting in degree. The finest of the five is on the north side, and flows at first in a northerly direction, then curves toward the west, and descends into a small blue glacier lake, whose banks around more than half its circumference are buried beneath perpetual snow. The outcropping edges of "the blue veins" are presented on the lower portion of this glacier, sweeping across the snout in fine concentric curves, scarcely marred by the rocky *débris* with which the glacier is laden. This beautiful glacier forms one of the highest sources of the North Fork of the San Joaquin.

Another of the Ritter glaciers, situated on the northeastern slopes of the mountain, is drained by a branch of Rush Creek, which flows into Mono Lake on the east side of the range. All the sixty-five Sierra glaciers that I have observed are a survival of the best fed and most favorably situated.

The Sierra granite is admirably fitted for the reception and preservation of glacial records, and from these it is plain that the Sierra ice once covered the whole range continuously as one sheet, which gradually broke up into individual glaciers, and these again into small residual glaciers arranged with reference to shadows. These last were very numerous; several thousand existed on the western flank alone, differing in no way from those that still linger in the highest and coolest fountains.

All the glaciers of California occur upon the north sides of mountains, and flow northward; or if they flow in an easterly or westerly direction, they are contained between protecting ridges trending in the same direction.

Furthermore, because the main axis of the Sierra extends in a north-northwesterly direction, the east side of the range is longer in shadow, and the greater number of the glaciers that occur along the immediate axis are on the east side.

The transformation of snow into glacier ice varies as to place and rapidity with the climate and with the form of the basin in which the fountain snow is collected. In the Sierra there is no definite snow-line, and therefore no fields of fountain snow extending to determinate elevations above the glaciers for the true glacier ice gradually to merge into. The change, therefore, of snow to flowing ice is more abrupt in the Sierra Nevada than in the Alps or in any mountain range possessed of perpetual snow not dependent upon shadows.

The whole number of active glaciers in the Alps is, according to the Schlagintweit brothers, 1100, of which one hundred may be regarded as primary. The total surface of snow, *névé*, and ice is estimated at 1177 square miles, or an average area of about one square mile per glacier. Some of the Sierra glaciers are as large; as, for example, the Lyell, North Ritter, and several that are nameless on the head of the South and Middle forks of the San Joaquin.

The main cause that has prevented the earlier discovery of Sierra Nevada glaciers is simply the want of explorations in the regions where they occur. The labors of the State Geological Survey in this connection amounted to a slight reconnaissance, while the common tourist, ascending the range only as far as Yosemite Valley, sees no portion of the true Alps containing the glaciers excepting a few peak clusters in the distance.

In the Swiss Alps carriage roads approach within a few hundred yards of some of the low-descending glaciers, while the comparative remoteness and inaccessibility of the Sierra glaciers may be inferred from the fact that, during the prosecution of my own explorations in five summers, I never met a single human being, not even an Indian or a hunter.

Harper's Monthly, November 1875

God's First Temples

HOW SHALL WE PRESERVE OUR FORESTS?

EDS. RECORD-UNION: The forests of coniferous trees growing on our mountain ranges are by far the most destructible of the natural resources of California. Our gold, and silver, and cinnabar are stored in the rocks, locked up in the safest of all banks, so that notwithstanding the world has been making a run upon them for the last twenty-five years, they still pay out steadily, and will probably continue to do so centuries hence, like rivers pouring from perennial mountain fountains. The riches of our magnificent soil-beds are also comparatively safe, because even the most barbarous methods of wildcat farming cannot effect complete destruction, and however great the impoverishment produced, full restoration of fertility is always possible to the enlightened farmer. But our forest belts are being burned and cut down and wasted like a field of unprotected grain, and once destroyed can never be wholly restored even by centuries of persistent and pains-taking cultivation.

The practical importance of the preservation of our forests is augmented by their relations to climate, soil and streams. Strip off the woods with their underbrush from the mountain flanks, and the whole State, the lowlands as well as the highlands, would gradually change into a desert. During rainfalls, and when the winter snow was melting, every stream would become a destructive torrent, overflowing its banks, stripping off and carrying away the fertile soils, filling up the lower river channels, and overspreading the lowland fields with detritus to a vastly more destructive degree than all the washings from hydraulic mines concerning which we now hear so much. Dripping forests give rise to moist sheets and currents of air, and the sod of grasses and underbrush thus fostered, together with the roots of trees themselves, absorb and hold back rains and melting snow, yet allowing them to ooze and percolate and flow gently in useful fertilizing streams. Indeed every pine needle and rootlet, as well as fallen trunks and large clasping roots, may be regarded as dams, hoarding the bounty of storm clouds, and dispensing it as blessings all through the summer, instead of allowing it to gather and rush headlong in short-lived devastating floods. Streams taking their rise in deep woods flow unfailingly as those derived from the eternal ice and snow of the Alps. So constant indeed and apparent is the relationship between forests and never-failing springs, that effect is frequently mistaken for cause, it being often asserted that fine forests will grow only along streamsides where their roots are well watered, when in fact the forests themselves produce many of the streams flowing through them.

The main forest belt of the Sierra is restricted to the western flank, and extends unbrokenly from one end of the range to the other at an elevation of from three to eight thousand feet above sea level. The great master-existence of these noble woods is sequoia gigantea, or big tree. Only two species of sequoia are known to exist in the world. Both belong to California, one being found only in the Sierra, the other (sequoia sempervirens) in the Coast Ranges, although no less than five distinct fossil species have been discovered in the tertiary and cretaceous rocks of Greenland. I would like to call attention to this noble tree, with special reference to its preservation. The species extends from the well known Calaveras groves on the north, to the head of Deer creek on the south, near the big bend of the Kern river, a distance of about two hundred miles, at an elevation above sea level of from about five to eight thousand feet. From the Calaveras to the South Fork of King's river it occurs only in small isolated groves, and so sparsely and irregularly distributed that two gaps occur nearly forty miles in width, the one between the Calaveras and Tuolumne groves, the other between those of the Fresno and King's rivers. From King's river the belt extends across the broad, rugged basins of the Kaweah and Tule rivers to its southern boundary on Deer creek, interrupted only by deep, rocky canyons, the width of this portion of the belt being from three to ten miles.

In the northern groves few young trees or saplings are found ready to take the places of the failing old ones, and because these ancient, childless sequoias are the only ones known to botanists, the species has been generally regarded as doomed to speedy extinction, as being nothing more than an expiring remnant of an ancient flora, and that therefore there is no use trying to save it or to prolong its few dying days. This, however, is in the main a mistaken notion, for the Sierra as it now exists never had an ancient flora. All the species now growing on the range have been planted since the close of the glacial period, and the Big Tree has never formed a greater part of these post-glacial forests than it does today, however widely it may have been distributed throughout preglacial forests.

In tracing the belt southward, all the phenomena bearing upon its history goes to show that the dominion of Sequoia Gigantea, as King of California trees, is not yet passing away. No tree in the woods seems more firmly established, or more safely settled in accordance with climate and soil. They fill the woods and form the principal tree, growing heartily on solid ledges, along water courses, in the deep, moist soil of meadows, and upon avalanche and glacial debris, with a multitude of thrifty seedlings and saplings crowding around the aged, ready to take their places and rule the woods.

Nevertheless Nature in her grandly deliberate way keeps up a rotation of forest crops. Species develop and die like individuals, animal as well as plant. Man himself will as surely become extinct as sequoia or mastodon, and be at length known only as a fossil. Changes of this kind are, however, exceedingly slow in their movements, and, as far as the lives of individuals are concerned, such changes have no appreciable effect. Sequoia seems scarcely further past prime as a species than its companion firs (*Picea amabilis* and *P. grandis*), and judging from its present condition and its ancient history, as far as I have been able to decipher it, our sequoia will live and flourish gloriously until A.D. 15,000 at least—probably for longer—that is, if it be allowed to remain in the hands of Nature.

But waste and pure destruction are already taking place at a terrible rate, and unless protective measures be speedily invented and enforced, in a few years this noblest tree-species in the world will present only a few hacked and scarred remnants. The great enemies of forests are fire and the ax. The destructive effects of these, as compared with those caused by the operations of nature, are instantaneous. Floods undermine and kill many a tree, storm winds bend and break, landslips and avalanches overwhelm whole groves, lightning shatters and burns, but the combined effects of all these amount only to a wholesome beauty-producing culture. Last summer I found some five saw mills located in or near the lower edge of the Sequoia belt, all of which saw more or less of the big tree into lumber. One of these (Hyde's), situated on the north fork of the Kaweah, cut no less than 2,000,000 feet of Sequoia lumber last season. Most of the Fresno big trees are doomed to feed the mills recently erected near them, and a company has been formed by Chas. Converse to cut the noble forest on the south fork of·King's river. In these milling operations waste far exceeds use. After the choice young manageable trees have been felled, the woods are cleared of limbs and refuse by burning, and in these clearing fires, made with reference to further operations, all the young seedlings and saplings are destroyed, together with many valuable fallen trees and old trees, too large to be cut, thus effectually cutting off all hopes of a renewal of the forest.

These ravages, however, of mill-fires and mill-axes are small as compared with those of the "sheep-men's" fires. Incredible numbers of sheep are driven to the mountain pastures every summer, and in order to make easy paths and to improve the pastures, running fires are set everywhere to burn off the old logs and underbrush. These fires are far more universal and destructive than would be guessed. They sweep through nearly the entire forest belt of the range from one extremity to the other, and in the dry weather, before the coming on of winter storms, are very destructive to all kinds of young trees, and especially to sequoia, whose loose, fibrous bark catches and burns at once. Excepting the Calaveras, I, last summer, examined every sequoia grove in the range, together with the main belt extending across the basins of Kaweah and Tule, and found everywhere the most deplorable waste from this cause. Indians burn off underbrush to facilitate deer-hunting. Campers of all kinds often permit fires to run, so also do mill-men, but the fires of "sheep-men" probably form more than 90 per cent. of all destructive fires that sweep the woods.

Fire, then, is the arch destroyer of our forests, and sequoia forests suffer most of all. The young trees are most easily fire killed; the old are most easily burned, and the prostrate trunks, which *never rot* and would remain valuable until our tenth centennial, are reduced to ashes.

In European countries, especially in France, Germany, Italy and Austria, the economies of forestry have been carefully studied under the auspices of Government, with the most beneficial results. Whether our loose-jointed Government is really able or willing to do anything in the matter remains to be seen. If our law makers were to discover and enforce any method tending to lessen even in a small degree the destruction going on, they would thus cover a multitude of legislative sins in the eyes of every tree lover. I am satisfied, however, that the question can be intelligently discussed only after a careful survey of our forests has been made, together with studies of the forces now acting upon them.

A law was constructed some years ago making the cutting down of sequoias over sixteen feet in diameter illegal. A more absurd and shortsighted piece of legislation could not be conceived. All the young trees might be cut and burned, and all the old ones might be burned but not cut.

Sacramento Daily Union,
February 5, 1876

Snow-Storm on Mount Shasta

MOUNT SHASTA, situated near the northern extremity of the Sierra Nevada, rises in solitary grandeur from a lightly sculptured lava plain, and maintains a far more impressive and commanding individuality than any other mountain within the limits of California.

Go where you will within a radius of from fifty to a hundred miles, there stands the colossal cone of Shasta, clad in perpetual snow, the one grand landmark that never sets. While Mount Whitney, situated near the southern extremity of the Sierra, notwithstanding it lifts its granite summit some four or five hundred feet higher than Shasta, is yet almost entirely snowless during the summer months, and is so feebly individualized, the traveller often searches for it in vain amid the thickets of rival peaks by which it is surrounded.

The elevation of the highest point of Mount Shasta, as determined by the State Geological Survey, is in round numbers 14,400 feet above mean tide. That of Mount Whitney, computed from fewer and perhaps less reliable observations, is about 14,900 feet. But inasmuch as the average elevation of the common plain out of which Shasta rises is only about 4000 feet above the sea, while the actual base of Mount Whitney lies at an elevation of 11,000 feet, the individual stature of the former is nearly two and a half times that of the latter; and while the circumference of Mount Shasta around the base is nearly seventy miles, that of Whitney is less than five.

All that has been observed of the internal frame-work of Mount Shasta goes to show that its entire bulk originated in successive eruptions of ashes and lava, which, pouring over the lips of craters, layer upon layer, grew upward and outward like the trunk of an exogenous tree.

The Shasta lavas are chiefly trachytic and basaltic, varying greatly in color, density, and age. A few tufaceous and brecciated beds are visible in eroded sections near the summit, but pumice and obsidian, usually so abundant in other volcanic regions throughout the State, are here remarkably rare.

During the glacial period Mount Shasta was a centre of

dispersal for the glaciers of the circumjacent region. The entire mountain was then loaded with ice, which, ever descending, grooved its sides and broke up its summit into a mass of ruins. But the whole quantity of denudation the mountain has undergone is not easily determined, its porous crumbling rocks being ill adapted for the reception and preservation of glacial inscriptions. All the finer striations have been effaced, while the extreme irregularity of its lavas, as regards erodibility, and the disturbances caused by inter and post glacial eruptions, have obscured or wholly obliterated those heavier characters of the glacial record found so clearly inscribed upon the granitic pages of the high Sierra between latitude 36° 30′ and 39°. This much, however, is plain, that when at length the ice period began to draw near a close, the Shasta ice cap was gradually melted off around the bottom, and, in receding and breaking up into its present condition, deposited the irregular heaps and rings of moraine soil upon which the Shasta forests are growing.

The Whitney glacier is the most important of the few fragmentary ice patches still remaining active. It takes its rise in extensive snow and *névé* fields on the summit, flows northward, and descends in a series of crevassed curves and cascades almost to the timber line—a distance of nearly three miles. Though not the very largest, this is perhaps the longest active glacier in the State. Glacial erosion of the Shasta lavas gives rise to light porous soils, largely made up of sandy detritus that yields very readily to the transporting power of running water. Several centuries ago immense quantities of this lighter material were washed down from the higher slopes by an extraordinary flood, giving rise to the simultaneous deposition of conspicuous delta-like beds, extending around the entire circumference of the base, their smooth gray surfaces offering a striking contrast to the rough scoriaceous lava flows that divide them. But notwithstanding the incalculable wear and tear and ruinous degradation that Shasta has undergone, the regularity and symmetry of its outlines remain unrivaled. The mountain begins to leave the plain in slopes scarcely perceptible, measuring from two to three degrees. These are continued by exquisitely drawn gradations, mile after mile, all the way to the truncated crater-like summit, where they attain a steepness of from twenty to thirty-five degrees. This grand simplicity is partially interrupted on the north by a subordinate cone that grows out of the side of the main cone about 3000 feet below the summit.

This side cone has been in a state of eruption subsequent to the breaking up of the main ice cap, as shown by the comparatively unwasted circular crater in which it terminates, and by numerous streams of fresh unglaciated lava that radiate from it as a centre.

The main summit is about one and a half miles in diameter from southwest to northeast, and consists mainly of two extensive snow and *névé* fields, bounded by crumbling peaks and ridges, among which we look in vain for any sure plan of an ancient crater. The extreme summit is situated upon the southern extremity of a narrow ridge that bounds the main summit on the east. As viewed from the north, it is an irregular blunt peaklet about ten feet high, fast disappearing before the stormy atmospheric erosion to which it is subjected. Hot sulphurous gases and vapors escape with a loud hissing noise from fissures in the lava near the base of the eastern ridge, opposite the highest peaklet. Several of the vents cast up a spray of clear bead-like drops of hot water, that rise repeatedly into the air and fall back until worn into vapor.

The steam and spray phenomena seem to be produced simply by melting snow coming in the way of the escaping gases, while the gases themselves are evidently derived from the heated interior, and may be regarded as the last feeble expression of that vast volcanic energy that builded the mountain.

Since the close of the ice period, nature has divided Mount Shasta into three distinct botanic zones. The first, which may be called the chaparral zone, has an average width of about four miles, and comprises the greater portion of the sandy flood beds noted above. They are densely overgrown with chaparral from three to six feet high, composed chiefly of manzanita, cherry, chincapin, and several species of ceanothus, forming when in full bloom one of the most glorious spectacles conceivable.

The continuity of these immense chaparral fields is grandly interrupted by wide swaths of coniferous trees, chiefly sugar and yellow pines, with Douglass spruce, silver-fir, and incense cedar, many specimens of which are over 200 feet high and six or seven feet in diameter at the base.

Golden-rods, asters, gilias, lilies, and lupines, with a multitude of less conspicuous herbaceous plants, occur in warm openings of the woods, with forms and colors in delightful accord, and enlivened with butterflies and bees.

The next higher is the fir zone, made up almost exclusively of the three silver-firs, viz., *Picea grandis*, *P. amabilis*, and *P. amabilis*, var. *nobilis*.

This zone is from two to three miles wide, has an average elevation above the sea on its lower edge of 6000 feet, on its upper of 8000, and is far the simplest and best defined of the three.

The Alpine zone is made up of dwarf pines, heath-worts, stiff wiry carices, lichens, and red snow.

The pines attain an elevation of 9500 feet, but at this height their summits rise only three or four feet into the frosty air, and are close-pressed and level, as if crushed by winter snow, and shorn off by the icy winds, yet flowering nevertheless, and sometimes producing cones and ripe nuts. Bryanthus, a beautiful flowering heath-wort, flourishes a few hundred feet higher, accompanied by kalmia and spiræa. Dwarf daisies and carices attain an elevation on favorable slopes of 11,000 feet, while beyond this a scanty growth of lichens and red snow composes the entire vegetation.

The following is a list of all the coniferous trees I have been able to find growing upon Mount Shasta, named downward in the order of their occurrence:

Pinus flexilis	. Dwarf pine.
Pinus monticola	. Mountain pine.
Pinus contorta	. Tamarack pine.
Picea amabilis	⎫
Picea amabilis, var. *nobilis* . . .	⎬ Silver-fir.
Picea grandis	⎭
Pinus ponderosa	. Yellow pine.
Pinus ponderosa, var. *jeffreyii* .	. Jeffrey pine.
Pinus lambertiana	. Sugar-pine.
Abies douglassii	. Douglass spruce.

> *Libocedrus decurrens*   .   .   .   . .Incense cedar.
> *Pinus tuberculata.*
> *Juniperus occidentalis* .   .   .   . .Cedar.

The bulk of the forest is made up of the three silver-firs, Douglass spruce, the yellow and sugar pines, and incense cedar, and of these *Picea amabilis* is at once the most abundant and the most beautiful.

The ascent of Mount Shasta is usually made in July or August, from Strawberry Valley, on the Oregon and California stage-road. Storms are then less common and less violent, and the deep snows are melted from the lower slopes, and the beautiful Alpine vegetation is then coming into bloom. The ordinary plan is to ride from Strawberry Valley to the upper edge of the timber line, a distance of ten miles, the first day, and camp; then, rising early next morning, push to the summit, and return to the valley on the evening of the second day.

In journeying up the valley of the Upper Sacramento one obtains frequent views of Mount Shasta, through the pine-trees, from the tops of hills and ridges; but at Strawberry Valley there is a grand out-opening of the forests, and Shasta stands revealed at just the distance to be seen most comprehensively and impressively.

Looking at outlines, there, in the immediate foreground, is a smooth green meadow with its crooked stream; then a zone of dark forest, its countless spires of fir and pine rising above one another higher and higher in luxuriant ranks; and above all the great white cone sweeping far into the cloudless blue—meadow, forest, and mountain inseparably blended and framed in by the arching sky. My last ascent of Shasta was made on the 30th of April, 1875, accompanied by Jerome Fay, a hardy and competent mountaineer, for the purpose of making barometrical observations on the summit, while Captain A. F. Rodgers, of the United States Coast Survey, made simultaneous observations with a compared barometer at the base.

In the cooler portions of the woods winter snow was still lying five feet deep, and we had a tedious time breaking through it with the pack animals. It soon became apparent that we would not be able to reach the summer camping ground; and after floundering and breaking trail in the drifts until near sundown, we were glad to camp for the night as best we could upon a rough lava ridge that protruded through the snow. From here we carried blankets and one day's provision on our backs over the snow to the extreme edge of the timber line, and made a second camp in the lee of a block of red trachyte. This, of course, was done with a view to lessening as much as possible the labor of completing the ascent, to be undertaken next day. Here, on our trachyte bed, we obtained two hours of shallow sleep, mingled with fine glimpses of the keen starry night. We rose at 2 A.M., warmed a tin-cupful of coffee, broiled a slice of frozen venison on the coals, and started for the summit at 3.20 A.M.

The crisp icy sky was without a cloud, and the stars lighted us on our way. Deep silence brooded the mountain, broken only by the night wind and an occasional rock falling from crumbling buttresses to the snow slopes below. The wild beauty of the morning stirred our pulses in glad exhilaration, and we strode rapidly onward, seldom stopping to take breath—over the broad red apron of lava that descends from the west side of the smaller of the two cone summits, across the gorge that divides them, up the majestic snow curves sweeping to the top of the ancient crater, around the broad icy fountains of the Whitney glacier, past the hissing fumaroles, and at 7.30 A.M. we attained the utmost summit.

Up to this time there was nothing discernible either in the wind tones or in the sky that betokened the near approach of a storm; but on gaining the summit we observed several hundred square miles of white cumuli spread out on the lava plain toward Lassen's Peak, squirming dreamily in the sunshine far beneath, and exciting no alarm.

The slight weariness of the ascent was soon rested away. The sky was of the thinnest, purest azure; spiritual life filled every pore of rock and cloud; and we reveled in the marvelous abundance and beauty of the landscapes by which we were encircled.

At 9 A.M. the dry thermometer stood at 34° in shade, and rose steadily until 1 P.M., when it stood at 50°, although no doubt strongly influenced by sun heat radiated from the adjacent cliffs. A vigorous bumble-bee zigzagged around our heads, filling the air with a summery hay-field drone, as if wholly unconscious of the fact that the nearest honey flower was a mile beneath him.

Clouds the mean while were growing down in Shasta Valley—massive swelling cumuli, colored gray and purple and close pearly white. These, constantly extending around southward on both sides of Mount Shasta, at length united with the older field lying toward Lassen's Peak, thus circling the mountain in one continuous cloud zone. Rhett and Klamath lakes were eclipsed in clouds scarcely less bright than their own silvery disks. The black lava beds made famous by the Modoc war; many a snow-laden peak far north in Oregon; the Scott and Trinity mountains; the blue Coast Range; Shasta Valley, dotted with volcanoes; the dark coniferous forests filling the valleys of the Upper Sacramento—were all in turn obscured, leaving our own lofty cone solitary in the sunshine, and contained between two skies—a sky of spotless blue above, a sky of clouds beneath. The creative sun shone gloriously upon the white expanse, and rare cloud-lands, hill and dale, mountain and valley, rose responsive to his rays, and steadily developed to higher beauty and individuality.

One colossal master-cone, corresponding to Mount Shasta, rose close alongside with a visible motion, its firm polished bosses seemingly so near and substantial we fancied we might leap down upon them from where we stood, and reach the ground by scrambling down their sides.

Storm clouds on the mountains—how truly beautiful they are!—floating fountains bearing water for every well; the angels of streams and lakes; brooding in the deep pure azure, or sweeping along the ground, over ridge and dome, over meadow, over forest, over garden and grove; lingering with cooling shadows, refreshing every flower, and soothing rugged rock brows with a gentleness of touch and gesture no human hand can equal!

The weather of spring and summer throughout the middle region of the Sierra is usually well flecked with rain-storms and light dustings of snow, most of which are far too obviously joyous and life-giving to be regarded as storms. In the case of the smallest and most perfectly individualized specimens, a richly modeled cumulus cloud is seen rising above the dark forests, about 11 o'clock A.M., directly upward into the calm sky, to a height of about four or five thousand feet above the ground, or ten or twelve thousand feet above the sea; its pearly bosses finely relieved by gray and purple shadows, and exhibiting outlines as keen as those of a glacier-polished dome. In less than an hour it attains full development, and stands poised in the blazing sunshine like some colossal fungus. Presently a vigorous thunder-bolt crashes through the crisp sunny air, ringing like steel on steel, its startling detonation breaking into a spray of echoes among the rocky cañons below. Then down comes a cataract of rain to the wild gardens and groves. The big crystal drops tingle the pine needles, plash and spatter on granite pavements, and pour adown the sides of ridges and domes in a net-work of gray bubbling rills. In a few minutes the firm storm cloud withers to a mesh of dim filaments and disappears, leaving the sky more sunful than before. Every bird and plant is invigorated, a steam of fragrance rises from the ground, and the storm is finished—one cloud, one lightning flash, one dash of rain. This is the California rain-storm reduced to its lowest terms. Snow-storms of the same tone and dimensions abound in the highest summits, but in spring they not unfrequently attain larger proportions, and assume a violence of expression scarcely surpassed by those bred in the depths of winter. Such was the storm now gathering close around us. It began to declare itself shortly after noon, and I entertained the idea of abandoning my purpose of making a 3 P.M. observation, as agreed on by Captain Rodgers and myself, and at once make a push down to our safe camp in the timber. Jerome peered at short intervals over the jagged ridge on which we stood, making anxious gestures in the rough wind, and becoming more and more emphatic in his remarks upon the weather, declaring that if we did not make a speedy escape, we should be compelled to pass the night on the summit. Anxiety, however, to complete my observations fixed me to the ridge. No inexperienced person was depending upon me, and I told Jerome that we two mountaineers could break down through any storm likely to fall. About half past 1 o'clock P.M. thin fibrous cloud films began to blow directly over the summit of the cone from north to south, drawn out in long fairy webs, like carded wool, forming and dissolving as if by magic. The wind twisted them into ringlets and whirled them in a succession of graceful convolutions, like the outside sprays of Yosemite falls; then sailing out in the pure azure over the precipitous brink of the cone, they were drifted together in light gray rolls, like foam wreaths on a river.

These higher cloud fabrics were evidently produced by the chilling of the air from its own expansion, caused by an upward deflection against the mountain slopes. They steadily increased on the north rim of the cone, forming a thick, opaque, ill-defined embankment, from whose icy meshes snow flowers began to fall, alternating with hail. The sky speedily darkened, and just after I had completed my observations and boxed the instruments, the storm broke in full vigor. The cliffs were covered with a remarkable net-work of hail rills that poured and rolled adown the gray and red lava slopes like cascades of rock-beaten water.

These hail-stones seemed to belong to an entirely distinct species from any I had before observed. They resembled small mushrooms both in texture and general form, their six straight sides widening upward from a narrow base to a wide dome-like crown.

A few minutes after 3 P.M. we began to force our way down the eastern ridge, past the group of hissing fumaroles. The storm at once became inconceivably violent, with scarce a preliminary scowl. The thermometer fell twenty-two degrees, and soon sank below zero. Hail gave place to snow, and darkness came on like night. The wind, rising to the highest pitch of violence, boomed and surged like breakers on a rocky coast. The lightnings flashed amid the desolate crags in terrible accord, their tremendous muffled detonations unrelieved by a single echo, and seeming to come thudding passionately forth from out the very heart of the storm.

Could we have begun at once to descend the snow-filled grooves leading to the timber, we might have made good our escape, however dark or violent the storm. As it was, we had first to make our way along a dangerous snow ridge nearly a mile and a half in length, flanked by steep ice slopes on one side, and by shattered precipices on the other. Fortunately I had taken the precaution ere the storm began, while apprehensive of this very darkness, to make the most dangerous points clear to my mind, and to mark their relations with reference to the direction of the wind. When, therefore, the storm broke, I felt confident we could urge our way through the darkness and uproar with no other guidance. After passing the "Hot Springs," I halted in the shelter of a lava block to let Jerome, who had fallen a little behind, come up. Here he opened a council, in which, amid circumstances sufficiently exciting, but without evincing any bewilderment, he maintained, in opposition to my views, that it was impossible to proceed: the ridge was too dangerous, the snow was blinding, and the frost too intense to be borne; and finally, that, even supposing it possible for us to grope our way through the darkness, the wind was sufficiently violent to hurl us bodily over the cliffs, and that our only hope was in wearing away the afternoon and night among the fumaroles, where we should at least avoid freezing.

I urged that the wind was chiefly at our backs, and that, once arrived at the western edge of the cone, we had but to slide or wallow down steep inclines whose topographical leadings would insure our finding camp in any case, and that if need be we could creep along the more dangerous portions of the ridge, and clear the ice and precipices on hands and feet. He positively refused, however, to entertain any thought of venturing into the storm in that direction, while I, aware of the real dangers that would beset our efforts, and conscious of being the cause of his being thus imperiled, decided not to leave him.

Our discussions ended, Jerome made a dash from behind the lava block, and began forcing his way back some twenty or thirty yards to the Hot Springs against the wind flood, wavering and struggling as if caught in a torrent of water; and after watching in vain for any flaw in the storm that might be urged as a new argument for attempting the descent, I was compelled to follow. "Here," said Jerome, as we stood shivering in the midst of the hissing, sputtering fumaroles, "we shall be safe from frost." "Yes," said I, "we can lie in this mud and gravel, hot at least on one side; but how shall we protect our lungs from the acid gases? and how, after our clothing is saturated with melting snow, shall we be able to reach camp without freezing, even after the storm is over? We shall have to await the sunshine; and when will it come?"

The patch of volcanic climate to which we committed ourselves has an area of about one-fourth of an acre, but it was only about an eighth of an inch in thickness, because the scalding gas jets were shorn off close to the ground by the oversweeping flood of frost wind.

The marvelous lavishness of the snow can be conceived only by mountaineers. The crystal flowers seemed to touch one another and fairly to thicken the blast. This was the blooming time, the summer of the storm, and never before have I seen mountain cloud flowering so profusely. When the bloom of the Shasta chaparral is falling, the ground is covered for hundreds of square miles to the depth of half an inch; but the bloom of our Shasta cloud grew and matured and fell to a depth of two feet in less than a single day. Some crystals caught on my sleeve, and, examined under a lens, presented all their rays exquisitely perfect; but most were more or less bruised by striking against one another, or by falling and rolling over and over on the ground and rising again. The storm blast, laden with this fine-ground Alpine snow dust, can not long be braved with impunity, and the strongest mountaineer is glad to turn and flee.

I was in my shirt sleeves, and in less than half an hour was wet to the skin: Jerome fortunately had on a close-fitting coat, and his life was more deeply imbedded in flesh than mine. Yet we both trembled and shivered in a weak, nervous way, as much, I suppose, from exhaustion brought on by want of food and sleep as from the sifting of the icy wind through our wet clothing.

The snow fell with unabated lavishness until an hour or two after the coming on of what appeared to be the natural darkness of night. The whole quantity would probably measure about two feet. Up to the time the storm first fell upon the mountain, its development was gentle in the extreme—the deliberate growth of cumulus clouds beneath, the weaving of translucent tissue above, then the roar of the wind, the crash of thunder, and the darkening flight of snow flowers. Its decay was not less sudden—the clouds broke and vanished, not a snow-flake was left in the sky, and the stars shone out with pure and tranquil radiance.

As our experiences were somewhat exceptional during the long strange night that followed, it may perhaps be interesting to record them.

In the early stages of the night, while our sufferings were less severe, I tried to induce Jerome, who is a hunter, to break out in bear stories or Indian adventures to lessen our consciousness of the cold. But although meeting the storm bravely, he was not in talking condition. Occasionally he would indulge in calculations as to how long the fire of life would burn, whether the storm would last all the night and the next day, and if so, whether Sisson would be able to come to the rescue ere we succumbed to the cold. Then, with a view to cheering myself as well as him, I pictured the morning breaking all cloudless and sunful, assuring him that no storm ever lasted continuously from day to day at this season of the year; that out of all this frost and weariness we would yet escape to our friends and homes, and then all that would be left of the trying night would be a clump of unrelated memories he would tell to his children.

We lay flat on our backs, so as to present as little surface as possible to the wind. The mealy snow gathered on our breasts, and I did not rise again to my feet for seventeen hours. We were glad at first to see the snow drifting into the hollows of our clothing, hoping it would serve to deaden the force of the ice wind; but, though soft at first, it soon froze into a stiff, crusty heap, rather augmenting our novel misery. "Last year," said Jerome, "I guided a minister up here. I wish he were here now to try some prayers. What do you really think, Muir—would they help a fellow in a time like this?" Yet, after all, he seemed to recognize the unflinching fair play of Nature, and her essential kindliness, though making no jot of allowance for ignorance or mistakes. The snow fell on us not a whit more harshly than warm rain on the grass.

The night wind rushed in wild uproar across the shattered cliffs, piercing us through and through, and causing violent convulsive shivering, while those portions of our bodies in contact with the hot lava were being broiled.

When the heat became unendurable, we scraped snow and bits of trachyte beneath us, or shifted from place to place by shoving an inch or two at a time with heels and elbows; for to stand erect in blank exposure to the wind seemed like certain death.

The acrid incrustations sublimed from the escaping gases frequently gave way, opening new vents, over which we were scalded; and fearing that if at any time the wind should fall, carbonic acid, which usually forms so considerable a portion of the gaseous exhalations of volcanoes, might collect in sufficient quantities to cause sleep and death, I warned Jerome against forgetting himself for a single moment, even should his sufferings admit of such a thing. Accordingly, when, during the long dreary watches of the night, we roused suddenly from a state of half consciousness, we called each other excitedly by name, each fearing the other was benumbed or dead.

The ordinary sensations of cold give but faint conceptions of that which comes on after hard exercise, with want of food and sleep, combined with wetness in a high frost wind. Life is then seen to be a mere fire, that now smoulders, now brightens, showing how easily it may be quenched.

The weary hours wore away like a mass of unnumbered and half-forgotten years, in which all our other years and experiences were strangely interblended. Yet the pain we suffered was not of that bitter kind that precludes thought and takes away all capacity for enjoyment. A sort of stupefaction came on at times, in which we fancied we saw dry resiny pine logs suitable for camp fires, just as when, after going days without food, we fancy we see bread.

The extreme beauty of the sky at times beguiled our sense of suffering. Ursa Major, with its thousand home associations, circled in glorious brightness overhead; the mysterious star clouds of the Milky Way arched over with marvelous distinctness, and every planet glowed with long lance rays like lilies within reach. Then imagination, coming suddenly into play, would present the beauties of the warm zone beneath us, mingled with pictures of other lands. With unnatural vividness we saw fine secluded valleys, haunts of the deer and bear, and rich fir woods with their wealth of fern-like branches and orange lichens adorning their tall brown trunks. Then the bitter moaning wind and the drifting snow would break the blissful vision, and our dreary pains would cover us like clouds.

"Muir," Jerome would inquire, with pitiful faintness, "are you suffering much?" "Yes," I would reply, straining to keep my voice brave, "the pains of a Scandinavian hell, at once frozen and burned. But never mind, Jerome; the night will wear away at last, and to-morrow we go a-Maying, and what camp fires we will make, and what sun baths we will take!"

The frost became more and more intense, and we were covered with frozen snow and icicles, as if we had lain castaway beneath all the storms of winter. In about thirteen hours day began to dawn, but it was long ere the highest points of the cone were touched by the sun. No clouds were visible from where we lay, yet the morning was dull and blue and bitterly frosty, and never did the sun move so slowly to strip the shadows from the peaks. We watched the pale heatless light stealing toward us down the sparkling snow, but hour after hour passed by without a trace of that warm flushing sunrise splendor we were so eager to welcome. The extinction of a life seemed a simple thing after being so gradually drained of vitality, and as the time to make an effort to reach camp drew near, we became concerned to know what quantity of strength remained, and whether it would be sufficient to carry us through the miles of cold wind and snow that lay between us and the timber.

Healthy mountaineers always discover in themselves a reserve of power after great exhaustion. It is a kind of second life only available in emergencies like this, and having proved its existence, I had no great dread that either Jerome or myself would fail, though my left arm was already benumbed and hung powerless.

In our soaked and steamed condition we dared not attempt the descent until the temperature was somewhat mitigated. At length, about eight o'clock on this rare 1st of May, we rose to our feet, some seventeen hours after lying down, and began to struggle homeward. Our frozen trousers could scarce be made to bend; we therefore waded the snow with difficulty. The horizontal summit ridge was fortunately wind-swept and nearly bare, so that we were not compelled to lift our feet very high; and on reaching the long home slopes laden with fresh snow, we made rapid progress sliding and shuffling, our feebleness rather accelerating than diminishing our speed. After making a descent of 3000 feet, we felt the warm sun on our backs, and at once began to revive; and at 10 o'clock A.M. we reached camp and were safe. Half an hour afterward we heard Sisson shouting down in the fir woods on his way to camp with horses to take us to the hotel.

We had been so long without food, we cared but little about eating, but eagerly drank the hot coffee prepared by Sisson. Thawing our frozen toes was a painful task, but no permanent harm was done.

We learned from Sisson that when our terrific storm was in progress, only a calm, mild-looking cloud cap was observed on the mountain, that excited no solicitude for our safety. We estimated the snow-fall on the summit at two feet or more; at camp, some 5000 feet lower, we found only three inches, while down on the sloping base only a light shower had fallen, sufficient to freshen the grass.

We were soon mounted, and on our way down into the thick sunshine—to "God's country," as Sisson calls the chaparral zone. In two hours' ride the last snow bank was left behind. Violets appeared along the edges of the trail, and the chaparral was coming into bloom, with young lilies and larkspurs in rich profusion. How beautiful seemed the golden sunbeams streaming through the woods, and warming the brown furrowed boles of the cedar and pine! The birds observed us as we passed, and we felt like speaking to every flower.

At four in the afternoon we reached Strawberry Valley, and went to bed. Next morning we seemed to have risen from the dead. My bedroom was flooded with living sunshine, and from the window I saw the great white Shasta cone wearing its clouds and forests, and holding them loftily in the sky. How fresh and sunful and new-born our beautiful world appeared! Sisson's children came in with wild flowers and covered my bed, and the sufferings of our long freezing storm period on the mountain-top seemed all a dream.

Harper's Monthly, September 1877

Alaska

THE great wilderness of Alaska, with its lofty mountains laden with glaciers and snow, its deep in-reaching fiords and flowery plains, and its boundless wealth of evergreen forests and islands, and shining, singing waters, offers a glorious field for lovers of fountain beauty, much of which is now within easy reach of the ordinary traveler.

The trip by steamer from Puget Sound to the head of the Alexander Archipelago is perfectly enchanting. Leaving scientific interests entirely out of the count, no excursion that I know of may be made into any other portion of the wilds of America where so much fine and grand and novel scenery is so freely unfolded to view. Gazing from the deck of the steamer one is borne smoothly over calm blue waters, on and on through the midst of a thousand islands densely clothed with well-watered evergreens. The common discomforts of a sea-voyage are not felt, because the way is through a network of sheltered channels that are usually about as free as rivers are from heaving waves, and were it not for the brimy odor in the air and the strip of brown algæ seen at low tide on either shore, it would be difficult to realize that we are sailing on salt ocean water; we seem rather to be tracing a succession of inland glacier-lakes. Day after day we float in the heart of true fairyland, each succeeding view seeming more and more beautiful.

Never, before making this trip, have I found myself embosomed in scenery so hopelessly beyond description. To sketch picturesque bits definitely bounded is comparatively an easy task—a lake in the woods, a glacier meadow, a cascade in its dell, or even a grand mountain landscape beheld from some clear outlook after climbing from height to height through veiling forests, these may be attempted and some picture more or less telling made of them; for in them we find place for beginnings, starting from which we may make efforts that we may hope to conclude. But in this web of scenery embroidering the northern coast there is such indefinite expansiveness, so great a multitude of features without any redundance that may be slighted or left out, so varied and at the same time so similar, their lines graduating delicately into one another in endless succession; while the whole is so fine, so tender, so ethereal in light and shade, that any pen-work seems coarse and unavailing. Tracing the shining ways through sound and strait, past forest and waterfall, island and mountain and far azure headland, it seems as if we must surely at length reach the very paradise of poets, the abode of the blessed.

Here you glide into a narrow channel hemmed in with mountains that are forested down to the water's edge. There is no distant view, and the attention is held to the objects close about. The forests are closely planted like a field of wheat, the steep slopes on which they are growing permitting almost every individual tree to be seen rising above one another like the individuals in an audience,—the blue-green sharply tapered spires of the Menzies spruce, the warm yellow-green Merten spruces with their finger-like tops all pointing in the same direction or drooping gracefully like leaves of grass, and the airy, feathery brownish-green Alaska cedar, blending in harmony; lichens and mosses on the branches, a fringe of bushes along the shores. Gaps of paler green are seen where winter avalanches have cleared away the trees and on the higher summits, revealing hollows with snow in the shadows, the fountains of ancient glaciers, and short steep glens carrying cascading streams that are mostly hidden beneath fringes of dogwood and alder, showing white here and there where they leap sheer mossy cliffs, or unseen until they emerge on the brown algæ of the shore. Perchance a few ducks shoot past over-head, a bald eagle may be seen leisurely dressing his feathers on the top of a dead spar, or a loon is heard uttering its intensely lonely cry, all the scenery being made up of wildness as closely shut in and withdrawn as the wildness of mountains.

In the meantime the steamer may be so near the shore that you may almost reach the purple cones of the spruces as you pass. But new scenes are brought into the view with magical rapidity. Rounding some bossy cape the eye is called away into far-reached vistas bounded by finely curved headlands in charming array, one dipping gracefully beyond the other and

growing fainter and more ethereal in the distance. The tranquil channel up which you are sailing stretches river-like between, stirred here and there by the flashes of leaping salmon
that rise a foot or two above the water like vivid jets of silver,
and by flocks of white gulls that float like lilies among the
sun-spangles; while the cool white sunshine, sifting over all,
blends sky, land and water, in pale misty blue. Then, while
you are gazing with vague, dreamy longing into the depths
of this leafy ocean lane the steamer, turning into some hitherto unseen passage, glides through into a wide expanse, a
sound filled with islands sprinkled or clustered in forms and
compositions such as only Nature can invent. Some sheer-
faced, plunge abruptly into the blue prairie of brine; others
are rounded off in smooth convex brows, or with hollow
curves terminate in level points tipped with sedge. Some are
so small that the trees growing on them seem like mere handfuls culled from the neighboring woods and set in the water
to keep them fresh, while here and there at wide intervals you
may notice a bare detached rock just above the water, like a
black dot punctuating the end of a full outswelling sentence
of islands, every line of which is reflected in the mirror water,
form and meaning duplicated.

  The variety we find, both as to the contours and collocation
of the land masses in the green archipelago, is due mainly to
differences in the structure and composition of the rocks out
of which they are made and the unequal amount of glaciation
different portions of the landscape have received, some sections having been deeply chiselled by the influx of large,
steeply inclined glaciers from the mountains of the mainland.
Especially heavy was this influence toward the close of the
Glacier Period, when the general ice-sheet, moving in a direction nearly parallel with the trend of the coast, was beginning to fail, allowing the local glaciers from the mountains to
push farther out to sea. And again, the higher mountains of
the islands nourished small lingering glaciers which sculptured
their summits and sides, giving rise in some instances to amphitheatres of considerable size with cañons or valleys leading
down from them to the sea. These causes have produced
much of the obscuring variety of which Nature seems so fond,
but none the less will the studious observer see the underlying

harmony, the general trend of the islands in the direction of the flow of the ice-sheet, nearly parallel to the coast-line where the influence of local glaciers from the mainland was light, and in an oblique direction where the local influence was the greatest. Furthermore all the islands, great and small, as well as the headlands and promontories of the mainland, are seen to have a rounded, over-rubbed appearance, a finish free from angles, produced by the over-sweeping ice-flood during the period of glacial abundance, delicate complying harmony being everywhere apparent in broad generalizations.

The canals, channels, straits, passages and sounds are of course subordinate in size and trend to the same forces as the land-masses and differ from them only in being portions of the general pre-glacial margin of the continent more deeply eroded and covered with the ocean waters, which flowed into them as the ice was melted out of them. Had the general glacial degradation been greatly less, then these ocean-ways would have been valleys, and the islands bounding them would have been rounded hills and ridges, forming landscapes with undulating features, like those found above the sea-level wherever the rocks and glacial conditions have been similar.

The extension of the domain of the sea in connection with glacial action has not yet ceased in Alaska. In many a mountain-walled fiord of the mainland the advance of the waters may still be seen, beating against the crystal fronts of the glaciers, pressing slowly inland and taking possession inch by inch, century after century, as the shrinking glaciers withdraw in compliance with conditions of climate slowly changing.

In a general way these inland-bound channels of the Archipelago are like rivers, not only in separate reaches as seen from the deck of a ship but for hundreds of miles in the case of the longest of them; the tide-currents, the fresh drift-wood brought down by avalanches, the inflowing tributary land-streams and luxuriant over-leaning foliage of the banks making the resemblance all the more complete. But their courses are more direct than those of rivers, because of the steadiness of the flow of the ice-sheet of which they were born.

The largest of the islands are continents in effect from whatever direction they may be viewed, but far the greater number are small and appreciable as islands, hundreds of them being less than a mile in length, dotting the shining levels in perennial beauty. In their relations to each other the individual members of a group have evidently been derived from our rock-mass, yet they seldom seem broken or abridged in any way as to their lines of contour however abruptly they may dip their fronts. Viewed one by one they seem detached beauties, like extracts from a fine poem, while from the completeness of their lines and their individual ornamentation with trees, each seems a finished stanza in itself. In contemplating the arrangement of the trees a distinct impression is produced of their having been sorted and harmonized as to size and correlation like a well-balanced bouquet. In some of the smaller tufted islets a group of tapering spruces is planted in the middle, and two smaller groups corresponding with each other are planted on the ends at about equal distances from the central group. Or the whole forms one group with marked fringing trees that match each other, spreading around the sides like flowers leaning outward against the rim of a vase. These harmonious relations in the island woods are so constant that they evidently are the result of design, as much so as the arrangement of the feathers of a bird or the scales of a fish. Thus thoughtfully beautiful are these blessed islands, and their beauty is the beauty of youth. For though the freshness of their verdure must be attributed to the copious moisture in which they are bathed from the warm ocean current coming from the sunny fountains of Japan, the portion of the Japan current that bathes these shores is itself young; while the very existence of the islands, their features, finish, and peculiar distribution, are all immediately referable to the creative action of flowing ice during the great winter of the Glacial Period just now drawing to a close.

The first important stop made by the Alaska steamers after coaling at Nanaimo, Vancouver Island, is usually at Fort Wrangel, the distance between the two points being about six hundred miles. The town of Wrangel is situated on Wrangel Island, near the mouth of the Stikeen River. It is a miry, dilapidated, forbidding place, but has many advantages, particularly as a center from which excursions may be made to some of the most interesting portions of the country. Its grim boulder-like huts and houses, varying wildly in size and shape, are

built in a wrangling, angling fashion around the boggy shore
of the harbor for a mile or so, without manifesting the
slightest subordination to the points of the compass or to
building laws of any kind. Stumps and logs block the two
crooked streets of the settlement, each stump and log, by reason of the dampness of the climate, moss-grown and grass-
tufted on the top, but muddy and decaying at the bottom
where the hogs, which do most of the street work of the place,
have dressed against them. These picturesque obstructions,
however, are not much in the way, as no wheel of carriage or
wagon ever turns here. At the time of my last visit there was
not a horse on the island.

Indians, mostly of the Stikeen tribe, occupy the two ends
of the town, the few whites the middle portion; but there is
no determinate line of demarcation between them, the dwellings of the natives being mostly as large and as solidly built
of logs as those of the whites. The fort is a quadrangular
stockade with a dozen block and frame buildings located on
rising ground just back of the business portion of the town.
It was built shortly after the purchase of Alaska in 1867, but
in a few years was abandoned and sold to private parties.
Wrangel is a tranquil place. During a residence of several
months I never heard a noisy brawl among the people, or a
stormy wind in the streets, or a clap of thunder, or anything
like a storm-sound in the waves along the beach. During the
summer the abundant rains come straight down into the lush
vegetation steamy and tepid. The clouds are usually united,
filling all the sky, not racing in threatening ranks suggesting
energy of a destructive kind, but settling down in the form of
a bland, muffling poultice. The clear days are usually intensely
calm, gray and brooding, inclining one to dreamy meditation.
The islands seem to float and drowse on the glassy waters, and
in the woods every tree is at rest. But the very brightest of
Wrangel days are not what Californians would call bright, for
the sunshine is tempered in sifting through the moisture-laden
atmosphere, preventing glare and dazzling brilliancy except
under rare conditions. After sunrise a few smoke columns may
be seen rising languidly to tell of the first stir of the people.
Then an Indian or two may be noticed here and there at the
doors of their big barn-like cabins, or a merchant getting

ready for trade; but scarcely a definite sound is heard, only a muffled stir which gradually deepens. Later you may hear the strokes of an axe on firewood and the croaking of ravens. About eight or nine o'clock the town is generally awake and in its boots and boats. Indians, mostly women and children, begin to gather on the front platforms of the half-dozen stores, sitting carelessly in their blankets, every other face blackened hideously, a naked circle about the eyes, and perhaps a spot over each cheek-bone and on the tip of the nose where the smut has been weathered off. Some of the children also are blackened, and none are overclad. The larger girls and young women are brilliantly arrayed in calico and ribbons and shine among the blackened and blanketed old crones like tanagers among blackbirds. Most of the women have berries to sell, basketfuls of huckleberries, red and black, and the large yellow salmon berries and bog raspberries, looking fresh and clean, in striking relief to the surrounding squalor. They sit and wait in patience for purchasers until hungry; then if they cannot sell their berries they wisely eat them and go to the hillside back of the town and gather more.

Yonder you see a canoe gliding out from the shore containing perhaps a man, a woman, and a child or two, all paddling together in easy rhythm. They are going to catch a fish, no difficult matter, and when that is done their day's work is over. Another party is putting out to glean driftwood, to procure fuel in this way being easier than to drag it down through the bushes from the edge of the woods. As the day advances there is quite a fleet of canoes along the shore, all fashioned after one pattern, with high and long beak-like prows and sterns, and lines as fine as those about the breast of a wild duck. What the mustang is to the Mexican vaquero the canoe is to these coast Indians. They skim over the glassy sheltered waters to fish and hunt and trade, or merely to visit their neighbors. They exhibit much family pride and are extremely sociable, meeting frequently to inquire after one another's health, to hold "potlaches" and dances, and to gossip concerning coming marriages, deaths, births, or the last murder, and what number of blankets should be demanded as blood-money. Some seem to sail for the mere pleasure of the thing and to keep themselves and the children in practice, their canoes decorated with handfuls of the purple epilobium. Yonder you may see a whole family, grandparents and all, making a direct course for some island or promontory five or six miles away. They are going to gather berries, as the baskets tell. Nowhere else in my travels, north or south, have I found so lavish an abundance of wild berries. The woods and meadows are full of them, along the banks of the glaciers on the mountains as well as on the lowlands—huckleberries of many species, salmon berries, blackberries, raspberries, currants, and gooseberries, with strawberries and service berries in the drier openings, and cranberries in the bogs, sufficient for every bird, beast and human being in the territory, and thousands of tons to spare. The huckleberries are specially abundant. Those that grow on the mountains, on bushes about a foot high, are the best. The berries of the commonest species are smaller and covered with a dusty bluish bloom. The bushes are from three to six or seven feet high, and grow almost everywhere about the margins of the woods. This is the species on which the Indians most depend, who gather them in large quantities, beating them into pulp, and pressing them into cakes about an inch thick for winter use. The salmon and service berries are preserved in the same way, the cakes being thoroughly dried before they are stored. The salmonberry is quite generally distributed through the opener portions of the forests and along stream banks, and when in bloom makes a glorious show of rose-like flowers. The berries are about an inch in diameter and so abundant that in many places a quart or more may be gathered without moving from the spot where one is standing.

Berries alone are sufficient to make a telling advertisement of the fruitfulness of this wilderness, without the aid of the forests or fertile foodful waters. The climate of the islands and of that portion of the coast bathed by the warm Japan current is remarkably bland and temperate and free from extremes of heat or cold throughout the year. It is rainy, however, so much so that haymaking will not be extensively engaged in, whatever future developments may reveal, unless, as in some parts of Norway, artificial means of drying be resorted to. But even this rainy weather is good of its kind, mild in temperature, gentle in its fall, filling the fountains of the deep, cool rivers, feeding the luxuriant vegetation, and keeping the whole land fresh and fruitful; while anything more delightful than the shining weather in the midst of the rain, the great round sun-days of June and July, can hardly be found elsewhere.

An Alaskan midsummer day is a day without night. In the extreme northern part of the territory the sun does not set for weeks, and even as far south as Sitka at its lowest point it is only a few degrees below the horizon, so that the colors of the sunset blend with those of the sunrise, leaving no gap of night-darkness between. What is called the midnight of di-vided days is here only a low noon, the middle point in the gloaming, with light enough to read by. The thin clouds that are almost always present are then colored orange and red, marking in a very striking way the progress of the sun around the northern horizon. The day opens slowly, a low arch of light steals round to the northeastward with gradual increase of height and span and intensity of tone; and when at length the sun appears above the horizon it is without much of that stirring pomp, that flashing, awakening, triumphant energy so suggestive of the bible imagery—a bridegroom coming out of his chamber and rejoicing like a strong man to run a race. The red clouds with yellow dissolving edges subside into a hazy dimness, the islands with ruffs of mist about them cast ill-defined shadows on the glistening waters, and the whole fir-mament becomes pale pearl-gray. For three or four hours after sunrise there is nothing particularly impressive to be felt in the landscape. The sun though seemingly unclouded may almost be looked in the face, and the islands and mountains, with all their wealth of wood and ice and varied beauty of nature's architecture, seem comparatively dull and silent.

As the day advances toward high noon the sun-flood streaming in full power through the damp atmosphere lights the water-levels and the sky to glowing silver. Brightly play the ripples about the edges of the islands and over the plume-shaped streaks between them, stirred by some passing breeze. On the mountain and in the high-walled fiords still grander is the work of the sunshine. The broad snowy bosoms of the glaciers glow in dense pressed white, and their crystal fronts and the multitude of bergs that linger about them are kindled into a perfect blaze of irised light. The warm air throbs and makes itself felt as a life-giving, energizing ocean, embracing all the world. Now we may contemplate the life and motion about us; it comes to mind of itself—the tides, the rivers, the flow of the light through the satiny sky, the marvelous abundance of fishes feeding in the lower ocean, misty flocks of insects in the air, the wild sheep and goats on a thousand grassy ridges above the forests, the beaver and mink and otter far back on many a rushing stream, Indians floating and basking along the shores, the leaves of the forest drinking the light, and the glaciers on the mountains tracing valleys for rivers and grinding earth-meal for every living creature. Through the afternoon all the way down to the sunset the day grows in beauty. The light seems to thicken and become more generously fruitful without losing its softness or smooth translucent glow. Everything appears to settle into conscious repose, while the winds breathe gently or are wholly at rest. The few clouds visible are downy and luminous and combed out fine on the edges. A white gull here and there winnows the air on easy wing, and Indian hunters in their canoes are seen gliding about the islands, every stroke of their paddles told by a quick glancing flash—sky, land and water meeting and blending in one inseparable scene of enchantment. Then comes the sunset with its purple and gold, not a narrow arch on the horizon but oftentimes filling the sky, while the glowing fountain of it all is well round to the north.

I have seen far more gorgeous sunsets than any I have yet witnessed in Alaska but none more impressive. The clouds that usually bar the horizon are fired on the edges, leaving a dull center in strong contrast, and the spaces of clear sky between are filled in with greenish yellow or pale amber. The orderly flocks of small over-lapping clouds that frequently are seen higher are mostly touched with crimson like the outleaning sprays of a maple grove in the beginning of Indian summer, while a soft mellow purple flushes the sky to the zenith and fills the air, fairly steeping and transfiguring the islands and making all the water look like wine. The glowing gold soon vanishes, but because the sun descends at a low angle even the glowing portion of the display lasts longer than in most southern latitudes, while the upper colors with gradually lessening intensity sweep around to the north and unite with those of the morning.

The most extravagant of the sunset effects I have yet seen in this moist north-land occurred about the middle of July, when we were sailing between Nanaimo and Wrangel, in a portion of the Archipelago where the islands are sown thickest. The day had been rainy, but toward the latter part of the afternoon the clouds cleared away from the west, all save a few that settled down mostly in level over-lapping bars near the horizon. It was a calm evening and the color came on gradually, increasing in extent of area and richness of tone by slow degrees, as if requiring more time than usual to ripen. At a height of about thirty degrees there was a heavy bank deeply reddened on its lower side and on the projecting portions of its face. Below this there were three horizontal belts of purple edged with gold, while a spreading fan of flame, vividly defined, radiated upward across the purple bars and faded in a feather edge of dull red. Then the whole body of the atmosphere was filled with a thin translucent haze of claret purple in which the islands and mountains with melting outlines seemed to float. Even the nearest objects were colored, and the Divines going to the missions seemed truly divine as they gazed, transfigured, in the glorious purple baptism.

About one-third of the days of the summer of 1879 were rainy or threatening, one-third cloudy with little or no rain, and one-third clear. Of one hundred and forty-seven days beginning May 17, rain fell on sixty-five days, while forty-three were cloudy and thirty-nine clear. Rain fell on eighteen days in June, eight in July, fifteen in August, and twenty in September. But on some of these days only light showers fell, scarcely enough to count, and very few could be called stormy or dismal. Even the bleakest and most bedraggled days usually have a dash of late or early color to cheer them, or some white illumination about the noon hours. Nowhere else have I seen so much rain fall with so little noise. There was no loud-rushing wind all summer, and no thunder, at least I heard none, and from all I can learn it is about as rare a phenomenon in Alaska as in the California lowlands. There is a fresh, sound wholesomeness about even the wettest of the weather, which seems generally conducive to health. There is no mildew in the houses or tendency to mouldiness in any nook or corner, however hidden from the sun; and neither among the people nor the plants do we fine that dropsical succulence that so soft and poultice-like an atmosphere might lead one to expect. On the summits of the California Sierra throughout the greater portion of the year the presence of the atmosphere is hardly recognized, and the thin, white, bodyless light of morning comes to the peaks and glaciers as an unmixed spiritual essence, the most impressive of all the material manifestations of the Creator. But the most transparent and most brilliantly lighted of Alaskan atmospheres is always appreciably substantial, and oftentimes it is so thick and velvety that it would seem as if one might test its quality by rubbing it between the thumb and fingers. The cause of the dampness of the climate is not far to seek. It is found in the vapor-laden winds from the warm ocean waters, and the condensing range of ice-laden mountains along the coast, the highest and iciest on the continent.

July was the brightest month of the summer, with fourteen days of sunshine, six of them in succession, with an average temperature of about 60°, and a maximum of 70°. The average temperature for June at 7 A.M. was 54° 33'; M. 57° 13'; for the same hours for July, 55° 53' and 61° 45'; for August, 54° 20' and 61° 50'; and for September, 52° 23' and 56° 21'. The highest temperature observed here during the summer was 76°. The winter storms along the coast are mostly rain, at a temperature of about thirty-five degrees, with strong winds which, sweeping the long straight channels, lash them into white waves and carry salt scud far into the woods. The long nights are then gloomy enough to most people, and everybody is driven to shelter. Snow falls frequently, but seldom to any great depth about the coast settlement, or to lie long. The ground about Wrangel has been covered to a depth of four feet once only since the town was built. The mercury seldom falls much below the freezing point unless the wind blows steadily from the mainland; then at Sitka and Wrangel a zero temperature may be reached. Back from the coast, however, beyond the mountains, the winter months are intensely cold. At Glenora on the Stikeen River, less than a thousand feet above sea level, a temperature of from thirty to forty degrees below zero is not uncommon. But none need be cold where wood is so plentiful and so easily obtained for house-building and fires. The bulk of the forests of Southeastern Alaska is made up of three species of spruce and cypress, all of which are of good size, and grow close together, covering almost every acre of the islands, however rocky, and the margin of the coast and the mountain-slopes up to a height of from one to two thousand feet above the sea. The most important of these as to timber is the Yellow Cedar or Cypress (*Cupressus Nootkaensis*), a truly noble tree, which attains a height of a hundred to a hundred and fifty feet and a diameter of three to five feet. The branches are flat, drooping and feathery, dividing into beautiful light-green sprays like those of the California *Libocedrus*, but with finer foliage and more delicate plumes. The wood of this tree is undoubtedly the best the country affords, and one of the most valuable to be found on the whole Pacific Coast. It is pale yellow, close-grained, tough, durable, and takes a good polish, besides being pleasantly fragrant. The only California wood that resembles it is the *Torreya*, which has the same delicate yellow color and close grain; but the Torreya is not abundant and the trees are small and generally grow in inaccessible cañons, and so are comparatively insignificant as timber. Some three or four ships have been built of yellow cedar, and small quantities, a few thousand feet at a time, have been sent to Portland and San Francisco from Sitka, Wrangel, Checan, and Port Simpson. Some goes to China, where it is highly prized in the manufacture of fancy boxes. It deserves to be better known, not only to ship builders, but to carpenters and furniture makers. The natives make their paddles of it, and weave matting and coarse cloth from its inner bark, which is of a fine brown color with a satiny lustre. It is also the favorite firewood of the coast region, burning freely, but of course not lasting long. A yellow cedar fire seen for the first time is quite a notable phenomenon. The flames quiver and rush up in a multitude of ragged-edged lances, while the burning surfaces snap and crackle and explode, and throw off showers of glowing coals, with so much noise that conversation in the ordinary voice is impossible around such firesides. Every open hearth on which this wood is burned has to be closely screened with wire netting, else the floor for a distance of fifteen or twenty feet from the fire would be quickly strewn with cinders. The durability of the timber is shown by the fallen trunks lying in the damp woods, many of the largest of them lasting for centuries, and retaining even their delicate color and fragrance unimpaired. Decay goes slowly on from the outside, never beginning in the heartwood, so far as I have noticed, though many of the living trees are rendered almost valueless as timber by a fungus which produces a dry rot similar to that found in *Thuja* and *Libocedrus*. The species is distributed pretty generally along the coast and among the islands from Vancouver to Chilcat. But though its range is extensive, it is not very abundant at any one place, nor does it occupy any considerable area to the exclusion of other species.

The White Spruce or "Sitka Pine" (*Abies Menziesii*) ranks second in value as timber, while it is far more abundant than the cedar. Perhaps one-half of all the forest trees in Southeastern Alaska are of this species. In the heaviest portions of the forests, on deep moraine soil near the sea-level, it grows to a height of from one hundred and fifty to one hundred and seventy-five feet, with a diameter of three to six feet, and is a remarkably beautiful and graceful tree. In habit and general appearance it resembles the well-known Douglass spruce of California, Oregon and the Puget Sound region; but it is somewhat less slender, the branches covering a larger portion of the trunk, and the bluish-green needles radiating all around the branchlets are stiffer and so sharp-pointed that the younger branches cannot well be handled without gloves. The timber is tough, close-grained, and looks like pine, and in general use takes the place of pine. It is said to be stronger than the Puget Sound spruce and quite as durable, and the best of it is probably as good for ship-timber. In a considerable portion of the forests, however, the trees are too small for the masts and spars of larger class vessels. The average height of full grown trees is about eighty or ninety feet, and the diameter at the ground two feet or a little less. The other species is the graceful Hemlock-spruce (*Abies Mertensiana*). It is more slender than its companion species, but nearly as tall, and the young trees are more graceful in habit. The timber is inferior, and though very abundant is seldom used where any other kind is to be had. Of the other species found in these forests, but forming a small portion of the whole, the most note-worthy is the large Arbor Vitæ, (*Thuja gigantea*), called "Red Cedar." It is distributed up the coast from California to the southern portion of Alaska. From the soft, easily worked trunks of this magnificent tree the Indians make their fine canoes, some of them large enough to carry fifty men. One made from a tree that grew on the west coast of Vancouver Island is said to be sixty feet long, eight feet wide, and four feet deep.

There are but few pines in Alaska. I have seen only one species, *P. contorta*, a few specimens of which, fifty or sixty feet high, may occasionally be found about the open margins of lakes and meadows. Beyond the mountains it forms extensive forests. In the cañons and fiords and along the banks of the glaciers the Williamson spruce and a species of fir are found. They are usually quite small and storm-beaten, though in sheltered spots the fir sometimes reaches a height of sixty or seventy feet. The only hard woods I have seen in Alaska are birch, maple, alder and wild apple, one species of each. The birch grows mostly on steep declivities well back in the mountain cañons in company with spruce and fir. The largest specimens are about forty feet high, and a foot in diameter. The other species are found mostly about the margins of the main forests. The trees are quite small, about eight or nine inches in diameter, and fifteen to thirty feet high. Cottonwoods forty to sixty feet high line the banks of the rivers, growing on beds of flood soil amid a tangle of willows, raspberries and wild roses.

It appears, therefore, that with the important exception of the yellow cedar, timber trees for every use as good or better than those of Alaska abound in California, Oregon, Washington and British Columbia; and it will be only when those sources of supply are exhausted on the more accessible portions of the coast that these grand Alaskan forests will be invaded to any appreciable extent by the lumberman. Seward expected Alaska to become the ship-yard of the world. So it may, a century hence. Meanwhile this supply will keep, and serve the higher use of beauty. These glorious woods are not threatened by fire, or any other destruction dependent on the agency of man. They are too wet to burn. The roots of the trees are set in a deep sponge of mosses kept saturated by the abundant rains and snows. Beyond the mountains, in the forests of the interior, greater summer heat and less rain and snow render the existence of the trees less secure from the ravages of fire. Immense areas have already been cleared and now appear as smooth, grassy plains. In the region drained by the Yukon the principal tree is the white spruce, (*Abies alba.*) It is an exceedingly slender tree, spiry, erect, and closely clad with short, leafy sprays, forming the sharpest and most arrow-like spires to be found in any forest. The tallest are about one hundred and twenty-five feet high. I saw it growing bravely on the banks of the rivers that flow into Kotzebue Sound, forming the extreme margin of the Arctic forests. Some time these sources of supply may be made available by way of the rivers; but, fortunately, it will be long ere a time of need will drive the lumberman so far.

The coast and island forests of this south end of Alaska wear a grayish, brownish color in the foreground, black in the middle-ground, and dark blue in the distance. The gray and brown colors are derived from lichens and mosses that grow on the boles and form large nest-like masses on the horizontal palmate portions of the main branches, fifty or even a hundred feet above the ground. Landing almost anywhere to take a walk in these woods, you have first to fight your way through a fringe of underbrush tediously intertangled, made up of rubus, huckleberry, dogwood, willow, elder, etc., and a strange looking woody plant about six feet high, with limber, rope-like stems and heads of broad leaves spread out horizontally like those of palms. Both stem and leaves are covered with long, needle-like spines, so that it is impossible to grasp the plant anywhere with impunity. This is the *Echinopanax horrida*, popularly known as "the Devil's Club." It is used by the Indians as an instrument of torture in thrashing witches, and well deserves its name. From its leaning, twisted stems and heads of large translucent leaves, it seems out of place here, as belonging to the tropics rather than to the cool north-woods. Back in the shady depths of the forest the ground is covered with a thick felt of mosses, but little roughened with bushes of any kind, and about as clean and trackless as the sky. On that yellow, elastic carpet no dust ever settles, and walking upon it we make no mark or sound. It clothes the raw earth, logs and trees, ice and rock, the living and the dead, lightly and kindly, stretching untorn to the Polar Sea. How fine its beauty, every leaf and spore-cup and tiny pedicel neat and shining as if trimmed and polished afresh every day! Bars of sunshine are laid here and there, seeming wondrous bright in the deep brooding shade, and at long intervals the silence is mellowed and sweetened by the song of a bird or the song of a stream, and occasionally a deer or a bear may be seen, deepening the tone of the wildness; but most of the animals keep near the outer margin of the dense woods and along the open shore.

The whole country is shining with perennial streams, that flow on, ever fresh and sweet, through plains and forests and cliff-bound glacial cañons, telling all the way down to the sea how bountiful are the clouds that fill their shadowy fountains. Some thirty or forty rivers have been discovered in Alaska, the number varying as the smaller ones are called creeks or rivers by the map-makers. But not one of them all, from the mighty Yukon, two thousand miles long, to the shortest of the mountain torrents falling white from the glaciers, has thus far been fully explored. Miners, trappers, traders, and a few ardent explorers have been over most of the country in a rambling way, each bringing in geographical fragments that have been put together in maps that give fair outline views. The coast line in particular has been carefully drawn, and the mouths and the lower reaches of most of the streams; but their upper courses are still in great part invisible, like mountains with their heads in clouds. Perhaps about twenty of the Alaskan rivers are a hundred miles or more in length. The Yukon drains as large an area as that drained by all the other streams of the territory combined. It flows in a general north-westerly direction through British territory for six or seven hundred miles, then, approaching the Alaskan boundary near Fort Yukon, it turns abruptly to the left and pursues a southwesterly course to Behring Sea. It is a broad, majestic flood, scarcely interrupted by rapids, miles in width in some places, and navigable for light draft steamers for a distance of one thousand five hundred miles from its mouth—a noble companion of the great Mackenzie, the two heading together on the smoothly sculptured northern plateau of the Rocky Mountains. The largest of the rivers whose sources all lie within the bounds of Alaska is the Kuskoquim, which flows into a bay of that name in lat. 60°, and is supposed to be five or six hundred miles long. To the north of the delta of the Yukon a considerable number of smaller streams fall into Norton and Kortzebue Sounds; but from the northernmost of this series, around the shore of the Arctic Ocean for a distance of nearly a thousand miles, there are only one or two rivers of considerable size. Southward from the Yukon to Mount St. Elias, creeks and rivers occur at short intervals, most of which flow quietly as they approach the sea through low bogs and beds of glacial drift. The principal streams are the Kuskoquim, Suchitna, Knik, and Copper rivers. On the last mentioned, which is supposed to be three or four hundred miles in length, masses of native copper have been found. The Indians were acquainted with this metal before the advent of the whites, and from this source probably obtained their supplies of it for the manufacture of weapons and ornaments.

From Mount St. Elias the Coast Range extends in a lofty, unbroken chain beyond the southern boundary of the territory, gashed with stupendous cañons, every one of which carries a stream deep enough and wide enough to be called a river, though comparatively short, drawing their sources from the glaciers back thirty or forty miles in the white solitudes of the range. A few of this foaming brotherhood—the Chilcat, Chilcoot, Tahkoo, and Stikeen—come from beyond the Coast Range, though flowing across it in cañons cut for them by the forerunning glaciers heading in the broad Rocky Mountain plateau, in company with the tributaries of the Mackenzie and the Yukon. The tributary branches of the main trunk cañons of all these rivers are still occupied by glaciers, which descend on both sides in glorious array, their massive bulging fronts terminating a little way back in the shadows, near the bottom of the main cañons, or they are pushed grandly forward among the cottonwoods lining the streams, or, blocking the way of the streams, compel them to flow beneath the ice in long arching tunnels.

The Stikeen is perhaps better known than any other river in Alaska, because of its marking the way back to the Cassiar gold mines. It is three hundred and fifty or four hundred miles long and is navigable for small steamers to Glenora, one hundred and fifty miles. It flows first in a general westerly direction, through grassy, undulating plains, darkened here and there with patches of forest; then, curving southward and receiving numerous tributaries from the north, it enters the Coast Range and sweeps across it to the sea through a cañon that is sculptured like Yosemite, and is more than a hundred miles long, one to three miles wide at the bottom, and from five to eight thousand feet deep, marvelously beautiful and inspiring from end to end. To the appreciative tourist sailing up the river, the cañon is revealed like a gallery of sublime pictures, an unbroken series of majestic mountains, glaciers, water-falls, cascades, groves, flowery garden-beds and grassy meadows, in endless variety of form and composition, with furniture enough for a dozen Yosemites. Back of the walls, and thousands of feet above them, innumerable peaks and spires and domes of ice and snow tower grandly into the deep blue sky. Sailing past the groves and bends of the river, the views change with magical rapidity. Wondrous, too, are the changes dependent on the weather—avalanches from the heights, booming and resounding from cliff to cliff, and storm-winds from the arctic highlands sweeping the cañon like a flood, filling the air with ice-dust, and robing rock, glacier and forest in spotless white. In spring there are the chanting of cascades, the gentle breathing of warm winds, the opening of leaves and flowers, the nest-building of birds, the hundred-acre fields of wild roses coming into bloom, and tangles of bramble and huckleberry; swaths of birch and willow creeping up the lower slopes of the walls after the melting snow, massive cumuli piled about the highest peaks, gray rain-clouds wreathing and bathing outstanding brows and battlements; then the breaking forth of the sun on it all, the shining of the wet leaves and the river and crystal glaciers, the looming of the white domes in the azure, the serene color-grandeur of the morning and evening changing in glorious harmony through all the seasons and years. It is not easy to give anything like a full description of such a place, or even to sketch it in outline. All who can should see it for themselves. It is readily accessible from Wrangel by steamer or canoe, and the necessary outfit is easily obtained.

Leaving Wrangel you notice that the water of the bay is milky for miles out from the mouth of the river, the cause being the glacier mud suspended in it, which is the finest portion of the grist ground from the rocks by hundreds of glaciers ranged along the cañon walls. Entering the river five or six miles from Wrangel, the smooth green islands of the archipelago are lost to view, and the cañon walls close at hand are seen sweeping sublimely to the sky, with their trees in showy array, and peaks seven to eight thousand feet high, with small glaciers between them, make their appearance over the tops of their arrowy spires. About fifteen miles above the mouth of the river you come to the first of the larger glaciers, which is seen pouring down through the forest in a shattered ice cascade nearly to the level of the river. Here the cañon is about two miles wide, with cottonwoods along the river banks, and spruce and fir and patches of wild rose and raspberry bushes extending back to the cliffs. Twelve miles above this point a noble view is opened along the tributary cañon of the Skoot River—a group of glacier-laden peaks from ten to twelve thousand feet high, the sources of the largest tributary of the Stikeen. A few miles farther on the walls are steeper and smoother, offering fine ways for avalanches and but little anchorage for trees, so that they are mostly bare like those of the Merced Yosemite. The granite, too, has here the same neutral gray tone, and the sculpture and general style of architecture are similar. Cascades are chanting everywhere, descending in white ribbons from the upper glaciers to the green river levels. On one massive rock-front, corniced with ice, you may count eight cascades that form a lace-work beautifully relieved in the small green willows that fringe their edges. The largest booms like the Yosemite Falls in the spring, pouring from the blue shattered edge of a glacier to the foot of the cliff in a snowy plume two thousand feet long.

Thirty-five miles above the mouth of the river the most striking object of all comes in sight. This is the lower expanded portion of the Big Glacier, or Ice Mountain, as it is sometimes called, said to measure nearly six miles around the front, which is pushed boldly forward into the middle of the wide floor of the cañon among the trees. It takes its rise in the heart of the mountains, thirty or forty miles away, but most of its upper sources are hidden from view. Compared with this, the Swiss *Mer de Glace* is a small thing, though many glaciers in Glacier Bay and elsewhere in the territory are many times larger. The great white front of the glacier is about three hundred feet high, but it rises gradually to a height of about one thousand feet a few miles back from the immediate front. Seen through gaps in the trees growing on the terminal moraines, as one sails slowly against the current, the marvellous beauty and grandeur of its caves and chasms and shattered pinnacles in varying light and shade are seen to good advantage, but tame indeed must be the observer who is satisfied with so cheap a view.

On the opposite side of the river there is another large glacier flowing river-like through the forested bosses of the wall. Some three hundred years ago, the Indians say, these two glaciers, now facing each other, with their fronts several miles apart, were united, thus blocking the channel of the river which then flowed beneath the ice in a grand tunnel, and through this tunnel the Indians sometimes ventured in their canoes. This tradition is interesting, as carrying a truth hundreds of years without much change. That these two glaciers were united is undoubtedly true, though more than three hundred years have elapsed since they were separated, and the river ran free, as the trees growing on the banks show. Between the threatening ice-walls of these two glaciers lives Choquette. Happy man! though perhaps somewhat blind to his glacial blessings. It was not, he says, without grave misgivings that he ventured to build his cabin here, fearing that something might happen in connection with the mysterious "Ice Mountains." He is an Indian trader, the only settler on the river up to within a few miles of Glenora. Some thirty-five miles above Choquette's the Hudson Bay Company had a trading post, which is now abandoned. The big glacier is hardly out of sight ere you come upon another that pours a majestic crystal flood through the evergreens, while almost every hollow and tributary cañon contains a smaller one, the size varying with the extent of the area drained. Some are like mere snowbanks; others with the blue ice apparent, depend in massive bulging curves and swells, and graduate into the river-like forms that maze through the lower forested regions and are so striking and beautiful that they are admired even by the passing miners with gold dust in their eyes. I counted one hundred and sixty-one of them in sight from the river, but the whole number drained by the Stikeen throughout its entire course is probably more than three hundred.

A comparatively short time ago this magnificent cañon was occupied by a grand trunk glacier that flowed to the sea, and to which all these residual glaciers were tributary. The river, which has taken the place of the trunk glacier, is still imperfect, like a half developed plant. The trunk of the river is well formed, but the branches are only short stumps, slowly growing upward right and left over a hundred mountains, as the side glaciers melt back under changes of climate. The trunks of some of the shorter rivers heading in the Coast Range are still as imperfect as the branches of the larger ones, while a few, predestined to take their places in the general river system of the country, have not yet begun to flow, the channels they are to occupy and the country they are to drain being yet covered by a continuous mantle of ice.

Another interesting excursion may be made from Wrangel to the old deserted village of the Stikeen Indians. It is fourteen miles to the south of Wrangel, situated on a gently rising ground, with a strip of gravel and a strip of tall grass in front, the dark evergreen forest behind it, and charming views to right and left among the islands and channels. Not a house in the village has its walls left standing. The place was deserted some eighty or ninety years ago; so said our guide, Kadachan, and his word is corroborated by the venerable aspect of the ruins. But though the climate is so destructive to wooden buildings, many of the timbers lying in a dense growth of weeds and bushes are still in a good state of preservation, particularly those hewn from the yellow cedar. The magnitude of the ruins and the excellence of the workmanship manifest in them is surprising, as being the work of Indians. The first that I examined had been a dwelling about forty feet square, with walls built of planks two feet wide, six inches thick, and forty feet long. The ridge pole, of yellow cedar, still perfectly sound, is two feet in diameter, forty feet long, and as true as if it had been turned in a lathe. The nibble-marks of the stone adzes are still visible on these timbers, though crusted over with lichens in most places, giving the surface the appearance of stone. The pillars that supported the ridge-poles are still standing in some of the ruins. They are all, so far as I observed, elaborately carved with figures of fishes, birds and various animals, such as the beaver, wolf or bear. Each plank has evidently been hewn out of a whole log, and must have required great patience and industry as well as skill. Their geometrical accuracy is admirable. With the same tools, not one civilized workman in a thousand, however skillful, would have done as good work; few, indeed, with steel tools. Compared with this, the bravest work of our hardy backwoodsman with chalk line and broad axe is feeble and bungling. There is a completeness about the form, finish and proportions of these timbers that suggests instinct of a wild and positive kind, like that which guides the woodpecker in drilling round holes and the bee in making its cells.

But the most striking and interesting objects to be seen about these deserted streets are the carved monuments standing in front of the ruined houses. The simplest of them consists of a smooth round pillar, fifteen or twenty feet high, and about eighteen inches in diameter, hewn from the trunk of a cedar, and set firmly erect, with the carved figure of some animal on top, such as a bear or whale, or an eagle or raven, these being the totems of the families that occupied the houses in front of which they stand. Others support the figure of a man or woman, of life size or larger, usually in a sitting posture, and said to resemble and represent the dead whose charred bones and ashes are contained in cavities made in the pillars to received them. Others consist of a massive pillar thirty or forty feet high, the whole body of which is deeply carved from top to bottom with human figures, one above the other, with limbs grotesquely doubled and folded. In some instances, the human figures are mixed with those of animals, and are said to have some mythological or historical significance. But family pride and dignity in a telling display of their several totems seems to be the prevailing motive. All the figures are more or less rude and some are broadly grotesque, but there never is any feebleness or obscurity in the expression. On the contrary, every figure shows grave force and decision, combined with manly strength of execution. Colored lichens and mosses give them a venerable air of antiquity, though few are more than one hundred years old, while the larger vegetation often found in such as are most decayed produces a picturesque effect. For example, there is a bear five or six feet long reposing on top of his lichen-frescoed pillar with paws comfortably folded, a tuft of grass in each ear, and rubus bushes along his back; and yonder is an old chief poised on a taller pillar, apparently gazing out over the beautiful landscape in contemplative mood, a tuft of bushes leaning back with a jaunty air from the top of his weather-beaten hat, and downy mosses about his massive lips, the whole figure sharply relieved against the sky. But no rudeness or grotesqueness that may appear in combination with the decorations that nature has added provokes mirth; the work is too serious in aspect for mirth, and brave and true in execution. Similar monuments are made by all the tribes of the archipelago. Those of the Haidahs of Queen Charlotte Island are said to surpass all others in size and excellence of workmanship.

The erection of one of these totem poles is made a grand affair, and is talked of for a year or two beforehand. A feast is held to which hundreds of neighbors and friends are invited, and the joyous time is spent in eating, dancing, speech-making and the bestowing of gifts. Some of the larger specimens cost a thousand dollars or more. From one to two hundred blankets, worth three dollars apiece, are paid to the genius who does the carving, while the presents and feast may cost twice as much as the blankets, so that only wealthy families can afford them. An old Indian pointed out to me one of the Wrangel totem poles, which he said he had made, and for which he had received forty blankets, a gun, a canoe, and other articles of less value. Mr. Swan, who has contributed much information concerning the Indian tribes of the northwest coast, mentions one specimen that cost two thousand five hundred dollars. They are planted firmly in the ground. Even those of the deserted village are nearly all standing, showing the strength of the backbones of the builders.

The moss-grown ruins of the deserted village seem to fore-shadow too surely the fate of the Stikeen tribe, and perhaps of all the allied tribes of this portion of Alaska. Contact with the whites has already reduced the numbers of the Stikeens more than one-half, and there are fewer births than deaths. Like snow in sunshine they are passing away. Will they perish utterly in this land of abundance? A few years will tell. Under present conditions their only hope seems to lie in the efforts that are made for them by missionaries and teachers, who stand between them and the degrading vices of civilization, and bestow what good they can. Thus a remnant may possibly be saved to gather fresh strength and grow up into the high place to which they seem so fully capable of attaining.

Most of the permanent residents of Wrangel are traders in fish, furs and mining supplies, but since the Cassiar gold mines beyond the head-waters of the Stikeen have been worked out, on which most of the business life of Wrangel depended, the place has become comparatively unimportant. The greater part of the mining business of the territory now centres at the new town of Juneau, one hundred and fifty miles up the coast, opposite Douglass Island. The gold of Alaska is still in the ground; all save a few tons of it, gathered here and there from the more accessible veins and gravel beds of the islands and the mountains near the coast. Probably not one vein or placer in a thousand has yet been touched by the miner's pick, while the vast interior region drained by the Yukon is comparatively a virgin wilderness, its mineral wealth about as darkly hidden as when it was covered by the ice-mantle of the glacier period. So far as the mines have been examined, the color of gold has been found on every considerable stream, and light sooner or later is sure to come. Thousands of sturdy miners, graduating from the ledges and gulches of California and Nevada, will push over the whole territory and make it tell its wealth in the face of every obstacle with encouraging results. Many have already made their way by the Chilcat Pass into the basin of the Yukon. The extent of the developments likely to be made we can only guess; but comparing this northern portion of the gold-bearing belt of the continent with corresponding portions to the southward, the richness of which has been proved, a good foundation is discovered for the opinion that the country as a whole will prove at least moderately rich in the precious metals, and that gold, notwithstanding disadvantages of climate, obscuring vegetation, etc., will come to be regarded as one of the most important and reliable of its resources.

Leaving Wrangel, the steamer proceeds up the coast to Juneau. After passing through the picturesque Wrangel Narrows into Souchoi Channel and Prince Frederick Sound, you may notice a few icebergs on the outer edge of the fleet that comes from a large glacier flowing into the head of a magnificent fiord about twenty miles above the mouth of the Stikeen. This is the southernmost, so far as I have observed, of the glaciers of the Pacific Coast that flow directly into the waters of the sea and send off bergs. It is well known to the Indians, who glide about among the bergs in the smallest of their canoes to hunt seals, but it is not known among the whites at Wrangel, though they are almost within hearing of the thunder of its falling bergs. For a distance of about twelve miles the fiord is fairly crowded with icebergs of every size and shape, and to make one's way through them in the larger canoes without disaster requires the utmost caution and vigilance. The Indian name of the fiord is Hutli, or Thunder Bay, from the noise made by the falling and rising of the bergs as they are detached from the snout of the glacier. Gliding northward on your shining way, the mountains of the mainland on one hand, Kuprianoff and innumerable smaller islands on the other, the views in bright, cloudless weather reach far into the glorious wilderness, and all are purely wild, without trace of touch or taint, stainless as the sky. At long intervals a party of Indians may be seen sailing on their long journeys, but they make no mark on the landscape and never seem to belong to it. Like travelers in the air, they vanish in the distance and leave no visible sign. Salmon are seen here and there, leaping three or four feet out of the water, showing their silvery sides for a moment and then falling with a plash among foambells and widening circles of ripples. Ducks, too, of many species, stir the water and gulls and eagles the air, pictures of glad wild life. The beauty of the islands, seen in ever changing combinations, is an unfailing source of delight; but chiefly your attention will be turned upon the mountains, now for the first time in full near view. Now some bold granite headland, plunging into the channel with fine arching instep, will hold the eye, or some peak of surpassing beauty of sculpture, or some one of the larger glaciers seen directly in front, its gigantic arms and fingers clasping entire groups of peaks, and its huge white trunk sweeping to the waters of the channel between lofty gray domes and ridges, its crystal current breaking here and there into shattered cascades, with azure light filling the crevasses and making the most dangerous and inaccessible portions of the glacier the most beautiful of all. Creeping along the coast the icy cañons are opened to view and closed in regular succession like the leaves of a book. About midway between the head of Wrangel Narrows and Cape Fanshaw you are opposite a noble group of glaciers flowing from a complicated chain of crater-like fountains, guarded and guided around their summits and well down their sides by black jagged peaks and crests and curving mural ridges. From each of the larger clusters of fountains a wide cañon like Yosemite opens down to the foot of the range, that is, to the level of the sea. Three of the trunk glaciers flowing in these main cañons descend nearly or quite to the sea-level, though none of them send off icebergs, their fronts being cut off from the water by mud-flats and terminal moraines. The largest of the three, fed by eight or ten tributary glaciers, and probably about fifteen or twenty miles long, terminates in the middle of a grand Yosemitic fiord and valley in an imposing wall of ice about two miles long and from three to five hundred feet high, forming a barrier across the valley from wall to wall. It was to this glacier that the ships of the Alaska Ice Company resorted for the ice they carried to San Francisco, the Sandwich Islands, and I believe also to China and Japan. They had only to sail up the deep fiord harbor within a short distance of the ice-wall, drop anchor in the moraine mud, and load to capital advantage.

Another glacier a few miles to the south of this one receives two large tributaries about equal in size, and then flows on down a forested valley in a grand sweep to within a hundred feet or so of the sea-level. The third of this low-descending group is still farther south, and though less imposing than either of the others is still a truly magnificent object, even as seen imperfectly from the deck of the passing steamer, and of itself would be well worth a visit to Alaska to any lowlander so unfortunate as never to have seen a glacier.

But it seems a sad and pitiful thing to pass by all these fine mountain mansions of rock and ice without making a single visit for nearer views. For grand as they appear at a distance of ten or twelve miles, few can guess the grandeur they display when one is in cordial contact with them. I will therefore try to describe the largest of the three mentioned above as it appeared to me, when, with a small party, I saw it one bright July day and climbed among its blue dazzling crags.

Arriving opposite the mouth of the fiord into which it flows, we steered straight inland between wooded shores surpassingly beautiful, and soon the lower portion of the broad, swelling trunk of the glacier came in sight, lying at home tranquil and sunful in its massive granite valley, and extending a most cordial invitation to come and see. After we were fairly between the two majestic mountain rocks that stand guard at the gate of the fiord, the view that was unfolded fixed every eye in wondering admiration. No written words, however put together, can convey anything like an adequate conception of its sublime grandeur, the noble simplicity and fineness of the sculpture of the walls, their magnificent proportions, their cascades, gardens and forest adornments, the placid water between them, the great white and blue ice-wall stretching across in the middle, and the snow-laden mountain peaks beyond. Still less are words capable of describing the peculiar awe one experiences in entering these virgin mansions of the icy north, notwithstanding they are only the perfectly natural effect of simple and appreciable manifestations of the presence of God.

By one standing in the gateway of this glorious temple and regarding it only as a picture, its outlines may be easily traced. There is the water foreground of a pale milky-blue color, derived from the suspended rock-particles issuing from beneath the ice, a smooth sheet sweeping back five or six miles like one of the lower reaches of a great river. At the head the water is bounded by a wall of pale blue ice five or six hundred feet high, a few mountain tops covered with snow appearing beyond it. On either hand stretches a series of majestic granite rocks from three to four thousand feet in height, in some parts bare, in some forested, all flecked with patches of yellow-green chaparral and flower gardens, especially about half way up from their bases, the whole built together in a general varied way into walls like those of Yosemite Valley. The walls extend far beyond the ice-barrier, one immense brow appearing beyond the other along the sides of the glacier, while their bases are buried beneath the ice. This is in fact a Yosemite Valley on a grander scale in process of formation. The modeling and sculpture of the cliffs is nearly completed, and they are already well planted in most places. But there are no groves as yet on the raw, unfinished bottom of the valley, nor meadows, nor flower beds. It is as if the traveler on entering Yosemite should find the walls nearly in their present condition, with trees and flowers in warm nooks and along the sunny portions of the moraine-covered brows, but the bottom of the valley still covered with water and beds of gravel and mud, and the grand trunk glacier that formed it slowly melting and receding, but still occupying the upper half of the valley, its rugged front stretching across from the Three Brothers to a point below the Sentinel.

Sailing directly up to the sunken brow of the terminal moraine, we seemed to be separated from the glacier only by a low tide-leveled margin of detritus about a hundred yards in width, but we afterwards found the distance to be a mile or more. Approaching the driest looking portion of the moraine front we stepped ashore, but gladly wallowed back into the canoe, for the fine gray mineral paste made out of granite flour ground beneath the ice, at once began to take us in, swallowing us feet foremost with glacial deliberation. Our next attempt, made nearer the middle of the valley, was successful, and we soon found ourselves on good gravelly ground beyond reach of the tides, and made haste in a direct line for the huge ice-wall which seemed to recede as we advanced. The only difficulty encountered on the way was a network of icy streams, many of which had to be forded. At length we reached the glorious crystal wall, along the foot of which we passed, admiring its marvelous architecture, the play of light in the blue rifts and angles, and the structure of the ice as displayed in the less fractured sections, finding fresh, exultant, rejoicing beauty at every step. By dint of patient zigzaging and doubling among the crevasses and a vigorous use of an axe in cutting steps on the ice-blades and ridges, we made our way up over the terminal wall and back a mile or so above the jagged cascading brow to a height of about seven hundred feet above the base of the wall. Here we obtained a glorious view. The whole front and brow of the glacier is gashed and sculptured into a maze of yawning chasms and crevasses and a bewildering variety of strange forms appalling to the strongest nerves but beautiful beyond description—clusters of glittering lance-shaped spires, gables and obelisks; bold outstanding bastions, and plain mural cliffs adorned along the top with fretted cornice and battlement; while every gorge and crevasse, pit and hollow, was filled with light, pulsing and shimmering in pale blue tones of ineffable tenderness and beauty. The day was warm, and back on the broad waving bosom of the glacier, where crevasses were less common, small streams of pure water were outspread in a complicated network, gleaming and glancing in frictionless channels worn into the solid blue ice, and flowing with a grace of motion and a glad ring and gurgle and flashing of light to be found only on the crystal hills and dales of a glacier. Every feature glowed with intention, reflecting the earth-plans of God. Along the sides we could see the mighty flood grinding against its granite walls with tremendous pressure, rounding the outstanding bosses, deepening and widening its grand valley channel, and fashioning every portion of its mountain walls into the forms they are destined to have in the fullness of time, when, all the ice-work accomplished, the glacier, like a tool no longer required, shall be withdrawn from its place by the sun.

Back two or three miles from the front the current is now perhaps about twelve hundred feet deep. But when we examine the walls, the grooved and rounded features so surely glacial show that in the earlier days of the Ice-Age they were all overswept, this glacier having once flowed at a height of from three to four thousand feet above its present level. Standing here with facts so fresh and telling, and held up so vividly before us, every seeing observer, not to say geologist, must readily apprehend the earth-sculpturing, landscape-making action of flowing ice. And here, too, one learns that the world, though made, is being made; that this is still the morning of creation, that mountains and valleys long since conceived are now being born, channels traced for rivers, basins hollowed for lakes; that moraine-soil is being ground and outspread for coming plants, coarse bowlders and gravel for forests, finer meal for grasses and flowers; while the finest water-bolted portion of the grist seen hastening out to sea is being stored away in the darkness, and builded particle on particle, cementing and crystalizing to make the mountains and valleys and plains of other landscapes, which, like fluent, pulsing water, rise and fall and pass on through the ages in endless rhythm and beauty.

We gladly would have remained on this rugged, living, savage old mill of God and studied its works and ways, but we had no store of bread, and the little steamer that brought us was screaming nervously for our return. Therefore, threading our way back through the crevasses, and down the blue cliffs, we snatched a few flowers from a warm spot on the edge of the ice, plashed across the moraine streams, and bade the glacier farewell.

Opposite this group the steamer passes around an outcurving bank of traveled bowlders and sand ten miles in length, which is pushed forward into the sound and is about half exposed at low tide. This curved embankment, of which Point Vanderpent is the most prominent portion, is the terminal moraine of a grand old glacier that was at least ten miles wide, and was once united with the ice-sheet that formerly filled all the channels along the coast. Its location and the general relationship it bears to the three large glaciers described above indicate that these three once flowed together as tributaries to form the vanished trunk to which the great moraine belonged. Making our visit a few centuries too late, we had missed the grandest feature of this part of the coast. Enough is left, however, to enable us to restore it in imagination, and see it about as vividly as if actually present, with fertile snow-clouds wreathing its fountains, sunshine on its broad, undulating bosom, and its lofty ten-mile ice-wall planted in the deep waters of the sound and sending off fleets of bergs with loud-resounding thunder in calm and storm through the long icy centuries.

At the mouth of the Tahkou Inlet, as you approach Juneau, drifting icebergs indicate the glacial wealth of the neighborhood. The Tahkou Indians have a small village here, which, at the time of my visit, was deserted. Not a single lawyer, doctor or policeman had been left to guard it. These people are so happily rich, that they have but little of a perishable kind to keep or to lose, nothing worth fretting about. The inhabitants were away catching salmon, so our Indians told us. All the Indian villages are thus abandoned at regular periods every year, while the people repair to fishing, berrying and hunting stations, occupying each in succession for a week or two at a time, coming and going to and from the substantially built villages. Then, after the summer's work is done—the winter's supply of salmon dried and packed, fish and seal oil stored in boxes, berries and spruce bark beaten and dried and pressed into cakes, their hunts after wild goats, deer and bears brought to a close, their trading trips completed, and the year's stock of quarrels with the neighboring tribes patched up in some way—then they devote themselves to feasting, dancing, visiting, and hootchenoo drinking. Hootchenoo is a vile, fiery liquor which they have learned to distil in the most primitive way from sugar, molasses, dried apples and flour. It keeps entire villages for weeks at a time in a state of frenzied, demoniac drunkenness. The Tahkous were once a powerful and warlike tribe, but this vile drinking and other vices have nearly swept them out of existence. They have a larger village on the Tahkou River, but according to the census taken eight years ago by the missionaries, the tribe numbers only 269 all told—109 men, 79 women, and 81 children. These figures show the vanishing condition of the tribe at a glance.

The Tahkou Inlet, or fiord, is about twenty miles long and from three to five miles wide, and extends back into the heart of the mountains, draining hundreds of glaciers, great and small, once tributary branches of the one grand glacier that formed and occupied the fiord for its channel. This fiord, more plainly than any other that I have examined, illustrates the mode of formation of the wonderful system of deep channels extending from Puget Sound; for it is a marked portion of that system, a branch of Stephen's Passage, still in process

of formation, while its trends and general sculpture are as distinctly glacial as those of the smaller fiords. I counted some
forty-five glaciers in sight from the canoe in sailing up the
middle of the fiord. Three of these come down to the level
of the sea at the head of the fiord from a group of lofty mountains, forming a glorious spectacle. The middle one of the
three belongs to the first class, pouring its majestic current
directly into the fiord and filling it with bergs. The next below
also sends off icebergs occasionally, though separated from the
tide-water by a narrow strip of moraine detritus. While I was
examining it a large mass fell from the snout, damming the
outlet, and when at length the dam gave way, a powerful flood
swept thousands of small bergs forward into the fiord with
exciting display of energy. In a short time all was quiet again,
the flood-waters were spent, and only a blue scar on the
rounded gray front of the glacier and a line of stranded bergs
on the overswept moraine flat were left to tell the event.

While I sat sketching among the drifting icebergs, where I
could see well back into their snowy fountains, two Tahkou
Indians, father and son, came gliding toward us in an extremely small cottonwood canoe. Coming alongside with a
good natured "saghaya," they inquired who we were, our objects, etc., while they in turn gave us information about the
river, their village, and two other large glaciers a few miles up
the river-cañon. They were hunting seals, and as they glided
away in pursuit of their prey, crouching in their tiny shell of
a boat among the great bergs, with barbed spear held in place,
they formed a picture as arctic and remote from anything to
be found in civilization as ever was sketched for us by the
explorers of the far north. Making our way through the
crowded bergs to the extreme head of the fiord, we entered
the river, but were soon forced back by the swift current. The
Tahkou is a large stream, and like the Stikeen, draws its
sources from far inland, crossing the Coast Range through a
magnificent cañon, and draining a multitude of glaciers on its
way. The Indians, with keen appreciation of the advantages of
their position for trade, hold possession of the river and compel the Indians of the interior to accept their services as mid-
dlemen, instead of allowing them to come down the river to
trade directly with the whites.

After leaving Juneau the steamer passes between Douglass and Admiralty Islands into the beautiful and spacious Lynn Canal, carrying supplies to the canneries at Pyramid Harbor, near the mouth of the Chilcat River, thus introducing the tourist to some of the grandest scenery of the northern extremity of the archipelago. The Auk and Eagle Glaciers are seen on the right as the steamer enters the canal, sweeping grandly through the forests, showing beauty and majesty, ever new and inspiring notwithstanding all that has been seen before. But it is on the left side of the canal as you go north, towards the head, that the most striking and beautiful feature of this northern landscape is seen,—the grand Davidson Glacier. It first appears as an immense ridge of ice thrust abruptly forward into the canal, but it is not until you have advanced to a position almost immediately in front of it that its sublime and simple beauty is fully displayed. Then it is seen sweeping smoothly forward in a broad flood, and issuing from its far white fountains, a massive granite gateway spreading then to right and left into an immense fan-shaped mass exquisitely symmetrical in all its lines. It measures more than three miles around the front, and on the terminal moraine built up out of the deep waters of the canal there is a fine growth of spruces, which forms a beautiful fringe for the front of the ice. This spruce fringe so evidently belongs to the glacier and is so neatly applied to its broad, curving front, that it appears almost conventional. No one who has seen the Davidson Glacier will ever forget it, however icy his after travels may be.

Shortly after passing the glacier, the northmost point of the trip is reached, a little beyond lat. 59°. Here among the salmon at the canning establishment one may learn something of the population of these beautiful waters. Whatever may be said of other resources of the territory, its timber, minerals and furs, it is hardly possible to exaggerate the importance of the fisheries. Besides whales in the far north, and the cod, herring, halibut, and other fish that swarm over immense areas along the shores and inlets, there are probably not less than a thousand salmon streams in Alaska, filled with fine salmon every season. Their number is beyond conception. At certain seasons there are in the smaller streams more salmon, bulk for bulk, than water. In fording the lower portions of some of the streams, when they are shallowed by the fall of the tides, the wriggling, struggling multitudes crowding against one another in tens of thousands are unable to get out of one's way. On one occasion one of my men waded out into the midst of a crowded run and amused himself by picking up the fish and throwing them over his head. Thousands could thus be taken by hand on rocky shallows. In a single hour an Indian may capture salmon enough to last a year. Sailing up these streams in a dark night when the salmon are running and the waters are phosphorescent, a very beautiful and exciting effect is produced; for then the myriad fins of the onrushing multitude churn all the water into silver fire, making a glorious glow in the darkness.

It is through the cañon of the Chilcat River, opening into the head of Lynn Canal, that the best way lies across the mountains into the basin of the Yukon, and over this pass an ever increasing stream of prospectors and miners push their way every season, though it is only a few years since the Chilcat tribe holding possession of the pass allowed either traders or miners to use it. These Yukon gold-seekers have been fairly successful as far as known, and the wealth of that wilderness is being gradually revealed.

The prow of the steamer is now turned southward down the canal, along Cross Sound, and into the wonderful Glacier Bay. All the voyage thus far has been lavishly icy, but this is preeminently the Ice-land not only of Alaska, but of the whole Pacific Coast, from California to the shores of the frozen Polar Sea.

Glancing for a moment at the results of a general exploration of the mountain ranges of the coast, we have shown in other portions of this work that there are between sixty and seventy small residual glaciers in the Sierra Nevada. Northward, through Oregon and Washington, groups of active glaciers still exist on all the highest mountains—the Three Sisters, Mts. Jefferson, Hood, Adams, St. Helens, Rainier, Baker and others; one of the largest of the Rainier group descends nearly to the level of the sea. On through British Columbia and the southeastern portion of Alaska, the broad, sustained chain of mountains extending along the coast is generally glacier-bearing. The upper branches of nearly all of the main cañons are occupied by glaciers, which gradually increase in size and descend lower, until the lofty region between Mt. Fairweather and Mt. St. Elias is reached, where a considerable number are found that discharge into the waters of the ocean. This is the region of greatest glacial abundance on the west side of the continent. Westward from Icy Bay, around Prince William Sound and Cook's Inlet, the Alaska Peninsula and Aleutian Islands, the size and number of the glaciers gradually diminish, while to the north of latitude 62° few, if any, glaciers remain in existence, the ground being comparatively low, and the snowfall light. In Glacier Bay the traveler is introduced to the iciest portion of the Alaskan Alps, where he may spend a whole summer without reaching the upper fountains of the five great glaciers that flow into the bay and discharge icebergs.

The largest of these is the Muir Glacier, which enters the bay on the northeast side, at the head of a fiord with lofty, massive granite walls. The steamer sails up the fiord with its load of wondering tourists, making a way through the drifting icebergs with which the waters are crowded, and drops anchor within half a mile of the blue, shining ice-wall in which the glacier terminates. When first observed at a distance of eight or ten miles, the ice-wall appears as an abrupt, sharply defined barrier about fifty feet high, stretching across from side to side of the fiord, a distance of several miles. Its height above the water is probably three or four hundred feet, but far the greater portion is below the water and terminal moraine. If the water and the rock-detritus of the bottom were drained and cleared away, this magnificent wall of pale blue ice would probably be found to be not less than a thousand feet in height. Though in general views it seems massive and regular in form, it is by no means smooth. Deep rifts and hollows alternate with broad, plain bastions, while it is roughened along the top with innumerable spires and pyramids, and sharp, jagged blades leaning and toppling; and when the slanting sunbeams are pouring through the midst of all this angular cut-glass of ice, the effect is a perfect glory of rainbow colors. Added to this and mingling with it is the irised spray ever and anon rising from the plunging bergs as they fall from the wall or rise from the bottom of it with loud-resounding roar, while the countless bergs floating in front are shining also and sifting the sunbeams, making a very paradise of light in full rainbow bloom.

Impressive, too, are the nights along these crystal cliffs—the shining of the moon and stars, projecting buttresses and battlements seemingly far higher than by day, standing forward resplendant in the moonlight, vividly relieved amid the shadows of the hollows, the thunder of the falling masses at intervals of three or four minutes, and the lunar bows with faint iris colors in the up-dashing spray. But it is in the darkest nights when storms are blowing that the grandest views are to be had. Then the ghostly bergs, grating and crashing against one another, seem like living creatures, dancing in mad delight with the phosphorescent water, which laves them all with silver light; while the great crystal wall is illumined by a glowing fringe of foam beating against its base.

The steamer lies at anchor long enough for short excursions on shore. Two or three miles above the front, on the left bank, one may easily get upon the surface of the glacier, where it is so smooth and free from cracks and chasms that a hundred horsemen might ride abreast up stream for ten miles or more, though the middle of the glacier for several miles back from the front is shattered into a perfect labyrinth of yawning crevasses and splintered ridges hopelessly inaccessible. From the top of an icy mountain, about three thousand feet high, and six miles from the end of the ice-wall, may be obtained a grand, comprehensive view, embracing most of the glacier and its tributaries. It then appears as a vast reservoir of ice, fed by a hundred tributary glaciers, pouring into it from the snowy recesses of an immensely high range of mountains, which, in clear weather, display themselves over the vast expanse of ice in all their glory. But unless one is willing to remain a month or two, comparatively little of this glacial wilderness will be seen.

From Glacier Bay and Cross Sound, the steamer now passes through the picturesque Peril Straits to Sitka, the capital of the territory. Here the traveler may spend an interesting day amid the old Russian ruins and along the beautiful shores of the bay.

Leaving Sitka, Fort Wrangel is again touched for the mails,

and thence turning southward, the home voyage is speedily accomplished, and you find yourself again on common ways with many pictures of wild north-land beauty that will remain apart from all others, and enrich your life forever.

from *Picturesque California*, 1888

Features of the Proposed
Yosemite National Park

THE upper Tuolumne Valley is the widest, smoothest, most serenely spacious, and in every way the most delightful summer pleasure park in all the high Sierra. And since it is connected with Yosemite by two good trails, and with the levels of civilization by a broad, well-graded carriage-road that passes between Yosemite and Mount Hoffman, it is also the most accessible. It lies in the heart of the high Sierra at a height of from 8500 to 9000 feet above the level of the sea, at a distance of less than ten miles from the northeastern boundary of the Yosemite reservation. It is bounded on the southwest by the gray, jagged, picturesque Cathedral range, which extends in a southeasterly direction from Cathedral Peak to Mount Lyell and Mount Ritter, the culminating peaks of the grand mass of icy mountains that form the "crown of the Sierra"; on the northeast, by a similar range or spur, the highest peak of which is Mount Conness; on the east, by the smooth, majestic masses of Mount Dana, Mount Gibbs, Mount Ord, and others, nameless as yet, on the axis of the main range; and on the west by a heaving, billowy mass of glacier-polished rocks, over which the towering masses of Mount Hoffman are seen. Down through the open sunny levels of the valley flows the bright Tuolumne River, fresh from many a glacial fountain in the wild recesses of the peaks, the highest of which are the glaciers that lie on the north sides of Mount Lyell and Mount McClure.

Along the river are a series of beautiful glacier meadows stretching, with but little interruption, from the lower end of the valley to its head, a distance of about twelve miles. These form charming sauntering grounds from which the glorious mountains may be enjoyed as they look down in divine seren-ity over the majestic swaths of forest that clothe their bases. Narrow strips of pine woods cross the meadow-carpet from side to side, and it is somewhat roughened here and there by groves, moraine boulders, and dead trees brought down from the heights by avalanches; but for miles and miles it is so smooth and level that a hundred horsemen may ride abreast over it.

The main lower portion of the meadow is about four miles long and from a quarter to half a mile wide; but the width of the valley is, on an average, about eight miles. Tracing the river we find that it forks a mile above the Soda Springs, which are situated on the north bank opposite the point where the Cathedral trail comes in—the main fork turning southward to Mount Lyell, the other eastward to Mount Dana and Mount Gibbs. Along both forks strips of meadow extend almost to their heads. The most beautiful portions of the meadows are spread over lake basins, which have been filled up by deposits from the river. A few of these river-lakes still exist, but they are now shallow and are rapidly approaching extinction. The sod in most places is exceedingly fine and silky and free from rough weeds and bushes; while charming flowers abound, especially gentians, dwarf daisies, ivesias, and the pink bells of dwarf vaccinium. On the banks of the river and its tributaries Cassiope and Bryanthus may be found where the sod curls over in bosses, and about piles of boulders. The principal grass of these meadows is a delicate Calamagrostis with very slender leaves, and when it is in flower the ground seems to be covered with a faint purple mist, the stems of the spikelets being so fine that they are almost invisible, and offer no appreciable resistance in walking through them. Along the edges of the meadows beneath the pines and throughout the greater part of the valley tall ribbon-leaved grasses grow in abundance, chiefly Bromus, Triticum, and Agrostis.

In October the nights are frosty, and then the meadows at sunrise, when every leaf is laden with crystals, are a fine sight. The days are warm and calm, and bees and butterflies continue to waver and hum about the late-blooming flowers until the coming of the snow, usually late in November. Storm then follows storm in close succession, burying the meadows to a depth of from ten to twenty feet, while magnificent avalanches descend through the forests from the laden heights, depositing huge piles of snow mixed with uprooted trees and boulders. In the open sunshine the snow lasts until June, but the new season's vegetation is not generally in bloom until late in July. Perhaps the best time to visit this valley is in August. The snow is then melted from the woods, and the meadows are dry and warm, while the weather is mostly sunshine, reviving and exhilarating in quality; and the few clouds that rise and the showers they yield are only enough for freshness, fragrance, and beauty.

The groves about the Soda Springs are favorite camping-grounds on account of the pleasant-tasting, ice-cold water of the springs, charged with carbonic acid, and because of the fine views of the mountains across the meadow—the Glacier Monument, Cathedral Peak, Cathedral Spires, Unicorn Peak, and their many nameless companions rising in grand beauty above a noble swath of forest that is growing on the left lateral moraine of the ancient Tuolumne Glacier, which, broad and deep and far-reaching, exerted vast influence on the scenery of this portion of the Sierra. But there are fine camping-grounds all along the meadows, and one may move from grove to grove every day all summer enjoying a fresh home and finding enough to satisfy every roving desire for change.

There are four capital excursions to be made from here— to the summits of Mounts Dana and Lyell; to Mono Lake and the volcanoes, through Bloody Cañon; and to the great Tuolumne Cañon as far as the foot of the main cascades. All of these are glorious, and sure to be crowded with joyful and exciting experiences; but perhaps none of them will be remembered with keener delight than the days spent in sauntering in the broad velvet lawns by the river, sharing the pure air and light with the trees and mountains, and gaining something of the peace of nature in the majestic solitude.

The excursion to the top of Mount Dana is a very easy one; for though the mountain is 13,000 feet high, the ascent from the west side is so gentle and smooth that one may ride a mule to the very summit. Across many a busy stream, from meadow to meadow, lies your flowery way, the views all sublime; and they are seldom hidden by irregular foregrounds. As you gradually ascend, new mountains come into sight, enriching the landscape; peak rising above peak with its individual architecture, and its masses of fountain snow in endless variety of position and light and shade. Now your attention is turned to the moraines, sweeping in beautiful curves from the hollows and cañons of the mountains, regular in form as

railroad embankments, or to the glossy waves and pavements
of granite rising here and there from the flowery sod, polished
a thousand years ago and still shining. Towards the base of
the mountain you note the dwarfing of the trees, until at a
height of about 11,000 feet you find patches of the tough
white-barked pine pressed so flat by the ten or twenty feet of
snow piled upon them every winter for centuries that you may
walk over them as if walking on a shaggy rug. And, if curious
about such things, you may discover specimens of this hardy
mountaineer of a tree, not more than four feet high and about
as many inches in diameter at the ground, that are from two
hundred to four hundred years old, and are still holding on
bravely to life, making the most of their short summers, shaking their tasseled needles in the breeze right cheerily, drinking
the thin sunshine, and maturing their fine purple cones as if
they meant to live forever. The general view from the summit
is one of the most extensive and sublime to be found in all
the range. To the eastward you gaze far out over the hot
desert plains and mountains of the "Great Basin," range beyond range extending with soft outlines blue and purple in
the distance. More than six thousand feet below you lies Lake
Mono, overshadowed by the mountain on which you stand.
It is ten miles in diameter from north to south and fourteen
from east to west, but appears nearly circular, lying bare in
the treeless desert like a disk of burnished metal, though at
times it is swept by storm-winds from the mountains and
streaked with foam. To the south of the lake there is a range
of pale-gray volcanoes, now extinct, and though the highest
of them rise nearly two thousand feet above the lake, you can
look down into their well-defined circular, cup-like craters,
from which, a comparatively short time ago, ashes and cinders
were showered over the surrounding plains and glacier-laden
mountains.

To the westward the landscape is made up of gray glaciated
rocks and ridges, separated by a labyrinth of cañons and darkened with lines and broad fields of forest, while small lakes
and meadows dot the foreground. Northward and southward
the jagged peaks and towers that are marshaled along the axis
of the range are seen in all their glory, crowded together in
some places like trees in groves, making landscapes of wild,

extravagant, bewildering magnificence, yet calm and silent as the scenery of the sky.

Some eight glaciers are in sight. One of these is the Dana Glacier on the northeast side of the mountain, lying at the foot of a precipice about a thousand feet high, with a lovely pale-green lake in the general basin a little below the glacier. This is one of the many small shrunken remnants of the vast glacial system of the Sierra that once filled all the hollows and valleys of the mountains and covered all the lower ridges below the immediate summit fountains, flowing to right and left away from the axis of the range, lavishly fed by the snows of the glacial period.

In the excursion to Mount Lyell the immediate base of the mountain is easily reached on horseback by following the meadows along the river. Turning to the southward above the forks of the river you enter the Lyell branch of the valley, which is narrow enough and deep enough to be called a cañon. It is about eight miles long and from 2000 to 3000 feet deep. The flat meadow bottom is from about 300 to 200 yards wide, with gently curved margins about 50 yards wide, from which rise the simple massive walls of gray granite at an angle of about thirty-three degrees, mostly timbered with a light growth of pine and streaked in many places with avalanche channels. Towards the upper end of the cañon the grand Sierra crown comes into sight, forming a sublime and finely balanced picture, framed by the massive cañon walls. In the foreground you have the purple meadow fringed with willows; in the middle distance, huge swelling bosses of granite that form the base of the general mass of the mountain, with fringing lines of dark woods marking the lower curves, but smoothly snow-clad except in the autumn.

There is a good camping-ground on the east side of the river about a mile above. A fine cascade comes down over the cañon wall in telling style and makes fine camp music. At one place near the top careful climbing is necessary, but it is not so dangerous or difficult as to deter any climber of ordinary strength and skill, while the views from the summit are glorious. To the northward are Mammoth Mountain, Mounts Gibbs, Dana, Warren, Conness, and many others, unnumbered and unnamed; to the southeast the indescribably wild and jagged range of Mount Ritter and the Minarets; south-westward stretches the dividing ridge between the North Fork of the San Joaquin and the Merced, uniting with the Obelisk or Merced group of peaks that form the main fountains of the Illilouette branch of the Merced River; and to the northwest-ward extends the Cathedral spur. All these spurs, like distinct ranges, meet at your feet. Therefore you look over them mostly in the direction of their extension, and their peaks seem to be massed and crowded together in bewildering combinations; while immense amphitheaters, cañons, and subordinate masses, with their wealth of lakes, glaciers, and snow-fields, maze and cluster between them. In making the ascent in June or October the glacier is easily crossed, for then its snow mantle is smooth or mostly melted off. But in mid-summer the climbing is exceedingly tedious, because the snow is then weathered into curious and beautiful blades, sharp and slender, and set on edge in a leaning position. They lean to-wards the head of the glacier, and extend across from side to side in regular order in a direction at right angles to the di-rection of greatest declivity, the distance between the crests being about two or three feet, and the depth of the troughs between them about three feet. No more interesting problem is ever presented to the mountaineer than a walk over a glacier thus sculptured and adorned.

The Lyell Glacier is about a mile wide and less than a mile long, but presents, nevertheless, all the more characteristic features of large, river-like glaciers—moraines, earth-bands, blue-veins, crevasses, etc., while the streams that issue from it are turbid with rock-mud, showing its grinding action on its bed. And it is all the more interesting since it is the highest and most enduring remnant of the great Tuolumne Glacier, whose traces are still distinct fifty miles away, and whose in-fluence on the landscape was so profound. The McClure Gla-cier, once a tributary of the Lyell, is much smaller. Eighteen years ago I set a series of stakes in it to determine its rate of motion, which towards the end of summer, in the middle of the glacier, I found to be a little over an inch in twenty-four hours.

The trip to Mono from the Soda Springs can be made in a day, but Bloody Cañon will be found rough for animals. The scenery of the cañon, however, is wild and rich, and many days may profitably be spent around the shores of the lake and out on its islands and about the volcanoes.

In making the trip down the Big Tuolumne Cañon animals may be led as far as a small, grassy, forested lake basin that lies below the crossing of the Virginia Creek trail. And from this point any one accustomed to walk on earthquake boulders, carpeted with cañon chaparral, can easily go down the cañon as far as the big cascades and return to camp in one day. Many, however, are not able to do this, and it is far better to go leisurely, prepared to camp anywhere, and enjoy the marvelous grandeur of the place.

The cañon begins near the lower end of the meadows and extends to the Hetch Hetchy Valley, a distance of about eighteen miles, though it will seem much longer to any one who scrambles through it. It is from 1200 to about 5000 feet deep, and is comparatively narrow, but there are several fine, roomy, park-like openings in it, and throughout its whole extent Yosemite features are displayed on a grand scale—domes, El Capitan rocks, gables, Sentinels, Royal Arches, glacier points, Cathedral Spires, etc. There is even a Half Dome among its wealth of rock forms, though less sublime and beautiful than the Yosemite Half Dome. It also contains falls and cascades innumerable. The sheer falls, except when the snow is melting in early spring, are quite small in volume as compared with those of Yosemite and Hetch Hetchy; but many of them are very beautiful, and in any other country would be regarded as great wonders. But it is the cascades or sloping falls on the main river that are the crowning glory of the cañon, and these in volume, extent, and variety surpass those of any other cañon in the Sierra. The most showy and interesting of the cascades are mostly in the upper part of the cañon, above the point where Cathedral Creek and Hoffman Creek enter. For miles the river is one wild, exulting, on-rushing mass of snowy purple bloom, spreading over glacial waves of granite without any definite channel, and through avalanche taluses, gliding in silver plumes, dashing and foaming through huge boulder-dams, leaping high into the air in glorious wheel-like whirls, tossing from side to side, doubling, glinting, singing in glorious exuberance of mountain energy.

Every one who is anything of a mountaineer should go on through the entire length of the cañon, coming out by Hetch Hetchy. There is not a dull step all the way. With wide variations it is a Yosemite Valley from end to end.

THE HETCH HETCHY VALLEY.

Most people who visit Yosemite are apt to regard it as an exceptional creation, the only valley of its kind in the world. But nothing in Nature stands alone. She is not so poor as to have only one of anything. The explorer in the Sierra and elsewhere finds many Yosemites, that differ not more than one tree differs from another of the same species. They occupy the same relative positions on the mountain flanks, were formed by the same forces in the same kind of granite, and have similar sculpture, waterfalls, and vegetation. The Hetch Hetchy Valley has long been known as the Tuolumne Yosemite. It is said to have been discovered by Joseph Screech, a hunter, in 1850, a year before the discovery of the great Merced Yosemite. It lies in a northwesterly direction from Yosemite, at a distance of about twenty miles, and is easily accessible to mounted travelers by a trail that leaves the Big Oak Flat road at Bronson's Meadows, a few miles below Crane Flat. But by far the best way to it for those who have useful limbs is across the divide direct from Yosemite. Leaving the valley by Indian Cañon or Fall Cañon, you cross the dome-paved basin of Yosemite Creek, then bear to the left around the head fountains of the South Fork of the Tuolumne to the summit of the Big Tuolumne Cañon, a few miles above the head of Hetch Hetchy. Here you will find a glorious view. Immediately beneath you, at a depth of more than 4000 feet, you see a beautiful ribbon of level ground, with a silver thread in the middle of it, and green or yellow according to the time of year. That ribbon is a strip of meadow, and the silver thread is the main Tuolumne River. The opposite wall of the cañon rises in precipices, steep and angular, or with rounded brows like those of Yosemite, and from this wall as a base extends a fine wilderness of mountains, rising dome above dome, ridge above ridge, to a group of snowy peaks on the summit of the range. Of all this sublime congregation of mountains Castle Peak is king: robed with snow and light, dipping unnumbered points and spires into the thin blue sky, it maintains amid noble companions a perfect and commanding individuality.

You will not encounter much difficulty in getting down into the cañon, for bear trails may readily be found leading from the upper feeding-grounds to the berry gardens and acorn orchards of Hetch Hetchy, and when you reach the river you have only to saunter by its side a mile or two down the cañon before you find yourself in the open valley. Looking about you, you cannot fail to discover that you are in a Yosemite valley. As the Merced flows through Yosemite, so does the Tuolumne through Hetch Hetchy. The bottom of Yosemite is about 4000 feet above sea level, the bottom of Hetch Hetchy is about 3800 feet, and in both the walls are of gray granite and rise abruptly in precipices from a level bottom, with but little debris along their bases. Furthermore it was a home and stronghold of the Tuolumne Indians, as Ahwahne was of the grizzlies. Standing boldly forward from the south wall near the lower end of the valley is the rock Kolana, the outermost of a picturesque group corresponding to the Cathedral Rocks of Yosemite, and about the same height. Facing Kolana on the north side of the valley is a rock about 1800 feet in height, which presents a bare, sheer front like El Capitan, and over its massive brow flows a stream that makes the most graceful fall I have ever seen. Its Indian name is Tu-ee-u-la-la, and no other, so far as I have heard, has yet been given it. From the brow of the cliff it makes a free descent of a thousand feet and then breaks up into a ragged, foaming web of cascades among the boulders of an earthquake talus. Towards the end of summer it vanishes, because its head streams do not reach back to the lasting snows of the summits of the range, but in May and June it is indescribably lovely. The only fall that I know with which it may fairly be compared is the Bridal Veil, but it excels even that fall in peaceful, floating, swaying gracefulness. For when we attentively observe the Bridal Veil, even towards the middle of summer when its waters begin to fail, we may discover, when the winds blow aside the outer folds of spray, dense comet-shaped masses shooting through the air with terrible energy; but from the top of the cliff, where the Hetch Hetchy veil first floats free, all the way to the bottom it is in perfect repose. Again, the Bridal Veil is in a shadow-haunted nook inaccessible to the main wind currents of the valley, and has to depend for many of its gestures on irregular, teasing side currents and whirls, while Tu-ee-u-la-la, being fully exposed on the open cliff, is sun drenched all day, and is ever ready to yield graceful compliance to every wind that blows. Most people unacquainted with the behavior of mountain streams fancy that when they escape the bounds of their rocky channels and launch into the air they at once lose all self-control and tumble in confusion. On the contrary, on no part of their travels do they manifest more calm self-possession. Imagine yourself in Hetch Hetchy. It is a sunny day in June, the pines sway dreamily, and you are shoulder-deep in grass and flowers. Looking across the valley through beautiful open groves you see a bare granite wall 1800 feet high rising abruptly out of the green and yellow vegetation and glowing with sunshine, and in front of it the fall, waving like a downy scarf, silver bright, burning with white sun-fire in every fiber. In coming forward to the edge of the tremendous precipice and taking flight a little hasty eagerness appears, but this is speedily hushed in divine repose. Now observe the marvelous distinctness and delicacy of the various kinds of sun-filled tissue into which the waters are woven. They fly and float and drowse down the face of that grand gray rock in so leisurely and unconfused a manner that you may examine their texture and patterns as you would a piece of embroidery held in the hand. It is a flood of singing air, water, and sunlight woven into cloth that spirits might wear.

The great Hetch Hetchy Fall, called Wa-páma by the Tuolumnes, is on the same side of the valley as the Veil, and so near it that both may be seen in one view. It is about 1800 feet in height, and seems to be nearly vertical when one is standing in front of it, though it is considerably inclined. Its location is similar to that of the Yosemite Fall, but the volume of water is much greater. No two falls could be more unlike than Wa-páma and Tu-ee-u-la-la, the one thundering and beating in a shadowy gorge, the other chanting in deep, low tones, and with no other shadows about it than those of its own waters, pale-gray mostly, and violet and pink delicately graded. One whispers, "He dwells in peace," the other is the thunder of his chariot wheels in power. This noble pair are the main falls of the valley, though there are many small ones essential to the perfection of the general harmony.

The wall above Wa-páma corresponds, both in outlines and in details of sculpture, with the same relative portion of the Yosemite wall. Near the Yosemite Fall the cliff has two conspicuous benches extending in a horizontal direction 500 and 1500 feet above the valley. Two benches similarly situated, and timbered in the same way, occur on the same relative position on the Hetch Hetchy wall, and on no other portion. The upper end of Yosemite is closed by the great Half Dome, and the upper end of Hetch Hetchy is closed in the same way by a mountain rock. Both occupy angles formed by the confluence of two large glaciers that have long since vanished. In front of this head rock the river forks like the Merced in Yosemite. The right fork as you ascend is the main Tuolumne, which takes its rise in a glacier on the north side of Mount Lyell and flows through the Big Cañon. I have not traced the left fork to its highest source, but, judging from the general trend of the ridges, it must be near Castle Peak. Upon this left or North Fork there is a remarkably interesting series of cascades, five in number, ranged along a picturesque gorge, on the edges of which we may saunter safely and gain fine views of the dancing spray below. The first is a wide-spreading fan of white, crystal-covered water, half leaping half sliding over a steep polished pavement, at the foot of which it rests and sets forth clear and shining on its final flow to the main river. A short distance above the head of this cascade you discover the second, which is as impressively wild and beautiful as the first, and makes you sing with it as though you were a part of it. It is framed in deep rock walls that are colored yellow and red with lichens, and fringed on the jagged edges by live-oaks and sabine pines, and at the bottom in damp nooks you may see ferns, lilies, and azaleas.

Three or four hundred yards higher you come to the third of the choir, the largest of the five. It is formed of three smaller ones inseparably combined, which sing divinely, and make spray of the best quality for rainbows. A short distance beyond this the gorge comes to an end, and the bare stream, without any definite channel, spreads out in a thin, silvery sheet about 150 feet wide. Its waters are throughout almost

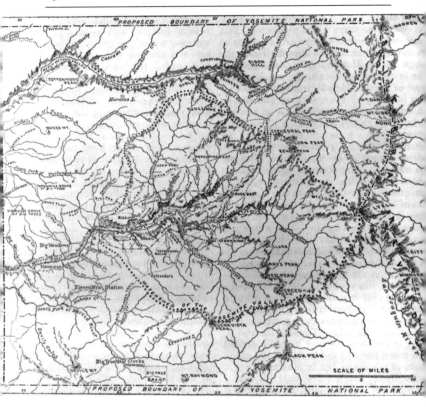

Map of the Yosemite region, showing present reservation, water-shed of the valley, and approximate limits of the proposed national park.*

its whole extent, drawn out in overlapping folds of lace, thick sown with diamond jets and sparks that give an exceedingly rich appearance. Still advancing, you hear a deep muffled booming, and you push eagerly on through flowery thickets

*The above map represents the limits of the park as proposed by Mr. Muir and as advocated before the Committee on Public Lands of the House of Representatives. As we go to press, the Committee seems disposed to extend the north and south limits eastward to the Nevada line, thus adding an equal amount to the area here indicated. The honor of introducing the National Park bill belongs to General William Vandever of California.—EDITOR.

until the last of the five appears through the foliage. The precipice down which it thunders is fretted with projecting knobs, forming polished keys upon which the wild waters play.

The bottom of the valley is divided by a low, glacier-polished bar of granite, the lower portion being mostly meadow land, the upper dry and sandy, and planted with fine Kellogg oaks, which frequently attain a diameter of six or seven feet. On the talus slopes the pines give place to the mountain live-oak, which forms the shadiest groves in the valley and the greatest in extent. Their glossy foliage, warm yellow-green and closely pressed, makes a kind of ceiling, supported by bare gray trunks and branches gnarled and picturesque. A few specimens of the sugar pine and tamarack pine are found in the valley, also the two silver firs. The Douglas spruce and the libocedrus attain noble dimensions in certain favorable spots, and a few specimens of the interesting *Torreya Californica* may be found on the south side. The brier-rose occurs in large patches, with tall, spiky mints and arching grasses. On the meadows lilies, larkspurs, and lupines of several species are abundant, and in some places reach above one's head. Rock-ferns of rare beauty fringe and rosette the walls from top to bottom—*Pellæa densa*, *P. mucronata* and *P. Bridgesii*, *Cheilanthes gracillima*, *Allosorus*, etc. *Adiantum pedatum* occurs in a few mossy corners that get spray from the falls. *Woodwardia radicans* and *Asplenium felix-fœmina* are the tallest ferns of the valley—six feet high, some of them. The whole valley was a charming garden when I last saw it, and the huts of the Indians and a lone cabin were the only improvements.

As will be seen by the map, I have thus briefly touched upon a number of the chief features of a region which it is proposed to reserve out of the public domain for the use and recreation of the people. A bill has already been introduced in Congress by Mr. Vandever creating a national park about the reservation which the State now holds in trust for the people. It is very desirable that the new reservation should at least extend to the limits indicated by the map, and the bill cannot too quickly become a law. Unless reserved or protected the whole region will soon or late be devastated by lumbermen and sheepmen, and so of course be made unfit for use as a pleasure ground. Already it is with great difficulty that campers, even in the most remote parts of the proposed reservation and in those difficult of access, can find grass enough to keep their animals from starving; the ground is already being gnawed and trampled into a desert condition, and when the region shall be stripped of its forests the ruin will be complete. Even the Yosemite will then suffer in the disturbance effected on the water-shed, the clear streams becoming muddy and much less regular in their flow. It is also devoutly to be hoped that the Hetch Hetchy will escape such ravages of man as one sees in Yosemite. Ax and plow, hogs and horses, have long been and are still busy in Yosemite's gardens and groves. All that is accessible and destructible is being rapidly destroyed—more rapidly than in any other Yosemite in the Sierra, though this is the only one that is under the special protection of the Government. And by far the greater part of this destruction of the fineness of wildness is of a kind that can claim no right relationship with that which necessarily follows use.

Century Magazine, September 1890

The American Forests

THE forests of America, however slighted by man, must have been a great delight to God; for they were the best he ever planted. The whole continent was a garden, and from the beginning it seemed to be favored above all the other wild parks and gardens of the globe. To prepare the ground, it was rolled and sifted in seas with infinite loving deliberation and forethought, lifted into the light, submerged and warmed over and over again, pressed and crumpled into folds and ridges, mountains, and hills, subsoiled with heaving volcanic fires, ploughed and ground and sculptured into scenery and soil with glaciers and rivers,—every feature growing and changing from beauty to beauty, higher and higher. And in the fullness of time it was planted in groves, and belts, and broad, exuberant, mantling forests, with the largest, most varied, most fruitful, and most beautiful trees in the world. Bright seas made its border, with wave embroidery and icebergs; gray deserts were outspread in the middle of it, mossy tundras on the north, savannas on the south, and blooming prairies and plains; while lakes and rivers shone through all the vast forests and openings, and happy birds and beasts gave delightful animation. Everywhere, everywhere over all the blessed continent, there were beauty and melody and kindly, wholesome, foodful abundance.

These forests were composed of about five hundred species of trees, all of them in some way useful to man, ranging in size from twenty-five feet in height and less than one foot in diameter at the ground to four hundred feet in height and more than twenty feet in diameter,—lordly monarchs proclaiming the gospel of beauty like apostles. For many a century after the ice-ploughs were melted, nature fed them and dressed them every day,—working like a man, a loving, devoted, painstaking gardener; fingering every leaf and flower and mossy furrowed bole; bending, trimming, modeling, balancing; painting them with the loveliest colors; bringing over them now clouds with cooling shadows and showers, now sunshine; fanning them with gentle winds and rustling their leaves; exercising them in every fibre with storms, and pruning them; loading them with flowers and fruit, loading them with snow, and ever making them more beautiful as the years rolled by. Wide-branching oak and elm in endless variety, walnut and maple, chestnut and beech, ilex and locust, touching limb to limb, spread a leafy translucent canopy along the coast of the Atlantic over the wrinkled folds and ridges of the Alleghanies,—a green billowy sea in summer, golden and purple in autumn, pearly gray like a steadfast frozen mist of interlacing branches and sprays in leafless, restful winter.

To the southward stretched dark, level-topped cypresses in knobby, tangled swamps, grassy savannas in the midst of them like lakes of light, groves of gay, sparkling spice-trees, magnolias and palms, glossy-leaved and blooming and shining continually. To the northward, over Maine and Ottawa, rose hosts of spiry, rosiny evergreens,—white pine and spruce, hemlock and cedar, shoulder to shoulder, laden with purple cones, their myriad needles sparkling and shimmering, covering hills and swamps, rocky headlands and domes, ever bravely aspiring and seeking the sky; the ground in their shade now snow-clad and frozen, now mossy and flowery; beaver meadows here and there, full of lilies and grass; lakes gleaming like eyes, and a silvery embroidery of rivers and creeks watering and brightening all the vast glad wilderness.

Thence westward were oak and elm, hickory and tupelo, gum and liriodendron, sassafras and ash, linden and laurel, spreading on ever wider in glorious exuberance over the great fertile basin of the Mississippi, over damp level bottoms, low dimpling hollows, and round dotting hills, embosoming sunny prairies and cheery park openings, half sunshine, half shade; while a dark wilderness of pines covered the region around the Great Lakes. Thence still westward swept the forests to right and left around grassy plains and deserts a thousand miles wide: irrepressible hosts of spruce and pine, aspen and willow, nut-pine and juniper, cactus and yucca, caring nothing for drought, extending undaunted from mountain to mountain, over mesa and desert, to join the darkening multitudes of pines that covered the high Rocky ranges and the glorious forests along the coast of the moist and balmy Pacific, where new species of pine, giant cedars and spruces, silver firs and Sequoias, kings of their race, growing close together like grass in a meadow, poised their brave domes and spires in the sky, three hundred feet above the ferns and the lilies that enameled the ground; towering serene through the long centuries, preaching God's forestry fresh from heaven.

Here the forests reached their highest development. Hence they went wavering northward over icy Alaska, brave spruce and fir, poplar and birch, by the coasts and the rivers, to within sight of the Arctic Ocean. American forests! the glory of the world! Surveyed thus from the east to the west, from the north to the south, they are rich beyond thought, immortal, immeasurable, enough and to spare for every feeding, sheltering beast and bird, insect and son of Adam; and nobody need have cared had there been no pines in Norway, no cedars and deodars on Lebanon and the Himalayas, no vine-clad selvas in the basin of the Amazon. With such variety, harmony, and triumphant exuberance, even nature, it would seem, might have rested content with the forests of North America, and planted no more.

So they appeared a few centuries ago when they were rejoicing in wildness. The Indians with stone axes could do them no more harm than could gnawing beavers and browsing moose. Even the fires of the Indians and the fierce shattering lightning seemed to work together only for good in clearing spots here and there for smooth garden prairies, and openings for sunflowers seeking the light. But when the steel axe of the white man rang out on the startled air their doom was sealed. Every tree heard the bodeful sound, and pillars of smoke gave the sign in the sky.

I suppose we need not go mourning the buffaloes. In the nature of things they had to give place to better cattle, though the change might have been made without barbarous wickedness. Likewise many of nature's five hundred kinds of wild trees had to make way for orchards and cornfields. In the settlement and civilization of the country, bread more than timber or beauty was wanted; and in the blindness of hunger, the early settlers, claiming Heaven as their guide, regarded God's trees as only a larger kind of pernicious weeds, extremely hard to get rid of. Accordingly, with no eye to the future, these pious destroyers waged interminable forest wars; chips flew thick and fast; trees in their beauty fell crashing by

millions, smashed to confusion, and the smoke of their burning has been rising to heaven more than two hundred years.
After the Atlantic coast from Maine to Georgia had been
mostly cleared and scorched into melancholy ruins, the overflowing multitude of bread and money seekers poured over
the Alleghanies into the fertile middle West, spreading ruthless
devastation ever wider and farther over the rich valley of the
Mississippi and the vast shadowy pine region about the Great
Lakes. Thence still westward, the invading horde of destroyers
called settlers made its fiery way over the broad Rocky Mountains, felling and burning more fiercely than ever, until at last
it has reached the wild side of the continent, and entered the
last of the great aboriginal forests on the shores of the Pacific.

Surely, then, it should not be wondered at that lovers of
their country, bewailing its baldness, are now crying aloud,
"Save what is left of the forests!" Clearing has surely now
gone far enough; soon timber will be scarce, and not a grove
will be left to rest in or pray in. The remnant protected will
yield plenty of timber, a perennial harvest for every right use,
without further diminution of its area, and will continue to
cover the springs of the rivers that rise in the mountains and
give irrigating waters to the dry valleys at their feet, prevent
wasting floods and be a blessing to everybody forever.

Every other civilized nation in the world has been compelled to care for its forests, and so must we if waste and
destruction are not to go on to the bitter end, leaving America
as barren as Palestine or Spain. In its calmer moments, in the
midst of bewildering hunger and war and restless over-industry, Prussia has learned that the forest plays an important part
in human progress, and that the advance in civilization only
makes it more indispensable. It has, therefore, as shown by
Mr. Pinchot, refused to deliver its forests to more or less
speedy destruction by permitting them to pass into private
ownership. But the state woodlands are not allowed to lie idle.
On the contrary, they are made to produce as much timber
as is possible without spoiling them. In the administration of
its forests, the state righteously considers itself bound to treat
them as a trust for the nation as a whole, and to keep in view
the common good of the people for all time.

In France no government forests have been sold since 1870.

On the other hand, about one half of the fifty million francs spent on forestry has been given to engineering works, to make the replanting of denuded areas possible. The disappearance of the forests in the first place, it is claimed, may be traced in most cases directly to mountain pasturage. The provisions of the Code concerning private woodlands are substantially these: no private owner may clear his woodlands without giving notice to the government at least four months in advance, and the forest service may forbid the clearing on the following grounds,—to maintain the soil on mountains, to defend the soil against erosion and flooding by rivers or torrents, to insure the existence of springs and watercourses, to protect the dunes and seashore, etc. A proprietor who has cleared his forest without permission is subject to heavy fine, and in addition may be made to replant the cleared area.

In Switzerland, after many laws like our own had been found wanting, the Swiss forest school was established in 1865, and soon after the federal forest law was enacted, which is binding over nearly two thirds of the country. Under its provisions, the cantons must appoint and pay the number of suitably educated foresters required for the fulfillment of the forest law; and in the organization of a normally stocked forest, the object of first importance must be the cutting each year of an amount of timber equal to the total annual increase, and no more.

The Russian government passed a law in 1888, declaring that clearing is forbidden in protected forests, and is allowed in others "only when its effects will not be to disturb the suitable relations which should exist between forest and agricultural lands."

Even Japan is ahead of us in the management of her forests. They cover an area of about twenty-nine million acres. The feudal lords valued the woodlands, and enacted vigorous protective laws; and when, in the latest civil war, the Mikado government destroyed the feudal system, it declared the forests that had belonged to the feudal lords to be the property of the state, promulgated a forest law binding on the whole kingdom, and founded a school of forestry in Tokio. The forest service does not rest satisfied with the present proportion of woodland, but looks to planting the best forest trees it can find in any country, if likely to be useful and to thrive in Japan.

In India systematic forest management was begun about forty years ago, under difficulties—presented by the character of the country, the prevalence of running fires, opposition from lumbermen, settlers, etc.—not unlike those which confront us now. Of the total area of government forests, perhaps seventy million acres, fifty-five million acres have been brought under the control of the forestry department,—a larger area than that of all our national parks and reservations. The chief aims of the administration are effective protection of the forests from fire, an efficient system of regeneration, and cheap transportation of the forest products; the results so far have been most beneficial and encouraging.

It seems, therefore, that almost every civilized nation can give us a lesson on the management and care of forests. So far our government has done nothing effective with its forests, though the best in the world, but is like a rich and foolish spendthrift who has inherited a magnificent estate in perfect order, and then has left his rich fields and meadows, forests and parks, to be sold and plundered and wasted at will, depending on their inexhaustible abundance. Now it is plain that the forests are not inexhaustible, and that quick measures must be taken if ruin is to be avoided. Year by year the remnant is growing smaller before the axe and fire, while the laws in existence provide neither for the protection of the timber from destruction nor for its use where it is most needed.

As is shown by Mr. E. A. Bowers, formerly Inspector of the Public Land Service, the foundation of our protective policy, which has never protected, is an act passed March 1, 1817, which authorized the Secretary of the Navy to reserve lands producing live-oak and cedar, for the sole purpose of supplying timber for the navy of the United States. An extension of this law by the passage of the act of March 2, 1831, provided that if any person should cut live-oak or red cedar trees or *other timber* from the lands of the United States for any other purpose than the construction of the navy, such person should pay a fine not less than triple the value of the timber cut, and be imprisoned for a period not exceeding twelve months. Upon this old law, as Mr. Bowers points out, having the construction of a wooden navy in view, the United States government has to-day chiefly to rely in protecting its timber throughout the arid regions of the West, where none of the naval timber which the law had in mind is to be found.

By the act of June 3, 1878, timber can be taken from public lands not subject to entry under any existing laws except for minerals, by *bona fide* residents of the Rocky Mountain states and territories and the Dakotas. Under the timber and stone act, of the same date, land in the Pacific States and Nevada, valuable mainly for timber, and unfit for cultivation if the timber is removed, can be purchased for two dollars and a half an acre, under certain restrictions. By the act of March 3, 1875, all land-grant and right-of-way railroads are authorized to take timber from the public lands adjacent to their lines for construction purposes; and they have taken it with a vengeance, destroying a hundred times more than they have used, mostly by allowing fires to run into the woods. The settlement laws, under which a settler may enter lands valuable for timber as well as for agriculture, furnish another means of obtaining title to public timber.

With the exception of the timber culture act, under which, in consideration of planting a few acres of seedlings, settlers on the treeless plains got 160 acres each, the above is the only legislation aiming to protect and promote the planting of forests. In no other way than under some one of these laws can a citizen of the United States make any use of the public forests. To show the results of the timber-planting act, it need only be stated that of the thirty-eight million acres entered under it, less than one million acres have been patented. This means that less than fifty thousand acres have been planted with stunted, woebegone, almost hopeless sprouts of trees, while at the same time the government has allowed millions of acres of the grandest forest trees to be stolen or destroyed, or sold for nothing. Under the act of June 3, 1878, settlers in Colorado and the Territories were allowed to cut timber for mining and educational purposes from mineral land, which in the practical West means both cutting and burning anywhere and everywhere, for any purpose, on any sort of public land. Thus, the prospector, the miner, and mining and railroad companies are allowed by law to take all the timber they like for their mines and roads, and the forbidden settler, if there are no mineral lands near his farm or stock-ranch, or none that he knows of, can hardly be expected to forbear taking what he needs wherever he can find it. Timber is as necessary as bread, and no scheme of management failing to recognize and properly provide for this want can possibly be maintained. In any case, it will be hard to teach the pioneers that it is wrong to steal government timber. Taking from the government is with them the same as taking from nature, and their consciences flinch no more in cutting timber from the wild forests than in drawing water from a lake or river. As for reservation and protection of forests, it seems as silly and needless to them as protection and reservation of the ocean would be, both appearing to be boundless and inexhaustible.

The special land agents employed by the General Land Office to protect the public domain from timber depredations are supposed to collect testimony to sustain prosecution and to superintend such prosecution on behalf of the government, which is represented by the district attorneys. But timber thieves of the Western class are seldom convicted, for the good reason that most of the jurors who try such cases are themselves as guilty as those on trial. The effect of the present confused, discriminating, and unjust system has been to place almost the whole population in opposition to the government; and as conclusive of its futility, as shown by Mr. Bowers, we need only state that during the seven years from 1881 to 1887 inclusive, the value of the timber reported stolen from the government lands was $36,719,935, and the amount recovered was $478,073, while the cost of the services of special agents alone was $455,000, to which must be added the expense of the trials. Thus for nearly thirty-seven million dollars' worth of timber the government got less than nothing; and the value of that consumed by running fires during the same period, without benefit even to thieves, was probably over two hundred millions of dollars. Land commissioners and Secretaries of the Interior have repeatedly called attention to this ruinous state of affairs, and asked Congress to enact the requisite legislation for reasonable reform. But, busied with tariffs, etc., Congress has given no heed to these or other appeals, and our forests, the most valuable and the most destructible of all the natural resources of the country, are being robbed and burned more rapidly than ever. The annual appropriation for so-called "protection service" is hardly sufficient to keep twenty-five timber agents in the field, and as far as any efficient protection of timber is concerned these agents themselves might as well be timber.*

That a change from robbery and ruin to a permanent rational policy is urgently needed nobody with the slightest knowledge of American forests will deny. In the East and along the northern Pacific coast, where the rainfall is abundant, comparatively few care keenly what becomes of the trees as long as fuel and lumber are not noticeably dear. But in the Rocky Mountains and California and Arizona, where the forests are inflammable, and where the fertility of the lowlands depends upon irrigation, public opinion is growing stronger every year in favor of permanent protection by the federal government of all the forests that cover the sources of the streams. Even lumbermen in these regions, long accustomed to steal, are now willing and anxious to buy lumber for their mills under cover of law: some possibly from a late second growth of honesty, but most, especially the small mill-owners, simply because it no longer pays to steal where all may not only steal, but also destroy, and in particular because it costs about as much to steal timber for one mill as for ten, and, therefore, the ordinary lumberman can no longer compete with the large corporations. Many of the miners find that timber is already becoming scarce and dear on the denuded hills around their mills, and they, too, are asking for protection of forests, at least against fire. The slow-going, unthrifty farmers, also, are beginning to realize that when the timber is stripped from the mountains the irrigating streams dry up in summer, and are destructive in winter; that soil, scenery, and everything slips off with the trees: so of course they are coming into the ranks of tree-friends.

Of all the magnificent coniferous forests around the Great Lakes, once the property of the United States, scarcely any belong to it now. They have disappeared in lumber and smoke, mostly smoke, and the government got not one cent for them; only the land they were growing on was considered valuable, and two and a half dollars an acre was charged for

*A change for the better, compelled by public opinion, is now going on,—1901.

it. Here and there in the Southern States there are still considerable areas of timbered government land, but these are comparatively unimportant. Only the forests of the West are significant in size and value, and these, although still great, are rapidly vanishing. Last summer, of the unrivaled redwood forests of the Pacific Coast Range, the United States Forestry Commission could not find a single quarter-section that remained in the hands of the government.*

Under the timber and stone act of 1878, which might well have been called the "dust and ashes act," any citizen of the United States could take up one hundred and sixty acres of timber land, and by paying two dollars and a half an acre for it obtain title. There was some virtuous effort made with a view to limit the operations of the act by requiring that the purchaser should make affidavit that he was entering the land exclusively for his own use, and by not allowing any association to enter more than one hundred and sixty acres. Nevertheless, under this act wealthy corporations have fraudulently obtained title to from ten thousand to twenty thousand acres or more. The plan was usually as follows: A mill company, desirous of getting title to a large body of redwood or sugar-pine land, first blurred the eyes and ears of the land agents, and then hired men to enter the land they wanted, and immediately deed it to the company after a nominal compliance with the law; false swearing in the wilderness against the government being held of no account. In one case which came under the observation of Mr. Bowers, it was the practice of a lumber company to hire the entire crew of every vessel which might happen to touch at any port in the redwood belt, to enter one hundred and sixty acres each and immediately deed the land to the company, in consideration of the company's paying all expenses and giving the jolly sailors fifty dollars apiece for their trouble.

By such methods have our magnificent redwoods and much of the sugar-pine forests of the Sierra Nevada been absorbed by foreign and resident capitalists. Uncle Sam is not often

*The State of California recently appropriated two hundred and fifty thousand dollars to buy a block of redwood land near Santa Cruz for a state park. A much larger national park should be made in Humboldt or Mendocino county.

called a fool in business matters, yet he has sold millions of acres of timber land at two dollars and a half an acre on which a single tree was worth more than a hundred dollars. But this priceless land has been patented, and nothing can be done now about the crazy bargain. According to the everlasting laws of righteousness, even the fraudulent buyers at less than one per cent of its value are making little or nothing, on account of fierce competition. The trees are felled, and about half of each giant is left on the ground to be converted into smoke and ashes; the better half is sawed into choice lumber and sold to citizens of the United States or to foreigners: thus robbing the country of its glory and impoverishing it without right benefit to anybody,—a bad, black business from beginning to end.

The redwood is one of the few conifers that sprout from the stump and roots, and it declares itself willing to begin immediately to repair the damage of the lumberman and also that of the forest-burner. As soon as a redwood is cut down or burned it sends up a crowd of eager, hopeful shoots, which, if allowed to grow, would in a few decades attain a height of a hundred feet, and the strongest of them would finally become giants as great as the original tree. Gigantic second and third growth trees are found in the redwoods, forming magnificent temple-like circles around charred ruins more than a thousand years old. But not one denuded acre in a hundred is allowed to raise a new forest growth. On the contrary, all the brains, religion, and superstition of the neighborhood are brought into play to prevent a new growth. The sprouts from the roots and stumps are cut off again and again, with zealous concern as to the best time and method of making death sure. In the clearings of one of the largest mills on the coast we found thirty men at work, last summer, cutting off redwood shoots "in the dark of the moon," claiming that all the stumps and roots cleared at this auspicious time would send up no more shoots. Anyhow, these vigorous, almost immortal trees are killed at last, and black stumps are now their only monuments over most of the chopped and burned areas.

The redwood is the glory of the Coast Range. It extends along the western slope, in a nearly continuous belt about ten miles wide, from beyond the Oregon boundary to the south of Santa Cruz, a distance of nearly four hundred miles, and in massive, sustained grandeur and closeness of growth surpasses all the other timber woods of the world. Trees from ten to fifteen feet in diameter and three hundred feet high are not uncommon, and a few attain a height of three hundred and fifty feet or even four hundred, with a diameter at the base of fifteen to twenty feet or more, while the ground beneath them is a garden of fresh, exuberant ferns, lilies, gaultheria, and rhododendron. This grand tree, Sequoia sempervirens, is surpassed in size only by its near relative, Sequoia gigantea, or Big Tree, of the Sierra Nevada, if, indeed, it is surpassed. The sempervirens is certainly the taller of the two. The gigantea attains a greater girth, and is heavier, more noble in port, and more sublimely beautiful. These two Sequoias are all that are known to exist in the world, though in former geological times the genus was common and had many species. The redwood is restricted to the Coast Range, and the Big Tree to the Sierra.

As timber the redwood is too good to live. The largest sawmills ever built are busy along its seaward border, "with all the modern improvements," but so immense is the yield per acre it will be long ere the supply is exhausted. The Big Tree is also, to some extent, being made into lumber. It is far less abundant than the redwood, and is, fortunately, less accessible, extending along the western flank of the Sierra in a partially interrupted belt, about two hundred and fifty miles long, at a height of from four to eight thousand feet above the sea. The enormous logs, too heavy to handle, are blasted into manageable dimensions with gunpowder. A large portion of the best timber is thus shattered and destroyed, and, with the huge, knotty tops, is left in ruins for tremendous fires that kill every tree within their range, great and small. Still, the species is not in danger of extinction. It has been planted and is flourishing over a great part of Europe, and magnificent sections of the aboriginal forests have been reserved as national and State parks,—the Mariposa Sequoia Grove, near Yosemite, managed by the State of California, and the General Grant and Sequoia national parks on the Kings, Kaweah, and Tule rivers, efficiently guarded by a small troop of United States cavalry under the direction of the Secretary of the Interior.

But there is not a single specimen of the redwood in any national park. Only by gift or purchase, so far as I know, can the government get back into its possession a single acre of this wonderful forest.

The legitimate demands on the forests that have passed into private ownership, as well as those in the hands of the government, are increasing every year with the rapid settlement and upbuilding of the country, but the methods of lumbering are as yet grossly wasteful. In most mills only the best portions of the best trees are used, while the ruins are left on the ground to feed great fires, which kill much of what is left of the less desirable timber, together with the seedlings, on which the permanence of the forest depends. Thus every mill is a centre of destruction far more severe from waste and fire than from use. The same thing is true of the mines, which consume and destroy indirectly immense quantities of timber with their innumerable fires, accidental or set to make open ways, and often without regard to how far they run. The prospector deliberately sets fires to clear off the woods just where they are densest, to lay the rocks bare and make the discovery of mines easier. Sheep-owners and their shepherds also set fires everywhere through the woods in the fall to facilitate the march of their countless flocks the next summer, and perhaps in some places to improve the pasturage. The axe is not yet at the root of every tree, but the sheep is, or was before the national parks were established and guarded by the military, the only effective and reliable arm of the government free from the blight of politics. Not only do the shepherds, at the driest time of the year, set fire to everything that will burn, but the sheep consume every green leaf, not sparing even the young conifers, when they are in a starving condition from crowding, and they rake and dibble the loose soil of the mountain sides for the spring floods to wash away, and thus at last leave the ground barren.

Of all the destroyers that infest the woods, the shake-maker seems the happiest. Twenty or thirty years ago, shakes, a kind of long, boardlike shingles split with a mallet and a frow, were in great demand for covering barns and sheds, and many are used still in preference to common shingles, especially those made from the sugar-pine, which do not warp or crack in the hottest sunshine. Drifting adventurers in California, after harvest and threshing are over, oftentimes meet to discuss their plans for the winter, and their talk is interesting. Once, in a company of this kind, I heard a man say, as he peacefully smoked his pipe: "Boys, as soon as this job's done I'm goin' into the duck business. There's big money in it, and your grub costs nothing. Tule Joe made five hundred dollars last winter on mallard and teal. Shot 'em on the Joaquin, tied 'em in dozens by the neck, and shipped 'em to San Francisco. And when he was tired wading in the sloughs and touched with rheumatiz, he just knocked off on ducks, and went to the Contra Costa hills for dove and quail. It's a mighty good business, and you're your own boss, and the whole thing's fun."

Another of the company, a bushy-bearded fellow, with a trace of brag in his voice, drawled out: "Bird business is well enough for some, but bear is my game, with a deer and a California lion thrown in now and then for change. There's always market for bear grease, and sometimes you can sell the hams. They're good as hog hams any day. And you are your own boss in my business, too, if the bears ain't too big and too many for you. Old grizzlies I despise,—they want cannon to kill 'em; but the blacks and browns are beauties for grease, and when once I get 'em just right, and draw a bead on 'em, I fetch 'em every time." Another said he was going to catch up a lot of mustangs as soon as the rains set in, hitch them to a gang-plough, and go to farming on the San Joaquin plains for wheat. But most preferred the shake business, until something more profitable and as sure could be found, with equal comfort and independence.

With a cheap mustang or mule to carry a pair of blankets, a sack of flour, a few pounds of coffee, and an axe, a frow, and a cross-cut saw, the shake-maker ascends the mountains to the pine belt where it is most accessible, usually by some mine or mill road. Then he strikes off into the virgin woods, where the sugar pine, king of all the hundred species of pines in the world in size and beauty, towers on the open sunny slopes of the Sierra in the fullness of its glory. Selecting a favorable spot for a cabin near a meadow with a stream, he unpacks his animal and stakes it out on the meadow. Then he chops into one after another of the pines, until he finds one that he feels sure will split freely, cuts this down, saws off a section four feet long, splits it, and from this first cut, perhaps seven feet in diameter, he gets shakes enough for a cabin and its furniture,—walls, roof, door, bedstead, table, and stool. Besides his labor, only a few pounds of nails are required. Sapling poles form the frame of the airy building, usually about six feet by eight in size, on which the shakes are nailed, with the edges overlapping. A few bolts from the same section that the shakes were made from are split into square sticks and built up to form a chimney, the inside and interspaces being plastered and filled in with mud. Thus, with abundance of fuel, shelter and comfort by his own fireside are secured. Then he goes to work sawing and splitting for the market, tying the shakes in bundles of fifty or a hundred. They are four feet long, four inches wide, and about one fourth of an inch thick. The first few thousands he sells or trades at the nearest mill or store, getting provisions in exchange. Then he advertises, in whatever way he can, that he has excellent sugar-pine shakes for sale, easy of access and cheap.

Only the lower, perfectly clear, free-splitting portions of the giant pines are used,—perhaps ten to twenty feet from a tree two hundred and fifty in height; all the rest is left a mass of ruins, to rot or to feed the forest fires, while thousands are hacked deeply and rejected in proving the grain. Over nearly all of the more accessible slopes of the Sierra and Cascade mountains in southern Oregon, at a height of from three to six thousand feet above the sea, and for a distance of about six hundred miles, this waste and confusion extends. Happy robbers! dwelling in the most beautiful woods, in the most salubrious climate, breathing delightful odors both day and night, drinking cool living water,—roses and lilies at their feet in the spring, shedding fragrance and ringing bells as if cheering them on in their desolating work. There is none to say them nay. They buy no land, pay no taxes, dwell in a paradise with no forbidding angel either from Washington or from heaven. Every one of the frail shake shanties is a centre of destruction, and the extent of the ravages wrought in this quiet way is in the aggregate enormous.

It is not generally known that, notwithstanding the immense quantities of timber cut every year for foreign and home markets and mines, from five to ten times as much is destroyed as is used, chiefly by running forest fires that only the federal government can stop. Travelers through the West in summer are not likely to forget the fire-work displayed along the various railway tracks. Thoreau, when contemplating the destruction of the forests on the east side of the continent, said that soon the country would be so bald that every man would have to grow whiskers to hide its nakedness, but he thanked God that at least the sky was safe. Had he gone West he would have found out that the sky was not safe; for all through the summer months, over most of the mountain regions, the smoke of mill and forest fires is so thick and black that no sunbeam can pierce it. The whole sky, with clouds, sun, moon, and stars, is simply blotted out. There is no real sky and no scenery. Not a mountain is left in the landscape. At least none is in sight from the lowlands, and they all might as well be on the moon, as far as scenery is concerned.

The half-dozen transcontinental railroad companies advertise the beauties of their lines in gorgeous many-colored folders, each claiming its as the "scenic route." "The route of superior desolation"—the smoke, dust, and ashes route—would be a more truthful description. Every train rolls on through dismal smoke and barbarous, melancholy ruins; and the companies might well cry in their advertisements: "Come! travel our way. Ours is the blackest. It is the only genuine Erebus route. The sky is black and the ground is black, and on either side there is a continuous border of black stumps and logs and blasted trees appealing to heaven for help as if still half alive, and their mute eloquence is most interestingly touching. The blackness is perfect. On account of the superior skill of our workmen, advantages of climate, and the kind of trees, the charring is generally deeper along our line, and the ashes are deeper, and the confusion and desolation displayed can never be rivaled. No other route on this continent so fully illustrates the abomination of desolation." Such a claim would be reasonable, as each seems the worst, whatever route you chance to take.

Of course a way had to be cleared through the woods. But the felled timber is not worked up into firewood for the engines and into lumber for the company's use; it is left lying in vulgar confusion, and is fired from time to time by sparks from locomotives or by the workmen camping along the line. The fires, whether accidental or set, are allowed to run into the woods as far as they may, thus assuring comprehensive destruction. The directors of a line that guarded against fires, and cleared a clean gap edged with living trees, and fringed and mantled with the grass and flowers and beautiful seedlings that are ever ready and willing to spring up, might justly boast of the beauty of their road; for nature is always ready to heal every scar. But there is no such road on the western side of the continent. Last summer, in the Rocky Mountains, I saw six fires started by sparks from a locomotive within a distance of three miles, and nobody was in sight to prevent them from spreading. They might run into the adjacent forests and burn the timber from hundreds of square miles; not a man in the State would care to spend an hour in fighting them, as long as his own fences and buildings were not threatened.

Notwithstanding all the waste and use which have been going on unchecked like a storm for more than two centuries, it is not yet too late—though it is high time—for the government to begin a rational administration of its forests. About seventy million acres it still owns,—enough for all the country, if wisely used. These residual forests are generally on mountain slopes, just where they are doing the most good, and where their removal would be followed by the greatest number of evils; the lands they cover are too rocky and high for agriculture, and can never be made as valuable for any other crop as for the present crop of trees. It has been shown over and over again that if these mountains were to be stripped of their trees and underbrush, and kept bare and sodless by hordes of sheep and the innumerable fires the shepherds set, besides those of the millmen, prospectors, shake-makers, and all sorts of adventurers, both lowlands and mountains would speedily become little better than deserts, compared with their present beneficent fertility. During heavy rainfalls and while the winter accumulations of snow were melting, the larger streams would swell into destructive torrents, cutting deep, rugged-edged gullies, carrying away the fertile humus and soil as well as sand and rocks, filling up and overflowing their lower channels, and covering the lowland fields with raw detritus. Drought and barrenness would follow.

In their natural condition, or under wise management, keeping out destructive sheep, preventing fires, selecting the trees that should be cut for lumber, and preserving the young ones and the shrubs and sod of herbaceous vegetation, these forests would be a never failing fountain of wealth and beauty. The cool shades of the forest give rise to moist beds and currents of air, and the sod of grasses and the various flowering plants and shrubs thus fostered, together with the network and sponge of tree roots, absorb and hold back the rain and the waters from melting snow, compelling them to ooze and percolate and flow gently through the soil in streams that never dry. All the pine needles and rootlets and blades of grass, and the fallen, decaying trunks of trees, are dams, storing the bounty of the clouds and dispensing it in perennial life-giving streams, instead of allowing it to gather suddenly and rush headlong in short-lived devastating floods. Everybody on the dry side of the continent is beginning to find this out, and, in view of the waste going on, is growing more and more anxious for government protection. The outcries we hear against forest reservations come mostly from thieves who are wealthy and steal timber by wholesale. They have so long been allowed to steal and destroy in peace that any impediment to forest robbery is denounced as a cruel and irreligious interference with "vested rights," likely to endanger the repose of all ungodly welfare.

Gold, gold, gold! How strong a voice that metal has!

"O wae for the siller, it is sae preva'lin'!"

Even in Congress a sizable chunk of gold, carefully concealed, will outtalk and outfight all the nation on a subject like forestry, well smothered in ignorance, and in which the money interests of only a few are conspicuously involved. Under these circumstances, the bawling, blethering oratorical stuff drowns the voice of God himself. Yet the dawn of a new day in forestry is breaking. Honest citizens see that only the rights of the government are being trampled, not those of the settlers. Only what belongs to all alike is reserved, and every acre that is left should be held together under the federal government as a basis for a general policy of administration for the public good. The people will not always be deceived by selfish opposition, whether from lumber and mining corporations or from sheepmen and prospectors, however cunningly brought forward underneath fables and gold.

Emerson says that things refuse to be mismanaged long. An exception would seem to be found in the case of our forests, which have been mismanaged rather long, and now come desperately near being like smashed eggs and spilt milk. Still, in the long run the world does not move backward. The wonderful advance made in the last few years, in creating four national parks in the West, and thirty forest reservations, embracing nearly forty million acres; and in the planting of the borders of streets and highways and spacious parks in all the great cities, to satisfy the natural taste and hunger for landscape beauty and righteousness that God has put, in some measure, into every human being and animal, shows the trend of awakening public opinion. The making of the far-famed New York Central Park was opposed by even good men, with misguided pluck, perseverance, and ingenuity; but straight right won its way, and now that park is appreciated. So we confidently believe it will be with our great national parks and forest reservations. There will be a period of indifference on the part of the rich, sleepy with wealth, and of the toiling millions, sleepy with poverty, most of whom never saw a forest; a period of screaming protest and objection from the plunderers, who are as unconscionable and enterprising as Satan. But light is surely coming, and the friends of destruction will preach and bewail in vain.

The United States government has always been proud of the welcome it has extended to good men of every nation, seeking freedom and homes and bread. Let them be welcomed still as nature welcomes them, to the woods as well as to the prairies and plains. No place is too good for good men, and still there is room. They are invited to heaven, and may well be allowed in America. Every place is made better by them. Let them be as free to pick gold and gems from the hills, to cut and hew, dig and plant, for homes and bread, as the birds are to pick berries from the wild bushes, and moss and leaves for nests. The ground will be glad to feed them, and the pines will come down from the mountains for their homes as willingly as the cedars came from Lebanon for Solomon's temple. Nor will the woods be the worse for this use, or their benign influences be diminished any more than the sun is diminished by shining. Mere destroyers, however, tree-killers, wool and mutton men, spreading death and confusion in the fairest groves and gardens ever planted,—let the government hasten to cast them out and make an end of them. For it must be told again and again, and be burningly borne in mind, that just now, while protective measures are being deliberated languidly, destruction and use are speeding on faster and farther every day. The axe and saw are insanely busy, chips are flying thick as snowflakes, and every summer thousands of acres of priceless forests, with their underbrush, soil, springs, climate, scenery, and religion, are vanishing away in clouds of smoke, while, except in the national parks, not one forest guard is employed.

All sorts of local laws and regulations have been tried and found wanting, and the costly lessons of our own experience, as well as that of every civilized nation, show conclusively that the fate of the remnant of our forests is in the hands of the federal government, and that if the remnant is to be saved at all, it must be saved quickly.

Any fool can destroy trees. They cannot run away; and if they could, they would still be destroyed,—chased and hunted down as long as fun or a dollar could be got out of their bark hides, branching horns, or magnificent bole backbones. Few that fell trees plant them; nor would planting avail much towards getting back anything like the noble primeval forests. During a man's life only saplings can be grown, in the place of the old trees—tens of centuries old—that have been destroyed. It took more than three thousand years to make some of the trees in these Western woods,—trees that are still standing in perfect strength and beauty, waving and singing in the mighty forests of the Sierra. Through all the wonderful, eventful centuries since Christ's time—and long before that—God has cared for these trees, saved them from drought, disease, avalanches, and a thousand straining, leveling tempests and floods; but he cannot save them from fools,—only Uncle Sam can do that.

from *Our National Parks*, 1901

The Wild Parks and Forest Reservations of the West

"Keep not standing fix'd and rooted,
    Briskly venture, briskly roam;
Head and hand, where'er thou foot it,
    And stout heart are still at home.
In each land the sun does visit
    We are gay, whate'er betide:
To give room for wandering is it
    That the world was made so wide."

THE tendency nowadays to wander in wildernesses is delightful to see. Thousands of tired, nerve-shaken, over-civilized people are beginning to find out that going to the mountains is going home; that wildness is a necessity; and that mountain parks and reservations are useful not only as fountains of timber and irrigating rivers, but as fountains of life. Awakening from the stupefying effects of the vice of over-industry and the deadly apathy of luxury, they are trying as best they can to mix and enrich their own little ongoings with those of Nature, and to get rid of rust and disease. Briskly venturing and roaming, some are washing off sins and cobweb cares of the devil's spinning in all-day storms on mountains; sauntering in rosiny pinewoods or in gentian meadows, brushing through chaparral, bending down and parting sweet, flowery sprays; tracing rivers to their sources, getting in touch with the nerves of Mother Earth; jumping from rock to rock, feeling the life of them, learning the songs of them, panting in whole-souled exercise, and rejoicing in deep, long-drawn breaths of pure wildness. This is fine and natural and full of promise. So also is the growing interest in the care and preservation of forests and wild places in general, and in the half wild parks and gardens of towns. Even the scenery habit in its most artificial forms, mixed with spectacles, silliness, and kodaks; its devotees arrayed more gorgeously than scarlet tanagers, frightening the wild game with red umbrellas,—even this is encouraging, and may well be regarded as a hopeful sign of the times.

All the Western mountains are still rich in wildness, and by means of good roads are being brought nearer civilization every year. To the sane and free it will hardly seem necessary to cross the continent in search of wild beauty, however easy the way, for they find it in abundance wherever they chance to be. Like Thoreau they see forests in orchards and patches of huckleberry brush, and oceans in ponds and drops of dew. Few in these hot, dim, strenuous times are quite sane or free; choked with care like clocks full of dust, laboriously doing so much good and making so much money,—or so little,—they are no longer good for themselves.

When, like a merchant taking a list of his goods, we take stock of our wildness, we are glad to see how much of even the most destructible kind is still unspoiled. Looking at our continent as scenery when it was all wild, lying between beautiful seas, the starry sky above it, the starry rocks beneath it, to compare its sides, the East and the West, would be like comparing the sides of a rainbow. But it is no longer equally beautiful. The rainbows of to-day are, I suppose, as bright as those that first spanned the sky; and some of our landscapes are growing more beautiful from year to year, notwithstanding the clearing, trampling work of civilization. New plants and animals are enriching woods and gardens, and many landscapes wholly new, with divine sculpture and architecture, are just now coming to the light of day as the mantling folds of creative glaciers are being withdrawn, and life in a thousand cheerful, beautiful forms is pushing into them, and new-born rivers are beginning to sing and shine in them. The old rivers, too, are growing longer, like healthy trees, gaining new branches and lakes as the residual glaciers at their highest sources on the mountains recede, while the rootlike branches in their flat deltas are at the same time spreading farther and wider into the seas and making new lands.

Under the control of the vast mysterious forces of the interior of the earth all the continents and islands are slowly rising or sinking. Most of the mountains are diminishing in size under the wearing action of the weather, though a few are increasing in height and girth, especially the volcanic ones, as fresh floods of molten rocks are piled on their summits and spread in successive layers, like the wood-rings of trees, on their sides. New mountains, also, are being created from time to time as islands in lakes and seas, or as subordinate cones on the slopes of old ones, thus in some measure balancing the waste of old beauty with new. Man, too, is making many far-reaching changes. This most influential half animal, half angel is rapidly multiplying and spreading, covering the seas and lakes with ships, the land with huts, hotels, cathedrals, and clustered city shops and homes, so that soon, it would seem, we may have to go farther than Nansen to find a good sound solitude. None of Nature's landscapes are ugly so long as they are wild; and much, we can say comfortingly, must always be in great part wild, particularly the sea and the sky, the floods of light from the stars, and the warm, unspoilable heart of the earth, infinitely beautiful, though only dimly visible to the eye of imagination. The geysers, too, spouting from the hot underworld; the steady, long-lasting glaciers on the mountains, obedient only to the sun; Yosemite domes and the tremendous grandeur of rocky cañons and mountains in general,—these must always be wild, for man can change them and mar them hardly more than can the butterflies that hover above them. But the continent's outer beauty is fast passing away, especially the plant part of it, the most destructible and most universally charming of all.

Only thirty years ago, the great Central Valley of California, five hundred miles long and fifty miles wide, was one bed of golden and purple flowers. Now it is ploughed and pastured out of existence, gone forever,—scarce a memory of it left in fence corners and along the bluffs of the streams. The gardens of the Sierra, also, and the noble forests in both the reserved and unreserved portions are sadly hacked and trampled, notwithstanding the ruggedness of the topography,—all excepting those of the parks guarded by a few soldiers. In the noblest forests of the world, the ground, once divinely beautiful, is desolate and repulsive, like a face ravaged by disease. This is true also of many other Pacific Coast and Rocky Mountain valleys and forests. The same fate, sooner or later, is awaiting them all, unless awakening public opinion comes forward to stop it. Even the great deserts in Arizona, Nevada, Utah, and New Mexico, which offer so little to attract settlers, and which a few years ago pioneers were afraid of, as places of desolation and death, are now taken as pastures at the rate of one or two square miles per cow, and of course their plant treasures are passing away,—the delicate abronias, phloxes, gilias, etc. Only a few of the bitter, thorny, unbitable shrubs are left, and the sturdy cactuses that defend themselves with bayonets and spears.

Most of the wild plant wealth of the East also has vanished,—gone into dusty history. Only vestiges of its glorious prairie and woodland wealth remain to bless humanity in boggy, rocky, unploughable places. Fortunately, some of these are purely wild, and go far to keep Nature's love visible. White water-lilies, with rootstocks deep and safe in mud, still send up every summer a Milky Way of starry, fragrant flowers around a thousand lakes, and many a tuft of wild grass waves its panicles on mossy rocks, beyond reach of trampling feet, in company with saxifrages, bluebells, and ferns. Even in the midst of farmers' fields, precious sphagnum bogs, too soft for the feet of cattle, are preserved with their charming plants unchanged,—chiogenes, Andromeda, Kalmia, Linnæa, Arethusa, etc. Calypso borealis still hides in the arbor vitæ swamps of Canada, and away to the southward there are a few unspoiled swamps, big ones, where miasma, snakes, and alligators, like guardian angels, defend their treasures and keep them as pure as paradise. And beside a' that and a' that, the East is blessed with good winters and blossoming clouds that shed white flowers over all the land, covering every scar and making the saddest landscape divine at least once a year.

The most extensive, least spoiled, and most unspoilable of the gardens of the continent are the vast tundras of Alaska. In summer they extend smooth, even, undulating, continuous beds of flowers and leaves from about lat. 62° to the shores of the Arctic Ocean; and in winter sheets of snowflowers make all the country shine, one mass of white radiance like a star. Nor are these Arctic plant people the pitiful frost-pinched unfortunates they are guessed to be by those who have never seen them. Though lowly in stature, keeping near the frozen ground as if loving it, they are bright and cheery, and speak Nature's love as plainly as their big relatives of the South. Tenderly happed and tucked in beneath downy snow to sleep through the long, white winter, they make haste to bloom in the spring without trying to grow tall, though some rise high enough to ripple and wave in the wind, and display masses of color,—yellow, purple, and blue,—so rich that they look like beds of rainbows, and are visible miles and miles away.

As early as June one may find the showy Geum glaciale in flower, and the dwarf willows putting forth myriads of fuzzy catkins, to be followed quickly, especially on the dryer ground, by mertensia, eritrichium, polemonium, oxytropis, astragalus, lathyrus, lupinus, myosotis, dodecatheon, arnica, chrysanthemum, nardosmia, saussurea, senecio, erigeron, matrecaria, caltha, valeriana, stellaria, Tofieldia, polygonum, papaver, phlox, lychnis, cheiranthus, Linnæa, and a host of drabas, saxifrages, and heathworts, with bright stars and bells in glorious profusion, particularly Cassiope, Andromeda, ledum, pyrola, and vaccinium,—Cassiope the most abundant and beautiful of them all. Many grasses also grow here, and wave fine purple spikes and panicles over the other flowers,—poa, aira, calamagrostis, alopecurus, trisetum, elymus, festuca, glyceria, etc. Even ferns are found thus far north, carefully and comfortably unrolling their precious fronds,—aspidium, cystopteris, and woodsia, all growing on a sumptuous bed of mosses and lichens; not the scaly lichens seen on rails and trees and fallen logs to the southward, but massive, round-headed, finely colored plants like corals, wonderfully beautiful, worth going round the world to see. I should like to mention all the plant friends I found in a summer's wanderings in this cool reserve, but I fear few would care to read their names, although everybody, I am sure, would love them could they see them blooming and rejoicing at home.

On my last visit to the region about Kotzebue Sound, near the middle of September, 1881, the weather was so fine and mellow that it suggested the Indian summer of the Eastern States. The winds were hushed, the tundra glowed in creamy golden sunshine, and the colors of the ripe foliage of the heathworts, willows, and birch—red, purple, and yellow, in pure bright tones—were enriched with those of berries which were scattered everywhere, as if they had been showered from the clouds like hail. When I was back a mile or two from the shore, reveling in this color-glory, and thinking how fine it would be could I cut a square of the tundra sod of conventional picture size, frame it, and hang it among the paintings on my study walls at home, saying to myself, "Such a Nature painting taken at random from any part of the thousand-mile bog would make the other pictures look dim and coarse," I heard merry shouting, and, looking round, saw a band of Eskimos—men, women, and children, loose and hairy like wild animals—running towards me. I could not guess at first what they were seeking, for they seldom leave the shore; but soon they told me, as they threw themselves down, sprawling and laughing, on the mellow bog, and began to feast on the berries. A lively picture they made, and a pleasant one, as they frightened the whirring ptarmigans, and surprised their oily stomachs with the beautiful acid berries of many kinds, and filled sealskin bags with them to carry away for festive days in winter.

Nowhere else on my travels have I seen so much warm-blooded, rejoicing life as in this grand Arctic reservation, by so many regarded as desolate. Not only are there whales in abundance along the shores, and innumerable seals, walruses, and white bears, but on the tundras great herds of fat reindeer and wild sheep, foxes, hares, mice, piping marmots, and birds. Perhaps more birds are born here than in any other region of equal extent on the continent. Not only do strong-winged hawks, eagles, and water-fowl, to whom the length of the continent is merely a pleasant excursion, come up here every summer in great numbers, but also many short-winged warblers, thrushes, and finches, repairing hither to rear their young in safety, reinforce the plant bloom with their plumage, and sweeten the wilderness with song; flying all the way, some of them, from Florida, Mexico, and Central America. In coming north they are coming home, for they were born here, and they go south only to spend the winter months, as New Englanders go to Florida. Sweet-voiced troubadours, they sing in orange groves and vine-clad magnolia woods in winter, in thickets of dwarf birch and alder in summer, and sing and chatter more or less all the way back and forth, keeping the whole country glad. Oftentimes, in New England, just as the last snow-patches are melting and the sap in the maples begins to flow, the blessed wanderers may be heard about orchards and the edges of fields where they have stopped to glean a scanty meal, not tarrying long, knowing they have far to go. Tracing the footsteps of spring, they arrive in their tundra homes in June or July, and set out on the return journey in September, or as soon as their families are able to fly well.

This is Nature's own reservation, and every lover of wildness will rejoice with me that by kindly frost it is so well defended. The discovery lately made that it is sprinkled with gold may cause some alarm; for the strangely exciting stuff makes the timid bold enough for anything, and the lazy destructively industrious. Thousands at least half insane are now pushing their way into it, some by the southern passes over the mountains, perchance the first mountains they have ever seen,—sprawling, struggling, gasping for breath, as, laden with awkward, merciless burdens of provisions and tools, they climb over rough-angled boulders and cross thin miry bogs. Some are going by the mountains and rivers to the eastward through Canada, tracing the old romantic ways of the Hudson Bay traders; others by Bering Sea and the Yukon, sailing all the way, getting glimpses perhaps of the famous fur-seals, the ice-floes, and the innumerable islands and bars of the great Alaska river. In spite of frowning hardships and the frozen ground, the Klondike gold will increase the crusading crowds for years to come, but comparatively little harm will be done. Holes will be burned and dug into the hard ground here and there, and into the quartz-ribbed mountains and hills; ragged towns like beaver and muskrat villages will be built, and mills and locomotives will make rumbling, screeching, disenchanting noises; but the miner's pick will not be followed far by the plough, at least not until Nature is ready to unlock the frozen soil-beds with her slow-turning climate key. On the other hand, the roads of the pioneer miners will lead many a lover of wildness into the heart of the reserve, who without them would never see it.

In the meantime, the wildest health and pleasure grounds accessible and available to tourists seeking escape from care and dust and early death are the parks and reservations of the West. There are four national parks,*—the Yellowstone, Yosemite, General Grant, and Sequoia,—all within easy reach,

*There are now five parks and thirty-eight reservations.

and thirty forest reservations, a magnificent realm of woods, most of which, by railroads and trails and open ridges, is also fairly accessible, not only to the determined traveler rejoicing in difficulties, but to those (may their tribe increase) who, not tired, not sick, just naturally take wing every summer in search of wildness. The forty million acres of these reserves are in the main unspoiled as yet, though sadly wasted and threatened on their more open margins by the axe and fire of the lumberman and prospector, and by hoofed locusts, which, like the winged ones, devour every leaf within reach, while the shepherds and owners set fires with the intention of making a blade of grass grow in the place of every tree, but with the result of killing both the grass and the trees.

In the million acre Black Hills Reserve of South Dakota, the easternmost of the great forest reserves, made for the sake of the farmers and miners, there are delightful, reviving sauntering-grounds in open parks of yellow pine, planted well apart, allowing plenty of sunshine to warm the ground. This tree is one of the most variable and most widely distributed of American pines. It grows sturdily on all kinds of soil and rocks, and, protected by a mail of thick bark, defies frost and fire and disease alike, daring every danger in firm, calm beauty and strength. It occurs here mostly on the outer hills and slopes where no other tree can grow. The ground beneath it is yellow most of the summer with showy Wythia, arnica, applopappus, solidago, and other sun-loving plants, which, though they form no heavy entangling growth, yet give abundance of color and make all the woods a garden. Beyond the yellow pine woods there lies a world of rocks of wildest architecture, broken, splintery, and spiky, not very high, but the strangest in form and style of grouping imaginable. Countless towers and spires, pinnacles and slender domed columns, are crowded together, and feathered with sharp-pointed Engelmann spruces, making curiously mixed forests,—half trees, half rocks. Level gardens here and there in the midst of them offer charming surprises, and so do the many small lakes with lilies on their meadowy borders, and bluebells, anemones, daisies, castilleias, comandras, etc., together forming landscapes delightfully novel, and made still wilder by many interesting animals,—elk, deer, beavers, wolves, squirrels, and birds. Not very long ago this was the richest of all the red man's hunting-grounds hereabout. After the season's buffalo hunts were over,—as described by Parkman, who, with a picturesque cavalcade of Sioux savages, passed through these famous hills in 1846,—every winter deficiency was here made good, and hunger was unknown until, in spite of most determined, fighting, killing opposition, the white gold-hunters entered the fat game reserve and spoiled it. The Indians are dead now, and so are most of the hardly less striking free trappers of the early romantic Rocky Mountain times. Arrows, bullets, scalping-knives, need no longer be feared; and all the wilderness is peacefully open.

The Rocky Mountain reserves are the Teton, Yellowstone, Lewis and Clark, Bitter Root, Priest River and Flathead, comprehending more than twelve million acres of mostly unclaimed, rough, forest-covered mountains in which the great rivers of the country take their rise. The commonest tree in most of them is the brave, indomitable, and altogether admirable Pinus contorta, widely distributed in all kinds of climate and soil, growing cheerily in frosty Alaska, breathing the damp salt air of the sea as well as the dry biting blasts of the Arctic interior, and making itself at home on the most dangerous flame-swept slopes and ridges of the Rocky Mountains in immeasurable abundance and variety of forms. Thousands of acres of this species are destroyed by running fires nearly every summer, but a new growth springs quickly from the ashes. It is generally small, and yields few sawlogs of commercial value, but is of incalculable importance to the farmer and miner; supplying fencing, mine timbers, and firewood, holding the porous soil on steep slopes, preventing landslips and avalanches, and giving kindly, nourishing shelter to animals and the widely outspread sources of the life-giving rivers. The other trees are mostly spruce, mountain pine, cedar, juniper, larch, and balsam fir; some of them, especially on the western slopes of the mountains, attaining grand size and furnishing abundance of fine timber.

Perhaps the least known of all this grand group of reserves is the Bitter Root, of more than four million acres. It is the wildest, shaggiest block of forest wildness in the Rocky Mountains, full of happy, healthy, storm-loving trees, full of streams that dance and sing in glorious array, and full of Nature's animals,—elk, deer, wild sheep, bears, cats, and innumerable smaller people.

In calm Indian summer, when the heavy winds are hushed, the vast forests covering hill and dale, rising and falling over the rough topography and vanishing in the distance, seem lifeless. No moving thing is seen as we climb the peaks, and only the low, mellow murmur of falling water is heard, which seems to thicken the silence. Nevertheless, how many hearts with warm red blood in them are beating under cover of the woods, and how many teeth and eyes are shining! A multitude of animal people, intimately related to us, but of whose lives we know almost nothing, are as busy about their own affairs as we are about ours: beavers are building and mending dams and huts for winter, and storing them with food; bears are studying winter quarters as they stand thoughtful in open spaces, while the gentle breeze ruffles the long hair on their backs; elk and deer, assembling on the heights, are considering cold pastures where they will be farthest away from the wolves; squirrels and marmots are busily laying up provisions and lining their nests against coming frost and snow foreseen; and countless thousands of birds are forming parties and gathering their young about them for flight to the southlands; while butterflies and bees, apparently with no thought of hard times to come, are hovering above the late-blooming goldenrods, and, with countless other insect folk, are dancing and humming right merrily in the sunbeams and shaking all the air into music.

Wander here a whole summer, if you can. Thousands of God's wild blessings will search you and soak you as if you were a sponge, and the big days will go by uncounted. If you are business-tangled, and so burdened with duty that only weeks can be got out of the heavy-laden year, then go to the Flathead Reserve; for it is easily and quickly reached by the Great Northern Railroad. Get off the track at Belton Station, and in a few minutes you will find yourself in the midst of what you are sure to say is the best care-killing scenery on the continent,—beautiful lakes derived straight from glaciers, lofty mountains steeped in lovely nemophila-blue skies and clad with forests and glaciers, mossy, ferny waterfalls in their hollows, nameless and numberless, and meadowy gardens abounding in the best of everything. When you are calm enough for discriminating observation, you will find the king of the larches, one of the best of the Western giants, beautiful, picturesque, and regal in port, easily the grandest of all the larches in the world. It grows to a height of one hundred and fifty to two hundred feet, with a diameter at the ground of five to eight feet, throwing out its branches into the light as no other tree does. To those who before have seen only the European larch or the Lyall species of the eastern Rocky Mountains, or the little tamarack or hackmatack of the Eastern States and Canada, this Western king must be a revelation.

Associated with this grand tree in the making of the Flathead forests is the large and beautiful mountain pine, or Western white pine (Pinus monticola), the invincible contorta or lodge-pole pine, and spruce and cedar. The forest floor is covered with the richest beds of Linnæa borealis I ever saw, thick fragrant carpets, enriched with shining mosses here and there, and with Clintonia, pyrola, moneses, and vaccinium, weaving hundred-mile beds of bloom that would have made blessed old Linnæus weep for joy.

Lake McDonald, full of brisk trout, is in the heart of this forest, and Avalanche Lake is ten miles above McDonald, at the feet of a group of glacier-laden mountains. Give a month at least to this precious reserve. The time will not be taken from the sum of your life. Instead of shortening, it will indefinitely lengthen it and make you truly immortal. Nevermore will time seem short or long, and cares will never again fall heavily on you, but gently and kindly as gifts from heaven.

The vast Pacific Coast reserves in Washington and Oregon—the Cascade, Washington, Mount Rainier, Olympic, Bull Run, and Ashland, named in order of size—include more than 12,500,000 acres of magnificent forests of beautiful and gigantic trees. They extend over the wild, unexplored Olympic Mountains and both flanks of the Cascade Range, the wet and the dry. On the east side of the Cascades the woods are sunny and open, and contain principally yellow pine, of moderate size, but of great value as a cover for the irrigating streams that flow into the dry interior, where agriculture on a grand scale is being carried on. Along the moist, balmy, foggy, west flank of the mountains, facing the sea, the woods reach their highest development, and, excepting the California redwoods, are the heaviest on the continent. They are made up mostly of the Douglas spruce (Pseudotsuga taxifolia), with the giant arbor vitæ, or cedar, and several species of fir and hemlock in varying abundance, forming a forest kingdom unlike any other, in which limb meets limb, touching and overlapping in bright, lively, triumphant exuberance, two hundred and fifty, three hundred, and even four hundred feet above the shady, mossy ground. Over all the other species the Douglas spruce reigns supreme. It is not only a large tree, the tallest in America next to the redwood, but a very beautiful one, with bright green drooping foliage, handsome pendent cones, and a shaft exquisitely straight and round and regular. Forming extensive forests by itself in many places, it lifts its spiry tops into the sky close together with as even a growth as a well-tilled field of grain. No ground has been better tilled for wheat than these Cascade Mountains for trees: they were ploughed by mighty glaciers, and harrowed and mellowed and outspread by the broad streams that flowed from the ice-ploughs as they were withdrawn at the close of the glacial period.

In proportion to its weight when dry, Douglas spruce timber is perhaps stronger than that of any other large conifer in the country, and being tough, durable, and elastic, it is admirably suited for ship-building, piles, and heavy timbers in general; but its hardness and liability to warp when it is cut into boards render it unfit for fine work. In the lumber markets of California it is called "Oregon pine." When lumbering is going on in the best Douglas woods, especially about Puget Sound, many of the long, slender boles are saved for spars; and so superior is their quality that they are called for in almost every shipyard in the world, and it is interesting to follow their fortunes. Felled and peeled and dragged to tide-water, they are raised again as yards and masts for ships, given iron roots and canvas foliage, decorated with flags, and sent to sea, where in glad motion they go cheerily over the ocean prairie in every latitude and longitude, singing and bowing responsive to the same winds that waved them when they were in the woods. After standing in one place for centuries they thus go round the world like tourists, meeting many a friend from the old home forest; some traveling like themselves, some standing head downward in muddy harbors, holding up the platforms of wharves, and others doing all kinds of hard timber work, showy or hidden.

This wonderful tree also grows far northward in British Columbia, and southward along the coast and middle regions of Oregon and California; flourishing with the redwood wherever it can find an opening, and with the sugar pine, yellow pine, and libocedrus in the Sierra. It extends into the San Gabriel, San Bernardino, and San Jacinto Mountains of southern California. It also grows well on the Wasatch Mountains, where it is called "red pine," and on many parts of the Rocky Mountains and short interior ranges of the Great Basin. But though thus widely distributed, only in Oregon, Washington, and some parts of British Columbia does it reach perfect development.

To one who looks from some high standpoint over its vast breadth, the forest on the west side of the Cascades seems all one dim, dark, monotonous field, broken only by the white volcanic cones along the summit of the range. Back in the untrodden wilderness a deep furred carpet of brown and yellow mosses covers the ground like a garment, pressing about the feet of the trees, and rising in rich bosses softly and kindly over every rock and mouldering trunk, leaving no spot uncared for; and dotting small prairies, and fringing the meadows and the banks of streams not seen in general views, we find, besides the great conifers, a considerable number of hardwood trees,—oak, ash, maple, alder, wild apple, cherry, arbutus, Nuttall's flowering dogwood, and in some places chestnut. In a few favored spots the broad-leaved maple grows to a height of a hundred feet in forests by itself, sending out large limbs in magnificent interlacing arches covered with mosses and ferns, thus forming lofty sky-gardens, and rendering the underwoods delightfully cool. No finer forest ceiling is to be found than these maple arches, while the floor, ornamented with tall ferns and rubus vines, and cast into hillocks by the bulging, moss-covered roots of the trees, matches it well.

Passing from beneath the heavy shadows of the woods, almost anywhere one steps into lovely gardens of lilies, orchids, heathworts, and wild roses. Along the lower slopes, especially in Oregon, where the woods are less dense, there are miles of rhododendron, making glorious masses of purple in the spring, while all about the streams and the lakes and the beaver meadows there is a rich tangle of hazel, plum, cherry, crab-apple, cornel, gaultheria, and rubus, with myriads of flowers and abundance of other more delicate bloomers, such as erythronium, brodiæa, fritillaria, calochortus, Clintonia, and the lovely hider of the north, Calypso. Beside all these bloomers there are wonderful ferneries about the many misty waterfalls, some of the fronds ten feet high, others the most delicate of their tribe, the maidenhair fringing the rocks within reach of the lightest dust of the spray, while the shading trees on the cliffs above them, leaning over, look like eager listeners anxious to catch every tone of the restless waters. In the autumn berries of every color and flavor abound, enough for birds, bears, and everybody, particularly about the streamsides and meadows where sunshine reaches the ground: huckleberries, red, blue, and black, some growing close to the ground, others on bushes ten feet high; gaultheria berries, called "sal-al" by the Indians; salmon berries, an inch in diameter, growing in dense prickly tangles, the flowers, like wild roses, still more beautiful than the fruit; raspberries, gooseberries, currants, blackberries, and strawberries. The underbrush and meadow fringes are in great part made up of these berry bushes and vines; but in the depths of the woods there is not much underbrush of any kind,—only a thin growth of rubus, huckleberry, and vine-maple.

Notwithstanding the outcry against the reservations last winter in Washington, that uncounted farms, towns, and villages were included in them, and that all business was threatened or blocked, nearly all the mountains in which the reserves lie are still covered with virgin forests. Though lumbering has long been carried on with tremendous energy along their boundaries, and home-seekers have explored the woods for openings available for farms, however small, one may wander in the heart of the reserves for weeks without meeting a human being, Indian or white man, or any conspicuous trace of one. Indians used to ascend the main streams on their way to the mountains for wild goats, whose wool furnished them clothing. But with food in abundance on the coast there was little to draw them into the woods, and the monuments they have left there are scarcely more conspicuous than those of birds and squirrels; far less so than those of the beavers, which have dammed streams and made clearings that will endure for centuries. Nor is there much in these woods to attract cattle-keepers. Some of the first settlers made farms on the small bits of prairie and in the comparatively open Cowlitz and Chehalis valleys of Washington; but before the gold period most of the immigrants from the Eastern States settled in the fertile and open Willamette Valley of Oregon. Even now, when the search for tillable land is so keen, excepting the bottom-lands of the rivers around Puget Sound, there are few cleared spots in all western Washington. On every meadow or opening of any sort some one will be found keeping cattle, raising hops, or cultivating patches of grain, but these spots are few and far between. All the larger spaces were taken long ago; therefore most of the newcomers build their cabins where the beavers built theirs. They keep a few cows, laboriously widen their little meadow openings by hacking, girdling, and burning the rim of the close-pressing forest, and scratch and plant among the huge blackened logs and stumps, girdling and killing themselves in killing the trees.

Most of the farm lands of Washington and Oregon, excepting the valleys of the Willamette and Rogue rivers, lie on the east side of the mountains. The forests on the eastern slopes of the Cascades fail altogether ere the foot of the range is reached, stayed by drought as suddenly as on the west side they are stopped by the sea; showing strikingly how dependent are these forest giants on the generous rains and fogs so often complained of in the coast climate. The lower portions of the reserves are solemnly soaked and poulticed in rain and fog during the winter months, and there is a sad dearth of sunshine, but with a little knowledge of woodcraft any one may enjoy an excursion into these woods even in the rainy season. The big, gray days are exhilarating, and the colors of leaf and branch and mossy bole are then at their best. The mighty trees getting their food are seen to be wide-awake, every needle thrilling in the welcome nourishing storms, chanting and bowing low in glorious harmony, while every raindrop and snowflake is seen as a beneficent messenger from the sky. The snow that falls on the lower woods is mostly soft, coming through the trees in downy tufts, loading their branches, and bending them down against the trunks until they look like arrows, while a strange muffled silence prevails, making everything impressively solemn. But these lowland snowstorms and their effects quickly vanish. The snow melts in a day or two, sometimes in a few hours, the bent branches spring up again, and all the forest work is left to the fog and the rain. At the same time, dry snow is falling on the upper forests and mountain tops. Day after day, often for weeks, the big clouds give their flowers without ceasing, as if knowing how important is the work they have to do. The glinting, swirling swarms thicken the blast, and the trees and rocks are covered to a depth of ten to twenty feet. Then the mountaineer, snug in a grove with bread and fire, has nothing to do but gaze and listen and enjoy. Ever and anon the deep, low roar of the storm is broken by the booming of avalanches, as the snow slips from the overladen heights and rushes down the long white slopes to fill the fountain hollows. All the smaller streams are hushed and buried, and the young groves of spruce and fir near the edge of the timber-line are gently bowed to the ground and put to sleep, not again to see the light of day or stir branch or leaf until the spring.

These grand reservations should draw thousands of admiring visitors at least in summer, yet they are neglected as if of no account, and spoilers are allowed to ruin them as fast as they like.* A few peeled spars cut here were set up in London, Philadelphia, and Chicago, where they excited wondering attention; but the countless hosts of living trees rejoicing at home on the mountains are scarce considered at all. Most travelers here are content with what they can see from car windows or the verandas of hotels, and in going from place

*The outlook over forest affairs is now encouraging. Popular interest, more practical than sentimental in whatever touches the welfare of the country's forests, is growing rapidly, and a hopeful beginning has been made by the Government in real protection for the reservations as well as for the parks. From July 1, 1900, there have been 9 superintendents, 39 supervisors, and from 330 to 445 rangers of reservations.

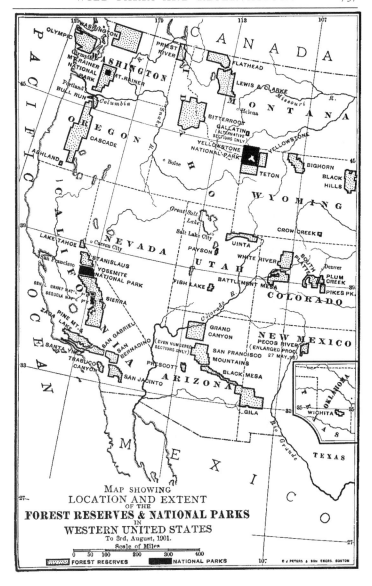

MAP SHOWING
LOCATION AND EXTENT
OF THE
FOREST RESERVES & NATIONAL PARKS
IN
WESTERN UNITED STATES
To 3rd, August, 1901.
Scale of Miles

FOREST RESERVES   NATIONAL PARKS

to place cling to their precious trains and stages like wrecked
sailors to rafts. When an excursion into the woods is proposed,
all sorts of dangers are imagined,—snakes, bears, Indians. Yet
it is far safer to wander in God's woods than to travel on black
highways or to stay at home. The snake danger is so slight it
is hardly worth mentioning. Bears are a peaceable people, and
mind their own business, instead of going about like the devil
seeking whom they may devour. Poor fellows, they have been
poisoned, trapped, and shot at until they have lost confidence
in brother man, and it is not now easy to make their acquaintance. As to Indians, most of them are dead or civilized into
useless innocence. No American wilderness that I know of is
so dangerous as a city home "with all the modern improvements." One should go to the woods for safety, if for nothing
else. Lewis and Clark, in their famous trip across the continent
in 1804–1805, did not lose a single man by Indians or animals,
though all the West was then wild. Captain Clark was bitten
on the hand as he lay asleep. That was one bite among more
than a hundred men while traveling nine thousand miles. Log-
gers are far more likely to be met than Indians or bears in the
reserves or about their boundaries, brown weather-tanned
men with faces furrowed like bark, tired-looking, moving
slowly, swaying like the trees they chop. A little of everything
in the woods is fastened to their clothing, rosiny and smeared
with balsam, and rubbed into it, so that their scanty outer
garments grow thicker with use and never wear out. Many a
forest giant have these old woodmen felled, but, round-shoul-
dered and stooping, they too are leaning over and tottering
to their fall. Others, however, stand ready to take their places,
stout young fellows, erect as saplings; and always the foes of
trees outnumber their friends. Far up the white peaks one can
hardly fail to meet the wild goat, or American chamois,—an
admirable mountaineer, familiar with woods and glaciers as
well as rocks,—and in leafy thickets deer will be found; while
gliding about unseen there are many sleek furred animals enjoying their beautiful lives, and birds also, notwithstanding
few are noticed in hasty walks. The ousel sweetens the glens
and gorges where the streams flow fastest, and every grove
has its singers, however silent it seems,—thrushes, linnets,
warblers; humming-birds glint about the fringing bloom of

the meadows and peaks, and the lakes are stirred into lively pictures by water-fowl.

The Mount Rainier Forest Reserve should be made a national park and guarded while yet its bloom is on;* for if in the making of the West Nature had what we call parks in mind,—places for rest, inspiration, and prayers,—this Rainier region must surely be one of them. In the centre of it there is a lonely mountain capped with ice; from the ice-cap glaciers radiate in every direction, and young rivers from the glaciers; while its flanks, sweeping down in beautiful curves, are clad with forests and gardens, and filled with birds and animals. Specimens of the best of Nature's treasures have been lovingly gathered here and arranged in simple symmetrical beauty within regular bounds.

Of all the fire-mountains which, like beacons, once blazed along the Pacific Coast, Mount Rainier is the noblest in form, has the most interesting forest cover, and, with perhaps the exception of Shasta, is the highest and most flowery. Its massive white dome rises out of its forests, like a world by itself, to a height of fourteen thousand to fifteen thousand feet. The forests reach to a height of a little over six thousand feet, and above the forests there is a zone of the loveliest flowers, fifty miles in circuit and nearly two miles wide, so closely planted and luxuriant that it seems as if Nature, glad to make an open space between woods so dense and ice so deep, were economizing the precious ground, and trying to see how many of her darlings she can get together in one mountain wreath, —daisies, anemones, geraniums, columbines, erythroniums, larkspurs, etc., among which we wade knee-deep and waist-deep, the bright corollas in myriads touching petal to petal. Picturesque detached groups of the spiry Abies lasiocarpa stand like islands along the lower margin of the garden zone, while on the upper margin there are extensive beds of bryan-

*This was done shortly after the above was written. "One of the most important measures taken during the past year in connection with forest reservations was the action of Congress in withdrawing from the Mount Rainier Forest Reserve a portion of the region immediately surrounding Mount Rainier and setting it apart as a national park." (*Report of Commissioner of General Land Office*, for the year ended June, 1899.) But the park as it now stands is far too small.

thus, Cassiope, Kalmia, and other heathworts, and higher still saxifrages and drabas, more and more lowly, reach up to the edge of the ice. Altogether this is the richest subalpine garden I ever found, a perfect floral elysium. The icy dome needs none of man's care, but unless the reserve is guarded the flower bloom will soon be killed, and nothing of the forests will be left but black stump monuments.

The Sierra of California is the most openly beautiful and useful of all the forest reserves, and the largest, excepting the Cascade Reserve of Oregon and the Bitter Root of Montana and Idaho. It embraces over four million acres of the grandest scenery and grandest trees on the continent, and its forests are planted just where they do the most good, not only for beauty, but for farming in the great San Joaquin Valley beneath them. It extends southward from the Yosemite National Park to the end of the range, a distance of nearly two hundred miles. No other coniferous forest in the world contains so many species or so many large and beautiful trees,—Sequoia gigantea, king of conifers, "the noblest of a noble race," as Sir Joseph Hooker well says; the sugar pine, king of all the world's pines, living or extinct; the yellow pine, next in rank, which here reaches most perfect development, forming noble towers of verdure two hundred feet high; the mountain pine, which braves the coldest blasts far up the mountains on grim, rocky slopes; and five others, flourishing each in its place, making eight species of pine in one forest, which is still further enriched by the great Douglas spruce, libocedrus, two species of silver fir, large trees and exquisitely beautiful, the Paton hemlock, the most graceful of evergreens, the curious tumion, oaks of many species, maples, alders, poplars, and flowering dogwood, all fringed with flowery underbrush, manzanita, ceanothus, wild rose, cherry, chestnut, and rhododendron. Wandering at random through these friendly, approachable woods, one comes here and there to the loveliest lily gardens, some of the lilies ten feet high, and the smoothest gentian meadows, and Yosemite valleys known only to mountaineers. Once I spent a night by a camp-fire on Mount Shasta with Asa Gray and Sir Joseph Hooker, and, knowing that they were acquainted with all the great forests of the world, I asked whether they knew any coniferous forest that rivaled that of the Sierra. They unhesitatingly said: "No. In the beauty and grandeur of individual trees, and in number and variety of species, the Sierra forests surpass all others."

This Sierra Reserve, proclaimed by the President of the United States in September, 1893, is worth the most thoughtful care of the government for its own sake, without considering its value as the fountain of the rivers on which the fertility of the great San Joaquin Valley depends. Yet it gets no care at all. In the fog of tariff, silver, and annexation politics it is left wholly unguarded, though the management of the adjacent national parks by a few soldiers shows how well and how easily it can be preserved. In the meantime, lumbermen are allowed to spoil it at their will, and sheep in uncountable ravenous hordes to trample it and devour every green leaf within reach; while the shepherds, like destroying angels, set innumerable fires, which burn not only the undergrowth of seedlings on which the permanence of the forest depends, but countless thousands of the venerable giants. If every citizen could take one walk through this reserve, there would be no more trouble about its care; for only in darkness does vandalism flourish.*

The reserves of southern California,—the San Gabriel, San Bernardino, San Jacinto, and Trabuco,—though not large, only about two million acres altogether, are perhaps the best appreciated. Their slopes are covered with a close, almost impenetrable growth of flowery bushes, beginning on the sides of the fertile coast valleys and the dry interior plains. Their higher ridges, however, and mountains are open, and fairly well forested with sugar pine, yellow pine, Douglas spruce, libocedrus, and white fir. As timber fountains they amount to little, but as bird and bee pastures, cover for the precious streams that irrigate the lowlands, and quickly available retreats from dust and heat and care, their value is incalculable. Good roads have been graded into them, by which in a few hours lowlanders can get well up into the sky and find refuge in hospitable camps and club-houses, where, while breathing

*See note, p. 736.

reviving ozone, they may absorb the beauty about them, and look comfortably down on the busy towns and the most beautiful orange groves ever planted since gardening began.

The Grand Cañon Reserve of Arizona, of nearly two million acres, or the most interesting part of it, as well as the Rainier region, should be made into a national park, on account of their supreme grandeur and beauty. Setting out from Flagstaff, a station on the Atchison, Topeka, and Santa Fé Railroad, on the way to the cañon you pass through beautiful forests of yellow pine,—like those of the Black Hills, but more extensive,—and curious dwarf forests of nut pine and juniper, the spaces between the miniature trees planted with many interesting species of eriogonum, yucca, and cactus. After riding or walking seventy-five miles through these pleasure-grounds, the San Francisco and other mountains, abounding in flowery parklike openings and smooth shallow valleys with long vistas which in fineness of finish and arrangement suggest the work of a consummate landscape artist, watching you all the way, you come to the most tremendous cañon in the world. It is abruptly countersunk in the forest plateau, so that you see nothing of it until you are suddenly stopped on its brink, with its immeasurable wealth of divinely colored and sculptured buildings before you and beneath you. No matter how far you have wandered hitherto, or how many famous gorges and valleys you have seen, this one, the Grand Cañon of the Colorado, will seem as novel to you, as unearthly in the color and grandeur and quantity of its architecture, as if you had found it after death, on some other star; so incomparably lovely and grand and supreme is it above all the other cañons in our fire-moulded, earthquake-shaken, rain-washed, wave-washed, river and glacier sculptured world. It is about six thousand feet deep where you first see it, and from rim to rim ten to fifteen miles wide. Instead of being dependent for interest upon waterfalls, depth, wall sculpture, and beauty of parklike floor, like most other great cañons, it has no waterfalls in sight, and no appreciable floor spaces. The big river has just room enough to flow and roar obscurely, here and there groping its way as best it can, like a weary, murmuring, overladen traveler trying to escape from the tremendous, bewildering labyrinthic abyss, while its roar serves only to deepen the silence. Instead of being filled with air, the vast space between the walls is crowded with Nature's grandest buildings,—a sublime city of them, painted in every color, and adorned with richly fretted cornice and battlement spire and tower in endless variety of style and architecture. Every architectural invention of man has been anticipated, and far more, in this grandest of God's terrestrial cities.

from *Our National Parks*, 1901

The Yellowstone National Park

O F the four national parks of the West, the Yellowstone is far the largest. It is a big, wholesome wilderness on the broad summit of the Rocky Mountains, favored with abundance of rain and snow,—a place of fountains where the greatest of the American rivers take their rise. The central portion is a densely forested and comparatively level volcanic plateau with an average elevation of about eight thousand feet above the sea, surrounded by an imposing host of mountains belonging to the subordinate Gallatin, Wind River, Teton, Absaroka, and Snowy ranges. Unnumbered lakes shine in it, united by a famous band of streams that rush up out of hot lava beds, or fall from the frosty peaks in channels rocky and bare, mossy and bosky, to the main rivers, singing cheerily on through every difficulty, cunningly dividing and finding their way east and west to the two far-off seas.

Glacier meadows and beaver meadows are outspread with charming effect along the banks of the streams, parklike expanses in the woods, and innumerable small gardens in rocky recesses of the mountains, some of them containing more petals than leaves, while the whole wilderness is enlivened with happy animals.

Beside the treasures common to most mountain regions that are wild and blessed with a kind climate, the park is full of exciting wonders. The wildest geysers in the world, in bright, triumphant bands, are dancing and singing in it amid thousands of boiling springs, beautiful and awful, their basins arrayed in gorgeous colors like gigantic flowers; and hot paintpots, mud springs, mud volcanoes, mush and broth caldrons whose contents are of every color and consistency, plash and heave and roar in bewildering abundance. In the adjacent mountains, beneath the living trees the edges of petrified forests are exposed to view, like specimens on the shelves of a museum, standing on ledges tier above tier where they grew, solemnly silent in rigid crystalline beauty after swaying in the winds thousands of centuries ago, opening marvelous views back into the years and climates and life of the past. Here, too, are hills of sparkling crystals, hills of sulphur, hills of glass, hills of cinders and ashes, mountains of every style of architecture, icy or forested, mountains covered with honey-bloom sweet as Hymettus, mountains boiled soft like potatoes and colored like a sunset sky. A' that and a' that, and twice as muckle's a' that, Nature has on show in the Yellowstone Park. Therefore it is called Wonderland, and thousands of tourists and travelers stream into it every summer, and wander about in it enchanted.

Fortunately, almost as soon as it was discovered it was dedicated and set apart for the benefit of the people, a piece of legislation that shines benignly amid the common dust-and-ashes history of the public domain, for which the world must thank Professor Hayden above all others; for he led the first scientific exploring party into it, described it, and with admirable enthusiasm urged Congress to preserve it. As delineated in the year 1872, the park contained about 3344 square miles. On March 30, 1891, it was to all intents and purposes enlarged by the Yellowstone National Park Timber Reserve, and in December, 1897, by the Teton Forest Reserve; thus nearly doubling its original area, and extending the southern boundary far enough to take in the sublime Teton range and the famous pasture-lands of the big Rocky Mountain game animals. The withdrawal of this large tract from the public domain did no harm to any one; for its height, 6000 to over 13,000 feet above the sea, and its thick mantle of volcanic rocks, prevent its ever being available for agriculture or mining, while on the other hand its geographical position, reviving climate, and wonderful scenery combine to make it a grand health, pleasure, and study resort,—a gathering-place for travelers from all the world.

The national parks are not only withdrawn from sale and entry like the forest reservations, but are efficiently managed and guarded by small troops of United States cavalry, directed by the Secretary of the Interior. Under this care the forests are flourishing, protected from both axe and fire; and so, of course, are the shaggy beds of underbrush and the herbaceous vegetation. The so-called curiosities, also, are preserved, and the furred and feathered tribes, many of which, in danger of extinction a short time ago, are now increasing in numbers,

—a refreshing thing to see amid the blind, ruthless destruction that is going on in the adjacent regions. In pleasing contrast to the noisy, ever changing management, or mismanagement, of blundering, plundering, money-making vote-sellers who receive their places from boss politicians as purchased goods, the soldiers do their duty so quietly that the traveler is scarce aware of their presence.

This is the coolest and highest of the parks. Frosts occur every month of the year. Nevertheless, the tenderest tourist finds it warm enough in summer. The air is electric and full of ozone, healing, reviving, exhilarating, kept pure by frost and fire, while the scenery is wild enough to awaken the dead. It is a glorious place to grow in and rest in; camping on the shores of the lakes, in the warm openings of the woods golden with sunflowers, on the banks of the streams, by the snowy waterfalls, beside the exciting wonders or away from them in the scallops of the mountain walls sheltered from every wind, on smooth silky lawns enameled with gentians, up in the fountain hollows of the ancient glaciers between the peaks, where cool pools and brooks and gardens of precious plants charmingly embowered are never wanting, and good rough rocks with every variety of cliff and scaur are invitingly near for outlooks and exercise.

From these lovely dens you may make excursions whenever you like into the middle of the park, where the geysers and hot springs are reeking and spouting in their beautiful basins, displaying an exuberance of color and strange motion and energy admirably calculated to surprise and frighten, charm and shake up the least sensitive out of apathy into newness of life.

However orderly your excursions or aimless, again and again amid the calmest, stillest scenery you will be brought to a standstill hushed and awe-stricken before phenomena wholly new to you. Boiling springs and huge deep pools of purest green and azure water, thousands of them, are plashing and heaving in these high, cool mountains as if a fierce furnace fire were burning beneath each one of them; and a hundred geysers, white torrents of boiling water and steam, like inverted waterfalls, are ever and anon rushing up out of the hot, black underworld. Some of these ponderous geyser columns are as large as sequoias,—five to sixty feet in diameter, one hundred and fifty to three hundred feet high,—and are sustained at this great height with tremendous energy for a few minutes, or perhaps nearly an hour, standing rigid and erect, hissing, throbbing, booming, as if thunderstorms were raging beneath their roots, their sides roughened or fluted like the furrowed boles of trees, their tops dissolving in feathery branches, while the irised spray, like misty bloom is at times blown aside, revealing the massive shafts shining against a background of pine-covered hills. Some of them lean more or less, as if storm-bent, and instead of being round are flat or fan-shaped, issuing from irregular slits in silex pavements with radiate structure, the sunbeams sifting through them in ravishing splendor. Some are broad and round-headed like oaks; others are low and bunchy, branching near the ground like bushes; and a few are hollow in the centre like big daisies or water-lilies. No frost cools them, snow never covers them nor lodges in their branches; winter and summer they welcome alike; all of them, of whatever form or size, faithfully rising and sinking in fairy rhythmic dance night and day, in all sorts of weather, at varying periods of minutes, hours, or weeks, growing up rapidly, uncontrollable as fate, tossing their pearly branches in the wind, bursting into bloom and vanishing like the frailest flowers,—plants of which Nature raises hundreds or thousands of crops a year with no apparent exhaustion of the fiery soil.

The so-called geyser basins, in which this rare sort of vegetation is growing, are mostly open valleys on the central plateau that were eroded by glaciers after the greater volcanic fires had ceased to burn. Looking down over the forests as you approach them from the surrounding heights, you see a multitude of white columns, broad, reeking masses, and irregular jets and puffs of misty vapor ascending from the bottom of the valley, or entangled like smoke among the neighboring trees, suggesting the factories of some busy town or the camp-fires of an army. These mark the position of each mush-pot, paint-pot, hot spring, and geyser, or gusher, as the Icelandic words mean. And when you saunter into the midst of them over the bright sinter pavements, and see how pure and white and pearly gray they are in the shade of the mountains, and how radiant in the sunshine, you are fairly enchanted. So numerous they are and varied, Nature seems to have gathered them from all the world as specimens of her rarest fountains, to show in one place what she can do. Over four thousand hot springs have been counted in the park, and a hundred geysers; how many more there are nobody knows.

These valleys at the heads of the great rivers may be regarded as laboratories and kitchens, in which, amid a thousand retorts and pots, we may see Nature at work as chemist or cook, cunningly compounding an infinite variety of mineral messes; cooking whole mountains; boiling and steaming flinty rocks to smooth paste and mush,—yellow, brown, red, pink, lavender, gray, and creamy white,—making the most beautiful mud in the world; and distilling the most ethereal essences. Many of these pots and caldrons have been boiling thousands of years. Pots of sulphurous mush, stringy and lumpy, and pots of broth as black as ink, are tossed and stirred with constant care, and thin transparent essences, too pure and fine to be called water, are kept simmering gently in beautiful sinter cups and bowls that grow ever more beautiful the longer they are used. In some of the spring basins, the waters, though still warm, are perfectly calm, and shine blandly in a sod of overleaning grass and flowers, as if they were thoroughly cooked at last, and set aside to settle and cool. Others are wildly boiling over as if running to waste, thousands of tons of the precious liquids being thrown into the air to fall in scalding floods on the clean coral floor of the establishment, keeping onlookers at a distance. Instead of holding limpid pale green or azure water, other pots and craters are filled with scalding mud, which is tossed up from three or four feet to thirty feet, in sticky, rank-smelling masses, with gasping, belching, thudding sounds, plastering the branches of neighboring trees; every flask, retort, hot spring, and geyser has something special in it, no two being the same in temperature, color, or composition.

In these natural laboratories one needs stout faith to feel at ease. The ground sounds hollow underfoot, and the awful subterranean thunder shakes one's mind as the ground is shaken, especially at night in the pale moonlight, or when the sky is overcast with storm-clouds. In the solemn gloom, the geysers, dimly visible, look like monstrous dancing ghosts, and their wild songs and the earthquake thunder replying to the storms overhead seem doubly terrible, as if divine government were at an end. But the trembling hills keep their places. The sky clears, the rosy dawn is reassuring, and up comes the sun like a god, pouring his faithful beams across the mountains and forest, lighting each peak and tree and ghastly geyser alike, and shining into the eyes of the reeking springs, clothing them with rainbow light, and dissolving the seeming chaos of darkness into varied forms of harmony. The ordinary work of the world goes on. Gladly we see the flies dancing in the sunbeams, birds feeding their young, squirrels gathering nuts, and hear the blessed ouzel singing confidingly in the shallows of the river,—most faithful evangel, calming every fear, reducing everything to love.

The variously tinted sinter and travertine formations, outspread like pavements over large areas of the geyser valleys, lining the spring basins and throats of the craters, and forming beautiful coral-like rims and curbs about them, always excite admiring attention; so also does the play of the waters from which they are deposited. The various minerals in them are rich in colors, and these are greatly heightened by a smooth, silky growth of brilliantly colored confervæ which lines many of the pools and channels and terraces. No bed of flower-bloom is more exquisite than these myriads of minute plants, visible only in mass, growing in the hot waters. Most of the spring borders are low and daintily scalloped, crenelated, and beaded with sinter pearls. Some of the geyser craters are massive and picturesque, like ruined castles or old burned-out sequoia stumps, and are adorned on a grand scale with outbulging, cauliflower-like formations. From these as centres the silex pavements slope gently away in thin, crusty, overlapping layers, slightly interrupted in some places by low terraces. Or, as in the case of the Mammoth Hot Springs, at the north end of the park, where the building waters issue from the side of a steep hill, the deposits form a succession of higher and broader terraces of white travertine tinged with purple, like the famous Pink Terrace at Rotomahana, New Zealand, draped in front with clustering stalactites, each terrace having a pool of indescribably beautiful water upon it in a basin with a raised rim that glistens with confervæ,—the whole, when viewed at a distance of a mile or two, looking like a broad, massive cascade pouring over shelving rocks in snowy purpled foam.

The stones of this divine masonry, invisible particles of lime or silex, mined in quarries no eye has seen, go to their appointed places in gentle, tinkling, transparent currents or through the dashing turmoil of floods, as surely guided as the sap of plants streaming into bole and branch, leaf and flower. And thus from century to century this beauty-work has gone on and is going on.

Passing through many a mile of pine and spruce woods, toward the centre of the park you come to the famous Yellowstone Lake. It is about twenty miles long and fifteen wide, and lies at a height of nearly 8000 feet above the level of the sea, amid dense black forests and snowy mountains. Around its winding, wavering shores, closely forested and picturesquely varied with promontories and bays, the distance is more than 100 miles. It is not very deep, only from 200 to 300 feet, and contains less water than the celebrated Lake Tahoe of the California Sierra, which is nearly the same size, lies at a height of 6400 feet, and is over 1600 feet deep. But no other lake in North America of equal area lies so high as the Yellowstone, or gives birth to so noble a river. The terraces around its shores show that at the close of the glacial period its surface was about 160 feet higher than it is now, and its area nearly twice as great.

It is full of trout, and a vast multitude of birds—swans, pelicans, geese, ducks, cranes, herons, curlews, plovers, snipe—feed in it and upon its shores; and many forest animals come out of the woods, and wade a little way in shallow, sandy places to drink and look about them, and cool themselves in the free flowing breezes.

In calm weather it is a magnificent mirror for the woods and mountains and sky, now pattered with hail and rain, now roughened with sudden storms that send waves to fringe the shores and wash its border of gravel and sand. The Absaroka Mountains and the Wind River Plateau on the east and south pour their gathered waters into it, and the river issues from the north side in a broad, smooth, stately current, silently gliding with such serene majesty that one fancies it knows the vast journey of four thousand miles that lies before it, and the work it has to do. For the first twenty miles its course is in a level, sunny valley lightly fringed with trees, through which it flows in silvery reaches stirred into spangles here and there by ducks and leaping trout, making no sound save a low whispering among the pebbles and the dipping willows and sedges of its banks. Then suddenly, as if preparing for hard work, it rushes eagerly, impetuously forward rejoicing in its strength, breaks into foam-bloom, and goes thundering down into the Grand Cañon in two magnificent falls, one hundred and three hundred feet high.

The cañon is so tremendously wild and impressive that even these great falls cannot hold your attention. It is about twenty miles long and a thousand feet deep,—a weird, unearthly-looking gorge of jagged, fantastic architecture, and most brilliantly colored. Here the Washburn range, forming the northern rim of the Yellowstone basin, made up mostly of beds of rhyolite decomposed by the action of thermal waters, has been cut through and laid open to view by the river; and a famous section it has made. It is not the depth or the shape of the cañon, nor the waterfall, nor the green and gray river chanting its brave song as it goes foaming on its way, that most impresses the observer, but the colors of the decomposed volcanic rocks. With few exceptions, the traveler in strange lands finds that, however much the scenery and vegetation in different countries may change, Mother Earth is ever familiar and the same. But here the very ground is changed, as if belonging to some other world. The walls of the cañon from top to bottom burn in a perfect glory of color, confounding and dazzling when the sun is shining,—white, yellow, green, blue, vermilion, and various other shades of red indefinitely blending. All the earth hereabouts seems to be paint. Millions of tons of it lie in sight, exposed to wind and weather as if of no account, yet marvelously fresh and bright, fast colors not to be washed out or bleached out by either sunshine or storms. The effect is so novel and awful, we imagine that even a river might be afraid to enter such a place. But the rich and gentle beauty of the vegetation is reassuring. The lovely Linnæa borealis hangs her twin bells over the brink of the cliffs, forests and gardens extend their treasures in smiling

confidence on either side, nuts and berries ripen well whatever
may be going on below; blind fears vanish, and the grand
gorge seems a kindly, beautiful part of the general harmony,
full of peace and joy and good will.

The park is easy of access. Locomotives drag you to its
northern boundary at Cinnabar, and horses and guides do the
rest. From Cinnabar you will be whirled in coaches along the
foaming Gardiner River to Mammoth Hot Springs; thence
through woods and meadows, gulches and ravines along
branches of the Upper Gallatin, Madison, and Firehole rivers
to the main geyser basins; thence over the Continental Divide
and back again, up and down through dense pine, spruce, and
fir woods to the magnificent Yellowstone Lake, along its
northern shore to the outlet, down the river to the falls and
Grand Cañon, and thence back through the woods to Mammoth Hot Springs and Cinnabar; stopping here and there at
the so-called points of interest among the geysers, springs,
paint-pots, mud volcanoes, etc., where you will be allowed a
few minutes or hours to saunter over the sinter pavements,
watch the play of a few of the geysers, and peer into some of
the most beautiful and terrible of the craters and pools. These
wonders you will enjoy, and also the views of the mountains,
especially the Gallatin and Absaroka ranges, the long, willowy
glacier and beaver meadows, the beds of violets, gentians,
phloxes, asters, phacelias, goldenrods, eriogonums, and many
other flowers, some species giving color to whole meadows
and hillsides. And you will enjoy your short views of the great
lake and river and cañon. No scalping Indians will you see.
The Blackfeet and Bannocks that once roamed here are gone;
so are the old beaver-catchers, the Coulters and Bridgers, with
all their attractive buckskin and romance. There are several
bands of buffaloes in the park, but you will not thus cheaply
in tourist fashion see them nor many of the other large animals
hidden in the wilderness. The song-birds, too, keep mostly
out of sight of the rushing tourist, though off the roads
thrushes, warblers, orioles, grosbeaks, etc., keep the air sweet
and merry. Perhaps in passing rapids and falls you may catch
glimpses of the water-ouzel, but in the whirling noise you will
not hear his song. Fortunately, no road noise frightens the
Douglas squirrel, and his merry play and gossip will amuse

you all through the woods. Here and there a deer may be seen crossing the road, or a bear. Most likely, however, the only bears you will see are the half tame ones that go to the hotels every night for dinner-table scraps,—yeast-powder biscuit, Chicago canned stuff, mixed pickles, and beefsteaks that have proved too tough for the tourists.

Among the gains of a coach trip are the acquaintances made and the fresh views into human nature; for the wilderness is a shrewd touchstone, even thus lightly approached, and brings many a curious trait to view. Setting out, the driver cracks his whip, and the four horses go off at half gallop, half trot, in trained, showy style, until out of sight of the hotel. The coach is crowded, old and young side by side, blooming and fading, full of hope and fun and care. Some look at the scenery or the horses, and all ask questions, an odd mixed lot of them: "Where is the umbrella? What is the name of that blue flower over there? Are you sure the little bag is aboard? Is that hollow yonder a crater? How is your throat this morning? How high did you say the geysers spout? How does the elevation affect your head? Is that a geyser reeking over there in the rocks, or only a hot spring?" A long ascent is made, the solemn mountains come to view, small cares are quenched, and all become natural and silent, save perhaps some unfortunate expounder who has been reading guidebook geology, and rumbles forth foggy subsidences and upheavals until he is in danger of being heaved overboard. The driver will give you the names of the peaks and meadows and streams as you come to them, call attention to the glass road, tell how hard it was to build,— how the obsidian cliffs naturally pushed the surveyor's lines to the right, and the industrious beavers, by flooding the valley in front of the cliff, pushed them to the left.

Geysers, however, are the main objects, and as soon as they come in sight other wonders are forgotten. All gather around the crater of the one that is expected to play first. During the eruptions of the smaller geysers, such as the Beehive and Old Faithful, though a little frightened at first, all welcome the glorious show with enthusiasm, and shout, "Oh, how wonderful, beautiful, splendid, majestic!" Some venture near enough to stroke the column with a stick, as if it were a stone pillar or a tree, so firm and substantial and permanent it seems.

While tourists wait around a large geyser, such as the Castle or the Giant, there is a chatter of small talk in anything but solemn mood; and during the intervals between the preliminary splashes and upheavals some adventurer occasionally looks down the throat of the crater, admiring the silex formations and wondering whether Hades is as beautiful. But when, with awful uproar as if avalanches were falling and storms thundering in the depths, the tremendous outburst begins, all run away to a safe distance, and look on, awestricken and silent, in devout, worshiping wonder.

The largest and one of the most wonderfully beautiful of the springs is the Prismatic, which the guide will be sure to show you. With a circumference of 300 yards, it is more like a lake than a spring. The water is pure deep blue in the centre, fading to green on the edges, and its basin and the slightly terraced pavement about it are astonishingly bright and varied in color. This one of the multitude of Yellowstone fountains is of itself object enough for a trip across the continent. No wonder that so many fine myths have originated in springs; that so many fountains were held sacred in the youth of the world, and had miraculous virtues ascribed to them. Even in these cold, doubting, questioning, scientific times many of the Yellowstone fountains seem able to work miracles. Near the Prismatic Spring is the great Excelsior Geyser, which is said to throw a column of boiling water 60 to 70 feet in diameter to a height of from 50 to 300 feet, at irregular periods. This is the greatest of all the geysers yet discovered anywhere. The Firehole River, which sweeps past it, is, at ordinary stages, a stream about 100 yards wide and 3 feet deep; but when the geyser is in eruption, so great is the quantity of water discharged that the volume of the river is doubled, and it is rendered too hot and rapid to be forded.

Geysers are found in many other volcanic regions,—in Iceland, New Zealand, Japan, the Himalayas, the Eastern Archipelago, South America, the Azores, and elsewhere; but only in Iceland, New Zealand, and this Rocky Mountain park do they display their grandest forms, and of these three famous regions the Yellowstone is easily first, both in the number and in the size of its geysers. The greatest height of the column of the Great Geyser of Iceland actually measured was 212 feet, and of the Strokhr 162 feet.

In New Zealand, the Te Pueia at Lake Taupo, the Waikite at Rotorna, and two others are said to lift their waters occasionally to a height of 100 feet, while the celebrated Te Tarata at Rotomahana sometimes lifts a boiling column 20 feet in diameter to a height of 60 feet. But all these are far surpassed by the Excelsior. Few tourists, however, will see the Excelsior in action, or a thousand other interesting features of the park that lie beyond the wagon-roads and the hotels. The regular trips—from three to five days—are too short. Nothing can be done well at a speed of forty miles a day. The multitude of mixed, novel impressions rapidly piled on one another make only a dreamy, bewildering, swirling blur, most of which is unrememberable. Far more time should be taken. Walk away quietly in any direction and taste the freedom of the mountaineer. Camp out among the grass and gentians of glacier meadows, in craggy garden nooks full of Nature's darlings. Climb the mountains and get their good tidings. Nature's peace will flow into you as sunshine flows into trees. The winds will blow their own freshness into you, and the storms their energy, while cares will drop off like autumn leaves. As age comes on, one source of enjoyment after another is closed, but Nature's sources never fail. Like a generous host, she offers here brimming cups in endless variety, served in a grand hall, the sky its ceiling, the mountains its walls, decorated with glorious paintings and enlivened with bands of music ever playing. The petty discomforts that beset the awkward guest, the unskilled camper, are quickly forgotten, while all that is precious remains. Fears vanish as soon as one is fairly free in the wilderness.

Most of the dangers that haunt the unseasoned citizen are imaginary; the real ones are perhaps too few rather than too many for his good. The bears that always seem to spring up thick as trees, in fighting, devouring attitudes before the frightened tourist whenever a camping trip is proposed, are gentle now, finding they are no longer likely to be shot; and rattlesnakes, the other big irrational dread of over-civilized people, are scarce here, for most of the park lies above the snake-line. Poor creatures, loved only by their Maker, they are timid and bashful, as mountaineers know; and though perhaps not possessed of much of that charity that suffers long and is kind, seldom, either by mistake or by mishap, do harm to any one. Certainly they cause not the hundredth part of the pain and death that follow the footsteps of the admired Rocky Mountain trapper. Nevertheless, again and again, in season and out of season, the question comes up, "What are rattlesnakes good for?" As if nothing that does not obviously make for the benefit of man had any right to exist; as if our ways were God's ways. Long ago, an Indian to whom a French traveler put this old question replied that their tails were good for toothache, and their heads for fever. Anyhow, they are all, head and tail, good for themselves, and we need not begrudge them their share of life.

Fear nothing. No town park you have been accustomed to saunter in is so free from danger as the Yellowstone. It is a hard place to leave. Even its names in your guidebook are attractive, and should draw you far from wagon-roads,—all save the early ones, derived from the infernal regions: Hell Roaring River, Hell Broth Springs, The Devil's Caldron, etc. Indeed, the whole region was at first called Coulter's Hell, from the fiery brimstone stories told by trapper Coulter, who left the Lewis and Clark expedition and wandered through the park, in the year 1807, with a band of Bannock Indians. The later names, many of which we owe to Mr. Arnold Hague of the U.S. Geological Survey, are so telling and exhilarating that they set our pulses dancing and make us begin to enjoy the pleasures of excursions ere they are commenced. Three River Peak, Two Ocean Pass, Continental Divide, are capital geographical descriptions, suggesting thousands of miles of rejoicing streams and all that belongs to them. Big Horn Pass, Bison Peak, Big Game Ridge, bring brave mountain animals to mind. Birch Hills, Garnet Hills, Amethyst Mountain, Storm Peak, Electric Peak, Roaring Mountain, are bright, bracing names. Wapiti, Beaver, Tern, and Swan lakes, conjure up fine pictures, and so also do Osprey and Ouzel falls. Antelope Creek, Otter, Mink, and Grayling creeks, Geode, Jasper, Opal, Carnelian, and Chalcedony creeks, are lively and sparkling names that help the streams to shine; and Azalea,

Stellaria, Arnica, Aster, and Phlox creeks, what pictures these bring up! Violet, Morning Mist, Hygeia, Beryl, Vermilion, and Indigo springs, and many beside, give us visions of fountains more beautifully arrayed than Solomon in all his purple and golden glory. All these and a host of others call you to camp. You may be a little cold some nights, on mountain tops above the timber-line, but you will see the stars, and by and by you can sleep enough in your town bed, or at least in your grave. Keep awake while you may in mountain mansions so rare.

If you are not very strong, try to climb Electric Peak when a big bossy, well-charged thunder-cloud is on it, to breathe the ozone set free, and get yourself kindly shaken and shocked. You are sure to be lost in wonder and praise, and every hair of your head will stand up and hum and sing like an enthusiastic congregation.

After this reviving experience, you should take a look into a few of the tertiary volumes of the grand geological library of the park, and see how God writes history. No technical knowledge is required; only a calm day and a calm mind. Perhaps nowhere else in the Rocky Mountains have the volcanic forces been so busy. More than ten thousand square miles hereabouts have been covered to a depth of at least five thousand feet with material spouted from chasms and craters during the tertiary period, forming broad sheets of basalt, andesite, rhyolite, etc., and marvelous masses of ashes, sand, cinders, and stones now consolidated into conglomerates, charged with the remains of plants and animals that lived in the calm, genial periods that separated the volcanic outbursts.

Perhaps the most interesting and telling of these rocks, to the hasty tourist, are those that make up the mass of Amethyst Mountain. On its north side it presents a section two thousand feet high of roughly stratified beds of sand, ashes, and conglomerates coarse and fine, forming the untrimmed edges of a wonderful set of volumes lying on their sides,—books a million years old, well bound, miles in size, with full-page illustrations. On the ledges of this one section we see trunks and stumps of fifteen or twenty ancient forests ranged one above another, standing where they grew, or prostrate and broken like the pillars of ruined temples in desert sands,—a forest fifteen or twenty stories high, the roots of each spread above the tops of the next beneath it, telling wonderful tales of the bygone centuries, with their winters and summers, growth and death, fire, ice, and flood.

There were giants in those days. The largest of the standing opal and agate stumps and prostrate sections of the trunks are from two or three to fifty feet in height or length, and from five to ten feet in diameter; and so perfect is the petrifaction that the annual rings and ducts are clearer and more easily counted than those of living trees, centuries of burial having brightened the records instead of blurring them. They show that the winters of the tertiary period gave as decided a check to vegetable growth as do those of the present time. Some trees favorably located grew rapidly, increasing twenty inches in diameter in as many years, while others of the same species, on poorer soil or overshadowed, increased only two or three inches in the same time.

Among the roots and stumps on the old forest floors we find the remains of ferns and bushes, and the seeds and leaves of trees like those now growing on the southern Alleghanies,—such as magnolia, sassafras, laurel, linden, persimmon, ash, alder, dogwood. Studying the lowest of these forests, the soil it grew on and the deposits it is buried in, we see that it was rich in species, and flourished in a genial, sunny climate. When its stately trees were in their glory, volcanic fires broke forth from chasms and craters, like larger geysers, spouting ashes, cinders, stones, and mud, which fell on the doomed forest like hail and snow; sifting, hurtling through the leaves and branches, choking the streams, covering the ground, crushing bushes and ferns, rapidly deepening, packing around the trees and breaking them, rising higher until the topmost boughs of the giants were buried, leaving not a leaf or twig in sight, so complete was the desolation. At last the volcanic storm began to abate, the fiery soil settled; mud floods and boulder floods passed over it, enriching it, cooling it; rains fell and mellow sunshine, and it became fertile and ready for another crop. Birds, and the winds, and roaming animals brought seeds from more fortunate woods, and a new forest grew up on the top of the buried one. Centuries of genial growing seasons passed. The seedling trees became giants, and with strong outreaching branches spread a leafy canopy over the gray land.

The sleeping subterranean fires again awake and shake the mountains, and every leaf trembles. The old craters, with perhaps new ones, are opened, and immense quantities of ashes, pumice, and cinders are again thrown into the sky. The sun, shorn of his beams, glows like a dull red ball, until hidden in sulphurous clouds. Volcanic snow, hail, and floods fall on the new forest, burying it alive, like the one beneath its roots. Then come another noisy band of mud floods and boulder floods, mixing, settling, enriching the new ground, more seeds, quickening sunshine and showers; and a third noble magnolia forest is carefully raised on the top of the second. And so on. Forest was planted above forest and destroyed, as if Nature were ever repenting, undoing the work she had so industriously done, and burying it

Of course this destruction was creation, progress in the march of beauty through death. How quickly these old monuments excite and hold the imagination! We see the old stone stumps budding and blossoming and waving in the wind as magnificent trees, standing shoulder to shoulder, branches interlacing in grand varied round-headed forests; see the sunshine of morning and evening gilding their mossy trunks, and at high noon spangling on the thick glossy leaves of the magnolia, filtering through translucent canopies of linden and ash, and falling in mellow patches on the ferny floor; see the shining after rain, breathe the exhaling fragrance, and hear the winds and birds and the murmur of brooks and insects. We watch them from season to season; see the swelling buds when the sap begins to flow in the spring, the opening leaves and blossoms, the ripening of summer fruits, the colors of autumn, and the maze of leafless branches and sprays in winter; and we see the sudden oncome of the storms that overwhelmed them.

One calm morning at sunrise I saw the oaks and pines in Yosemite Valley shaken by an earthquake, their tops swishing back and forth, and every branch and needle shuddering as if in distress like the frightened screaming birds. One may imagine the trembling, rocking, tumultuous waving of those ancient Yellowstone woods, and the terror of their inhabitants when the first foreboding shocks were felt, the sky grew dark, and rock-laden floods began to roar. But though they were close pressed and buried, cut off from sun and wind, all their happy leaf-fluttering and waving done, other currents coursed through them, fondling and thrilling every fibre, and beautiful wood was replaced by beautiful stone. Now their rocky sepulchres are partly open, and show forth the natural beauty of death.

After the forest times and fire times had passed away, and the volcanic furnaces were banked and held in abeyance, another great change occurred. The glacial winter came on. The sky was again darkened, not with dust and ashes, but with snow which fell in glorious abundance, piling deeper, deeper, slipping from the overladen heights in booming avalanches, compacting into glaciers, that flowed over all the landscape, wiping off forests, grinding, sculpturing, fashioning the comparatively featureless lava beds into the beautiful rhythm of hill and dale and ranges of mountains we behold to-day; forming basins for lakes, channels for streams, new soils for forests, gardens, and meadows. While this ice-work was going on, the slumbering volcanic fires were boiling the subterranean waters, and with curious chemistry decomposing the rocks, making beauty in the darkness; these forces, seemingly antagonistic, working harmoniously together. How wild their meetings on the surface were we may imagine. When the glacier period began, geysers and hot springs were playing in grander volume, it may be, than those of to-day. The glaciers flowed over them while they spouted and thundered, carrying away their fine sinter and travertine structures, and shortening their mysterious channels.

The soils made in the down-grinding required to bring the present features of the landscape into relief are possibly no better than were some of the old volcanic soils that were carried away, and which, as we have seen, nourished magnificent forests, but the glacial landscapes are incomparably more beautiful than the old volcanic ones were. The glacial winter has passed away, like the ancient summers and fire periods, though in the chronology of the geologist all these times are recent. Only small residual glaciers on the cool northern slopes of the highest mountains are left of the vast all-embracing ice-mantle, as solfataras and geysers are all that are left of the ancient volcanoes.

Now the post-glacial agents are at work on the grand old palimpsest of the park region, inscribing new characters; but still in its main telling features it remains distinctly glacial. The moraine soils are being leveled, sorted, refined, and reformed, and covered with vegetation; the polished pavements and scoring and other superficial glacial inscriptions on the crumbling lavas are being rapidly obliterated; gorges are being cut in the decomposed rhyolites and loose conglomerates, and turrets and pinnacles seem to be springing up like growing trees; while the geysers are depositing miles of sinter and travertine. Nevertheless, the ice-work is scarce blurred as yet. These later effects are only spots and wrinkles on the grand glacial countenance of the park.

Perhaps you have already said that you have seen enough for a lifetime. But before you go away you should spend at least one day and a night on a mountain top, for a last general, calming, settling view. Mount Washburn is a good one for the purpose, because it stands in the middle of the park, is unencumbered with other peaks, and is so easy of access that the climb to its summit is only a saunter. First your eye goes roving around the mountain rim amid the hundreds of peaks: some with plain flowing skirts, others abruptly precipitous and defended by sheer battlemented escarpments; flat-topped or round; heaving like sea-waves or spired and turreted like Gothic cathedrals; streaked with snow in the ravines, and darkened with files of adventurous trees climbing the ridges. The nearer peaks are perchance clad in sapphire blue, others far off in creamy white. In the broad glare of noon they seem to shrink and crouch to less than half their real stature, and grow dull and uncommunicative,—mere dead, draggled heaps of waste ashes and stone, giving no hint of the multitude of animals enjoying life in their fastnesses, or of the bright bloom-bordered streams and lakes. But when storms blow they awake and arise, wearing robes of cloud and mist in majestic speaking attitudes like gods. In the color glory of morning and evening they become still more impressive; steeped in the divine light of the alpenglow their earthiness disappears, and, blending with the heavens, they seem neither high nor low.

Over all the central plateau, which from here seems level, and over the foothills and lower slopes of the mountains, the forest extends like a black uniform bed of weeds, interrupted only by lakes and meadows and small burned spots called parks,—all of them, except the Yellowstone Lake, being mere dots and spangles in general views, made conspicuous by their color and brightness. About eighty-five per cent of the entire area of the park is covered with trees, mostly the indomitable lodge-pole pine (*Pinus contorta*, var. *Murrayana*), with a few patches and sprinklings of Douglas spruce, Engelmann spruce, silver fir (*Abies lasiocarpa*), Pinus flexilis, and a few alders, aspens, and birches. The Douglas spruce is found only on the lowest portions, the silver fir on the highest, and the Engelmann spruce on the dampest places, best defended from fire. Some fine specimens of the flexilis pine are growing on the margins of openings,—wide-branching, sturdy trees, as broad as high, with trunks five feet in diameter, leafy and shady, laden with purple cones and rose-colored flowers. The Engelmann spruce and sub-alpine silver fir also are beautiful and notable trees,—tall, spiry, hardy, frost and snow defying, and widely distributed over the West, wherever there is a mountain to climb or a cold moraine slope to cover. But neither of these is a good fire-fighter. With rather thin bark, and scattering their seeds every year as soon as they are ripe, they are quickly driven out of fire-swept regions. When the glaciers were melting, these hardy mountaineering trees were probably among the first to arrive on the new moraine soil beds; but as the plateau became drier and fires began to run, they were driven up the mountains, and into the wet spots and islands where we now find them, leaving nearly all the park to the lodge-pole pine, which, though as thin-skinned as they and as easily killed by fire, takes pains to store up its seeds in firmly closed cones, and holds them from three to nine years, so that, let the fire come when it may, it is ready to die and ready to live again in a new generation. For when the killing fires have devoured the leaves and thin resinous bark, many of the cones, only scorched, open as soon as the smoke clears away; the hoarded store of seeds is sown broadcast on the cleared ground, and a new growth immediately springs up triumphant out of the ashes. Therefore, this tree not only holds its ground, but extends its conquests farther after every fire. Thus the evenness and closeness of its growth are accounted for. In one part of the forest that I examined, the growth was about as close as a cane-brake. The trees were from four to eight inches in diameter, one hundred feet high, and one hundred and seventy-five years old. The lower limbs die young and drop off for want of light. Life with these close-planted trees is a race for light, more light, and so they push straight for the sky. Mowing off ten feet from the top of the forest would make it look like a crowded mass of telegraph-poles; for only the sunny tops are leafy. A sapling ten years old, growing in the sunshine, has as many leaves as a crowded tree one or two hundred years old. As fires are multiplied and the mountains become drier, this wonderful lodge-pole pine bids fair to obtain possession of nearly all the forest ground in the West.

How still the woods seem from here, yet how lively a stir the hidden animals are making; digging, gnawing, biting, eyes shining, at work and play, getting food, rearing young, roving through the underbrush, climbing the rocks, wading solitary marshes, tracing the banks of the lakes and streams! Insect swarms are dancing in the sunbeams, burrowing in the ground, diving, swimming,—a cloud of witnesses telling Nature's joy. The plants are as busy as the animals, every cell in a swirl of enjoyment, humming like a hive, singing the old new song of creation. A few columns and puffs of steam are seen rising above the treetops, some near, but most of them far off, indicating geysers and hot springs, gentle-looking and noiseless as downy clouds, softly hinting at the reaction going on between the surface and the hot interior. From here you see them better than when you are standing beside them, frightened and confused, regarding them as lawless cataclysms. The shocks and outbursts of earthquakes, volcanoes, geysers, storms, the pounding of waves, the uprush of sap in plants, each and all tell the orderly love-beats of Nature's heart.

Turning to the eastward, you have the Grand Cañon and reaches of the river in full view; and yonder to the southward lies the great lake, the largest and most important of all the high fountains of the Missouri-Mississippi, and the last to be discovered.

In the year 1541, when De Soto, with a romantic band of adventurers, was seeking gold and glory and the fountain of youth, he found the Mississippi a few hundred miles above its mouth, and made his grave beneath its floods. La Salle, in 1682, after discovering the Ohio, one of the largest and most beautiful branches of the Mississippi, traced the latter to the sea from the mouth of the Illinois, through adventures and privations not easily realized now. About the same time Joliet and Father Marquette reached the "Father of Waters" by way of the Wisconsin, but more than a century passed ere its highest sources in these mountains were seen. The advancing stream of civilization has ever followed its guidance toward the west, but none of the thousand tribes of Indians living on its banks could tell the explorer whence it came. From those romantic De Soto and La Salle days to these times of locomotives and tourists, how much has the great river seen and done! Great as it now is, and still growing longer through the ground of its delta and the basins of receding glaciers at its head, it was immensely broader toward the close of the glacial period, when the ice-mantle of the mountains was melting: then with its three hundred thousand miles of branches outspread over the plains and valleys of the continent, laden with fertile mud, it made the biggest and most generous bed of soil in the world.

Think of this mighty stream springing in the first place in vapor from the sea, flying on the wind, alighting on the mountains in hail and snow and rain, lingering in many a fountain feeding the trees and grass; then gathering its scattered waters, gliding from its noble lake, and going back home to the sea, singing all the way! On it sweeps, through the gates of the mountains, across the vast prairies and plains, through many a wild, gloomy forest, cane-brake, and sunny savanna; from glaciers and snowbanks and pine woods to warm groves of magnolia and palm; geysers dancing at its head keeping time with the sea-waves at its mouth; roaring and gray in rapids, booming in broad, bossy falls, murmuring, gleaming in long, silvery reaches, swaying now hither, now thither, whirling, bending in huge doubling, eddying folds, serene, majestic, ungovernable, overflowing all its metes and bounds, frightening the dwellers upon its banks; building, wasting, uprooting, planting; engulfing old islands and making new ones, taking away fields and towns as if in sport, carrying canoes and ships of commerce in the midst of its spoils and drift, fertilizing the continent as one vast farm. Then, its work done, it gladly vanishes in its ocean home, welcomed by the waiting waves.

Thus naturally, standing here in the midst of its fountains, we trace the fortunes of the great river. And how much more comes to mind as we overlook this wonderful wilderness! Fountains of the Columbia and Colorado lie before us, interlaced with those of the Yellowstone and Missouri, and fine it would be to go with them to the Pacific; but the sun is already in the west, and soon our day will be done.

Yonder is Amethyst Mountain, and other mountains hardly less rich in old forests, which now seem to spring up again in their glory; and you see the storms that buried them,—the ashes and torrents laden with boulders and mud, the centuries of sunshine, and the dark, lurid nights. You see again the vast floods of lava, red-hot and white-hot, pouring out from gigantic geysers, usurping the basins of lakes and streams, absorbing or driving away their hissing, screaming waters, flowing around hills and ridges, submerging every subordinate feature. Then you see the snow and glaciers taking possession of the land, making new landscapes. How admirable it is that, after passing through so many vicissitudes of frost and fire and flood, the physiognomy and even the complexion of the landscape should still be so divinely fine!

Thus reviewing the eventful past, we see Nature working with enthusiasm like a man, blowing her volcanic forges like a blacksmith blowing his smithy fires, shoving glaciers over the landscapes like a carpenter shoving his planes, clearing, ploughing, harrowing, irrigating, planting, and sowing broadcast like a farmer and gardener, doing rough work and fine work, planting sequoias and pines, rosebushes and daisies; working in gems, filling every crack and hollow with them; distilling fine essences; painting plants and shells, clouds, mountains, all the earth and heavens, like an artist,—ever working toward beauty higher and higher. Where may the mind find more stimulating, quickening pasturage? A thousand Yellowstone wonders are calling, "Look up and down and round about you!" And a multitude of still, small voices may be heard directing you to look through all this transient, shifting show of things called "substantial" into the truly substantial, spiritual world whose forms flesh and wood, rock and water, air and sunshine, only veil and conceal, and to learn that here is heaven and the dwelling-place of the angels.

The sun is setting; long, violet shadows are growing out over the woods from the mountains along the western rim of the park; the Absaroka range is baptized in the divine light of the alpenglow, and its rocks and trees are transfigured. Next to the light of the dawn on high mountain tops, the alpenglow is the most impressive of all the terrestrial manifestations of God.

Now comes the gloaming. The alpenglow is fading into earthy, murky gloom, but do not let your town habits draw you away to the hotel. Stay on this good fire-mountain and spend the night among the stars. Watch their glorious bloom until the dawn, and get one more baptism of light. Then, with fresh heart, go down to your work, and whatever your fate, under whatever ignorance or knowledge you may afterward chance to suffer, you will remember these fine, wild views, and look back with joy to your wanderings in the blessed old Yellowstone Wonderland.

from *Our National Parks*, 1901

The Forests of the Yosemite Park

THE coniferous forests of the Yosemite Park, and of the Sierra in general, surpass all others of their kind in America or indeed in the world, not only in the size and beauty of the trees, but in the number of species assembled together, and the grandeur of the mountains they are growing on. Leaving the workaday lowlands, and wandering into the heart of the mountains, we find a new world, and stand beside the majestic pines and firs and sequoias silent and awestricken, as if in the presence of superior beings new arrived from some other star, so calm and bright and godlike they are.

Going to the woods is going home; for I suppose we came from the woods originally. But in some of nature's forests the adventurous traveler seems a feeble, unwelcome creature; wild beasts and the weather trying to kill him, the rank, tangled vegetation, armed with spears and stinging needles, barring his way and making life a hard struggle. Here everything is hospitable and kind, as if planned for your pleasure, ministering to every want of body and soul. Even the storms are friendly and seem to regard you as a brother, their beauty and tremendous fateful earnestness charming alike. But the weather is mostly sunshine, both winter and summer, and the clear sunny brightness of the park is one of its most striking characteristics. Even the heaviest portions of the main forest belt, where the trees are tallest and stand closest, are not in the least gloomy. The sunshine falls in glory through the colossal spires and crowns, each a symbol of health and strength, the noble shafts faithfully upright like the pillars of temples, upholding a roof of infinite leafy interlacing arches and fretted skylights. The more open portions are like spacious parks, carpeted with small shrubs, or only with the fallen needles sprinkled here and there with flowers. In some places, where the ground is level or slopes gently, the trees are assembled in groves, and the flowers and underbrush in trim beds and thickets as in landscape gardens or the lovingly planted grounds of homes; or they are drawn up in orderly rows around meadows and lakes and along the brows of cañons.

But in general the forests are distributed in wide belts in accordance with climate and the comparative strength of each kind in gaining and holding possession of the ground, while anything like monotonous uniformity is prevented by the grandly varied topography, and by the arrangement of the best soilbeds in intricate patterns like embroidery; for these soilbeds are the moraines of ancient glaciers more or less modified by weathering and stream action, and the trees trace them over the hills and ridges, and far up the sides of the mountains, rising with even growth on levels, and towering above one another on the long rich slopes prepared for them by the vanished glaciers.

Had the Sierra forests been cheaply accessible, the most valuable of them commercially would ere this have fallen a prey to the lumberman. Thus far the redwood of the Coast Mountains and the Douglas spruce of Oregon and Washington have been more available for lumber than the pine of the Sierra. It cost less to go a thousand miles up the coast for timber, where the trees came down to the shores of navigable rivers and bays, than fifty miles up the mountains. Nevertheless, the superior value of the sugar pine for many purposes has tempted capitalists to expend large sums on flumes and railroads to reach the best forests, though perhaps none of these enterprises has paid. Fortunately, the lately established system of parks and reservations has put a stop to any great extension of the business hereabouts in its most destructive forms. And as the Yosemite Park region has escaped the millmen, and the all-devouring hordes of hoofed locusts have been banished, it is still in the main a pure wilderness, unbroken by axe clearings except on the lower margin, where a few settlers have opened spots beside hay meadows for their cabins and gardens. But these are mere dots of cultivation, in no appreciable degree disturbing the grand solitude. Twenty or thirty years ago a good many trees were felled for their seeds; traces of this destructive method of seed-collecting are still visible along the trails; but these as well as the shingle-makers' ruins are being rapidly overgrown, the gardens and beds of underbrush once devastated by sheep are blooming again in all their wild glory, and the park is a paradise that makes even the loss of Eden seem insignificant.

On the way to Yosemite Valley, you get some grand views over the forests of the Merced and Tuolumne basins and glimpses of some of the finest trees by the roadside without leaving your seat in the stage. But to learn how they live and behave in pure wildness, to see them in their varying aspects through the seasons and weather, rejoicing in the great storms, in the spiritual mountain light, putting forth their new leaves and flowers when all the streams are in flood and the birds are singing, and sending away their seeds in the thoughtful Indian summer when all the landscape is glowing in deep calm enthusiasm,—for this you must love them and live with them, as free from schemes and cares and time as the trees themselves.

And surely nobody will find anything hard in this. Even the blind must enjoy these woods, drinking their fragrance, listening to the music of the winds in their groves, and fingering their flowers and plumes and cones and richly furrowed boles. The kind of study required is as easy and natural as breathing. Without any great knowledge of botany or wood-craft, in a single season you may learn the name and something more of nearly every kind of tree in the park.

With few exceptions all the Sierra trees are growing in the park,—nine species of pine, two of silver fir, one each of Douglas spruce, libocedrus, hemlock, juniper, and sequoia,—sixteen conifers in all, and about the same number of round-headed trees, oaks, maples, poplars, laurel, alder, dogwood, tumion, etc.

The first of the conifers you meet in going up the range from the west is the digger nut-pine (*Pinus Sabiniana*), a remarkably open, airy, wide-branched tree, forty to sixty feet high, with long, sparse, grayish green foliage and large cones. At a height of fifteen to thirty feet from the ground the trunk usually divides into several main branches, which, after bearing away from one another, shoot straight up and form separate heads as if the axis of the tree had been broken, while the secondary branches divide again and again into rather slender sprays loosely tasseled, with leaves eight to twelve inches long. The yellow and purple flowers are about an inch long, the staminate in showy clusters. The big, rough, burly cones, five to eight or ten inches in length and five or six in diameter, are rich brown in color when ripe, and full of hard-shelled nuts that are greatly prized by Indians and squirrels. This strange-looking pine, enjoying hot sunshine like a palm, is sparsely distributed along the driest part of the Sierra among small oaks and chaparral, and with its gray mist of foliage, strong trunk and branches, and big cones seen in relief on the glowing sky, forms the most striking feature of the foothill vegetation.

Pinus attenuata is a small, slender, arrowy tree, with pale green leaves in threes, clustered flowers half an inch long, brownish yellow and crimson, and cones whorled in conspicuous clusters around the branches and also around the trunk. The cones never fall off or open until the tree dies. They are about four inches long, exceedingly strong and solid, and varnished with hard resin forming a waterproof and almost worm and squirrel proof package, in which the seeds are kept fresh and safe during the lifetime of the tree. Sometimes one of the trunk cones is overgrown and imbedded in the heart wood like a knot, but nearly all are pushed out and kept on the surface by the pressure of the successive layers of wood against the base.

This admirable little tree grows on brushy, sunbeaten slopes, which from their position and the inflammable character of the vegetation are most frequently fire-swept. These grounds it is able to hold against all comers, however big and strong, by saving its seeds until death, when all it has produced are scattered over the bare cleared ground, and a new generation quickly springs out of the ashes. Thus the curious fact that all the trees of extensive groves and belts are of the same age is accounted for, and their slender habit; for the lavish abundance of seed sown at the same time makes a crowded growth, and the seedlings with an even start rush up in a hurried race for light and life.

Only a few of the attenuata and Sabiniana pines are within the boundaries of the park, the former on the side of the Merced Cañon, the latter on the walls of Hetch-Hetchy Valley and in the cañon below it.

The nut-pine (*Pinus monophylla*) is a small, hardy, contented-looking tree, about fifteen or twenty feet high and a foot in diameter. In its youth the close radiating and aspiring branches form a handsome broad-based pyramid, but when fully grown it becomes round-topped, knotty, and irregular, throwing out crooked divergent limbs like an apple tree. The leaves are pale grayish green, about an inch and a half long, and instead of being divided into clusters they are single, round, sharp-pointed, and rigid like spikes, amid which in the spring the red flowers glow brightly. The cones are only about two inches in length and breadth, but nearly half of their bulk is made up of sweet nuts.

This fruitful little pine grows on the dry east side of the park, along the margin of the Mono sage plain, and is the commonest tree of the short mountain ranges of the Great Basin. Tens of thousands of acres are covered with it, forming bountiful orchards for the Red-man. Being so low and accessible, the cones are easily beaten off with poles, and the nuts procured by roasting until the scales open. To the tribes of the desert and sage plains these seeds are the staff of life. They are eaten either raw or parched, or in the form of mush or cakes after being pounded into meal. The time of nut harvest in the autumn is the Indian's merriest time of all the year. An industrious squirrelish family can gather fifty or sixty bushels in a single month before the snow comes, and then their bread for the winter is sure.

The white pine (*Pinus flexilis*) is widely distributed through the Rocky Mountains and the ranges of the Great Basin, where in many places it grows to a good size, and is an important timber tree where none better is to be found. In the park it is sparsely scattered along the eastern flank of the range from Mono Pass southward, above the nut-pine, at an elevation of from eight to ten thousand feet, dwarfing to a tangled bush near the timber-line, but under favorable conditions attaining a height of forty or fifty feet, with a diameter of three to five. The long branches show a tendency to sweep out in bold curves, like those of the mountain and sugar pines to which it is closely related. The needles are in clusters of five, closely packed on the ends of the branchlets. The cones are about five inches long,—the smaller ones nearly oval, the larger cylindrical. But the most interesting feature of the tree is its bloom, the vivid red pistillate flowers glowing among the leaves like coals of fire.

The dwarfed pine or white-barked pine (*Pinus albicaulis*) is sure to interest every observer on account of its curious low matted habit, and the great height on the snowy mountains at which it bravely grows. It forms the extreme edge of the timber-line on both flanks of the summit mountains—if so lowly a tree can be called timber—at an elevation of ten to twelve thousand feet above the level of the sea. Where it is first met on the lower limit of its range it may be thirty or forty feet high, but farther up the rocky wind-swept slopes, where the snow lies deep and heavy for six months of the year, it makes shaggy clumps and beds, crinkled and pressed flat, over which you can easily walk. Nevertheless in this crushed, down-pressed, felted condition it clings hardily to life, puts forth fresh leaves every spring on the ends of its tasseled branchlets, blooms bravely in the lashing blasts with abundance of gay red and purple flowers, matures its seeds in the short summers, and often outlives the favored giants of the sun lands far below. One of the trees that I examined was only about three feet high, with a stem six inches in diameter at the ground, and branches that spread out horizontally as if they had grown up against a ceiling; yet it was four hundred and twenty-six years old, and one of its supple branchlets, about an eighth of an inch in diameter inside the bark, was seventy-five years old, and so tough that I tied it into knots. At the age of this dwarf many of the sugar and yellow pines and sequoias are seven feet in diameter and over two hundred feet high.

In detached clumps never touched by fire the fallen needles of centuries of growth make fine elastic mattresses for the weary mountaineer, while the tasseled branchlets spread a roof over him, and the dead roots, half resin, usually found in abundance, make capital camp-fires, unquenchable in thickest storms of rain or snow. Seen from a distance the belts and patches darkening the mountain sides look like mosses on a roof, and bring to mind Dr. Johnson's remarks on the trees of Scotland. His guide, anxious for the honor of Mull, was still talking of its woods and pointing them out. "Sir," said Johnson, "I saw at Tobermory what they called a wood, which I unluckily took for heath. If you show me what I shall take for furze, it will be something."

The mountain pine (*Pinus monticola*) is far the largest of

the Sierra tree mountaineers. Climbing nearly as high as the dwarf albicaulis, it is still a giant in size, bold and strong, standing erect on the storm-beaten peaks and ridges, tossing its cone-laden branches in the rough winds, living a thousand years, and reaching its greatest size—ninety to a hundred feet in height, six to eight in diameter—just where other trees, its companions, are dwarfed. But it is not able to endure burial in snow so long as the albicaulis and flexilis. Therefore, on the upper limit of its range it is found on slopes which, from their steepness or exposure, are least snowy. Its soft graceful beauty in youth, and its leaves, cones, and outsweeping feathery branches constantly remind you of the sugar pine, to which it is closely allied. An admirable tree, growing nobler in form and size the colder and balder the mountains about it.

The giants of the main forest in the favored middle region are the sequoia, sugar pine, yellow pine, libocedrus, Douglas spruce, and the two silver firs. The park sequoias are restricted to two small groves, a few miles apart, on the Tuolumne and Merced divide, about seventeen miles from Yosemite Valley. The Big Oak Flat road to the valley runs through the Tuolumne Grove, the Coulterville through the Merced. The more famous and better known Mariposa Grove, belonging to the state, lies near the southwest corner of the park, a few miles above Wawona.

The sugar pine (*Pinus Lambertiana*) is first met in the park in open, sunny, flowery woods, at an elevation of about thirty-five hundred feet above the sea, attains full development at a height between five and six thousand feet, and vanishes at the level of eight thousand feet. In many places, especially on the northern slopes of the main ridges between the rivers, it forms the bulk of the forest, but mostly it is intimately associated with its noble companions, above which it towers in glorious majesty on every hill, ridge, and plateau from one extremity of the range to the other, a distance of five hundred miles,— the largest, noblest, and most beautiful of all the seventy or eighty species of pine trees in the world, and of all the conifers second only to King Sequoia.

A good many are from two hundred to two hundred and twenty feet in height, with a diameter at four feet from the ground of six to eight feet, and occasionally a grand patriarch, seven or eight hundred years old, is found that is ten or even twelve feet in diameter and two hundred and forty feet high, with a magnificent crown seventy feet wide. David Douglas, who discovered "this most beautiful and immensely grand tree" in the fall of 1826 in southern Oregon, says that the largest of several that had been blown down, "at three feet from the ground was fifty-seven feet nine inches in circumference" (or fully eighteen feet in diameter); "at one hundred and thirty-four feet, seventeen feet five inches; extreme length, two hundred and forty-five feet." Probably for *fifty-seven* we should read *thirty-seven* for the base measurement, which would make it correspond with the other dimensions; for none of this species with anything like so great a girth has since been seen. A girth of even thirty feet is uncommon. A fallen specimen that I measured was nine feet three inches in diameter inside the bark at four feet from the ground, and six feet in diameter at a hundred feet from the ground. A comparatively young tree, three hundred and thirty years old, that had been cut down, measured seven feet across the stump, was three feet three inches in diameter at a height of one hundred and fifty feet, and two hundred and ten feet in length.

The trunk is a round, delicately tapered shaft with finely furrowed purplish-brown bark, usually free of limbs for a hundred feet or more. The top is furnished with long and comparatively slender branches, which sweep gracefully downward and outward, feathered with short tasseled branchlets, and divided only at the ends, forming a palmlike crown fifty to seventy-five feet wide, but without the monotonous uniformity of palm crowns or of the spires of most conifers. The old trees are as tellingly varied and picturesque as oaks. No two are alike, and we are tempted to stop and admire every one we come to, whether as it stands silent in the calm balsam-scented sunshine or waving in accord with enthusiastic storms. The leaves are about three or four inches long, in clusters of five, finely tempered, bright lively green, and radiant. The flowers are but little larger than those of the dwarf pine, and far less showy. The immense cylindrical cones, fifteen to twenty or even twenty-four inches long and three in diameter, hang singly or in clusters, like ornamental tassels, at the ends of the long branches, green, flushed with purple on the sunward side. Like those of almost all the pines they ripen in the autumn of the second season from the flower, and the seeds of all that have escaped the Indians, bears, and squirrels take wing and fly to their places. Then the cones become still more effective as ornaments, for by the spreading of the scales the diameter is nearly doubled, and the color changes to a rich brown. They remain on the tree the following winter and summer; therefore few fertile trees are ever found without them. Nor even after they fall is the beauty work of these grand cones done, for they make a fine show on the flowery, needle-strewn ground. The wood is pale yellow, fine in texture, and deliciously fragrant. The sugar, which gives name to the tree, exudes from the heart wood on wounds made by fire or the axe, and forms irregular crisp white candy-like masses. To the taste of most people it is as good as maple sugar, though it cannot be eaten in large quantities.

No traveler, whether a tree lover or not, will ever forget his first walk in a sugar-pine forest. The majestic crowns approaching one another make a glorious canopy, through the feathery arches of which the sunbeams pour, silvering the needles and gilding the stately columns and the ground into a scene of enchantment.

The yellow pine (*Pinus ponderosa*) is surpassed in size and nobleness of port only by its kingly companion. Full-grown trees in the main forest, where it is associated with the sugar pine, are about one hundred and seventy-five feet high, with a diameter of five to six feet, though much larger specimens may easily be found. The largest I ever measured was a little over eight feet in diameter four feet above the ground, and two hundred and twenty feet high. Where there is plenty of sunshine and other conditions are favorable, it is a massive symmetrical spire, formed of a strong straight shaft clad with innumerable branches, which are divided again and again into stout branchlets laden with bright shining needles and green or purple cones. Where the growth is at all close half or more of the trunk is branchless. The species attains its greatest size and most majestic form in open groves on the deep, well-drained soil of lake basins at an elevation of about four thousand feet. There nearly all the old trees are over two hundred feet high, and the heavy, leafy, much-divided branches sumptuously clothe the trunk almost to the ground. Such trees are easily climbed, and in going up the winding stairs of knotty limbs to the top you will gain a most telling and memorable idea of the height, the richness and intricacy of the branches, and the marvelous abundance and beauty of the long shining elastic foliage. In tranquil weather, you will see the firm outstanding needles in calm content, shimmering and throwing off keen minute rays of light like lances of ice; but when heavy winds are blowing, the strong towers bend and wave in the blast with eager wide-awake enthusiasm, and every tree in the grove glows and flashes in one mass of white sunfire.

Both the yellow and sugar pines grow rapidly on good soil where they are not crowded. At the age of a hundred years they are about two feet in diameter and a hundred feet or more high. They are then very handsome, though very unlike: the sugar pine, lithe, feathery, closely clad with ascending branches; the yellow, open, showing its axis from the ground to the top, its whorled branches but little divided as yet, spreading and turning up at the ends with magnificent tassels of long stout bright needles, the terminal shoot with its leaves being often three or four feet long and a foot and a half wide, the most hopeful looking and the handsomest treetop in the woods. But instead of increasing, like its companion, in wildness and individuality of form with age, it becomes more evenly and compactly spiry. The bark is usually very thick, four to six inches at the ground, and arranged in large plates, some of them on the lower part of the trunk four or five feet long and twelve to eighteen inches wide, forming a strong defense against fire. The leaves are in threes, and from three inches to a foot long. The flowers appear in May: the staminate pink or brown, in conspicuous clusters two or three inches wide; the pistillate crimson, a fourth of an inch wide, and mostly hidden among the leaves on the tips of the branchlets. The cones vary from about three to ten inches in length, two to five in width, and grow in sessile outstanding clusters near the ends of the upturned branchlets.

Being able to endure fire and hunger and many climates this grand tree is widely distributed: eastward from the coast

across the broad Rocky Mountain ranges to the Black Hills
of Dakota, a distance of more than a thousand miles, and
southward from British Columbia, near latitude 51°, to Mexico, about fifteen hundred miles. South of the Columbia River
it meets the sugar pine, and accompanies it all the way down
along the Coast and Cascade mountains and the Sierra and
southern ranges to the mountains of the peninsula of Lower
California, where they find their southmost homes together.
Pinus ponderosa is extremely variable, and much bother it
gives botanists who try to catch and confine the unmanage-
able proteus in two or a dozen species,—Jeffreyi, deflexa, Apa-
checa latifolia, etc. But in all its wanderings, in every form, it
manifests noble strength. Clad in thick bark like a warrior in
mail, it extends its bright ranks over all the high ranges of the
wild side of the continent: flourishes in the drenching fog and
rain of the northern coast at the level of the sea, in the snow-
laden blasts of the mountains, and the white glaring sunshine
of the interior plateaus and plains, on the borders of mirage-
haunted deserts, volcanoes, and lava beds, waving its bright
plumes in the hot winds undaunted, blooming every year for
centuries, and tossing big ripe cones among the cinders and
ashes of nature's hearths.

The Douglas spruce grows with the great pines, especially
on the cool north sides of ridges and cañons, and is here
nearly as large as the yellow pine, but less abundant. The
wood is strong and tough, the bark thick and deeply furrowed, and on vigorous, quick-growing trees the stout,
spreading branches are covered with innumerable slender,
swaying sprays, handsomely clothed with short leaves. The
flowers are about three fourths of an inch in length, red or
greenish, not so showy as the pendulous bracted cones. But
in June and July, when the young bright yellow leaves appear,
the entire tree seems to be covered with bloom.

It is this grand tree that forms the famous forests of western
Oregon, Washington, and the adjacent coast regions of British
Columbia, where it attains its greatest size and is most abundant, making almost pure forests over thousands of square
miles, dark and close and almost inaccessible, many of the
trees towering with straight, imperceptibly tapered shafts to a
height of three hundred feet, their heads together shutting

out the light,—one of the largest, most widely distributed, and most important of all the Western giants.

The incense cedar (*Libocedrus decurrens*), when full grown, is a magnificent tree, one hundred and twenty to nearly two hundred feet high, five to eight and occasionally twelve feet in diameter, with cinnamon-colored bark and warm yellow-green foliage, and in general appearance like an arbor vitæ. It is distributed through the main forest from an elevation of three to six thousand feet, and in sheltered portions of cañons on the warm sides to seven thousand five hundred. In mid-winter, when most trees are asleep, it puts forth its flowers. The pistillate are pale green and inconspicuous; but the staminate are yellow, about one fourth of an inch long, and are produced in myriads, tingeing all the branches with gold, and making the tree as it stands in the snow look like a gigantic goldenrod. Though scattered rather sparsely amongst its companions in the open woods, it is seldom out of sight, and its bright brown shafts and warm masses of plumy foliage make a striking feature of the landscape. While young and growing fast in an open situation no other tree of its size in the park forms so exactly tapered a pyramid. The branches, outspread in flat plumes and beautifully fronded, sweep gracefully downward and outward, except those near the top, which aspire; the lowest droop to the ground, overlapping one another, shedding off rain and snow, and making fine tents for storm-bound mountaineers and birds. In old age it becomes irregular and picturesque, mostly from accidents: running fires, heavy wet snow breaking the branches, lightning shattering the top, compelling it to try to make new summits out of side branches, etc. Still it frequently lives more than a thousand years, invincibly beautiful, and worthy its place beside the Douglas spruce and the great pines.

This unrivaled forest is still further enriched by two majestic silver firs, Abies magnifica and Abies concolor, bands of which come down from the main fir belt by cool shady ridges and glens. Abies magnifica is the noblest of its race, growing on moraines, at an elevation of seven thousand to eight thousand five hundred feet above the sea, to a height of two hundred or two hundred and fifty feet, and five to seven in diameter; and with these noble dimensions there is a richness and symmetry and perfection of finish not to be found in any other tree in the Sierra. The branches are whorled, in fives mostly, and stand out from the straight red purple bole in level or, on old trees, in drooping collars, every branch regularly pinnated like fern fronds, and clad with silvery needles, making broad plumes singularly rich and sumptuous.

The flowers are in their prime about the middle of June: the staminate red, growing on the underside of the branchlets in crowded profusion, giving a rich color to nearly all the tree; the pistillate greenish yellow tinged with pink, standing erect on the upper side of the topmost branches; while the tufts of young leaves, about as brightly colored as those of the Douglas spruce, push out of their fragrant brown buds a few weeks later, making another grand show.

The cones mature in a single season from the flowers. When full grown they are about six to eight inches long, three or four in diameter, blunt, massive, cylindrical, greenish gray in color, covered with a fine silvery down, and beaded with transparent balsam, very rich and precious-looking, standing erect like casks on the topmost branches. If possible, the inside of the cone is still more beautiful. The scales and bracts are tinged with red, and the seed wings are purple with bright iridescence.

Abies concolor, the white silver fir, grows best about two thousand feet lower than the magnifica. It is nearly as large, but the branches are less regularly pinnated and whorled, the leaves are longer, and instead of standing out around the branchlets or turning up and clasping them they are mostly arranged in two horizontal or ascending rows, and the cones are less than half as large. The bark of the magnifica is reddish purple and closely furrowed, that of the concolor is gray and widely furrowed,—a noble pair, rivaled only by the Abies grandis, amabilis, and nobilis of the forests of Oregon, Washington, and the Northern California Coast Range. But none of these northern species form pure forests that in extent and beauty approach those of the Sierra.

The seeds of the conifers are curiously formed and colored, white, brown, purple, plain or spotted like birds' eggs, and excepting the juniper they are all handsomely and ingeniously winged with reference to their distribution. They are a sort of

cunningly devised flying machines,—one-winged birds, birds
with but one feather,—and they take but one flight, all save
those which, after flying from the cone-nest in calm weather,
chance to alight on branches where they have to wait for a
wind. And though these seed wings are intended for only a
moment's use, they are as thoughtfully colored and fashioned
as the wings of birds, and require from one to two seasons to
grow. Those of the pine, fir, hemlock, and spruce are curved
in such manner that, in being dragged through the air by the
seeds, they are made to revolve, whirling the seeds in a close
spiral, and sustaining them long enough to allow the winds
to carry them to considerable distances,—a style of flying full
of quick merry motion, strikingly contrasted to the sober dignified sailing of seeds on tufts of feathery pappus. Surely no
merrier adventurers ever set out to seek their fortunes. Only
in the fir woods are large flocks seen; for, unlike the cones of
the pine, spruce, hemlock, etc., which let the seeds escape
slowly, one or two at a time, by spreading the scales, the fir
cones when ripe fall to pieces, and let nearly all go at once in
favorable weather. All along the Sierra for hundreds of miles,
on dry breezy autumn days, the sunny spaces in the woods
among the colossal spires are in a whirl with these shining
purple-winged wanderers, notwithstanding the harvesting
squirrels have been working at the top of their speed for weeks
trying to cut off every cone before the seeds were ready to
swarm and fly. Sequoia seeds have flat wings, and glint and
glance in their flight like a boy's kite. The dispersal of juniper
seeds is effected by the plum and cherry plan of hiring birds
at the cost of their board, and thus obtaining the use of a pair
of extra good wings.

Above the great fir belt, and below the ragged beds and
fringes of the dwarf pine, stretch the broad dark forests of
Pinus contorta, var. Murrayana, usually called tamarack pine.
On broad fields of moraine material it forms nearly pure forests at an elevation of about eight or nine thousand feet above
the sea, where it is a small, well proportioned tree, fifty or
sixty feet high and one or two in diameter, with thin gray
bark, crooked much-divided straggling branches, short needles in clusters of two, bright yellow and crimson flowers, and
small prickly cones. The very largest I ever measured was

ninety feet in height, and a little over six feet in diameter four feet above the ground. On moist well-drained soil in sheltered hollows along streamsides it grows tall and slender with ascending branches, making graceful arrowy spires fifty to seventy-five feet high, with stems only five or six inches thick.

The most extensive forest of this pine in the park lies to the north of the Big Tuolumne Meadows,—a famous deer pasture and hunting ground of the Mono Indians. For miles over wide moraine beds there is an even, nearly pure growth, broken only by glacier meadows, around which the trees stand in trim array, their sharp spires showing to fine advantage both in green flowery summer and white winter. On account of the closeness of its growth in many places, and the thinness and gumminess of its bark, it is easily killed by running fires, which work widespread destruction in its ranks; but a new generation rises quickly from the ashes, for all or a part of its seeds are held in reserve for a year or two or many years, and when the tree is killed the cones open and the seeds are scattered over the burned ground like those of the attenuata.

Next to the mountain hemlock and the dwarf pine this species best endures burial in heavy snow, while in braving hunger and cold on rocky ridgetops it is not surpassed by any. It is distributed from Alaska to Southern California, and inland across the Rocky Mountains, taking many forms in accordance with demands of climate, soil, rivals, and enemies; growing patiently in bogs and on sand dunes beside the sea where it is pelted with salt scud, on high snowy mountains and down in the throats of extinct volcanoes; springing up with invincible vigor after every devastating fire and extending its conquests farther.

The sturdy storm-enduring red cedar (*Juniperus occidentalis*) delights to dwell on the tops of granite domes and ridges and glacier pavements of the upper pine belt, at an elevation of seven to ten thousand feet, where it can get plenty of sunshine and snow and elbow-room without encountering quick-growing overshadowing rivals. They never make anything like a forest, seldom come together even in groves, but stand out separate and independent in the wind, clinging by slight joints to the rock, living chiefly on snow and thin air, and maintaining tough health on this diet for two thousand years or more, every feature and gesture expressing steadfast dogged endurance. The largest are usually about six or eight feet in diameter, and fifteen or twenty in height. A very few are ten feet in diameter, and on isolated moraine heaps forty to sixty feet in height. Many are mere stumps, as broad as high, broken by avalanches and lightning, picturesquely tufted with dense gray scalelike foliage, and giving no hint of dying. The staminate flowers are like those of the libocedrus, but smaller; the pistillate are inconspicuous. The wood is red, fine-grained, and fragrant; the bark bright cinnamon and red, and in thrifty trees is strikingly braided and reticulated, flaking off in thin lustrous ribbons, which the Indians used to weave into matting and coarse cloth. These brown unshakable pillars, standing solitary on polished pavements with bossy masses of foliage in their arms, are exceedingly picturesque, and never fail to catch the eye of the artist. They seem sole survivors of some ancient race, wholly unacquainted with their neighbors.

I have spent a good deal of time, trying to determine their age, but on account of dry rot which honeycombs most of the old ones, I never got a complete count of the largest. Some are undoubtedly more than two thousand years old; for though on good moraine soil they grow about as fast as oaks, on bare pavements and smoothly glaciated overswept granite ridges in the dome region they grow extremely slowly. One on the Starr King ridge, only two feet eleven inches in diameter, was eleven hundred and forty years old. Another on the same ridge, only one foot seven and a half inches in diameter, had reached the age of eight hundred and thirty-four years. The first fifteen inches from the bark of a medium-sized tree—six feet in diameter—on the north Tenaya pavement had eight hundred and fifty-nine layers of wood, or fifty-seven to the inch. Beyond this the count was stopped by dry rot and scars of old wounds. The largest I examined was thirty-three feet in girth, or nearly ten in diameter; and though I failed to get anything like a complete count, I learned enough from this and many other specimens to convince me that most of the trees eight to ten feet thick standing on pavements are more than twenty centuries of age rather than less. Barring accidents, for all I can see, they would live forever. When killed, they waste out of existence about as slowly as granite.

Even when overthrown by avalanches, after standing so long, they refuse to lie at rest, leaning stubbornly on their big elbows as if anxious to rise, and while a single root holds to the rock putting forth fresh leaves with a grim never-say-die and never-lie-down expression.

As the juniper is the most stubborn and unshakable of trees, the mountain hemlock (*Tsuga Mertensiana*) is the most graceful and pliant and sensitive, responding to the slightest touches of the wind. Until it reaches a height of fifty or sixty feet it is sumptuously clothed down to the ground with drooping branches, which are divided into countless delicate waving sprays, grouped and arranged in most indescribably beautiful ways, and profusely sprinkled with handsome brown cones. The flowers also are peculiarly beautiful and effective: the pistillate very dark rich purple; the staminate blue of so fine and pure a tone that the best azure of the high sky seems to be condensed in them.

Though apparently the most delicate and feminine of all the mountain trees, it grows best where the snow lies deepest, at an elevation of from nine thousand to nine thousand five hundred feet, in hollows on the northern slopes of mountains and ridges. But under all circumstances and conditions of weather and soil, sheltered from the main currents of the winds or in blank exposure to them, well fed or starved, it is always singularly graceful in habit. Even at its highest limit in the park, ten thousand five hundred feet above the sea on exposed ridgetops, where it crouches and huddles close together in low thickets like those of the dwarf pine, it still contrives to put forth its sprays and branches in forms of irrepressible beauty, while on moist well-drained moraines it displays a perfectly tropical luxuriance of foliage, flower, and fruit.

In the first winter storms the snow is oftentimes soft, and lodges in the dense leafy branches, pressing them down against the trunk, and the slender drooping axis bends lower and lower as the load increases, until the top touches the ground and an ornamental arch is made. Then, as storm succeeds storm and snow is heaped on snow, the whole tree is at last buried, not again to see the light or move leaf or limb until set free by the spring thaws in June or July. Not the young saplings only are thus carefully covered and put to sleep in the whitest of white beds for five or six months of the year, but trees thirty and forty feet high. From April to May, when the snow is compacted, you may ride over the prostrate groves without seeing a single branch or leaf of them. In the autumn they are full of merry life, when Clark crows, squirrels, and chipmunks are gathering the abundant crop of seeds while the deer rest beneath the thick concealing branches. The finest grove in the park is near Mount Conness, and the trail from the Tuolumne soda springs to the mountain runs through it. Many of the trees in this grove are three to four or five feet in diameter and about a hundred feet high.

The mountain hemlock is widely distributed from near the south extremity of the high Sierra northward along the Cascade Mountains of Oregon and Washington and the coast ranges of British Columbia to Alaska, where it was first discovered in 1827. Its northmost limit, so far as I have observed, is in the icy fiords of Prince William's Sound in latitude 61°, where it forms pure forests at the level of the sea, growing tall and majestic on the banks of the great glaciers, waving in accord with the mountain winds and the thunder of the falling icebergs. Here as in the Sierra it is ineffably beautiful, the very loveliest evergreen in America.

Of the round-headed dicotyledonous trees in the park the most influential are the black and goldcup oaks. They occur in some parts of the main forest belt, scattered among the big pines like a heavier chaparral, but form extensive groves and reach perfect development only in the Yosemite valleys and flats of the main cañons. The California black oak (*Quercus Californica*) is one of the largest and most beautiful of the Western oaks, attaining under favorable conditions a height of sixty to a hundred feet, with a trunk three to seven feet in diameter, wide-spreading picturesque branches, and smooth lively green foliage handsomely scalloped, purple in the spring, yellow and red in autumn. It grows best in sunny open groves on ground covered with ferns, chokecherry, brier rose, rubus, mints, goldenrods, etc. Few, if any, of the famous oak groves of Europe, however extensive, surpass these in the size and strength and bright, airy beauty of the trees, the color and fragrance of the vegetation beneath them, the quality of the light that fills their leafy arches, and in the grandeur of the surrounding scenery. The finest grove in the park is in one of the little Yosemite valleys of the Tuolumne Cañon, a few miles above Hetch-Hetchy.

The mountain live-oak, or goldcup oak (*Quercus chrysolepis*), forms extensive groves on earthquake and avalanche taluses and terraces in cañons and Yosemite valleys, from about three to five thousand feet above the sea. In tough, sturdy, unwedgeable strength this is the oak of oaks. In general appearance it resembles the great live-oak of the Southern states. It has pale gray bark, a short, uneven, heavily buttressed trunk which usually divides a few feet above the ground into strong wide-reaching limbs, forming noble arches, and ending in an intricate maze of small branches and sprays, the outer ones frequently drooping in long tresses to the ground like those of the weeping willow, covered with small simple polished leaves, making a canopy broad and bossy, on which the sunshine falls in glorious brightness. The acorn cups are shallow, thick-walled, and covered with yellow fuzzy dust. The flowers appear in May and June with a profusion of pollened tresses, followed by the bronze-colored young leaves.

No tree in the park is a better measure of altitude. In cañons, at an elevation of four thousand feet, you may easily find a tree six or eight feet in diameter; and at the head of a side cañon, three thousand feet higher, up which you can climb in less than two hours, you find the knotty giant dwarfed to a slender shrub, with leaves like those of huckleberry bushes, still bearing acorns, and seemingly contented, forming dense patches of chaparral, on the top of which you may make your bed and sleep softly like a Highlander in heather. About a thousand feet higher it is still smaller, making fringes about a foot high around boulders and along seams in pavements and the brows of cañons, giving hand-holds here and there on cliffs hard to climb. The largest I have measured were from twenty-five to twenty-seven feet in girth, fifty to sixty feet high, and the spread of the limbs was about double the height.

The principal riverside trees are poplar, alder, willow, broad-leaved maple, and Nuttall's flowering dogwood. The poplar (*Populus trichocarpa*), often called balm of Gilead from the gum on its buds, is a tall, stately tree, towering above its companions and gracefully embowering the banks of the main streams at an elevation of about four thousand feet. Its abundant foliage turns bright yellow in the fall, and the Indian-summer sunshine sifts through it in delightful tones over the slow-gliding waters when they are at their lowest ebb.

The flowering dogwood is brighter still in these brooding days, for every branch of its broad head is then a brilliant crimson flame. In the spring, when the streams are in flood, it is the whitest of trees, white as a snow bank with its magnificent flowers four to eight inches in width, making a wonderful show, and drawing swarms of moths and butter-flies.

The broad-leaved maple is usually found in the coolest boulder-choked cañons, where the streams are gray and white with foam, over which it spreads its branches in beautiful arches from bank to bank, forming leafy tunnels full of soft green light and spray,—favorite homes of the water ousel. Around the glacier lakes, two or three thousand feet higher, the common aspen grows in fringing lines and groves which are brilliantly colored in autumn, reminding you of the color glory of the Eastern woods.

Scattered here and there or in groves the botanist will find a few other trees, mostly small,—the mountain mahogany, cherry, chestnut-oak, laurel, and nutmeg. The California nutmeg (*Tumion Californicum*) is a handsome evergreen, belonging to the yew family, with pale bark, prickly leaves, fruit like a green-gage plum, and seed like a nutmeg. One of the best groves of it in the park is at the Cascades below Yosemite.

But the noble oaks and all these rock-shading, stream-embowering trees are as nothing amid the vast abounding billowy forests of conifers. During my first years in the Sierra I was ever calling on everybody within reach to admire them, but I found no one half warm enough until Emerson came. I had read his essays, and felt sure that of all men he would best interpret the sayings of these noble mountains and trees. Nor was my faith weakened when I met him in Yosemite. He seemed as serene as a sequoia, his head in the empyrean; and forgetting his age, plans, duties, ties of every sort, I proposed an immeasurable camping trip back in the heart of the mountains. He seemed anxious to go, but considerately mentioned his party. I said: "Never mind. The mountains are calling; run away, and let plans and parties and dragging lowland duties all 'gang tapsal-teerie.' We'll go up a cañon singing your own song, 'Good-by, proud world! I'm going home,' in divine earnest. Up there lies a new heaven and a new earth; let us go to the show." But alas, it was too late,—too near the sundown of his life. The shadows were growing long, and he leaned on his friends. His party, full of indoor philosophy, failed to see the natural beauty and fullness of promise of my wild plan, and laughed at it in good-natured ignorance, as if it were necessarily amusing to imagine that Boston people might be led to accept Sierra manifestations of God at the price of rough camping. Anyhow, they would have none of it, and held Mr. Emerson to the hotels and trails.

After spending only five tourist days in Yosemite he was led away, but I saw him two days more; for I was kindly invited to go with the party as far as the Mariposa big trees. I told Mr. Emerson that I would gladly go to the sequoias with him, if he would camp in the grove. He consented heartily, and I felt sure that we would have at least one good wild memorable night round a sequoia camp-fire. Next day we rode through the magnificent forests of the Merced basin, and I kept calling his attention to the sugar pines, quoting his wood-notes, "Come listen what the pine tree saith," etc., pointing out the noblest as kings and high priests, the most eloquent and commanding preachers of all the mountain forests, stretching forth their century-old arms in benediction over the worshiping congregations crowded about them. He gazed in devout admiration, saying but little, while his fine smile faded away.

Early in the afternoon, when we reached Clark's Station, I was surprised to see the party dismount. And when I asked if we were not going up into the grove to camp they said: "No; it would never do to lie out in the night air. Mr. Emerson might take cold; and you know, Mr. Muir, that would be a dreadful thing." In vain I urged, that only in homes and hotels were colds caught, that nobody ever was known to take cold camping in these woods, that there was not a single cough or sneeze in all the Sierra. Then I pictured the big climate-changing, inspiring fire I would make, praised the beauty and fragrance of sequoia flame, told how the great trees would stand about us transfigured in the purple light, while the stars looked down between the great domes; ending by urging them to come on and make an immortal Emerson night of it. But the house habit was not to be overcome, nor the strange dread of night air, though it is only cooled day air with a little dew in it. So the carpet dust and unknowable reeks were preferred. And to think of this being a Boston choice! Sad commentary on culture and the glorious transcendentalism.

Accustomed to reach whatever place I started for, I was going up the mountain alone to camp, and wait the coming of the party next day. But since Emerson was so soon to vanish, I concluded to stop with him. He hardly spoke a word all the evening, yet it was a great pleasure simply to be near him, warming in the light of his face as at a fire. In the morning we rode up the trail through a noble forest of pine and fir into the famous Mariposa Grove, and stayed an hour or two, mostly in ordinary tourist fashion,—looking at the biggest giants, measuring them with a tape line, riding through prostrate fire-bored trunks, etc., though Mr. Emerson was alone occasionally, sauntering about as if under a spell. As we walked through a fine group, he quoted, "There were giants in those days," recognizing the antiquity of the race. To commemorate his visit, Mr. Galen Clark, the guardian of the grove, selected the finest of the unnamed trees and requested him to give it a name. He named it Samoset, after the New England sachem, as the best that occurred to him.

The poor bit of measured time was soon spent, and while the saddles were being adjusted I again urged Emerson to stay. "You are yourself a sequoia," I said. "Stop and get acquainted with your big brethren." But he was past his prime, and was now as a child in the hands of his affectionate but sadly civilized friends, who seemed as full of old-fashioned conformity as of bold intellectual independence. It was the afternoon of the day and the afternoon of his life, and his course was now westward down all the mountains into the sunset. The party mounted and rode away in wondrous contentment, apparently, tracing the trail through ceanothus and dogwood bushes, around the bases of the big trees, up the slope of the sequoia basin, and over the divide. I followed to the edge of the grove. Emerson lingered in the rear of the train, and when he reached the top of the ridge, after all the rest of the party were over and out of sight, he turned his horse, took off his hat and waved me a last good-by. I felt lonely, so sure had I been that Emerson of all men would be the quickest to see the mountains and sing them. Gazing awhile on the spot where he vanished, I sauntered back into the heart of the grove, made a bed of sequoia plumes and ferns by the side of a stream, gathered a store of firewood, and then walked about until sundown. The birds, robins, thrushes, warblers, etc., that had kept out of sight, came about me, now that all was quiet, and made cheer. After sundown I built a great fire, and as usual had it all to myself. And though lonesome for the first time in these forests, I quickly took heart again,—the trees had not gone to Boston, nor the birds; and as I sat by the fire, Emerson was still with me in spirit, though I never again saw him in the flesh. He sent books and wrote, cheering me on; advised me not to stay too long in solitude. Soon he hoped that my guardian angel would intimate that my probation was at a close. Then I was to roll up my herbariums, sketches, and poems (though I never knew I had any poems), and come to his house; and when I tired of him and his humble surroundings, he would show me to better people.

But there remained many a forest to wander through, many a mountain and glacier to cross, before I was to see his Wachusett and Monadnock, Boston and Concord. It was seventeen years after our parting on the Wawona ridge that I stood beside his grave under a pine tree on the hill above Sleepy Hollow. He had gone to higher Sierras, and, as I fancied, was again waving his hand in friendly recognition.

from *Our National Parks*, 1901

The Grand Cañon of the Colorado

HAPPY nowadays is the tourist, with earth's wonders, new and old, spread invitingly open before him, and a host of able workers as his slaves making everything easy, padding plush about him, grading roads for him, boring tunnels, moving hills out of his way, eager, like the devil, to show him all the kingdoms of the world and their glory and foolishness, spiritualizing travel for him with lightning and steam, abolishing space and time and almost everything else. Little children and tender, pulpy people, as well as storm-seasoned explorers, may now go almost everywhere in smooth comfort, cross oceans and deserts scarce accessible to fishes and birds, and, dragged by steel horses, go up high mountains, riding gloriously beneath starry showers of sparks, ascending like Elijah in a whirlwind and chariot of fire.

First of the wonders of the great West to be brought within reach of the tourist were the Yosemite and the Big Trees, on the completion of the first transcontinental railway; next came the Yellowstone and icy Alaska, by the Northern roads; and last the Grand Cañon of the Colorado, which, naturally the hardest to reach, has now become, by a branch of the Santa Fé, the most accessible of all.

Of course with this wonderful extension of steel ways through our wildness there is loss as well as gain. Nearly all railroads are bordered by belts of desolation. The finest wilderness perishes as if stricken with pestilence. Bird and beast people, if not the dryads, are frightened from the groves. Too often the groves also vanish, leaving nothing but ashes. Fortunately, nature has a few big places beyond man's power to spoil—the ocean, the two icy ends of the globe, and the Grand Cañon.

When I first heard of the Santa Fé trains running to the edge of the Grand Cañon of Arizona, I was troubled with thoughts of the disenchantment likely to follow. But last winter, when I saw those trains crawling along through the pines of the Cocanini Forest and close up to the brink of the chasm at Bright Angel, I was glad to discover that in the presence of such stupendous scenery they are nothing. The locomotives and trains are mere beetles and caterpillars, and the noise they make is as little disturbing as the hooting of an owl in the lonely woods.

In a dry, hot, monotonous forested plateau, seemingly boundless, you come suddenly and without warning upon the abrupt edge of a gigantic sunken landscape of the wildest, most multitudinous features, and those features, sharp and angular, are made out of flat beds of limestone and sandstone forming a spiry, jagged, gloriously colored mountain-range countersunk in a level gray plain. It is a hard job to sketch it even in scrawniest outline; and try as I may, not in the least sparing myself, I cannot tell the hundredth part of the wonders of its features—the side-cañons, gorges, alcoves, cloisters, and amphitheaters of vast sweep and depth, carved in its magnificent walls; the throng of great architectural rocks it contains resembling castles, cathedrals, temples, and palaces, towered and spired and painted, some of them nearly a mile high, yet beneath one's feet. All this, however, is less difficult than to give any idea of the impression of wild, primeval beauty and power one receives in merely gazing from its brink. The view down the gulf of color and over the rim of its wonderful wall, more than any other view I know, leads us to think of our earth as a star with stars swimming in light, every radiant spire pointing the way to the heavens.

But it is impossible to conceive what the cañon is, or what impression it makes, from descriptions or pictures, however good. Naturally it is untellable even to those who have seen something perhaps a little like it on a small scale in this same plateau region. One's most extravagant expectations are indefinitely surpassed, though one expect much from what is said of it as "the biggest chasm on earth"—"so big is it that all other big things,—Yosemite, the Yellowstone, the Pyramids, Chicago,—all would be lost if tumbled into it." Naturally enough, illustrations as to size are sought for among other cañons like or unlike it, with the common result of worse confounding confusion. The prudent keep silence. It was once said that the "Grand Cañon could put a dozen Yosemites in its vest pocket."

The justly famous Grand Cañon of the Yellowstone is, like

the Colorado, gorgeously colored and abruptly countersunk in a plateau, and both are mainly the work of water. But the Colorado's cañon is more than a thousand times larger, and as a score or two new buildings of ordinary size would not appreciably change the general view of a great city, so hundreds of Yellowstones might be eroded in the sides of the Colorado Cañon without noticeably augmenting its size or the richness of its sculpture. But it is not true that the great Yosemite rocks would be thus lost or hidden. Nothing of their kind in the world, so far as I know, rivals El Capitan and Tissiack, much less dwarfs or in any way belittles them. None of the sandstone or limestone precipices of the cañon that I have seen or heard of approaches in smooth, flawless strength and grandeur the granite face of El Capitan or the Tenaya side of Cloud's Rest. These colossal cliffs, types of permanence, are about three thousand and six thousand feet high; those of the cañon that are sheer are about half as high, and are types of fleeting change; while glorious-domed Tissiack, noblest of mountain buildings, far from being overshadowed or lost in this rosy, spiry cañon company, would draw every eye, and, in serene majesty, "aboon them a'" she would take her place—castle, temple, palace, or tower. Nevertheless a noted writer, comparing the Grand Cañon in a general way with the glacial Yosemite, says: "And the Yosemite—ah, the lovely Yosemite! Dumped down into the wilderness of gorges and mountains, it would take a guide who knew of its existence a long time to find it." This is striking, and shows up well above the levels of commonplace description; but it is confusing, and has the fatal fault of not being true. As well try to describe an eagle by putting a lark in it. "And the lark—ah, the lovely lark! Dumped down the red, royal gorge of the eagle, it would be hard to find." Each in its own place is better, singing at heaven's gate, and sailing the sky with the clouds.

Every feature of nature's big face is beautiful,—height and hollow, wrinkle, furrow, and line,—and this is the main master furrow of its kind on our continent, incomparably greater and more impressive than any other yet discovered, or likely to be discovered, now that all the great rivers have been traced to their heads.

The Colorado River rises in the heart of the continent on

the dividing ranges and ridges between the two oceans, drains thousands of snowy mountains through narrow or spacious valleys, and thence through cañons of every color, sheer-walled and deep, all of which seem to be represented in this one grand cañon of cañons.

It is very hard to give anything like an adequate conception of its size, much more of its color, its vast wall-sculpture, the wealth of ornate architectural buildings that fill it, or, most of all, the tremendous impression it makes. According to Major Powell, it is about two hundred and seventeen miles long, from five to fifteen miles wide from rim to rim, and from about five thousand to six thousand feet deep. So tremendous a chasm would be one of the world's greatest wonders even if, like ordinary cañons cut in sedimentary rocks, it were empty and its walls were simple. But instead of being plain, the walls are so deeply and elaborately carved into all sorts of recesses—alcoves, cirques, amphitheaters, and side-cañons—that were you to trace the rim closely around on both sides your journey would be nearly a thousand miles long. Into all these recesses the level, continuous beds of rock in ledges and benches, with their various colors, run like broad ribbons, marvelously beautiful and effective even at a distance of ten or twelve miles. And the vast space these glorious walls in-close, instead of being empty, is crowded with gigantic archi-tectural rock forms gorgeously colored and adorned with towers and spires like works of art.

Looking down from this level plateau, we are more im-pressed with a feeling of being on the top of everything than when looking from the summit of a mountain. From side to side of the vast gulf, temples, palaces, towers, and spires come soaring up in thick array half a mile or nearly a mile above their sunken, hidden bases, some to a level with our stand-point, but none higher. And in the inspiring morning light all are so fresh and rosy-looking that they seem new-born; as if, like the quick-growing crimson snow-plants of the California woods, they had just sprung up, hatched by the warm, brood-ing, motherly weather.

In trying to describe the great pines and sequoias of the Sierra, I have often thought that if one of those trees could be set by itself in some city park, its grandeur might there be impressively realized; while in its home forests, where all magnitudes are great, the weary, satiated traveler sees none of them truly. It is so with these majestic rock structures.

Though mere residual masses of the plateau, they are dowered with the grandeur and repose of mountains, together with the finely chiseled carving and modeling of man's temples and palaces, and often, to a considerable extent, with their symmetry. Some, closely observed, look like ruins; but even these stand plumb and true, and show architectural forms loaded with lines strictly regular and decorative, and all are arrayed in colors that storms and time seem only to brighten. They are not placed in regular rows in line with the river, but "a' through ither," as the Scotch say, in lavish, exuberant crowds, as if nature in wildest extravagance held her bravest structures as common as gravel-piles. Yonder stands a spiry cathedral nearly five thousand feet in height, nobly symmetrical, with sheer buttressed walls and arched doors and windows, as richly finished and decorated with sculptures as the great rock temples of India or Egypt. Beside it rises a huge castle with arched gateway, turrets, watch-towers, ramparts, etc., and to right and left palaces, obelisks, and pyramids fairly fill the gulf, all colossal and all lavishly painted and carved. Here and there a flat-topped structure may be seen, or one imperfectly domed; but the prevailing style is ornate Gothic, with many hints of Egyptian and Indian.

Throughout this vast extent of wild architecture—nature's own capital city—there seem to be no ordinary dwellings. All look like grand and important public structures, except perhaps some of the lower pyramids, broad-based and sharp-pointed, covered with down-flowing talus like loosely set tents with hollow, sagging sides. The roofs often have disintegrated rocks heaped and draggled over them, but in the main the masonry is firm and laid in regular courses, as if done by square and rule.

Nevertheless they are ever changing: their tops are now a dome, now a flat table or a spire, as harder or softer strata are reached in their slow degradation, while the sides, with all their fine moldings, are being steadily undermined and eaten away. But no essential change in style or color is thus effected. From century to century they stand the same. What seems confusion among the rough earthquake-shaken crags nearest one comes to order as soon as the main plan of the various structures appears. Every building, however complicated and laden with ornamental lines, is at one with itself and every one of its neighbors, for the same characteristic controlling belts of color and solid strata extend with wonderful constancy for very great distances, and pass through and give style to thousands of separate structures, however their smaller characters may vary.

Of all the various kinds of ornamental work displayed,— carving, tracery on cliff-faces, moldings, arches, pinnacles,— none is more admirably effective or charms more than the webs of rain-channeled taluses. Marvelously extensive, without the slightest appearance of waste or excess, they cover roofs and dome-tops and the base of every cliff, belt each spire and pyramid and massy, towering temple, and in beautiful continuous lines go sweeping along the great walls in and out around all the intricate system of side-cañons, amphitheaters, cirques, and scallops into which they are sculptured. From one point hundreds of miles of this fairy embroidery may be traced. It is all so fine and orderly that it would seem that not only had the clouds and streams been kept harmoniously busy in the making of it, but that every raindrop sent like a bullet to a mark had been the subject of a separate thought, so sure is the outcome of beauty through the stormy centuries. Surely nowhere else are there illustrations so striking of the natural beauty of desolation and death, so many of nature's own mountain buildings wasting in glory of high desert air—going to dust. See how steadfast in beauty they all are in their going. Look again and again how the rough, dusty boulders and sand of disintegration from the upper ledges wreathe in beauty the next and next below with these wonderful taluses, and how the colors are finer the faster the waste. We oftentimes see nature giving beauty for ashes,—as in the flowers of a prairie after fire,—but here the very dust and ashes are beautiful.

Gazing across the mighty chasm, we at last discover that it is not its great depth nor length, nor yet these wonderful buildings, that most impresses us. It is its immense width, sharply defined by precipitous walls plunging suddenly down from a flat plain, declaring in terms instantly apprehended that the vast gulf is a gash in the once unbroken plateau, made by slow, orderly erosion and removal of huge beds of rocks. Other valleys of erosion are as great,—in all their dimensions some are greater,—but none of these produces an effect on the imagination at once so quick and profound, coming without study, given at a glance. Therefore by far the greatest and most influential feature of this view from Bright Angel or any other of the cañon views is the opposite wall. Of the one beneath our feet we see only fragmentary sections in cirques and amphitheaters and on the sides of the outjutting promontories between them, while the other, though far distant, is beheld in all its glory of color and noble proportions—the one supreme beauty and wonder to which the eye is ever turning. For while charming with its beauty it tells the story of the stupendous erosion of the cañon—the foundation of the unspeakable impression made on everybody. It seems a gigantic statement for even nature to make, all in one mighty stone word, apprehended at once like a burst of light, celestial color its natural vesture, coming in glory to mind and heart as to a home prepared for it from the very beginning. Wildness so godful, cosmic, primeval, bestows a new sense of earth's beauty and size. Not even from high mountains does the world seem so wide, so like a star in glory of light on its way through the heavens.

I have observed scenery-hunters of all sorts getting first views of yosemites, glaciers, White Mountain ranges, etc. Mixed with the enthusiasm which such scenery naturally excites, there is often weak gushing, and many splutter aloud like little waterfalls. Here, for a few moments at least, there is silence, and all are in dead earnest, as if awed and hushed by an earthquake—perhaps until the cook cries "Breakfast!" or the stable-boy "Horses are ready!" Then the poor unfortunates, slaves of regular habits, turn quickly away, gasping and muttering as if wondering where they had been and what had enchanted them.

Roads have been made from Bright Angel Hotel through the Cocanini Forest to the ends of outstanding promontories, commanding extensive views up and down the cañon. The nearest of them, three or four miles east and west, are

McNeil's Point and Rowe's Point; the latter, besides commanding the eternally interesting cañon, gives wide-sweeping
views southeast and west over the dark forest roof to the San
Francisco and Mount Trumbull volcanoes—the bluest of
mountains over the blackest of level woods.

Instead of thus riding in dust with the crowd, more will be
gained by going quietly afoot along the rim at different times
of day and night, free to observe the vegetation, the fossils in
the rocks, the seams beneath overhanging ledges once inhabited by Indians, and to watch the stupendous scenery in the
changing lights and shadows, clouds, showers, and storms.
One need not go hunting the so-called "points of interest."
The verge anywhere, everywhere, is a point of interest beyond
one's wildest dreams.

As yet, few of the promontories or throng of mountain
buildings in the cañon are named. Nor among such exuberance of forms are names thought of by the bewildered,
hurried tourist. He would be as likely to think of names for
waves in a storm. The Eastern and Western Cloisters, Hindu
Amphitheater, Cape Royal, Powell's Plateau, and Grand View
Point, Point Sublime, Bissell and Moran points, the Temple
of Set, Vishnu's Temple, Shiva's Temple, Twin Temples,
Tower of Babel, Hance's Column—these fairly good names
given by Dutton, Holmes, Moran, and others are scattered
over a large stretch of the cañon wilderness.

All the cañon rock-beds are lavishly painted, except a few
neutral bars and the granite notch at the bottom occupied by
the river, which makes but little sign. It is a vast wilderness of
rocks in a sea of light, colored and glowing like oak and maple
woods in autumn, when the sun-gold is richest. I have just
said that it is impossible to learn what the cañon is like from
descriptions and pictures. Powell's and Dutton's descriptions
present magnificent views not only of the cañon but of all the
grand region round about it; and Holmes's drawings, accom-
panying Dutton's report, are wonderfully good. Surely faithful
and loving skill can go no further in putting the multitudinous
decorated forms on paper. But the *colors*, the living, rejoicing
colors, chanting morning and evening in chorus to heaven!
Whose brush or pencil, however lovingly inspired, can give us

these? And if paint is of no effect, what hope lies in pen-work? Only this: some may be incited by it to go and see for themselves.

No other range of mountainous rock-work of anything like the same extent have I seen that is so strangely, boldly, lavishly colored. The famous Yellowstone Cañon below the falls comes to mind; but, wonderful as it is, and well deserved as is its fame, compared with this it is only a bright rainbow ribbon at the roots of the pines. Each of the series of level, continuous beds of carboniferous rocks of the cañon has, as we have seen, its own characteristic color. The summit limestone-beds are pale yellow; next below these are the beautiful rose-colored cross-bedded sandstones; next there are a thousand feet of brilliant red sandstones; and below these the red wall lime-stones, over two thousand feet thick, rich massy red, the greatest and most influential of the series, and forming the main color-fountain. Between these are many neutral-tinted beds. The prevailing colors are wonderfully deep and clear, changing and blending with varying intensity from hour to hour, day to day, season to season; throbbing, wavering, glowing, responding to every passing cloud or storm, a world of color in itself, now burning in separate rainbow bars streaked and blotched with shade, now glowing in one smooth, all-pervading ethereal radiance like the alpenglow, uniting the rocky world with the heavens.

The dawn, as in all the pure, dry desert country, is ineffably beautiful; and when the first level sunbeams sting the domes and spires, with what a burst of power the big, wild days begin! The dead and the living, rocks and hearts alike, awake and sing the new-old song of creation. All the massy head-lands and salient angles of the walls, and the multitudinous temples and palaces, seem to catch the light at once, and cast thick black shadows athwart hollow and gorge, bringing out details as well as the main massive features of the architecture; while all the rocks, as if wild with life, throb and quiver and glow in the glorious sunburst, rejoicing. Every rock temple then becomes a temple of music; every spire and pinnacle an angel of light and song, shouting color halleluiahs.

As the day draws to a close, shadows, wondrous, black, and thick, like those of the morning, fill up the wall hollows, while the glowing rocks, their rough angles burned off, seem soft and hot to the heart as they stand submerged in purple haze, which now fills the cañon like a sea. Still deeper, richer, more divine grow the great walls and temples, until in the supreme flaming glory of sunset the whole cañon is transfigured, as if all the life and light of centuries of sunshine stored up and condensed in the rocks was now being poured forth as from one glorious fountain, flooding both earth and sky.

Strange to say, in the full white effulgence of the midday hours the bright colors grow dim and terrestrial in common gray haze; and the rocks, after the manner of mountains, seem to crouch and drowse and shrink to less than half their real stature, and have nothing to say to one, as if not at home. But it is fine to see how quickly they come to life and grow radiant and communicative as soon as a band of white clouds come floating by. As if shouting for joy, they seem to spring up to meet them in hearty salutation, eager to touch them and beg their blessings. It is just in the midst of these dull midday hours that the cañon clouds are born.

A good storm-cloud full of lightning and rain on its way to its work on a sunny desert day is a glorious object. Across the cañon, opposite the hotel, is a little tributary of the Colorado called Bright Angel Creek. A fountain-cloud still better deserves the name "Angel of the Desert Wells"—clad in bright plumage, carrying cool shade and living water to countless animals and plants ready to perish, noble in form and gesture, seeming able for anything, pouring life-giving, wonder-working floods from its alabaster fountains, as if some sky-lake had broken. To every gulch and gorge on its favorite ground is given a passionate torrent, roaring, replying to the rejoicing lightning—stones, tons in weight, hurrying away as if frightened, showing something of the way Grand Cañon work is done. Most of the fertile summer clouds of the cañon are of this sort, massive, swelling cumuli, growing rapidly, displaying delicious tones of purple and gray in the hollows of their sun-beaten bosses, showering favored areas of the heated landscape, and vanishing in an hour or two. Some, busy and thoughtful-looking, glide with beautiful motion along the middle of the cañon in flocks, turning aside here and there, lingering as if studying the needs of particular spots, exploring side-cañons, peering into hollows like birds seeking nest-places, or hovering aloft on outspread wings. They scan all the red wilderness, dispensing their blessings of cool shadows and rain where the need is the greatest, refreshing the rocks, their offspring as well as the vegetation, continuing their sculpture, deepening gorges and sharpening peaks. Sometimes, blending all together, they weave a ceiling from rim to rim, perhaps opening a window here and there for sunshine to stream through, suddenly lighting some palace or temple and making it flare in the rain as if on fire.

Sometimes, as one sits gazing from a high, jutting promontory, the sky all clear, showing not the slightest wisp or penciling, a bright band of cumuli will appear suddenly, coming up the cañon in single file, as if tracing a well-known trail, passing in review, each in turn darting its lances and dropping its shower, making a row of little vertical rivers in the air above the big brown one. Others seem to grow from mere points, and fly high above the cañon, yet following its course for a long time, noiseless, as if hunting, then suddenly darting lightning at unseen marks, and hurrying on. Or they loiter here and there as if idle, like laborers out of work, waiting to be hired.

Half a dozen or more showers may oftentimes be seen falling at once, while far the greater part of the sky is in sunshine, and not a raindrop comes nigh one. These thunder-showers from as many separate clouds, looking like wisps of long hair, may vary greatly in effects. The pale, faint streaks are showers that fail to reach the ground, being evaporated on the way down through the dry, thirsty air, like streams in deserts. Many, on the other hand, which in the distance seem insignificant, are really heavy rain, however local; these are the gray wisps well zigzagged with lightning. The darker ones are torrent rain, which on broad, steep slopes of favorable conformation give rise to so-called "cloud-bursts"; and wonderful is the commotion they cause. The gorges and gulches below them, usually dry, break out in loud uproar, with a sudden downrush of muddy, boulder-laden floods. Down they all go in one simultaneous gush, roaring like lions rudely awakened, each of the tawny brood actually kicking up a dust at the first onset.

During the winter months snow falls over all the high plateau, usually to a considerable depth, whitening the rim and
the roofs of the cañon buildings. But last winter, when I arrived at Bright Angel in the middle of January, there was no
snow in sight, and the ground was dry, greatly to my disap-
pointment, for I had made the trip mainly to see the cañon
in its winter garb. Soothingly I was informed that this was an
exceptional season, and that the good snow might arrive at
any time. After waiting a few days, I gladly hailed a broad-
browed cloud coming grandly on from the west in big promising blackness, very unlike the white sailors of the summer
skies. Under the lee of a rim-ledge, with another snow-lover,
I watched its movements as it took possession of the cañon
and all the adjacent region in sight. Trailing its gray fringes
over the spiry tops of the great temples and towers, it gradually settled lower, embracing them all with ineffable kindness
and gentleness of touch, and fondled the little cedars and
pines as they quivered eagerly in the wind like young birds
begging their mothers to feed them. The first flakes and crystals began to fly about noon, sweeping straight up the middle
of the cañon, and swirling in magnificent eddies along the
sides. Gradually the hearty swarms closed their ranks and all
the cañon was lost in gray gloom except a short section of the
wall and a few trees beside us, which looked glad with snow
in their needles and about their feet as they leaned out over
the gulf. Suddenly the storm opened with magical effect to
the north over the cañon of Bright Angel Creek, inclosing a
sunlit mass of the cañon architecture, spanned by great white
concentric arches of cloud like the bows of a silvery aurora.
Above these and a little back of them was a series of upboiling
purple clouds, and high above all, in the background, a range
of noble cumuli towered aloft like snow-laden mountains,
their pure pearl bosses flooded with sunshine. The whole noble picture, calmly glowing, was framed in thick gray gloom,
which soon closed over it; and the storm went on, opening
and closing until night covered all.

Two days later, when we were on a jutting point about
eighteen miles east of Bright Angel and one thousand feet
higher, we enjoyed another storm of equal glory as to cloud
effects, though only a few inches of snow fell. Before the

storm began we had a magnificent view of this grander upper part of the cañon and also of the Cocanini Forest and Painted Desert. The march of the clouds with their storm-banners flying over this sublime landscape was unspeakably glorious, and so also was the breaking up of the storm next morning— the mingling of silver-capped rock, sunshine, and cloud.

Most tourists make out to be in a hurry even here; therefore their few days or hours would be best spent on the promontories nearest the hotel. Yet a surprising number go down the Bright Angel trail to the brink of the inner gloomy granite gorge overlooking the river. Deep cañons attract like high mountains; the deeper they are, the more surely are we drawn into them. On foot, of course, there is no danger whatever, and, with ordinary precautions, but little on animals. In comfortable tourist faith, unthinking, unfearing, down go men, women, and children on whatever is offered, horse, mule, or burro, as if saying with Jean Paul, "fear nothing but fear"— not without reason, for these cañon trails down the stairways of the gods are less dangerous than they seem, less dangerous than home stairs. The guides are cautious, and so are the experienced, much-enduring beasts. The scrawniest Rosinantes and wizened-rat mules cling hard to the rocks endwise or sidewise, like lizards or ants. From terrace to terrace, climate to climate, down one creeps in sun and shade, through gorge and gully and grassy ravine, and, after a long scramble on foot, at last beneath the mighty cliffs one comes to the grand, roaring river.

To the mountaineer the depth of the cañon, from five thousand to six thousand feet, will not seem so very wonderful, for he has often explored others that are about as deep. But the most experienced will be awe-struck by the vast extent of strange, countersunk scenery, the multitude of huge rock monuments of painted masonry built up in regular courses towering above, beneath, and round about him. By the Bright Angel trail the last fifteen hundred feet of the descent to the river has to be made afoot down the gorge of Indian Garden Creek. Most of the visitors do not like this part, and are content to stop at the end of the horse-trail and look down on the dull-brown flood from the edge of the Indian Garden Plateau. By the new Hance trail, excepting a few daringly steep spots, you can ride all the way to the river, where there is a good spacious camp-ground in a mesquit-grove. This trail, built by brave Hance, begins on the highest part of the rim, eight thousand feet above the sea, a thousand feet higher than the head of Bright Angel trail, and the descent is a little over six thousand feet, through a wonderful variety of climate and life. Often late in the fall, when frosty winds are blowing and snow is flying at one end of the trail, tender plants are blooming in balmy summer weather at the other. The trip down and up can be made afoot easily in a day. In this way one is free to observe the scenery and vegetation, instead of merely clinging to his animal and watching its steps. But all who have time should go prepared to camp awhile on the riverbank, to rest and learn something about the plants and animals and the mighty flood roaring past. In cool, shady amphitheaters at the head of the trail there are groves of white silver fir and Douglas spruce, with ferns and saxifrages that recall snowy mountains; below these, yellow pine, nut-pine, juniper, hop-hornbeam, ash, maple, holly-leaved berberis, cowania, spiræa, dwarf oak, and other small shrubs and trees. In dry gulches and on taluses and sun-beaten crags are sparsely scattered yuccas, cactuses, agave, etc. Where springs gush from the rocks there are willow thickets, grassy flats, and bright flowery gardens, and in the hottest recesses the delicate abronia, mesquit, woody compositæ, and arborescent cactuses.

The most striking and characteristic part of this widely varied vegetation are the cactaceæ—strange, leafless, old-fashioned plants with beautiful flowers and fruit, in every way able and admirable. While grimly defending themselves with innumerable barbed spears, they offer both food and drink to man and beast. Their juicy globes and disks and fluted cylindrical columns are almost the only desert wells that never go dry, and they always seem to rejoice the more and grow plumper and juicier the hotter the sunshine and sand. Some are spherical, like rolled-up porcupines, crouching in rock hollows beneath a mist of gray lances, unmoved by the wildest winds. Others, standing as erect as bushes and trees or tall branchless pillars crowned with magnificent flowers, their prickly armor sparkling, look boldly abroad over the glaring desert, making the strangest forests ever seen or dreamed of.

Cereus giganteus, the grim chief of the desert tribe, is often thirty or forty feet high in southern Arizona. Several species of tree yuccas in the same deserts, laden in early spring with superb white lilies, form forests hardly less wonderful, though here they grow singly or in small lonely groves. The low, almost stemless *Yucca baccata*, with beautiful lily-flowers and sweet banana-like fruit, prized by the Indians, is common along the cañon rim, growing on lean, rocky soil beneath mountain-mahogany, nut-pines, and junipers, beside dense flowery mats of *Spiræa cæspitosa* and the beautiful pinnate-leaved *Spiræa millefolium*. The nut-pine, *Pinus edulis*, scattered along the upper slopes and roofs of the cañon buildings, is the principal tree of the strange Dwarf Cocanini Forest. It is a picturesque stub of a pine about twenty-five feet high, usually with dead, lichened limbs thrust through its rounded head, and grows on crags and fissured rock tables, braving heat and frost, snow and drought, and continues patiently, faithfully fruitful for centuries. Indians and insects and almost every desert bird and beast come to it to be fed.

To civilized people from corn and cattle and wheat-field countries the cañon at first sight seems as uninhabitable as a glacier crevasse, utterly silent and barren. Nevertheless it is the home of a multitude of our fellow-mortals, men as well as animals and plants. Centuries ago it was inhabited by tribes of Indians, who, long before Columbus saw America, built thousands of stone houses in its crags, and large ones, some of them several stories high, with hundreds of rooms, on the mesas of the adjacent regions. Their cliff-dwellings, almost numberless, are still to be seen in the cañon, scattered along both sides from top to bottom and throughout its entire length, built of stone and mortar in seams and fissures like swallows' nests, or on isolated ridges and peaks. The ruins of larger buildings are found on open spots by the river, but most of them aloft on the brink of the wildest, giddiest precipices, sites evidently chosen for safety from enemies, and seemingly accessible only to the birds of the air. Many caves were also used as dwelling-places, as were mere seams on cliff-fronts formed by unequal weathering and with or without outer or side walls; and some of them were covered with colored pictures of animals. The most interesting of these cliff-dwellings had pathetic little ribbon-like strips of garden on narrow terraces, where irrigating-water could be carried to them—most romantic of sky-gardens, but eloquent of hard times.

In recesses along the river and on the first plateau flats above its gorge were fields and gardens of considerable size, where irrigating-ditches may still be traced. Some of these ancient gardens are still cultivated by Indians, descendants of cliff dwellers, who raise corn, squashes, melons, potatoes, etc., to reinforce the produce of the many wild food-furnishing plants, nuts, beans, berries, yucca and cactus fruits, grass and sunflower seeds, etc., and the flesh of animals, deer, rabbits, lizards, etc. The cañon Indians I have met here seem to be living much as did their ancestors, though not now driven into rock dens. They are able, erect men, with commanding eyes, which nothing that they wish to see can escape. They are never in a hurry, have a strikingly measured, deliberate, bearish manner of moving the limbs and turning the head, are capable of enduring weather, thirst, hunger, and over-abundance, and are blessed with stomachs which triumph over everything the wilderness may offer. Evidently their lives are not bitter.

The largest of the cañon animals one is likely to see is the wild sheep, or Rocky Mountain bighorn, a most admirable beast, with limbs that never fail, at home on the most nerve-trying precipices, acquainted with all the springs and passes and broken-down jumpable places in the sheer ribbon cliffs, bounding from crag to crag in easy grace and confidence of strength, his great horns held high above his shoulders, wild red blood beating and hissing through every fiber of him like the wind through a quivering mountain pine.

Deer also are occasionally met in the cañon, making their way to the river when the wells of the plateau are dry. Along the short spring streams beavers are still busy, as is shown by the cottonwood and willow timber they have cut and peeled, found in all the river drift-heaps. In the most barren cliffs and gulches there dwell a multitude of lesser animals, well-dressed, clear-eyed, happy little beasts—wood-rats, kangaroo-rats, gophers, wood-mice, skunks, rabbits, bob cats, and many others, gathering food, or dozing in their sun-warmed dens. Lizards, too, of every kind and color are here enjoying life on the hot cliffs, and making the brightest of them brighter.

Nor is there any lack of feathered people. The golden eagle may be seen, and the osprey, hawks, jays, humming-birds, the mourning-dove, and cheery familiar singers—the black-headed grosbeak, robin, bluebird, Townsend's thrush, and many warblers, sailing the sky and enlivening the rocks and bushes through all the cañon wilderness.

Here at Hance's river-camp or a few miles above it brave Powell and his brave men passed their first night in the cañon on their adventurous voyage of discovery thirty-three years ago. They faced a thousand dangers, open or hidden, now in their boats gladly sliding down swift, smooth reaches, now rolled over and over in back-combing surges of rough, roaring cataracts, sucked under in eddies, swimming like beavers, tossed and beaten like castaway drift—stout-hearted, un-daunted, doing their work through it all. After a month of this they floated smoothly out of the dark, gloomy, roaring abyss into light and safety two hundred miles below. As the flood rushes past us, heavy-laden with desert mud, we natu-rally think of its sources, its countless silvery branches out-spread on thousands of snowy mountains along the crest of the continent, and the life of them, the beauty of them, their history and romance. Its topmost springs are far north and east in Wyoming and Colorado, on the snowy Wind River, Front, Park, and Sawatch ranges, dividing the two ocean waters, and the Elk, Wasatch, Uinta, and innumerable spurs streaked with streams, made famous by early explorers and hunters. It is a river of rivers—the Du Chesne, San Rafael, Yampa, Dolores, Gunnison, Cotchetopa, Uncompahgre, Eagle, and Roaring rivers, the Green and the Grand, and scores of others with branches innumerable, as mad and glad a band as ever sang on mountains, descending in glory of foam and spray from snow-banks and glaciers through their rocky moraine-dammed, beaver-dammed channels. Then, all emerging from dark balsam and pine woods and coming to-gether, they meander through wide, sunny park valleys, and at length enter the great plateau and flow in deep cañons, the beginning of the system culminating in this grand cañon of cañons.

Our warm cañon camp is also a good place to give a thought to the glaciers which still exist at the heads of the highest tributaries. Some of them are of considerable size, especially those on the Wind River and Sawatch ranges in Wyoming and Colorado. They are remnants of a vast system of glaciers which recently covered the upper part of the Colorado basin, sculptured its peaks, ridges, and valleys to their present forms, and extended far out over the plateau region—how far I cannot now say. It appears, therefore, that, however old the main trunk of the Colorado may be, all its wide-spread upper branches and the landscapes they flow through are new-born, scarce at all changed as yet in any important feature since they first came to light at the close of the glacial period.

The so-called Grand Colorado Plateau, of which the Grand Cañon is only one of its well-proportioned features, extends with a breadth of hundreds of miles from the flanks of the Wasatch and Park Mountains to the south of the San Francisco Peaks. Immediately to the north of the deepest part of the cañon it rises in a series of subordinate plateaus, diversified with green meadows, marshes, bogs, ponds, forests, and grovy park valleys, a favorite Indian hunting-ground, inhabited by elk, deer, beaver, etc. But far the greater part of the plateau is good sound desert, rocky, sandy, or fluffy with loose ashes and dust, dissected in some places into a labyrinth of stream-channel chasms like cracks in a dry clay-bed, or the narrow slit crevasses of glaciers,—blackened with lava-flows, dotted with volcanoes and beautiful buttes, and lined with long continuous escarpments,—a vast bed of sediments of an ancient sea-bottom, still nearly as level as when first laid down after being heaved into the sky a mile or two high.

Walking quietly about in the alleys and byways of the Grand Cañon City, we learn something of the way it was made; and all must admire effects so great from means apparently so simple: rain striking light hammer-blows or heavier in streams, with many rest Sundays; soft air and light, gentle sappers and miners, toiling forever; the big river sawing the plateau asunder, carrying away the eroded and ground waste, and exposing the edges of the strata to the weather; rain torrents sawing cross-streets and alleys, exposing the strata in the same way in hundreds of sections, the softer, less resisting beds weathering and receding faster, thus undermining the harder beds, which fall, not only in small weathered particles, but in heavy sheer-cleaving masses, assisted down from time to time by kindly earthquakes, rain torrents rushing the fallen material to the river, keeping the wall rocks constantly exposed. Thus the cañon grows wider and deeper. So also do the side-cañons and amphitheaters, while secondary gorges and cirques gradually isolate masses of the promontories, forming new buildings, all of which are being weathered and pulled and shaken down while being built, showing destruction and creation as one. We see the proudest temples and palaces in stateliest attitudes, wearing their sheets of detritus as royal robes, shedding off showers of red and yellow stones like trees in autumn shedding their leaves, going to dust like beautiful days to night, proclaiming as with the tongues of angels the natural beauty of death.

Every building is seen to be a remnant of once continuous beds of sediments—sand and slime on the floor of an ancient sea, and filled with the remains of animals, and that every particle of the sandstones and limestones of these wonderful structures was derived from other landscapes, weathered and rolled and ground in the storms and streams of other ages. And when we examine the escarpments, hills, buttes, and other monumental masses of the plateau on either side of the cañon, we discover that an amount of material has been carried off in the general denudation of the region compared with which even that carried away in the making of the Grand Cañon is as nothing. Thus each wonder in sight becomes a window through which other wonders come to view. In no other part of this continent are the wonders of geology, the records of the world's auld lang syne, more widely opened, or displayed in higher piles. The whole cañon is a mine of fossils, in which five thousand feet of horizontal strata are exposed in regular succession over more than a thousand square miles of wall-space, and on the adjacent plateau region there is another series of beds twice as thick, forming a grand geological library—a collection of stone books covering thousands of miles of shelving tier on tier conveniently arranged for the student. And with what wonderful scriptures are their pages filled—myriad forms of successive floras and faunas, lavishly illustrated with colored drawings, carrying us back into the midst of the life of a past infinitely remote. And as we go on and on, studying this old, old life in the light of the life beating warmly about us, we enrich and lengthen our own.

Century Magazine, November 1902

Hetch Hetchy Valley

YOSEMITE is so wonderful that we are apt to regard it as an exceptional creation, the only valley of its kind in the world; but Nature is not so poor as to have only one of anything. Several other yosemites have been discovered in the Sierra that occupy the same relative positions on the Range and were formed by the same forces in the same kind of granite. One of these, the Hetch Hetchy Valley, is in the Yosemite National Park about twenty miles from Yosemite and is easily accessible to all sorts of travelers by a road and trail that leaves the Big Oak Flat road at Bronson Meadows a few miles below Crane Flat, and to mountaineers by way of Yosemite Creek basin and the head of the middle fork of the Tuolumne.

It is said to have been discovered by Joseph Screech, a hunter, in 1850, a year before the discovery of the great Yosemite. After my first visit to it in the autumn of 1871, I have always called it the "Tuolumne Yosemite," for it is a wonderfully exact counterpart of the Merced Yosemite, not only in its sublime rocks and waterfalls but in the gardens, groves and meadows of its flowery park-like floor. The floor of Yosemite is about 4000 feet above the sea; the Hetch Hetchy floor about 3700 feet. And as the Merced River flows through Yosemite, so does the Tuolumne through Hetch Hetchy. The walls of both are of gray granite, rise abruptly from the floor, are sculptured in the same style and in both every rock is a glacier monument.

Standing boldly out from the south wall is a strikingly picturesque rock called by the Indians, Kolana, the outermost of a group 2300 feet high, corresponding with the Cathedral Rocks of Yosemite both in relative position and form. On the opposite side of the Valley, facing Kolana, there is a counterpart of the El Capitan that rises sheer and plain to a height of 1800 feet, and over its massive brow flows a stream which makes the most graceful fall I have ever seen. From the edge of the cliff to the top of an earthquake talus it is perfectly free in the air for a thousand feet before it is broken into cascades among talus boulders. It is in all its glory in June, when the snow is melting fast, but fades and vanishes toward the end of summer. The only fall I know with which it may fairly be compared is the Yosemite Bridal Veil; but it excels even that favorite fall both in height and airy-fairy beauty and behavior. Lowlanders are apt to suppose that mountain streams in their wild career over cliffs lose control of themselves and tumble in a noisy chaos of mist and spray. On the contrary, on no part of their travels are they more harmonious and self-controlled. Imagine yourself in Hetch Hetchy on a sunny day in June, standing waist-deep in grass and flowers (as I have often stood), while the great pines sway dreamily with scarcely perceptible motion. Looking northward across the Valley you see a plain, gray granite cliff rising abruptly out of the gardens and groves to a height of 1800 feet, and in front of it Tueeulala's silvery scarf burning with irised sun-fire. In the first white outburst at the head there is abundance of visible energy, but it is speedily hushed and concealed in divine repose, and its tranquil progress to the base of the cliff is like that of a downy feather in a still room. Now observe the fineness and marvelous distinctness of the various sun-illumined fabrics into which the water is woven; they sift and float from form to form down the face of that grand gray rock in so leisurely and unconfused a manner that you can examine their texture, and patterns and tones of color as you would a piece of embroidery held in the hand. Toward the top of the fall you see groups of booming, comet-like masses, their solid, white heads separate, their tails like combed silk interlacing among delicate gray and purple shadows, ever forming and dissolving, worn out by friction in their rush through the air. Most of these vanish a few hundred feet below the summit, changing to varied forms of cloud-like drapery. Near the bottom the width of the fall has increased from about twenty-five feet to a hundred feet. Here it is composed of yet finer tissues, and is still without a trace of disorder—air, water and sunlight woven into stuff that spirits might wear.

So fine a fall might well seem sufficient to glorify any valley; but here, as in Yosemite, Nature seems in nowise moderate, for a short distance to the eastward of Tueeulala booms and thunders the great Hetch Hetchy Fall, Wapama, so near that you have both of them in full view from the same standpoint.

It is the counterpart of the Yosemite Fall, but has a much greater volume of water, is about 1700 feet in height, and appears to be nearly vertical, though considerably inclined, and is dashed into huge outbounding bosses of foam on projecting shelves and knobs. No two falls could be more unlike—Tueeulala out in the open sunshine descending like thistledown; Wapama in a jagged, shadowy gorge roaring and thundering, pounding its way like an earthquake avalanche.

Besides this glorious pair there is a broad, massive fall on the main river a short distance above the head of the Valley. Its position is something like that of the Vernal in Yosemite, and its roar as it plunges into a surging trout-pool may be heard a long way, though it is only about twenty feet high. On Rancheria Creek, a large stream, corresponding in position with the Yosemite Tenaya Creek, there is a chain of cascades joined here and there with swift flashing plumes like the one between the Vernal and Nevada Falls, making magnificent shows as they go their glacier-sculptured way, sliding, leaping, hurrahing, covered with crisp clashing spray made glorious with sifting sunshine. And besides all these a few small streams come over the walls at wide intervals, leaping from ledge to ledge with birdlike song and watering many a hidden cliff-garden and fernery, but they are too unshowy to be noticed in so grand a place.

The correspondence between the Hetch Hetchy walls in their trends, sculpture, physical structure, and general arrangement of the main rock-masses and those of the Yosemite Valley has excited the wondering admiration of every observer. We have seen that the El Capitan and Cathedral rocks occupy the same relative positions in both valleys; so also do their Yosemite points and North Domes. Again, that part of the Yosemite north wall immediately to the east of the Yosemite Fall has two horizontal benches, about 500 and 1500 feet above the floor, timbered with golden-cup oak. Two benches similarly situated and timbered occur on the same relative portion of the Hetch Hetchy north wall, to the east of Wapama Fall, and on no other. The Yosemite is bounded at the head by the great Half Dome. Hetch Hetchy is bounded in the same way, though its head rock is incomparably less wonderful and sublime in form.

The floor of the Valley is about three and a half miles long, and from a fourth to half a mile wide. The lower portion is mostly a level meadow about a mile long, with the trees restricted to the sides and the river banks, and partially separated from the main, upper, forested portion by a low bar of glacier-polished granite across which the river breaks in rapids.

The principal trees are the yellow and sugar pines, digger pine, incense cedar, Douglas spruce, silver fir, the California and golden-cup oaks, balsam cottonwood, Nuttall's flowering dogwood, alder, maple, laurel, tumion, etc. The most abundant and influential are the great yellow or silver pines like those of Yosemite, the tallest over two hundred feet in height, and the oaks assembled in magnificent groves with massive rugged trunks four to six feet in diameter, and broad, shady, wide-spreading heads. The shrubs forming conspicuous flowery clumps and tangles are manzanita, azalea, spiræa, brier-rose, several species of ceanothus, calycanthus, philadelphus, wild cherry, etc.; with abundance of showy and fragrant herbaceous plants growing about them or out in the open in beds by themselves—lilies, Mariposa tulips, brodiaeas, orchids, iris, spraguea, draperia, collomia, collinsia, castilleja, nemophila, larkspur, columbine, goldenrods, sunflowers, mints of many species, honeysuckle, etc. Many fine ferns dwell here also, especially the beautiful and interesting rock-ferns—pellaea, and cheilanthes of several species—fringing and rosetting dry rock-piles and ledges; woodwardia and asplenium on damp spots with fronds six or seven feet high; the delicate maiden-hair in mossy nooks by the falls, and the sturdy, broad-shouldered pteris covering nearly all the dry ground beneath the oaks and pines.

It appears, therefore, that Hetch Hetchy Valley, far from being a plain, common, rock-bound meadow, as many who have not seen it seem to suppose, is a grand landscape garden, one of Nature's rarest and most precious mountain temples. As in Yosemite, the sublime rocks of its walls seem to glow with life, whether leaning back in repose or standing erect in thoughtful attitudes, giving welcome to storms and calms alike, their brows in the sky, their feet set in the groves and gay flowery meadows, while birds, bees, and butterflies help the river and waterfalls to stir all the air into music—things frail and fleeting and types of permanence meeting here and blending, just as they do in Yosemite, to draw her lovers into close and confiding communion with her.

Sad to say, this most precious and sublime feature of the Yosemite National Park, one of the greatest of all our natural resources for the uplifting joy and peace and health of the people, is in danger of being dammed and made into a reservoir to help supply San Francisco with water and light, thus flooding it from wall to wall and burying its gardens and groves one or two hundred feet deep. This grossly destructive commercial scheme has long been planned and urged (though water as pure and abundant can be got from sources outside of the people's park, in a dozen different places), because of the comparative cheapness of the dam and of the territory which it is sought to divert from the great uses to which it was dedicated in the Act of 1890 establishing the Yosemite National Park.

The making of gardens and parks goes on with civilization all over the world, and they increase both in size and number as their value is recognized. Everybody needs beauty as well as bread, places to play in and pray in, where Nature may heal and cheer and give strength to body and soul alike. This natural beauty-hunger is made manifest in the little window-sill gardens of the poor, though perhaps only a geranium slip in a broken cup, as well as in the carefully tended rose and lily gardens of the rich, the thousands of spacious city parks and botanical gardens, and in our magnificent National parks—the Yellowstone, Yosemite, Sequoia, etc.—Nature's sublime wonderlands, the admiration and joy of the world. Nevertheless, like anything else worth while, from the very beginning, however well guarded, they have always been subject to attack by despoiling gain-seekers and mischief-makers of every degree from Satan to Senators, eagerly trying to make everything immediately and selfishly commercial, with schemes disguised in smug-smiling philanthropy, industriously, shampiously crying, "Conservation, conservation, panutilization," that man and beast may be fed and the dear Nation made great. Thus long ago a few enterprising merchants utilized the Jerusalem temple as a place of business instead of a place of prayer, changing money, buying and selling cattle and sheep and doves; and earlier still, the first forest reservation, including only one tree, was likewise despoiled. Ever since the establishment of the Yosemite National Park, strife has been going on around its borders and I suppose this will go on as part of the universal battle between right and wrong, however much its boundaries may be shorn, or its wild beauty destroyed.

The first application to the Government by the San Francisco Supervisors for the commercial use of Lake Eleanor and the Hetch Hetchy Valley was made in 1903, and on December 22nd of that year it was denied by the Secretary of the Interior, Mr. Hitchcock, who truthfully said:

> Presumably the Yosemite National Park was created such by law because of the natural objects of varying degrees of scenic importance located within its boundaries, inclusive alike of its beautiful small lakes, like Eleanor, and its majestic wonders, like Hetch Hetchy and Yosemite Valley. It is the aggregation of such natural scenic features that makes the Yosemite Park a wonderland which the Congress of the United States sought by law to reserve for all coming time as nearly as practicable in the condition fashioned by the hand of the Creator— a worthy object of National pride and a source of healthful pleasure and rest for the thousands of people who may annually sojourn there during the heated months.

In 1907 when Mr. Garfield became Secretary of the Interior the application was renewed and granted; but under his successor, Mr. Fisher, the matter has been referred to a Commission, which as this volume goes to press still has it under consideration.

The most delightful and wonderful camp grounds in the Park are its three great valleys—Yosemite, Hetch Hetchy, and Upper Tuolumne; and they are also the most important places with reference to their positions relative to the other great features—the Merced and Tuolumne Cañons, and the High Sierra peaks and glaciers, etc., at the head of the rivers. The main part of the Tuolumne Valley is a spacious flowery lawn four or five miles long, surrounded by magnificent snowy mountains, slightly separated from other beautiful meadows, which together make a series about twelve miles in length, the highest reaching to the feet of Mount Dana, Mount Gibbs, Mount Lyell and Mount McClure. It is about 8500 feet above the sea, and forms the grand central High Sierra camp ground from which excursions are made to the noble mountains, domes, glaciers, etc.; across the Range to the Mono Lake and volcanoes and down the Tuolumne Cañon to Hetch Hetchy. Should Hetch Hetchy be submerged for a reservoir, as proposed, not only would it be utterly destroyed, but the sublime cañon way to the heart of the High Sierra would be hopelessly blocked and the great camping ground, as the watershed of a city drinking system, virtually would be closed to the public. So far as I have learned, few of all the thousands who have seen the park and seek rest and peace in it are in favor of this outrageous scheme.

One of my later visits to the Valley was made in the autumn of 1907 with the late William Keith, the artist. The leaf-colors were then ripe, and the great godlike rocks in repose seemed to glow with life. The artist, under their spell, wandered day after day along the river and through the groves and gardens, studying the wonderful scenery; and, after making about forty sketches, declared with enthusiasm that although its walls were less sublime in height, in picturesque beauty and charm Hetch Hetchy surpassed even Yosemite.

That any one would try to destroy such a place seems incredible; but sad experience shows that there are people good enough and bad enough for anything. The proponents of the dam scheme bring forward a lot of bad arguments to prove that the only righteous thing to do with the people's parks is to destroy them bit by bit as they are able. Their arguments are curiously like those of the devil, devised for the destruction of the first garden—so much of the very best Eden fruit going to waste; so much of the best Tuolumne water and Tuolumne scenery going to waste. Few of their statements are even partly true, and all are misleading.

Thus, Hetch Hetchy, they say, is a "low-lying meadow." On the contrary, it is a high-lying natural landscape garden, as the photographic illustrations show.

"It is a common minor feature, like thousands of others."

On the contrary it is a very uncommon feature; after Yosemite, the rarest and in many ways the most important in the National Park.

"Damming and submerging it 175 feet deep would enhance its beauty by forming a crystal-clear lake." Landscape gardens, places of recreation and worship, are never made beautiful by destroying and burying them. The beautiful sham lake, forsooth, would be only an eyesore, a dismal blot on the landscape, like many others to be seen in the Sierra. For, instead of keeping it at the same level all the year, allowing Nature centuries of time to make new shores, it would, of course, be full only a month or two in the spring, when the snow is melting fast; then it would be gradually drained, exposing the slimy sides of the basin and shallower parts of the bottom, with the gathered drift and waste, death and decay of the upper basins, caught here instead of being swept on to decent natural burial along the banks of the river or in the sea. Thus the Hetch Hetchy dam-lake would be only a rough imitation of a natural lake for a few of the spring months, an open sepulcher for the others.

"Hetch Hetchy water is the purest of all to be found in the Sierra, unpolluted, and forever unpollutable." On the contrary, excepting that of the Merced below Yosemite, it is less pure than that of most of the other Sierra streams, because of the sewerage of camp grounds draining into it, especially of the Big Tuolumne Meadows camp ground, occupied by hundreds of tourists and mountaineers, with their animals, for months every summer, soon to be followed by thousands from all the world.

These temple destroyers, devotees of ravaging commercialism, seem to have a perfect contempt for Nature, and, instead of lifting their eyes to the God of the mountains, lift them to the Almighty Dollar.

Dam Hetch Hetchy! As well dam for water-tanks the people's cathedrals and churches, for no holier temple has ever been consecrated by the heart of man.

from *The Yosemite*, 1912

Cedar Keys

OCTOBER 23. To-day I reached the sea. While I was yet many miles back in the palmy woods, I caught the scent of the salt sea breeze which, although I had so many years lived far from sea breezes, suddenly conjured up Dunbar, its rocky coast, winds and waves; and my whole childhood, that seemed to have utterly vanished in the New World, was now restored amid the Florida woods by that one breath from the sea. Forgotten were the palms and magnolias and the thousand flowers that enclosed me. I could see only dulse and tangle, long-winged gulls, the Bass Rock in the Firth of Forth, and the old castle, schools, churches, and long country rambles in search of birds' nests. I do not wonder that the weary camels coming from the scorching African deserts should be able to scent the Nile.

How imperishable are all the impressions that ever vibrate one's life! We cannot forget anything. Memories may escape the action of will, may sleep a long time, but when stirred by the right influence, though that influence be light as a shadow, they flash into full stature and life with everything in place. For nineteen years my vision was bounded by forests, but to-day, emerging from a multitude of tropical plants, I beheld the Gulf of Mexico stretching away unbounded, except by the sky. What dreams and speculative matter for thought arose as I stood on the strand, gazing out on the burnished, treeless plain!

But now at the seaside I was in difficulty. I had reached a point that I could not ford, and Cedar Keys had an empty harbor. Would I proceed down the peninsula to Tampa and Key West, where I would be sure to find a vessel for Cuba, or would I wait here, like Crusoe, and pray for a ship. Full of these thoughts, I stepped into a little store which had a considerable trade in quinine and alligator and rattlesnake skins, and inquired about shipping, means of travel, etc.

The proprietor informed me that one of several sawmills near the village was running, and that a schooner chartered to carry a load of lumber to Galveston, Texas, was expected at the mills for a load. This mill was situated on a tongue of land a few miles along the coast from Cedar Keys, and I determined to see Mr. Hodgson, the owner, to find out particulars about the expected schooner, the time she would take to load, whether I would be likely to obtain passage on her, etc.

Found Mr. Hodgson at his mill. Stated my case, and was kindly furnished the desired information. I determined to wait the two weeks likely to elapse before she sailed, and go on her to the flowery plains of Texas, from any of whose ports, I fancied, I could easily find passage to the West Indies. I agreed to work for Mr. Hodgson in the mill until I sailed, as I had but little money. He invited me to his spacious house, which occupied a shell hillock and commanded a fine view of the Gulf and many gems of palmy islets, called "keys," that fringe the shore like huge bouquets—not too big, however, for the spacious waters. Mr. Hodgson's family welcomed me with that open, unconstrained cordiality which is characteristic of the better class of Southern people.

At the sawmill a new cover had been put on the main driving pulley, which, made of rough plank, had to be turned off and smoothed. He asked me if I was able to do this job and I told him that I could. Fixing a rest and making a tool out of an old file, I directed the engineer to start the engine and run slow. After turning down the pulley and getting it true, I put a keen edge on a common carpenter's plane, quickly finished the job, and was assigned a bunk in one of the employees' lodging-houses.

The next day I felt a strange dullness and headache while I was botanizing along the coast. Thinking that a bath in the salt water might refresh me, I plunged in and swam a little distance, but this seemed only to make me feel worse. I felt anxious for something sour, and walked back to the village to buy lemons.

Thus and here my long walk was interrupted. I though that a few days' sail would land me among the famous flower-beds of Texas. But the expected ship came and went while I was helpless with fever. The very day after reaching the sea I began to be weighed down by inexorable leaden numbness, which I resisted and tried to shake off for three days, by bathing in the Gulf, by dragging myself about among the palms, plants, and strange shells of the shore, and by doing a little mill work. I did not fear any serious illness, for I never was sick before, and was unwilling to pay attention to my feelings.

But yet heavier and more remorselessly pressed the growing fever, rapidly gaining on my strength. On the third day after my arrival I could not take any nourishment, but craved acid. Cedar Keys was only a mile or two distant, and I managed to walk there to buy lemons. On returning, about the middle of the afternoon, the fever broke on me like a storm, and before I had staggered halfway to the mill I fell down unconscious on the narrow trail among dwarf palmettos.

When I awoke from the hot fever sleep, the stars were shining, and I was at a loss to know which end of the trail to take, but fortunately, as it afterwards proved, I guessed right. Subsequently, as I fell again and again after walking only a hundred yards or so, I was careful to lie with my head in the direction in which I thought the mill was. I rose, staggered, and fell, I know not how many times, in delirious bewilderment, gasping and throbbing with only moments of consciousness. Thus passed the hours till after midnight, when I reached the mill lodging-house.

The watchman on his rounds found me lying on a heap of sawdust at the foot of the stairs. I asked him to assist me up the steps to bed, but he thought my difficulty was only intoxication and refused to help me. The mill hands, especially on Saturday nights, often returned from the village drunk. This was the cause of the watchman's refusal. Feeling that I must get to bed, I made out to reach it on hands and knees, tumbled in after a desperate struggle, and immediately became oblivious to everything.

I awoke at a strange hour on a strange day to hear Mr. Hodgson ask a watcher beside me whether I had yet spoken, and when he replied that I had not, he said: "Well, you must keep pouring in quinine. That's all we can do." How long I lay unconscious I never found out, but it must have been many days. Some time or other I was moved on a horse from the mill quarters to Mr. Hodgson's house, where I was nursed about three months with unfailing kindness, and to the skill and care of Mr. and Mrs. Hodgson I doubtless owe my life.

Through quinine and calomel—in sorry abundance—with other milder medicines, my malarial fever became typhoid. I had night sweats, and my legs became like posts of the temper and consistency of clay on account of dropsy. So on until January, a weary time.

As soon as I was able to get out of bed, I crept away to the edge of the wood, and sat day after day beneath a moss-draped live-oak, watching birds feeding on the shore when the tide was out. Later, as I gathered some strength, I sailed in a little skiff from one key to another. Nearly all the shrubs and trees here are evergreen, and a few of the smaller plants are in flower all winter. The principal trees on this Cedar Key are the juniper, long-leafed pine, and live-oak. All of the latter, living and dead, are heavily draped with tillandsia, like those of Bonaventure. The leaf is oval, about two inches long, three fourths of an inch wide, glossy and dark green above, pale beneath. The trunk is usually much divided, and is extremely unwedgeable. The specimen on the opposite page* is growing in the dooryard of Mr. Hodgson's house. It is a grand old king, whose crown gleamed in the bright sky long ere the Spanish shipbuilders felled a single tree of this noble species.

The live-oaks of these keys divide empire with the long-leafed pine and palmetto, but in many places on the mainland there are large tracts exclusively occupied by them. Like the Bonaventure oaks they have the upper side of their main spreading branches thickly planted with ferns, grasses, small saw palmettos, etc. There is also a dwarf oak here, which forms dense thickets. The oaks of this key are not, like those of the Wisconsin openings, growing on grassy slopes, but stand, sunk to the shoulders, in flowering magnolias, heathworts, etc.

During my long sojourn here as a convalescent I used to lie on my back for whole days beneath the ample arms of these great trees, listening to the winds and the birds. There is an extensive shallow on the coast, close by, which the receding tide exposes daily. This is the feeding-ground of thousands of waders of all sizes, plumage, and language, and they make a

*Of the original journal.

lively picture and noise when they gather at the great family board to eat their daily bread, so bountifully provided for them.

Their leisure in time of high tide they spend in various ways and places. Some go in large flocks to reedy margins about the islands and wade and stand about quarrelling or making sport, occasionally finding a stray mouthful to eat. Some stand on the mangroves of the solitary shore, now and then plunging into the water after a fish. Some go long journeys inland, up creeks and inlets. A few lonely old herons of solemn look and wing retire to favorite oaks. It was my delight to watch those old white sages of immaculate feather as they stood erect drowsing away the dull hours between tides, curtained by long skeins of tillandsia. White-bearded hermits gazing dreamily from dark caves could not appear more solemn or more becomingly shrouded from the rest of their fellow beings.

One of the characteristic plants of these keys is the Spanish bayonet, a species of yucca, about eight or ten feet in height, and with a trunk three or four inches in diameter when full grown. It belongs to the lily family and develops palmlike from terminal buds. The stout leaves are very rigid, sharp-pointed and bayonet-like. By one of these leaves a man might be as seriously stabbed as by an army bayonet, and woe to the luckless wanderer who dares to urge his way through these armed gardens after dark. Vegetable cats of many species will rob him of his clothes and claw his flesh, while dwarf palmettos will saw his bones, and the bayonets will glide to his joints and marrow without the smallest consideration for Lord Man.

The climate of these precious islets is simply warm summer and warmer summer, corresponding in time with winter and summer in the North. The weather goes smoothly over the points of union betwixt the twin summers. Few of the storms are very loud or variable. The average temperature during the day, in December, was about sixty-five degrees in the shade, but on one day a little damp snow fell.

Cedar Key is two and one half or three miles in diameter and its highest point is forty-four feet above mean tide-water. It is surrounded by scores of other keys, many of them looking like a clump of palms, arranged like a tasteful bouquet, and placed in the sea to be kept fresh. Others have quite a sprinkling of oaks and junipers, beautifully united with vines. Still others consist of shells, with a few grasses and mangroves, circled with a rim of rushes. Those which have sedgy margins furnish a favorite retreat for countless waders and divers, especially for the pelicans that frequently whiten the shore like a ring of foam.

It is delightful to observe the assembling of these feathered people from the woods and reedy isles; herons white as wave-tops, or blue as the sky, winnowing the warm air on wide quiet wing; pelicans coming with baskets to fill, and the multitude of smaller sailors of the air, swift as swallows, gracefully taking their places at Nature's family table for their daily bread. Happy birds!

The mockingbird is graceful in form and a fine singer, plainly dressed, rather familiar in habits, frequently coming like robins to door-sills for crumbs—a noble fellow, beloved by everybody. Wild geese are abundant in winter, associated with brant, some species of which I have never seen in the North. Also great flocks of robins, mourning doves, bluebirds, and the delightful brown thrashers. A large number of the smaller birds are fine singers. Crows, too, are here, some of them cawing with a foreign accent. The common bob-white quail I observed as far south as middle Georgia.

Lime Key, sketched on the opposite page, is a fair specimen of the Florida keys on this part of the coast. A fragment of cactus, *Opuntia*, sketched on another page,* is from the above-named key, and is abundant there. The fruit, an inch in length, is gathered, and made into a sauce, of which some people are fond. This species forms thorny, impenetrable thickets. One joint that I measured was fifteen inches long.

The mainland of Florida is less salubrious than the islands, but no portion of this coast, nor of the flat border which sweeps from Maryland to Texas, is quite free from malaria. All the inhabitants of this region, whether black or white, are liable to be prostrated by the ever-present fever and ague, to

---

*Of the original journal.

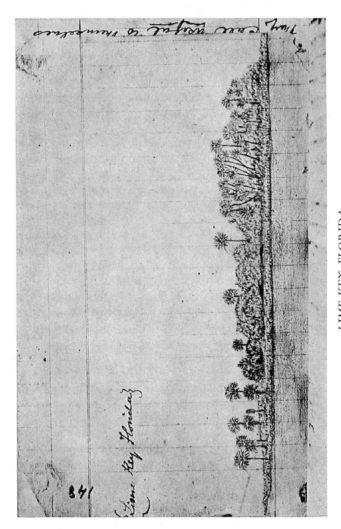

LIME KEY, FLORIDA
From Mr. Muir's sketch in the original journal

say nothing of the plagues of cholera and yellow fever that come and go suddenly like storms, prostrating the population and cutting gaps in it like hurricanes in woods.

The world, we are told, was made especially for man—a presumption not supported by all the facts. A numerous class of men are painfully astonished whenever they find anything, living or dead, in all God's universe, which they cannot eat or render in some way what they call useful to themselves. They have precise dogmatic insight of the intentions of the Creator, and it is hardly possible to be guilty of irreverence in speaking of *their* God any more than of heathen idols. He is regarded as a civilized, law-abiding gentleman in favor either of a republican form of government or of a limited monarchy; believes in the literature and language of England; is a warm supporter of the English constitution and Sunday schools and missionary societies; and is as purely a manufactured article as any puppet of a half-penny theater.

With such views of the Creator it is, of course, not surprising that erroneous views should be entertained of the creation. To such properly trimmed people, the sheep, for example, is an easy problem—food and clothing "for us," eating grass and daisies white by divine appointment for this predestined purpose, on perceiving the demand for wool that would be occasioned by the eating of the apple in the Garden of Eden.

In the same pleasant plan, whales are storehouses of oil for us, to help out the stars in lighting our dark ways until the discovery of the Pennsylvania oil wells. Among plants, hemp, to say nothing of the cereals, is a case of evident destination for ships' rigging, wrapping packages, and hanging the wicked. Cotton is another plain case of clothing. Iron was made for hammers and ploughs, and lead for bullets; all intended for us. And so of other small handfuls of insignificant things.

But if we should ask these profound expositors of God's intentions, How about those man-eating animals—lions, tigers, alligators—which smack their lips over raw man? Or about those myriads of noxious insects that destroy labor and drink his blood? Doubtless man was intended for food and drink for all these? Oh, no! Not at all! These are unresolvable difficulties connected with Eden's apple and the Devil. Why does water drown its lord? Why do so many minerals poison him? Why are so many plants and fishes deadly enemies? Why is the lord of creation subjected to the same laws of life as his subjects? Oh, all these things are satanic, or in some way connected with the first garden.

Now, it never seems to occur to these far-seeing teachers that Nature's object in making animals and plants might possibly be first of all the happiness of each one of them, not the creation of all for the happiness of one. Why should man value himself as more than a small part of the one great unit of creation? And what creature of all that the Lord has taken the pains to make is not essential to the completeness of that unit—the cosmos? The universe would be incomplete without man; but it would also be incomplete without the smallest transmicroscopic creature that dwells beyond our conceitful eyes and knowledge.

From the dust of the earth, from the common elementary fund, the Creator has made *Homo sapiens.* From the same material he has made every other creature, however noxious and insignificant to us. They are earth-born companions and our fellow mortals. The fearfully good, the orthodox, of this laborious patchwork of modern civilization cry "Heresy" on every one whose sympathies reach a single hair's breadth beyond the boundary epidermis of our own species. Not content with taking all of earth, they also claim the celestial country as the only ones who possess the kind of souls for which that imponderable empire was planned.

This star, our own good earth, made many a successful journey around the heavens ere man was made, and whole kingdoms of creatures enjoyed existence and returned to dust ere man appeared to claim them. After human beings have also played their part in Creation's plan, they too may disappear without any general burning or extraordinary commotion whatever.

Plants are credited with but dim and uncertain sensation, and minerals with positively none at all. But why may not even a mineral arrangement of matter be endowed with sensation of a kind that we in our blind exclusive perfection can have no manner of communication with?

But I have wandered from my object. I stated a page or two back that man claimed the earth was made for him, and I was going to say that venomous beasts, thorny plants, and deadly diseases of certain parts of the earth prove that the whole world was not made for him. When an animal from a tropical climate is taken to high latitudes, it may perish of cold, and we say that such an animal was never intended for so severe a climate. But when man betakes himself to sickly parts of the tropics and perishes, he cannot see that he was never intended for such deadly climates. No, he will rather accuse the first mother of the cause of the difficulty, though she may never have seen a fever district; or will consider it a providential chastisement for some self-invented form of sin.

Furthermore, all uneatable and uncivilizable animals, and all plants which carry prickles, are deplorable evils which, according to closet researches of clergy, require the cleansing chemistry of universal planetary combustion. But more than aught else mankind requires burning, as being in great part wicked, and if that transmundane furnace can be so applied and regulated as to smelt and purify us into conformity with the rest of the terrestrial creation, then the tophetization of the erratic genus Homo were a consummation devoutly to be prayed for. But, glad to leave these ecclesiastical fires and blunders, I joyfully return to the immortal truth and immortal beauty of Nature.

from A Thousand-Mile Walk to the Gulf, 1916

Save the Redwoods

W E ARE often told that the world is going from bad to worse, sacrificing everything to mammon. But this righteous uprising in defense of God's trees in the midst of exciting politics and wars is telling a different story, and every Sequoia, I fancy, has heard the good news and is waving its branches for joy. The wrongs done to trees, wrongs of every sort, are done in the darkness of ignorance and unbelief, for when light comes the heart of the people is always right. Forty-seven years ago one of these Calaveras King Sequoias was laboriously cut down, that the stump might be had for a dancing-floor. Another, one of the finest in the grove, more than three hundred feet high, was skinned alive to a height of one hundred and sixteen feet from the ground and the bark sent to London to show how fine and big that Calaveras tree was—as sensible a scheme as skinning our great men would be to prove their greatness. This grand tree is of course dead, a ghastly disfigured ruin, but it still stands erect and holds forth its majestic arms as if alive and saying, "Forgive them; they know not what they do." Now some millmen want to cut all the Calaveras trees into lumber and money. But we have found a better use for them. No doubt these trees would make good lumber after passing through a sawmill, as George Washington after passing through the hands of a French cook would have made good food. But both for Washington and the tree that bears his name higher uses have been found.

Could one of these Sequoia kings come to town in all its god-like majesty so as to be strikingly seen and allowed to plead its own cause, there would never again be any lack of defenders. And the same may be said of all the other Sequoia groves and forests of the Sierra with their companions and the noble *Sequoia sempervirens*, or redwood, of the coast mountains.

In a general view we find that the *Sequoia gigantea*, or Big Tree, is distributed in a widely interrupted belt along the west flank of the Sierra, from a small grove on the middle fork of the American River to the head of Deer Creek, a distance of about two hundred and sixty miles, at an elevation of about five thousand to a little over eight thousand feet above the sea. From the American River grove to the forest on Kings River the species occurs only in comparatively small isolated patches or groves so sparsely distributed along the belt that three of the gaps in it are from forty to sixty miles wide. From Kings River southward the Sequoia is not restricted to mere groves, but extends across the broad rugged basins of the Kaweah and Tule rivers in majestic forests a distance of nearly seventy miles, the continuity of this portion of the belt being but slightly broken save by the deep cañons.

In these noble groves and forests to the southward of the Calaveras Grove the axe and saw have long been busy, and thousands of the finest Sequoias have been felled, blasted into manageable dimensions, and sawed into lumber by methods destructive almost beyond belief, while fires have spread still wider and more lamentable ruin. In the course of my explorations twenty-five years ago, I found five sawmills located on or near the lower margin of the Sequoia belt, all of which were cutting more or less Big Tree lumber, which looks like the redwood of the coast, and was sold as redwood. One of the smallest of these mills in the season of 1874 sawed two million feet of Sequoia lumber. Since that time other mills have been built among the Sequoias, notably the large ones on Kings River and the head of the Fresno. The destruction of these grand trees is still going on.

On the other hand, the Calaveras Grove for forty years has been faithfully protected by Mr. Sperry, and with the exception of the two trees mentioned above is still in primeval beauty. The Tuolumne and Merced groves near Yosemite, the Dinky Creek grove, those of the General Grant National Park and the Sequoia National Park, with several outstanding groves that are nameless on the Kings, Kaweah, and Tule river basins, and included in the Sierra forest reservation, have of late years been partially protected by the Federal Government; while the well-known Mariposa Grove has long been guarded by the State.

For the thousands of acres of Sequoia forest outside of the reservation and national parks, and in the hands of lumbermen, no help is in sight. Probably more than three times as

many Sequoias as are contained in the whole Calaveras Grove
have been cut into lumber every year for the last twenty-six
years without let or hindrance, and with scarce a word of protest on the part of the public, while at the first whisper of the
bonding of the Calaveras Grove to lumbermen most everybody rose in alarm. This righteous and lively indignation on
the part of Californians after the long period of deathlike apathy, in which they have witnessed the destruction of other
groves unmoved, seems strange until the rapid growth that
right public opinion has made during the last few years is
considered and the peculiar interest that attaches to the Calaveras giants. They were the first discovered and are best
known. Thousands of travelers from every country have come
to pay them tribute of admiration and praise, their reputation
is world-wide, and the names of great men have long been
associated with them—Washington, Humboldt, Torrey and
Gray, Sir Joseph Hooker, and others. These kings of the forest, the noblest of a noble race, rightly belong to the world,
but as they are in California we cannot escape responsibility
as their guardians. Fortunately the American people are equal
to this trust, or any other that may arise, as soon as they see
it and understand it.

Any fool can destroy trees. They cannot defend themselves
or run away. And few destroyers of trees ever plant any; nor
can planting avail much toward restoring our grand aboriginal
giants. It took more than three thousand years to make some
of the oldest of the Sequoias, trees that are still standing in
perfect strength and beauty, waving and singing in the mighty
forests of the Sierra. Through all the eventful centuries since
Christ's time, and long before that, God has cared for these
trees, saved them from drought, disease, avalanches, and a
thousand storms; but he cannot save them from sawmills and
fools; this is left to the American people. The news from
Washington is encouraging. On March third [1905?] the
House passed a bill providing for the Government acquisition
of the Calaveras giants. The danger these Sequoias have been
in will do good far beyond the boundaries of the Calaveras
Grove, in saving other groves and forests, and quickening interest in forest affairs in general. While the iron of public sen-
timent is hot let us strike hard. In particular, a reservation or

national park of the only other species of Sequoia, the *sempervirens*, or redwood, hardly less wonderful than the *gigantea*, should be quickly secured. It will have to be acquired by gift or purchase, for the Government has sold every section of the entire redwood belt from the Oregon boundary to below Santa Cruz.

Sierra Club Bulletin, January 1920

Chronology

shore and countryside, exploring caves and Dunbar Castle, and playing war with friends. Twin sisters Mary and Annie are born in 1846. Father joins Campbellite Disciples of Christ and around the end of 1848 plans to migrate to Canada.

1849   Parents sell their house and property. Muir leaves with father, David, and Sarah for America on February 19 (mother remains in Scotland until new home is established). Father learns of a proposed canal in southern Wisconsin that would link the St. Lawrence Seaway with the Gulf of Mexico, providing wide markets for farmers, and decides to settle there. Buys 80-acre tract of isolated land by a small lake in Marquette County, Wisconsin, near the Fox River; names it Fountain Lake Farm and constructs a shanty as temporary housing. Muir spends much of the summer stalking local wildlife and roaming the nearby forest, meadows, streams, and lake; later writes: "I was set down in the midst of pure wildness where every object excited endless admiration and wonder." With hired help, father clears the area, plants crops, and by the end of October completes eight-room, two-and-a-half-story house. Mother arrives in November with Margaret, Dan, Mary, and Annie.

1850–54   Sister Joanna is born in 1850. Required by father to work on the farm up to 16 hours a day, Muir labors nearly every day of the year but the Sabbath, and except for brief periods his formal schooling ends. Leaves the farm only rarely, traveling occasionally to Portage, 16 miles away, to help get supplies. Feels increasingly trapped by father's cruel discipline and constant religious discourse, finding relief only when father is away distributing religious books or delivering sermons as an itinerant preacher. Chosen in autumn of 1854 to help build a corduroy road through the township along with young Scots immigrants David Gray and David Taylor, Muir comes to share their taste for poetry. "I remember as a great and sudden discovery that the poetry of the Bible, Shakespeare, and Milton was a source of inspiring, exhilarating, uplifting pleasure," he later writes, "and I became anxious to know all the poets, and saved up small sums to buy as many of their books as possible." Reads voraciously in his spare time, including histories, ancient classics, the works of Scott, Burns, Cow-

per, and others, borrowing some of the books from neighbors. Father disapproves of most non-religious books, and
mother and siblings help Muir to conceal this reading
from him.

1855–59   Finds little time to read before his prescribed bedtime and
gains father's permission to rise early; begins getting up at
1 A.M. to study until dawn. With soil fertility at Fountain
Lake Farm rapidly diminishing, father buys a new tract of
land nearby that he calls Hickory Hill. Work of clearing
the land, plowing, planting crops, and establishing a new
home falls primarily upon Muir. Without water nearby,
Muir is also assigned to dig a well and spends months
chiseling away at a vein of sandstone. When the well
reaches 80 feet, he is overcome by carbon dioxide and
pulled unconscious from the hole; soon recovers and returns to digging, but the incident leaves him with a permanent throat irritation. In winter, when it is too cold to
read in early hours without the use of firewood, Muir
tinkers in cellar with father's tools and some of his own
design. Having constructed miniature waterwheels and
windmills at Fountain Lake Farm, he turns to more elaborate designs; creates numerous devices including a self-
setting sawmill, complex clocks, thermometers, an
"early-rising machine" (a bed balanced on a fulcrum and
connected to a clock that tilts to a 45-degree angle at a
given hour, tipping the sleeper to his feet), and a "field
thermometer" large enough to be read from the surrounding hills and able to measure the increase in temperature caused by a person approaching within about five
feet of it.

1860   At urging of neighbor William Duncan, Muir decides
(against his father's wishes) to exhibit at the State Agricultural Fair in Madison in September; exhibits clocks and
a thermometer fashioned from a washboard whose sensi-
tivity is equal to that of his larger field thermometer, and
demonstrates his early-rising machine. Meets Jeanne Smith
Carr, a judge of the exhibits, whose husband teaches
science at the nearby University of Wisconsin. Receives
honorarium of $15 and is commended as "a genius" by
the judges. Accepts offer of employment from fellow ex-
hibitor Norman Wiard, who claims to have invented a

steam-powered iceboat capable of operating on a frozen river. Travels with Wiard to Prairie du Chien in fall; while caring for the boat, supports himself by tending livestock and doing chores in return for board at a local hotel. Wiard's boat proves a failure, and Muir receives little of the formal training in mechanical drawing he had been promised.

1861   Returns to Madison in January hoping to enroll at the University of Wisconsin. Finds only small jobs as a coachman and assistant to an insurance agent. Learning that it is possible to attend classes with little money by boarding oneself, Muir quits jobs and gains admission during spring semester. Takes geology and chemistry classes with Ezra Slocum Carr, Jeanne Carr's husband, and is exposed for the first time to precepts and empirical methods of science. Studies Latin and Greek with James Davie Butler. Invents a study desk that retrieves a book, holds it in place for reading for a period of time, and then automatically replaces it with another. Subsists on a sparse diet, sometimes only graham mush and an occasional potato. Walks the 35 miles home to work on family farm during summer. Returns to classes in fall, but lack of money soon forces him to suspend his education. Takes job during winter as a district school teacher 10 miles south of Madison.

1862   Returns to classes in spring with new confidence, having won local renown as lecturer and science teacher. Introduced by fellow student Milton S. Griswold to botany, in which he becomes keenly interested. During summer vacation works at Fountain Lake Farm, now owned by sister Sarah and husband David Galloway. Uses free time to collect, catalog, and classify specimens of local plant life. With his acceptance of scientific methodology, Muir grows further away from father's religious beliefs and the two find it increasingly difficult to get along.

1863   Depressed by the Civil War, wants nothing to do with the conflict; makes plans to attend medical school and become a doctor, but by spring the war threatens to disrupt them. "This war seems farther from a close than ever," he writes. "How strange that a country with so many schools and churches should be desolated by so unsightly a monster." Takes extended botanical trip in summer, traveling down the Wisconsin River, across the Mississippi, and roaming along the Iowa Bluffs before returning home. Lives with Sarah and David Galloway over fall and winter.

1864   A new draft order is signed by President Lincoln, to become effective in March. Muir takes a train heading north on March 1; walks through part of Michigan and crosses Canadian border, seeking to lose himself in the forests and swamps surrounding Lake Huron. Spends summer tramping along an unplanned, zigzagging route through the islands and inland swamps near Lake Huron and Georgian Bay; collects botanical samples. Lives for a time with a family of Scots immigrants, doing chores in return for board; at other times camps outdoors. In June, deeply moved when he comes upon the rare white orchid *Calypso borealis* alone next to a stream in deep woods: "I never before saw a plant so full of life; so perfectly spiritual," he later writes, "it seemed pure enough for the throne of its Creator. I felt as if I were in the presence of superior beings who loved me and beckoned me to come. I sat down beside them and wept for joy." Travels to Niagara Falls in September to meet brother Dan, who had fled to Canada in 1862. Continues traveling, eventually stopping at Meaford on the southern end of Georgian Bay where he and Dan take jobs at Trout and Jay woodworking factory for winter.

1865   Works as machinist at the factory. In free time continues collecting and naming plant species. When asked to teach a Sunday school class in the community, offers his students instruction in botany instead of the Bible as a means of understanding creation. With few people to talk to about nature, writes to Ezra Carr, his former professor; Carr's wife, Jeanne, responds and the two begin a correspondence that will last for the next decade. Brother Dan returns to the United States in May after the war ends, and Muir's loneliness deepens. Without money and uncertain of his future direction, signs contract in September to use his inventing talents to increase Trout and Jay's productivity; agrees to produce 30,000 broom handles and 12,000 rakes, in return for half the profits. Working 18-hour days, Muir succeeds in increasing output; invents a self-feeding lathe and other automatic devices to improve production of rakes.

1866   Has completed broom handles and 6,000 rakes, but not
            yet been paid, when the factory is destroyed by a fire in
            March. Declining offer of a partnership in return for help-
            ing to rebuild the plant, accepts a note for $200 and a
            small amount of cash and returns to the United States.
            Wanders through New York, Ohio, Indiana, and Illinois
            before stopping in Indianapolis, where he finds work as a
            sawyer at Osgood, Smith & Co., a factory making wagon
            parts. Is quickly promoted to supervisor and spends long
            hours tinkering with gadgets and machines, but regrets
            suspending his studies of nature and botany.

1867   Working late at night on the factory's belt system in early
            March, Muir loses his grip on a file, which flies up and
            pierces his right eye, temporarily blinding it; loses sight in
            left eye from sympathetic nervous shock. Although vision
            in the left eye returns quickly and vision is restored in the
            right eye over the next several weeks, the incident causes
            Muir to reconsider his priorities. While recuperating with
            family during summer, decides "to make and take one
            more grand sabbath day three years long," a trip "suffi-
            cient to lighten and brighten my after life in the gloom
            and hunger of civilization's defrauding duties." Intending
            to go to South America to botanize, takes train from In-
            dianapolis to Louisville in September and from there walks
            to the Gulf of Mexico; carries with him in a waterproof
            bag the New Testament, Milton's *Paradise Lost*, a collec-
            tion of Robert Burns' poems, and a journal he will keep
            on the trip (posthumously published in 1916 as *A Thou-
            sand-Mile Walk to the Gulf*). Tramps through Kentucky
            into the Cumberland Mountains of Tennessee, then con-
            tinues into Georgia. Arrives in Savannah and camps for
            nearly a week in a cemetery in nearby Bonneville, subsist-
            ing on crackers and stale water. Travels by boat for Fer-
            nandina, Florida, then walks from the Atlantic Coast
            southwest across the state to the Gulf. In Cedar Keys,
            while waiting for a boat to Galveston, Texas, takes a job
            at a local sawmill. Several days later, is stricken with fever
            and remains bedridden for several weeks, desperately ill, at
            the home of the mill's owner.

1868   Altering his plans, takes a schooner to Havana in January
            and spends nearly a month exploring the harbor and coast-
            line surrounding the city; still too weak to investigate

mountains of the interior, decides to return to a more northerly climate. Takes an orange boat to New York in February, but feels overwhelmed by the size of the city and its crowds. Travels to California by steamer in March by way of the Isthmus of Panama, arriving in San Francisco at the end of the month; decides to remain in California for a few months before re-embarking for South America. Spends summer wandering through the Central Valley region; investigates local plant life and works at odd jobs, including breaking horses, shearing sheep, and serving as a farm laborer. In autumn, takes a job as a shepherd for 1,800 sheep.

1869   Returns to the valley in spring and contracts as chief shepherd with Patrick Delaney; follows his flock into the Sierra Nevada mountains in search of good grazing. Continues into the high country and eventually into the Yosemite Valley, where he explores the region thoroughly for the first time. Returns to the low country as fall approaches and works on Delaney's ranch; goes back to Yosemite in November. Contracts with James Hutchings, one of the valley's original white settlers, to build and operate a sawmill on condition that no living trees will be cut. Becomes a good friend of Hutchings' wife, Elvira Sproat Hutchings, who shares an interest in botany.

1870   Muir continues to operate the sawmill, using Sundays to explore the valley. Maintains correspondence with Jeanne Carr, now living in Oakland where Ezra is teaching at University of California. When she begins directing important persons to the Yosemite with notes to Muir requesting that he guide them through the valley, he becomes known to a wider circle. Finds himself embroiled in scientific controversy over the geologic origins of the Yosemite area when his theory that glaciers were responsible for carving out the area's landscape is contradicted by California state geologist Josiah D. Whitney, who holds random catastrophic forces responsible; wins many converts to his theory while leading tours of the region.

1871   Ralph Waldo Emerson arrives in Yosemite on vacation in May. Initially too timid to approach him, Muir leaves a note at Emerson's hotel: "I invite you to join me in a month's worship with Nature in the high temples of the great Sierra Crown beyond our holy Yosemite." Emerson declines Muir's repeated offers to join him on a camping trip but does meet Muir at his cabin near Yosemite Falls and tours parts of the valley with him. In late summer Muir quits his job at the mill in order to devote more time to his search for evidence of glacial activity (he eventually succeeds in finding a small living glacier high in the mountains). Urged to publish the results by Clinton L. Merriam (a New York congressman interested in geology) and John Daniel Runkle (president of Massachusetts Institute of Technology), he adapts several of his letters about glaciers into article form. His first published essay, "Yosemite Glaciers," appears in the *New-York Tribune* in December.

1872   Spends winter working on his writing, putting together accounts of life and nature in the Yosemite. *The Overland Monthly*, a California literary magazine, publishes "Yosemite Valley in Flood" (April), "Twenty Hill Hollow" (July), and "Living Glaciers of California" (December). Despite his accomplishment, Muir confronts a growing loneliness. "In all God's mountain mansions," he writes, "I find no human sympathy, and I hunger." Through Jeanne Carr, in October meets artist William Keith, with whom he forms close friendship. Travels to San Francisco near the end of the year; spends two weeks visiting the Carrs and other friends, and meets a host of celebrated literary figures. Returning to Yosemite, goes into the mountains and embarks on extended exploration of Tenaya Canyon.

1873   By April is working on 15 different articles; becomes a regular contributor to *The Overland Monthly*, which publishes an article on his Tenaya trip in April, a piece on Hetch Hetchy Valley in July, and another on the Tuolumne Canyon in August. He embarks on another extended exploration, this time intending to investigate the entire length of the Sierra. On returning late in the year, he leaves again for Oakland to pursue his writing during the winter.

1874   Resides at the home of friend J. B. McChesney, Oakland superintendent of schools, whom he met through Jeanne Carr. Grows more accustomed to life in civilization, delighting in old friendships and attending occasional social affairs. At the Carrs', meets Louie Wanda Strentzel, 27-

year-old daughter of Louisiana Irwin Strentzel and Dr. John Theophil Strentzel, a Polish immigrant who owns a prosperous fruit farm near Martinez; she shares Muir's interest in botany. Also forms close friendship with State Superintendent of Schools John Swett and his wife, Mary Tracy Swett. Muir completes the last of his glacier articles for *The Overland Monthly* in September and returns briefly to Yosemite. Although pleased to be in the wild again, finds that he no longer feels at home: "No one of the rocks seems to call me now," he writes to Jeanne Carr, "nor any of the distant mountains. Surely this Merced and Tuolumne chapter of my life is done."

1875–79   Moves in with the Swetts; enjoys company of the couple and their four children and feels less lonely. In "God's First Temples: How Shall We Preserve Our Forests?" (published in the *Sacramento Record-Union*, February 1876), urges that the government take responsibility for the forests. Becomes a popular local lecturer, overcoming stage fright in order to preach the spiritual value of wilderness. Extends his wanderings farther during summer and fall of 1877, traveling to Utah and the mountains surrounding the Great Salt Lake, and later exploring the San Gabriel Mountains in the southern part of the state. Takes a river journey in fall, traveling down the Merced and the San Joaquin to the Sacramento; visits Strentzel household in Martinez. Sees them more frequently in spring of 1878 and considers marrying Louie. Travels to Nevada during summer; spends winter writing in San Francisco. In June 1879, shortly before he leaves on his first voyage to Alaska, Muir and Louie agree to marry upon his return. Spends six months in Alaska.

1880   On return journey, arrives in Portland in early January. Explores the Columbia and delivers several lectures in Portland, then spends two weeks in San Francisco before visiting the Strentzels in mid-February. Muir and Louie Strentzel marry on April 14 (her parents give them their house as a wedding gift and build another for themselves). Muir spends three months working on the farm, and in July departs again for Alaska; Louie, who is one month pregnant, remains at home. On the journey, Muir explores glaciers with missionary S. Hall Young; Young's dog, Stickeen, accompanies them, displaying intelligence and stubborn will that Muir admires despite his usual disdain for domesticated animals. On August 30, Muir and Stickeen find themselves trapped while exploring Taylor Glacier; they make a narrow escape on a thin band of ice stretching across a 70-foot chasm. Returns to Martinez to await the birth of his child.

1881–88   Daughter Anna Wanda (called Wanda) Muir is born on March 25, 1881. Muir leaves again for Alaska in May. On returning to Martinez in October, takes over responsibility for the farm and settles into a comfortable family life. Sharply curtails wilderness trips for several years, visiting Yosemite only briefly in 1884 and 1885, and does little writing. Father, who has lived apart from mother since 1874, dies in October 1885 with Muir at his bedside. Daughter Helen Muir is born on January 23, 1886; concerned about her fragile health, Muir rarely leaves the ranch for 18 months after her birth. Prodded by wife and friends to take up writing again, accepts offer to edit and contribute to proposed collection of California nature studies (published by the J. Dewing Co. as *Picturesque California* in 1888). Travels with William Keith to the Cascade Mountains in Washington in summer of 1888 and finds that forest destruction caused by commercial logging has grown more severe. Agrees with Louie to shed some of his responsibilities by selling and leasing portions of their land.

1889   Meets Robert Underwood Johnson, associate editor of the prestigious *Century* magazine, when he visits California in the spring. Travels with Johnson to Yosemite in early June to explore the valley and the high country along the Tuolumne River; they find substantial damage caused by lumbering, tourists, and grazing sheep. Johnson proposes creation of a national park to incorporate both the Yosemite Valley and the surrounding region. Muir agrees to write two articles for *The Century Magazine*, while Johnson undertakes to lobby for the park in Washington.

1890–91   Completes "The Treasures of the Yosemite" and "Features of the Proposed Yosemite National Park" for *The Century Magazine* by the early summer and embarks on another trip to Alaska. Articles (published in August and September 1890) help precipitate debate in Congress over the proposed park. Muir returns from Alaska in September in time to see Congress pass a bill creating a national park even larger than he himself had outlined (law goes into effect October 1). Muir's role in publicizing the park reinvigorates his literary career, and he continues to write and lobby for government protection of wilderness. Father-in-law John Strentzel dies in October 1890; Muir moves with family into the Strentzel home so mother-in-law will not be alone. Sister Margaret and husband John Reid settle in Martinez in 1891 and Reid takes over supervision of Muir's land.

1892   Approached by Henry Senger, a professor of philology at Berkeley, with the idea of forming a local club for mountain lovers, Muir agrees to meet with a small group of enthusiasts in late May, and they form the Sierra Club. Muir is elected president, a post he will hold for the rest of his life. With Muir granting newspaper interviews and sending telegrams to Washington, the club helps prevent passage of a bill in the Senate aimed at reducing Yosemite's boundaries.

1893–94   Plans trip to Europe with William Keith. Goes to New York in May and is introduced by Robert Underwood Johnson to New York society, meeting Mark Twain, Rudyard Kipling, Nicola Tesla, and John Burroughs, among others. During brief trip to Boston, Cambridge, and Concord, lays flowers on Thoreau's and Emerson's graves, visits Walden Pond, and meets Sarah Orne Jewett, Francis Parkman, and Josiah Royce. Embarks for Europe in late June; returns to Dunbar, his boyhood home in Scotland, then visits Norway, England, Switzerland, and Italy. After returning in fall goes to Washington, D.C., at his wife's suggestion to assess the new political situation. Accompanied by Johnson, visits Interior Secretary Hoke Smith and other persons influential in conservation policy. Back home, reworks essays first published 1875–81 for his first book (published in 1894 by Century Company as *The Mountains of California*). Sends first of what will become annual Christmas donations to cousin in Dunbar for distribution to the poor.

1896   Johnson, botanist Charles Sprague Sargent, and forester Gifford Pinchot persuade Hoke Smith to help create a public forest commission through the National Academy of Sciences, thus bypassing Congressional opposition. The six-man commission, including both Sargent and Pinchot, plans a tour of the nation's forest reserves during summer and asks Muir to join them as adviser. Muir visits mother in Portage in June, then goes to Cambridge to accept honorary degree from Harvard (will also receive honorary degrees from University of Wisconsin in 1897, Yale, 1911, and University of California, 1913). Mother dies on June 23. Joining the forest commission in Chicago, Muir travels with them through South Dakota, Wyoming, Montana, Washington, Oregon, and California, and to the Grand Canyon in Arizona and the forest reserves of Colorado. Having observed the poor condition of many forests, commission members agree that more formal protection is necessary, but differ on the means to use. Muir follows Sargent in arguing that forest reserves should be inviolate, and that their protection should be under the control of the Army, and thus outside the corrupting influence of politics; Pinchot favors less severe restrictions, arguing for regulated use along guidelines established by a professional forest service.

1897   The forestry commission releases a preliminary version of its report to President Grover Cleveland in February, calling for the creation of 13 new reserves. Just prior to leaving office, Cleveland approves these reserves and places more than 21 million acres under federal protection. Outraged western politicians attempt to reverse the action in Congress, but their effort stalls and the debate continues. Muir campaigns for wilderness protection; sends letters to politicians and helps organize the Sierra Club to lobby for the reserves. Writes story about Stickeen for *The Century Magazine* (published in September as "An Adventure With a Dog and a Glacier"). Annoyed that Robert Johnson has abridged the piece, Muir agrees to write articles for *The Atlantic Monthly*; the first, "The American Forests" (August), is an impassioned plea for the protection of America's wilderness. Congress suspends all but two of the new reserves in June. With Sargent and botanist William Canby, Muir takes brief trip to Alaska in August. Later that summer, on Pinchot's recommendation, the new Secretary of the Interior, Cornelius Bliss, allows the grazing of sheep in the Oregon and Washington reserves; Muir and Sargent, who had helped to launch Pinchot's

career, feel betrayed. Mother-in-law Louisiana Strentzel
dies.

1898   Second *Atlantic Monthly* article, "Wild Parks and Forest
        Reservations of the West" (January), helps to ignite public
        sympathy for the forest reserves; a renewed effort to abol-
        ish President Cleveland's reserves in March fails in Con-
        gress. Muir travels with Sargent through North Carolina
        and Tennessee, revisiting part of the route he had traveled
        on his 1867 walk to the Gulf of Mexico. Spends late fall
        roaming about New England and parts of Canada. Tours
        Washington, D.C., and travels to Florida, where he visits
        several friends.

1899   Participates in summer expedition to Alaska organized by
        New York financier and railroad magnate Edward H. Har-
        riman. At first mistrustful of Harriman, Muir comes to
        admire him during the voyage and the two become
        friends. The expedition, which includes more than 20 sci-
        entists, travels along the Alaska coastline, stopping occa-
        sionally to explore glaciers and conduct experiments.

1900–2 Enjoys visits from friends made on Alaska expedition, in-
        cluding biologist C. Hart Merriam and geographer Henry
        Gannett. Finishes last of ten articles for *Atlantic Monthly*
        and prepares them for book version (published 1901 by
        Houghton Mifflin as *Our National Parks*). Leads first of
        annual trips to the mountains sponsored by the Sierra
        Club, guiding nearly 100 club members around Yosemite
        for a month.

1903–4 Agrees to guide President Theodore Roosevelt on a trip
        through the Sierra high country; joins Roosevelt in May
        in San Francisco and travels with him to Yosemite. Spurn-
        ing a banquet organized by local politicians and park of-
        ficials, Roosevelt instead spends three nights camping
        alone with Muir; they explore Glacier Point, the head of
        Nevada Falls, and other points. Roosevelt departs Yosem-
        ite persuaded that the federal government should assume
        full control of the park. Muir accompanies Sargent in sum-
        mer 1903 on a trip to Europe and Asia; they travel through
        Paris and on to Finland and Russia. After exploring Siberia
        and then sailing to Shanghai, Muir parts company with
        Sargent in order to visit India; from there, takes a steam-

ship to Egypt where he sees the pyramids and journeys up the Nile. Takes a southerly route home through the Far East, stopping along the way to visit Australia, New Zealand, the Philippines, China, Japan, and Hawaii. Arrives in San Francisco near the end of May 1904.

1905–6   At Muir's request, William Colby, a lawyer belonging to the Sierra Club, drafts a bill to cede the Yosemite Valley back to federal control. Introduced in the state legislature in January 1905, the bill unleashes another round of debate. Muir makes several trips to Sacramento campaigning for the bill; appeals to Edward H. Harriman for help. With the aid of Harriman's railroad lobby, the bill passes in February. The struggle then moves to Congress, where its passage is delayed for another year. Muir again appeals to Harriman, who plays a critical role in ensuring the measure's success (Yosemite Valley is added officially to the national park in June 1906). Daughter Helen is stricken with pneumonia and on doctor's advice in May 1905 Muir takes her to Arizona to aid her recovery. Learns in late June that Louie is seriously ill and returns home; she dies on August 6, 1905, from a lung tumor. Grief-stricken, Muir is unable to write for the next year. Daughter Wanda marries Thomas Rae Hanna, a civil engineer who studied with her at Berkeley, in June 1906. Helen returns home in August.

1907–9   Learns that the city of San Francisco (with assistance from Gifford Pinchot and the new Secretary of the Interior, James Garfield) may succeed in an application to dam the Hetch Hetchy Valley (which lies within Yosemite National Park) in order to obtain water for the city. Muir and the Sierra Club launch a campaign to arouse public opinion against the dam, but fail to rally enough support. In May 1908, Garfield grants permission to dam the valley, subject to Congressional approval. Hetch Hetchy dam approval stalls in Congress due to adverse public opinion; new president William Howard Taft and Secretary of the Interior Richard A. Ballinger also help to delay the project. Taft and Ballinger visit Yosemite in October 1909; Muir, serving as presidential guide, takes the opportunity to argue that San Francisco could find alternative water supplies without violating the park's boundaries. *Stickeen*, published by Houghton Mifflin in March, becomes Muir's most popular book.

1910–12   Daughter Helen is married to Buell A. Funk, son of a cattle rancher. Muir stays for long visits with friends Katharine and John D. Hooker of Los Angeles and Henry F. Osborne and his family at Garrison's-on-the-Hudson. Revises his early Sierra journals (published by Houghton Mifflin in 1911 as *My First Summer in the Sierra*); completes the manuscripts for *The Yosemite* (published by Century Company in 1912) and *The Story of My Boyhood and Youth* (Houghton Mifflin, 1913). Saddened by death of close friend Willam Keith in April 1911. Decides to fulfill a lifelong dream by exploring the Amazon River. Ignoring protests of family and friends, he departs in August. Sails up the Amazon and investigates the surrounding forests, exploring lagoon at Rio Negro before returning to the mouth of the river. Sails down coast to Buenos Aires and takes train across continent to Santiago, Chile. Treks to Montevideo and boards ship bound for Africa, intent on locating and examining a baobab tree. Finds the trees near Victoria Falls ("one of the greatest of the great tree days of my lucky life"); journeys on to explore the Nile valley. Arrives back in New York in late March 1912.

1913   Muir once again campaigns to save Hetch Hetchy after President Woodrow Wilson appoints dam supporter Franklin K. Lane as Secretary of the Interior. Writes letters and newspaper articles and rallies Sierra Club to defeat the proposal; the effort begins to take a toll on Muir, and he falls ill several times. With the new administration backing the proposal, a bill granting San Francisco permission to dam Hetch Hetchy passes Congress in December (Muir later writes to a friend: "it is a monumental mistake, but it is more, it is a monumental crime").

1914   Hampered by failing health, attempts to finish account of his Alaska journeys (published posthumously by Houghton Mifflin as *Travels in Alaska* in 1915). Visits daughter Helen in Daggett in December; develops pneumonia and on December 23 is admitted to California Hospital in Los Angeles. Dies December 24. Buried in family plot on the Martinez ranch.

Note on the Texts

This volume presents the texts of four books by John Muir, *The Story of My Boyhood and Youth* (1913), *My First Summer in the Sierra* (1911), *The Mountains of California* (1894), and *Stickeen* (1909), followed by a selection of 18 essays, 16 of which were published between 1871 and 1912 and two of which were published posthumously.

The Story of My Boyhood and Youth is a memoir of the years 1838 to 1863. Muir was persuaded to dictate his recollections to a stenographer while visiting with his friend Edward H. Harriman in August 1908, and several years later he drew on the resulting typescript to compose his memoir. It was published by Houghton Mifflin Company in March 1913. Portions of the memoir appeared in *The Atlantic Monthly* (Nov. 1912–Feb. 1913), and before the book came out Muir received a letter from a childhood friend who objected to a passage concerning the cruelty of his father. To spare his friend's feelings, Muir revised the section; the changes were not received by Houghton Mifflin in time for the first printing but were made in all subsequent ones. This volume presents the text of the 1913 first printing; Muir's revisions are shown in the notes.

My First Summer in the Sierra is an account of Muir's 1869 stay in the Yosemite and its environs. Muir used part of his 1869 journal as the basis for the book, but he significantly revised and rearranged it, adding episodes that occurred in later years. It was published by Houghton Mifflin Company in 1911. The text printed here is of the Houghton Mifflin first edition.

In writing *The Mountains of California*, his first book, Muir drew on 18 essays published between 1875 and 1882. He revised and wove together the essays, adding new material primarily for Chapters I and XII. Chapter II is based on "Living Glaciers of California" (*Harper's Monthly Magazine*, Nov. 1875); Chapter III on "Snow Banners of the California Alps" (*Harper's Monthly Magazine*, July 1877); Chapter IV on "In the Heart of the California Alps" (*Scribner's Monthly*, July 1880); Chapter V on "The Passes of the Sierra" (*Scribner's Monthly*, Feb. 1879); Chapter VI on "The Mountain Lakes of California" (*Scribner's Monthly*, Jan. 1879); Chapter VII on "The Glacier Meadows of the Sierra" (*Scribner's Monthly*, Feb. 1879); Chapter VIII on "On the Post-Glacial History of Sequoia Gigantea" (*Proceedings of the American Association for the Advancement of Science*, Salem, Mass., May 1877), "The New Sequoia Forests of California" (*Harper's Monthly Magazine*, Nov. 1878), and "Coniferous Forests of the Sierra Nevada" (*Scribner's Monthly*, Sept.–Oct. 1881); Chapter IX on

"The Douglass Squirrel of California," (*Scribner's Monthly*, Dec. 1878); Chapter X on "A Wind-Storm in the Forests of the Yuba" (*Scribner's Monthly*, Nov. 1878); Chapter XI on "Flood-Storm in the Sierra" (*The Overland Monthly*, June 1875); Chapter XIII on "The Humming-Bird of the California Water-Falls" (*Scribner's Monthly*, Feb. 1878); Chapter XIV on "Wild Sheep of the Sierra," (*Scribner's Monthly*, May 1881); Chapter XV on "Summering in the Sierra: Ancient River Channels" (*San Francisco Daily Evening Bulletin*, July 26, 1876) and "Summering in the Sierra: A Sierra Cave" (*San Francisco Daily Evening Bulletin*, Aug. 12, 1876); and Chapter XVI on "The Bee-Pastures of California" (*The Century Magazine*, June–July 1882). The book was published by The Century Company in 1894. The text printed here is that of the first Century Company edition.

Stickeen is the story of Muir's experiences with a dog in 1880 at Taylor Bay, Alaska. He wrote about the dog Stickeen in his journal in August 1880 and in subsequent years often recounted the incident and made notes for a story about it. He continued to refine and enlarge the story after his first version appeared in *The Century Magazine* as "An Adventure With a Dog And a Glacier" (Sept. 1897). *Stickeen* was published by Houghton Mifflin in 1909 and became Muir's most popular book. The text printed here is of the first Houghton Mifflin edition.

The texts of the 18 essays included in this volume are arranged in the order of their initial appearances and are taken from their first publications, with the exceptions noted below. The following is a list of the sources:

"Yosemite Glaciers," *New-York Tribune*, December 5, 1871.

"Yosemite Valley in Flood," *The Overland Monthly*, April 1872.

"A Geologist's Winter Walk," *The Overland Monthly*, April 1873. (This was an excerpt from a letter to Jeanne Carr that she submitted for publication without Muir's knowledge.)

"Wild Wool," *The Overland Monthly*, April 1875.

"Flood-Storm in the Sierra," *The Overland Monthly*, June 1875 (later published in substantially revised form as Chapter XI, "The River Floods," in *The Mountains of California*).

"Living Glaciers of California," *Harper's Monthly Magazine*, November 1875 (later published in substantially revised form as Chapter II, "The Glaciers," in *The Mountains of California*).

"God's First Temples: How Shall We Preserve Our Forests?," *Sacramento Daily Union*, February 5, 1876. Courtesy of the John Muir Papers, Holt-Atherton Department of Special Collections, University of the Pacific Libraries.

"Snow-Storm on Mount Shasta," *Harper's Monthly Magazine*, September 1877.

"Alaska," *Picturesque California and the Region West of the Rocky Mountains, from Alaska to Mexico* (San Francisco and New York: The J. Dewing Company, 1888), an illustrated collection of travel writings by Muir and others, edited by Muir.

"Features of the Proposed Yosemite National Park," *The Century Magazine*, September 1890.

"The American Forests" first appeared in *The Atlantic Monthly*, August 1897, and was revised by Muir for Chapter X of *Our National Parks* (Boston: Houghton Mifflin Company, 1901), a collection of his essays. The text presented in this volume is taken from *Our National Parks*.

"The Wild Parks and Forest Reservations of the West" first appeared in *The Atlantic Monthly*, January 1898, and was revised by Muir for Chapter I of *Our National Parks*. The text presented in this volume is taken from *Our National Parks*.

"The Yellowstone National Park" first appeared in *The Atlantic Monthly*, April 1898, and was revised by Muir for Chapter II of *Our National Parks*. The text presented in this volume is taken from *Our National Parks*.

"The Forests of the Yosemite Park" first appeared in *The Atlantic Monthly*, April 1900, and was revised by Muir for Chapter IV of *Our National Parks*. The text presented in this volume is taken from *Our National Parks*.

"The Grand Cañon of the Colorado," *The Century Magazine*, November 1902.

"Hetch Hetchy Valley" appeared as Chapter XV of *The Yosemite* (New York: The Century Co., 1912), a collection of otherwise previously published essays by Muir. In writing "Hetch Hetchy Valley," a plea for the preservation of the valley, Muir drew on the closing section of his 1890 essay, "Features of the Proposed Yosemite National Park" (see above).

"Cedar Keys" appeared posthumously as Chapter VI of *A Thousand-Mile Walk to the Gulf* (Boston: Houghton Mifflin Company, 1916), edited by William Badè. The published version is drawn from the journal Muir kept during his 1867 walk from Indianapolis to the Gulf of Mexico. Muir had planned to publish his journal of the walk but died before he completed editing it; his friend Badè prepared the published version. A portion of Muir's original journal is printed in the notes to pages 825–27 of this volume.

"Save the Redwoods" was first published in the *Sierra Club Bulletin*, January 1920. The passage was found among Muir's papers after his death.

This volume presents the texts of the printings chosen for inclusion here but does not attempt to reproduce features of their typographic design. Spelling, punctuation, and capitalization often are expressive features and they are not altered, even when inconsistent or irregular. The following is a list of typographical errors corrected, cited by page and line number: 135.28, admirably,; 194.29, plant; 202.16, others; 244.35, Cathderal; 250.34, currus; 258.31, though; 437.23, *Marrayana*; 459.22, First; 578.24, hight; 582.31, as the; 586.18, of all; 586.33, death,; 595.20, "benmost bore"; 621.12, *coulairs*; 632.21, sheepmens'; 683.10, phosporescent; 683.36, Ranier; 734.21, ground; 744.11, snowy; 775.27, forest where.

Notes

In the notes below, the reference numbers denote page and line of this volume (the line count includes titles, headings, and captions). No note is made for material included in standard desk-reference books such as Webster's *Collegiate, Biographical,* and *Geographical* dictionaries. Biblical references are keyed to the King James Version. Footnotes in the text were in the originals. For further background and references to other studies, see: William Frederic Badè, *The Life and Letters of John Muir* (Boston: Houghton Mifflin Company, 1924); *John of the Mountains: The Unpublished Journals of John Muir,* ed. Linnie Marsh Wolfe (Boston: Houghton Mifflin Company, 1938); Linnie Marsh Wolfe, *Son of the Wilderness: The Life of John Muir* (New York: Alfred Knopf, 1945); Stephen Fox, *John Muir and His Legacy: The American Conservation Movement* (Boston: Little Brown and Company, 1981); Michael P. Cohen, *The Pathless Way: John Muir and the American Wilderness* (Madison: University of Wisconsin Press, 1984); Frederick Turner, *Rediscovering America: John Muir in His Time and Ours* (New York: Viking, 1985); William F. Kimes and Maymie B. Kimes, *John Muir: A Reading Bibliography* (Fresno: Panorama West Books, 1986).

The editor acknowledges Gregory Summers for his work in preparing the Chronology.

THE STORY OF MY BOYHOOD AND YOUTH

1.1–2   THE STORY . . . YOUTH]   Edward H. Harriman persuaded Muir to allow a stenographer to take down his recollections of his life during a visit to Harriman's Pelican Bay Lodge in Klamath Lake, Oregon, in August 1908. The resulting triple-spaced typescript was more than a thousand pages long, and this book, pared down as a series of episodes and published five years later, was the eventual result.

8.23   "Llewellyn's Dog,"]   Traditional story of Llewelyn the Great, prince of Wales, (d. 1240) and the greyhound given him by King John.

9.1–2   "The Inchcape Bell,"]   Actually, "The Inchcape Rock" (1802).

9.24–28   the keeper . . . medical school.]   William Hare, an Irishman living in Edinburgh, in 1827 sold the body of a person who died in his lodging house to Dr. Robert Knox, a prominent anatomist at the Edinburgh College of Surgeons, and then in 1828 with William Burke, his lodger, lured to the house and murdered, usually by suffocation, about 15 persons to procure more bodies for Knox; the doctor evidently did not inquire into the nature of the deaths. When one of the victims was traced to Hare's home the murderers were apprehended. Hare turned king's evidence and Burke was convicted of the murders and executed by hanging in 1829. Hare is believed to have fled to England to escape lynching.

15.8–9   Tam . . . witches]   In Robert Burns' "Tam o' Shanter" (1791).

29.11   Scotch ornithologist Wilson]   Alexander Wilson (1766–1813), known as the founder of American ornithology, immigrated to the United States in 1794, worked as a schoolteacher in New Jersey and Pennsylvania and, with William Bartram's encouragement, began the serious study of ornithology. His major work is *American Ornithology* (9 vols., 1808–14); he also wrote poetry, including *The Foresters* (1805), an account of his walk from Philadelphia to Niagara Falls and back.

32.34   Fort Winnebago]   Built 1828 near the site of present Portage, Wisconsin, and abandoned by the military in 1846. The Muir homestead was about 16 miles south of Portage, the closest town.

60.4–5   Fountain . . . Muir Lake]   At present John Muir Memorial Park in Columbia County, Wisconsin. Nothing remains of the original Muir farmstead.

60.38   "oak openings"]   Nineteenth-century phrase for oak savannahs in which prairie grasses mingled with widely separated trees, most commonly shagbark hickories and white and bur oaks.

66.40–67.1   The best . . . agley,"]   Cf. Robert Burns, "To a Mouse" (1785), stanza 7: "The best laid schemes o' Mice an' Men, / Gang aft agley."

78.22–23   passenger pigeons]   Passenger pigeons became extinct by 1920, and the last great nestings in Wisconsin took place in the 1870s, shortly after Muir arrived in California.

80.17   Pokagon's]   Simon Pokagon (1830–99), author of the posthumously published novel *O-gi-maw-kwe-ki Mit-i-gwa-ki (Queen of the Woods)* (1899), was the son of a Potawatomi chief. He studied at Oberlin College.

102.14   Todleben]   Russian military engineer Count Frants Eduard Ivanovich Totleben, or Todleben (1818–84).

102.17   terrible war]   The Crimean War (1853–56).

103.35–105.17   One of the saddest deaths . . . jaw.]   In later printings, Muir made changes in this section in deference to the sensibilities of a childhood friend who objected to the depiction of his father, the "blacksmith and preacher"; some of the changes are shown below.

103.37   blacksmith and preacher, etc.]   In later printings, this reads: "devout, severe puritan."

104.11–13   The brawny . . . shortcoming.]   In later printings, this reads: "His guardian brother, delighting in hard work and able for anything, was as remarkable for strength of body and mind as poor Charlie for childishness."

104.20   he ran away]   In later printings, "he ran gladly."

104.22   punishment]   In later printings, "illness."

104.24–25   was beaten every day]   In later printings, "was tired of life."

105.3–8   bring the reproach . . . brother then walked]   In later printings, this reads: "bring harm to religion. Though snatched from the lake to his bed, poor Charlie lived only a few days longer. A physician who was called when his health first became seriously impaired reported that he was suffering from Bright's disease. After all was over, the stoical brother walked."

105.15–17   in all that excessively . . . blacksmith's jaw.]   In later printings, this reads: "the brother who had faithfully cared for him controlled and concealed all his natural affection as incompatible with sound faith."

106.22–23   "they should take . . . who can,"]   Cf. "Rob Roy's Grave" (1807), lines 39–40.

118.5   Dick's "Christian Philosopher,"]   Thomas Dick (1774–1857) was a Scottish Secessionist minister who became a schoolteacher and author; the book (1823) is subtitled: *or the Connection of Science with Religion.*

123.22   Burns's wee mousie]   In "To a Mouse."

124.35   "All flesh is grass."]   Isaiah 40:6.

139.29   I invented a desk]   The desk-clock has been placed on permanent display at the State Historical Society of Wisconsin in Madison.

MY FIRST SUMMER IN THE SIERRA

147.1–2   MY FIRST . . . SIERRA]   For this book Muir significantly revised the diary that he kept during his first visit to the Yosemite and its environs in 1869, linking entries with carefully constructed transitional passages and adding episodes from other summers.

163.10–11   "wee, . . . beasties"]   Cf. Robert Burns, "To a Mouse," line 1.

179.24   "bank to brae."]   Robert Burns, "Winter": "While, tumbling brown, the Burn comes down, / And roars frae bank to brae"; a "burn" is a rivulet and a "brae," the slope of a hill.

198.22–23   Once I . . . Bonaventure graveyard]   During his walk to the Gulf of Mexico in 1867.

204.23–34   "He giveth his beloved sleep."]   Psalm 127:2.

213.36–37   Samson's riddle . . . sweetness."]   Cf. Judges 14:5–8, 14–18; the solution to the riddle is: "What is sweeter than honey? And what is stronger than a lion?"

239.6   "I sift . . . mountains below."]   "The Cloud," line 7.

249.11   Grip]   A parrot in Charles Dickens' *Barnaby Rudge* (1841).

250.9–10   Tenaya . . . company of soldiers]   Tenaya was chief of the Ah-wahneechee Indians who were removed from Yosemite in 1851; he was killed in 1853.

257.9   Professor J. D. Butler]   James Davie Butler was professor of classics. He helped to introduce Muir to the works of Emerson.

259.9   Mrs. Hutchings]   Elvira Hutchings, who became a close friend of Muir's.

259.34   General Alvord]   Benjamin Alvord (1813–84), a career soldier, was brevetted brigadier general of the Union Army in 1862 and served as paymaster general for the U.S. Army, 1872–80. He taught mathematics and physics at West Point early in his career, served in numerous conflicts, including the Seminole War, 1835–37, and was the author of many articles, notably on math and geography.

278.28–29   "still singing . . . for joy."]   Cf. Job 38:7.

282.11–13   "It's coming yet . . . a' that."]   From Burns' untitled song that begins: "The Honest Man the best of Men."

THE MOUNTAINS OF CALIFORNIA

311.1–2   THE MOUNTAINS OF CALIFORNIA]   This volume established Muir's reputation as a writer. In it, he revised and wove together essays that had been published previously in national periodicals such as *Scribner's Monthly*, its successor *The Century Magazine*, and *Harper's New Monthly Magazine*. For the 1911 printing, Muir added the following dedication: "To the Memory of Louiza Strentzel, this ninth edition of The Mountains of California is affectionately dedicated."

316.7   When I first]   In 1868.

318.28–31   miners . . . left their marks.]   The landscape was altered principally through placer mining, in which gold miners worked the gravel of Sierra streambeds and river valleys by hand, using water to wash away earth and gravel from the gold they hoped to find in their pans and sluices. Placer mining created pits in gravel beds, but far more devastating was hydraulic mining, in which high-pressure jets of water were used to wash away whole hillsides in order to extract their gold. Hydraulic mining so silted up the Sacramento Valley and altered its drainage patterns that in the 1870s and 1880s farmers successfully lobbied to ban it.

318.34   quartz-mining]   Underground mining for gold embedded in quartz veins.

320.12–14   lava . . . granite]   The Sierra Nevadas are in fact underlain by an enormous batholith—a huge intrusion of volcanic magma that did not breach the surface but instead cooled underground—which is the source of the granite for which they are famous.

320.20   Mount Shasta]   Mount Shasta, like Mount Lassen, is considered part of the series of volcanic peaks that make up the Cascade Range.

326.29–30   Schlagintweit brothers]   German naturalists, explorers, and writers Hermann von Schlagintweit (1826–82) and Adolf Schlagintweit (1829–57); they explored the Alps in 1846–53.

326.31   *névé*]   Or firn, the granular, partially compacted snow located at the upper end of a glacier.

333.18–23   lateral moraines . . . terminal moraines]   Moraines are the piles of gravel that accumulate along the front and sides of glaciers as their ice moves forward. Every glacier is always moving forward as the weight of snow and ice renders its base plastic, even when the front of the glacier remains fixed at a stable location (the front will remain fixed as long as the rate at which snow and ice accumulate in the winter matches the rate at which they melt in the summer). Moraines form as the forward moving ice transports rock to the stable front of the glacier, where the load is deposited to form heaps of gravel on the margins of the ice. Terminal moraines lie at the outward leading edge of the glacier, marking its farthest forward extent; lateral moraines lie along its edges.

334.6   "bergschrund,"]   A crevasse, a fissure extending deep into the ice of a glacier.

337.26–28   As the snaw . . . sang Burns]   In "Tam o' Shanter."

361.17   mining regions of Nevada]   The most famous of the Nevada mines were those of the Comstock Lode, in the vicinity of Virginia City. Building and fueling the mines, which required an immense amount of timber from the nearby mountains, resulted in extensive deforestation.

364.36   supplies of acorns]   Acorns were a principal foodstuff for native peoples in many parts of California.

377.37–38   terrible fate . . . Donner party]   A group of 82 emigrants under the leadership of Jacob and George Donner of Illinois were trapped in the Sierra Nevada mountains by an eight-day snowstorm at the end of October 1846 and reached the brink of starvation by mid-December. The first rescuers from Sutter's Fort (present-day Sacramento) reached the Donner party's camps through deep snow on February 18 and began bringing survivors down into the valley settlements. The last emigrant left camp on April 21; by that time many in the main party had died from exhaustion and malnutrition and their flesh had been eaten by the others as a last resort. Of the 82 emigrants, 47 survived.

387.31   money-changers . . . temple]   Cf. Matthew 2:12, Mark 11:15.

403.37–404.1   "boundless contiguity of shade,"]   William Cowper, *The Task* (1785): Bk. 2—"The Timepiece," line 2.

404.9   openness . . . Sierra woods]   The openness of the forests in Muir's time was in part attributable to Indian burning, which helped clear the undergrowth. The valley floor of Yosemite would become more densely forested because of subsequent suppression of these fires.

405.24   moraines vanish]   Moraines consist of unconsolidated gravel, often deposited in such a way as to create very steep slopes that erode easily.

436.6   Heer and Lesquereux]   Swiss naturalists Oswald Heer (1809–83) and (Charles) Leo Lesquereux (1806–89); Lesquereux immigrated to the United States in 1848.

436.25–26   forest reservations]   First established by the Forest Reserves Act of 1891, which provided for the setting aside of forested public land to protect watersheds and timber supplies. In the early 20th century these reserves became known as the national forests.

463.22   "Old Hundredth,"]   Dignified tune so-named for its use as the setting for Psalm 100 in the 1563 Sternhold and Hopkins *Psalter*.

512.1–7   high-walled corral . . . dummy hunters]   Archaeological records for this hunting technique, which was used in many parts of North America, go back thousands of years.

516.15   Micawber-like]   The impecunious Wilkins Micawber, always waiting for "something to turn up," in Charles Dickens' *David Copperfield* (1849–50).

STICKEEN

549.1   STICKEEN]   Muir's earliest-known writing about the dog Stickeen is in a journal entry dated August 30, 1880, made during his second trip to Alaska; it reads:

> An Indian Cur. What labyrinth of relationship Stickeen had, I never tried to trace; probably he came from the Stickeen tribes.
>
> Indian curs are all solemn, even when puppies, I suppose from having to work hard. They are made beasts of burden as soon as they can carry a pound or two. Those of the interior of the country are all thus used, old and young. Each has its pair of saddle-bags, according to size, marching solemnly. Hiding, Stickeen probably learned in trying to avoid his load.
>
> When we came to the Indian villages, he hardly noticed other dogs, being wholly unlike those kingly, magisterial dogs that ever draw a company of dependents at their heels. Rather he was a hermit—a wandering star beyond the influence of any of his kind.
>
> A good-natured sailor and vagabond, he was fond of wandering but

without visible enthusiasm, nosing among logs and trees with sober, unhasting industry, now and then shaking the rain from his hair or the dew from the huckleberry bushes, heeding no kind of weather, never in a hurry or fuss, eating as if it were a sad duty.

Never cat-like with the small game he killed, without yelp or growl he did the job with official decorum, like a dull boy doing his chores.

He was smooth and glossy as a berry. His little round feet made no sound on the moss carpet of the woods, turf and moss, nor on the glacier that never before felt the foot of man or dog. From most of dog sins he was free—didn't fuss, steal, whine, or get in the way. He never offered his head to be patted as an affectionate terrier would, or a loving collie; neither did he refuse a caress—he just didn't care. He was cold and unemotional as a glacier curled up in a blue shadow on the mountains. Yet his eyes puzzled me—aye, those eyes! They were deep, calm, fateful, suggesting the unfathomable wells of the glaciers.

But at first he seemed to me a small dim dull sluggish unromantic nobody . . . as unfussy as a tree. Even the minister knew him not. He was just a little dog that followed him.

No mark of years was on him—he seemed neither old nor young. He always looked grave, no matter how playful you might be with him; scratch his ears, pat his head, set him up on hind legs, or cuddle him on your lap, he was still irresistibly grave—not a tail-wag. A little black horizontal philosopher, calm, pensive, silently watchful. . . .

He was particular about his beds, and no dog had better ones, for the woods down to the tide-line are not simply carpeted with mosses, but richly plushed with them, so that all the ground was a bed, fresher and finer far than any king could buy of fluffy down silk. Only sticks and roots woven into the yellow fronds had to be avoided. A mossy hollow—not too damp—at the foot of a spruce tree between bulging roots was the favorite place where he curled up comfortably, himself like a little boss of moss, swelled up over a boulder.

He was an adventurous swimmer, as much at home on the waves as a seal. And he could make his way through any wind like a salmon through swift water.

(*John of the Mountains: The Unpublished Journals of John Muir*, ed. Linnie Marsh Wolfe, pp. 275–77. Reprinted by permission.)

551.2   J. G. HOLLAND]   Josiah Gilbert Holland (1819–81), author and editor of magazines including *Scribner's Monthly* and its successor *The Century Magazine*.

566.31   wee . . . beastie]   See note 163.10–11.

SELECTED ESSAYS

577.1   *Yosemite Glaciers*]   Aside from a very brief botanical listing in the Boston *Recorder* in 1866, this was Muir's first publication.

588.23–26   Hutching's . . . Black's] James M. Hutching's and A. G. Black's hotels.

589.6   Hill's painting] Thomas Hill (1829–1908) emigrated from England in 1840 and settled in California around 1871; he was famous for his landscapes of the Yosemite Valley region.

592.1   *A Geologist's Winter Walk*] This was an excerpt from a letter to Jeanne Carr. She submitted it to *The Overland Monthly* without Muir's knowledge.

595.20   'benmost bore'] Robert Burns, *The Jolly Beggars. A Cantata*, 2nd recitative; the words mean "inmost crevice (or cranny)."

607.1   *Flood-Storm in the Sierra*] Muir later revised this essay for *The Mountains of California*, Chapter XI (pp. 474–82 in this volume).

617.28   "it is . . . for a' that"] From Robert Burns' "The Honest Man."

618.1   *Living Glaciers of California*] Muir revised this essay for *The Mountains of California*, Chapter II (pp. 326–35 in this volume).

619.1–7   The first Sierra glacier . . . my discovery] The bulk of Muir's writings about his geological "discoveries" appeared, like this essay, in popular journals. But at a time when science was just beginning to professionalize itself into the academic disciplines that characterized it in the 20th century, Muir was taken quite seriously as an amateur geologist, principally for his work in applying Louis Agassiz's theories of glaciation to the mountain landscapes of the American West. His more explicitly "scientific" work appeared in the *Proceedings of the Boston Society of Natural History* with the help of Dr. Samuel Kneeland, who shared Muir's interest in Yosemite geology. Muir also published his work in the *Proceedings of the American Association for the Advancement of Science*.

621.14–19   lateral moraines . . . channel.] See note 333.18–23.

622.14   *névé*] See note 326.31.

622.15   *Bergschrund*] See note 334.6.

624.38   Professor Joseph Leconte] Le Conte (1823–1901) was a leading geologist at the University of California at Berkeley.

626.18   Schlagintweit brothers] See note 326.29–30.

626.25   Clarence King] King (1842–1901) was considered the leading geologist of his generation; he served as the first director of the U.S. Geological Survey, 1879–81.

629.1   *God's First Temples*] This is the first article in which Muir protests the destruction of natural resources and wild country in the mountain West.

629.20–630.10   The practical importance . . . them.] Muir's argument about the role of forests in regulating streamflow was already familiar to many 19th-century readers from the work of George Perkins Marsh (1801–82), whose

Man and Nature (1864) ascribed the fall of ancient Greece and Rome to the environmental degradation resulting from their indiscriminate cutting of Mediterranean forests. *Man and Nature* was crucial in building a national consensus about the need to protect American forests, leading eventually to the establishment of the Adirondack State Park in New York and to the 1891 Forest Reserves Act which laid the foundation for the national forests. Muir's efforts to defend wilderness areas in the West were a part of this national movement.

645.13   Sisson]   Proprietor of the hotel at which Muir was staying.

649.1   *Alaska*]   For the material in this essay, Muir drew on a series of articles written during his first trip to Alaska in the second half of 1879 and published in the San Francisco *Daily Evening Bulletin.* The trip gave Muir the opportunity to view for the first time glacial landscapes on a much larger and more active scale than he had been exploring for the past decade in the Sierra Nevada.

657.5–658.2   An Alaskan midsummer day . . . all the world.]   Muir often reworked the material in his journals to produce his essays; for this passage he used an entry from his journal of July 10, 1879, which reads:

> I should like to sketch one of these Alaska summer days, however imperfect the sketch must be. It is a day without night, for it begins and ends at midnight, which is the low noon of the great round day. The sky is red and orange then, for clouds more or less distinct are almost always present. The day opens slowly, the center of greatest light insensibly increasing and circling round the horizon's rim; and when at length the sun appears, it is without much of that stirring, impressive pomp, that flashing awakening energy so suggestive of the Bible image of a strong man coming forward to run a race. The colored clouds with their dissolving edges seem to vanish as their color leaves them, sinking into a hazy dimness around the horizon. The islands, some of them with ruffs of mist about their bases, cast black ill-defined shadows over the glistening water, and the whole dome of the sky becomes pale, whitish gray. For three or four hours after sunrise there is no striking feature to be felt or seen. The sun may be looked in the face though seemingly unclouded, and the islands full in the light, and the mainland mountains are seen in the distance. Yet in all their beauty of form and wealth of woods they seem to be yet asleep, rather dull and uncommunicative. As the day advances towards high noon, the light of the sun shining down in full power lights the water levels to silver. Brightly play the ripples about the bushy edges of the warm shores, inzoning every island with a white-glowing girdle. The bland air beats now and makes itself felt as a life-giving ocean of energy through the all-pervading, sifting, drenching, luminous mist of pearl sunshine.

(*John of the Mountains: The Unpublished Journals of John Muir*, ed., Wolfe, pp. 252–53. Reprinted by permission.)

657.20–21   a bridegroom . . . race.]   Cf. Psalm 19:5.

672.35–37   Mr. Swan . . . coast]   James G. Swan, a native of Boston, wrote of his 1852–55 stay on the coast in *The North West Coast: or Three Years in Washington Territory* (1857).

683.14–22   through the cañon . . . gradually revealed.]   This would in 1898 become the principal route that prospectors followed during the Klondike gold rush.

684.16   Muir Glacier]   Named for John Muir in 1880.

685.36–38   Sitka . . . Russian ruins]   Sitka, founded 1799, was the capital of Russian America and continued as the capital of Alaska when the territory came under U.S. rule in 1867; the capital was transferred to Juneau in 1906.

687.1–2   *Features . . . National Park*]   Muir began to emerge during the 1890s as the leading proponent of permanent federal protection of Yosemite as a national park. In 1864 the United States had given the Yosemite Valley to the state of California. It was the nation's first wild land park, and leading landscape architect Frederick Law Olmsted (1822–1903) had played a key role in designing that park. Muir was among those who by the 1890s were arguing for setting aside a much larger tract of land than just Yosemite Valley itself and in 1892 he became a founder of the Sierra Club as part of the lobbying effort to protect the Yosemite and other parts of the Sierra high country.

701.1   *The American Forests*]   This is Muir's most sustained essay on the lands that eventually became the core of the national forests. It is an outgrowth of his service as a consultant to the National Forestry Commission, chaired by Harvard botanist Charles Sprague Sargent (1841–1927) and with members such as as Yale scientist William H. Brewer (1828–1910), Alexander Agassiz (1835–1910), and Gifford Pinchot (1865–1946). The essay, which was commissioned in 1897 by *Atlantic Monthly* editor Walter Hines Page, is essentially a précis of the Forestry Report's major arguments, rendered livelier and more accessible by Muir's prose. In arguing for government ownership and regulation of forested lands throughout the nation, Muir aligned himself with the work that Gifford Pinchot (who would become Theodore Roosevelt's Chief Forester and founder of the United States Forest Service) was beginning to pursue in promoting permanent federal management of forests on public lands. The echoes of Marsh's *Man and Nature* (see note 629.20–630.10) also are evident here. Pinchot and Muir would soon diverge in their visions of how such forests should be managed and used, with the struggle over Hetch Hetchy providing the occasion for a final break that in fact reflected longstanding philosophical tensions between the two men; the two actually came into conflict over grazing policy in the western forests not long after this piece was written.

707.19   timber culture act]   Passed in 1873, the act was another legacy of George Perkins Marsh's *Man and Nature*, the theory being that by encouraging settlers to plant trees in grassland and desert environments, "rain would follow the plow" and barren land would be made fertile for agriculture.

709.39–40   *A change . . . 1901.]   "The American Forests" was first published in August 1897.

721.1–2   *The Wild Parks and Forest Reservations of the West*]   This essay was originally published in *The Atlantic Monthly* as the first in a series of nine articles on wild parks of the American West that Walter Hines Page commissioned from Muir following the success of "The American Forests"; all ten essays were collected, with some revisions, in *Our National Parks.*

729.2–3   buffalo . . . described by Parkman]   In Francis Parkman's *The Oregon Trail* (1849).

741.38   p. 736]   The page number has been changed to conform to the present volume.

745.5–6   A' that . . . muckle's a' that]   Robert Burns, *The Jolly Beggars: A Cantata*, Song VII; muckle means "great," "much," "big."

745.34   guarded . . . United States cavalry.]   Management of the national parks passed from the U.S. Army to the modern Park Service after passage of the National Park Service Act in 1916.

746.22   scaur]   Scottish: A bare spot on the side of a steep hill; a precipice; a cliff.

764.11–12   Joliet and Father Marquette]   The French explorers passed between the Great Lakes and Mississippi watersheds at Portage, Wisconsin, not far from the spot where the Muir family settled.

772.34–39   Dr. Johnson's . . . something."]   In James Boswell, *Journal of a Tour of the Hebrides* (1785), entry of October 19, 1773.

786.33   Emerson came.]   This is Muir's first published account of his 1871 meeting with Emerson, who was vacationing in the West as part of a cross-country railroad trip with family and friends. Emerson had become exhausted by his teaching and writing schedule and the trip has been credited with prolonging his life.

787.3   'gang tapsal-teerie.']   Go topsy-turvey, from Burns' "Green grow the Rashes."

787.4   'Good-by . . . home,']   "Good-Bye," line 1, in *Poems* (1847).

787.24   "Come listen . . . saith,"]   Cf. "Woodnotes II" in *Poems* (1847).

788.24   Galen Clark]   Clark was appointed California's state guardian of the Yosemite Grant in 1866. He was heavily involved in promoting the area for tourist use.

793.9–10   Major Powell]   Explorer, geologist, conservationist, and teacher John Wesley Powell (1834–1902), a Union Army veteran who had lost his lower right arm at the battle of Shiloh, organized the first descent of the Grand Canyon in 1869.

794.13 "'a' through ither,"] All through one another.

803.3 Hance] John Hance was one of the earliest promoters of the canyon for tourists and was responsible for some of its earliest trails.

810.1 *Hetch Hetchy Valley*] This essay is Muir's most important single piece on the Hetch Hetchy controversy. For it, Muir edited and expanded the closing section of his 1890 article "Features of the Proposed Yosemite National Park" (pp. 694–700 in this volume).

818.2 OCTOBER 23.] In 1867. Muir's journal account of his walk to the Gulf of Mexico was posthumously edited and published by his friend, William Badè.

825.4–827.25 The world . . . beauty of Nature.] This is Muir's most systematic and explicit attack on an anthropocentric view of the creation. In Muir's own journal, the passage reads:

> The world we are told was made for man. A presumption that is totally unsupported by facts.
> There is a very numerous class of men who are cast into painfully fits of astonishment whenever they find anything living or dead in all Gods universe which they cannot eat or in some way render what they call useful to themselves. They have ~~very~~ precise ~~& very~~ dogmatic insight of the "intentions" of the Creator. It is ~~not more~~ hardly possible to be guilty of irreverence in speaking of their God any more than of ~~the~~ heathen idols institutions of the Hindoos. He is regarded as a civilized & law-abiding gentleman, in favor of a Republican form of government or ~~of~~ a limited monarchy, believes in the literature & language of England & is a warm supporter of the English constitution & of all wellgotten sabbath schools and missionary societies, & in all respects is a purely a manufactured article as any puppet of a halfpenny theatre & of course, with such views of the Creator, it is not surprising that ~~very~~ erroneous views should be entertained of the creation.
> To such properly trimmed people the sheep for example is an easy problem,—"food & clothing for us." Eating grass & daises white by Divine appointment, for this predestined purpose on perceiving the demand for wool that would be occasioned by the apple Fall
> The horse also "to carry us" & to work & the ox for ~~roast~~ beef & the cow "to mother us" with milk, all this is plain, but the countless herds of wild horses & buffalo ought to be dragging gashing plowshares behind them "to conquer the stubborn evil."
> Dogs too to follow our foxes, & to bark for & preserve us, the good & bright & the wicked. Among birds we have hens for albumen for our puddings and cakes. All managed nicely "for us" ~~by predestined intention~~ in proper order etc.

Whales are storehouses of oil "for us" to help out the stars in lighting our nights, until the discovery of the Pennsylvania wells.

Among plants, to say nothing of the cereals, hemp is a plain case for the ships rigging wrapping of our packages, hanging the wicker & cotton is another plain case, of clothing.

Iron was made for hammers & plows & lead for bullets, All intended "for us" & so of another small handful of insignificant things. But if we should ask these profound expositors of Gods intentions, How about those maneating animals the lion, tiger, alligator, who smack their ~~palates after eating~~ lips over raw men, creations lords, or about those myriads of "noxious" insects that destroy his labors, & drink his blood, Doubtless man was "intended" food & drink for all these, Oh no! Not at all! These are unresolvable difficulties of Edens apples & the devil.

Why does water drown its load Why do so many minerals poison him, Why are so many plants & fishes deadly enemys to him Why is the lord of creation subjected to the same laws of life as his subjects. Oh! All these things are Satanic, or in some way connected with the first garden. Now it does not occur to these farseeing intentionists that the Lords primary object in constructing all of his creatures was at least might be the happiness first of all of each one, not the mere provident creation of all for the happiness of one. Why ought man to value himself as more than an infinitely small ~~composing~~ unit of the one great unit of creation, & what creature of all that the Lord has taken the pains to make, is ~~less~~ not essential to the grand completeness of that unit.

The universe would be incomplete without lord man but it would also be incomplete without the smallest transmicroscopic creature that dwells beyond our conceitful eyes. "From the dust of the earth,"— from the common elementary fund The Creator has made lord homo From the same material he has made every creature however noxious & insignificant to us. They are "earthborn companions & fellow mortals.

The fearfully good—the orthodox Godlikes of this laborious patchwork of modern civilization cry Heresy! upon every one whose sympathies are allowed to reach out a single hairsbreadth beyond the boundary epidermis of ~~their~~ our own species, Not content with taking all of earth—they also claim the celestial country, as they of course are the only possessors of the kind of souls for which that imponderable empire was planned.

This star made many a successful journey around the heavens ere man was made, & entire kingdoms of creatures enjoyed existence & returned to dust ere man appeared to claim them & when human beings have also played their little part in creations plan. They too ~~shall~~ may disappear without any general burning or extraordinary commotion whatever.

Plants are credited with but dim & uncertain sensation, & minerals with positively none at all, but why may not even mineral arrangements of matter be endowed with sensation of a kind that we in our exclusive perfection can have no manner of communication with.

Well I have wandered from my object,— I stated a page or two back that man claimed that the earth was made for him & I was going to say that enormous beasts & thorny plants & deadly malarias dwelling in certain portions of the earth prove that the whole earth was not made from him. When an animal from a tropic clime is taken to high latitudes & ~~they~~ it perishes of cold we say "That animal was "never intended" for so severe a climate. But when ~~but when~~ man is taken to humid portions of the tropics & perishes amid deadly malarias, he cannot see that he was "never intended" for such climates. No, he will rather accuse his first mother of the difficulty who never once beheld a fever district. Or will consider it as providential chastisement for some ~~self invented form of what is called~~ sin & all uneatable & uncivilizable animals & all plants which carry prickles are deplorable evils, which according to closet researches of clergy require the cleansing chemistry of universal planetary combustion. But only mankind require burning & if that transmundane furnace can be so applied & regulated as to smelt us to conformity with the rest of the terrestrial creation, the tophetization of the erratic genus were a consumation devoutly to be prayed for,—but, glad to leave these ecclesiastical fires, & joyfully return to the immortal truth & immortal beauty of ~~unmanageable~~ Nature.

(*The John Muir Papers, 1858–1954. Series Two, Journals and Sketchbooks, 1867–1873, Reel No. 23* [Alexandria: Chadwyck-Healey Inc. with The University of the Pacific, 1986], ed. Ronald H. Limbaugh and Kirsten E. Lewis. Reprinted by permission of John Muir Papers, Holt-Atherton Department of Special Collections, University of the Pacific. Copyright 1984 Muir-Hanna Trust.)

828.19–20   "Forgive . . . do."]   Cf. Luke 23:34.

Index

LIBRARY OF CONGRESS CATALOGING-IN-PUBLICATION DATA

Muir, John, 1838–1914.
    [Selections. 1997]
    Nature writings / John Muir.
    888 p.   cm. —(The Library of America ; 92)
    Includes index.
    Contents: The story of my boyhood and youth — My
first summer in the Sierra — The mountains of California
— Stickeen — Selected essays.
    ISBN 1–883011–24–8
    1. Muir, John, 1838–1914.   2. Natural history—United
States.   3. Naturalists—United States—Biography.
4. Conservationists—United States—Biography.
I. Title.   II. Series.
QH31.M9A3   1997
508.74'092—dc20   96-9664
[B] M41   CIP

THE LIBRARY OF AMERICA SERIES

This book is set in 10 point Linotron Galliard,
a face designed for photocomposition by Matthew Carter
and based on the sixteenth-century face Granjon. The paper is
acid-free Ecusta Nyalite and meets the requirements for permanence
of the American National Standards Institute. The binding
material is Brillianta, a woven rayon cloth made by
Van Heek-Scholco Textielfabrieken, Holland.
The composition is by The Clarinda
Company. Printing and binding by
R.R.Donnelley & Sons Company.
Designed by Bruce Campbell.

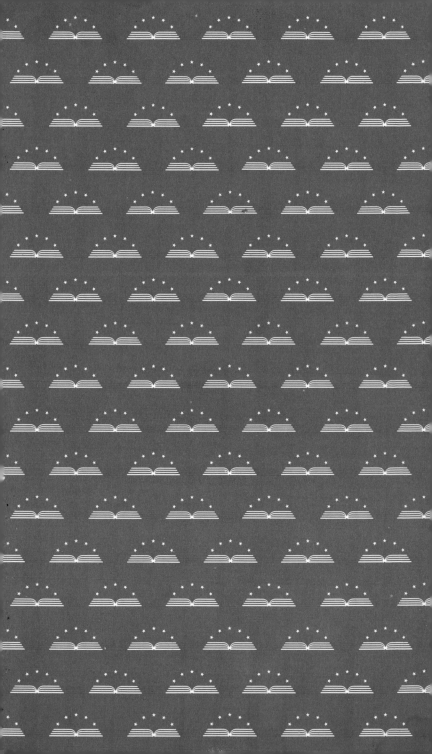